WITHDRAWN

Urban Renewal:
The Record and the Controversy

A Publication of the Joint Center for Urban Studies of the Massachusetts Institute of Technology and Harvard University

This book is one of a series published under the auspices of the Joint Center for Urban Studies, a cooperative venture of the Massachusetts Institute of Technology and Harvard University. The Joint Center was founded in 1959 to organize and encourage research on urban and regional problems. Participants have included scholars from the fields of anthropology, architecture, business, city planning, economics, education, engineering, history, law, philosophy, political science, and sociology.

The findings and conclusions of this book are, as with all Joint Center publications, solely the responsibility of the contributors.

Other books published in the Joint Center series include:

CHARLES ABRAMS, *Man's Struggle for Shelter in an Urbanizing World.* The M.I.T. Press, 1964.

WILLIAM ALONSO, *Location and Land Use.* Harvard University Press, 1964.

MARTIN ANDERSON, *The Federal Bulldozer.* The M.I.T. Press, 1964.

DONALD APPLEYARD, KEVIN LYNCH, and JOHN R. MYER, *The View from the Road.* The M.I.T. Press, 1964.

EDWARD C. BANFIELD and JAMES Q. WILSON, *City Politics.* Harvard University Press and the M.I.T. Press, 1963.

JOHN E. BURCHARD and OSCAR HANDLIN, editors, *The Historian and the City.* The M.I.T. Press, 1963.

RALPH W. CONANT, editor, *The Public Library and the City.* The M.I.T. Press, 1965.

BERNARD J. FRIEDEN, *The Future of Old Neighborhoods.* The M.I.T. Press, 1964.

NATHAN GLAZER and DANIEL P. MOYNIHAN, *Beyond the Melting Pot.* The M.I.T. Press, 1963.

CHARLES HAAR, *Law and Land: Anglo-American Planning Practice.* Harvard University Press, 1964.

KEVIN LYNCH, *The Image of the City.* The M.I.T. Press, 1960.

LLOYD RODWIN, *Housing and Economic Progress.* The M.I.T. Press, 1961.

STEPHAN THERNSTROM, *Poverty and Progress.* Harvard University Press, 1964.

SAM B. WARNER, JR., *Streetcar Suburbs.* Harvard University Press, 1962.

MORTON AND LUCIA WHITE, *The Intellectual Versus the City: From Thomas Jefferson to Frank Lloyd Wright.* Harvard University Press, 1962.

Urban Renewal:
The Record and the
Controversy

edited by James Q. Wilson

The M.I.T. Press
Massachusetts Institute of Technology
Cambridge, Massachusetts, and London, England

Acknowledgments

The editor wishes to acknowledge with gratitude the invaluable assistance of Mrs. Janet Eckstein in the preparation of this volume. She bore the principal burden of preparing the manuscript for the press.

Advice and assistance also came from the editor's colleagues at the Joint Center for Urban Studies, especially William Alonso, Ralph Conant, William Doebele, Bernard J. Frieden, John T. Howard, Kevin Lynch, and Lloyd Rodwin. The responsibility for the selection and arrangement of materials is, of course, wholly the editor's.

List of Contributors

CHARLES ABRAMS *Chairman, City Planning Department, Columbia University*

WILLIAM ALONSO *Associate Professor of Regional Planning, Graduate School of Design, Harvard University*

MARTIN ANDERSON *Associate Professor of Business, Graduate School of Business, Columbia University*

OTTO A. DAVIS *Assistant Professor of Economics, Graduate School of Industrial Administration, Carnegie Institute of Technology*

HILBERT FEFFERMAN *Associate General Counsel, Operations, Housing and Home Finance Agency*

ASHLEY A. FOARD *Associate General Counsel, Legislation, Housing and Home Finance Agency*

MARC FRIED *Research Professor and Director, Institute of Human Sciences, Boston College*

BERNARD FRIEDEN *Associate Professor of City Planning, Massachusetts Institute of Technology*

HERBERT J. GANS *Associate Professor of Sociology, Teachers College, Columbia University*

WILLIAM G. GRIGSBY *Associate Professor of City Planning, University of Pennsylvania*

ROBERT P. GROBERG *Assistant Director, National Association of Housing and Redevelopment Officials*

CHESTER HARTMAN *Research Fellow in Sociology, Harvard Medical School, and Fellow, Joint Center for Urban Studies of the Massachusetts Institute of Technology and Harvard University*

HAROLD KAPLAN *Associate Professor of Political Science, York University*

HUBERT KAY *Fortune Magazine*

NORTON E. LONG *Professor of Community Government, Brandeis University*

WALTER MCQUADE *Associate Editor, Fortune Magazine*

ROGER MONTGOMERY *Director, Urban Renewal Design Center, School of Architecture, Washington University*

WILLIAM L. SLAYTON *Commissioner, Urban Renewal Administration*

WALLACE F. SMITH *Center for Real Estate and Urban Economics, University of California at Berkeley*

WILTON S. SOGG *Gottfried, Ginsburg, Guren and Merritt, Cleveland, Ohio*

RAYMOND VERNON *Professor of International Trade and Investment, Graduate School of Business Administration, Harvard University*

ROBERT C. WEAVER *Administrator, Housing and Home Finance Agency*

WARREN WERTHEIMER *Law Offices of Charles W. Tuckman, San Francisco, California*

ANDREW B. WHINSTON *Associate Professor of Economics, University of Virginia*

JAMES Q. WILSON *Associate Professor of Government, Harvard University, and Director, Joint Center for Urban Studies of the Massachusetts Institute of Technology and Harvard University*

BASIL G. ZIMMER *Professor of Sociology, Brown University*

Contents

Introduction   xiii
James Q. Wilson

I.   The Economics of Cities and Renewal   1

   1. The Changing Economic Function of the
Central City   3
Raymond Vernon

   2. Housing Markets and Public Policy   24
William G. Grigsby

   3. The Economics of Urban Renewal   50
Otto A. Davis and Andrew B. Whinston

II.   Urban Renewal: Background and Goals   69

   4. Federal Urban Renewal Legislation   71
Ashley A. Foard and Hilbert Fefferman

   5. Legal and Governmental Issues in Urban
Renewal   126
Wilton S. Sogg and Warren Wertheimer

   6. The Operation and Achievements of the
Urban Renewal Program   189
William L. Slayton

III.   Urban Renewal in Practice: Three Cases   231

   7. Urban Renewal in Newark   233
Harold Kaplan

8. Urban Renewal in Boston   259
   Walter McQuade

9. The Industrial Corporation in Urban
   Renewal   278
   Hubert Kay

IV Relocation and Community Life   291

10. The Housing of Relocated Families   293
    Chester Hartman

11. The Housing of Relocated Families:
    Summary of a Census Bureau Survey   336
    U.S. Housing and Home Finance Agency

12. A Comment on the HHFA Study of
    Relocation   353
    Chester Hartman

13. Grieving for a Lost Home: Psychological
    Costs of Relocation   359
    Marc Fried

14. The Small Businessman and Relocation   380
    Basil Zimmer

V. Government and Citizen Participation in
    Urban Renewal   405

15. Planning and Politics: Citizen Participation
    in Urban Renewal   407
    James Q. Wilson

16. Local Government and Renewal Policies   422
    Norton E. Long

VI. Planning and Design   435

17. Cities, Planners, and Urban Renewal   437
    William Alonso

18. Improving the Design Process in Urban
    Renewal   454
    Roger Montgomery

VII. Challenges and Responses   489

19. The Federal Bulldozer   491
Martin Anderson

20. Urban Renewal Realistically Reappraised   509
Robert P. Groberg

21. *The Federal Bulldozer:* A Review   532
Wallace F. Smith

22. The Failure of Urban Renewal   537
Herbert J. Gans

23. Some Blessings of Urban Renewal   558
Charles Abrams

VIII. The Future of Urban Renewal   583

24. Policies for Rebuilding   585
Bernard Frieden

25. A General Strategy for Urban Renewal   624
William G. Grigsby

26. New Directions in Urban Renewal   663
Robert C. Weaver

Index   673

Introduction

JAMES Q. WILSON

Urban renewal is not the most expensive or the most far-reaching domestic governmental program of our time, yet it is one of the most widely-discussed and perhaps the most controversial. We spend far more on farm subsidies and highways, yet these programs—except for an occasional scandal—are rarely debated outside the circle of immediate participants and their scholarly observers. There are other federal housing programs—especially the FHA mortgage guarantee program—the collective impact of which has, in the past at least, been considerably greater than urban renewal, yet only rarely in recent years have they been the objects of general public discussion. The decisions of a variety of obscure regulatory commissions in Washington probably affect the lives of more people than does urban renewal, yet seldom does one encounter in print the names of these agencies, much less an argument over their policies. Urban renewal, on the other hand, has been the object of the closest scrutiny in the pages of both popular and esoteric magazines, in books both scholarly and polemical, and in newspaper editorials as well as news accounts of citizen meetings and city council hearings.

The controversy about the program has not slowed its progress—nearly 1,600 renewal projects are underway in more than 770 communities in 44 states. Nor has the progress silenced the arguments—the books and articles which criticize or defend the program continue to multiply.

One reason for this continuing tempest may simply be that the intellectual has characteristically displayed an ambivalent attitude toward the city. On the one hand, the city since Jefferson's time has been viewed with suspicion and anxiety—it seems to breed poverty and despair, to dehumanize its citizens, and to strangle its residents in traffic snarls, crime waves, and polluted air. On the other hand, the city is the source of urbanity and civility, of the diversity and specialization which enhance the quality of life. For some, the meaning of urbanity is limited to the central business district and the high-brow cultural institutions found in or near it; the city is a market place for transacting business and exercising choices with respect to leisure-time activities. For others, urbanity includes the diversity of life styles found in any heterogeneous settlement; the city is a collection of neighborhoods and "subcultures" with distinctive and desirable (or at least inevitable) ways of life which ought to be preserved. The extreme partisans of all views tend to suffuse their attachments with romantic certitude, and yet there is truth in each.

These intellectual differences lead to different policy concerns. Those who dislike the artifacts of urban life—the highway, the automobile, congestion—seek to abolish them by calling for the creation of new towns and garden cities where careful planning can recapture small-town pleasantries without sacrificing the diversity of big-city life. The devotees of the central city strive for its economic and cultural rejuvenation, even at the expense of the fringe and especially at the expense of those who settle in the decaying parts of the central area, thereby reducing its attraction for the economic and intellectual elite. Adherents of this view sometimes curse the alleged homogeneity, banality, and conformity of suburban life. Finally, those who cherish the variety and opportunities afforded by the various neighborhoods and corresponding life styles of the city seek to defend such natural areas against planned change; as for the economic vitality of the central city, that can perhaps be preserved by means short of renewal or, failing that, allowed to decline, in the hope that the market will provide substitutes elsewhere.

Urban renewal is a program which raises so many of the questions which intellectuals find relevant about cities that every project seems to require a re-examination of first principles: What is the purpose of a city? Whose values are to be served? What sacrifices should citizens make for the common good, somehow defined? To whose benefit should government subsidies be paid, and with what justification? To what extent does democracy require citizen participation in—and a veto over—decisions about the future of neighborhoods and the disposition of private property? No political system—least of all ours—is well suited to a continuing debate over first principles. If only principles were at stake and intellectuals interested, however, the controversy would have long since become academic in every sense of the word. But vital interests are at stake as well, and urban renewal happens to be a program which affects interests in a visible, highly dramatic fashion. Government usually takes money impersonally, through taxes, to support programs which those taxed rarely see; benefits conferred similarly arrive impersonally, through the beneficence of a half-hidden agency. Urban renewal, like selective service, physically takes things and turns them, before our eyes, to new uses. Homes are destroyed or rehabilitated; new structures rise or the uses of old structures are changed; streets and community facilities are rearranged. The citizens—both those who benefit and those who suffer—see their government at work in the most vivid way. The spirit of the republic is made visible by urban renewal in a way that few other programs can match. And it all must be done with some degree of local consent. Small wonder that the full range of human passions is unleashed, producing, in every project area, hope, discontent, bitterness, prudence, and suspicion as, from plans to maps to workmen to relocation to new construction, change unfolds.

It is often forgotten in the midst of all this that urban renewal is not a goal, but a tool. It is a method whereby a great variety of ends can be served, some good, some bad. Since the use of that tool is left largely in the hands of local communities, the number of different goals which will be served, and the probability that not all will be judged ideal, is rather large. In some places, renewal has meant erecting a civic monument in a downtown plaza; in others, rehabilitating sound but decaying homes to improve living conditions for residents; in others, getting "undesirables" out of "desirable" neighborhoods by spot clearance; in others, stabilizing blighted neighborhoods and encouraging residents to improve their properties; in others, developing land that will attract new businesses into the community or clearing land that will get unpopular businesses out of the community; and in still others, assembling tracts on which subsidized low- or middle-income housing might be built. Given this welter of aims and achievements, it is understandable that urban renewal should mean very different things to different people. And it is also clear that neither blanket condemnations nor blanket defenses are appropriate.

Because of the complexities of the program as well as the many different levels on which the argument can proceed, a book which attempts to offer a representative selection of writings on urban renewal must perforce contain materials from many points of view, written in both scholarly and journalistic styles, and addressed to different aspects of the program. Furthermore, it seems that a program over which there have been so many arguments cannot be discussed without the assumption that the speaker is engaging in special pleading. This book, let it be understood, makes no argument and pleads no cause; its sole purpose is to provide a ready source in which the reader can find the best materials on the history of the program; its theory and practice; the legal, political, social, economic, and design issues involved; and both sides of some of the controversies surrounding the program. Not everyone will agree with the selections made; in partial defense, let it be understood that for some points of view a satisfactory article could not be found, either because it had not been written, or had been badly written, or could not be reprinted.

The Joint Center for Urban Studies of M.I.T. and Harvard, under whose aegis this volume was prepared, is a research center whose purpose is to encourage and support studies on urban affairs by scholars and students at M.I.T. and Harvard. It, like the two universities of which it is a part, takes no position on public issues, including urban renewal. Several present and former members of the Joint Center—Charles Abrams, William Alonso, Martin Anderson, Bernard Frieden, Chester Hartman, Norton Long, Raymond Vernon, and the editor—are represented in this book by selections from their writings. Their views are entirely their own responsibility.

The book is divided into eight parts. The economics of cities is dealt with first because, whatever else a city may be, it is primarily a collection of people and enterprises brought together to create and distribute goods and services. The central city—the downtown business and industrial districts—is the place where this activity is principally carried on. Since urban renewal is at least in part an effort to maintain the economic function of the central city, Raymond Vernon discusses the changes which have occurred in that function. Although people are brought to a city in search of jobs and markets, their presence in the city gives rise to a special kind of market: the market for land and housing. Urban renewal is in part a method for intervening in that market to change its operation or eliminate its frictions. William G. Grigsby describes the housing market from the standpoint of public policy. Finally, the peculiar economics of urban renewal itself—how it seeks to improve on the free market mechanism in allocating land and buildings—is analyzed by Otto A. Davis and Andrew B. Whinston.

The history, goals, methods, and accomplishments of urban renewal are discussed in Part II. The development of the legislation and the early debates over the purposes of the program are described by Ashley A. Foard and Hilbert Fefferman. The legal issues raised by renewal—condemnation and transfer of property, control of reuse, and compensation—are discussed by Wilton S. Sogg and Warren Wertheimer in the context of other techniques (zoning, building and housing codes, abatement of nuisances) traditionally used to regulate the use of land. An official government summary of the aims and accomplishments of the renewal program is provided by the Commissioner of the Urban Renewal Administration, William L. Slayton. This review, first given in 1963 as testimony before a Congressional committee, has been updated to June 1965 by the URA especially for this volume.

In order to provide a clear understanding of how renewal works in practice, Part III contains three accounts—one by a scholar, two by journalists—of the development of local renewal programs. The first, by Harold Kaplan, describes Newark, New Jersey, one of the first cities to adopt renewal, and emphasizes the political context of renewal decisions. The second, by an editor of *Fortune* magazine, describes the evolution of a program in a city (Boston) which has emphasized rehabilitation rather than clearance. Finally, the role of the private developer—especially the large industrial corporation—in renewal is described in another article from *Fortune*. In all three cases, a common theme emerges: the need for strong, vigorous executive action in order to develop and sustain a renewal program.

Relocation of families and businesses from renewal sites is perhaps the most controversial aspect of the program. In Part IV, Chester

Hartman reviews studies of relocation in various cities from 1930 (long before the renewal program began) to 1963. Prompted in part by the criticisms of people such as Hartman, the Housing and Home Finance Agency requested the United States Census Bureau to survey the relocation experience of families in 132 cities; the HHFA report of the study is printed here. Hartman returns to the issue by raising questions about the HHFA study. A clinical psychologist, Marc Fried, draws attention to the psychological, rather than the economic or physical, impact of renewal by reporting on a study he did of an early Boston renewal project which involved complete land clearance (subsequent projects have not generally been of this character). The experiences of small businessmen, rather than families, with relocation are discussed by Basil Zimmer on the basis of a careful study of the dislocation in Providence, Rhode Island, resulting from both renewal and highway programs.

Urban renewal occupies a unique place in American political experience in two senses: first, it has increasingly sought to involve the participation of citizens in affected neighborhoods (in addition to their representatives on city councils), and second, it has been one of the programs that have begun to change the shape of American federalism by emphasizing direct federal-city relations instead of the earlier pattern of federal-state relations. In Part V, James Q. Wilson discusses the first phenomenon, Norton Long (in an article written especially for this volume), the second.

Important opportunities have been afforded city planners and urban designers, as well as architects, by the urban renewal program. Whatever its social costs and benefits, the manifest consequence of the program is to change, often radically, some visual aspect of our urban environment. In Part VI, William Alonso discusses how city planners in America have viewed the city and how they have responded to urban renewal as a technique for remaking the city. Roger Montgomery, who has been a design consultant to the Urban Renewal Administration, feels that most renewal projects "have been executed with slight concern for design," and on the basis of a case study of renewal design in Detroit, explains this failure and indicates how it can be overcome.

One root-and-branch critique of the renewal program was published in 1964. Written by Martin Anderson while a student of industrial management at M.I.T., the book—*The Federal Bulldozer*

—aroused a storm of controversy, in part because it called for the abolition of the program on the grounds that the free market had accomplished more at less social cost. An article by Anderson summarizing his views appears in Part VII, followed by a critical rejoinder prepared by a staff member of the National Association of Housing and Redevelopment Officials and a review article written by Wallace Smith of the University of California. Another challenge to renewal—differing from Anderson's in that it places less faith in the free market—was written by Herbert J. Gans. Charles Abrams, while admitting defects in the programs, seeks to meet both kinds of criticisms in a chapter on "Some Blessings of Urban Renewal."

Finally, three experts on renewal—two scholars and one government official—look to the future. Bernard J. Frieden suggests new policies for planning renewal efforts which will achieve certain benefits (clearing surplus structures and increasing social choice for residents) at minimum cost in terms of relocation. William G. Grigsby calls for new criteria for federal assistance to local communities so that *national* urban renewal goals (which emphasize improving housing opportunities for people) more completely guide local renewal programs (which often emphasize the maintenance of the economic values of the central business district). Robert C. Weaver, the Administrator of the Housing and Home Finance Agency and a member of the Visiting Committee of the Joint Center for Urban Studies, describes the directions in which, at the federal level, the program now seems to be moving.

PART I

THE ECONOMICS

OF CITIES AND RENEWAL

1 The Changing Economic Function of the Central City *

RAYMOND VERNON

By almost any objective standard, the major central cities of our nation over the past fifty years or more, have been developing more slowly than the suburban areas that surround them. By many such standards, this *relative* decline has lately begun to appear as an *absolute* decline as well.

Neither the relative nor the absolute decline, considered by itself, is conclusively a sign of deterioration in the central city's economic or social life. But the signs of an absolute decline do raise questions which the relative decline did not. They suggest the possibility of a flight from an environment whose deterioration might conceivably be arrested. They suggest the abandonment of public and private ·capital which might conceivably still have economic use. They suggest also the possibility that precious space may be available in the central city for conversion to new uses, if only the processes of abandonment were understood and the new uses defined. Our job here is to try to understand the forces which lie behind these trends.

POPULATION MOVEMENT

The placement of American cities has typically been dominated by problems of transportation—problems of servicing the movement of

* Reprinted from *The Changing Economic Function of the Central City*, New York, Committee for Economic Development, 1959, pp. 40–62.

goods and people across oceans, down rivers, and through mountain passes. Sheer chance also played a part, no doubt, in their original placement: sheer chance reflected in the sequence by which various land areas were explored and settled or by the special enterprise of some individual or group.

At any event, almost from the moment the first house was erected, the first street laid, and the first drainage ditch dug in any of these embryo cities, a process of obsolescence took hold which dominated the pattern of subsequent development. This obsolescence, one should note, developed not only in the private structures but also in the public domain. It was not only that the first dwellings soon became inadequate by the standards of the people who lived in the city, but also that the street layouts, the sewage systems, and the water supply systems also became obsolescent. Almost from the first, then, there was rebuilding as well as building: a tearing down and reordering of structures and public facilities. "New York will be a great city," a visiting Englishman remarked a century ago, "when it gets built."

In the course of this building and rebuilding, however, the general tendency was to add to the ossification of the structure: to surface the public streets more permanently and to cram their sub-surface with more and more cables, mains, and transit conveyances; to replace wood dwellings with stone, and one-story structures with three- and four-story dwellings and factories. Each rebuilding, therefore, tended to make the next one a little more difficult than the last.

But the obsolescence process went on. In middle income homes, sanitary facilities and water supplies were brought into the home; gas mantles were replaced by electricity; the servant's bedroom gave way to the utility closet and the dishwasher; the private automobile supplemented shank's mare, the bicycle, the horse trolley and the subway.

The response of families who could afford it, at one stage or another in most central cities, was to abandon the original residential neighborhoods and to build new neighborhoods elsewhere at points further removed from the city center. Step by step, Bostonians retreated from the Common, Philadelphians from Independence Hall, New Yorkers from Astor Place. By 1881, Henry James—speaking through one of his fictional characters—was saying:

". . . At the end of three or four years we'll move. That's the way to live in New York—to move every three or four years. Then you always get the last thing. . . . So you see we'll always have a new house; you get all the latest improvements. . . ."[1]

By the beginning of the twentieth century, the electric trolley and the suburban railway were quickening the moving process. By the 1930's, the automobile and the bus had speeded the movement even more.

This tendency produced a typical growth pattern around our central cities. At any stage, one could discern points outside the older areas—points where the rail lines and public conveyances ran—where new residential construction was at a peak and populations were increasing at a rapid rate. As time went on, these points where maximum growth rates were being registered were further and further removed from the center of the city, and when the automobile came they were no longer isolated points but a continuous band of maximum growth ringing the central city.

Thus, during the decade of 1900 to 1910, the most rapidly growing parts of metropolitan areas were the central cities themselves. In 1910 to 1920, the maximum growth rates occurred in a five-mile wide ring surrounding the edges of the central cities. In the next three decades, the high growth rates had moved outward still further to a ring 5 to 10 miles from the central city.[2] By 1956, the outward tendency was so marked that over three-quarters of the major metropolitan areas' new dwelling units, measured by number or value, were scheduled for construction outside the central cities.[3]

The result of this pattern of development is suggested by Table 1. In every case, it will be noted, populations in the central city depicted in the table tended to decline in relation to the metropolitan area of which it was a part. This, of course, reflects relative rather than absolute decline. After 1950, however, New York City's populations declined in absolute terms. The odds are high that a few others may also have done so.

[1] Morris Townsend speaking in Henry James' *Washington Square*, reprinted in *Modern Library* Series (1950), p. 38.

[2] Amos H. Hawley, *The Changing Shape of Metropolitan America*, (Glencoe, Ill., 1956), pp. 14–16.

[3] Based on Baltimore, Boston, Buffalo, Chicago, Cleveland, Detroit, Los Angeles, New York Northeastern New Jersey, San Francisco–Oakland metropolitan areas. U.S. Bureau of Labor Statistics, *Monthly Labor Review*, June 1957, p. 690. U.S. Dept. of Commerce and U.S. Dept. of Labor *Construction Review*, May 1956 to April 1957.

TABLE 1. *Central Cities' Proportion of Population in Thirteen Standard Metropolitan Areas, 1900–1950*

Central cities as % of corresponding standard metropolitan areas

Central Cities	1900	1910	1920	1930	1940	1950
Baltimore	79.6	77.5	86.1	81.7	79.3	71.0
Boston, Lowell, Lawrence[a]	42.6	42.6	41.3	37.0	36.0	34.0
Buffalo	69.3	68.2	67.3	62.9	60.1	53.3
Chicago	81.2	79.4	76.7	72.2	70.4	65.9
Cincinnati	61.8	61.6	63.8	59.7	57.9	55.7
Cleveland	82.8	84.9	82.0	72.4	69.3	62.4
Detroit	66.9	75.9	76.1	72.0	68.3	61.3
Los Angeles	53.9	59.3	57.8	53.2	51.6	45.1
N.Y. City, Jersey City, Newark	77.0	76.4	74.6	70.8	70.2	66.8
Philadelphia	68.4	68.3	67.2	62.2	60.4	56.4
Pittsburgh	41.7	36.3	33.4	33.1	32.3	30.6
St. Louis	71.8	68.4	67.8	60.5	57.0	51.0
San Francisco, Oakland	75.5	73.3	71.6	68.1	64.1	51.8
Total, Listed Central Cities	69.1	68.6	67.7	63.7	62.1	57.2

SOURCE: Donald J. Bogue, *Population Growth in Standard Metropolitan Areas 1900–1950*, Appendix.

[a] As percent of area consisting of the counties of Essex, Middlesex, Norfolk, and Suffolk in Massachusetts. The sum of the four counties differs slightly from the corresponding town-delimited standard metropolitan areas.

To account for the absolute decline in New York City's populations and to appreciate why other cities are likely to experience a similar pattern, one must return to a consideration of the process of growth and structural obsolescence which dominates the central cities. Earlier, we carried the story to the point at which the middle-income groups moved to new neighborhoods further removed from the city's center. But this was not typically the end of the economic life of the structures vacated by them.

The next stage was the familiar one, almost universally observed in the nation's central cities. Most of the structures abandoned by one income group were filled by another group several rungs lower on the income ladder. The new tenants crowded the old structures much more than their predecessors had done. Maintenance and repair standards deteriorated. Ultimately, the middle class areas became slums.

But a careful observation of the neighborhood patterns within central cities indicates that the slums, in turn, are having a population cycle of their own. An initial heavy crowding is eventually followed by a tapering off of populations in the slum areas. The ring of slum population growth crawls outward from the center of the city in a belated imitation of the middle-income group that preceded. The pattern is illustrated by developments in Philadelphia in recent years. The greatest concentration of old dilapidated structures in that city is found in its southeast section, bounded by the Schuylkill and Delaware rivers. Seven out of eight of the one-family dwelling units in this area had been built before 1919 and 26 per cent of the dwelling units in the area were substandard by 1950. In the rest of the city, such dwelling units were much less aged and less dilapidated on the average. The differences were reflected in population changes during the 1940–1950 decade. While the southeast area's population declined by 3 per cent, that of the rest of the city rose by 10 per cent.

The same pattern appeared in Manhattan's lower East Side, at an even earlier date. Here, about two-thirds of the dwelling units had been erected before 1919 and about half of the dwelling units were classified as substandard in the 1940 census. From 1930 to 1940, population on the lower East Side declined 19 per cent while that in the rest of the borough rose 3 per cent. To be sure, some razing of slum structures has occurred in these old areas and elsewhere, a fact which has either hastened the population decline of deteriorated areas or tended to reclaim depopulated areas for other uses. On the whole, however, such razing has commonly failed to match the population decline in the slum districts where it occurred. The picture is one of the reduced use of old slum dwellings and the development of new slums to replace them.

RETAIL JOB MOVEMENT

Inevitably, the number of retail jobs in central cities has changed with the changing pattern of their populations. As households have shifted outward toward the suburbs, the neighborhood retail trade has gone along. This is illustrated by Table 2, which shows how the central city's proportion of retail trade in their respective metropolitan areas has changed in the past quarter century.

But something more than a simple proportionate shift in retail trade has occurred, as evidenced by trends in retail trade in the central business districts of these cities. These districts, as delineated

TABLE 2. *Central Cities' Proportion of Retail Trade*[a] *Employment in Thirteen Standard Metropolitan Areas, 1929–1954* *(paid employees only)*

Central cities as % of corresponding standard metropolitan areas

Central Cities	1929	1939	1948	1954
Baltimore	94.8	91.4	88.3	81.9
Boston, Lowell, Lawrence[b]	61.3	54.5	52.4	48.7
Buffalo	78.9	73.2	70.3	64.5
Chicago	81.7	78.3	75.6	69.1
Cincinnati	79.8	76.8	73.8	69.6
Cleveland	87.7	83.4	80.6	73.5
Detroit	82.2	77.9	72.6	63.3
Los Angeles	70.0	61.7	54.4	48.3
N.Y. City, Jersey City, Newark	79.8	76.1	74.6	67.8
Philadelphia	79.2	70.4	67.8	61.1
Pittsburgh	61.0	55.3	52.5	45.7
St. Louis	79.9	73.1	67.6	61.3
San Francisco, Oakland	85.2	80.7	72.3	63.5
Total, Listed Central Cities	78.0	72.8	69.4	62.7

SOURCES: U.S. Census of Business, 1929, 1939, 1948, 1954.

[a] Coverage varies for the several years. 1948 & 1954 data exclude "Milk Dealers" which are included in the 1929 & 1939 figures. 1929 data also include "automobile garage, repair services" which are covered by the census of Selected Services for the later years. 1929 data are based on full-time employees only.

[b] As percent of area consisting of the counties of Essex, Middlesex, Norfolk, and Suffolk in Massachusetts. The sum of the four counties differs slightly from the corresponding town-delimited standard metropolitan areas.

by the United States Bureau of the Census, typically embrace the main city shopping centers and typically draw their trade from all corners of their respective metropolitan areas. From 1948 to 1954— while the central cities as a whole were slipping in relative positions as retail trade centers—the central business districts of these cities were slipping even faster. Whereas 13 central cities registered a decline of one-tenth in their share of the 13 metropolitan area's retail trade employment in which they were located, the 13 central business districts' share fell by one-quarter. Indeed in seven of these central business districts, there was not only a relative decline in retail sales but an absolute decline as well, a decline all the more remarkable because it occurred during a period when retail sales in the nation were growing prodigiously.

Behind this decline in the central business district's role as a retail shopping center, there lie three main forces. One of these already has been mentioned—the fact that populations in the oldest portions of the central city have tended to grow more slowly than for the city in total or have actually declined in absolute number in some neighborhoods. Another force has been the relatively slower rate of growth of the number of jobs of all kinds in the central cities, a tendency which has reduced the number of prospective "downtown" shoppers; we shall have more to say about this tendency at a later point. Finally—perhaps most importantly—there has been the almost universal preference of the shopper to use the automobile instead of mass transit facilities in the journey from home to bargain counter.

There is not much need to labor the point that a revolutionary shift in transportation preferences has been occurring. The shift has been documented copiously in other sources.[4] The implications of the shift are pointed up by the experience recorded in New York City's central business district. Between 1940 and 1956, the number of persons entering the district on a typical business day had barely changed; it was 3,271,000 on the earlier date and 3,316,000 on the later. Yet during this same period, the number of motor vehicles entering the district had risen from 351,200 to 519,300 daily, a rise of 48 per cent. One can also be reasonably certain that the number of cars circulating entirely within the central business district rose by something like the same magnitude during the 16-year period.

This rise, one need hardly point out, has taxed the obsolescent street system of the area almost beyond endurance. Congestion has always been characteristic of some obsolescent sections in most central cities; Boston's narrow crooked street system in the neighborhoods of Scollay Square and the Washington Street area, New York's street system in the Greenwich Village district, and the narrow north-south streets of Philadelphia's and Baltimore's downtown grids were never designed for the automobile and could scarcely accommodate the horse-drawn dray. But the revolutionary shift away from mass transit has made congestion throughout these and other central city areas widespread and endemic; and some of the results are seen in the decline of shopping in the central city.

[4] See particularly Wilfred Owen, *The Metropolitan Transportation Problem* (Washington, 1956).

WHOLESALE JOB MOVEMENT

From the ancient days when central cities were principally market towns, wholesaling has been a significant feature of city activity. Goods carried overseas by ships to Atlantic or Pacific ports; articles floated on rivers and lakes or dragged overland to St. Louis, Chicago, Pittsburgh and Denver; these formed the nucleus for the wholesaling function in the towns which were to become our great central cities. Here, the goods were weighed, inspected and bought on the spot.

The ties between wholesaling and the institutions of the city grew more and more firm with the passage of time. In the 19th century, the city was the mecca where the wholesaler from distant markets arranged his financing, indulged his more exotic appetites, and acquired his trade intelligence. Reminiscing about that period in New York, Jacob Knickerbocker says:

> In the 50's [the 1850's], the wholesale business was located in the lower sections of the city. . . . The position and activities of the salesmen were rather unique. Each had his list of customers from the various sections of the country. When they came to New York to purchase most of them also expected to have a "good time" and looked to the salesmen to provide it for them. Sometimes the entertainment graded the extent of the purchases. . . .[5]

So dominant was the central city in this type of activity that even as late as 1929, the central cities in 13 metropolitan areas accounted for over 93 per cent of the wholesaling jobs in those areas. From that date on, however, there was a rapid decline in the relative importance of wholesaling jobs in all these cities, as Table 3 shows.

Once again, the forces which lie behind this shift can be traced in part to transportation changes and to the advanced state of obsolescence of the central city. On the transport side, the shift in goods movement from rail to truck has freed wholesalers from the compelling need to be on a rail line and has weakened the advantage of being close to a rail junction. As long as wholesalers relied principally on the rail lines in our principal central cities, the fact that the point of convergence of different lines was typically within the central city acted as an attractive force. Once the truck began to be

[5] Jacob Knickerbocker, *Then and Now* (Boston, 1939), p. 39.

TABLE 3. *Central Cities' Proportion of Wholesale Employment*[a]
in Thirteen Standard Metropolitan Areas, 1929–1954
(paid employees only)

Central cities as % of corresponding standard metropolitan areas

Central Cities	1929	1939	1948	1954
Baltimore	99.5	97.4	94.7	94.2
Boston, Lowell, Lawrence[b]	82.9	79.7	75.1	66.6
Buffalo	93.4	91.0	90.0	85.4
Chicago	96.9	94.1	91.6	86.6
Cincinnati	96.2	92.7	87.8	86.5
Cleveland	97.1	97.9	96.4	93.5
Detroit	94.8	92.0	90.1	76.8
Los Angeles	80.7	70.1	71.9	66.3
N.Y. City, Jersey City, Newark	95.1	93.1	90.4	84.6
Philadelphia	93.6	91.0	88.3	81.8
Pittsburgh	88.6	83.6	82.9	75.6
St. Louis	89.7	92.7	90.7	85.5
San Francisco, Oakland	96.1	95.0	94.4	85.1
Total, Listed Central Cities	93.1	90.3	88.1	81.7

SOURCES: U.S. Census of Business, 1929, 1939, 1948, 1954.

[a] Data for the several years are not strictly comparable due to the various changes in coverage.

[b] As percent of area consisting of the counties of Essex, Middlesex, Norfolk, and Suffolk in Massachusetts. The sum of the four counties differs slightly from the corresponding town-delimited standard metropolitan areas.

used, however, the attraction of the central city as the preferred distribution point for wholesalers was weakened.

Yet it should not be assumed that the shift from rail to truck is the only transportation force which is pushing wholesalers with stocks from locations in the central cty. As we indicated earlier, the best location for distribution to local markets is not necessarily at the center of the market. As the proportion of the total market outside the congested center grows, and as the relative level of congestion in the center area increases, the case for locating outside the center progressively improves. This is one of the elements which has produced the trend shown in Table 3.

Some of the forces which have pushed wholesaling and distribution from the city centers, however, stem from changes within the warehouse. Goods-handling has been undergoing a technological revolution in recent decades. In some instances, the city-style multistory warehouse has been readily adaptable to these changes. But for the most part, the palletizing of goods and the use of fork-lift trucks and drag lines have created a substantial demand for horizontal warehousing space, with wide bays and high ceilings. These are developments which have not yet spent their full force.

MANUFACTURING JOB MOVEMENT

For as long as the record can be constructed, the major central cities of the nation have been declining in importance as manufacturing centers relative to their suburban hinterlands. As Table 4 shows, virtually every one of the 13 metropolitan areas depicted there experienced this relative decline of the central city.

Once again, it is well to make a distinction between a *relative* decline and an *absolute* decline in the jobs contained in the central city limits. In recent years—from 1947 to 1954, for example—the cities of Boston, Chicago, Detroit, Pittsburgh, St. Louis, and San Francisco recorded not only a *relative* decline but also an *absolute* decline in the number of these jobs.

Manufacturing enterprises can differ so much from one another in their locational needs that one hesitates to generalize about the movement of these jobs out of the central cities. Some industries have been quite invulnerable to the creeping obsolescence of the central city's environment; others have been highly sensitive to it. Some have departed from their central city location at a precipitate rate; a few are still as highly concentrated in central city locations as they were a quarter century ago. Nevertheless, there are a few generalizations which apply in some degree to most of the manu-facturing economy found in large metropolitan areas.

To understand the forces which determined industrial location in our major central cities a century or two ago, one has to turn once again to the overwhelming restraints imposed by problems of transportation. When these cities were in their embryo state, such industry as existed—the mills and metal-working shops, and even the tanneries and abattoirs—necessarily lay inside or close by the city. For the city itself typically sat athwart the natural transporta-tion routes of the area, such as the rivers, lakes and mountain passes. And the city typically provided much of the market and all the labor which the factory employed.

By the middle of the 19th century, however, the problem of industrial location had grown rather more complex. By this time, large manufacturing plants were no longer a rarity and the development of the railroad and the horse trolley were offering them a little more latitude in the choice of a site suitable for the construction of substantial factory structures. Still, these plants were as reliant as ever on rail or water for their transport needs. And since the major rail junctures had commonly developed within the limits of the larger cities, special advantages still existed in remaining in the vicinity of the cities. What is more, homes and factories still could not be too far apart—no further than an hour's journey by foot, ferry or trolley. This, too, contributed to the cohesive development of the city.

In the course of time, however, some of the more noisome industries began to feel the pressures to locate in less constricted spaces. Abattoirs, smelters, and other unsocial industries began to look for sites where no inhibitions would exist to polluting the air or water. Industries of this sort accordingly began to locate in what was then regarded as the far outskirts of the growing cities.

Nevertheless, though the sites which they selected in the late 19th century often seemed remote from the city limits at the time, the cities' growth over the next several decades soon engulfed them. Today, these industries often sit in little enclaves surrounded by urban development; within these enclaves they share a blight perpetuated by the sometimes unavoidable by-products of their operations. Yet in many cases, these industries have little apparent choice but to remain where they are. For their next move—overleaping and locating beyond the urban development which surrounds them —would frequently carry them into territory well removed from their markets or their labor force.

Most of the movement from the central city, however, came later and was spurred by other factors. As time went on, manufacturing structures, like residential structures, became obsolescent. The process of obsolescence was greatly accelerated by the introduction of assembly line techniques in manufacture and by revolutionary developments in materials handling to which we earlier referred. As a result of these changes, as we now all know, the old multi-story mill-style building became increasingly inappropriate for many operations which it had previously housed. The preferred type of structure became the elongated one-story building, laid out on large sites with the easy possibility of expansion in any direction. The ad-

TABLE 4. *Central Cities' Proportion of Manufacturing Production Workers*[a]
in Thirteen Metropolitan Areas, 1899–1954

Central cities as % of corresponding metropolitan areas

Central Cities	BASED ON INDUSTRIAL AREAS[b]				BASED ON STANDARD METROPOLITAN AREAS[c]			
	1899	1909	1919	1929	1929	1939	1947	1954
Baltimore	91.8	87.1	88.0	86.0	85.5	72.0	70.4	62.9
Boston, Lowell, Lawrence	22.3	22.3	23.9	26.6[e]	40.6[e]	40.4	40.5	34.7
Buffalo	74.7	68.7	65.1	59.8	59.8	49.8	47.9	43.1
Chicago	88.0	82.0	77.7	73.6	73.6	71.9	70.4	65.2
Cincinnati	75.4	65.9	61.8	56.1[d]	67.7[d]	72.6	71.3	59.8
Cleveland	91.0	82.5	85.3	83.1[d]	89.1[d]	86.3	83.0	69.5
Detroit	83.6	88.1	63.2	75.6	75.2	57.7	60.3	53.5
Los Angeles	83.4	80.2	70.5	66.4[e]	66.6[e]	55.4	46.9	42.3
N.Y. City, Jersey City, Newark	69.9	67.5	61.7	61.3[e]	69.8[e]	67.9	66.3	63.0
Philadelphia	78.4	74.1	60.4	65.7	65.7	61.0	61.3	56.0
Pittsburgh	53.1	35.4	34.0	27.1	27.1	22.6	23.0	22.6
St. Louis	80.6	72.7	70.6	70.6	69.9	69.7	70.6	63.9
San Francisco, Oakland	81.2	60.5	46.1	48.5[e]	68.2[e]	62.3	55.9	50.4
Total, Listed Central Cities[f]	69.3	64.8	60.4	61.7	66.1	61.9	60.8	55.5
Total, 48 Central Cities[g]					66.5	62.3	62.1	57.5

SOURCES: Based on the manufacturing censuses of the U.S. Bureau of the Census. The 1899–1929 series of central cities as percentages of their corresponding industrial areas were taken from Glenn E. McLaughlin, *Growth of American Manufacturing Areas* (Pittsburgh, 1938), pp. 98, 129. The 1929–1939 series of central cities as percentages of their corresponding standard metropolitan areas were based on data given in Evelyn M. Kitagawa and Donald J. Bogue, *Suburbanization of Manufacturing Activity within Standard Metropolitan Areas* (Oxford, Ohio, 1955), pp. 132–139. The 1947 and 1954 data are those reported in the State Bulletins of the *1954 Census of Manufactures*.

a The coverage of industries is not strictly comparable from year to year due to the various changes in industry classifications and definitions of the several censuses. No adjustment other than those made by McLaughlin and Bogue has been attempted. For details, see McLaughlin, p. 99, footnote, and Bogue, pp. 4–5.

b For definition of the industrial areas, see U.S. Bureau of the Census, *15th Census of the U.S., Manufactures, 1929*, Vol. III, p. 11, and McLaughlin, p. 11.

c For definition and area covered by the various standard metropolitan areas (S.M.A.), see Kitagawa and Bogue, p. 13, and U.S. Bureau of the Census, *Census of Manufactures, 1947*, Vol. III, p. 32. The Boston area given here is based on whole counties while the census since 1939 has delimited the New England areas along town boundaries. (See Kitagawa and Bogue, pp. 13, 139, 140.)

d In general, for the 13 areas given here, with the exception of Cincinnati and Cleveland, the various S.M.A.'s are either identical with or larger than the corresponding industrial areas. The industrial area of Cincinnati includes one more county; namely, Butler County, Ohio, than the Cincinnati S.M.A. The Cleveland S.M.A. is substituting Lake County (Ohio) for the industrial area's Lorain County (Ohio). In terms of manufacturing, Lorain County was more important than Lake County in 1929.

e For the central cities of Boston, New York, and San Francisco, more than one city is considered as the central city in the 1929–1954 S.M.A. series. According to the 1899–1929 industrial area series, only one single city is taken as the central city. For the central city of Los Angeles, the discrepancy between the two 1929 figures is due to the fact that the S.M.A. series is based on the 1932 expanded boundaries of the city of Los Angeles.

f These are the 13 large areas selected by McLaughlin. See McLaughlin, pp. 13–15.

g These are the S.M.A.'s with at least 40,000 manufacturing employees in 1947. The 1947 census reports listed 53 S.M.A.'s with this qualification. For three of the 53, 1954 data are not complete. 1954 census also combined four of the New England S.M.A.'s into two.

vent of trucking was of course of considerable importance in this development. No longer confined to railside or waterside locations, manufacturers were free to look for sites over much more extensive areas.

There were times, to be sure, when the manufacturer replaced his obsolescent old structure on the very site where his original plant had stood or on a site nearby. There were numerous advantages in such a course: Some of the sunk capital in the old site could be salvaged by such a process; some of the old labor force could be retained; some of the neighborhood contacts in the central city, such as repair services and supply sources, could still be utilized.

By and large, the possibility of carving out a new site or greatly enlarging an old site in the central city became increasingly difficult with the passage of time. Zoning regulations were a part of the problem; these regulations, which first appeared in American cities to any extent in the 1920's, often inhibited the expansion of manufacturing in neighborhoods where some manufacturing already existed. To be sure, such restraints ordinarily did not apply to plants in existence prior to the adoption of the zoning requirements. But they did operate to discourage the radical expansion or total replacement of plants in many city areas.

Even where zoning ordinances played no role, however, the assembly of a city site was a formidable operation. As the city developed, most of its land was cut up in small parcels and covered with durable structures of one kind or another. The problem of assembling these sites, in the absence of some type of condemnation power, required a planning horizon of many years and a willingness to risk the possibility of price gouging by the last holdout. Moreover, once a site was acquired, razing costs alone could easily run on the order of $50,000 an acre in current dollar terms. All told, the value of the site could amount to 20 or 30 times more than that of an equivalent area in a developed suburban location. In these circumstances, it was small wonder that many manufacturing establishments chose a suburban location in replacing their obsolescent structures.

Other factors were also operating to push manufacturing into the suburbs. Some of the main forces which previously had drawn manufacturing plants to the centers of the old cities were being weakened by technological change. We have already observed how the truck and the automobile were providing a new mobility to goods and to the labor force, allowing manufacturers to locate at greater distances from existing clusters of homes and factories. In addition, some of the other features unique to the old cities—some of the "external economies" of such cities—were being found over increasingly wider areas. Special power facilities, special transportation services, a variety of repair services, all of these were being extended in the course of time to an increasing number of points outside the older industrial districts.

In tracing the outward movement of manufacturing plants for the central city, one must not overlook the special problems of the plant which operates from industrial lofts and other multi-tenanted quarters. Plants of this sort, anxious to avoid any investment in bricks and mortar, typically have had to take their space where they found it. Accordingly, they have been limited in their locational choices either to industrial buildings constructed for multiple tenancy or to obsolete factory buildings abandoned by their original users.

Establishments of this sort also have tended to move outward from the central city. For with the passage of time, factory buildings have become available to an increasing extent for subdivision and rental in suburban industrial areas. And the scale of existing rentals for such space has been sufficiently low to prevent the construction of new industrial loft structures either in the central cities' confines or elsewhere.[6] Besides, the fact that some of the "external economies" unique to the old cities were appearing on the outskirts as well, removed a major obstacle to suburban locations for many small firms.

The net effect of these outward tendencies has been to delineate more sharply the special characteristics of the central city as a site for manufacturing operations. More and more, the central city has come to specialize in the "communications-oriented" segment of manufacturing. More and more, too, the emphasis has been on the "unstandardized," the uncertain, and the exotic type of manufacturing specialization. And there is every reason to expect that, to the

[6] Calculations based on the cost structure in the New York Metropolitan Region suggest that new multi-tenanted industrial structures—even if built on sites acquired at no cost—would have to command an annual rental of more than $3 per square foot whereas the prevailing rental rate in existing structures tends to be less than $1.00.

extent that manufacturing remains in the central city, these forms of specialization will grow more pronounced still.

OFFICE JOB MOVEMENT

Those who are concerned with analyzing the economic future of central cities are dogged at the outset with special problems of data gathering. For enough has been written here to underline the point that the business of cities is of a kind which tends to evade the census-taker and which, once detected, resists statistical classification—namely, the new, shifting, different, "unstandardized" operation. The problem reaches new intensity with respect to the activities which go on in the offices of the nation's great central cities.

Whereas manufacturing, transportation, retail trade, and wholesale trade are economic activities whose existence is easily recognized and catalogued, many aspects of office activity are more difficult to classify. Where the work of a firm or an institution is such that all of it is performed in an office setting—as is the case with banks, insurance companies, securities dealers, and related institutions—the problem is not so difficult. But most office activities—most record-keeping, data-processing, purchasing, routing, billing, controlling, expediting, designing, scheduling, and researching—have developed as adjuncts of producing, transporting, and selling and are not ordinarily identified and enumerated as an independent operation. Yet because the central cities are coming more and more to be reliant for their economic existence upon office activity, it is indispensable to probe into this amorphous group of operations and to draw what generalizations can be pulled out of the unstructured and unsatisfying data.

The financial institutions, we have observed, were among the more easily recognized office activities. From their earliest beginnings, these activities sought out central city locations. We have dwelt upon the forces conducive to central city growth enough by this time to have indicated why banks and security markets should have gravitated toward the very heart of the old cities. "Information" was the greatest stock-in-trade of the security dealer and the banker—information about the credit of an individual, the affairs of an enterprise, the condition of a trade, the politics of a nation; in the ordinary course, such information could best be acquired at the points where ships arrived and departed, where travelers congregated, where news was gathered, and where the posts were swiftest and most frequent.

Besides, the most critical business of these financial entities ordinarily was that of negotiation—the subtle jockeying between buyer and seller, borrower and lender. This is a type of activity which one could scarcely leave to the mails, to the telegraph, or even to the telephone, except where the negotiations were perfunctory, routinized and repetitive.

The pull of the big cities was not due solely to these factors, however. Some aspects of the financial community's activities were indeed sufficiently routinized and standardized that a central city location would not have been absolutely compelling. Insurance company activities, for instance, are largely of a routine and repetitive character. Where such companies chose to centralize their record keeping activities in a single office, the problem was to find a large enough pool of literate clerks to handle the volume of work generated by such an office. In general, women did better than men at this sort of work. Accordingly, the problem became one of locating at a point where a large number of literate women would be assembled daily. The obvious location indicated was a large city, where literacy rates were high, at a point in the city close by mass transit facilities.

The affinity of the financial institutions for the central city was so marked in 1947 that in eight metropolitan areas every major branch of the financial community—banking, insurance, and securities dealers—had more than four-fifths of its employment in the central cities.

As the nation's larger manufacturing, transport, and utility companies developed central offices sufficiently large to make a separate establishment feasible, they too were pulled to the downtown areas of the cities, reacting to much the same forces as had drawn the financial institutions to such locations. One of the functions of these central offices as they developed was to be close to the trade currents—to know what was going on in markets, in technology, in finance. Another was the subtle business of negotiation. Besides, like the insurance companies, their labor requirements were large quantities of literate clerks and stenographers. Their indicated locations, therefore, were the downtown sections of the nation's great cities.

In the end, this use of the central business district tended to elbow out competing uses. The capacity of the office to preempt the downtown area stemmed in part from the relative intensity of its need for central locations. It arose in part also from the special insensitivity of many office activities to the cost of space. Office space costs constitute an incidental fraction of the total costs of manufacturing companies; they involve the prestige center of the enterprise; they affect the daily surroundings and contacts of the firm's elite; accordingly, their location is less prone to determination on a dry-as-dust least-cost calculation than a manufacturing facility or than a warehousing location would be.

As a major fount of employment for a variety of related services, the central offices and the financial institutions managed to draw to the downtown portions of central cities a considerable variety of appended activities. Advertising agencies, employment agencies, management advisory services, addressing and mailing services, all were drawn to the area, where they might provide the type of service which their customers demanded. In 1948, the 13 central cities covered earlier accounted for 94 per cent of the employment in their metropolitan areas' business services.

Nevertheless, although all of these activities have grown in the central city, they have also shared to some degree in the general outward redistribution of population and jobs. In the first place, a considerable proportion of the financial community's activities has come to be oriented to residential neighborhoods. With the much more widespread ownership of personal savings and checking accounts and with the growing use of consumer credit, a considerable segment of banking activity has taken on the locational attributes of any consumer-oriented service. The outward shift of residences, coupled with that of manufacturing, wholesaling and retail trade, has accordingly led to a redistribution of the financial facilities which service them. In the brief period from 1947 to 1956, for eight selected metropolitan areas, there was a modest outward shift in each category of financial facilities except insurance carriers.

This still leaves a significant nub of office employment, located in the central city, which has no obvious reason for dispersal to the suburbs. Just how large this cluster may be is quite unclear, since the statistics seem hopelessly incomplete on this score. But many central offices, business service offices, insurance companies, and "downtown" financial institutions must probably be counted in this category.

By all the signs, the activities of this sector of the nation's economy should continue to grow, perhaps at a rate much faster than of the economy as a whole. Yet even here—even in this stronghold of big city employment—there are certain factors to be taken into account in appraising the future ties to the central city.

One of these is the fact that as central cities decline in population, and as Negroes and other groups with more restricted job opportunities constitute a larger proportion of the population that remains, the young women who have constituted so large a proportion of the labor force of these office installations will become more and more remote from the downtown portions of the central cities. With commuting distances lengthening and mass transit facilities deteriorating in most cities, the question is raised whether the downtown area will continue to be the optimum point at which to collect the preferred office labor force.

A second factor which could affect the growth of central city office employment is the impact of new data-processing and communication techniques on employment. One must be careful not to exaggerate the speed or extent of the shifts which these developments will produce. The introduction of new data-processing systems is a slow and costly business. Besides, its introduction often stimulates the demand for new and timelier data in the firm, thus blunting its labor-displacing effects. Yet there is no denying that such innovations can suppress the growth in office manpower, change the nature of required office skills, and shift the preferred location of some office functions out of the central city. The repetitive, standardized processes of the office are likely to be most amenable to an out-of-city location, while the elite functions are unlikely to be much affected.

The introduction of mass-data processing equipment has another implication for location. It opens up the possibility of central data-handling for the multi-plant or multi-warehouse firm which previously had been performing many of its office functions on a regional or local basis. This in turn creates the possibility of a redelegation of decisions to the central office—decisions on inventories, shipments, production schedules and the like. To the extent that the office function grows, therefore, the growth may well occur to a disproportionate extent in the office districts of the larger central cities, at the expense of the regional centers.

The possibility that only the largest cities may be the principal beneficiaries of continued office growth—indeed, the possibility that they may be the only beneficiaries—is raised also by the increased use of air travel by business executives. All of the locational implications of such travel are not yet clear. But one of the consequences of the use of such travel is that far-flung plants, warehouses and sales offices are no longer so remote from head-quarters as they used to be. Accordingly, the risks of operating through absentee management and the need to delegate decision-making to the field may seem somewhat reduced.

Of course the development of air travel may be read two ways. For the availability of such air travel opens up the possibility of stationing key corporate offices in the field, yet being able to summon them to headquarters on a few hours' notice. But the odds seem heavy that the increased mobility among executives will not be exploited by dispersing them to the field but rather by gathering them in to central points; that in the rival pulls for more face-to-face contact among top executives and more face-to-face contact with plant managers, the former pull will be the stronger. This, too, suggests that "central office cities" may grow more so, at the expense of the lesser regional office centers. But it would be comforting if hard data could be brought to bear to test these conjectures.

SUMMARY

As one fits these various trends into a coherent whole, they suggest the possibility that we may have entered upon a new phase in the development of the large central cities of the nation. At the very center of such cities—more so in the larger than in the smaller ones—there is every reason to expect continued vitality. Office activities in the nation are expanding and will continue to expand. The central cities may not capture quite as high a proportion of such activity as they have in the past, but there is not much doubt that absolute increases in such employment will occur. Nor is there much doubt that, to the extent that they occur, they will offer a continued stimulus to some central business districts.

This activity aside, one sees only a growing obsolescence in the rest of the central city beyond its central business district. There is nothing in view calculated to interrupt the cycle so far evident in the old cities. When middle-income structures reach an advanced stage of obsolescence, they will be converted to intensive low-income use. The ancient slums will be partially abandoned, as they have been in the past, for the newer ones; populations will thin out in the former and rise in the latter, in a wave which moves gradually outward to the edges of the city and into the older portions of the suburban towns.

The outward movement of people will be matched by an outward movement of jobs. Retail trade will follow the populations. Manufacturing and wholesaling establishments will continue to respond to obsolescence by looking for new quarters and by renting in structures in the suburban industrial areas where obsolescence is less advanced. The movement of jobs will reinforce the movement of residences.

Beyond the central business district, therefore, but within the confines of the central city, there is likely to be a long-run decline in the intensive use of space as sites for jobs and homes. Will such space be converted to other uses? It is difficult to detect any actual or incipient private demand for city space which is of a magnitude calculated to replace such prior uses. Modern factory space is ruled out by the high costs of recapturing the site; new multi-story lofts face a poor market, since they will be competing with obsolescent factories vacated by their prior owners; office space, however greatly it expands, can scarcely be expected to fill more than a minuscule area, largely concentrated toward the city center; high-income renters may fill a little more space, but not much.

This leaves two possibilities: that middle-income families may decide to return to the cities in great numbers; or that subsidized governmental intervention, such as low-income housing or open-space projects, may be expanded to such levels as to constitute a significant space-using force. The first possibility would fly in the face of deep-seated historical trends, based on powerful sociological forces. The latter demands a scale of intervention much larger than any which heretofore has been contemplated.

2 Housing Markets and Public Policy *

WILLIAM G. GRIGSBY

From the standpoint of public policy, perhaps the most critical aspect of housing market dynamics concerns the seeming inability of even the best neighborhoods either to resist permanently the forces of decay and obsolescence or to regenerate themselves without public intervention once these forces have set in. With a few notable exceptions,[1] the *residential* real estate market works only once. It creates, alters, maintains, and improves, and eventually discards assets, but seems incapable of providing for their replacement on the site. The invisible hand, which only infrequently produces the optimum spatial deployment of land uses, with respect to renewal typically produces nothing at all. The impotence of the market mechanism, however, is only partial. Although incapable of overcoming the basic barriers to continuous renewal, namely the immobility of buildings and abutting rights of way, the diversity of ownership in real property, and the low income of families in areas most in need of attention, business enterprise is constantly at work revitalizing the urban structure within the constraints imposed upon

* Reprinted from *Housing Markets and Public Policy*, Philadelphia, University of Pennsylvania Press, 1963, pp. 251–283.
[1] Examples are luxury high-rise apartments on Manhattan's East Side which replaced rundown structures in a variety of uses, the Georgetown section in Washington, D.C., and many of the residential blocks in downtown Philadelphia.

24

it by law and lack of full knowledge as to the possible consequences of various decisions. Urban redevelopment will reshape in several important ways the dynamics of the housing market. At the same time, however, the mechanics of the market process are such as to impose certain strictures on redevelopment itself. For federal and local agencies to maximize the full potential of private investment, there must be a more adequate understanding of the consequences for the entire housing supply of particular forms of public intervention. This in turn means better comprehension of the underlying needs and desires which seek expression in the market place.

It is the purpose of this chapter to provide some of the knowledge necessary for effective governmental action in this area. Four general questions will be explored. What is the size and location of the urban housing problem? Is it improving or becoming worse? What are the barriers to the elimination of substandard living accommodations? What steps, other than those already being taken, might hasten a solution to this vexing social dilemma? Although complete agreement with the views expressed here is unlikely, it is hoped that the facts that will be presented will resolve some of the controversy over residential renewal that has persisted up to the present moment.

SIZE AND LOCATION OF THE PROBLEM

Despite the much publicized opulence of the United States, a large proportion of American families reside in substandard housing. At the time of the 1960 Census, fully one-sixth of the country's 53,000,000 households lived in dwellings which were dilapidated or lacking in plumbing facilities or both (Table 1). An additional but unknown number of families were in dwelling units that were not classified as deficient by Census enumerators, but which have been found to be in serious violation of local building codes.[2] Still other households live in structures which themselves are adequate, but which are overcrowded or in undesirable surroundings. As a rough

[2] For example, in some Census Tracts in Philadelphia, the number of dwelling units not in conformance with the local code has exceeded the Census figure for deficient units by as much as two to one. In Philadelphia, and probably in most other cities, local inspectors are more thoroughly trained than Census enumerators, and, unlike the latter who may obtain all their information at the front door, personally examine the interior of each dwelling unit. More important, the Census reports only two or three types of deficiencies.

TABLE 1. *Occupied Dwelling Units Dilapidated or Lacking Facilities**
By Type of Tenure, United States, 1950, 1956, and 1960

Type of Tenure	1950	1956	1960	NET ATTRITION OF SUBSTANDARD UNITS		ANNUAL RATE OF ATTRITION OF SUBSTANDARD UNITS	
				April '50– Dec. '56	*Jan. '57– April '60*	*April '50– Dec. '56*	*Jan. '57– April '60*
Owner-Occupied—Total	23,559,996	30,120,509	32,796,000				
Not dilapidated, lacking facilities	5,746,779	3,720,743	2,986,000				
Dilapidated	1,377,493	1,072,010	886,000				
Total substandard	7,124,272	4,792,753	3,872,000	2,331,519	1,050,000	345,410	323,000
Substandard as a % of all owner-occupied	31	16	12				
Renter-Occupied—Total	19,266,315	19,753,414	20,224,000				
Not dilapidated, lacking facilities	5,268,455	3,491,023	3,440,000				
Dilapidated	2,400,915	1,954,580	1,495,000				
Total substandard	7,669,370	5,445,603	4,935,000	2,223,767	700,000	329,446	215,000
Substandard as a % of all renter-occupied	41	29	25				
Total Occupied	42,826,281	49,873,923	53,020,000				
Not dilapidated, lacking facilities	11,015,234	7,211,766	6,426,000				
Dilapidated	3,778,508	3,026,590	2,381,000				
Total substandard	14,793,642	10,238,356	8,807,000	4,555,286	1,750,000	674,856	538,000
Substandard as a % of all occupied	35	21	17				

SOURCE: *1950 Census of Housing, NHI,* and preliminary report from *1960 Census of Housing.*
* Data for 1960, but not 1950 and 1956, include an estimate of the number of substandard units in structures for which no information was obtained. Attrition figures for 1957–60 have been adjusted to reflect this difference.
NOTE: There were two changes in definition between 1950 and 1960 which must be recognized in making any comparisons between years. These changes are explained in the text.

approximation, it appears that at least one-quarter of our population is not in a decent home or suitable living environment.

Area Variations

It is illuminating to observe not only the over-all magnitude of the current problem, but also its spatial distribution. First of all, housing conditions[3] in the central cities of metropolitan areas do not appear to be appreciably worse than in the suburban rings (Table 2). The proportions of substandard units in the two areas are 13 per cent and 11 per cent, respectively. The small difference hardly accords with popular conceptions. What is forgotten is that nearly every declining central city has its decaying satellites: the Newarks, Garys, and Camdens.

TABLE 2. *Changes in the Number of Occupied Substandard Dwelling Units Inside and Outside Standard Metropolitan Areas, 1950–56*

	1950		1956	
Area	Number*	Per Cent of Occupied Inventory	Number*	Per Cent of Occupied Inventory
Inside SMA's—In Central Cities				
Dilapidated	....	..	669,767	4
Nondilapidated, lacking facilities ..	....	..	1,308,255	9
Total occupied substandard	....	..	1,978,022	13
Inside SMA's—Outside Central Cities				
Dilapidated	....	..	441,563	3
Nondilapidated, lacking facilities ..	....	..	1,107,415	8
Total occupied substandard	....	..	1,548,978	11
Inside SMA's—Total				
Dilapidated	1,404,112	6	1,111,330	4
Nondilapidated, lacking facilities ..	3,814,211	16	2,415,670	8
Total occupied substandard	5,218,323	22	3,527,000	12
Outside SMA's				
Dilapidated	2,374,296	13	1,915,260	10
Nondilapidated, lacking facilities ..	7,201,023	40	4,796,096	25
Total occupied substandard	9,575,319	54	6,711,356	35
United States—Total				
Dilapidated	3,778,408	9	3,026,590	6
Nondilapidated, lacking facilities ..	11,015,234	26	7,211,766	15
Total occupied substandard	14,793,642	35	10,238,356	21

SOURCE: *1950 Census of Housing* and the *NHI.*

* Does not include an estimate of the number of substandard units in structures for which no information was obtained.

[3] Excluding for the moment neighborhood environment and overcrowding.

Second, and much more striking, the worst housing is not concentrated in the metropolitan areas where all the attention is focused, but is equally a problem in the smaller towns and rural areas. In fact, only 35 per cent of the occupied substandard housing in 1956 was in metropolitan centers.

Or, to put it in terms of rates, only one-eighth of the occupied metropolitan housing stock, as compared with almost three-eighths of the nonmetropolitan inventory, was substandard. This is not, as might be supposed, solely a reflection of the relative lack in nonmetropolitan areas of facilities which are not a requisite to a decent living environment in rural homes. The nonmetropolitan areas do account, as would be expected, for almost two-thirds of all occupied dwelling units lacking facilities, but they have an equal proportion of the occupied dilapidated housing as well.[4] If homes that lack facilities are excluded from the nonmetropolitan, but not from the metropolitan count of substandard units, the rate of substandardness in both areas is about the same.

In addition to the differences between metropolitan and non-metropolitan areas, there are huge variations among metropolitan areas themselves. Of the nine Standard Metropolitan Areas (SMA's) surveyed in the 1956 *National Housing Inventory* (*NHI*), the proportion of occupied substandard housing ranged from a high of almost 20 per cent in Atlanta to less than 5 per cent in Los Angeles. The proportion of substandard units in all the SMA's showed declines from 1950 to 1956, but absolute change varied greatly. Dallas, Detroit, Los Angeles, and Philadelphia lost almost half of their substandard units, whereas the improvement in other areas was more modest. These variations reflect both income and market differences which must be carefully analyzed in formulating renewal programs for specific cities.

Finally, there are significant regional differences in the amount and rate of substandardness. The South, with 1,240,000 dwellings that were dilapidated and another 3,097,000 that lacked the basic plumbing facilities, accounted for almost half of the total occupied substandard inventory in the nation in 1960. It also had the highest proportion of deficient units, 28 per cent, as compared with 10 per

---

[4] Separate figures for urban and rural sectors of nonmetropolitan areas are not available, but judging from 1950 Census figures, it would appear that the rate of substandardness is probably still over one-half in rural sections, as compared with only one-fourth or one-fifth in urban places outside of SMA's.

cent, 15 per cent, and 8 per cent in the Northeast, North Central, and West, respectively.

Tenure Variations

In formulating strategy for the elimination of substandard housing, it is essential to distinguish between the owner-occupied and rental stock, because the response of landlords to various housing programs is quite different from that of a family living in its own home. It can be seen in Table 3 that 56 per cent of unsatisfactory units in the United States in 1956 were occupied by renters, and that the percentage of dwellings with deficiencies was almost twice as high in the rental as in the owner-occupied inventory. This difference between the two sectors is even greater inside metropolitan areas. Here almost two-thirds of the substandard occupied housing in 1956 were rental units. The discrepancy increases still further inside the central cities of SMA's, where over 80 per cent of the occupied substandard stock was in rental tenure. By contrast, this

TABLE 3. *Incidence of Substandard Occupied Dwelling Units** By Area and Tenure, 1956

Substandard Dwelling Units	United States	INSIDE SMA'S		Outside SMA's
		Total	Inside Central Cities	
Owner-Occupied				
Number	4,792,753	1,216,870	369,153	3,575,883
Per cent of total owner-occupied	16	7	5	29
Per cent of total occupied substandard	44	34	19	53
Renter-Occupied				
Number	5,445,603	2,310,130	1,608,869	3,135,473
Per cent of total renter-occupied	28	19	19	46
Per cent of total occupied substandard	56	66	81	47
Total				
Number	10,238,356	3,527,000	1,978,022	6,711,356
Per cent of total occupied ..	21	12	13	35

SOURCE: *NHI.*
* Does not include an estimate of substandard units in structures for which no information was obtained.

figure drops to 47 per cent outside SMA's. These figures, it will be remembered, do not include dwellings which met Census standards but which were overcrowded or in violation of local codes or in an unhealthful environment. Similar differences between the rental and owner-occupied sectors would be expected among these units also. Thus, in the areas we normally think of in discussions of urban renewal, the housing problem is primarily in the rental stock.

Racial Variations

The problem of slums has frequently been described as one of racial minorities. For example, over 70 per cent of families displaced from Title I clearance projects have been nonwhite.[5] Bureau of the Census data for 1960 do not, however, indicate such a pronounced correlation between housing conditions and race. Nonwhite families living in substandard housing numbered 2,309,000, but this figure was little more than one-quarter of the national total. The proportion of nonwhites with inadequate shelter was double that for whites, but even so, over two-thirds of the nonwhite population resided in standard units. In urban areas, the picture was no different; a majority of substandard dwellings were occupied by white households.

In the cities represented by the 70 per cent figure above, Negroes and other racial minorities may account for a higher proportion of substandard housing than in urban areas generally. For example, in Philadelphia, 60 per cent of the deficient units in 1956 were in nonwhite occupancy.[6] Even so, it appears that Negro neighborhoods may have been the targets of redevelopment more often than white areas of like quality.[7]

PROGRESS WITHOUT A RENEWAL PROGRAM

The cost of renewal, residential and nonresidential, for the country as a whole has been calculated to range into the trillions of dollars,

[5] Martin Millspaugh, "Problems and Opportunities of Relocation," *Law and Contemporary Problems,* School of Law, Duke University, XXVI (Winter, 1961), 20.

[6] Unpublished data from *NHI,* Philadelphia Supplement.

[7] For a similar conclusion in the case of Chicago, see Beverly Duncan and Philip Hauser, *Housing a Metropolis* (Glencoe: The Free Press, 1960), pp. 85–86.

of which a substantial proportion (about one-fifth) must come from the public sector.[8] When these estimates are matched against the available resources and competing needs of society, the nation's renewal goals appear impossible to attain for at least several decades. It is astonishing to find, therefore, that considerable progress toward the originally announced goals has been made in the last decade with very little federal and even less state and local financial assistance under the various redevelopment programs.

It will be remembered that two of the stated purposes of the Housing Act of 1949 were relief of the housing shortage and the provision of a decent living environment for every American family. From the adoption of the program until the 1960 Census, the net vacancy rate among nondilapidated units rose from 1.6 per cent to over 3 per cent and the number of families living in overcrowded conditions decreased substantially.[9] Even more striking, occupied substandard housing dropped by 6,000,000 units.[10] Whereas in 1950, 14,800,000 units, representing 35 per cent of the national occupied stock, were dilapidated or lacking in facilities or both, by 1960 this figure had dropped to 8,800,000, or only 17 per cent of the occupied inventory (Table 1). It is quite probable that there was more improvement in housing accommodations from 1950 to 1960 than in the prior two decades combined.

This impressive record is in sharp contrast to the postwar forecasts of most housing analysts of a steadily expanding substandard inventory. More significant, it was achieved with virtually no assistance from the federal urban renewal program. By the end of 1956, when occupied substandard housing had already dropped by

[8] John W. Dyckman and Reginald R. Isaacs, *Capital Requirements for Urban Development and Renewal* (New York: McGraw-Hill, 1961), Chapter 2.

[9] See Grigsby, *op. cit.*, introduction to Chapter V.

[10] Two definitional changes between 1950 and 1960 may affect these figures. The inclusion in 1960 of accommodations previously classified as nondwelling unit living quarters would tend to understate the amount of improvement since most of these units are thought to be substandard. On the other hand, the new category of "deteriorating" may include dwelling units that under the old system would have been classified as "dilapidated." Comparison of the recorded decline of occupied substandard housing from 1950 to 1956, when the former definitions were still used, with the apparently slower rate of progress from 1957 to 1960 suggests that the record of improvement has not been exaggerated by the change of definition. It can be seen in Table 1, however, that the rate of reduction of the two components of substandardness —dilapidation and lacking facilities—probably has been affected. The former shows a much greater annual rate of decline from 1957 to 1960, and the latter from 1950 to 1956.

more than 4,500,000 units, only one Title I project had been finished.[11] Three years later, completions still numbered only a handful. Many projects were in progress, but the number of substandard units demolished by renewal action was nominal beside the attrition resulting from other sources. It would appear, therefore, rather hazardous to estimate the extent to which the public purse must be tapped in the future when the catalytic power of current public renewal expenditures on private investment remains to be fully tested.

An Illusion of Progress?

It is difficult to reconcile these findings with the repeated assertions that slums are spreading. Much of the discrepancy may be explained by the fact that, although substandard structures are being vacated, they remain standing and continue to blight an ever-expanding portion of the landscape. Nationally, about one-fifth of the substandard units are not occupied.[12] In small sections of some cities, the vacancy rate, including abandonments, is reputed to be double that amount. It is also possible that depressing exterior appearance has been erroneously accepted as a measure of the inadequacy of both building and environment. It is conceivable too that unconsciously we have been raising our own standards of acceptability. In any event, it seems probable that our thinking has been unduly burdened with data applicable to an earlier period and, as a result, that plans have been geared to conditions which no longer exist to the same extent and degree as formerly. Certainly the widespread belief that housing conditions are deteriorating is in need of serious re-examination.

Variations in Rate of Progress

The rate of improvement in housing conditions was quite uneven throughout the various sectors of the stock. It did not differ greatly between the rental and owner-occupied sectors nor between housing inside and outside SMA's (Tables 1 and 2). Considerable diver-

[11] By comparison, 200,000 units of federally aided public housing (other than Capehart housing) costing more than two billion dollars were completed between 1950 and 1956, and would appear to have been a much more potent renewal force than the renewal program itself. At the end of 1958, only ten renewal projects had been completed, and the total expenditure for projects which had reached the execution stage was less than one billion dollars. Housing and Home Finance Agency, *Twelfth Annual Report*, 1958, p. 20.
[12] *NHI.*

sity, however, existed among individual metropolitan areas. Most interesting were the notable variations by race, with the nonwhite population either exceeding or lagging far behind the over-all pace of the country, depending upon the measure used. In terms of changes in the percentage of substandard dwelling units occupied by each racial group, Negroes and other racial minorities made greater progress than the rest of the country. The proportion of nonwhites living in substandard housing dropped from almost three-fourths in 1950 to less than one-half in 1960. The corresponding figures for the white population were approximately one-third and one-seventh, respectively, indicating a substantial but not equivalent gain.

Most of the improvement for the nonwhite population is explained statistically by an expansion in the number of nonwhite households. As a result, when their housing progress is measured in terms of the change in the number of substandard dwellings which they occupy, a quite different picture emerges. While the inventory of occupied substandard units in the nation as a whole was almost halved between 1950 and 1960, the number of nonwhite households in inadequate shelter fell by only 17 per cent, from 2,770,000 to 2,309,000. Nearly all of this improvement took place in the South, possibly as a result of outmigration. The Northeast actually showed a rise in the number of substandard dwellings occupied by Negroes and other racial minorities. Among the challenges of the 1960's, surely the housing problem of these families is one that should rank very high.

Perhaps the most startling feature in the pattern of improvement was the remarkable amount of quality change both up and down. Thus, there was a gross reduction in occupied substandard units of 8,760,000 from 1950 to 1956, but this huge gain was cut almost in half by simultaneous increases in substandard housing in other structures. It is particularly dismaying to find that although 5,000,000 occupied substandard units in 1950 had been brought up to a satisfactory level by the end of 1956, more than 2,200,000 occupied units which were standard in 1950 were added to the substandard inventory.[13] These slippages, presumably permitted by inadequate codes and lax enforcement at the local level, substantially restricted

[13] There is a questionable group of 752,000 units which had all facilities in 1950, but were lacking them in 1956. This would suggest either sampling error in the *NHI* or a large increase in shared facilities in some sections of the inventory.

the rate of progress.[14] Nevertheless, the net elevation of quality represents a remarkable accomplishment. Equally significant, it is precisely opposite to the trend predicted by critics of national housing policy who have used their own anticipation of an increase in substandard units to "prove" that the level of production is inadequate.[15]

Progress Explained

What explains the remarkable improvement in housing conditions with so little in the way of direct federal grants? Although renovation and repair were statistically the most important explanation, the principal cause seems to have been what is usually described in negative terms as the flight to the suburbs. This outward movement permitted lower-income families to vacate slum areas and acquire somewhat better quarters within the city. It also indirectly provided accommodations for inmigrants from rural areas, thus ensuring that the huge improvement in the housing situation in these sections would not be matched by a concomitant degeneration of conditions in the metropolitan centers. It was not by chance that new construction from 1950 to 1956 exceeded household formation by an amount—3,873,000 units—that almost equaled the 4,567,000 decline in the number of occupied substandard dwellings.

The so-called flight was in reality simply part of the continuing flow of families into better homes. For the first time in our history, however, insufficient vacant land for new construction was available within the boundaries of the central cities, and the flow, therefore, had to find an outlet in the peripheral areas. Were it not for this fact, the entire trend would probably have gone largely unnoticed and uncriticized. If it had been commented upon at all, most of the observations no doubt would have been quite favorable. But regard-

---

[14] The point has been made by other authors that substandard new construction was also a material negative factor, but it will be noted in Table 4 that most of this was outside SMA's and nearly all outside central cities. Furthermore, five-sixths of these units were not dilapidated, but were lacking in facilities. All this suggests that most of the dwellings were erected in rural or semirural areas, where indoor plumbing is not so important. In fact, the new homes, despite their substandard classification, probably were a considerable improvement over what they replaced. See, for example, the description of LaForge, a Farm Security Administration housing project of single-family homes without either indoor water or toilet, in Stuart Chase, *Goals for America* (New York: The Twentieth Century Fund, 1942), Chapter 5.

[15] In defense of these critics it must be pointed out that they were misled in part by underestimates of home-building activity by the Bureau of Labor Statistics.

TABLE 4. *Changes in Number of Standard and Substandard Occupied Units by Cause of Change, United States and Selected Areas, 1950–56*

Cause of Change	United States	INSIDE SMA'S			Outside SMA'S
		Total	Inside Central Cities	Outside Central Cities	
In Standard Occupied Units					
Net gain through improvement of substandard "same" units	2,750,000†	1,000,000*	400,000†	600,000†	1,750,000*
Plus construction of standard units	9,008,000	6,089,000	1,682,000	4,407,000	2,919,000
Plus addition of standard units from other sources	439,000	245,000	150,000	95,000	194,000
Plus gain of standard units via conversions and mergers	303,000	224,000	132,000	92,000	79,000
Less net increase in vacancies in standard "same" units	−265,000	−85,000	−77,000	−8,000	−180,000
Less losses of standard units by demolition and other means	−620,000	−467,000	−326,000	−141,000	−153,000
Net Increase	11,615,000	7,006,000	1,961,000	5,045,000	4,609,000
In Occupied Substandard Units					
Net reduction through improvement of substandard "same" units	2,750,000*	1,000,000*	400,000†	600,000†	1,750,000*
Less substandard units created by new construction	−780,000	−212,000	−23,000	−189,000	−568,000
Less substandard units created by other sources	−327,000	−150,000	−86,000	−64,000	−177,000
Plus reduction of substandard units via conversions and mergers	362,000	212,000	144,000	68,000	150,000
Plus net increase in vacancies in substandard "same" units	1,086,000	200,000	121,000	79,000	886,000
Plus reduction of substandard units via demolition and other means	1,476,000	690,000	495,000	195,000	786,000
Net Reduction	4,567,000	1,740,000	1,051,000	689,000	2,827,000

SOURCE: Derived from data in the *NHI* and the *1950 Census of Housing*.
* By subtraction. Column total derived independently.
† Estimated.

less of how the movement may be described, its effect on housing quality was generally beneficial, and all factors which facilitated the process contributed in turn to better living conditions for the entire community.

The most important elements behind the suburban trend were probably the extremely liberal federal credit programs from 1950 to 1955, rising incomes, and an aging housing stock. Improved highway facilities also contributed, not only directly by opening up areas for residential development, but also indirectly by accelerating the suburbanization of employment opportunities.

It should be pointed out that, although most of the improvement in housing conditions is explained by the suburban expansion, the bulk of the new construction in the outlying areas was undertaken to accommodate population and household growth. This is demonstrated by the fact that the increase in the number of suburban households has been much greater than the decline in the number of occupied substandard dwellings. Central cities have not, with few exceptions, experienced significant absolute losses to the suburbs, as the terms "exodus" and "flight" imply.[16] Rather, they have encountered a shift in the structure of population as metropolitan expansion has been forced increasingly to vacant land in the suburbs, where the growth market is limited primarily to families who can afford new homes. It has been the ability of the suburban market to accommodate to the pressure of population growth and to provide additional housing as well that has prevented growth from resulting in a deterioration of housing conditions.

Migration to the suburbs, though undoubtedly the most important national trend associated with improved housing conditions, was not the principal factor in all areas. . . . Nevertheless, it appears clear that in most localities a rejection of the older inlying housing stock by those families who could afford something better in the suburbs has been the primary immediate cause of improved housing for the population generally.[17]

16 This result, however, stems to some degree from defining "suburbs" to include only those areas beyond the city limits. Inlying areas of some central cities *have* experienced significant population losses, either because of transition to nonresidential use or as a result of declines in the size or number of households.

17 In the Philadelphia SMA, to cite one example, the city in 1956 had one-half of the total housing inventory in the metropolitan area, but only one-

If the decentralization of population has been instrumental in effecting so beneficial a result, why the concern about flight to the suburbs? One might object to the unplanned sprawl, the lack of public open spaces, the unnecessarily low densities, or to the architectural monotony of some of the developments. These, however, are criticisms of the absence of direction in the process rather than of the process itself. The real reason for the despair is, of course, quite obvious. As a result of the multiplicity of governmental jurisdictions within urbanized areas, some of the social and financial costs of the improved living conditions have been unfairly distributed. National progress has been achieved partially at the expense of older central cities. Correction of this inequity, however, through a clearance and rebuilding program intended, as many are, to attract medium- and high-income families back to the city is fraught with difficulties, and in many cases is not even the proper approach. Indeed, a wrongly conceived program may compound the problem. More is said of this later.

THE FUTURE PROBLEM

Will the remarkable pace of improvement between 1950 and 1960 continue without a massive renewal program, or is the progress that has come about through the market process on the verge of losing its momentum? If the latter is true, how much and what kinds of intervention are required by public agencies?

There are conflicting forces at work. Incomes continue to rise and the housing inventory of central cities grows older. Improved highways and expressways are being added at a pace even more rapid than that of the previous decade. The desire for low densities by users of both residential and nonresidential space persists and is being satisfied in the market. All these factors, to one degree or another, favor abandonment of the lower quality stock in the denser sections near the metropolitan core.

On the other hand, a number of elements are working to reduce outmigration. Interest rates have risen and the easy mortgage terms

---

quarter of the homes valued over $10,000 and only one-third of the apartments renting for over $100 a month. Thus, the vast majority of middle- and upper-income families have no suitable alternative to a suburban residence.

of the mid-fifties are not likely to reappear in the foreseeable future. Moreover, residential mobility is likely to be diminished now that many of the families who were forced to take temporary quarters at the end of World War II have moved into permanent residences. This reduction in mobility will tend to cut the market supply and thus the available housing opportunities of those who might wish to move out of older neighborhoods. Finally, it has been suggested by one analyst that home repairs, which played an important part in raising the quality of the housing stock between 1950 and 1956, are not likely to continue at the same pace. The cheap and easy improvements have been made. The more expensive jobs, as well as those which would have to be handled by very low-income families, probably constitute the bulk of the remainder.[18] This view is supported by the decline in the rate of progress from 1957 to 1960.[19]

The weight of evidence favors continued improvement, but at a steadily decreasing pace. The annual rate of attrition of substandard units, which dropped from 675,000 during the 1950–56 period to 540,000 in the succeeding three years, will continue to fall, but no doubt more sharply. Projecting this trend, the yearly rate in the decade of the sixties will average around 200,000. If this assumption is reasonably correct, the question arises as to what measures might be taken to eliminate the residual substandard units at an earlier date than would otherwise be possible. It is the purpose of the remaining sections of the chapter to illuminate this general area of policy concern.

The Bottleneck in Renewal

A comprehensive program of residential renewal must cope with five separate and distinct problems. The first is the dilemma of the low-income family living in substandard accommodations. The second relates to inadequate housing occupied by families who can afford something better. The third concerns structures which are not substandard, but which must be demolished because they are either surrounded by substandard buildings or are in areas to be renewed for nonresidential use. The fourth has to do with improve-

---

[18] Frank S. Kristof, "Components of Change in the Nation's Housing Inventory in Relation to the 1960 Census." Paper presented at the Annual Meeting of the American Statistical Association, December 28, 1959.

[19] Assuming that the apparent change of rate was not the result of the changes in definitions discussed earlier.

ments to neighborhood environments. The fifth and final problem involves the improvement of areas in which neither the individual structures nor the surrounding yards and common spaces are in violation of local ordinances, but where the over-all quality is still substandard by other criteria. Historically, the entire program of urban renewal evolved from a serious concern over the first problem on this list. It is paradoxical, therefore, that this is the area where legislative progress has been least. Yet if the restoration of our cities is ever to be achieved, it is here that a solution must be found. Although we can proceed independently on the other four fronts for a time, ultimately the pace of renewal will be set by the speed with which the low-income population is adequately rehoused.

The Low-Income—Substandard Housing Nexus

Despite the frequently heard observation that slum areas are filled with families who can afford better housing, the bulk of substandard units in the United States is occupied by households with low incomes. In fact, of the 10,000,000 families living in substandard housing in 1956, over three-quarters earned less than $4,000 a year. Inside metropolitan areas, the proportion was two-thirds.[20] By contrast, only three-eighths of the families with standard accommodations had such low incomes. The association of low income with inadequate housing is even more striking in the group earning less than $2,000. Over 45 per cent of the families in this group were ill-housed, and, equally, they accounted for over 45 per cent of the occupied substandard inventory.[21] Some of these families, particularly the one- and two-person households, may have the assets, if not

[20] Conversely, only one-third of all families earning less than $4,000 a year but one-ninth of those earning between $4,000 and $5,999 lived in substandard dwelling units. Inside metropolitan areas, the figures were one-quarter and one-twelfth, respectively. It would seem that analysts who use the number of low-income families as a measure of housing need grossly exaggerate the housing problem of this group. Equally guilty are those who compare the distribution of family income with the distribution of prices and rents of *new* housing to illustrate the seriousness of the current situation. Analyses of the relationship of income to housing expenditures would be much improved if some adjustment were made for the transitory income component and also for variations in the asset position of household heads with similar earnings.

[21] Inside SMA's the concentration was less pronounced. Only one-third of the "Under $2,000" group lived in substandard housing, and they accounted for only one-third of the occupied substandard inventory.

the income, to acquire better housing. It is probable, however, that the vast majority do not.

A projection of the number of low-income families, together with a calculation of the proportion who are likely to be forced to live in inadequate accommodations, provides the basis for estimating the public cost of the major segment of the residential renewal program. Such a computation is performed below in order to give the reader an appreciation of the general magnitudes involved. The costs of implementing programs in the other four problem areas described above will not be calculated here. It is doubtful whether they would be very large in comparison with the expenses involved in meeting the low-income problem. Thus the estimate to be presented here might be viewed as the major portion of the public expense which must be incurred in order to achieve our housing goals.

Four brief explanatory comments about the calculations. First, since this volume is concerned with urban housing markets, only the renewal problem within metropolitan areas will be considered. This delimitation excludes some urban housing that is outside of SMA's and includes a small number of rural homes that are within metropolitan area borders. Absence of current data on urbanized areas forces this compromise, but it is not a serious one. In 1950, urbanized areas contained 28,500,000 occupied dwellings and 6,100,000 occupied substandard units. The corresponding figures for SMA's were not greatly different: 24,500,000 and 5,300,000. Moreover, the addition of new SMA's since 1950 has probably reduced the discrepancy. Thus metropolitan area figures provide a good approximation of the urban housing problem. Exclusion of rural housing from this analysis is not meant to imply that inadequate shelter is any less a problem because it is not in an urban environment. Some of the deleterious effects of substandard housing in farm areas have been well documented. The solutions to the rural problem, however, are quite different, and it could only confuse the issues to merge the two areas of concern.

Second, because metropolitan area data for 1960 were not yet available at the time of this writing, the projection is made from 1957 with the 1956 *NHI* figures used as the point of departure. To facilitate comparisons with other forecasts, the terminal date of the projection is set at 1970.

Third, the reader will note as the discussion proceeds that a number of the assumptions on which the calculations are based are at best informed guesses. It will be found, however, that rather large shifts in these assumptions do not alter the final results enough to change the policy implications to any significant degree.

Fourth, the projections carry an implicit assumption of substantially full employment. Recent trends place this assumption in question. In fact, even now a fairly high proportion of substandard housing may be occupied by families whose major wage earner is in need of work a good share of the time. Certainly progress in housing is heavily dependent upon the effectiveness with which we are able to deal with this more basic difficulty. The presumption here is that the problem of excess unemployment will be solved.

With these caveats and qualifications in mind, we can now proceed with the calculation. Out of approximately 15,000,000 low-income households that lived inside SMA's in 1956, 3,000,000, or 20 per cent, resided in accommodations that were found by Census enumerators to be dilapidated or lacking in facilities.[22] These families accounted for five-sixths of the occupied substandard inventory. As pointed out earlier, the Census figures on substandard dwelling units understate the total problem of inadequate shelter. They do not include families in standard but overcrowded quarters, nor some structures which are in serious violation of local housing codes. To adjust for these two sources of error, the 3,000,000 figure was arbitrarily raised by 20 per cent to 3,600,000.

Available to this group at prices or rents which they could afford were only about 300,000 vacant dwelling units which had all basic facilities.[23] Judging from current value and rent-income relationships, however, a majority of these units would, in the normal course of events, be taken by families with somewhat higher earnings. Thus, about 3,500,000 households were burdened with

[22] Low income was defined as the bottom half of the income distribution. There may be some households who have earnings in excess of the median figure of $4,900 who cannot afford and do not have an adequate home. Equally, however, a portion of the families that have been classified as low-income no doubt have the means to acquire standard housing even though they have not chosen to do so. Of the 3,000,000 low-income families living in substandard accommodations, 2,500,000 had earnings below $4,000. Thus very little would be changed by drawing the low-income line at $4,000 instead of $4,900.

[23] It was assumed that this group could afford contract rents under $80 per month and sales prices under $8,000.

both low incomes and unavailability of adequate housing. It would seem reasonable to presume that nearly all of them had no immediate way out of this dilemma, for even if it were assumed that many of these families could afford standard accommodations (which is doubtful), if they actually elected to move to better quarters, the resulting housing shortage would quickly boost rents beyond their reach.

By 1970, rising real incomes will have considerably reduced the proportion of low-income families, but population expansion inside SMA's will fully counteract the income effect, leaving the figure of 3,500,000 virtually unchanged in so far as these two variables are concerned.[24] The number of families trapped in substandard housing will, however, be lowered substantially by the operation of the private market. For the United States as a whole, including all substandard dwellings regardless of the income of the occupants, the attrition from 1957 to 1970 should equal roughly 4,500,000 units. This figure includes 1,750,000 already lost by 1960 plus the previously estimated 200,000 units per year from 1960 to 1970 plus a 20 per cent upward adjustment, just explained, necessary to bring the Census figures in line with the concept of inadequate shelter used here. Of the 4,500,000 units, about 1,500,000 may be expected to be within metropolitan areas, and of this latter figure, in the neighborhood of 1,000,000 should be units occupied by low-income families.[25] Thus in 1970, barring significant shifts in the forms of public intervention, the low-income—substandard housing nexus will involve 2,500,000 (3,500,000 minus 1,000,000) households.

Here then is a hard core of familes which constitute a sizable problem for urban renewal, particularly since concern for this group seems to have lost its priority in the thinking of most of those

[24] This amounts to a projection of the trend from 1950 to 1956. The *NHI* figures indicate that the absolute number of low-income families did not decline materially between these two years, and thus suggest that this group either had more assets or a better array of housing alternatives in 1956 than in 1950. For a discussion of the probable effect of rising incomes on the income structure, see Chester Rapkin and William G. Grigsby, *The Demand for Housing in Eastwick* (Philadelphia: Institute for Urban Studies, 1960), Chapter III.

[25] Adjusting for changes in the value of the dollar, it appeared that of the total decline in occupied substandard housing from 1950 to 1956, one-third was associated with abandonment of substandard housing by upper-income families and two-thirds with whatever factors were responsible for enabling low-income families to obtain better housing. It is this experience which is projected forward to 1970.

now initiating redevelopment policy. The Gordian knot of low-income families in substandard housing can be cut only by more rapidly rising incomes or some form of public assistance.

The Illusion of Prohibitive Expense

The foregoing estimate may seem depressingly large, particularly if one transforms the bare figure into a visual picture of human privation and misery. It also appears enormous when juxtaposed against the only federal tool being used to solve the problem—public housing. To accommodate the 2,500,000 families in public units would necessitate the construction within SMA's of five times as many subsidized dwellings during the thirteen-year period from 1957 to 1970 as were built throughout the United States in the prior twenty years combined.

Yet, if the public costs of a solution are analyzed independently of any specific approach, they may be seen to be astonishingly low. The 2,500,000 households are after all not devoid of resources. On the average, they are probably able to devote one-fifth of their earnings to housing. Assuming that in 1970 the median income of this group is around $2,500, they could, therefore, contribute $500 a year toward adequate shelter. This in turn would mean that an annual government subsidy averaging as little as $300 per family would put a large supply of acceptable housing within their reach, for within SMA's there are currently over 6,000,000 standard units having annual carrying costs of less than $800 a year, and according to our projections, this figure should increase somewhat by the end of the decade. Thus, ignoring for the moment the very basic problem that nearly all of the 6,000,000 dwellings are currently occupied, the annual public contribution under these assumptions would be only $750,000,000. This figure is not much larger than the total current renewal program, residential and nonresidential, and somewhat less than the yearly federal outlay for farm subsidies. Moreover, . . . a large portion of the cost could be avoided if the federal government pushed for more vigorous code enforcement at the local level. In addition, as will be shown, some of the expense would in a sense be recouped through lower writedown costs in redevelopment areas. Finally, to the extent that the federal contribution was in the form of a subsidized interest rate, it would, under certain conditions that will be explained later, not involve a corresponding expense to the taxpayer. Thus, it is conceivable that the total public expenditure would run well below $500,000,000 a year, of which two-thirds, or only about $300,000,000, would come from the federal treasury. This amount would not make our cities beautiful nor would it provide for our other urban needs, such as transportation and open space, but it would meet a minimum requirement which in fact is requisite to realizing some of our other goals.

BARRIERS TO A SOLUTION

If the expense of housing the low-income population is indeed so small, why then has this not been done? There are several reasons, each of which impedes progress toward a solution.

Lack of a Satisfactory Formula

The major source of difficulty has been the failure to find a subsidy formula that is both politically acceptable and in consonance with the private market mechanism. The casual observer might conclude that several such methods are already in existence, for the federal government possesses an array of weapons designed to improve housing conditions. Liberal mortgage insurance, public housing, and several different devices for urban renewal focus on various aspects of the problem. Yet in the entire arsenal of housing and urban renewal programs, there is not today a single tool that comes to grips with the basic dilemma—low income.

The present public housing program is certainly not equal to the task. In twenty–five years, it has produced only a handful of units (about 500,000). It is not permitted in a few states, has not been tried in many cities which are legally authorized to participate in the federal program, and is not widely accepted, even by those for whom it was intended, in a large share of the localities which do have projects in operation.[26] A considerable number of families have incomes which are too *low* to enable them to enter public projects. Unrelated individuals living in one household, most single persons, and certain types of problem families are also excluded.

[26] See Robert M. Fisher, *Twenty Years of Public Housing* (New York: Harper & Bros., 1959), Chapter 8.

The costs of producing public units are in many areas exorbitant.[27] An exclusively rental program, it is operating at cross-purposes with the basic aspirations of most American families. Although experimentation in public housing has frequently been urged and now seems to be under way, it is doubtful whether any plan in which government is the landlord will receive the political acceptance necessary to cope with the housing problem of 2,500,000 families.

The urban renewal program, despite its specific goal of a decent home and suitable living environment for every American family, has been equally ineffective and possibly even harmful in so far as its stated purpose is concerned. Redevelopment projects have caused a substantial *reduction* in the supply of low-cost housing—standard as well as substandard—as dwellings in blighted areas have been razed and replaced by nonresidential uses or homes for higher-income families.[28] The plight of the low-income family has been abandoned to the filtering process, a particularly unfortunate circumstance since renewal has thus far reduced not only the supply of low-cost units, but the total supply of housing as well. Partially in recognition of this problem, a shift in emphasis to rehabilitation has gradually developed. However, since public subsidy for the improvement of individual dwellings is lacking, this program also has none of the basic requirements for solving the housing problem of low-income groups.

The most obvious solution might seem to be some form of direct cash subsidy for specified low-income families.[29] Such a plan faces two major difficulties. The first concerns the issue of eligiblity. If all low-income families, including those living in standard accommodations, were permitted to receive payments, the relatively modest public costs computed in the previous section would have to be increased fivefold. If the entire low-income population were not

[27] In Philadelphia, three new public housing projects will have an average cost per dwelling unit fully 80 per cent above the average sale price of a new six-room brick row house, and about 30 to 50 per cent more than several new private apartment structures. This experience is not atypical.

[28] See the annual reports of the Housing and Home Finance Agency and also various issues of *Urban Renewal Project Characteristics* (Housing and Home Finance Agency, Urban Renewal Administration).

[29] The subsidy would not have to be in the form of a rent certificate if other administrative checks were used to ensure that the families who received the payments obtained satisfactory housing. [Such a subsidy was authorized by Congress in 1965.—Ed.]

made eligible, questions of inequitable treatment of equal classes would arise. This problem could be partially solved by departing from the basic income criterion to include consideration of assets as well.

The second and more serious difficulty relates to the impact of the subsidy on the private market. The amount of assistance received by needy families would not be sufficient to enable them to purchase or rent new construction. Virtually all of the funds which they received, therefore, would go toward the acquisition of better accommodations in the existing stock. Thus an enormous rise in the market demand for low-priced units would be created without any direct corresponding increase in market supply. Home prices would be bid up, and although this might have some favorable impact on both rehabilitation and housing starts, it seems unlikely that beneficial results would compare favorably with the costs. Clearly, if buyers and renters are channeled upward in the used supply, other families have to be drawn out of this sector into the new construction market. At present there is no device to accomplish this phase of the task. A subsidy for middle-income families would no doubt provide the answer in so far as the market problem is concerned, but aid to this group is hard to justify when well over 90 per cent are adequately housed. Similarly, it would be possible to increase the assistance to the low-income households enough for some of them to acquire new rather than used dwellings. Although this in effect is what is done in the case of public housing, the idea may be criticized on the ground that the recipient families would be provided with shelter superior to that available to households with higher income.

All proposals for meeting the low-income housing problem are confronted with various combinations of these stumbling blocks. Some plans are too expensive; others, politically impossible; still others, likely to disrupt the market. This in itself, however, does not explain our failure to resolve the issues and come forth with a solution. There are several other factors which will be briefly noted.

Lack of Support

Basically, the failure to find an effective way of handling the problem of slums stems from the fact that public and political opinion on the subject varies, for the most part, between apathy and widespread antagonism. There has always been strong resistance to and lack of support for any form of shelter subsidy for low-income groups. This situation apparently is part of a more general pattern. All ideas for public assistance, whether for better housing or other purposes, that are based on income or means criteria alone seem to have been more widely opposed than programs in which the benefits were tied to some other variable. Aid for veterans, farmers, business, old people, and others is legislated with relative ease even in the face of statistics indicating that a large proportion of the recipients in a particular group have no need for it, and in fact may be the beneficiaries of enormous windfall profits. If this analysis is correct, it suggests that the rate of progress might be accelerated if it were possible to develop programs for special segments within the low- and middle-income population for whom public support might be more readily forthcoming. A few such programs are already in existence. For example, financing under Sections 220 and 221, as well as housing aids for the elderly, is probably utilized primarily by families and individuals in the lower-income strata. These programs touch only part of the total problem, but are, nevertheless, illustrative of one possible type of strategy which might be more widely employed.

Limited Capacity of the Building Industry

Although an annual subsidy of the magnitude described (under $500,000,000 a year) is modest relative to other government aid programs, its potential impact on capital investment is awesome. Assuming that aid to the 2,500,000 hard-core families led directly or indirectly to the construction of an equivalent number of dwelling units over a ten-year period, this would represent an 18 per cent increase in home starts and an annual increment to residential wealth of about three billion dollars. The impact of such a large volume of investment might easily create difficulties in the building industry and the economy generally.

As many authors have reminded us, during periods of full employment, with the home-building industry operating at capacity, a program that increased demand still further would only create additional problems. Throughout most of the first twenty years of federal activity in the field of low-income housing, the question of capacity was certainly a critical one and is known to have influenced some of the thinking on housing assistance. Only since 1956 has the situation changed, and the shift was not widely recognized until about 1960. Looking ahead, a return to peak levels of output is, according to all predictions, certain to occur by 1965. At that time, limited productive capacity will again constitute a formidable obstacle to any solution. With the construction industry and the existing supply of housing straining to accommodate new demand, continued abandonment of low-quality dwelling units and large-scale relocation through urban renewal may become extremely difficult. It seems clear, therefore, that if the entire low-income population is to be adequately housed by 1970, programs to expand housing starts must be initiated while there is still slack in the economy.

Problem Families

Nearly all of the suggestions for housing subsidies have one fundamental limitation. They are based on an image of the potential client which may soon be rendered obsolete by continued prosperity and by other government housing programs.

Federal housing assistance for low-income groups was launched in the thirties when most poor families were, in a social sense, part of the middle class. Occupants of public housing were not readily distinguishable from other families except with respect to income. This situation continued through World War II and the early postwar period because of the housing shortage. More than a decade of prosperity, however, has sharply changed the clientele until now most of the occupants are members of special deprived groups with chronically low income: the Negro faced with discrimination in the job market; the aged unable to work or on small pensions; the broken family; and the family with no wage earner.

As a result of gains in education and employment opportunities and greater freedom in the housing market, Negroes, who now constitute more than half of the occupants of public units, will begin to improve their income and housing position much faster than whites in the coming decade, and the proportion needing public assistance will drop sharply. The aged are now being helped by two additional government housing programs which are being vigorously pushed. Accordingly, by 1970 it is possible that the vast majority of low-income families and individuals living in substandard housing will be multiple-problem cases whose most serious difficulty is not housing at all. If so, the solution for this group will certainly far exceed the cost estimates calculated here and be considerably more complex than our discussion has implied.

3 The Economics of Urban Renewal *†

Otto A. Davis and Andrew B. Whinston

INTRODUCTION

In light of two implications of urban renewal, it is not at all
surprising that this phenomenon provides an excellent area for the
application of welfare economics. These implications are: First, that
the market mechanism has not functioned "properly" in urban
property; and second, that positive action can "improve" the situation. The propositions of welfare economics provide some tools for
judging public policy measures such as urban renewal. But since
these propositions themselves are based upon ethical postulates, it
seems desirable that we begin our discussion of urban renewal by
stating explicitly what we consider the role of the economist to be
in this situation.

* Reprinted from a symposium, *Urban Renewal: Part II,* Vol. 26, No. 1
(Winter 1961), pp. 105–117, by permission from *Law and Contemporary
Problems,* published by the Duke University School of Law, Durham, North
Carolina. Copyright © 1961 by Duke University.
   † The authors would like to express their appreciation to Professors Donald
A. Fink and Merton Miller, both of Carnegie Institute of Technology, and to
Edgar M. Hoover and Melvin K. Bers, both of the Pittsburgh Regional Plan-
ning Association, for reading and criticizing the manuscript. Conversations
with Professor W. W. Cooper, of the Carnegie Institute of Technology, were
also beneficial.

I. WELFARE ECONOMICS AND URBAN RENEWAL

Welfare economics itself provides one criterion, the Pareto condition, for judging public policy measures. The Pareto condition states that a social policy measure can be judged "desirable" if it results in either (1) everyone being made better off, or (2) someone being made better off without anyone being made worse off. This rule is, of course, an ethical proposition, but it requires a minimum of premises and should command wide assent.

On the other hand, the economist need not be limited solely to the Pareto condition in giving policy advice. This becomes especially true when the objective ambiguity of the terms "better off" and "worse off" is considered. Indeed, the role of the economist in the formation of social policy may be compared to that of the consultant to an industrial firm. The consultant to a firm serves two functions. First, given the goals of the firm, he tries to find the best or most efficient means of achieving these goals. The second function of the consultant is equally important; he must try to clarify vague goals by pointing out possible inconsistencies and determining implications in order that re-evaluations and explicit statements can be made.

We conceive of the role of the economist as quite similar to that outlined for the consultant. First, the economist may try to clarify social goals by pointing out inconsistencies and determining implications of possible social rules. Second, if a goal happens to be given and agreed upon—*i.e.*, if a social welfare function is defined—then the economist might try to advise the body politic by proposing politics for the attainment of the defined goals.

It is in the above spirit that we consider the problem of urban renewal. Granted the individualistic basis of western civilization, it seems reasonable to assume that any action which satisfies the Pareto condition would improve social welfare and, therefore, should be desired by society. On the other hand, society might desire, granted the institutional form of political decision-making, certain actions which violate the narrowly conceived Pareto condition.[1] Certainly

---

[1] It is worthy of note that it can be argued very convincingly, if the individualistic ethic is adopted, that any social welfare function must satisfy a broadly conceived Pareto condition—that is, a Pareto condition defined by political consensus. See, *e.g.*, Buchanan, *Positive Economics, Welfare Economics, and Political Economy*, 2 J. LAW & ECONOMICS 124 (1959).

income redistribution would fit this category. And so may urban renewal.

Specifically, the social welfare function which we use has the following properties: If the sum of the benefits, measured by changes in capital values, exceeds the sum of the costs, then the action is termed desirable. While this welfare criterion may not seem clear at this point, it is appropriate to note here that a major portion of the remainder of the paper will be devoted to determining how benefits and costs are to be measured. What is important here is to make clear the basis upon which our judgments will be made.

Several characteristics of this welfare criterion should be noted here. First, any action which satisfies the narrowly conceived Pareto condition will satisfy this criterion. On the other hand, any action which satisfies the welfare criterion need not meet the Pareto condition unless compensation is required. Second, our criterion is concerned with the efficient allocation of resources. The question of the ethically desirable distribution of income will not be considered here, although some might hold that urban renewal is concerned with income redistribution. We merely point out that income redistribution can be more efficiently achieved through other means than urban renewal.

II. THE PRICE MECHANISM AND URBAN BLIGHT

Having stated the position from which we shall make policy judgments, we now must examine the question of why urban renewal is necessary. In other words, why do "blighted" areas develop and persist? Why do individuals fail to keep their properties in "acceptable" states of repair?

Several arguments may be advanced as answers to the above questions. For example, it has been asserted that property owners have exaggerated notions of the extent and timing of municipal expansion. Hence they may neglect possible improvements of existing structures in anticipation of the arrival of more intensive uses which might bring capital gains.[2] Note that even if this argument is accepted as plausible—and the reason why property owners might

---

[2] Fisher, *Economic Aspects of Zoning, Blighted Areas, and Rehabilitation Laws*, 3 AM. ECON. REV. 334 (1942).

have exaggerated notions about municipal expansion is by no means evident—it does not constitute an argument for urban renewal. Instead, one might infer that, given sufficient time, a transition to intensive and profitable uses would take place.[3] Then too, it can be argued that there is no reason to expect governmental authorities to have better judgment than individual entrepreneurs.

Aside from the previous "mistaken judgments" argument, it might seem plausible at first glance to believe on the basis of price theory and the profit maximization assumption that urban blight could not occur. After all, would not profit-maximizing individuals find it to their advantage to keep their property in a state of repair? Certainly it seems reasonable to suppose that if individual benefits from repair or redevelopment exceed individual costs, then individual action could be expected and no social action would be necessary. We shall now attempt to demonstrate why rational individual action might allow property to deteriorate and blight to occur.

First of all, the fact that the value of any one property depends in part upon the neighborhood in which it is located seems so obvious as hardly to merit discussion. Yet, since this simple fact is the villain of the piece, further elaboration is warranted. Pure introspective evidence seems sufficient to indicate that persons consider the neighborhood when deciding to buy or rent some piece of urban property.[4] If this is the case, then it means that externalities are present in utility functions; that is to say, the subjective utility or enjoyment derived from a property depends not only upon the design, state of repairs, and so on of that property, but also upon the characteristics of nearby properties. This fact will, of course, be reflected in both capital and rental values. This is the same as saying that it is also reflected in the return on investment.

---

[3] Indeed, it can even be argued that this line of reasoning considered alone leads to the conclusion that urban renewal expenditures are wasteful. See, *e.g.*, Davis, *A Pure Theory of Urban Renewal*, 36 LAND ECONOMICS 221 (1960).

[4] This interdependence of urban property values has, of course, long been recognized. See, for example, the discussion in ALFRED MARSHALL, PRINCIPLES OF ECONOMICS bk. 5, ch. 11 (8th ed. 1920). The following quote is especially interesting in this regard. "But the general rule holds that the amount and character of the building put upon each plot of land is, in the main (subject to the local building bylaws), that from which the most profitable results are anticipated, with little or no reference to its reaction on the situation value of the neighborhood. In other words, the site value of the plot is governed by causes which are mostly beyond the control of him who determines what buildings shall be put on it." *Id.* at 445.

In order to explain how interdependence can cause urban blight, it seems appropriate to introduce a simple example from the theory of games. This example, which has been developed in an entirely different context and is commonly known as "The Prisoner's Dilemma," appears to contain the important points at issue here.[5] For the sake of simplicity, let us consider only two adjacent properties. More general situations do not alter the result but do complicate the reasoning. Let us use the labels Owner I and Owner II. Suppose that each owner has made an initial investment in his property from which he is reaping a return, and is now trying to determine whether to make the additional investment for redevelopment. The additional investment will, of course, alter the return which he receives, and so will the decision of the other owner.

The situation which they might face can be summarized in the following game matrix:

$$
\begin{array}{cc}
 & \text{Owner II} \\
 & \begin{array}{cc} \text{Invest} & \text{Not Invest} \end{array} \\
\text{Owner I} \begin{array}{c} \text{Invest} \\ \text{Not Invest} \end{array} &
\begin{pmatrix}
(.07, .07) & (.03, .10) \\
(.10, .03) & (.04, .04)
\end{pmatrix}
\end{array}
$$

The matrix game is given the following interpretation: Each property owner has made an initial investment and has an additional sum which is invested in, say, corporate bonds. At present, the average return on both these investments, the property and the corporate bonds considered together, is four per cent. Thus if neither owner makes the decision to sell his corporate bonds and make a new investment in the redevelopment of his property, each will continue to get the four per cent average return. This situation is represented by the entries within brackets in the lower right of

[5] For an explanation of the "game theoretic" points of interest in the Prisoner's Dilemma example, see R. DUNCAN LUCE & HOWARD RAIFFA, GAMES AND DECISIONS 94–102 (1957). The reason for the intriguing title of this type of game theory analysis is interesting in itself. The name is derived from a popular interpretation. The district attorney takes two suspects into custody and keeps them separated. He is sure they are guilty of a specific crime but does not have adequate evidence for a conviction. He talks to each separately and tells them that they can confess or not confess. If neither confesses, then he will book them on some minor charge and both will receive minor punishment. If both confess, then they will be prosecuted but he will recommend less than the most severe sentence. If either one confesses and the other does not, then the confessor will receive lenient treatment for turning state's evidence, whereas the latter will get "the book" slapped at him. The Prisoner's Dilemma is that without collusion between them, the individually rational action for each is to confess.

the matrix where each individual has made the decision "Not Invest." The left hand figure in the brackets always refers to the average return which Owner I receives, and the right hand figure reflects the return of Owner II. Thus for the "Not Invest, Not Invest" decisions, the matrix entry reflects the fact that both owners continue to get a four per cent return.

On the other hand, if both individuals made the decision to sell their bonds and invest the proceeds in redevelopment of their property, it is assumed that each would obtain an average return of seven per cent on his total investment. Therefore, the entry in the upper left of the matrix, the entry for the "Invest, Invest" decisions, has a seven per cent return for each owner.

The other two entries in the matrix, which represent the situation when one owner invests and the other does not, are a little more complicated. We assumed, as was mentioned earlier, that externalities, both external economies and diseconomies, are present. These interdependencies are reflected in the returns from investment. For example, consider the entries in the brackets in the lower left corner of the matrix. In this situation, Owner I would have decided to "Not Invest" and Owner II would have decided to "Invest."

Owner I is assumed to obtain some of the benefits from Owner II's investment, the redevelopment contributing something to a "better neighborhood." For example, if the two properties under consideration happened to be apartment buildings, the decision of Owner II to invest might mean that he would demolish his "outdated" apartment building and construct a new one complete with off-street parking and other amenities. But this would mean that the tenants of Owner I would now have an easier time finding parking spaces on the streets, their children might have the opportunity of associating with the children of the "higher class" people who might be attracted to the modern apartment building, and so forth. All this means that (as soon as leases allow) Owner I can edge up his rents. Thus his return is increased without having to make an additional investment. We assume that his return becomes ten per cent in this case, and this figure is appropriately centered in the matrix. Owner II, on the other hand, would find that, since his renters also consider the "neighborhood" (which includes the ill effects of Owner I's "outdated" structure), his level of rents would have to be less than would be the case if his apartment building were in an alternative location. Thus we assume that the return on his total investment (the investment in the now-demolished structure plus the investment in the new structure) falls to three per cent. This figure is also appropriately entered in the matrix. For simplicity, the reverse situation, where Owner I decided to invest and Owner II decides not to invest, is taken to be similar. Thus the reverse entries are made in the upper right corner of the matrix.[6]

Having described the possible situations which the two owners face, consider now the decision-making process. Both owners are assumed to be aware of the returns which are available to themselves in the hypothesized situations. Owner I will be considered first. Owner I must decide whether to invest or not invest. Remember that the left hand entries in the brackets represent the possible returns for Owner I. Two possible actions of Owner II are relevant for Owner I in his effort to make his own decision. Therefore, Owner I might use the following decision process: Assume, first, that Owner II decides to invest. Then what decision would be the most advantageous? A decision to invest means only a seven per cent return on Owner I's capital, whereas the decision not to invest would yield an average return of ten per cent of the total relevant amount of capital. Therefore, if Owner II were to decide to invest, it would certainly be individually advantageous to Owner I not to invest. But suppose that Owner II decided not to invest. Then what would be the most advantageous decision for Owner I? Once again the results can be seen from the matrix. For Owner I the decision to invest now means that he will receive only a three per cent return on his capital, whereas the decision not to invest means that he can continue to receive the four per cent average return. Therefore, if Owner II were to decide not to invest, it would still be individually advantageous to Owner I not to invest.

[6] Economists might think that we have used inappropriate and sleight-of-hand methods by lumping together old and new investments, and also by considering the average rate of return instead of marginal rates. Actually these methods are completely appropriate here due to the way we have simplified the problem to make the exposition of the game theory easier. The old investment does not represent a sunk cost, since it is yielding a return and thus has economic value. Both owners are assumed to have precisely the amount of money in bonds that is required for the redevelopment of their property. The rate of return on the bonds can be assumed to be the "social rate of return" and the best alternative available to the two individuals. Since the owners are interested in maximizing the total income from their capital, the above assumptions allow us to lump together and to use average rates.

The situation for Owner II is similar. If Owner I is assumed to invest, then Owner II can gain a ten per cent average return on his capital by not investing and only a seven per cent return by investing. If Owner I is assumed not to invest, then Owner II can gain only a three per cent return by investing, but a four per cent average return by not investing. Therefore, the individually rational action for Owner II is also not to invest.

The situation described above means, of course, that neither Owner I nor Owner II will decide to invest in redevelopment. Therefore, we might conclude that the interdependencies summarized in the Prisoner's Dilemma example can explain why blighted areas can develop[7] and persist. Before concluding the analysis, however, we might try to answer some questions which may at this point be forthcoming.

First of all, it might be suggested that we have imposed an unrealistic condition by not allowing the two owners to coordinate their decisions.[8] After all, does it not seem likely that the two owners would get together and mutually agree to invest in the redevelopment of their properties? Not only would such action be socially desirable, but it would seem to be individually advantageous. Note that while it might be easy for the two property owners in our simple example to communicate and coordinate their decisions,[9] this would not appear to be the case as the number of individuals increased. If any single owner were to decide not to invest while all other owners decided to redevelop, then the former would stand to gain by such action. The mere presence of many owners would seem to make coordination more difficult and thus

[7] It is to be emphasized that these results depend upon the interdependencies or neighborhood effects being "sufficiently strong" to get a combination of returns similar to those which we used in the example. It is unlikely that this condition would be satisfied for all urban property. Our point is that similar combinations seem possible, and if they do occur, then they can explain one peculiar phenomenon of urban property. The explanation is presented later in the paper.

[8] It is worthy of note that experimental data concerning the prisoner's dilemma in other contexts tend to indicate that, if communication does not take place, players continually choose individually rational strategies. For the results of these laboratory experiments, see Scodel, Minas, Ratoosh & Lipetz, *Some Descriptive Aspects of Two-Person Non-Zero-Sum Games*, 3 J. CONFLICT RESOLUTION 114 (1959).

[9] It will be recalled that we made the example overly simple only for the purpose of exposition. While the consideration of many individuals would make the example more realistic, it would only make the game theory more complicated and not alter the result as far as this case is concerned.

make our assumption more realistic. Yet, this is precisely the point; it is the objective of social policy to encourage individuals in such situations to coordinate their decisions so that interdependencies will not prevent the achievement of a Pareto welfare point. In this regard, it is worthwhile to note that, if coordination and redevelopment do take place voluntarily, then no problem exists, and urban renewal is not needed.

Second it might be observed that, if coordinated action does not take place, incentive exists for either Owner I, Owner II, or some third party to purchase the properties and develop both of them in order that the seven per cent return can be obtained. And certainly, it cannot be denied that this often occurs in reality. However, it is necessary to point out here that, because of the institutional peculiarities of urban property, there is no assurance that such a result will always take place. Consider, for example, an area composed of many holdings. Suppose that renewal or redevelopment would be feasible if coordination could be achieved, but that individual action alone will not result in such investment due to the interdependencies. In other words, the situation is assumed to be similar to the previous example except that many owners are present. Incentive exists for some entrepreneur to attempt to purchase the entire area and invest in redevelopment or renewal.

Now suppose that one or more of the owners of the small plots in the area became aware of the entrepreneur's intentions. If the small plots were so located as to be important for a successful project, then the small holders might realize that it would be possible to gain by either (1) using their position to expropriate part of the entrepreneur's expected profits by demanding a very high price for their properties, or (2) refusing to sell in order to enjoy the external economies generated by the redevelopment. If several of the small holders become aware of the entrepreneur's intentions, then it is entirely possible, with no communication or collusion between these small holders, for a situation to result where each tries to expropriate as much of the entrepreneur's profit as possible by either of the above methods. This competition can result in a Prisoner's Dilemma type of situation for the small holders. Individually rational action on their part may result in the cancellation of the project by the entrepreneur. Indeed, anyone familiar with the functioning of the urban property market must be aware of such difficulties and of the care that must be taken to prevent price-gouging when an effort is made to assemble some tract of land.[10]

If the above analysis is correct, then it is clear that situations may exist where individually rational action may not allow for socially desirable investment in the redevelopment of urban properties. Now such situations need not—indeed, in general will not—exist in all urban properties. The results of the analysis not only required special assumptions about the nature of investment returns caused by interdependencies, but it was also shown that, due to the special institutional character of tract assembly, the presence of numerous small holdings can block entrepreneurial action for redevelopment. These two conditions may or may not be filled for any given tract of land. However, we now may use the above results to *define* urban blight.[11] Blight is said to exist whenever (1) strictly individual action does not result in redevelopment, (2) the coordination of decision-making via some means would result in redevelopment, and (3) the sum of benefits from renewal could exceed the sum of costs. These conditions must be filled. We shall devote a major portion of the latter part of the paper to making this definition operational; but, for the moment, let it suffice for us to point out two factors. First, it is a problem of social policy to develop methods whereby blighted areas can be recognized and positive action can be taken to facilitate either redevelopment or renewal. Second, and this point may be controversial, blight is not necessarily associated with the outward appearance of properties in any area.

Since this second point may be subtle and seem contrary to intuitive ideas about blight, further discussion may be warranted. Note that we have defined blight strictly in relation to the allocation of resources. The fact that the properties in an area have a "poor" appearance may or may not be an indication of blight and the

[10] For example, Raymond Vernon states, "As the city developed, most of its land was cut up in small parcels and covered with durable structures of one kind or another. The problem of assembling these sites, in the absence of some type of condemnation power, required a planning horizon of many years and a willingness to risk the possibility of price gouging by the last holdout." RAYMOND VERNON, THE CHANGING ECONOMIC FUNCTION OF THE CENTRAL CITY 53 (1959). [Reprinted in Chapter 1 of this volume.—Ed.]

[11] It is to be pointed out and emphasized that our definition of the term "blight" does not seem to be what is meant by the term in common usage where it has a connotation of absolute obsolescence. Our definition refers to the misuse of land in general and carries no such connotation. The difference in meanings is unfortunate, but we could not find a more appropriate term.

malallocation of resources. For several factors, aside from tastes, help to determine the appearance of properties. The situation which we have described, where individually rational action may lead to no investment and deterioration, is only one type of case. Another may be based on the distribution of incomes. Poor classes can hardly be expected to afford the spacious and comfortable quarters of the well-to-do. Indeed, given the existence of low income households, a slum area *may* represent an efficient use of resources. If the existence of slums per se violates one's ethical standards, then, as economists, we can only point out that for elimination of slums the main economic concern must be with the distribution of income, and urban renewal is not sufficient to solve that problem. Indeed, unless some action is taken to alter the distribution of income, the renewal of slum areas is likely to lead to the creation of slum areas elsewhere.[12] It is to be emphasized that slums may or may not satisfy the definition of a blighted area. On the other hand, the mere fact that the properties in some given area appear "nice" to the eye is not sufficient evidence to indicate that blight (by our definition) is absent.

One additional remark of clarification seems warranted. It is obvious that not all individuals are free to purchase or rent property in all areas of the metropolis. Discrimination—e.g., by race—may create two or more "separate" markets, and there seems to be no reason to suspect short-run equilibrium in the sense of investment return *between* markets. We simply note here that, granted the discrimination, this fact does not affect our definition of blight, nor does it alter the proposals which we shall present.

III. A BRIEF CRITIQUE OF PRESENT PRACTICES

Having seen that, due to externalities or interdependencies and the difficulty of tract assembly, individually rational action may allow

---

[12] It is a curious fact that renewal seems to be regarded as a "cure" for slum areas. For, granted the distribution of income and the fact that the poor classes simply cannot afford to pay high enough rents to warrant the more spacious and comfortable quarters, the renewal of all slum areas, unless accompanied by an income-subsidy program, would only be self-defeating and lead to social waste. Renewal of all slum areas could cause rents for the "nicer" quarters to fall temporarily within the possible range of the poor classes, but the rents would not be sufficiently high to warrant expenditures by the landlord to maintain the structure. New slums would appear, calling for more renewal activity. This process would simply continue. On the other hand, efficient slum-removal programs are possible, and one will be presented at a later point in this paper.

blight to develop, we now turn our attention to questions of public policy. It bears repeating that wherever our definition of blight is satisfied, then resources are misallocated in the sense that some institutional arrangement—some means—exists under which redevelopment or renewal could profitably be carried out. The problem is to discover that institutional arrangement. We begin our search by examining briefly the relevant aspects of the present practices.

Title I of the Housing Act of 1949[13] seems to have set the general pattern for urban renewal practices. While the Act of 1954[14] broadened the concept, the general formula for urban redevelopment remains essentially unchanged. Both federal loans and capital grants are provided for the projects. Loans are generally for the purpose of providing working capital. The capital grants may cover up to two-thirds of the net cost of the project, with the remainder of the funds being provided by either state or local sources.[15]

The striking fact about the present program, and also about many of the proposals for extending that program, is the utter lack of a relevant criterion for expenditures. How much should be invested in urban renewal? How does one determine whether projects are really worthwhile? Does the present program attempt to "correct" the allocation of resources or does it simply result in further misallocation? There seems to have been little or no serious effort to find answers to these questions. In fact, it is widely admitted that there is a lack of adequate criteria even to determine what projects should be undertaken.[16]

It seems evident from the statements of mayors and others who propose expansions of the present program that the need approach to governmental expenditures underlies their suggestions. That is to say, a certain project "needs" to be carried out; and, granted this requirement, money is sought for the project. It should be evident that this approach to governmental expenditures may not result in

[13] 63 Stat. 413, 42 U.S.C. §§ 1441–60 (1958).
[14] 68 Stat. 622, as amended, 42 U.S.C. §§ 1450–62 (1958); 68 Stat. 596, as amended, 12 U.S.C. §§ 1715k, 1715l (1958).
[15] There are, of course, conditions which must be satisfied before a community can be eligible for federal funds. See, e.g., COMM'N ON INTERGOVERNMENTAL RELATIONS, TWENTY-FIVE FEDERAL GRANT-IN-AID PROGRAMS (1955).
[16] A remark by Morton J. Schussheim, Deputy Director of the Area Development Division of the Committee for Economic Development, is interesting in this respect. Mr. Schussheim writes, "It is true . . . that local officials responsible for urban renewal programs do not have adequate criteria for determining what projects to undertake and on what scale." A Pure Theory of Urban Renewal: A Comment, 34 LAND ECONOMICS 395 (1960).

the correct allocation of resources. The need approach obscures budgetary considerations and makes comparison of alternatives difficult, since a need is simply assumed without reference to other possible areas of expenditure. The need approach is arbitrary and overlooks the return on investment, an extremely important consideration for the problem of a rational allocation of resources.[17]

IV. REDISTRIBUTION, THE COST-BENEFIT CRITERION, AND URBAN RENEWAL

Having pointed out that the existing institutional arrangements concerning urban renewal contain no explicit criterion for determining either the amount of such expenditure or when a project is desirable, we now propose the previously introduced benefits-cost criterion and will discuss later the institutional arrangements under which it could be applied. First, however, let us detail more fully our use of this criterion and the reasons for its selection.

We assume that income and utility are positively correlated. This means that if potential benefits, appropriately-defined, exceed costs, then the conditions for Pareto optimality, in the absence of corrective measures, are not filled. It is possible for some action to be taken which will make one or more persons better off without making anyone worse off.[18] In this context, the action will take the form of investment in urban renewal.

It is to be emphasized again that the benefits-cost criterion refers only to the problem of efficiency—*i.e.*, to the allocation of resources on the basis of a given distribution of income. However, it is possible to design programs which do redistribute income but which still are completely compatible with the benefit-cost criterion. The point is that the two problems—distribution and allocation—must be kept conceptually separate.

[17] It may be commonplace to point out that there exists for any given social action a social welfare function which is maximal for that action, and by definition this resource allocation is optimal. Our point is simply that it seems dubious that a type of need approach to forming criteria is reasonable, given that urban problems are not unique as a social problem.

[18] It is easy to see the exact relation between benefits-costs and the Pareto condition. If the sum of benefits exceeds the sum of costs for some particular action, then although some individual might be made worse off by the action, it is theoretically possible to pay compensation to that individual so that the Pareto condition will be satisfied.

Given the fact that interdependencies are a cause of blight, two kinds of actions are possible—preventive and reconstructive. We consider first preventive action.

As was pointed out earlier, the problem in preventing the development of blight consists essentially in finding methods of coordinating the decisions about investment in repair and upkeep so that the socially and individually desirable choices are equated. One step in this direction can be made through the development and use of a special type of building code which bears a superficial resemblance to municipal zoning.[19] It can be seen from the Prisoner's Dilemma example discussed earlier that it is individually desirable to invest *if there is assurance that all individuals will be constrained to make a similar decision.* The special building code specifying minimum levels of repair and upkeep can provide a rough approximation toward optimal levels of coordination.

A brief outline of the scheme follows: Since it is intuitively obvious that different types of property require different kinds of repair and types of upkeep, it would seem desirable that these building codes differ according to the type property under consideration. The role of the planner would be to try to determine the proper restrictions for each type of property. He could try to gather information on interaction effects through the use of statistical sampling techniques and questionnaires. He then could draw up districts and try to estimate the proper level of the building code for each district. A crude approximation to the benefit-cost criterion is easily supplied. It is advantageous to property owners mutually to constrain themselves to make "appropriate" repair expenditures, for this coordinates decisions. Therefore, the planner can simply submit the proposed code for each district to the property owners of that district; if the planner has proposed an appropriate code, then mutual consent should be forthcoming. If mutual consent is not obtained, then it would seem suitable to

[19] It is to be emphasized that the building code envisioned here bears only a superficial resemblance to zoning. The two tools are aimed at different problems. Municipal zoning tries to prevent the establishment of "undesirable" properties in specified neighborhoods. These special building codes would be aimed at the elimination of interdependencies affecting repair and upkeep decisions. For an elaboration on the complexities involved in municipal zoning, see Davis & Whinston, *The Economics of Complex Systems: The Case of Municipal Zoning* (O.N.R. Research Memorandum, Graduate School of Industrial Administration, Carnegie Institute of Technology, 1961).

assume that the proper code for the district has not been proposed and that a new proposal would be necessary.[20]

While codes adopted via the above scheme should be helpful in preventing blight, it must be noted that implementation of this plan would require the selection of an appropriate institutional and legal framework. As economists, we do not pretend to know the legal difficulties which might be involved; but a joint effort by the two professions to set up the framework for such a scheme seems to us to be desirable.

Let us now turn our attention to the policy problem when blight is already in existence. Present practices provide something of a framework here; what is missing is a relevant criterion. Of course, it should be noted that it may sometimes be possible to obtain redevelopment through individual effort via the previously-stated special-building-code method. In other instances, the optimal property uses may have changed from what they formerly were. The area may be composed of lots too small to obtain an orderly transition of property uses by means of the building code. It may be desirable to replan streets, or other reasons may be advanced for the usual type of urban renewal effort. Therefore, let us try to determine the appropriate comparison of costs and benefits when the usual type renewal activity takes place.

Let us assume that the city government has marked some blighted area for redevelopment. Taking the property tax rate as given, suppose that the city has raised funds for the project by selling bonds. With the money thus raised, the city has purchased the blighted area, using the right of eminent domain wherever needed. Suppose that the city has demolished the outdated structures, made adequate provision for public services, and then, having finished its part of the operation, sold lots to entrepreneurs who have agreed in advance to build, say, modern apartment buildings.

Note what city action has accomplished. It has removed the obstacles to private renewal. The right of eminent domain has removed the possibility of price-gouging and stubborn property

[20] Our use of the term "mutual consent" may represent something of a subterfuge. In actuality, it may not be desirable to insist on unanimity nor would it seem desirable to use a simple majority. Something on the order of eighty to ninety per cent may be reasonable. For a discussion of the problems involved in voting and the difficulties associated with the selection of political decision rules, see JAMES M. BUCHANAN & GORDON TULLOCK, THE CALCULUS OF CONSENT (1962).

owners acting so as to prevent the assembly of a large enough tract. Each entrepreneur who buys the lots from the city is assured that adjoining lots will also be suitably developed, so that interaction difficulties are eliminated.

One fact needs great emphasis here. *The elimination of externalities or interaction effects causes social and private products to be equated.* Therefore, if possible redistribution is left aside; and if for the moment problems are waived which arise from public projects where the market mechanism does not serve as an adequate guide, then it can be stated that revenues and expenditures can be made identical to costs and benefits. Therefore, renewal projects are warranted if, and only if, revenues exceed expenditures. And, even where problems associated with redistribution and public projects are not waived, it is still possible to make the revenue-expenditure criterion approximate the benefit-cost criterion, although some administrative difficulties are involved.

What are the appropriate comparisons of costs and benefits? Consider first the case without the complications. The costs of the local government include the acquisition of land, demolition and improvements, aiding the relocation of displaced families, and interest expenses.[21] The measurement of revenues is slightly more complicated. The primary item, of course, would be receipts from the sale of lots. Since we are dealing with local government, however, a tax on real property will exist. Since the discounted value of the tax is likely to be shifted onto the immobile resource—land—it is necessary to account for this factor. If the project is successful, the new structures should have a higher value than the old; so there should be a net addition to tax revenues. This net addition should be discounted to a present value and counted as a receipt from the project. Thus, a comparison of revenues and expenses is possible, and the project is warranted only if revenues exceed expenses.

We now consider the second case with the additional complications. Note that the previous discussion still applies here, with the following qualifications upon the administrative rules involved. If public projects such as parks, playgrounds, public buildings, and so

---

[21] Peculiarly enough, the present-day requirement that individuals be paid for their property and the administrative rule of aiding individuals who may be dislocated to find new quarters affords a method of approximate compensation so that the Pareto condition can be satisfied.

forth, are planned in conjunction with the renewal effort, then estimates of the social benefit to be derived from these projects must be made by the governmental unit or units which ordinarily pay for them.[22] These estimated benefits are to be considered as revenues from the renewal effort, and the appropriate governmental units are to be required to contribute these amounts to the authority which administers the renewal activity. Thus the revenue-expenditure criterion should very closely approximate the benefits-cost criterion, depending, of course, upon how well the governmental units estimate the social benefits derived from the special public projects.

If there happens to exist some agreed-upon ethical distribution of income, then we point out first that urban renewal is not an efficient method of achieving redistribution. Possible benefits might accrue to special groups instead of the low-income classes. Other methods for simple redistribution exist which should be preferred to urban renewal. However, if the ethical distribution is connected with some arbitrary housing standard below which conditions are viewed as inadequate for "decent living," the cost-benefit criterion need not be rendered useless. Conditional subsidies could be granted to the low-income households living in substandard housing. These subsidies would make it possible for the cost-benefit criterion to work effectively for renewal purposes.

Several corollaries to the cost-benefit criterion should be pointed out. If problems of ethical income distribution are waived, then from the standpoint of a rational allocation of resources, no federal or state subsidies are needed for urban renewal purposes per se. Of course, the adjustments made for the second case may have to be accomplished, but note that in reality these are based upon considerations not directly dependent upon urban renewal. Renewal projects should not lose money. Indeed, they should result in a profit. On the other hand, granted the fact that constitutional and/or statutory debt limits have often been imposed upon local governments, these should be waived for borrowing for urban renewal purposes. Finally, the local governments should be granted the power of eminent domain for urban renewal purposes.

[22] We assume that the units which ordinarily pay for this type of public projects are identical to the units which derive the benefits from these projects. If this is not the case, then further administrative adjustments have to be made, but these adjustments should be made anyway and should not be dependent upon possible urban renewal projects.

CONCLUSION

In arriving at these indications for the use of the cost-benefit criterion in urban renewal, we started with the Pareto condition. However, it was suggested that other social welfare functions, which allow for income redistribution or even minimum condition housing, need not affect the usefulness of this criterion as long as the rational allocation of resources is viewed as a *conceptually separate* problem. It is to be emphasized that for the purpose of urban renewal, conceptual separation of the two problems can be achieved through the methods outlined above.

PART II

URBAN RENEWAL: BACKGROUND
AND GOALS

4 Federal Urban Renewal Legislation*

ASHLEY A. FOARD AND HILBERT FEFFERMAN†

This article outlines the early origins, the struggle for enactment, and the development of federal urban renewal legislation. It also discusses separately two of several major issues which recurringly give rise to changes in that legislation. One concerns restrictions in the federal law which direct federal urban renewal aids toward the betterment of housing, as distinguished from the betterment of cities and of urban life in general. The other concerns the statutory formula for apportioning the cost of the program between the federal government and local governments.

. . . No one . . . would expect a major federal program such as urban renewal, even though it may be urgently needed and broadly supported, to be quickly formulated in detail adequate for enactment and swiftly enacted into law. A few might, however, underestimate the pitfalls and the time required. Some delays are inherent in the routine operations of the democratic legislative process, but the greatest delays in obtaining the enactment of legislation are to be

* Reprinted, with some revisions, from a symposium, *Urban Renewal: Part I*, Vol. 25, No. 4 (Autumn 1960), pp. 635–684, by permission from *Law and Contemporary Problems*, published by the Duke University School of Law, Durham, North Carolina. Copyright © 1960 by Duke University.

† The views expressed are those of the writers, who in no way purport in this article to speak for the Housing and Home Finance Agency, with which agency they are presently employed.

expected when there are many diverse and important interests involved; and this may be true even after there is much agreement that the legislation's underlying purpose is good. The history of the basic federal urban renewal statute—Title I of the Housing Act of 1949[1]—was not exceptional in this regard. It involved very many diverse interests and extended over a period of many years.[2]

I. EARLY ORIGINS OF THE FEDERAL LAW

The major outlines of the 1949 legislation were distinctly visible in proposals made as early as 1941.[3] *A Handbook on Urban Redevelopment for Cities in the United States,* published in November

[1] 63 Stat. 413, 414, 42 U.S.C. § 1441 *et seq.* (1958).

[2] Because the lengthy legislative history is crowded with many bills, hearings, and reports, this article will be burdened with many references and dates which are included largely to fill the needs of readers who may wish to consult the inadequately indexed primary sources. However, it is not possible within the space available to describe the history of detailed provisions of the law. Neither would it be very helpful, even if possible, to trace the basic provisions of the statute to the first person or persons who may have proposed them. As is so often true when problems are widely felt, similar solutions often occur at about the same time to many persons independently. The writers have not infrequently drafted laws to conform to legislative solutions hammered out in their presence, only to hear strangers later claim, obviously in good faith, to be the authors of the proposals. In some cases work, while unknown to the writers as draftsmen, had influenced their principals; and in other cases, work, though done earlier, had gone unnoticed when the legislation was written.

[3] Proposals for eliminating slums and blight were, of course, made much earlier. See, for example, the early suggestions made or referred to in the following publications: 3 THE PRESIDENT'S [HOOVER] CONFERENCE ON HOME BUILDING AND HOME OWNERSHIP ch. 1, app. VII (1932); Symposium, *Low Cost Housing and Slum Clearance,* 1 LAW & CONTEMP. PROB. 135–256 (1934); II JAMES FORD, SLUMS AND HOUSING chs. 27, 30, 35 (1936); Engle, *The British Housing Program,* 190 ANNALS 191 (1937); Keppler, *Housing in the Netherlands, id.* at 205; MABEL L. WALKER, URBAN BLIGHT AND SLUMS chs. 25, 28, 29 (12 Harvard City Planning Studies 1938). The earlier proposals are not reviewed here because they did not receive the direct attention of the congressional committees which considered urban redevelopment legislation, or because they relate to experience in other countries, or are not directed to federally-aided programs, or are not stated in much detail. Also, many earlier and detailed proposals for federal aid are not within the scope of this article because they approach the problem of eliminating slums and blight primarily through federal aid for low-rent housing construction, thereby conforming to the pattern of the United States Housing Act of 1937, rather than of the 1949 legislation. For example, in NATIONAL RESOURCES COMMITTEE, OUR CITIES—THEIR ROLE IN THE NATIONAL ECONOMY (1937), contrast the very general reference to cooperation by the federal government under the heading "Abolition of the Slum" (*id.* at 75) with the specific recommendations for federal action under the headings "Housing" (*id.* at 76) and "Six" (*id.* at xi).

1941, by the Federal Housing Administration, dealt with the problems of urban slums and blight and with the need for municipal rehabilitation and redevelopment. It recommended a planning agency for each city and also a corporate arm of local government to be known as a "city realty corporation" with broad powers to acquire, hold, and dispose of real property for redevelopment, including the power to acquire sites through eminent domain. This proposal contemplated the long-term leasing of tracts, before or after clearance of buildings, to privately-financed redevelopment corporations for construction in accordance with approved plans conforming to the master plan of the city. The possible need for federal financial aid to the community was suggested.

In December of the same year, 1941, a proposal conforming in more details to the federal urban redevelopment program as later authorized was made in an article, *Urban Redevelopment and Housing*, by Guy Greer and Alvin H. Hansen.[4] It opens with the following statement:

With few exceptions, our American cities and towns have drifted into a situation, both physically and financially, that is becoming intolerable. Their plight, moreover, is getting progressively worse.

The authors listed as the two chief obstacles in the way of replanning by the cities and of rebuilding by private enterprise: first, the lack of adequate powers in local governments to control the use of land; and secondly, the frozen status of high land costs in slum and blighted areas. The following are features of their proposal for removing these two obstacles:

1. Federal loans or subsidies to communities for the elimination of slums and blighted areas, and technical aid to planning agencies of the communities.

2. Comprehensive state enabling legislation granting necessary powers to the city or a "special unit" of local government, especially to authorize the acquisition of land through eminent domain where necessary.

3. Requirements that the proposed redevelopment plan (i) be in accordance with a master plan for the community, and (ii) indicate the future use of each portion of the acquired area, whether to be for public or private purposes.

[4] Published as a pamphlet by the National Planning Association.

4. Acquisition by local governments of land in slum and blighted areas with funds advanced from the federal government, as a step preliminary to demolition and redevelopment.

5. Use of land for redevelopment to be independent of acquisition cost to the community, and recognition that acquisition cost of slum and blighted areas would normally exceed the direct dollar return to the community for use of the land.

6. Repayment of federal advances, to the extent possible, from proceeds from use of the land, but recognition of need for federal loss of funds.

7. Provision of public works in relation to the undertaking.

8. Demolition and rebuilding or rehabilitation to proceed as rapidly as feasible.

9. The *quid pro quo* of federal financial aid should be the initiation by the urban community of a long-range program of replanning and rebuilding.

With one important modification, the first eight of these features are to be found in the federally-aided program as contemplated by the 1949 Act, and the ninth is strikingly similar to the requirement enacted in 1954 that the locality shall, in return for the federal aid, adopt a long-range "workable program" for dealing with its overall problem of slums and blight.

The major difference between the 1941 proposal and the 1949 Act relates to the type of federal subsidy. The Greer-Hansen proposal contemplated a subsidy, indefinite in amount, which would be made available over a long period of time.[5] This form of subsidy appears to be geared to the expectation (which Greer and Hansen shared

---

[5] Thus, it was suggested that federal advances for land acquisition might be repaid, with some interest, but only to the extent that this could be done by paying during a period of 50 years or so, something like two-thirds of the proceeds received by the municipality from leasing the land to redevelopers. See also three other suggestions described in Hansen, *Three Plans for Financing Urban Redevelopment*, appearing in *Hearings Before the Subcommittee on Housing and Urban Redevelopment of the Senate Special Committee on Post-War Economic Policy and Planning*, 79th Cong., 1st Sess. pt. 9, at 1622 (1945) [hereinafter cited as *Taft Subcommittee Hearings*]. One plan called for federal loans amortized over 100 years and bearing 1% interest, the federal subsidy consisting of the low interest rate. The city's general credit would be pledged to the repayment. A second plan called for full federal guaranties of tax-exempt revenue bonds sold by the city to private investors. Revenues would consist of income from leased project land, and to the extent that the revenues were inadequate for retiring the bonds, the difference would be contributed, two-thirds by the federal government and one-third by the local government. The third plan would simply obligate the city to repay federal advances, with 1% interest, utilizing revenues from leasing project land, the general credit of the

with the authors of the 1941 FHA Handbook) that the land would normally be made available to private redevelopers under long-term leases, which would make the net loss on each project depend upon rentals paid over a long period of years. The 1949 Act, on the other hand, provided for a lump sum federal capital grant which would defray two-thirds of the net loss or "net project cost" as that highly technical term is defined in the statute. Quite clearly, the act contemplates that the land would generally be sold to redevelopers in fee.[6] When this is done, the major actual receipts are known, and it is much easier, without excessive artificiality, to calculate the federal grant as a percentage of the "net project cost." Thus, the expectation that project land would generally be sold in fee tends to reinforce the use of a "capital grant" type of federal subsidy in preference to other forms of subsidy, payable over long terms.

On April 2, 1943, Senator Thomas of Utah introduced S. 953, Seventy-eighth Congress, which closely paralleled the Greer-Hansen proposal.[7] The bill would have provided for federal advances to municipalities for acquiring land to be redeveloped pursuant to local plans which had been federally approved. The advances were to be repayable, with two per cent annual interest, from rentals received by the municipality from leasing to private redevelopers project land not retained for public improvements. A later draft of the bill substituted a one per cent interest rate.[8] No federal grant was proposed, the federal "subsidy" consisting of the low interest rate and the risk of loss which would result from the indefinite period for

city not being pledged. The federal "subsidy" would consist of the low interest rate and the high risk of loss.

Similar proposals for long-term loans (99 years) bearing very low interest rates, or even no interest, or for federal guarantees, were made by National Housing Administrator John B. Blandford, Jr., during these Hearings. *Taft Subcommittee Hearings*, pt. 4, at 1052, pt. 6, at 1305.

[6] The 1949 Act also makes provision for cases where all or some of the land will be leased. § 102(a) provides for "definitive" (long-term) federal loans which become necessary when the leasing of project land by the city eliminates or reduces sales proceeds available for immediate repayment of "temporary" federal loans. 63 Stat. 414, 42 U.S.C. § 1452(a) (1958). § 110(f) provides for imputing a value to land which is leased, this value being treated, for purposes of calculating the federal capital grant, as though it were sales proceeds. 63 Stat. 421, 42 U.S.C. § 1460(f) (1958).

[7] Professor Hansen participated in the drafting, done largely by Alfred Bettman of Cincinnati, then Chairman of the Legislative Committee of the American Institute of Planners and also of the American Bar Association Committee on Planning Law and Legislation.

[8] Draft dated Dec. 10, 1943, printed for Committee use and reprinted in *Taft Subcommittee Hearings* pt. 9, at 1625.

repayment and from not pledging the general credit of the city to repayment. Also, federal advances which the bill would have authorized for preparing a master city plan and for planning specific redevelopment projects would apparently have been repayable only if a loan were later made for land acquisition. Senator Wagner of New York, on June 4, 1943, introduced, at the request of the Urban Land Institute, S. 1163, Seventy-eighth Congress, which would have provided for ninety-nine year federal loans to municipalities for acquisition. The loans would have been repayable only from the proceeds of the lease or sale of the project land, with interest to be determined by the National Housing Agency.[9] Federal grants were to be limited to the locality's planning expenses.

The Thomas bill, while technically pending before the Senate Committee on Education and Labor, actually received instead the attention of the Subcommittee on Housing and Urban Redevelopment of the Senate Special Committee on Post-War Economic Policy and Planning.[10] Under the very active chairmanship of Senator Taft, the Subcommittee conducted extensive and unusually searching hearings and studies between mid-1944 and mid-1945 on a very broad range of housing and urban development problems. Its report on *Postwar Housing*, dated August 1, 1945, and printed for the use of the full Committee, recommended:[11]

[9] Predecessor of the Housing and Home Finance Agency.

[10] This was so because clearly any new federal aid program involving the tearing down of many structures would have to await the winning of World War II. Meanwhile, many thought it important to formulate such a program in advance of the war's end so that it would be available to help take up an expected slack in economic activity while industry converted from war to peace production. In introducing his bill, Senator Thomas stated: "It is of the highest importance that, in the reconversion from a wartime to a peacetime economy and the absorption of labor and resources which will be released by the termination of the war, the public expenditures which will be made shall be placed in projects which are both socially useful and economically sound." Senator Thomas in no way implied that the proposed slum-clearance program was a temporary one for the postwar period, and Senator Wagner, in introducing his bill, denied that it was a "postwar" or "public-works" or "relief" or "pump-priming" bill. He emphasized that it was instead a program of federal aid for land development and redevelopment by private enterprise, and that the problem should be faced before the war is over in order for industry, finance, and state and local governments to be "ready to act when the war is over."

[11] See p. 23, para. (g), and pp. 17–19. The recommendation that the program be established "on a provisional basis" is explained in the report by the need for experimentation resulting from lack of information as to the size of the task, the extent of the losses to be incurred from acquiring, clearing, and disposing of land, and the amount and nature of the aid which should be provided by the federal government.

The establishment, on a provisional basis, of a new form of assistance to cities in ridding themselves of unhealthful housing conditions and of restoring blighted areas to productive use by private enterprise.

The Subcommittee recommended that the National Housing Agency be authorized to undertake a program of loans and annual contributions to assist municipalities in acquiring and clearing slum or blighted areas and disposing of them through sale or lease for public or private purposes. Redevelopment would be in accordance with a plan for the specific project area and consistent with "a general guiding plan, prepared by an official local planning agency, for the clearance of all slums in the city." The federal annual contributions would be made for a period not exceeding forty-five years and would have the purpose "of covering the financial charges on the estimated or actual amount (whichever is the lesser) of the difference between (a) the total acquisition and demolition costs and (b) the recovery through sale or lease." The federal contributions would not exceed a fixed percentage of the financing costs involved. The municipality would be required to contribute an amount at least equal to one-half of the federal contributions, thereby in effect limiting the federal contributions to two-thirds of the net cost. The federal government would "retain the power of election to substitute a capital payment in lieu of its outstanding annual contributions commitment at any time." Federal loans for site acquisition and demolition would be authorized with maximum maturities of twenty years and at an interest rate not exceeding the "going rate" paid by the federal government on its own obligations.

The proposed federal aid formula parallels the program of loans and annual contributions for low-rent public housing authorized in the United States Housing Act of 1937.[12] Both included federal loans to the locality (at interest rates based on a "going rate" paid by the federal treasury) to cover capital outlays; federal annual contributions over long periods of time to help defray a major portion of net losses; and local contributions to help defray a lesser portion of the net losses. Both programs also contemplated that there would be a definite upper limit on the federal contributions but that the assured federal contributions would be sufficient to make it possible to turn to the private market for a major share of the financing. Both also made provision for an alternate type of

12 50 Stat. 888, 42 U.S.C. § 1401 (1958).

federal subsidy in the form of a lump-sum capital grant.[13] The similarities between the Taft Subcommittee's proposal and the 1937 Act are to a considerable extent traceable to experience under the 1937 Act. This is especially true of the proposal to make federal contributions over a long period of years. More important, however, are the basic underlying forces which shaped both the act and the proposal. The Subcommittee report stated that "an essential feature of any plan of Federal assistance should be provision for limiting the extent of the loss to be borne by the Federal Government and for sharing . . . costs by the municipality." The report also stated that the Subcommittee did not find in the testimony any proposals that fully conformed to these principles. Senator Taft, during the course of the hearings, had previously revealed by his questions and comments that he would oppose an indefinite subsidy such as that involved in a very low interest rate and that he would seek a federal assistance formula that involved some definite contribution from the local community or a state.[14]

In emphasizing the many similarities between the Taft Subcommittee's proposal and the United States Housing Act of 1937, it is important not to lose sight of the basic difference between the two. Whereas the 1937 Act was intended to help clear slums[15] through

[13] In fact, this authority was not used under the 1937 Act, whereas it was later adopted as the sole form of basic subsidy under the 1949 Act.

[14] *Taft Subcommittee Hearings* pt. 9, at 1612, 1613.

[15] The title of the 1937 Act was "An Act to provide financial assistance to the States and political subdivisions thereof *for the elimination of unsafe and insanitary housing conditions, for the eradication of slums,* for the provision of decent, safe and sanitary dwellings for families of low income, and for the reduction of unemployment and the stimulation of business activity, to create a United States Housing Authority, and for other purposes." (Emphasis added.) The Act itself required the elimination by demolition, effective closing, or compulsory improvement of unsafe or insanitary dwellings in the locality substantially equal in number to the dwellings provided with the federal aid. Under earlier authority, the federal government itself constructed low-rent housing projects through the Housing Division of the Public Works Administration. These were known as low-cost housing and "slum clearance" projects. See authority in § 202(d) of the National Industrial Recovery Act, 48 Stat. 195, 201 (1933). The emphasis on slum clearance purposes in the public housing legislation was thought necessary in order to justify the taking of private property through eminent domain. The elimination of slums was considered to be more clearly a "public purpose" involving the public health than was the construction of low-rent housing. Some may regard it as a paradox that, while the slum clearance purpose was emphasized by the courts during the 1930's in cases upholding the taking of private land for public housing projects, these early housing cases (some involving slum clearance only indirectly) were sometimes the decisive factor during the 1950's in obtaining

federal loans and annual contributions for the provision of low-rent housing, the new proposal contemplated that the federal subsidy would be addressed directly to the loss from assembling, clearing, and disposing of the land, with "the same degree of assistance" being given regardless of the type of redevelopment.

Another recommendation by the Subcommittee foreshadowed a significant provision of the 1949 Act. The Subcommittee recommended that in estimating the municipality's contribution, credit be given not only for the value of land transferred to the project and the cost of streets, public utilities, and other site facilities incident to the project, but also for expenditures on "public buildings made necessary by the project." Finally, the Subcommittee contemplated, as does the 1949 Act, that land would be disposed of through sale or lease, whereas many earlier proposals were predicated on leasing as the normal, or even sole, method of disposal.[16]

II. THE STRUGGLE FOR ENACTMENT

The history of the specific legislation which became Title I of the Housing Act of 1949 begins in 1945 in the Seventy-ninth Congress.

---

judicial approval for the taking of land by a city for purposes of direct slum clearance and private redevelopment.

See also § 201(a) (2) of the Emergency Relief and Construction Act of 1932, 47 Stat. 709, 711, under which the Reconstruction Finance Corporation was authorized "to make loans to corporations formed wholly for the purpose of providing housing for families of low income, or for reconstruction of slum areas, which are regulated by State or municipal law as to rents, charges, capital structure, rate of return, and areas and methods of operation, to aid in financing projects, undertaken by such corporations which are self-liquidating in character." One such loan financed a large privately-owned rental housing project (Knickerbocker Village) built on a slum-cleared site in New York City.

[16] During the hearings, Alfred Bettman testified that the leasing policy embodied in Senator Thomas's bill was "debatable" and "should perhaps be changed so as to permit sales." He stated: "While there is much to be said in favor of a lease land tenure policy as promotive of the stabilizing of the plans upon which the Federal aid would be based, nevertheless the time may not have as yet arrived for the adoption of that policy." Other proponents of leasing may have been motivated not only by the tighter municipal control over land use, but also by the possibility of capturing for the municipality long-range increases in land value, thereby offsetting losses due to clearance. However, members of the Subcommittee apparently felt that neither of these considerations warranted a displacement of private ownership and control (subject to restrictions in the redevelopment plan) over large areas of urban real property. In any event, it was felt that a federal law should certainly not be written so as to preclude the municipality from selling project land. *Taft Subcommittee Hearings* pt. 9, at 1611.

The bill which was enacted in 1949 was one of a long series of companion or rival bills which successively and almost continuously received the attention of the Banking and Currency Committees of the House and Senate during three Congresses. On August 1, 1945, Senator Wagner of New York, for himself and for Senator Ellender of Louisiana, introduced S. 1342, Seventy-ninth Congress. Its urban redevelopment provisions very closely followed the recommendations of the Taft Subcommittee report, which was dated that same day. On November 14, S. 1592, Seventy-ninth Congress, containing similar provisions, was introduced as a substitute bill by Senator Wagner of New York, for himself and Senators Ellender and Taft. Senators Wagner and Ellender had served on the Taft Subcommittee; Senator Wagner was also Chairman of the regular Committee on Banking and Currency to which S. 1592 was referred; and Senator Taft was the second ranking minority member of that Committee.

Title VI of the bill was headed "Land Assembly for Participation by Private Enterprise in Development or Redevelopment Programs." Other titles of S. 1592 provided for the establishment of a permanent national housing agency; a housing research program; grants to localities for urban planning; substantial changes in the operations of the Federal Home Loan Bank Board and the Federal Savings and Loan Insurance Corporation; extensive changes in the mortgage insurance operations of the Federal Housing Administration, including special programs for moderate income families and for cooperative housing; a new program under which the FHA would insure the annual yield on mortgage-free private investment in rental housing projects; the disposition of federally-owned war housing; a new program of loans and grants by the Secretary of Agriculture for farm housing; and authorization over a period of years for 500,000 additional low-rent public housing units. Many of these proposals were highly controversial. During the sixteen days of committee hearings held between November 27, 1945, and January 25, 1946, especially bitter opposition was expressed by the home-building, mortgage-lending, and real estate industries to the proposed enlargement of the low-rent public housing program. While more narrowly based, there was equally vigorous opposition to many other provisions of the bill. For example, the savings-and-loan segment of the mortgage-lending industry objected strongly to the inclusion of the Federal Home Loan Bank Board and the Federal Savings and Loan Insurance Corporation as subordinate agencies in the proposed permanent National Housing Agency. Although more than a little criticism was directed at the urban redevelopment title, it was clear to observers at the hearings that this title was not generating really heated objections. Indeed, the National Association of Real Estate Boards and the United States Savings and Loan League endorsed the principle of federal aid for slum clearance and urban redevelopment, while objections expressed by the National Association of Home Builders and the Mortgage Bankers of America were stated rather mildly.[17]

[17] A representative of the National Association of Real Estate Boards (which had once itself proposed federal loans for urban redevelopment) suggested that the enactment of federal aid for slum clearance and private redevelopment would enable private enterprise to do the job that public housing was supposed to do. He also testified as follows: "The National Association of Real Estate Boards strongly favors a program for urban redevelopment. . . . We would want to see legislation that would assure local control of the projects from start to finish, and Federal financial assistance made in lump sum grants on a 50-50 matching basis for land assembly purposes. . . . We favor putting the Federal contribution into an outright grant, because in that way you know exactly what it will cost the United States Treasury. . . . The annual contribution is vicious, also, in that it insures Federal domination of the municipality." *Hearings Before the Senate Committee on Banking and Currency on S. 1592, General Housing Act of 1945*, 79th Cong., 1st Sess. 454–55, 480–81 (1945–46). It is true that the Association by 1947 had reversed its position and opposed federal aid for urban redevelopment. *Hearings Before the Senate Committee on Banking and Currency on S. 866 Housing*, 80th Cong., 1st Sess. 345, 363, 368 (1947). However, the main grounds for the objection at that time seemed to be that state and local aids were sufficient for such a program and that large-scale redevelopment was not likely while housing conditions were tight. By 1949, even these objections by the Association were weakened when its representative, in opposing enactment of Title I of the Housing Act of 1949, stated that he was "not necessarily" opposed to federal money for slum clearance by local redevolpment agencies, but that he was opposed to Title I "as presently written." On the same occasion, another representative of the Association, when pressed for the grounds of his objections to Title I, referred to a provision for developing "open urban land" and stated "that is our objection to the bill." *Hearings Before the Senate Committee on Banking and Currency on S. 138, General Housing Legislation*, 81st Cong., 1st Sess. 411, 413 (1949). By 1954, the Association had come a long way around toward its original position, expressing approval of the Title I program if major emphasis were placed on conservation and rehabilitation, with clearance being focused on the very worst slum pockets that cannot be rehabilitated. *Hearings Before the Senate Committee on Banking and Currency on S. 2889, Housing Act of 1954*, 83d Cong., 2d Sess. 440–41 (1954).

Testimony presented on behalf of the United States Savings and Loan League included the following statements: "Our people have studied the problem of slum clearance for some years and agree that it is an appropriate field for public action and public expenditure. We have felt that the procedure could be carried out largely by local governments and that, after the land so

The omnibus bill was reported by the Senate Banking and Currency Committee on April 8, 1946, with many amendments, but with its major proposals retained.[18] Despite the widespread opposition, chiefly flowing from trade associations, but with vigorous support for the bill from many professional, municipal, religious, and labor organizations,[19] the bill was passed by the Senate on April 15, 1946 with overwhelming bipartisan support. There was no record vote, but during the voice vote, observers in the gallery noted that, in a well-attended chamber, not a single senator voted against final passage.

The opposition made itself far more strongly felt in the House,

---

acquired was written down to a reasonable use value, it should be used for its highest and best use, public or private. We have clearly felt that it should not be used exclusively for public housing. We think it is appropriate for the Federal Government to furnish money to be used along with funds of States and municipalities for such land assembly in the slum areas of our cities." Criticisms of the provisions were addressed to matters of detail. The League testified that the provisions were unnecessarily complex; that the proposed annual contributions "involve a complicated and expensive approach" and that the transaction "could better be handled by direct grants at the outset"; and that the law should make it completely clear that land could be redeveloped for other than public housing purposes and that local public housing authorities would not necessarily administer the program locally. *Hearings Before the Senate Committee on Banking and Currency on S. 1592, General Housing Act of 1945*, 79th Cong., 1st Sess. 837–38, 844–45 (1945–46).

The President of the National Association of Home Builders testified against "Federal subsidies for public housing and slum clearance" in S. 1592, but, except for reference to the funds involved, his entire discussion was directed to the public housing provisions and not to the slum clearance provisions. *Id.* at 599–602. Testimony which was offered against the slum clearance provisions of S. 1592 on behalf of the Mortgage Bankers of America consisted of the following relatively mild objection: "We cannot say that these provisions are the best answer to this important problem. We believe, however, that the expenditure of federal funds *at this time* is inflationary and inopportune." *Id.* at 404–05. (Emphasis added.)

[18] Senate Comm. on Banking and Currency, *General Housing Act of 1946*, S. Rep. No. 1131, 79th Cong., 2d Sess. (1946). The report contains both a brief summary and a detailed section-by-section analysis of the bill as reported. (The bill was debated in the Senate on April 11 and 15, 1946.)

[19] Organizations supporting the bill included the American Association of Social Workers, American Association of University Women, American Federation of Labor, American Public Health Association, American Veterans of World War II (AMVETS), Congress of Industrial Organizations, Federal Council of Churches of Christ in America, National Association of Housing Officials, National Board of the Young Women's Christian Association, National Catholic Welfare Council, National Conference of Catholic Charities, National Council of Jewish Women, National Institute of Municipal Law Officers, United States Conference of Mayors, and Veterans of Foreign Wars of the United States.

where opponents of the more controversial features were able to gain the support of many representatives from rural districts. Opponents of the Wagner-Ellender-Taft bill in the House rallied around a rival bill, H.R. 6205, Seventy-ninth Congress, introduced on April 18, 1946, by Representative Wolcott of Michigan, ranking Republican member of the House Committee on Banking and Currency. His bill, unlike the Senate bill, made no provision for a permanent over-all housing agency, additional low-rent public housing, special FHA mortgage insurance aids for moderate-income families and cooperatives, FHA yield insurance on rental housing, and farm housing aids. However, the Wolcott bill did propose a federal urban redevelopment program, perhaps in recognition of the fact that this was a far less controversial proposal than those excluded from the bill.[20] Although the proposal differed greatly from that in the Senate bill, it gave support to the principle that substantial federal aid was warranted for this purpose. Thus, the Wolcott bill would have authorized the Reconstruction Finance Corporation to make $1 billion of federal loan funds and $1 billion of federal capital grants available to localities for slum clearance projects. The major difference in the federal formula under the two bills was that federal grants under the Wolcott bill would have been limited to one-half, rather than two-thirds, of the net project cost.[21]

Hearings on general housing legislation were scheduled in the House Committee on Banking and Currency on June 28 and 29, and on July 1, 3, and 5, 1946. On each occasion, the Committee adjourned on a point of order raised by opponents of the Wagner-Ellender-Taft bill on the grounds that the House was in session. The House hearings were neither completed nor published and the Seventy-ninth Congress adjourned on August 2, 1946, without the bill having reached the floor of the House. This was only the beginning of a long series of similar disappointments to be suffered by the sponsors of general housing legislation and of federal aid for urban redevelopment.

[20] Senator Ellender recognized this fact when he inserted in the *Congressional Record* twelve questions and answers which were later printed as a pamphlet, *Objections to the Wagner-Ellender-Taft Bill Are Not Valid*. Not one of the questions or objections was addressed to the urban redevelopment program. See 92 CONG. REC. 3699 (1946).

[21] Perhaps a motive for assigning the program to the RFC was to avoid giving aid and comfort to the proponents of a permanent national housing agency.

A successor bill, S. 866, was introduced in the Eightieth Congress on March 10, 1947, by Senator Taft, for himself and Senators Ellender and Wagner, and came to be known as the Taft-Ellender-Wagner bill. Its urban redevelopment provisions did not differ much from those in S. 1592.[22] S. 866 was reported by the Senate Banking and Currency Committee in April, 1947 after hearings during March and April.[23]

The battle lines which had formed in 1945 and 1946 around the Wagner-Ellender-Taft bill shifted very little during 1947, 1948, and the first six months of 1949, as the Taft-Ellender-Wagner bill was considered, modified, and superseded by other comprehensive housing bills. The intensive legislative battles during this entire period involved no important new positions, even though many skirmishes were fought over new terrain under new leaders utilizing new tactics. For example, the terrain was changed when a special Joint Committee on Housing was appointed in July 1947 to make a new study and investigation of housing. Its Chairman, Representative Gamble of New York, and its Vice Chairman, Senator McCarthy of Wisconsin, opposed many of the important provisions in the Wagner-Ellender-Taft bill. The Committee held very extensive hearings from September 1947 through January 1948, while proponents of comprehensive housing legislation charged that this was a delaying tactic by the Chairman and Vice Chairman. However, a majority of the Committee did in fact favor the Taft-Ellender-Wagner bill, and its Final Majority Report of March 15, 1948, reflected that fact.[24] Here again, urban redevelopment proposals were not the subject of major differences of opinion concerning basic principles.[25]

Amendments to conform S. 866 to the recommendations of the Joint Committee were introduced by Senator Flanders of Vermont,

[22] A detailed comparison of the two bills appears in Part 6 of a pamphlet prepared by the Legislative Reference Service of the Library of Congress for the use of the Senate Committee on Banking and Currency, THE GENERAL HOUSING BILL—ARGUMENTS FOR AND AGAINST SENATE BILL 1592, 80TH CONG., 1ST SESS. (Comm. Print 1947).

[23] Senate Comm. on Banking and Currency, *National Housing Commission Act*, S. REP. No. 140, 80th Cong., 1st Sess. (1947).

[24] Joint Comm. on Housing, *Final Majority Report, Housing Study and Investigation*, H.R. REP. No. 1564, 80th Cong., 2d Sess. (1948).

[25] *Compare* Joint Comm. on Housing, *Housing Study and Investigation*, S. REP. No. 1019, 80th Cong., 2d Sess. 6–7, 18, 20 (1948), *with* Joint Comm. on Housing, *Final Majority Report*, H.R. REP. No. 1564, 80th Cong., 2d Sess., at 24–25 (1948) (individual views of Senator McCarthy).

simultaneously with the publication of the final report of the Joint Committee on March 15. Hearings on these amendments were held on March 31 and April 1 by the Senate Banking and Currency Committee, and the amendments were reported on April 8.[26] They included a number of significant changes in the urban redevelopment provisions.[27] The most noteworthy from a long-range viewpoint was the change from a system of federal annual contributions for slum clearance to a system of capital grants. This change had been recommended during the hearings in the Seventy-ninth Congress by the National Association of Real Estate Boards and the United States Savings and Loan League.[28] During the Eightieth Congress, it was concurred in by the Housing Administrator, who stated: "This seems to be a desirable improvement, since the amount of the subsidy necessary would become fixed when the land in a project area had been assembled, cleared, and sold or leased for redevelopment, and there would not appear to be any possibility of savings to the Government through the use of a system of annual contributions. Further, of course, Senator Flanders' amendments . . . would reduce very substantially the period when substantial Federal supervision of project accounts and revenues would be required."[29] Another change was the new requirement that the Housing Administrator, in extending financial aid under the urban redevelopment title, "give consideration" to the extent to which the locality has undertaken a program to encourage housing cost reductions through the adoption and improvement of building and other local codes.[30]

The Senate debated the bill at great length and passed it by voice vote on April 22, 1948, again with overwhelming bipartisan sup-

[26] Senate Comm. on Banking and Currency, *Housing Act,* S. REP. No. 140, 80th Cong., 2d Sess. pt. 2 (1948).

[27] See Senate Comm. on Banking and Currency, *Housing Act,* S. REP. No. 140, 80th Cong., 1st Sess. pt. 2 (1948), for a section-by-section analysis of S. 866 as reported in 1948; a comparison with the legislative recommendations of the Joint Committee on Housing; and a comparison with the bill as previously reported in 1947. See also *Hearings Before the Senate Committee on Banking and Currency on Perfecting Amendments to S. 866,* 80th Cong., 2d Sess. 179–81 (1948), for the Housing Administrator's analysis of the changes in the urban redevelopment provisions.

[28] See *Hearings, supra* note 17.

[29] *Hearings Before the Senate Committee on Banking and Currency on Perfecting Amendments to S. 866,* 80th Cong., 2d Sess. 180 (1948).

[30] This was a forerunner of the so-called "workable program" requirement of the 1954 legislation referred to below.

port.[31] It nevertheless died in the Eightieth Congress after extensive hearings by the House Banking and Currency Committee between May 3 and June 8; the collection meanwhile of about 120 signatures on a petition by members of the House to discharge that Committee of further consideration of the bill so that it could be brought to an early vote on the floor; the introduction by Chairman Wolcott on June 8 of H.R. 6841, a substitute bill which did not contain public housing, slum clearance, and farm housing provisions; a fourteen-to-thirteen vote within the Committee on June 10 to restore the omitted provisions in the form in which they appeared in the Taft-Ellender-Wagner bill; the introduction on June 11 by Chairman Wolcott, at the request of the Committee, of H.R. 6888, a clean bill, containing those provisions, which was reported three days later;[32] the tabling of the bill by the House Rules Committee on June 16; the introduction, reporting,[33] and passage by the House[34] on June 16, 17, and 18, respectively, of Chairman Wolcott's new bill, H.R. 6959, which omitted these provisions; the adjournment of the Congress for the 1948 national political conventions shortly after Senator Ellender, with the support of Senator Tobey, objected on June 19 to a unanimous consent request for the consideration of the House-passed bill; a special congressional session which started July 26, and which was called by the President primarily for the consideration of the Taft-Ellender-Wagner bill and of legislation "to check inflation";[35] the reporting of H.R. 6959 by the Senate,

[31] Along with Senators Taft and Ellender, active supporters of the bill included Senator Tobey of New Hampshire, Chairman of the Banking and Currency Committee during the Republican Eightieth Congress and a member of the Joint Committee on Housing; Senator Flanders of Vermont, Republican member of both Committees and sponsor of the 1948 amendments to the bill; Senator Maybank of South Carolina, member of the Banking and Currency Committee during the Eightieth Congress and its Chairman in the following Democratic Congress; and Senator Sparkman of Alabama, a member of both Committees and Chairman of the Housing and Rents Subcommittee of the Banking and Currency Committee during the Eighty-first Congress. The bill was debated in the Senate on April 14, 15, 20, 21, and 22, 1948.

[32] House Comm. on Banking and Currency, *Housing Act of 1948*, H.R. REP. No. 2340, 80th Cong., 2d Sess. (1948).

[33] House Comm. on Banking and Currency, *Housing Act of 1948*, H.R. REP. No. 2389, 80th Cong., 2d Sess. (1948).

[34] Under suspension of the rules, with no amendments allowed.

[35] The President's Proclamation No. 2796, July 15, 1948, 13 FED. REG. 4057 (1948), and Address by the President before a Joint Session of the Senate and the House of Representatives, *Urgent Needs of the American People*, H.R. Doc. No. 734, 80th Cong., 2d Sess. (1948).

amended so that it was in substantially the same form as the Taft-Ellender-Wagner bill;[36] the reluctant passage of that bill by the Senate after a floor amendment had removed the public housing, slum clearance and farm housing provisions;[37] and the reluctant approval by the President of the Housing Act of 1948 without these major provisions.[38]

The considerations[39] which led to the omission in mid-1948 of urban redevelopment provisions from House-originated legislation were different from those which led to the omission of public housing and farm housing provisions. The public housing provisions continued to be the target of uncompromising attack, and the farm housing provisions were often characterized as wrong in principle. The urban redevelopment provisions, however, continued to escape direct attack from most of the opponents of the Taft-Ellender-Wagner bill, although latent or disguised general opposition was evident in some of the objections to matters of detail and in the fact that the provisions were omitted entirely when an unusually good opportunity to do so presented itself. The opportunity in mid-1948 for jettisoning the urban redevelopment proposal consisted of the pressure to enact, prior to the 1948 presidential elections, noncontroversial provisions for the encouragement of private housing construction during a period of severe housing shortage. This shortage had led to the inclusion in the Taft-Ellender-Wagner bill, as reported to the Senate in April 1948, of provisions postponing the purchase of any urban-redevelopment-project land until July 1, 1949, and also postponing the demoliton of any residential structures on such land until July 1, 1950. In the light of these provisions,

[36] Sen. Comm. on Banking and Currency, *National Housing Act*, S. Rep. No. 1773, 80th Cong., 2d Sess. (1948).

[37] The Senate debate on August 5 and 6, 1948, made it abundantly clear that the Senate had reluctantly omitted these provisions only because there was insufficient time, prior to the 1948 presidential elections, to overcome the parliamentary hurdles which a minority of the membership of the House of Representatives would certainly place in the way of the broader legislation.

[38] Pub. L. No. 901, 80th Cong., 2d Sess. (Aug. 10, 1948), and accompanying statement by the President.

[39] Evidence of these considerations may be found both in the Senate debate of August 5 and 6, 1948 and in a report (Special Subcomm. of the Senate Comm. on Banking and Currency, *Housing Act of 1948*, S. Doc. No. 202, 80th Cong., 2d Sess. (1948)) which was made on August 7 to the Senate Committee on Banking and Currency by three of its members who were designated by the Chairman to confer informally with members of the House of Representatives concerning housing legislation which could be enacted during the special session of Congress.

members of Congress motivated by some degree of opposition to the program were able to contend that no great harm would result from delaying enactment of the provisions until early in 1949, while substantial harm could result from the failure to enact a "half-loaf" measure. Some proponents of the urban redevelopment provisions countered that enactment was necessary in 1948 in order for land acquisition to be possible by July 1, 1949; but other proponents, recognizing that the housing shortage was not (as contemplated by the postponement provisions in their bill) likely to disappear by the summer of 1950, were willing to overlook the mote in the eye of the opposition in view of the beam in their own.

The Eighty-first Congress convened on January 3, 1949, and two days later witnessed an apparent breach in the Senate's record of bipartisan cooperation in the field of housing when Senator Ellender, for himself, Senator Wagner, and six other Democratic Senators, introduced S. 138, a comprehensive housing bill which consisted substantially of the unenacted parts of the Taft-Ellender-Wagner bill.[40] A roughly similar[41] bill, S. 709, was introduced on January 27 by Republican Senator Baldwin of Connecticut for himself, Senator Taft, and fourteen other Republican Senators, thereby making up in numbers what they had lost in time, and revealing the continued presence of bipartisan support, though not cooperation. After the Senate Banking and Currency Committee had held hearings on these and other housing bills during most of February, the Committee was prepared to report out a compromise bill.[42] Accordingly, in a symmetrical flourish of resumed cooperation, S.

[40] A section-by-section summary of S. 138, 81st Cong., 1st Sess. (1949), and a list of the major differences between it and S. 866, as passed by the Senate in the Eightieth Congress, may be found in 95 CONG. REC. 48–55 (1949). Among these differences were a proposed reduction in the maximum maturity of the federal urban redevelopment loans from 45 to 40 years; a new provision for federal loans for surveys and plans in preparation of urban redevelopment projects; and a new provision under which the President could, within prescribed limits, accelerate the availability of the $500 million urban redevelopment capital grant authorization which would otherwise become available in five equal annual installments.

[41] The most talked about difference between the Democratic and Republican bills was in the number of low-rent public housing units authorized—1,050,000 in the former and 600,000 in the latter. In the urban redevelopment provisions, the differences were minor, with the Democratic bill providing for 40-year maximum federal loans as against 45 years in the Republican bill and with other differences relating to merely temporary provisions governing the dates when land purchases and demolition could begin.

[42] The compromise consisted in large part of an 810,000 unit public housing authorization, as against either 1,050,000 or 600,000.

1070, Eighty-first Congress, was introduced on February 25 under the joint sponsorship of eleven Democratic and eleven Republican Senators, including Senators Ellender, Wagner and Taft, and was reported to the Senate that same day.[43] The bill was passed by the Senate on April 21 by a roll call vote of fifty-seven to thirteen. The opposition was led by Senators Bricker of Ohio and Cain of Washington, both of whom spoke chiefly against the public housing provisions.[44] Senator Bricker apparently expressed the prevailing views of opponents in both the Senate and the House when he stated: "I am in favor of the slum elimination section. I am opposed to the public housing section. I favor the research section, and I am opposed to the farm housing section."[45]

In the meantime, Representative Spence of Kentucky, Chairman of the House Committee on Banking and Currency, had on April 4, 1949, introduced a comprehensive housing bill, H.R. 4009, Eighty-first Congress. The Committee held hearings during April and the early part of May and then, during three days of executive sessions, adopted many amendments designed to reduce the number of differences between the House bill and the Senate-passed bill. On May 16, H.R. 4009 was reported by a vote of fourteen to seven.[46]

On June 7, the House Rules Committee voted seven to five to

[43] Senate Comm. on Banking and Currency, *Housing Act of 1949*, S. Rep. No. 84, 81st Cong., 1st Sess. pt. 1 (1949), and *id.* pt. 2 (section-by-section summary) (March 11, 1949). The Committee adopted the S. 138 provision which imposed a 40-year maximum on federal loans for urban redevelopment projects.

[44] See Senate debate on April 14, 19, 20, 21, 1949. A series of floor amendments to the bill were defeated by the Senate. These included an amendment by Senator Bricker to strike out the public housing and farm housing titles. They also included a series of eight amendments to the public housing title offered by Senator Bricker, either alone or with Senator Cain, which would have crippled or severely limited that program. In contrast, the only limiting amendment to the urban redevelopment provisions offered by the two Senators was one which would have required the Housing Administrator to obtain loan funds through the appropriations process, instead of by borrowing directly from the Treasury.

[45] 95 Cong. Rec. 4852 (1949). Compare the House debate on H.R. 4009, 81st Cong., 1st Sess. (1949), 95 Cong. Rec. 8128–67, 8223–69, 8341–84, 8451–82, 8534–60, 8615–87 (1949).

[46] See House Comm. on Banking and Currency, *Housing Act of 1949*, H.R. Rep. No. 590, 81st Cong., 1st Sess. (1949). Again, public attention was directed chiefly to the low-rent housing provisions, H.R. 4009 having proposed 1,050,000 dwelling units over a period of years instead of 810,000 units as in the Senate-passed bill. Differences in the urban redevelopment title between the House-reported and Senate bills were very minor, except that the House bill did not contain a provision, which had been added to the Senate bill by a floor amendment, requiring a public hearing prior to land acquisition by the local public agency. This difference was later eliminated by a House floor amendment which added a similar requirement to the House bill.

table the bill. Its opposition, as the year before, was centered on the public housing provisions. However, earlier actions taken by that Committee to block floor consideration of bills (such as the Taft-Ellender-Wagner bill) which had strong majority support in the House as a whole had led to the adoption of simplified procedures, which were in effect during the Eighty-first Congress, for bringing a bill to the floor of the House without the concurrence of the Rules Committee. Under threat of resorting to these procedures, proponents of H.R. 4009 persuaded the Rules Committee to reverse itself, and on June 16, the Committee voted eight to four to send the bill to the floor of the House.

The House debated the bill for several days, starting on June 22. As expected, the major attack was on the low-rent public housing provisions, which were narrowly sustained by a roll call vote of 209 to 204.[47] The entire bill was then passed on June 29 by a vote of 227 to 186.[48]

At no time during the debate were the urban redevelopment provisions seriously endangered. Representative Cole of Kansas (later to become the Housing Administrator and a strong proponent of urban redevelopment) offered an amendment to prohibit federal aid for urban redevelopment in any fiscal year unless the Secretary of the Treasury has estimated that the federal government's income for the year would not be less than its expenditures. This amendment was defeated by a division vote of 133 to 106.[49] Representative Phillips of California offered an amendment which would have required urban redevelopment loan funds and public housing annual contributions to be specifically authorized by Congress in appropriation acts before the federal government could enter into contracts to provide these forms of assistance. This amendment was defeated by a division vote of 131 to 119.[50]

[47] Roll Call No. 117, 95 CONG. REC. 8667 (1949). Prior to this vote, the House, sitting as a Committee of the Whole House, had approved an amendment offered by Chairman Spence to reduce the public housing authorization to 810,000 units, the same number proposed in the Senate-passed bill (95 CONG. REC. 8623–36 (1949)). However, the technical effect of the roll call vote was to retain in the bill as passed the 1,050,000 unit authorization proposed in the bill as introduced and reported.

[48] Roll Call No. 120, 95 CONG. REC. 8677 (1949). See also Roll Call No. 119, *ibid.*, rejecting a motion to recommit the bill and to substitute other legislation which included urban redevelopment, but not public housing, provisions. The bill was debated on June 22, 23, 24, 27, 28, and 29.

[49] 95 CONG. REC. 8548 (1949).

[50] *Id.* at 8549. Similar proposals in the field of housing and urban renewal have been made from time to time by the Eisenhower Administration.

Congressional action on the bill was completed on July 8, when the House and Senate each approved the Conference Report[51] resolving the few remaining differences between the two chambers. The Housing Act of 1949 was approved by the President on July 15, thereby ending a four-year struggle for enactment. During the history of this legislation, the major change in the basic proposal was the substitution of federal short term loans and capital grants, in connection with cleared land which would generally be sold by the local public agency, for long-term loans and annual subsidies payable over a long period of years, in connection with land which would generally be leased.

A number of factors had contributed to the length and intensity of the struggle. The most basic was that the opposing forces outside Congress were both highly influential and firmly committed to their positions. Organizations supporting the omnibus legislation included many civic, professional, municipal, religious, veteran, and labor organizations.[51a] Often, when legislative support is so widespread, it is also listless and intermittent. In this case, the supporting groups made an unusually sustained and vigorous effort in close cooperation with each other. Factual data and arguments were provided by the professional and municipal organizations and by the Executive Branch of the federal government. General public interest in housing and slum clearance legislation dated to the 1930's, but much wider interest was sparked and fanned by the severe nationwide housing shortage which prevailed during the years following the war. This shortage had resulted from the depression, wartime construction limitations, and construction material shortages immediately after the war. The housing shortage was universally

[51] Committee on Conference, *Conference Report on Housing Act of 1949*, H.R. REP. No. 975, 81st Cong., 1st Sess. (1949). The bill number was S. 1070, the House having inserted the text of H.R. 4009 as approved by the House after the enacting clause of S. 1070 as previously passed by the Senate. The differences confronting the conferees were relatively minor, as a practical matter, because the House had already indicated by its vote on the Spence amendment that it would accept the 810,000 low-rent housing units proposed in the Senate bill in place of the larger number of units approved by a narrow margin on the floor of the House. See note 47 *supra*. The conferees agreed to the elimination of a provision added on the floor of the House which would have required that preference in the selection of tenants for dwellings built in a redevelopment project area be given to families displaced from the area who were willing and able to pay the rents or prices charged for the new dwellings.

[51a] See note 19 *supra*. See also 95 CONG. REC. 8128 (1949) indicating endorsement of the legislation by 42 state governors.

recognized as a national emergency because of its special impact on returning veterans. Although this temporary emergency was not relevant to most of the omnibus legislation and although it actually furnished an argument against the slum clearance provisions, it was dealt with by some of the other provisions in the Taft-Ellender-Wagner bill, and during 1947 and 1948 (before these other provisions were separately enacted in the Housing Act of 1948), it added very volatile fuel to what might otherwise have been a slow-burning fire.

Objections to the comprehensive housing legislation as a whole, and particularly bitter objections to the public housing provisions, were expressed by every national trade organization whose members were primarily engaged in producing, financing, or dealing with residential property.[52] Although these organizations were handicapped by a "selfish special interest" label which was repeatedly pasted on them by the sponsors of the legislation and by President Truman, they nevertheless had certain counter-balancing advantages which were inherent in their being large yet specialized trade organizations. These advantages included their ability to coordinate their efforts even more closely than their opponents could; to mobilize local chapters and members more quickly; to testify on the basis of their detailed and practical knowledge of their own industries; and to concentrate all their legislative activity in this one field. Notwithstanding these advantages and the substantial support which they received from some rural Congressmen[53] and from the United

[52] In this connection, see *Hearings Before the House Select Committee on Lobbying Activities*, 81st Cong., 2d Sess. (1950), pursuant to H. Res. 298.

[53] For example, note the following statements: Congressman Vursell of Illinois: "Mr. Speaker, the $1,500,000,000 provided for in the bill for slum clearance will go, most of it, for the purchase of land in the heart of the big cities like Chicago, New York, and several other big cities. . . . Mr. Speaker, now after . . . city administrations and city politicians through the years have brought about these slum conditions because of neglect of their duty, and by waste and extravagance of public funds, the taxpayers in my district of southern Illinois, who have worked and saved to build their own homes, are called upon after they have paid their own taxes and kept their own homes in livable conditions, to contribute money in taxes and rentals. . . ." 95 CONG. REC. 7387 (1949). Congressman Herbert A. Meyer of Kansas: "Now what about the slum-clearance angle? Will these projects help in any way in southeastern Kansas? The answer is 'No; they will not.' The one and one-half billion dollars provided for slum clearance will be used mostly for the purchase of land in the heart of big cities such as Chicago, New York, etc. . . . If this legislation is passed the lowly taxpayers of southeastern Kansas will also have to contribute to the rebuilding of slums in New Jersey." Radio Address inserted in

States Chamber of Commerce and the National Association of Manufacturers, the several trade associations could not muster a majority of Congress on their side, particularly when the extremely wide public support which existed for the legislation was periodically intensified by bluntly worded presidential statements.[54] . . .

III. THE 1949 ACT AND AMENDMENTS[55]

A. *Original Provisions*

. . . The major outlines of Title I of the 1949 Act were essentially the same as proposals made in 1941, except as to the type of federal subsidy involved. Basically, Title I authorized financial assistance by the Housing and Home Finance Administrator to a local public agency for a project[56] consisting of the assembly, clearance, site-preparation, and sale or lease of land at its fair value

---

95 Cong. Rec. A3883 (1949). Congressman Scudder of California: "I feel that the slum-clearance program contained in this bill will not in any way benefit the first Congressional District [California] which is predominantly agricultural and with many small cities. With very few exceptions these small cities are inhabited by people who take pride in keeping up their homes regardless of how meager their means might be. Slums, in my opinion, are largely made by the people who live in them. . . . I feel the people in my district should not be compelled to pay the rentals for people residing in the large metropolitan areas." 95 Cong. Rec. 8663–64 (1949).

[54] See the following statements by President Truman calling for enactment of comprehensive housing legislation, including urban redevelopment provisions: *Message from the President Transmitting Outline of Plans Made for Reconversion Period*, H.R. Doc. No. 282, 79th Cong., 1st Sess. 18–20 (1945); *Message from the President of the United States Communicated to Congress*, H.R. Doc. No. 398, 79th Cong., 2d Sess. 34–35 (1946); *Address of the President Before Congress*, H.R. Doc. No. 1 80th Cong., 1st Sess. 6–7 (1947); *Veto Message on Housing and Rent Control Act of 1947*, H.R. Doc. No. 370, 80th Cong., 1st Sess. (1947); *Midyear Economic Report of the President*, H.R. Doc. No. 409, 80th Cong., 1st Sess. 44 (1947); *Message from the President of the United States Transmitting Program for Rent Control and Housing Legislation*, H.R. Doc. No. 547, 80th Cong., 2d Sess. (1948); *Address of President of United States on Urgent Need to Check Inflation and Meet Housing Shortage*, H.R. Doc. No. 734, 80th Cong., 2d Sess. (1948); Statement on Approval of Housing Act of 1948, Aug. 10, 1948; *Address of the President Before Congress*, H.R. Doc. No. 1, 81st Cong., 1st Sess. 6 (1949); *Economic Report of the President*, H.R. Doc. No. 36, 81st Cong., 1st Sess. 6, 16 (1949); 95 Cong.Rec. 144–45 (1949); *id.* at 8279–82.

[55] The provisions of Title I of the 1949 Act and summaries thereof are, of course, available at many sources, and, accordingly, the title will not be summarized in detail here. Provisions relating to subjects discussed in part IV of this article are explained in that part.

[56] See "The 'Predominantly Residential' Requirement," *infra* at IV (A).

for uses specified in a redevelopment plan for the area of the project. The project could not include the construction or improvement of any buildings contemplated by the redevelopment plan.[57]

Advances of funds to the local public agency were authorized for surveys and plans in preparation of the project, and temporary loans were authorized for land acquisition and other project costs, these loans to be repayable when the land was sold or leased for redevelopment. Long-term loans, up to forty years, were authorized with respect to the portions of any sites to be leased.[58]

Capital grants were authorized to help meet the loss involved in connection with the project.[59] The federal grants could not exceed two-thirds of the losses on all of these projects in the locality. The local government or other public body or entity had to furnish "grants-in-aid" equal to at least one-third of such losses. These local grants-in-aid could be in the form of cash, donation of land, the use of municipal labor and equipment to clear a project area, or the installation of streets, utilities, and other site improvements, or they could be made through the provision of parks or schools or other public facilities necessary to serve or support the new uses of land in the project areas.

An outline of the method of financing an urban redevelopment project under the act can be indicated by the following table.[60]

It was prescribed in the 1949 Act that contracts for loans or capital grants must require that: (1) the redevelopment plan be approved by the governing body of the locality; (2) the local governing body find, among other things, that the plan conforms to a general plan for the development of the locality as a whole; (3) the purchaser or lessee of the land be obligated to devote it to the uses specified in the redevelopment plan and to begin building his improvements on the land within a reasonable time; (4) there be a feasible method for the temporary relocation of the families displaced from the project area and for the permanent provision of

[57] In connection with any project on land which was open or predominantly open, the Housing Administrator was authorized to make loans, up to 10 years, for the provision of public buildings or facilities necessary to serve the new uses of such land.

[58] See note 6 *supra*.

[59] This loss, known as "net project cost," consisted of all project expenditures, plus the amount of non-cash local grants-in-aid, minus the proceeds of land disposition.

[60] The amounts used in this table are not intended to indicate average or typical amounts, but are assumed solely for the purpose of simplicity.

A. *Gross project cost* .... $10 million

Land acquisition	$ 8 million*
Demolition and relocation	1 million*
Provision of public facilities by city	1 million
TOTAL	$10 million

B. *Proceeds from sale of land* .... $ 4 million

C. *Net project cost* .... $ 6 million

D. *Grants*

Federal grant of ⅔ net cost	$ 4 million
Local grant of ⅓ net cost:	
Cash grant	1 million
Provision of public facilities by city	1 million
TOTAL	$ 6 million

E. *Loans repaid from:*

Proceeds of sale of land	$ 4 million
Federal grant	4 million
Local cash grant	1 million
TOTAL	$ 9 million

* Financed by $9 million of federal or private loans (planning costs excluded for purposes of simplicity).

decent, safe, and sanitary dwellings at prices and rents within the financial means of such families; and (5) none of the project land will be acquired by the local public agency until after a public hearing.

The 1949 Act authorized $1 billion in federal loans and $500 million in federal grants to become available over a five-year period. The grant authorization has been increased from time to time until it is now $2 billion.[61] It has become the measure of the volume of the program authorized by the Congress. This is so because the loan authorization is a revolving fund which is replenished as loans are repaid when projects are completed. Also, in some cases federal grants are used for projects without federal loans.[62]

[61] § 103(b) of the Housing Act of 1949, § 106(a) of the Housing Amendments of 1955, § 301 of the Housing Act of 1957, § 405(1) of the Housing Act of 1959, 73 Stat. 672, 42 U.S.C.A. § 1453 (Supp. 1959).

[62] Such projects, involving no contract for federal loans, must be distinguished from the typical projects where (as specifically authorized by § 102(c) of the Housing Act of 1949, 63 Stat. 414, 42 U.S.C. § 1452(c) (1958)) most of a federal loan is not disbursed because substitute private funds are obtained, with consent of the Housing Administrator, on better terms with a pledge of the federal loan contract. At present, just under 90% of the outstanding loans for projects are private rather than federal.

B. *The 1954 Revision*

The urban redevelopment legislation was not substantially changed until the Housing Act of 1954.[63] The revision in that act was primarily the result of recommendations by President Eisenhower's Advisory Committee on Government Housing Policies and Programs in its report made in December 1953. The dominant recommendations in this extensive report dealt with urban redevelopment. The principal motivations for these recommendations were apparently the desire of the Committee (1) to have private enterprise do a greater share of the total job of removing and preventing blight, especially through rehabilitation of existing structures; (2) to require cities to take greater responsibilities for meeting their over-all problems of slums and blight; and (3) to stimulate private residential redevelopment and the provision of private low-cost housing for families displaced by urban redevelopment and other governmental activities.

The basic change recommended was a shift from urban redevelopment to "urban renewal," which was then a term without common usage. It was described as a broader and more comprehensive approach to the problems of slums and blight, or as a redirection of the urban redevelopment program. More specifically, it meant a broadening of the program into blighted areas where the land would not be acquired by the local public agency. This was intended to permit blight in the area to be eliminated by private enterprise through rehabilitation, so that structures would be conserved before reaching a stage where demolition would be necessary. This was also intended to make the federal dollar go farther, as rehabilitation involved far less cost, especially to the federal government, than land acquisition and demolition. Most important of all, it was recognized that the vast job which needed to be done could not possibly be done solely through the very expensive method of clearance.

Major provisions of the 1954 Act relating to urban renewal are discussed in detail [elsewhere]. For purposes of this article, the writers believe it best merely to enumerate the following:

1. *Urban Renewal.* "Urban renewal" was substituted for "urban redevelopment," and the Title I program under the 1949 Act was broadened as recommended by the President's Advisory Committee. An urban renewal "project" was defined to include

[63] 68 Stat. 590, 622, 42 U.S.C. §§ 1451 *et seq.* (1958).

not only the previously authorized acquisition, clearance, and disposal of land by the local public agency, but the restoration of other blighted or deteriorating areas by "carrying out plans for a program of voluntary repair and rehabilitation of buildings or other improvements in accordance with the urban renewal plan."[64] An urban renewal project can be all redevelopment, or all rehabilitation, or a combination of the two.

Project functions which previously could be exercised by the local public agency on the land it acquired, such as installation of streets and utilities, were authorized to be exercised throughout the urban renewal area. This included the acquisition of individual parcels in a rehabilitation area for the purpose of demolishing the buildings if necessary to eliminate unhealthful conditions, lessen density, eliminate obsolete or other detrimental uses, or to otherwise remove or prevent blight or deterioration.

2. *The Workable Program.* Section 303 of the 1954 Act[65] prohibited any loan and grant contract for an urban renewal project until the locality presents to the Housing Administrator a "workable program" or plan of action for meeting its over-all problems of slums and blight and of community development generally. This program was also made a condition to federal financial assistance for low-rent public housing and for the new special FHA mortgage insurance programs authorized in the 1954 Act to assist urban renewal. . . .

3. *Special Mortgage Insurance Programs.* Section 123 of the 1954 Act[66] added new sections 220 and 221 to the National Housing Act to make FHA mortgage insurance available on liberal terms for private residential construction which would assist in meeting the objectives of the urban renewal program. The section 220 aid is available for new or rehabilitated sales and rental housing in urban renewal areas. The section 221 aid is available for these categories of housing provided for families displaced by urban renewal or other government action, and the housing may be located within an urban renewal area or elsewhere in the community. Because the purpose of section 220 is to encourage renewal of project areas for their most suitable housing

---

[64] 68 Stat. 626, 42 U.S.C. § 1460(5) (1958).
[65] 68 Stat. 623, 42 U.S.C. § 1451 (1958).
[66] 68 Stat. 596, 12 U.S.C. § 1715k, 1 (1958).

use, which is not necessarily low-cost housing, section-220-insured mortgages may be considerably larger in amount per dwelling unit than mortgages insured under section 221, which is designed to serve displaced persons who are generally of low or moderate income. These sections have been extensively amended from time to time for the purpose of increasing their use and effectiveness.

A basic factor in making these mortgage insurance programs workable was another provision in the 1954 Act[67] establishing the Special Assistance Functions of the Federal National Mortgage Association under which it was contemplated that mortgages insured by FHA under sections 220 and 221 would be purchased by the Association when not readily acceptable to private investors. The mortgages were made, and remain, eligible for purchase under the Special Assistance Functions.

4. *Matching Planning Grants.* Section 701 of the act[68] established a new program of federal matching grants (a) to state planning agencies for planning assistance to cities of less than 25,000 population, and (b) to state, metropolitan, and regional planning agencies for planning in metropolitan or regional areas. This section has been considerably expanded by a series of amendments.

5. *Demonstration Grants.* The act[69] authorized the Housing Administrator to make grants (from urban renewal capital grant funds) to cities and other public bodies to pay for up to two-thirds of the cost of developing, testing, and reporting methods and techniques, and carrying out demonstrations and other activities, for the prevention and elimination of slums and urban blight.

6. *Exception from Residential Requirement.* The act[70] made the first exception from the requirement that an urban redevelopment area must either be predominantly residential in character or be redeveloped for predominantly residential uses. An exception up to ten per cent of the total grant authorization was made for areas which are not appropriate for residential development, but contain a substantial number of slum, blighted, or deteriorating dwellings or other living accommodations, the elimination of

[67] 68 Stat. 616, 12 U.S.C. § 1720 (1958).
[68] 68 Stat. 640, 40 U.S.C. § 461 (1958).
[69] 68 Stat. 629, 42 U.S.C. § 1452a (1958).
[70] 68 Stat. 627, 42 U.S.C. § 1460 (1958).

which would tend to promote the public health, safety, and welfare. (Land not to be cleared and redeveloped was not made subject to the "predominantly residential" requirement by the 1954 Act.)

7. *Urban Renewal Service.* The Housing Administrator was authorized to establish facilities for furnishing an "urban renewal service" to communities to assist in the preparation of "workable programs" and to provide them with technical and professional assistance for planning and developing local urban renewal operations.[71]

8. *Public Housing for Urban Renewal.* The additional low-rent public housing units authorized by the 1954 Act were made available only for meeting the needs of families displaced by governmental activities in a community where an urban redevelopment or urban renewal project was being carried out.[72]

The 1954 Act applied the same financing provision to rehabilitation as applied to clearance and redevelopment. The following table[73] illustrates the application of the capital grant formula to both:

Project Activities	Urban Renewal Project Comprising Solely Redevelopment	Urban Renewal Project Comprising Solely Rehabilitation (Assumes a Larger Area)
Surveying and planning	$ 25,000	$ 25,000
Land acquisition	1,000,000	none
Demolition, clearance, and relocation ...	50,000	none
Installation of streets, sewers, water improvements, parks, etc.	200,000	720,000
Carrying out plans for a program of voluntary rehabilitation and repair of buildings	none	5,000
Gross project cost	$1,275,000	$750,000
Proceeds derived from sale of project land	525,000	none
Net project cost	750,000	750,000
Capital grant, ⅔ of net project cost	500,000	500,000
Local cash grant-in-aid	$ 250,000	$250,000

[71] 68 Stat. 624, 42 U.S.C. § 1451 (1958).

[72] This limitation on low-rent public housing was repealed by § 108 of the Housing Amendments of 1955, 69 Stat. 638.

[73] Prepared by Urban Renewal Administration. See *Hearings Before the Senate Committee on Banking and Currency on Housing Amendments of 1956*, 84th Cong., 2d Sess. 151 (1956).

C. *Other Amendments*

One of the most significant developments in the amendments following the 1954 Act related to urban renewal planning on a wider scale than the areas of specific projects about to be undertaken. The need for this broader type of planning was recognized in section 303(a) of the Housing Act of 1956,[74] which authorized the Housing Administrator to make advances to local public agencies for the preparation of General Neighborhood Renewal Plans for urban renewal areas of such scope that the urban renewal activities in the areas may have to be carried out in stages, over a period of not more than ten years, rather than as a single project. These Plans are preliminary plans outlining proposed urban renewal activities and providing a framework for the later preparation of several specific urban renewal plans. The advances for these Plans become repayable out of funds becoming available to the local public agency for the first urban renewal project in the area.

The Housing Act of 1959[75] authorized assistance for a much broader and more significant form of urban renewal planning—the preparation of long-range "community renewal programs," or preliminary plans with respect to all of the urban renewal needs of a city. The Housing Administrator was authorized to make grants for this planning, instead of advances. These grants may be made, up to two-thirds of cost, for the preparation of community-wide plans which include identification of slum or blighted areas in the community, measurement of blight, determination of resources needed and available to renew the areas, identification of potential project areas and types of action contemplated for each, and scheduling of urban renewal activities. This enables more effective use of federal and local funds by permitting the best scheduling of urban projects in the community. Eventually it may also help to furnish information on a national basis concerning urban renewal needs. It may be noted that community-wide renewal plans can encompass work previously authorized to be done with the aid of federal advances for General Neighborhood Renewal Plans and for surveys as to the feasibility of individual projects. However, the Congress did not repeal the earlier authority for advances to assist such Plans and surveys.

Other significant amendments enacted since the 1954 Act have

[74] 70 Stat. 1099, 42 U.S.C. § 1452(d) (1958).
[75] 73 Stat. 672, 42 U.S.C.A. § 1453 (Supp. 1959).

made federal funds available to local public agencies to compensate (if not otherwise compensated) individuals, families, and businesses for reasonable and necessary moving expenses and any direct losses of property, except good will, resulting from displacement by an urban renewal project. This was done in recognition of the fact that state eminent domain laws do not generally provide adequate compensation to all the persons materially affected by the public taking of property. The federal government bears one hundred per cent of the cost of these payments instead of the usual two-thirds of project costs. The Housing Act of 1956[76] permitted payments up to $100 in the cases of an individual or family, and up to $2,000 in the case of a business concern. The maximum statutory amount of these payments is now $200 in the case of an individual or family and $3,000 in the case of a business concern.[77] There has been almost continuous pressure in Congress further to increase these amounts, particularly the amount of payments to businesses, which may have actual moving expenses several times such amount. Legislation pending in the Eighty-sixth Congress when it recently adjourned would provide further increases.[78]

Up to the present time, urban renewal amendments have each year constituted one of the principal parts of omnibus housing legislation considered by Congress. For example, the length of the urban renewal amendments in the Housing Act of 1959 is about the same as the length of the original Title I of the 1949 Act. Other extensive amendments in the 1959 Act deal with programs having a direct relation to urban renewal, such as mortgage insurance for urban renewal housing, purchase of the mortgages by the Federal National Mortgage Association, and urban planning.

In addition to increases in grant authorizations there has been a general trend in the amendments toward greater federal benefits and more local discretion[79] in the urban renewal program. For example, the 1959 Act (Title IV):

[76] 70 Stat. 1100.
[77] 73 Stat. 674, 42 U.S.C. §§ 1456(f) (Supp. 1959).
[78] See § 801(a) of H.R. 12603, 86th Cong., 2d Sess. (1960) as reported by the House Committee on Banking and Currency, and § 403 of S. 3670, 86th Cong., 2d Sess. (1960), as passed by the Senate.
[79] One new restriction, § 407 of the 1959 Act, 73 Stat. 673, 42 U.S.C.A. § 1455 (Supp. 1959), prohibits any commitment for disposition of project land to a redeveloper unless the local public agency makes public certain information relating to the redeveloper and relating to any residential redevelopment or rehabilitation.

1. permits a community to count as a local grant-in-aid any eligible local public improvement started within three years prior to the execution of a loan and grant contract for the urban renewal project;

2. increases the maximum amount of relocation payments to persons and businesses displaced by urban renewal, and broadens the scope of those eligible for payments;

3. authorizes grants for community-wide urban renewal planning;

4. authorizes temporary loans, under certain conditions, for land acquisition by a local public agency before it is known that an urban renewal plan will be approved;

5. permits expenditures by a college or university in purchasing and clearing property near an urban renewal project to be counted as a local grant-in-aid, and waives the "predominantly residential" requirement in such cases;

6. defines the loans chargeable to the dollar limit on the urban renewal borrowing authorization in such a way as to make remote in time any restriction of lending activities by the limit;[80]

7. prohibits withholding available federal funds from an eligible urban renewal project except on the basis of urgency of need or feasibility of the project;

8. increases the amount of authorized exceptions from the requirement that an urban renewal project area be predominantly residential in character before redevelopment or else be developed for predominantly residential uses; and

9. simplifies the statutory requirements for an urban renewal plan.

Perhaps the most significant and novel proposal embodied in urban renewal legislation considered in the recent Eighty-sixth Congress was an amendment to enable a local public agency to carry out "pilot" rehabilitation efforts in urban renewal project areas. This amendment, contained in both the House and Senate versions

---

[80] The $1 billion ceiling on funds which can be borrowed from the Treasury for urban renewal loans is now applicable only to outstanding federal loan funds disbursed or committed and estimated to be disbursed from federal funds in the future, as of any one time under existing contracts. Under the law prior to the 1959 amendment, it applied to all loan funds contracted for without regard to whether they would ever be disbursed. The ratio of disbursed loans outstanding to private loans secured by the federal loan contracts has been as low as about 1 to 10.

of the "Housing Bill of 1960"[81] (which were pending when the Eighty-sixth Congress adjourned), would permit the local public agency to acquire a few dwellings, rehabilitate them as part of the urban renewal project at project expense, and sell them to private owners. The number of these dwellings involved in an urban renewal area could not exceed fifty dwelling units, nor two per cent of the number of units which are to be rehabilitated under the urban renewal plan. The proposal contemplates that the local public agency will, through this undertaking, demonstrate to property owners in the area that rehabilitation is feasible.

The Housing and Home Finance Agency has enthusiastically supported this proposal as a means of getting rehabilitation under way in urban renewal areas.[82] Rehabilitation of substantial numbers of existing houses in urban renewal areas has been carried out successfully in only a few cases, so that this important phase of urban renewal has been lagging. The Agency indicated that the "pilot" efforts should go a long way toward stimulating property owners to rehabilitate their properties.

As this proposal would permit certain rehabilitation work on buildings to be part of an urban renewal project, it would be the first exception, as a technical matter, from the prohibition in the 1949 Act against a project including construction or improvement of any building.[83] In principle, however, the proposal would not be a departure from the purposes for which federal grants are now used. As the proposed rehabilitation would serve as a demonstration for property owners throughout the urban renewal area, it would be similar in this respect to schools and other public buildings which serve the project. The costs of these buildings are counted as local grants-in-aid and are included in gross project cost and increase federal grants accordingly.

IV. TWO RECURRING ISSUES

Although the two issues discussed in this part are not perhaps the most important issues in federal urban renewal legislation, they were

[81] § 703 of H.R. 12603, 86th Cong., as reported by House Committee on Banking and Currency, and § 405 of S. 3670, as passed by the Senate.
[82] *Hearings Before the Senate Committee on Banking and Currency on Housing Legislation of 1960*, 86th Cong., 2d Sess. 990 (1960).
[83] 63 Stat. 420, 42 U.S.C. § 1460(c) (1958).

selected for discussion because each is important, currently controversial, has a way of appearing and reappearing in varying forms
and disguises, and is not likely to be finally settled soon.

A. The "Predominantly Residential" Requirement

Title I of the 1949 Act included a provision designed to direct
federal urban redevelopment aids toward the betterment of housing,
as distinguished from the betterment of cities and urban life in
general. In effect it limited an urban redevelopment project area to
one "which is predominantly residential in character" before redevelopment or "which is to be developed or redeveloped for
predominantly residential uses."[84] A similar limitation has been extended to all urban renewal projects and is the law today with
exceptions and modifications discussed below. The enactment of
these exceptions and modifications over a period of time reflects the
fact that the requirement has continued to be one of the most
important live issues in the field of urban renewal legislation.

The expression "predominantly residential" has had such general
and frequent usage throughout the operations under Title I that
some have come to regard it as a reference to an inherent characteristic of the program. Yet, it was not mentioned in the earlier urban
redevelopment proposals and is not a common concept in state laws
authorizing urban redevelopment or urban renewal projects.

The principal early advocates of a federal urban redevelopment
program, the planners, did not approach it from the standpoint of
housing. Their major objective was redevelopment in accord with a
general plan for the entire urban area. Slums were treated as but one
important phase of urban blight, and housing as but one important
form of redevelopment.[85] This position was forcefully presented

[84] § 110(c) of the 1949 Act defined "project" to include "acquisition of (i)
a slum area or a deteriorated or deteriorating area which is predominantly
residential in character, or (ii) any other deteriorated or deteriorating area
which is to be developed or redeveloped for predominantly residential uses,
or (iii) land which is predominantly open and which because of obsolete
platting, diversity of ownership, deterioration of structures or of site improvements, or otherwise substantially impairs or arrests the sound growth of the
community and which is to be developed for predominantly residential uses, or
(iv) open land necessary for sound community growth which is to be developed for predominantly residential uses (in which event the project thereon,
as provided in the proviso of section 103(a) hereof, shall not be eligible for
any capital grant). . . ." 63 Stat. 420.
[85] GUY GREER AND ALVIN HANSEN, URBAN REDEVELOPMENT AND HOUSING
(National Planning Ass'n, 1941).

before the Taft Subcommittee by Seward H. Mott, Director of the Urban Land Institute, and Alfred Bettman, representing the American Institute of Planners.[86] The latter's statement included:[87]

. . . a serious warning needs to be issued against conceiving urban redevelopment as a subject identical with housing or housing with little variations—housing the theme, urban redevelopment the variations. Of the uses of the land of an urban area, habitation is the largest, running, I believe, from 60 to 75 percent; but this is just as true of the unblighted as of the blighted areas, of the whole urban territory as of the blighted portion thereof. So, while housing construction will always form the larger proportion of all urban redevelopment or development, a costly mistake will be made if urban redevelopment be conceived of as the replanning and rebuilding of slum areas only or the replanning or rebuilding for housing only. The redevelopment or rehabilitation process needs to be applied to all areas which need it and for all the classes of uses which, according to good city planning principles, are appropriate to those areas. As urban redevelopment will prepare areas for reconstruction and will finance this preparation, housing, that is habitation, will be the greatest beneficiary of this process; but unless the legislation, planning and administration be understood to be for all kinds of blighted areas for all classes of urban uses, the process will not produce sound and stable results.

Objection to the above approach was voiced immediately by members of the Subcommittee, especially Senator Taft, who indicated his belief that any urban redevelopment project should involve housing.[88] He questioned the federal interest in any project going "beyond housing and beyond the elimination of slums." He argued that the federal government was committed to a policy of assisting housing, thereby relieving poverty and hardship, and that federally-aided urban redevelopment for this social welfare purpose was desirable, but projects going further merely improved the looks or financial status of local communities. Mr. Bettman contended, without being able to persuade Senator Taft, that the economic deterioration of cities affects the national economy, thereby justifying federal aid. Near the end of this discussion, the following exchange occurred:[89]

[86] *Taft Subcommittee Hearings* 1602–22.
[87] *Id.* at 1606.
[88] *Id.* at 1614, 1905.
[89] *Id.* at 1618. (Emphasis added.)

Senator TAFT. You tried to separate it [urban redevelopment] very clearly from housing. I wonder if there is not an intermediate step, an intermediate possibility? That is, that the federal government might finance the acquisition where, by doing so, they eliminate a comparatively large amount of slum housing, *where two-thirds of the place is residential*.

Mr. BETTMAN. That is right.

Senator TAFT. In order to do that, you might have to help the city finance a somewhat larger development plan. That seems to me a possible approach to it. I would regard that more favorably than a wide open plan.

Mr. BETTMAN. It would be *predominantly* housing, because all urban development is predominantly housing.

The Taft Subcommittee report recommended a predominantly residential requirement, saying "The Subcommittee is not convinced that the federal government should embark upon a general program of aid to cities looking to their rebuilding in more attractive and economical patterns."[90] As used here "predominantly residential" was taken to mean over half residential, not two-thirds. . . .

Throughout the controversy over the scope of the urban redevelopment program, its relationship to housing was recognized by all, and the differences of position arose from the degree of significance attached to that relationship. To the planners, housing was secondary—to be clearly distinguished from the basic function, the planned redevelopment of cities. To the Federal Works Agency (which in January 1949 lost its jurisdictional claim to the urban renewal program and in June 1949 its life), the urban renewal projects could have become primarily another type of public works, involving planning and engineering techniques similar to those used in other municipal improvements, but with additional housing problems requiring consultation with housing experts. Actually, little was presented to support the separation of urban redevelopment operations in whole or in part from housing operations. Such separation would undoubtedly have been a narrow approach, rather than the broad approach it was alleged to be.

On the other hand, it seems to us that a certain narrowness pervaded most of the discussion and consideration leading to enactment of the predominantly residential requirement. Urban redevel-

90 TAFT SUBCOMMITTEE REPORT ON POSTWAR HOUSING 17 (Aug. 1, 1945).

opment projects were generally viewed as though they existed in some detached or isolated spot. In viewing the housing significance of a redevelopment project, the discussion was focused on what would happen within its physical boundaries and on methods of relocating the residents. There was recognition of the need to conform a project plan to a current master city plan, but members of Congress apparently gave little attention to urban redevelopment as a step in the long and difficult, but continuous, journey toward the redevelopment of the city as a whole. Neither was much thought given by Congress to the potential effect of urban redevelopment on the people of the entire community in their day-to-day life at home, at work, at leisure, and in transit within the city.

There were occasional references in the congressional discussions to the fact that cities are largely made up of residential areas, but this was not offered to show that urban redevelopment would in any event have a residential orientation making unnecessary any statutory requirement relating to the character of the area of each project. Senator Taft made it clear that he felt that federal aid was justified only to avoid the harmful effect of substandard dwelling structures on the people living in them. In an unsuccessful attempt to find some common ground with the Senator, Mr. Bettman, in his very able presentation before the Taft Subcommittee in support of urban redevelopment, was driven to emphasize the role which nonresidential urban redevelopment projects can play in bettering the national economy by checking economic deterioration within cities. The Housing Agency, in an attempt to hasten the enactment of legislation which was politically achievable, often pointed out that most urban blighted areas consist of housing and that most cleared land would generally be used for housing. However, this was generally done in a context of minimizing the problems which would remain if federal aid were denied to projects involving the redevelopment of nonresidential areas for nonresidential uses. The Agency contended that these cases would be few; that federal assistance for them should be deferred; and (crossing over to the shadier side of the street) that in any case, it would frequently be possible to take care of the situation by simply enlarging the area until it becomes predominantly residential. In fairness to all concerned, the narrow tone of the discussions undoubtedly reflected the lack of widely-based popular support for a broader program, it being true that important legislation is not often brought into being by technicians and congressmen and executive officials alone. . . .

Parenthetically, it may be of interest that no significant controversy over the predominantly residential requirement arose during the period immediately following the enactment of the 1949 Act. Instead, all of the fire at that time seems to have been directed toward the Agency's interpretation of the related provision in the Act authorizing a project of "open land necessary for sound community growth which is to be developed for predominantly residential uses."[91] There the issue was whether an open land project involving no element of blight may be undertaken only if it provides housing as an adjunct to slum clearance projects in the community, as the Agency contended, or could be used to provide housing for other purposes such as "new towns" or satellite communities or public housing for any low-income families in the community. In defending its position, the Agency conceded that sound community development was a purpose of the act but contended that "the dog is slum clearance, and the tail is community development." The issue, while vigorously argued on both sides, was nevertheless somewhat academic in the absence of local pressure for specific federally-aided open land projects. However, it continued to be a subject of debate until Senator Douglas, in an address before the National Housing Conference on May 6, 1952, praised the Housing Agency for following legislative history and the intent of Congress instead of the recommendations of some of the prominent members of that organization.[92]

[91] See note 84 *supra*.

[92] The Act did not specify the more restrictive use of the open-land authority; that was promised in a letter from the Housing Agency requested and used on the Senate floor by Senator Douglas during debate on S. 1070, 81st Cong., 1st Sess. (1949). See 95 CONG. REC. 4876–77 (1949). It was contended by prominent counsel that there was no ambiguity in the law, and the Agency was therefore in error in going to the legislative history on the matter. This points up the distinction between the use of legislative history by a government agency administering discretionary authority and its use by a court or an administrative tribunal engaged in a judicial or quasi-judicial proceeding affecting the legal rights of parties who are reasonably entitled to rely on the plain meaning of a statute. To a government attorney, it seems quite unrealistic in the former case, to say the least, to expect an agency to ignore the clear intent of a vast majority of the Congress to limit the Agency's discretionary authority to a narrower scope than expressed in a statute. This footnote is not intended to imply that there were not also sound policy reasons for not exercising the suggested broader authority. Not the least of these was the absence of court decisions establishing the validity of open-land projects

The response of Congress to pressure for assistance to nonresidential projects (including several specific projects which were called to the attention of individual members of Congress by their constituents) is reflected in the authorized exceptions to the predominantly residential requirement. A major exception was enacted in the Housing Act of 1954, which permitted ten per cent of the authorized federal capital grant funds to be used for nonresidential projects.[93] However, a project was eligible only if it contained a substantial number of slum or deteriorating dwellings or other substandard living accommodations, the elimination of which would tend to promote the public health, safety, and welfare and only if the area "is not appropriate" for redevelopment for predominantly residential uses.[94] The general exception has grown to twenty per cent. The Housing Act of 1959 not only changed the ten per cent limitation to twenty per cent, but also removed the requirement that the project area have a substantial number of substandard dwellings.[95] Thus Congress has departed from the principle that

---

in any state; constitutional difficulties were anticipated in undertaking open-land projects, even though necessary as an adjunct to slum clearance operations. Subsequently, the validity of predominantly open-land projects where there is some element of blight has been upheld in three states. See the grounds for decision stated in Redevelopment Agency of City and County of San Francisco v. Hayes, 122 Cal. App.2d 777, 266 P.2d 105 (1954), *cert. denied sub nom.* Van Hoff v. Redevelopment Agency, 348 U.S. 897 (1954); People *ex rel.* Gutknecht v. City of Chicago, 414 Ill. 600, 111 N.E.2d 626 (1953); Oliver v. City of Clairton, 374 Pa. 333, 98 A.2d 47 (1953); and People *ex rel.* Adamowski v. Chicago Land Clearance Commission, 14 Ill.2d 74, 150 N.E.2d 792 (1958).

[93] 68 Stat. 627, 42 U.S.C. § 1460 (1958).

[94] The exception came to be known as the "skid row" amendment because it tended to affect areas which had a scattering of substandard rooming houses or "flop" houses. The Housing Agency administratively determined that the requirement that the area include a substantial number of dwellings or other living accommodations would be met if 20% of the ground area or floor area were devoted to residential uses scattered throughout the area. The Housing Act of 1954 continued the predominantly residential requirement with respect to the cleared area of a project, but did not extend it to other parts of the broader urban renewal area authorized in that act. The requirement was made applicable to the entire urban renewal area (instead of just the clearance area) by § 302 of the Housing Act of 1956 (70 Stat. 1097). This had the effect of relaxing the requirement where the rehabilitation portion of the area was residential. See also a minor exception for certain nonresidential projects, involving federal loans but not grants, in the last paragraph of § 110(c) of the Housing Act of 1949, as amended, 70 Stat. 1097, 42 U.S.C. § 1460 (1958). This minor exception was added by § 106(c) of the Housing Amendments of 1955, 69 Stat. 635, 637, 42 U.S.C. § 1460 (1958).

[95] § 413 of the Housing Act of 1959 (73 Stat. 675, 42 U.S.C.A. § 1460 (Supp. 1959)) changed the relevant language of § 110(c) of the Housing Act of 1949

each urban redevelopment project should involve the removal of substandard housing or the construction of housing in order to justify the federal aid. However, there has been no departure by Congress from the premise that the program as a whole should be housing-oriented and that restrictions should be included in the federal law for this purpose. In recommending the 1959 amendment, the report of the Senate Committee on Banking and Currency stated:[96]

The committee agrees that the basic objective of the program is to eliminate slums and blighted homes but also recognizes that no community can survive without an orderly plan for renewing its commercial and industrial areas. Urban renewal in its broadest sense would renew the entire living environment of the community including its commercial areas where families must shop and its industrial areas where families must work, as well as its residential areas where families live. It is appropriate, therefore, that a reasonable percentage of Federal assistance should be used to assist a community in renewing non-residential as well as residential areas.

When a statutory limitation is under basic attack, there is frequently, if not generally, an accommodation which avoids the complete removal of the limitation. It may be retained in modified form because of the belief that it has not yet outlived its usefulness or because of the legislature's reluctance to admit that a change in principle is involved or perhaps because of the legislature's instinctive reluctance to surrender a control. Sometimes general exceptions are provided, such as the ten per cent or twenty per cent exception to the predominantly residential requirement, and at other times

to read as follows: "Financial assistance shall not be extended under this title with respect to any urban renewal area which is not predominantly residential in character and which, under the urban renewal plan therefor, is not to be redeveloped for predominantly residential uses: *Provided,* That, if the governing body of the local public agency determines that the redevelopment of such an area for predominantly non-residential uses is necessary for the proper development of the community, the Administrator may extend financial assistance under this title for such a project: *Provided further,* That the aggregate amount of capital grants contracted to be made pursuant to this title with respect to such projects after the date of the enactment of the Housing Act of 1959 shall not exceed 20 per centum of the aggregate amount of grants authorized by this title to be contracted for after such date."

This language deleted a requirement that a predominantly residential project be "clearly" predominantly residential.

[96] Senate Comm. on Banking and Currency, *Housing Act of 1959,* S. REP. No. 41, 86th Cong., 1st Sess. 27 (1959).

exceptions are made for specific narrow purposes.[97] A number of the latter type of exceptions to the predominantly residential requirement have been enacted and others have been proposed. Taken together, they could represent a very substantial increase in the authorized volume of nonresidential projects and a substantial erosion of the basic limitation.

In 1956, the predominantly residential requirement was waived, along with other prescribed limitations, for urban areas which are in need of redevelopment or rehabilitation as the result of any catastrophe which the President finds, under other legislation, to be a major disaster.[98] In 1959, a more substantial waiver was enacted with respect to urban renewal projects which the local governing body finds will be of certain benefit to a college or university in or near the project area.[99] This 1959 exception would be extended to hospitals by bills pending in the Eighty-sixth Congress when it adjourned, one of which was passed by the Senate,[100] and the other of which was reported by the House Committee on Banking and Currency.[101] A number of recent bills, including some sponsored by the Eisenhower Administration and others sponsored by the Democratic congressional leadership, would also waive the predominantly residential requirement with respect to certain urban redevelopment projects in industrially depressed areas.[102]

If the trend to relax the predominantly residential requirement is continued, a point will soon be reached where it has no real limiting effect. Indeed, in the case of cities where the extent of industrial and

[97] Very frequently a proliferation of such statutory modifications, including some which are designed to take care of single cases, results in extremely complex legislation. This has happened in the field of urban renewal legislation. It is interesting that groups which have sponsored complicating changes, one by one, are often among those who complain vigorously about the resulting over-all complexity.

[98] § 111 of the Housing Act of 1949, as added by § 307 of the Housing Act of 1956, 70 Stat. 1101, 42 U.S.C. § 1462 (1958).

[99] § 112 of the Housing Act of 1949, as added by § 418 of the Housing Act of 1959, 73 Stat. 677, 42 U.S.C.A. § 1463 (Supp. 1959).

[100] S. 3670, 86th Cong., 2d Sess., passed by the Senate, June 16, 1960.

[101] H.R. 12603, 86th Cong., 2d Sess. (1960); House Comm. on Banking and Currency, *Housing Act of 1960*, H.R. REP. No. 1924, 86th Cong., 2d Sess. (1960).

[102] One such bill, S. 722, 86th Congress, 2d Sess. (1960), was vetoed by President Eisenhower on grounds unrelated to this provision. See also S. 1433, 86th Cong., 2d Sess. (1960), an Administration-sponsored bill, and S. 3569, and H.R. 12286, both 86th Cong., 2d Sess. (1960), compromise bills proposed on behalf of the Administration.

commercial blight does not constitute a disproportionate share of urban blight, a question may be raised as to whether this point has already not been reached. A 1955 analysis[103] of fifty-three municipalities shows the land use of developed areas as follows:

Residential .... About 73%
Commercial .... About 6%
Industrial & railroads .... About 21%

If about seventy-three per cent of municipal areas are residential, the twenty per cent exception, along with special purpose exceptions, should often be adequate to permit nonresidential urban renewal projects to be undertaken in about the same proportion to predominantly residential projects as nonresidential land use in the locality bears to residential land use. An additional factor which tends to make this true is that a project is charged against the exceptions only if it involves a predominantly nonresidential area to be developed for predominantly nonresidential uses. Thus, the volume of projects involving predominantly commercial or industrial areas can equal the volume permitted under the twenty per cent exception (and additional special exceptions) plus the volume of these projects which are developed for predominantly residential uses.

Although the form of future legislation on this particular subject cannot be predicted, the writers do venture to predict with some assurance that it will continue to be an active issue, with changes moving in the direction of greater freedom to undertake nonresidential projects. There is still a strong belief among many in Congress that the principal objective of the urban renewal program is the removal of slums and the improvement of housing, as distinguished from general city betterment. Others will continue to regard the predominantly residential requirement as a desirable economy measure, preventing added claims against federal grant funds. On the other side are the municipalities and local officials, ably represented in Congress and before its committees, who want more discretion in planning and deciding the type of projects to be undertaken. An added force which seems to be tipping the balance

[103] See HARLAND BARTHOLOMEW, LAND USES IN AMERICAN CITIES 121 (1955). The analysis covered cities of varying sizes. Developed areas considered here do not include streets, parks and playgrounds, and public and semipublic property.

in their favor is the position of business interests which normally tend to support restrictions on federal expenditures, but are increasingly in favor of reconstructing blighted business and industrial properties. Foremost among these are department store owners and mortgage and other lenders concerned about large outstanding investments in downtown retail properties now suffering competition from surburban shopping centers. Redevelopment to provide downtown commercial centers with parking space and attractive surroundings is a business necessity to them and a source of increased tax revenue to the city.

B. *Federal-Local Sharing of Costs*

The basic statutory formula[104] for sharing the costs of the urban renewal program as between the federal government and local governments has been under attack from opposite directions. Skipping over problems and statutory changes relating to technical methods of calculating the federal and the local share of program costs, it is the writers' intention to comment on attempts to change materially the relative size of the two shares.

In 1958, the Housing and Home Finance Administrator, as spokesman for the Eisenhower Administration, recommended the enactment of legislation[105] to reduce the federal share of net project costs to sixty per cent one year later, fifty-five per cent two years later, and fifty per cent three years later, with a resulting final increase in the local share to a matching fifty per cent. The change through gradual stages was intended to give localities, and possibly states, time to gear themselves to assuming the permanent larger burden. The Administrator stated:[106]

[104] See §§ 103(a), 104, 106(f), and 110(d), (e), (f) of the Housing Act of 1949, as amended, 71 Stat. 299, 300, 301, 42 U.S.C. §§ 1453(a), 1454, 1456(f), 1460(d), (e), (f) (1958).

[105] § 302 of S. 3399, 85th Cong., 2d Sess., Administration-sponsored bill introduced on March 4, 1958, by Senator Capehart of Indiana by request. A similar proposal was contained in § 304 of S. 612, 86th Cong., 1st Sess., Administration-sponsored bill introduced on January 21, 1959, by Senator Bennett of Utah for Senator Capehart.

[106] *Hearings Before the Subcommittee on Housing of the Senate Committee on Banking and Currency on the Housing Act of 1958*, 85th Cong., 2d Sess. 118–19 (1958). See also, the testimony by the Urban Renewal Commissioner, *id.* at 122–24, and in *Hearings Before the Subcommittee on Housing of the Senate Committee on Banking and Currency on the Housing Act of 1959*, 86th Cong., 1st Sess. 119–20 (1959).

The reasons for this recommendation are based, of course, upon considerations of the general fiscal policy of the Government and the need for greater participation on the part of States and localities in bearing the financial burden of undertakings having primarily local as well as national benefit. If essential programs such as urban renewal, which require large amounts of funds, are to be continued at their present levels, States and communities should bear a greater share of the financial burden. We do not know the total ultimate cost of eliminating all of the slums and blight in our country, but we can agree it is a staggering sum and that all of the Federal funds that could be made available would accomplish only a part of the job in the immediate future. Local expenditures should be of equal importance to the amount of work completed.

Unlike many other Federal-aid programs, urban-renewal projects result in direct financial benefits to communities, in addition to the immediate objective of the program. In addition to slum elimination and all of its benefits, cities receive an increased tax base of great and immediate financial value. In the long run, many cities may receive over a period of years sufficient increased taxes as a result of redevelopment and improvements in urban renewal areas to pay all of their local grants-in-aids—not only their cash contributions but their grants in the form of improvements and facilities. It is because of these facts, as well as other advantages of urban renewal, that so many cities are enthusiastically proceeding with their projects. Under the bill, communities would eventually pay one-sixth more of the net project cost than they pay with respect to projects now being undertaken. In view of the extent of present activities, it seems wholly unrealistic to assume that this modest increase would restrict our program.

During the course of the ensuing controversy, the Eisenhower Administration made it clear that its proposal was primarily motivated by its judgment concerning relative priorities of competing claims, including national defense and foreign aid, on a federal budget which it hoped to keep in balance. The Administration spokesmen argued that whatever upper limit might be placed on federal funds available for urban renewal, a larger total program could be supported if the local share of the cost were increased. This argument for making a given amount of federal funds stretch further was premised on the ability of localities gradually to assume the increased burden without undue hardship. The present level of activities was offered by the Administration as an indication that it was not unrealistic to expect that the cities could contribute even more. The Administration also felt that the states should participate in the program more than they had. Indeed, the proposal for reducing the federal share of urban renewal costs was part of an abortive Administration drive for returning to the states and localities greater responsibility for socially motivated programs generally.

In the meantime, local urban renewal officials, mayors, and other spokesmen for urban interests had been contending that even the present ⅔-⅓ formula placed undue hardship on the localities. From time to time, they proposed that the federal share of net project cost be increased to seventy-five or eighty per cent or even ninety per cent.[107] The President of the National Association of Housing and Redevelopment Officials made the following statement in opposition to any reduction in the federal two-thirds share and in support of increasing it to eighty per cent:[108]

I need only recite some of the financial problems with which American cities are faced today—declining tax bases, limited tax resources, substantial increases in the costs of providing essential municipal services, the necessity for providing new types of municipal services, and the demands of municipal growth—to explode the myth that our cities, or our States for that matter, can, or even should, absorb a greater proportionate part of the cost of urban renewal.

The Federal-local sharing formula is the price tag which the Federal Government places on the local participation in urban renewal. By raising the price, a substantial number of communities—many of those who are most in need of an aggressive urban renewal program—will either be priced out of the program completely or unable to buy as much of it as they need.

[107] These proposals for increasing the federal share should not be confused with a change which was enacted in the Housing Act of 1957. § 302 of that act, 71 Stat. 299, 42 U.S.C. § 1453 (1958), provided for the establishment of an alternative basis for calculating the federal capital grant. It permits a community to elect to receive either a two-thirds federal grant or a three-fourths federal grant with the higher percentage grant being based on gross project costs which do not include certain expenses of planning, surveys, legal services, and administrative overhead. The excluded costs are borne entirely by the local community. In effect, under the alternative formula, the federal government pays a *higher* percentage of a *reduced* project cost. In proposing the formula, the Housing Agency expressed the expectation that the federal share of the total costs would prove to be about the same under either formula, and stated that the purpose of the alternative formula is to make it possible to eliminate review and discussion at the federal level of survey, planning, and administrative costs.

[108] *Hearings Before the Subcommittee on Housing of the Senate Committee on Banking and Currency on the Housing Act of 1959*, 86th Cong., 1st Sess. 572 (1959). See also, *id.* at 582, and, for earlier recommendations by the Association, see *Hearings Before the Subcommittee on Housing of the House Committee on Banking and Currency on Slum Clearance and Related Housing Problems*, 85th Cong., 2d Sess. 90, 93 (1958).

The United States Conference of Mayors has also recommended that the federal share be increased to eighty per cent.[109] The Mayors of Boston, Milwaukee, and Gadsden, however, have suggested a ninety per cent federal contribution,[110] and the Mayor of New York, when asked what he thought about the suggestion, gave the following answer: "I mentioned that one of the recommendations at the Conference of Mayors was that the Federal contribution in redevelopment be increased from 66⅔ to eighty per cent. If anyone would want to sponsor going to ninety per cent, I am sure the cities would appreciate that too."[111]

Although he was addressing himself to a different though related issue, the Mayor of Philadelphia in 1958 argued as follows against asking the states to take over some of the responsibility for the urban renewal program:[112]

It takes no great political knowledge to realize that this could only result in a sharp reduction in the program—because of the rural domination of State legislatures as well as the lack of State resources.

Thirty-five years ago, 75 percent of the taxes went directly to the cities and the States. Today, the Federal Government takes 75 percent and the cities and States get only 25 percent. True, the Federal Government's responsibilities have grown in those years. But so have those of the cities and States.

Particularly is this true of the cities, with their vast influxes of population. We in Philadelphia have, in the past 5 years, increased our taxes by 35 percent, largely to meet this very problem. . . .

The third of a billion dollars allocated this year for urban renewal is less than one-half of 1 percent of our national budget. It would not even be enough to pay for a single aircraft carrier.

On a later occasion, the Mayor argued that the cities have been receiving a steady influx of lower-income groups, including disadvantaged nonwhite groups, with greater social needs and lower tax-paying ability, while higher-income families have tended to move across city lines to the suburbs.[113] Others have often pointed out

[109] *Hearings Before the Subcommittee on Housing of the House Committee on Banking and Currency on Slum Clearance and Related Housing Problems,* 85th Cong., 2d Sess. 188 (1958).

[110] *Id.* at 190, 192, 243.

[111] *Id.* at 254; see also *id.* at 255–56.

[112] *Id.* at 214.

[113] *Hearings Before the Subcommittee on Housing of the Senate Committee on Banking and Currency on Housing Legislation of 1960,* 86th Cong., 2d Sess. 392 (1960).

that states and cities must avoid increasing their taxes too sharply in relation to other states and cities in order to avoid driving industry across their borders.

Finally, an argument has been made that the federal tax structure is more productive and more equitable than state and local tax structures can possibly become in the foreseeable future, so that it is desirable to finance nationally-important programs largely with federal tax revenues. Senator Clark of Pennsylvania, in a lecture delivered at George Washington University on March 28, 1960,[114] stated that local budgets are inadequate partly because of an unwillingness to tax but more importantly because of a lack of real resources. He stated that federal revenues have risen by seventy-four per cent since 1946, but state and local revenues have more than tripled; that state and local tax rates have risen steadily, while federal taxpayers have enjoyed tax reductions; the federal indebtedness has risen five per cent since 1946, while state and local debt has risen 309 per cent; and finally that state and local tax burdens fall far more heavily on poor and moderate-income families than do federal tax burdens. Thus, Senator Clark argued that most local tax dollars are still collected from the real property tax, although the ownership of real estate has long ceased to be a good indication of relative wealth. That is, the owner of a heavily mortgaged home may be taxed on hardly any equity at all, whereas a man who is better off, with wealth largely in a safety deposit box, escapes local taxation on these assets, but is reached by federal taxation. On the further grounds that "over half of all State tax revenue now comes from sales and excise taxes," Senator Clark concluded that both "State and local taxes fall far more heavily upon the average- and lower-income families," whereas "the brunt of Federal taxation falls upon the corporations and the upper-income families."

It is apparent from the foregoing and from a reading of all the congressional discussions over a period of several years on the issue of the federal-local share of urban renewal costs that the arguments on both sides tend to be quite general and would just as logically support raising or lowering a fifty-five or seventy-five per cent federal grant as they would support raising or lowering a 66⅔ per cent federal grant. If objective studies have been made which would

---

[114] *Toward National Federalism,* 106 CONG. REC. A3007, A3008 (April 5, 1960) (reprinted at the request of Representative Bowles of Connecticut).

truly sharpen this issue quantitatively, they have, so far as we know, not been presented at any of the congressional hearings. Instead, both sides have presented their positions primarily in terms of what seems to them "equitable" and of the problems with which they are each faced in obtaining revenues needed for competing purposes. Under such circumstances, the congressional decision-making process necessarily tends to rest more heavily than is usual on visceral reactions. Indeed, this same tendency may be detected in the testimony by the Mayor of New York, quoted above, in which he recommended an eighty per cent federal grant, but thought that the cities would appreciate going to ninety per cent if anyone would want to sponsor the higher level. Similarly, in 1960 the Mayor of Philadelphia, testifying as President of the United States Conference of Mayors, stated that the recommendation of the Conference was for a four to one federal-local grant ratio, and then added: "I personally think that 3 to 1 would be a very fair figure. I mean, that is purely my personal position on it."[115]

It is interesting to note that the $\frac{2}{3}$-$\frac{1}{3}$ cost sharing formula was originally recommended by the Executive Branch without any pretense that a different ratio would be unreasonable. Recognizing that large sums of money would be involved which it would be difficult for cities to raise, and allowing for greater local resistance to newer forms of municipal expenditures, it was thought desirable to exceed substantially the fifty per cent matching grant formula which is customary in almost all federal aid programs, while at the same time requiring the locality to have a truly substantial stake in a program which would benefit it both socially and financially. The present ratio seemed about right for this two-fold objective. Ten years later, it still seemed about right to Mr. William Zeckendorf, Sr., the prominent redeveloper. During a congressional hearing in January 1958, the following exchange occurred between him and Representative McDonough of California:[116]

Mr. McDONOUGH.   What percentage should it be?
Mr. ZECKENDORF.   Well, I think if it got to be less than a third, it would be too much of a free ride, and I think there should be enough

[115] *Hearings, supra* note 113.
[116] *Hearings Before the Subcommittee on Housing of the House Committee on Banking and Currency on Slum Clearance and Related Housing Problems,* 85th Cong., 2d Sess. 336 (1958).

of a challenge to local pride to make sure they know they have got to pay something in, however substantial it may appear to them to be, or insubstantial it may appear to you to be.

I think this one-third is about as close to being good as you can get, and I think if you change it, and made it, let's say, 50–50, that it might have an end result that would be antithetical to urban renewal on a national scale.

The Eisenhower Administration has reasoned that a substantial local investment in the urban renewal program assures greater interest on the part of the local electorate and closer supervision by elected local officials, and that this in turn makes for more efficient and more economical operations. It is also often pointed out that federal supervision will inevitably tend to increase to a level which the localities will find onerous if ever the local share of the cost is reduced to a point where it represents no substantial burden on the community. This line of argument is almost always presented in the context of the supervision which is necessary to avoid wasteful administration and inefficient operations. It brings to mind possible losses in administrative and overhead costs which may in a few years run to hundreds of thousands of dollars in a single fair-sized city and to possible losses from unwise land assembly or land sale methods which may run to a few millions of dollars. However, more is at stake than financial losses from inefficient execution of projects. The absence of a substantial local investment may tempt localities to undertake projects which are basically undesirable because they involve a wasteful allocation of major economic resources. The danger would thereby be increased that, on some future swing to the right of the federal political pendulum, there would be enacted by the Congress inflexible limitations that could hobble the entire program. . . .

In the meantime, the recent direction of the congressional pendulum indicates a real possibility that the local share of urban renewal costs will actually be reduced too far. To understand why this is so we must consider, along with the pressures to reduce the statutory one-third local share to one-fourth or one-fifth or even one-tenth, other less obvious, but important, tendencies to lighten that share. These relate to the so-called "noncash grants-in-aid" which a locality may provide to assist its urban renewal projects and to certain project expenditures such as those for streets.

The noncash grants may take the form of schools, parks, playgrounds, or other public facilities, either on or off the project site, which are necessary for carrying out the project. If the public facility is of direct benefit to other areas as well as to the urban renewal project area, only a prorated portion of its cost is counted as a local grant. The eligible cost enters into the calculation of the gross project cost as well as of the local grant-in-aid so that the federal two-thirds and the local one-third shares are each calculated against a net project cost which reflects expenditures made for the public facilities.[117]

The Taft Subcommittee Report of August 1, 1945, had recommended that "expenditures on public buildings made necessary by the project" be recognized as local contributions "only to the extent that these expenditures exceed what the municipality would spend for the same purpose if there were no project."[118] The literal application of this hypothetical test was rejected as not being administratively practical. That is, no federal official should be required to guess what a municipality might have done under other circumstances. For example, from the very beginning of the urban redevelopment program under the 1949 Act, if an old school, no matter how dilapidated, were replaced by a new one which drew all of its pupils from the urban redevelopment project area, the entire cost of the new school would be credited as a local noncash grant-in-aid, even though it was reasonably certain that the old school would have had to be replaced before too long whether or not the surrounding slum area was cleared. Thus, it should be recognized that from the very beginning of the program, some local expendi-

[117] Informal proposals made in Congress that a public facility be counted as a local grant-in-aid but not as part of gross project cost were not strongly pressed because, in addition to placing a financial burden on the community, the exclusion from gross project cost would, as a practical matter, upset the financing arrangement of the program. Members of Congress who were not persuaded by the first reason were persuaded by the second. Thus, in the example in Part III of a project having a gross cost of $10 million, if the $1 million figure for provision of public facilities were excluded from the total in "A" (Gross project cost), to which the two-thirds federal and one-third local grants are applied, and if corresponding changes were made throughout the example, the total under "E" which is available for repaying the borrowings referred to in "A" would always, as a matter of arithmetic, be inadequate so long as the city continued to receive grant-in-aid credit for the public facilities.
[118] TAFT SUBCOMMITTEE REPORT 19 (Aug. 1, 1945).

tures which do not really represent an additional burden on the local community caused by the urban renewal program count as local urban renewal grants and also enter into gross project cost, thereby affecting the size of the federal grant. This fact is not cited with any intention of criticizing the policy, but it is relevant in evaluating the weight of the burden which the program places on the locality.

Similarly, expenditures for street improvements within an urban renewal area may be eligible as a direct project cost, even though there is a possibility that the improvements would have become necessary before too long anyway. This factor has become more significant since the 1954 amendments which extended the program to rehabilitation and conservation activities. Projects involving such activities generally cover larger areas than projects involving only clearance. Thus, there may be more streets to be improved, while at the same time there is less need for large outlays involved in land acquisition and the clearance of structures. Conservation and rehabilitation projects therefore tend to involve relatively greater use of federal funds for activities which have been traditionally carried out entirely at municipal expense.

In the early days of the program a problem arose under the requirement that a local grant-in-aid shall be "in connection with" a project "on which a contract for capital grant has been made." The requirement is reasonable but its application not always easy. Clearly, a locality ought not to be permitted to count the cost of a school if it had begun to lay the foundation before it even contemplated that there would ever be an urban redevelopment project in the vicinity. Obviously, too, the result would be unfair if a city were penalized because, before cold weather had set in, it had begun construction on a school needed for a redevelopment project without waiting until all the formalities involved in entering into a federal aid contract had been completed. Basically, the problem involved is one of finding an administratively workable test for determining the intended connection between the school or other public facility and the future urban redevelopment project. This problem was first met by having the local public agency obtain a written "prior approval" from the federal government which permitted the public facility to be started, without loss of local grant credit, before the federal aid contract was signed. In view of the long period of planning which may be involved in a project, the prior approval could be given several years before the federal urban redevelopment loan and grant contract. Although this particular device (and similar later devices based on identifying a project in a contract for planning advances) appeared to the Executive Branch to provide a reasonable way to meet the demand for flexibility and the need for establishing a "good faith" connection between the public facility and the future urban redevelopment project, many localities and Congress thought otherwise.

Section 413 of S. 57, Eighty-sixth Congress, which was vetoed by the President on July 7, 1959, would have provided that a public facility otherwise eligible as a local grant-in-aid shall not be deemed to be ineligible because of the absence of a federal "prior approval" provided that the construction of the facility was started not more than five years prior to the Housing Administrator's authorization of a contract for loan or capital grant for the urban renewal project. Even the failure to notify the Administrator that a public facility had been started could not, under the section, be used as a basis for declaring the facility ineligible as a local grant-in-aid. This provision would not have removed the substantive requirement that the eligible public facility be necessary to serve an urban renewal project, but it would have eliminated a workable method for determining that the municipality had originally provided the facility in order to serve a future renewal project rather than as a routine municipal improvement. The provision was criticized by the President in his veto message[119] as having the effect of reducing the local contribution.

A similar provision, but with the five-year period reduced to three, was later enacted in section 414 of the Housing Act of 1959. The Senate Committee report[120] stated that "it is the committee's intention that local public works be credited under this provision *only if the projects are clearly a part of, and contributory to, the urban renewal project.*" The reduction of the period from five years to three years and the statement in the Committee report removed some of the danger, which was inherent in the earlier provision, that substantial urban renewal funds would be diverted into a federal

119 Message from the President of the United States, *Housing Act of 1959— Veto Message*, S. Doc. No. 34, 86th Cong., 1st Sess. (1959).
120 Senate Comm. on Banking and Currency, *Housing Act of 1959*, S. REP. 715, 86th Cong., 1st Sess. 6 (1959). (Emphasis supplied by the Committee.)

program of aid for municipal public facilities. However, it still will result in credit being given for schools and other local facilities which were provided with no intention at the time to have them serve a future renewal project. While this provision represents a material chipping away of the local share of urban renewal costs, it will perhaps not cause as large a reduction in that share as another type of change which was made in the 1959 Act and which may be extended further.

In order to encourage urban renewal activities near the many colleges and universities which have been affected by blight in neighboring areas, section 418 of the 1959 Act added a new section 112 to the 1949 Act.[121] A major effect of this new section is to permit a local urban renewal agency to obtain noncash grant-in-aid credit for expenditures made by a college or university for acquiring land and buildings within or in the immediate vicinity of an urban renewal project area. The buildings may be acquired by the educational institution with the intention of rehabilitating or clearing them, and the clearance expenditures made by the educational institution would add to the local public agency's grant-in-aid credit. Expenditures made by the educational institution as long as five years prior to the authorization of an urban renewal loan and grant contract would be eligible. Also, unlike acquisition of land and buildings by the local public agency itself, there will be no disposition proceeds to offset the acquisition cost which enters into the noncash credit.

Where an educational institution has, within a five-year period, engaged in an extensive expansion program, the credit which the local public agency would receive could be very substantial indeed. Yet all of the expenditures would be made by the college or university and not by the city. The credit might well be large enough to provide the entire local grant-in-aid required for the later urban renewal project near the educational institution, and there may be enough left over to provide the local grant-in-aid required for several other local urban renewal projects having nothing to do with the college or university. Thus, the local public agency could retroactively receive a large credit which substantially shifts the financial burden of urban renewal activities in that locality as between the federal and local government.

[121] 73 Stat. 677, 42 U.S.C. § 1463 (Supp. 1959).

It is relevant to ask why such a departure from the federal-local cost-sharing formula should be available in order to give colleges and universities additional urban renewal benefits. As no urban renewal funds are furnished to the institution, the benefits consist of advantages flowing from the improvement of the neighboring area by a federally-aided urban renewal project and the opportunity to acquire in the vicinity additional land needed by the institution. Colleges and universities have an urgent need for expansion in the next few years, and the certainty of urban renewal in an area may be of considerable assistance to them in securing donors' funds required to carry out their building programs. The grant-in-aid credit would furnish a very strong incentive for a local public agency to undertake a nearby urban renewal project which would furnish these benefits to the institution, or to grant a higher priority than would otherwise be given to such a project over other urban renewal projects in the community.

However, it appears to the writers that urban renewal activities in the neighborhood of colleges and universities would generally be so commendable a means of accomplishing the two-fold purpose of furthering urban renewal and higher education in the locality that no special inducement should be held out to the local public agency to do what it ought to be doing anyway. Conversely, if the possibility of obtaining a large grant-in-aid credit at no direct cost to itself should induce a local public agency to plan an urban renewal project in the wrong place or at the wrong time, the federal treasury will have been called upon to underwrite a distortion of a federal program. It should be borne in mind that, as the responsibility for initiating urban renewal projects is solely that of the locality, the federal government is not in a practical position to reject an eligible project which has been presented to it for approval merely because other projects might more appropriately have been given a priority by the locality.

In any case, whatever the merits or faults of the amendment may be, it must be listed among the changes which tend to reduce the local share of the cost of urban renewal activities. Furthermore, as was predicted by some opponents, this change is being urged as a precedent for further similar changes in the law. Section 406 of S. 3670, Eighty-sixth Congress (Housing Bill of 1960), as passed by the Senate on June 16, 1960, and section 704 of H.R. 12603 (Housing

Bill of 1960), as reported by the House Committee on Banking and Currency on June 20, 1960, would extend these provisions to hospitals. Although no further action was taken in the Eighty-sixth Congress on legislation providing this extension, it will undoubtedly be considered in the Eighty-seventh Congress. It may be noted that universities often have extensive grounds and that many persons attached to a university live within its vicinity. Extensive grounds tend to make for a practical base from which to fight surrounding blight and the needs of students and faculty living on or near the grounds provide an additional motive for attacking surrounding blight. While similar considerations may reasonably be urged for hospitals, their force is greatly diminished by a major difference in degree. Thus, if hospitals are added to the 1959 provision, there will be little basis for rejecting the claims of a long list of other public institutions, thereby further reducing the local share of urban renewal costs. . . .

Additional light on the entire question of the burden on the localities which is represented by the local one-third share of the cost is revealed by an unpublished study which the Urban Renewal Administration made early in 1959. It estimated that up to December 31, 1958, local grants-in-aid averaged about thirty-six per cent, rather than 33⅓ per cent of net project costs, it being impossible exactly to gear the cost of grants-in-aid to future net project costs. This thirty-six per cent was estimated to be made up of cash grants averaging about fourteen per cent of net project costs, land donations averaging about two per cent, demolition averaging about 0.3 per cent, site improvements averaging a little under six per cent, and supporting public facilities averaging a little under fourteen per cent. . . .

It is too much to expect that pressures and counterpressures with respect to sharing the costs of urban renewal will cease or that the issue will be resolved without leaving some undesirable distortions in the program. However, it is not too much to hope that the pendulum will not swing so far in either direction as to result in major harm to the program.

5 Legal and Governmental Issues in Urban Renewal*†

WILTON S. SOGG AND WARREN WERTHEIMER

The rapid growth of American cities in the last six decades[1] has been accompanied by a substantial increase in the number and the size of slums and blighted areas,[2] and by a serious lack of adequate housing, greatly impaired economic values and tax revenues, an exodus of population and commerce from the central cities, dispro-

* Reprinted from the *Harvard Law Review*, Vol. 72 (January 1959), pp. 504–552, where it appeared as a Note under the title "Urban Renewal: Problems of Eliminating and Preventing Urban Deterioration." Copyright © 1962 by the Harvard Law Review Association.

† This Note was financed by a grant from the Harvard Law School. The editors interviewed housing, urban-renewal, and city-planning officials, members of private associations concerned with renewal, real-estate promoters and investors, and private attorneys. Interviews were conducted in Baltimore, Boston, Cambridge, Chicago, Cleveland, Detroit, Los Angeles, Newark (N.J.), New Haven, New Rochelle (N.Y.), New York City, Philadelphia, Portland (Me.), San Francisco, St. Louis, and Washington (D.C.). The editors wish to express their gratitude to the many persons who were interviewed or who responded to written inquiries.

[1] In 1890, one-third of the country's population was urban centered, while in 1956, slightly less than two-thirds of a population two-and-one-half times larger was so located. Address by Commissioner Richard L. Steiner of the Urban Renewal Administration, International Seminar on Urban Renewal, The Hague, Aug. 1958. The Urban Renewal Administration will hereinafter be cited "URA."

[2] For a discussion of the causes of slums and blight, see generally Seligman, *The Enduring Slums*, Fortune, Dec. 1957, p. 144; DETROIT CITY PLAN COMMISSION, PARKINS, NEIGHBORHOOD CONSERVATION 1 (1958); Johnstone, *The Federal Urban Renewal Program*, 25 U. CHI. L. REV. 301, 304 (1958).

portionate rates of crime, disease, poverty, and fire, and rapidly increasing costs of providing public services.[3] The earliest significant governmental efforts to deal with urban deterioration involved attempts to control the use of land through the creation of city plans[4] and the enactment of zoning ordinances, building codes, and housing codes.[5] More affirmative governmental action to improve housing conditions was taken subsequently through municipal construction of low-rent public housing with federal assistance.[6]

More recently, the states have turned increasingly to the clearance and redevelopment of sizable areas.[7] Although initially, private groups alone, utilizing only private capital, were authorized to accomplish these programs,[8] today such objectives are sought almost entirely by a system which combines the use of both public and private capital.[9] Such a program normally involves the acquisi-

---

[3] See generally DEWHURST & ASSOCIATES, AMERICA'S NEEDS AND RESOURCES 489–512 (1955); THE FUTURE OF CITIES AND URBAN REDEVELOPMENT (Woodbury ed. 1953); URBAN REDEVELOPMENT: PROBLEMS AND PRACTICES (Woodbury ed. 1953); THE EXPLODING METROPOLIS (Fortune ed. 1958).

[4] See Haar, The Master Plan: An Impermanent Constitution, 20 LAW & CONTEMP. PROB. 353 (1955). 35.3% of American cities with populations over 5,000 have or are developing city plans. Address by Commissioner Richard L. Steiner of the URA, International Seminar on Urban Renewal, The Hague, Aug. 1958. See also HOUSING AND HOME FINANCE AGENCY, PLANNING LAWS (2d ed. 1958). The Housing and Home Finance Agency will hereinafter be cited "HHFA." In 1953, 86% of cities over 10,000 had planning agencies. RHYNE, MUNICIPAL LAW 976 n.26 (1957).

[5] Building codes prescribe requirements for new construction, while housing codes set standards for existing structures. See generally URA, PROVISIONS OF HOUSING CODES (1956); NEW YORK STATE DIVISION OF HOUSING, HOUSING CODES (1958); Note, 69 HARV. L. REV. 1115 (1956). Lax enforcement of codes and the ease of securing variations and amendments to zoning ordinances have limited the effectiveness of these controls. Interview With Eastern Representative of Council of State Governments in New York City, July 1958.

[6] 48 Stat. 201 (1933), as amended, 42 U.S.C. § § 1401–33 (1952), as amended, 42 U.S.C. § § 1411d–35 (Supp. V, 1958); Mo. REV. STAT. § § 99.010–.230 (1949); see Johnstone, supra note 2, at 310 & n.38; City of Cleveland v. United States, 323 U.S. 329 (1945) (upholding validity of federal aid to public housing). See also cases on public housing collected in Annots., 10 A.L.R.2d 328 (1950); 172 A.L.R. 966 (1948); 130 A.L.R. 1069 (1941).

[7] Redevelopment, which lays primary emphasis upon the elimination of slums and usually employs both private and public capital, is to be distinguished from public housing, which has stressed the construction of new housing with public funds alone. Compare Mo. REV. STAT. § § 99.010–.230 (1949), with Mo. REV. STAT. § § 353.010–.180 (Supp. 1957).

[8] See, e.g., ILL. REV. STAT. ch. 67½, § § 251–94 (1957) (originally enacted in 1941).

[9] All but eight states now have statutes enabling public bodies to plan and spend for urban renewal. Address by Commissioner Richard L. Steiner of the URA, International Seminar on Urban Renewal, The Hague, Aug. 1958.

tion of all or most of the land within a designated area by a local public agency[10] through purchase or condemnation, the demolition of the structures on the land, and the conveyance of the cleared parcel to a private entrepreneur bound to redevelop it in accordance with a municipally approved plan.[11] Substantial redevelopment activity, however, commenced only after passage of the Housing Act of 1949,[12] which provided for federal aid to local public agencies undertaking redevelopment.

While redevelopment, that form of urban renewal which involves total clearance, remains the predominant mode of attack on urban deterioration, conservation, which involves the control of existing areas with a minimum of clearance, has begun to emerge as a potentially more effective technique.[13] A plan of conservation contemplates eliminating and preventing deterioration in an area not yet beyond reclamation through removal only of those buildings which cannot be salvaged; through reorganization and expansion of public facilities to provide the framework for a sound neighborhood; through the rehabilitation of private property—the remodeling and renovating of existing structures which do not conform to standards prescribed for the area;[14] and through the maintenance of all property in accordance with those standards.[15] As applied to sound portions of an area, a plan of conservation may require no rehabilitation and may be directed solely toward maintaining existing standards.[16] The Housing Act of 1954 extended to conservation

[10] In this Note, "local public agency" and "agency" mean "any State, county, municipality, or other governmental entity or public body, or two or more such entities or bodies," which are authorized to undertake renewal projects. See 68 Stat. 629 (1954), 42 U.S.C. § 1460(h) (Supp. V, 1958).

[11] Comparable large-scale private redevelopers are far less typical in Europe. Address by Dr. Ir. F. Bakker Schut, President of the Netherlands Institute for Housing and Town Planning, International Seminar on Urban Renewal, The Hague, Aug. 1958.

[12] 63 Stat. 413 (1949), 42 U.S.C. §§ 1441, 1451–60 (1952). For a discussion of the federal statutory pattern, see Johnstone, *supra* note 2, at 310–13.

[13] See p. 171 *infra*. In the future, the emphasis may be upon community-wide planning rather than upon planning neighborhoods or specific projects. See S. REP. No. 1732, 85th Cong., 2d Sess. 16–17 (1958). For a discussion of the more comprehensive British system, see HAAR, LAND PLANNING LAW IN A FREE SOCIETY (1951).

[14] For definitions of rehabilitation, see Slayton, *Conservation of Existing Housing*, 20 LAW & CONTEMP. PROB. 436, 438 (1955).

[15] See Slayton, *supra* note 14, at 436.

[16] Conservation and rehabilitation, which have no universally accepted meanings, will be used in this Note as above defined. *Compare* Slayton, *supra* note 14, at 436–39, *with* Johnstone, *supra* note 2, at 301 n.2.

programs, including those involving rehabilitation, assistance similar to that already offered in regard to redevelopment.[17] This Note will explore some of the legal and practical problems involved in accomplishing urban renewal through programs of redevelopment and conservation.[18]

I. ALLOCATION AND EXERCISE OF PUBLIC RESPONSIBILITY FOR RENEWAL

A. *Statutory Framework*

Although the authority of local public agencies to undertake renewal derives from state and local law, the federal government exerts a considerable influence on the nature of almost all renewal activities.[19] Federal aid takes four basic forms: (1) capital grants for the execution of renewal plans and for research in renewal; (2) loans to assist in the planning and execution of renewal projects; (3) insurance and purchase of mortgages on property in renewal areas and on property necessary for relocation of persons displaced by renewal; and (4) provision of technical assistance.[20] To qualify for most types of federal aid, a local public agency must present to the Housing and Home Finance Administrator a "workable program" of urban renewal for the community.[21] Upon approval of the program, the Administrator may certify to constituent agencies of the HHFA that federal assistance may be made available in such community. Because of the singular importance of federal financial assistance,[22] state enabling acts and local programs are oriented

---

[17] 68 Stat. 622 (1954), as amended, 42 U.S.C. § § 1450–62 (Supp. V, 1958).

[18] The term "urban renewal" may embrace programs of public housing and presupposes a program of general city planning. See Slayton, *supra* note 14, at 438.

[19] See Johnstone, *supra* note 2, at 301.

[20] 68 Stat. 622 (1954), as amended, 42 U.S.C. § § 1450–60 (Supp. V, 1958); 68 Stat. 596 (1954), as amended, 12 U.S.C. § § 1715 k, 1715*l* (Supp. V, 1958); see 11 HHFA ANN. REP. 235–49 (1958); HHFA, AIDS TO YOUR COMMUNITY (1958); URA, URBAN RENEWAL ADMINISTRATION, A BRIEF BACKGROUND (1958); URA, A REPORT ON URBAN RENEWAL DEMONSTRATIONS (1956).

[21] 68 Stat. 623 (1954), as amended, 42 U.S.C. § 1451(c) (Supp. V, 1958). See generally HHFA, THE WORKABLE PROGRAM—WHAT IT IS (1957).

[22] The failure of Congress to provide additional authorizations in 1958 has brought many projects to a stand-still. See, *e.g.*, New York City Department of City Planning, Newsletter, Oct. 1958, pp. 2–3 (four projects halted in New York City).

largely toward meeting federal requirements and toward promoting co-operation with federal agencies.[23]

The initial allocation of responsibility for the formulation and execution of an urban-renewal program is accomplished through the passage of general state enabling legislation.[24] The earliest statutes authorized the creation of privately financed redevelopment corporations and empowered them to acquire land by purchase or eminent domain and to redevelop it, subject to approval of a plan by a public agency.[25] Some such statutes granted tax abatement to the corporations,[26] and some imposed certain restrictions, including limitation of the return payable to security holders.[27] Few corporations have been formed under these statutes, apparently because the cost of acquiring, assembling, and clearing the land almost always exceeds its fair market value for the proposed re-use.[28] Current legislation,[29] therefore, permits local public agencies to bear, in conjunction with the federal government,[30] those project costs in excess of the price received on resale of the cleared land.

[23] The difficulty of meeting these federal requirements seems to be one of the major problems in urban renewal. See, e.g., Smith, *Surveying the Barriers to Local Redevelopment Progress*, American City, March 1956, pp. 154, 237.

[24] In some states, constitutional provisions specifically authorize urban-renewal legislation. See HHFA, STATE ENABLING LEGISLATION—URBAN REDEVELOPMENT AND URBAN RENEWAL summary III (1958). In Ohio, urban renewal proceeds under the "home rule" powers granted to municipalities by the constitution. OHIO CONST. art. XVIII, § 3; see DUGGAR & FORD, URBAN RENEWAL ADMINISTRATION 54 (1957). For a compilation of citations to the constitutional provisions and enabling statutes, see HHFA, *op. cit. supra*, at 1–21.

[25] See, e.g., PA. STAT. ANN. tit. 35, § § 1741–47 (1945, Supp. 1957).

[26] E.g., MASS. GEN. LAWS ANN. ch. 121A, § 10 (1958).

[27] E.g., MASS. GEN. LAWS ANN. ch. 121A, § 9 (1958).

[28] For example, although in 1941 Illinois enacted the Neighborhood Redevelopment Corporation Law, ILL. REV. STAT. ch. 67½, § § 251–94 (1957), very few redevelopment corporations have ever been formed pursuant to the act. One of these was formed to test the constitutionality of a 1953 amendment to the act and was dissolved without having fulfilled a renewal plan. Interview With Counsel in Department of City Planning in Chicago, Aug. 1958; Gray, Problems of Urban Redevelopment in a Declining Neighborhood 36, April 1, 1956 (unpublished thesis in Harvard Law School Library). The one active corporation is supported partly by a private university interested in improving its environment. Interview With Executive Director of South East Chicago Commission, in Chicago, Aug. 1958.

[29] In 1947, 23 states and the District of Columbia had some type of redevelopment legislation. Address by Commissioner Richard L. Steiner of the URA, International Seminar on Urban Renewal, The Hague, Aug. 1958. By 1958, all but 8 states had enabling legislation or constitutional provisions which authorized local public agencies to undertake redevelopment or renewal. HHFA, STATE ENABLING LEGISLATION—URBAN REDEVELOPMENT AND URBAN RENEWAL summaries I–IV (1958).

[30] Even with federal assistance, progress to date has been slow. See Wall Street Journal, May 7, 1958, p. 1, col. 6; Christian Science Monitor, Oct. 28,

State legislation may vest renewal powers in municipalities, housing authorities, housing-and-redevelopment authorities, or urban-renewal agencies, or in some combination of these.[31] Although the state, through a housing board or some other state agency, may maintain some minimum supervisory control over these public bodies, its role is usually limited to one of delegation of the necessary powers.[32] An effective enabling act should create the authority to prepare and execute a plan,[33] to relocate those displaced, and to contract for state and federal funds. State enabling acts usually provide for a determination as to whether the city needs a renewal agency, appointment and control of agency officials, designation of a project area, and plan initiation, review, and amendment.[34] Local public agencies are generally given the power to sue, to contract,[35] to take land by eminent domain, clear it,[36] and sell it to private redevelopers, to provide for the relocation of those displaced, and to co-operate with other agencies. The statutes further define the types of areas which may be renewed, specify techniques for disposition of the property, and prescribe the controls which must be imposed upon its re-use.[37]

State legislation provides several methods by which the adminis-

---

1958, p. 3, col. 1. Contracts have been completely fulfilled in only 10 projects, but the number should increase considerably, since there are now over 500 projects outstanding under some form of federal-aid contract. Substantial rehabilitation is being carried on in over 100 of these. Address by Commissioner Richard L. Steiner of the URA, International Seminar on Urban Renewal, The Hague, Aug. 1958; cf. Redevelopment Today, Architectural Forum, April 1958, p. 108.

[31] See HHFA, STATE ENABLING LEGISLATION—URBAN REDEVELOPMENT AND URBAN RENEWAL summaries VII–X (1958).

[32] Interview With Eastern Representative of Council of State Governments, in New York City, July 1958.

[33] Many administrators feel that planning should be kept separate from operational functions. E.g., Interview With Executive Director of Chicago Land Clearance Commission, in Chicago, Aug. 1958.

[34] See DUGGAR & FORD, URBAN RENEWAL ADMINISTRATION (1957).

[35] But cf. Parent v. Woonsocket Housing Authority, 143 A.2d 146 (R.I. 1958) (authority not bound by five-year employment contract).

[36] See URA, TECH. MEM. No. 5 (1956); URA, TECH. MEM. No. 13 (1957). See also URA, ADVISORY BULLETIN No. 3 (1958). Clearance of the entire area is usually undertaken after it has been totally vacated. This is a very expensive method. To reduce costs, the Kansas City Authority turned over individual buildings as they were vacated to contractors authorized to remove and sell, thereby decreasing the net cost of demolition from an estimated $169,000 to $5,165. LAND CLEARANCE FOR REDEVELOPMENT AUTHORITY OF KANSAS CITY, MO., THE STORY OF URBAN RENEWAL, THIRD ANNUAL REPORT 12 (1956).

[37] TENN. CODE ANN. § 13–813 (1955) (blighted area defined); PA. STAT. ANN. tit. 35, §§ 1710(g), (h), (j) (Supp. 1957) (techniques of disposition); PA. STAT. ANN. tit. 35, § 1711 (1949) (control of re-use).

trative machinery authorized by the statutes may be brought into operation. A determination of the need for renewal, a prerequisite to the activation of renewal agencies in most states, is ordinarily made by the enactment of an ordinance or resolution by the local governing body, which usually must be preceded by a public hearing.[38] In some states, application must then be made by the local body to a state agency for permission to begin operation.[39] Pursuant to final authorization, appointments to the agencies delegated the task of renewal must be made by municipal or county officials or by a state agency.

B. *Administrative Organization*

The trend in urban renewal, as in municipal government generally, toward proliferation of the number of agencies responsible in some way for a program, and toward increasing use of independent agencies has created problems of distribution of powers and coordination of local agencies.[40] In some cities, there is an overlap of the functions of one body and another. Each of several agencies may perform essentially the same functions with a consequent duplication of personnel.[41] Moreover, the creation of renewal agencies which are administratively and financially independent from city government[42] has been criticized on the ground that such bodies are not sufficiently responsive to the popular will.[43] On the

[38] *E.g.,* Mo. Rev. Stat. § 99.430(9) (Supp. 1957). Private groups play a material role under these statutes in creating the requisite interest to produce such a resolution. The American Council To Improve Our Neighborhoods (ACTION) is one of the large national organizations which undertake to assist groups interested in initiating local renewal activities. See generally ACTION, Urban Renewal Outline.

[39] Ill. Rev. Stat. ch. 67½, § 66 (1957).

[40] See Council of State Governments, The Book of the States 239–42 (1958); Dunham, *A Legal and Economic Basis for City Planning,* 58 Colum. L. Rev. 650 (1958). A reason for using independent agencies is to avoid municipal-debt limitations. Interview With Attorney in Newark, Aug. 1958. See also Woodbury, *The Background and Prospects of Urban Redevelopment in the United States,* in The Future of Cities and Urban Redevelopment 607, 649–70 (Woodbury ed. 1953).

[41] Urban Renewal Study Board of Baltimore, Report to the Mayor 5, 11, 35 (1956).

[42] See Jones, *Local Government Organization in Metropolitan Areas: Its Relation to Urban Redevelopment,* in The Future of Cities and Urban Redevelopment 477, 573–86 (Woodbury ed. 1953).

[43] Interview With Consultant, Department of City Planning, in Chicago, Aug. 1958. It is argued that power for renewal functions ought to be vested in the official upon whom public opprobrium is likely to fall. Interview With Executive Director of Northeastern Illinois Metropolitan Area Planning Commission, in Chicago, Aug. 1958.

other hand, the nonresponsiveness of such bodies is considered by some to be desirable to the extent that it insulates the task of renewal from those political pressures which are harmful.[44]

The need to satisfy the requirements of the workable program in order to qualify for federal aid[45] exerts considerable pressure on a community to co-ordinate its renewal activities toward a single end.[46] Consolidation of some renewal agencies may be accomplished through amendment of city charters or the passage of ordinances, but it often requires a change in the state enabling legislation.[47] Some cities have managed to integrate renewal activities into an existing department of city government.[48]

In addition to problems of internal organization, renewal is hindered by territorial limitations upon the powers of municipalities and municipal agencies.[49] In order to achieve optimum renewal planning and execution the entire metropolitan area must be considered.[50] Although several state statutes expressly authorize renewal agencies to co-operate with one another,[51] such authorization is likely to be of little use if a large city is surrounded by several

[44] Interview With Counsel to Chicago Land Clearance Commission, in Chicago, July 1958. An urban-renewal district may serve this purpose and in addition overcome territorial limitations upon municipal agencies. Interview with Executive Director, Chicago Land Clearance Commission, in Chicago, July 1958.

[45] See p. 135 *infra.*

[46] See Urie, *Organization and Management For Urban Renewal,* 39 PUBLIC MANAGEMENT 102, 103 (1957). See also Ross, *"Workable Program,"* 14 J. HOUSING 84–86 (1957); *City Government Changes Under Way in Support of Urban Renewal,* 14 J. HOUSING 15–20 (1957); American Society of Planning Officials, Planning Advisory Service, Information Report No. 100, at 3 (1957). In Philadelphia an Inter-Agency Committee on Housing held regular meetings of representatives of all major city agencies involved in urban-renewal activities. CITY OF PHILADELPHIA, WORKABLE PROGRAM FOR URBAN RENEWAL 1956, at 29 (1957).

[47] Interview With Executive Director of Chicago Land Clearance Commission, in Chicago, July 1958. State legislation, providing for a single renewal and housing agency has been suggested for several cities. See, *e.g.,* URBAN RENEWAL STUDY BOARD OF BALTIMORE, REPORT TO THE MAYOR 11 (1956); Boston Sunday Globe, June 29, 1958, p. A-3, col. 6.

[48] Interview With Director of Cleveland Urban Renewal Agency, in Cleveland, Aug. 1958.

[49] "Only a government with community-wide jurisdiction can plan and provide the services, physical facilities, guidance, and controls necessary to relate functional plans with areal plans. None of the metropolitan areas has such a government today." Jones, *supra* note 42, at 605. See also *id.* at 477–606.

[50] See Haar, *Regionalism and Realism in Land-Use Planning,* 105 U. PA. L. REV. 515 (1957).

[51] *E.g.,* CAL. HEALTH & SAFETY CODE §§ 33330, 33332.

small suburban communities which carry on no renewal activities.[52] Provisions authorizing co-operation between municipal and state bodies, however, have often been considerable help. In one city, for example, local renewal activities are co-ordinated with a state high-way program.[53] In addition, territorial limitations may be overcome by state authorization and incorporation of urban-renewal districts encompassing an entire metropolitan area and possessing powers to accomplish at least those renewal functions which an individual municipality cannot itself efficiently perform.[54] Although districts have been employed for other public-service purposes such as schools, drainage, and highways,[55] their use has not been generally accepted in urban renewal.

In selecting those areas which need renewal, the city must co-ordinate its choice with any existing city plan.[56] A public hearing may then be required to determine whether given areas to be designated for renewal satisfy the statutory definition. Several considerations generally influence the choice of an area. First, an area must be chosen in which the land will lend itself to advantageous re-use and will be readily salable.[57] Second, the need of the area for public facilities constitutes a persuasive reason for its designation,[58]

[52] The proposed 1958 Housing Act, S. 4035, 85th Cong., 2d Sess. § 314 (1958), would have provided planning assistance to any group of adjacent communities "having a total population of less than 25,000, and having common or related urban planning problems," similar to that already available to municipalities under 25,000. See S. REP. No. 1732, 85th Cong., 2d Sess. 22 (1958). See also note 247 *infra.*

[53] Logue, *Urban Ruin—Or Urban Renewal,* N.Y. Times, Nov. 9, 1958, § 6 (Magazine), p. 17.

[54] Interview With Executive Director of Northeastern Illinois Metropolitan Area Planning Commission, in Chicago, Aug. 1958; see Van Buskirk, *What Business Has Learned About Rebuilding a City,* in THE "LITTLE" ECONOMIES 25–30 (Committee for Economic Development ed. 1958).

[55] See generally COUNCIL OF STATE GOVERNMENTS, PUBLIC AUTHORITIES IN THE STATES (1953); Nehamkis, *The Public Authority: Some Legal and Practical Aspects,* 47 YALE L.J. 14 (1937).

[56] See Dunham, *A Legal and Economic Basis for City Planning,* 58 COLUM. L. REV. 650 (1958). Some statutes make the designation of renewal areas subject to review by the planning authority. *E.g.,* MICH. STAT. ANN. § 5.3523 (Supp. 1957).

[57] Interview With Redevelopment Director of New Rochelle, N.Y., in New York City, Aug. 1958.

[58] Interview With City Planning and Urban Renewal Consultants in Newark, Aug. 1958. Choice of area may also be influenced by the location of projects, such as highways, proposed by the state government. Interview With City Planner in New Haven, Aug. 1958; see Kaskel v. Impellitteri, 306 N.Y. 73, 82–95, 115 N.E.2d 659, 663–71 (1953) (dissenting opinion), *cert. denied,* 347 U.S. 934 (1954).

since the federal government may pay two-thirds of their cost. Third, an area which offers possibilities for dramatic demonstration of renewal is desirable, since, especially at the outset, a city depends heavily on public approval and support.[59] Fourth, an area which lends itself readily to the accomplishment of a plan is likely to be preferred over one which does not, so as to reduce expenditures of time and money.[60]

C. Public Financing

The cost to municipalities of conducting urban-renewal programs is considerable, especially when the local public agency must acquire and clear an entire area before disposing of the property to a redeveloper at its fair market value as unimproved land.[61] In order to encourage urban renewal, the federal government is authorized to pay up to two-thirds of the net project cost[62] if certain requirements are met by the city, including the submission of an acceptable workable program.[63] Net project cost includes project expenditures, such as the costs of planning, land acquisition, and demolition, plus the amount of local noncash grants-in-aid, less the amount received from the sale or lease of the land to private redevelopers.[64] Since local noncash grants-in-aid are included in the calculation of net project cost, the local agency may be able to finance its share of

[59] METROPOLITAN HOUSING AND PLANNING COUNCIL OF CHICAGO, THE ROAD BACK 1-2 (1954) (reprinted from the *Chicago Daily News*).

[60] Considerations such as the saving of historical sites may result in the drawing of area boundaries so as to exclude particular sites. Interview With Director of Cambridge Redevelopment Authority, in Cambridge, Mass., July 1958. See also N.Y. Times, Oct. 15, 1958, p. 1, col. 1 (Fulton Fish Market).

[61] For example, 10 redevelopment projects currently underway in New York City, covering 162 acres, have resulted in net project costs after resale of the land of about $84,000,000 of which the federal government will bear $56,000,-000 and the city $28,000,000. New York City, Slum Clearance Progress 1, 3, July 15, 1957.

[62] 63 Stat. 416, 421 (1949), as amended, 42 U.S.C. §§ 1453(a), 1460(e), (f) (Supp. V, 1958). Under a little-used alternative provision the federal government is authorized to pay three-fourths of net project cost calculated so as to include fewer items. 63 Stat. 416 (1949), as amended, 71 Stat. 300 (1957), as amended, 42 U.S.C. §§ 1453, 1460(e), (f) (Supp. V, 1958). Only 10% of the total amount of grants available for urban renewal can be for nonresidential projects. 68 Stat. 627 (1954), 42 U.S.C. § 1460(c) (Supp. V, 1958).

[63] 68 Stat. 623, 625 (1954), 42 U.S.C. §§ 1451(c), 1455(a) (Supp. V, 1958).

[64] 63 Stat. 421 (1949), as amended, 42 U.S.C. §§ 1460(e), (f) (Supp. V, 1958); HHFA, SLUM CLEARANCE AND URBAN REDEVELOPMENT PROGRAM, MANUAL OF POLICIES AND REQUIREMENTS FOR LOCAL PUBLIC AGENCIES pt. 2, ch. 10, §§ 1-2 (April 18, 1957), § 3 (March 13, 1958), § 4 (April 4, 1956).

the project by providing parks, buildings, and other public facilities, and by donating real property.[65] The inclusion of public facilities in the calculations encourages the city to select for renewal those areas in which such facilities are already planned.[66] Conversely, local expenditures planned for needed public facilities in an area may be deferred until a renewal plan for that area is approved.[67] The proposed 1958 Housing Bill would have reduced to some extent the incentive to defer by permitting facilities built within five years prior to federal approval of the renewal plan to be included in net project cost.[68]

The federal government may aid the city in at least two other ways. First, it may advance money to finance surveys and plans, the expense of which is included in calculating net project cost to determine the Government's two-thirds share.[69] If the project is dropped, apparently no attempt is made to recover the advance.[70] Second, it may make demonstration grants of two-thirds the cost of pilot projects or studies in the urban-renewal field which are of interest to other communities.[71]

Despite these federal grants, most cities face an acute problem in trying to finance their share of the cost of renewal programs.[72] Although an increase in tax revenues to be derived from the area is anticipated,[73] methods must be found for raising the funds immedi-

[65] For example, one California city financed its share without any cash outlay. Its contribution consisted of site improvements which had already been planned. Interview With a City Attorney in San Francisco, July 1958.

[66] However, if the property donated or facilities provided are of direct benefit both to the renewal area and to other areas, and the degree of benefit to the other areas exceeds 20% of the total benefits, the cost of the facility is allocated between the areas. 68 Stat. 628 (1954), 42 U.S.C. § 1460(d) (Supp. V, 1958).

[67] Sound areas which need public facilities may be benefited by the inclusion of such facilities in net project cost, since more local funds will be made available for such areas than if the city were required to pay the entire cost of facilities in renewal areas. This advantage, however, may be decreased to the extent that renewal areas are given more facilities than would normally be provided to them.

[68] S. 4035, 85th Cong., 2d Sess. § 309 (1958); see S. REP. No. 1732, 85th Cong., 2d Sess. 20 (1958).

[69] 68 Stat. 624 (1954), 42 U.S.C. § 1452(d) (Supp. V, 1958).

[70] Interview With Redevelopment Official in Los Angeles, July 1958.

[71] 68 Stat. 629 (1954), 42 U.S.C. § 1452(a) (Supp. V, 1958).

[72] See *Hearings Before a Subcommittee of the Senate Committee on Banking and Currency on Various Bills To Amend the Federal Housing Laws*, 85th Cong., 2d Sess. 495 (1958) [hereinafter cited as *1958 S. Hearings*].

[73] See NEW YORK CITY PLANNING COMMISSION, URBAN RENEWAL 92 (1958); Chicago Daily Tribune, Sept. 29, 1958, pt. 2, p. 2, col. 3.

ately. Sufficient funds usually cannot be raised solely out of current tax revenues.[74] The most common source of local funds for renewal is borrowing, which is subject, however, to municipal-debt limitations. Although the HHFA is empowered to lend money to the city at the going federal rate,[75] federal officials prefer that the local public agency pay its share as the project progresses.[76] Furthermore, the agency is frequently able to sell tax-exempt obligations at substantially below the going federal rate.[77] The general-obligation bond, backed by the full faith and credit of the city, is most likely to attract lenders,[78] but may impair the city's credit rating if used to excess.

California and Minnesota have authorized the use of tax-appreciation bonds, payable solely out of the anticipated increase in taxes to be derived from the redeveloped area.[79] Although interest rates on tax-appreciation bonds tend to be higher than those on general-obligation bonds because of the greater risk involved, the disparity in rates should decrease as more renewal projects are completed and produce a substantial increase in tax revenues.[80] The use of such bonds, however, conflicts with the giving of a tax abatement as an inducement to a redeveloper, although partial abatement may still be possible.[81] Furthermore, this method of financing may lead to an undue emphasis on producing a high tax base in the redeveloped area and a consequent disregard of the long-run advantages of good planning.[82]

State grants in some places further augment the city's ability to finance its one-third of the net project cost. A recent statute in Connecticut authorizes the state to pay one-half of the local share in

[74] To the extent that new public facilities constructed as part of the project benefit particular property, the city may be able to assess their cost against the owners of such property. See 3 METROPOLITAN PLANNING AND HOUSING COUNCIL OF CHICAGO, CONSERVATION 264 (1953). Such a method seems undesirable in that it is likely to antagonize area residents whose co-operation is of great importance. See Slayton, *supra* note 14, at 455–56.

[75] 63 Stat. 414 (1949), as amended, 42 U.S.C. § 1452(a) (Supp. V, 1958).

[76] Interview With Renewal Officials in Cambridge, Mass., Oct. 1958.

[77] *Ibid.*

[78] Interview With Investment Counselor in San Francisco, July 1958.

[79] CAL. HEALTH & SAFETY CODE § 33950; MINN. STAT. § 462.545 subd. 5 (1953). See also URA, TECH. MEM. No. 11, at 2–4 (1957).

[80] Interview With Investment Counselor in San Francisco, July 1958.

[81] See p. 163 *infra*.

[82] For example, there may be a temptation to build too many high-rise buildings, or to leave insufficient open space. Interview With Renewal Official in Los Angeles, July 1958.

urban-renewal projects, to pay one-half the cost of commercial or industrial redevelopment projects for which federal aid is unavailable, and to provide technical assistance in the preparation of capital-improvement programs by the cities.[83] However, perhaps in part because many state legislatures are controlled by rural interests,[84] only a few states provide financial assistance to urban renewal.[85] It is likely that greater state aid will be needed in order to continue redevelopment programs on a significant scale.[86]

II. ACCOMMODATION OF PUBLIC ACTIVITIES AND PRIVATE INTERESTS

A. *Notice and Hearing*

Communication between the public agency and those to be affected by the plan may serve one or more of three purposes: to enlist popular support,[87] to provide an opportunity for community participation in the plan, and to lay a foundation for the determination of legal rights. The holding of public hearings is directed toward the accomplishment of these objectives. It has been held that notice and a hearing on the issue of the legality of a plan are not constitutionally required prior to the institution of condemnation proceedings, provided the owner receives a hearing on the issue in the condemnation suit.[88] Nevertheless, it is desirable to inform the community about the program and to provide a means by which large numbers of people can express their views,[89] especially in view of the limited effectiveness of judicial review. State[90] and

[83] Conn. Public Acts Nos. 8, 18, 24, Special Sess., March 1958.

[84] See *1958 S. Hearings* 496.

[85] They are New York, Illinois, Pennsylvania, and Connecticut. See *1958 S. Hearings* 494–95.

[86] Interview With Regional Counsel of HHFA, in New York City, July 1958.

[87] This is accomplished through programs of education and public relations conducted both by the public agency and by privately sponsored groups. See pp. 172–73 *infra*.

[88] Ross v. Chicago Land Clearance Comm'n, 413 Ill. 377, 108 N.E.2d 776 (1952); State *ex rel*. Dalton v. Land Clearance for Redevelopment Authority, 364 Mo. 974, 994–95, 270 S.W.2d 44, 56 (1954); *cf*. City of Milwaukee v. Utech, 269 Wis. 132, 68 N.W.2d 719 (1955). See also Sullivan, *Administrative Procedure and the Advocatory Process in Urban Redevelopment*, 45 CALIF. L. REV. 134, 143–44 (1957).

[89] Town meetings, in those communities which hold them, provide a forum for such discussion. Interview With Temporary Executive Director of Brookline Redevelopment Commission, in Boston, July 1958.

[90] *E.g.*, Mo. REV. STAT. § 99.430(8) (Supp. 1957).

federal [91] statutes make provision for notice and public hearings at various stages in the accomplishment of a renewal program.[92] State statutes require hearings on various issues, including the need for a renewal agency, the designation of an area, the approval or amendment of a plan, and the disposition of land.[93] Such hearings are generally held before the agency responsible for the implementation of the renewal plan[94] or before the local governing body responsible for its approval.[95]

A public hearing is potentially more effective than a judicial proceeding in accommodating the needs of the program to private interests. Such a hearing provides an opportunity for the presentation of objections and suggestions bearing upon the desirability[96] as well as the legality of public action. Furthermore, while a court is not empowered to prescribe alternatives to official action declared unlawful, a public hearing before a body other than a court may result in the modification of proposed action or the adoption of a new plan. Hearings held at early stages in the plan are sometimes ineffective because of lack of public interest and insufficient development of issues. The likelihood of change, however, is greater during the earlier stages, while the plan is more flexible.[97] It is

[91] 63 Stat. 417 (1949), 42 U.S.C. § 1455(d) (1952).

[92] Generally, however, state statutes require notice to be given only by publication. See, e.g., ILL. REV. STAT. ch. 67½, § 268 (1957). In some states, execution of the plan is, in effect, conditioned upon approval by referendum of the bond issue required to finance the city's contribution to the project cost. Interview With Executive Director of Cambridge Redevelopment Authority, in Cambridge, Mass., July 1958.

[93] See, e.g., TENN. CODE ANN. §§ 13–901, –902, –906 (1955) (need for agency); OHIO REV. CODE ANN. § 725.03(E) (Page 1957) (designation of an area); MO. REV. STAT. § 99.430(9) (Supp. 1957) (approval of a plan); MICH. COMP. LAWS § 125.79 (1948) (amendment of plan); PA. STAT. ANN. tit. 35, § § 1710(g), (h), (j) (Supp. 1957) (terms of disposition).

[94] See, e.g., ILL. REV. STAT. ch. 67½, § 268 (1957).

[95] See, e.g., MICH. COMP. LAWS § 125.74 (1948). But see MASS. GEN. LAWS ANN. ch. 121, § 26kk (1958).

[96] Michigan provides by statute that all matters relevant to the renewal program may be presented and those presented in writing must be considered. MICH. COMP. LAWS § 125.74 (1948).

[97] It has been suggested that the hearings required by statute should be preceded by informal hearings with no legal significance, in order to make the final formal one more meaningful. Interview With Eastern Representative of Council of State Governments, in New York City, July 1958. In an attempt to solve this dilemma, California has provided for three hearings at various stages of the planning process. CAL. HEALTH & SAFETY CODE § § 33530, 33565, 33747. Some feel that three hearings are too many and prevent effective presentation and discussion at any one. Bill, Obstacles to Urban Renewal 3, May 20, 1958 (paper presented at California Statewide Conference on Urban Renewal and Redevelopment).

commonly believed that hearings, whenever they occur, in fact exert little or no influence on the decisions of the body before which they are held,[98] but provide only a forum for the venting of hostility toward the plan.[99] The failure of hearings to be more effective may be attributable to inadequate legal representation of small owners,[100] to unwillingness of administrators to modify a course of action once adopted, especially since hearings are usually held at a late stage in the progress of the plan,[101] and to the common absence of statutory provisions requiring findings and other procedural formalities.[102]

B. *Securing Judicial Review*

Since the raising of objections to renewal projects by way of defense in eminent-domain proceedings has generally succeeded only in delaying the projects, and because of a desire to halt progress before the actual taking of land, parties affected by a renewal plan have often sought affirmative judicial relief prior to condemnation. Suits based upon the theory that federal aid had been extended to carry out a plan which did not meet federal requirements, whether brought to enjoin the use of federal funds[103] or to invalidate the entire project,[104] have met with a nearly uniform lack of success. State courts have held that they are without power to review the actions of the Federal Adminis-

[98] Interview With Renewal Official in New Haven, Aug. 1958.

[99] Interview With Renewal Officials in Boston, July 1958.

[100] Counsel may use the hearings as an opportunity for making a display to impress their clients, rather than to present an effective case on the merits. Interview With Executive Director of South East Chicago Commission, in Chicago, Aug. 1958.

[101] See, *e.g.*, PA. STAT. ANN. tit. 35, § 1710(g) (Supp. 1957) (hearing held before local governing body after submission of redevelopment proposal by planning commission for approval). If the publication of the plan is undertaken too early, commercial and industrial tenants begin moving out, leaving landlords with sharply reduced income. Interview With Counsel to Redeveloper in Cleveland, Aug. 1958.

[102] One objection raised to hearings is that there is generally no right of cross-examination, but only one of rebuttal, which is far less effective in the face of glowing promises and generalized statements by city officials. Interview With Attorney for Owners and Tenants in Lincoln Square Project Area, in New York City, Aug. 1958.

[103] See Allied-City Wide, Inc. v. Cole, 230 F.2d 827 (D.C. Cir. 1956).

[104] See Hunter v. City of New York, 121 N.Y.S. 2d 841 (Sup. Ct. 1953). Even if the plaintiff had standing to question the lawfulness of the federal grant, a violation of federal law, while it might compel the withdrawal of federal funds, would not seem to affect the legality of the plan under state law.

trator,[105] and federal courts have held that a plaintiff does not have standing to challenge the lawfulness of a third party's action in providing money to a party whose expenditure of it will harm the plaintiff.[106] Although it thus appears that private parties have no right to challenge the compliance of a renewal plan with the requirements for federal aid in the absence of congressional action expressly conferring such a right,[107] they might have standing to sue to enforce substantial compliance by local officials with the terms of a validly certified plan, on the theory that action by the local officials in assuming an obligation in accordance with federal law confers upon private parties the right to enforce that obligation.[108]

Affirmative relief prior to condemnation proceedings has also been sought on the theory that state enabling legislation is unconstitutional, that a particular renewal plan is in violation of state law, or that administrative action is in excess of the authority conferred by the plan. Some courts have refused to entertain such actions on the ground that the administrative action taken was insufficient to permit adjudication.[109] Furthermore, the courts, although acknowledging the right of an owner whose property has been taken to raise such objections,[110] have generally held that prior to the commencement of condemnation proceedings, landowners have no standing to sue.[111] Certain states, however, have specifically permitted objections to be raised at an early stage by suit for declaratory judgment,[112] by a statutory procedure to review the planning board's

[105] See, e.g., Hunter v. City of New York, *supra* note 104; *cf.* Fieger v. Glen Oaks Village, Inc., 309 N.Y. 527, 132 N.E.2d 492 (1956).

[106] Allied-City Wide, Inc. v. Cole, 230 F.2d 827 (D.C. Cir. 1956); Taft Hotel Corp. v. HHFA, 162 F. Supp. 538 (D. Conn. 1958); *cf.* Alabama Power Co. v. Ickes, 302 U.S. 464 (1938).

[107] *Cf.* Choy v. Farragut Gardens 1, Inc., 131 F. Supp. 609 (S.D.N.Y. 1955) (tenants have no standing to challenge Housing Commissioner's determination of maximum rentals).

[108] *Cf.* Brinkmann v. Urban Realty Co., 10 N.J. 113, 89 A.2d 394 (1952) (tenants have standing to sue landlord for recovery of rent in excess of the maximum prescribed by the Housing Administrator).

[109] *E.g.*, Loebner v. City of New York, 162 N.Y.S.2d 233 (Sup. Ct. 1957); *cf.* Tate v. City of Eufaula, 165 F. Supp. 303 (M.D. Ala. 1958).

[110] See, e.g., McAuliffe & Burke Co. v. Boston Housing Authority, 334 Mass. 28, 133 N.E.2d 493 (1956).

[111] Ross v. Chicago Land Clearance Comm'n, 413 Ill. 377, 108 N.E.2d 776 (1952).

[112] *E.g.*, Foeller v. Housing Authority of Portland, 198 Ore. 205, 256 P.2d 752 (1953).

findings afforded any person who has previously filed written objections with the board or the local governing body,[113] or on the theory that the promulgation of a plan creates a cloud on the owner's title.[114]

Although typically the approval of a plan by the local governing body is subject to judicial review in the same manner as are ordinances generally,[115] in some states the procedure for securing review is defined by the renewal statute itself. For example, in California an individual seeking to contest the validity of proceedings for the adoption of a renewal plan must institute an action within ninety days after its approval by the local governing body.[116] Similarly, the Illinois Neighborhood Redevelopment Corporation Law provides that to initiate judicial review, written objections to the order of the Redevelopment Commission which has authorized the execution of the plan must be filed within twenty days,[117] and resort to the courts is thereafter to be regulated in accordance with the state's general provisions for administrative review.[118] It would be desirable to provide a means by which issues of the legality of a plan and action to be taken thereunder could be determined conclusively as early as possible. In achieving this objective, however, account must be taken of the right of an individual to receive, at some time, a judicial hearing on questions of the legality of official action which affects his property interests.[119] It seems to be within the power of the state to require all persons whose property interests are to be affected by the plan to seek, within a reasonable time after personal notice, a judicial determination of all justiciable issues pertaining to the legality of the plan and official

[113] N.J. STAT. ANN. § 40:55–21.9 (Supp. 1957); see Sorbino v. City of New Brunswick, 43 N.J. Super. 554, 129 A.2d 473 (Super. Ct. 1957).

[114] Miller v. City of Beaver Falls, 368 Pa. 189, 82 A.2d 34 (1951); see Cram, *Master Planning Creates Clouds on Title*, Mich. State B.J., April 1956, p. 9.

[115] See McQUILLEN, MUNICIPAL CORPORATIONS § 20.02 (1949). For a discussion of the difference between an ordinance and a resolution, see *id.* § 15.02.

[116] CAL. HEALTH & SAFETY CODE § § 33745–46. See generally Jacobs & Levine, *Redevelopment: Making Misused and Disused Land Available and Usable*, 8 HASTINGS L.J. 241, 254–56 (1957).

[117] ILL. REV. STAT. ch. 67½, § 268 (1957).

[118] ILL. REV. STAT. ch. 67½, § 280–1 (1957).

[119] See Prunk v. Indianapolis Redevelopment Comm'n, 228 Ind. 579, 93 N.E.2d 171 (1950), *appeal dismissed*, 340 U.S. 950 (1951).

action thereunder or to be foreclosed thereafter from raising such issues.[120] Under such a procedure, the only issue open for consideration in a later condemnation proceeding would be that of the amount of compensation.

C. *Scope of Review*

Courts have regarded not only the passage of enabling legislation but also the approval of a plan and the administrative action taken thereunder as "legislative" action,[121] and they have almost uniformly exercised a very limited scrutiny of such action.[122] Litigants have seldom urged successfully objections based upon the unconstitutionality of the enabling act,[123] the failure of the plan to comply with statutory requirements,[124] or of administrative action to comply with the plan.[125] The test is said to be whether the action of the agency was in bad faith, arbitrary, capricious, or an abuse of discretion.[126] For example, in *Kaskel v. Impellitteri*, the court

---

[120] *Cf.* CAL. HEALTH & SAFETY CODE § § 33745–46. Such a scheme is favored by some officials. *E.g.*, Interview With Housing and Redevelopment Director of Los Angeles, in Los Angeles, July 1958. However, if notice is given only by publication, the due-process requirements of the fourteenth amendment may not be satisfied. *Cf.* Walker v. City of Hutchinson, 352 U.S. 112 (1956), 43 IOWA L. REV. 295 (1958); Comment, *"Notice" in Proceedings to Condemn*, 4 ST. LOUIS U.L.J. 339 (1957).

[121] See Bristol Redevelopment Housing Authority v. Denton, 198 Va. 171, 93 S.E.2d 288 (1956).

[122] See Marquis, *Constitutional and Statutory Authority to Condemn*, 43 IOWA L. REV. 170, 182–86 (1958).

[123] See, *e.g.*, People *ex rel.* Gutknecht v. City of Chicago, 3 Ill. 2d 539, 121 N.E.2d 791 (1954) (statute not void for absence of public purpose); People *ex rel.* Gutknecht v. City of Chicago, 414 Ill. 600, 111 N.E.2d 626 (1953) (statute not void for inclusion of more than one subject); Herzinger v. Mayor & City Council of Baltimore, 203 Md. 49, 61–62, 98 A.2d 87, 93 (1953) (statute not void for vagueness); Wilson v. City of Long Branch, 27 N.J. 360, 378–81, 142 A.2d 837, 847–49 (1958), *cert. denied*, 27 U.S.L. WEEK 3134 (U.S. Oct. 27, 1958) (delegation to agency not unconstitutional). *But see* Richards v. City of Columbia, 227 S.C. 538, 88 S.E.2d 683 (1955) (statute void for vagueness of standards). See also Annot., 44 A.L.R.2d 1414 (1955).

[124] See, *e.g.*, Tate v. City of Eufaula, 165 F. Supp. 303 (M.D. Ala. 1958).

[125] One complaint alleged that the hearing on the plan was a sham, that no facts had been released to the public, that the agency had failed to make findings, that the area was not blighted, that the city was taking excellent land as an inducement to the redeveloper, that the expenses of relocation would exceed the statutory allowances, and that the agency had therefore acted arbitrarily and capriciously. See Complaint in Gilden's, Inc. v. O'Brion, No. 86640, Super. Ct., New Haven County, Oct. 10, 1957.

[126] See Babcock v. Community Redevelopment Agency, 148 Cal. App. 2d 38, 306 P.2d 513 (Dist. Ct. App. 1957); Worcester Knitting Realty Co. v.

rejected an allegation that the area in question did not meet statutory standards and refused to consider the contention that the real motive for the clearance of the area was other than that of slum eradication.[127] Similarly, courts have rejected the argument that because the city had negotiated with a private entrepreneur prior to the formal disposition procedure, the statutory requirements of bidding had not been met.[128] Finally, once a court has determined that the designation of a particular area is valid, it is generally unwilling to consider the validity of taking or leaving sound buildings within the area or the drawing of area boundaries so as to exclude blighted structures on the periphery.[129]

Furthermore, the courts have characteristically decided the validity of renewal statutes or of particular plans in terms broader than the controversies before them.[130] The resulting determinations of validity render it difficult to attack subsequent applications of the statute or the plan.[131] Significantly, in many states, only one case concerning the validity of official action has reached a court of last resort.[132]

Judicial reluctance to invalidate enabling legislation or to over-

---

Worcester Housing Authority, 335 Mass. 19, 138 N.E.2d 356 (1956); Oliver v. City of Clairton, 374 Pa. 333, 98 A.2d 47 (1953). *Compare* Kraushaar v. Zion, 135 N.Y.S.2d 491 (Sup. Ct. 1954), *with* In re Housing Authority of the City of Salisbury, 235 N.C. 463, 70 S.E.2d 500 (1952). See also Lavine, *Extent of Judicial Inquiry Into Power of Eminent Domain,* 28 So. CAL. L. REV. 369, 377, 380 (1955).

[127] 306 N.Y. 73, 115 N.E.2d 659 (1953), *cert. denied,* 347 U.S. 934 (1954). See also Business Week, April 28, 1956, pp. 86–90.

[128] See Bleecker Luncheonette, Inc. v. Wagner, 141 N.Y.S.2d 293, 298 (Sup. Ct.), *aff'd,* 286 App. Div. 828, 143 N.Y.S.2d 628 (1955).

[129] See Starr v. Nashville Housing Authority, 145 F. Supp. 498 (M.D. Tenn. 1956), *aff'd per curiam,* 354 U.S. 916 (1957); McAuliffe & Burke Co. v. Boston Housing Authority, 334 Mass. 28, 133 N.E.2d 493 (1956); Balsamo v. Providence Redevelopment Agency, 124 A.2d 238 (R.I. 1956).

[130] See, *e.g.,* Berman v. Parker, 348 U.S. 26 (1954).

[131] When the redevelopment technique first gained acceptance, officials were apprehensive of legal problems. As the conservation technique now gains acceptance, by contrast, many seem to be going ahead less cautiously. Interview With City Planning and Urban Renewal Consultants in Newark, Aug. 1958. See also Weiss, *Is the Power of Eminent Domain Dangerous Under the Urban Redevelopment Act?* 57 DICK. L. REV. 326 (1953); REGIONAL PLAN ASSOCIATION, INC., PLANNING AND COMMUNITY APPEARANCE 8, 86 (1958).

[132] See HHFA, STATE ENABLING LEGISLATION—URBAN REDEVELOPMENT AND URBAN RENEWAL (1958). It has been suggested that in view of the courts' limited supervision of local officials, federal administrators should assume that function, using the sanction of control over funds. Interview With Attorney for Redeveloper in Chicago, Aug. 1958.

turn the determinations of those bodies responsible for the formulation, approval, and execution of urban-renewal plans may be attributable to several factors. Such determinations often depend upon technical evaluations and data which are peculiarly within the knowledge and competence of the agency or legislative body.[133] Because of the nature of the facts upon which these determinations rest and because of the consideration of the facts by several separate bodies,[134] the courts generally regard it inappropriate to engage in substantial reappraisal. Another significant though unexpressed factor may be a distaste for upsetting, at the instance of a single party, a plan upon which considerable amounts of public funds have already been expended[135] and which is supported by all politically significant groups.[136] Although these obstacles to more effective judicial review might be alleviated to some extent by a requirement that the agencies make detailed findings of fact,[137] it seems likely that, as the complexity and comprehensiveness of renewal programs increase, individuals will be required to look more to nonjudicial devices for protection.[138]

III. PROBLEMS OF LAND ACQUISITION

A. *Limits of the Power to Acquire by Eminent Domain*

Since virtually any program of urban renewal involves the acquisition of private property by purchase or through exercise of the eminent-domain power, it becomes essential to define the extent to

[133] See, *e.g.*, Sorbino v. City of New Brunswick, 43 N.J. Super. 554, 576–78, 129 A.2d 473, 485 (Super. Ct. 1957). Recognition by the courts of the necessity of relying heavily on agency expertise may account both for their reluctance to strike down enabling legislation as an unconstitutional delegation of power and for their reluctance to inquire too closely into the agency's compliance with the standards under which the delegation is made. *Compare* Herzinger v. Mayor & City Council of Baltimore, 203 Md. 49, 61–62, 98 A.2d 87, 92–93 (1953), *with* Worcester Knitting Realty Co. v. Worcester Housing Authority, 335 Mass. 19, 138 N.E.2d 356 (1956).

[134] See Kaskel v. Impellitteri, 306 N.Y. 73, 80, 115 N.E.2d 659, 662 (1953), *cert. denied*, 347 U.S. 934 (1954).

[135] Interview With Official of ACTION in Cambridge, Mass., Oct. 1958.

[136] Interview With Attorney for Owners and Tenants in Lincoln Square Project Area, in New York City, Aug. 1958.

[137] Some states require such findings by statute. See, *e.g.*, MASS. GEN. LAWS ANN. ch. 121, § 26kk (1958).

[138] See Note, 68 HARV. L. REV. 1422, 1435–36 (1955).

which such acquisition is for a public use within the meaning of state and federal constitutions.[139] Because the exercise of the eminent-domain power brings into conflict the interest of the public and that of the private-property owner, limitations on its exercise should be formulated by a balancing of the degree of public necessity against the extent of private deprivation, and by a consideration of alternative means of accommodating the public need to private interests.[140]

The concept of public use is no longer confined, as it once was, to the notion of public ownership of and access to the property.[141] Rather, it has generally come to be synonymous with public purpose.[142] The states have traditionally had the power to intrude upon private interests on behalf of "public safety, public health, morality, peace and quiet, law and order. . . ."[143] Courts upholding renewal legislation have generally related the need of taking property to one or more of these traditional "police-power" objectives by viewing as the primary aim of the legislation the elimination or prevention of slum conditions, which breed crime, disease, and other social evils.[144] Although some courts upholding redevelopment statutes have indicated that clearance of the land is alone sufficient to constitute such a public purpose,[145] it seems that the

[139] See generally Note, 68 HARV. L. REV. 1422 (1955). Although some courts distinguish between the nature of public use necessary to sustain expenditure of public money generally and that necessary to sustain the use of the eminent-domain power, e.g., Crommett v. City of Portland, 150 Me. 217, 230, 107 A.2d 841, 849 (1954), most courts do not, e.g., Papadinis v. City of Somerville, 331 Mass. 627, 629, 121 N.E.2d 714, 715 (1954). In any event, it would seem that if a particular purpose justifies the use of eminent domain, it also justifies the expenditure of public funds. See Crommett v. City of Portland, *supra* at 230, 107 A.2d at 849.
[140] It is interesting to note that statutes authorizing renewal generally contain a legislative finding that the desired end can be accomplished only by the use of eminent domain. E.g., N.Y. UNCONSOL. LAWS § 3302 (McKinney 1949).
[141] E.g., Ferguson v. Illinois Cent. R.R., 202 Iowa 508, 512, 210 N.W. 604, 606 (1926).
[142] See, e.g., David Jeffrey Co. v. City of Milwaukee, 267 Wis. 559, 574, 66 N.W.2d 362, 371 (1954). This court, among others, maintains a distinction between public use or purpose and public benefit or advantage. Other courts do not. E.g., State ex rel. Dalton v. Land Clearance for Redevelopment Authority, 364 Mo. 974, 270 S.W.2d 44 (1954).
[143] Berman v. Parker, 348 U.S. 26, 32 (1954).
[144] See, e.g., Crommett v. City of Portland, 150 Me. 217, 107 A.2d 841 (1954).
[145] Papadinis v. City of Somerville, 331 Mass. 627, 632, 121 N.E.2d 714, 717 (1954); Nashville Housing Authority v. City of Nashville, 192 Tenn. 103, 237 S.W.2d 946 (1951).

public purpose is not fully accomplished until adequate provisions have been made to insure that the area does not return to the condition of a slum. Most courts have recognized the significance of some agency control over the reuse of the property.[146] Some courts have justified the taking of land in blighted open areas[147] as being directly related to slum clearance, in that such areas can be used to provide housing for those dislocated by redevelopment projects and to alleviate crowded living conditions in other parts of the community.[148] The taking of property in deteriorating areas not yet slums but likely to become such has been upheld on the ground that prevention of slums as well as their elimination is a valid public purpose.[149] Three courts, however, which have held redevelopment statutes unconstitutional,[150] viewed the statutes' primary objectives not as slum clearance but as the subsequent redevelopment of the area, which in each case was for commercial purposes. The taking of property and its conveyance to a private party with the expectation that he would profit from its redevelopment was held to be a public taking for private use, even though the redevelopers were bound to comply with a legislatively approved plan.[151] The courts, however, have generally rejected this argument, holding that the conveyance is merely a reasonable

[146] See, *e.g.*, Hunter v. Norfolk Redevelopment & Housing Authority, 195 Va. 326, 337, 78 S.E.2d 893, 900 (1953).

[147] Blighted open areas are defined by one statute as areas of "predominately open [land] . . . which, by reason of obsolete platting, diversity of ownership, deterioration of structures or site improvements, or taxes and special assessment delinquencies usually exceeding the fair value of the land, are unmarketable . . . for housing or other economic purposes. . . ." ILL. REV. STAT. ch. 67½, § 64 (1957).

[148] *E.g.*, People *ex rel.* Gutknecht v. City of Chicago, 414 Ill. 600, 111 N.E.2d 626 (1953). Although evils of blighted open areas may not be as closely related to police-power objectives as those of slums, the individual hardship of a taking in open areas is usually less.

[149] People *ex rel.* Gutknecht v. City of Chicago, 3 Ill. 2d 539, 121 N.E.2d 791 (1954); Zisook v. Maryland-Drexel Neighborhood Redevelopment Corp., 3 Ill. 2d 570, 121 N.E.2d 804 (1954). Other courts have indicated rehabilitation is a valid public purpose. *E.g.*, Boro Hall Corp. v. Impellitteri, 128 N.Y.S. 2d 804, 806 (Sup. Ct.) (dictum), *aff'd mem.*, 283 App. Div. 889, 130 N.Y.S.2d 6 (1954).

[150] Adams v. Housing Authority, 60 So. 2d 663 (Fla. 1952); Housing Authority v. Johnson, 209 Ga. 560, 74 S.E.2d 891 (1953) (new statute passed after constitutional amendment); Edens v. City of Columbia, 228 S.C. 563, 91 S.E.2d 280 (1956).

[151] See, *e.g.*, Adams v. Housing Authority, *supra* note 150.

incident to achieving the elimination of the slum, which is itself a valid purpose.[152]

Some courts have recognized that public purpose is a function of changing needs[153] and that the traditional police-power objectives serve to illustrate but not to delimit it.[154] For example, much existing commercial and industrial property does not produce enough tax revenue to justify either the services it requires or the choice location it occupies.[155] Moreover, inadequate facilities cause many sound business enterprises to leave a city,[156] resulting not only in a further impairment of the city's ability to provide needed services to all its residents but also in a depression of the prosperity of the entire community.[157] Recognizing the need to redevelop such areas, courts have upheld the acquisition of private commercial property for commercial redevelopment[158] and the taking of open areas because of the need for industrial expansion,[159] or because of "compelling economic community need."[160] The Supreme Court

[152] E.g., In re Slum Clearance in City of Detroit, 331 Mich. 714, 50 N.W.2d 340 (1951). But see Opinion to the Governor, 76 R.I. 365, 70 A.2d 817 (1950) (public purpose of condemning marina eliminated by leasing to private parties).

[153] See, e.g., Redevelopment Agency v. Hayes, 122 Cal. App. 2d 777, 802–03, 266 P.2d 105, 122 (Dist. Ct. App.), cert. denied, 348 U.S. 897 (1954); cf. Village of Euclid v. Ambler Realty Co., 272 U.S. 365, 387 (1926).

[154] E.g., Berman v. Parker, 348 U.S. 26, 32 (1954) (dictum).

[155] Interview With City Planner in Detroit, June 1958; Interview With Housing Official in New York City, Aug. 1958.

[156] See, e.g., BALTIMORE URBAN RENEWAL AND HOUSING AGENCY, HOUSING AUTHORITY OF BALTIMORE, IT'S HAPPENING IN BALTIMORE 1–2 (1957); Sullivan, Administrative Procedure and the Advocatory Process in Urban Redevelopment, 45 CALIF. L. REV. 134, 138 (1957); Interview With City Planner in St. Louis, Aug. 1958; cf. 1958 S. Hearings 497.

[157] See CITY PLANNING BOARD, GENERAL PLAN FOR BOSTON, PRELIMINARY REPORT 9–13 (1950). This would seem to be especially true of the smaller cities where the problem of slums is often minor compared with the problem of the deterioration of industrial and commercial facilities. Cf. 1958 S. Hearings 527–28.

[158] Schenck v. City of Pittsburgh, 364 Pa. 31, 70 A.2d 612 (1950).

[159] Oliver v. City of Clairton, 374 Pa. 333, 98 A.2d 47 (1953); cf. McConnell v. City of Lebanon, 314 S.W.2d 12 (Tenn. 1958), in which the court, upholding the leasing of a city-built factory to a foreign corporation, said that avoiding low wages and unemployment is a public purpose. Contra, Opinion to the Governor, 79 R.I. 305, 88 A.2d 167 (1952). See also MASS. GEN. LAWS ANN. ch. 121, § 26j (1958).

[160] Redevelopment Agency v. Hayes, 122 Cal. App. 2d 777, 266 P.2d 105 (Dist. Ct. App.), cert. denied, 348 U.S. 897 (1954). Other courts have indicated that the concept of public purpose is being expanded. See State v. Daytona Beach Racing & Recreational Facilities District, 89 So. 2d 34 (Fla. 1956) (tourist business so large that entertainment for tourists is a public use); Port of Umatilla v. Richmond, 212 Ore. 596, 321 P.2d 338 (1958) (condemnation by port authority and leasing to private parties for port development upheld).

has indicated that the taking of property for the attainment of aesthetic objectives may be a public purpose.[161] Although it is doubtful whether individual interests should be outweighed in all cases by aesthetic considerations, increased attractiveness in some cases reasonably may be considered essential to a city's survival.[162] Most courts, however, have not as yet avowedly included within the concept of public use considerations beyond those which would be considered traditional in regard to the exercise of the police power.[163]

Once the public purpose of a taking pursuant to statute has been established, courts have readily accepted the method by which the legislature has sought to accomplish that purpose.[164] They have held that the legislature may properly decide to accomplish the public purpose by formulating and applying a plan for the redevelopment of a delineated area as a whole so as to insure against the future occurrence of slum conditions there.[165] Thus a plan for total clearance of a slum area may include the taking of sound property.[166] If the prevention of slums is a valid public purpose, it would seem equally justifiable to take property in a deteriorating area likely to become a slum, regardless of the property's condition, when it does not conform to the uses contemplated by a plan for the

[161] Berman v. Parker, 348 U.S. 26, 33 (1954) (dictum). See also Brunacini v. Loomis, 177 N.Y.S.2d 954, 958 (Sup. Ct. 1958) (dictum); Bilbar Constr. Co. v. Board of Adjustment, 393 Pa. 62, 141 A.2d 851 (1958); State ex rel. Saveland Park Holding Corp. v. Weiland, 269 Wis. 262, 69 N.W.2d 217, cert. denied, 350 U.S. 841 (1955); Guandolo, Housing Codes in Urban Renewal, 25 Geo. Wash. L. Rev. 1, 38–42 (1956).

[162] Interviews With City Planners in Detroit and St. Louis, June & Aug. 1958. In Bowker v. City of Worcester, 334 Mass. 422, 430, 136 N.E.2d 208, 213 (1956) (dictum), the court said that the improvement of the appearance of a project area has been recognized as a public purpose.

[163] See, e.g., Crommett v. City of Portland, 150 Me. 217, 107 A.2d 841 (1954). To the extent that the subsequent use of the property is what constitutes the public purpose, it seems that control of reuse is vital.

[164] See, e.g., City & County of San Francisco v. Ross, 44 Cal. 2d 52, 279 P.2d 529 (1955).

[165] E.g., Berman v. Parker, 348 U.S. 26 (1954); Worcester Knitting Realty Co. v. Worcester Housing Authority, 335 Mass. 19, 138 N.E.2d 356 (1956).

[166] See, e.g., Starr v. Nashville Housing Authority, 145 F. Supp. 498 (M.D. Tenn. 1956), aff'd per curiam, 354 U.S. 916 (1957). By the same token, not all buildings in the area need be taken. McAuliffe & Burke Co. v. Boston Housing Authority, 334 Mass. 28, 133 N.E.2d 493 (1956). Although official abuses of discretion may occur through either the inclusion or exclusion of particular pieces of property for reasons unrelated to its condition or the needs of the plan, a court might be more reluctant to upset an entire plan because of such an exclusion than merely to prohibit a particular instance of such an inclusion.

area's conservation, provided the plan is reasonably related to the objective of arresting further deterioration. For similar reasons, the city should be able to take property which it is impossible to rehabilitate or which its owner is unwilling or financially unable to bring up to standards set for the area.[167] Although the exercise of power by an administrative official to select particular buildings to be taken because of noncompliance with area standards requires considerable discretion, the possibility of its abuse should not of itself impair the validity of such a delegation of power.[168] Moreover, as a practical matter, public officials are particularly dependent upon acceptance and support of conservation programs by area owners and residents.[169]

B. *Problems of Condemnation Litigation*

Once a basic decision has been reached as to when to start acquiring land,[170] the agency will ordinarily begin the negotiations for purchase, which are required in most states as a condition precedent to the institution of condemnation proceedings.[171] After a determination of value by its appraisers, the agency may make

[167] For examples of authorizations to take land for the foregoing purposes, see ILL. REV. STAT. ch. 67½, §§ 91.12–.13 (1957), upheld in People *ex rel.* Gutknecht v. City of Chicago, 3 Ill. 2d 539, 121 N.E.2d 791 (1954); WOOSTER SQUARE REDEVELOPMENT AND RENEWAL PLAN, CITY OF NEW HAVEN 2, 11–12 (rev. ed. 1958). Since the compliance of an owner who is willing but financially unable to rehabilitate might be secured by methods less drastic than taking the property, a court might require such a method to be used. *Cf.* Adams v. Housing Authority, 60 So. 2d 663 (Fla. 1952) (methods less drastic than eminent domain adequate to abate blighted area). Most courts, however, are unlikely to distinguish between an unwilling and a willing but impecunious owner. *Cf.* Randolph v. Wilmington Housing Authority, 139 A.2d 476 (Del. 1958) (legislative judgment that police power not adequate to remedy slums must stand). As a practical matter, it is desirable to avoid taking the property of this type of owner. See pp. 174–75 *infra.*

[168] See Gohld Realty Co. v. City of Hartford, 141 Conn. 135, 104 A.2d 365 (1954). Moreover, courts have not been entirely unwilling to hold that official action has exceeded the bounds of discretion. See *In re* Housing Authority of City of Salisbury, 235 N.C. 463, 70 S.E.2d 500 (1952) (housing authority found to have acted arbitrarily in selecting site on college campus for low-cost housing project); Winger v. Aires, 371 Pa. 242, 89 A.2d 521 (1952) (school board's exercise of power of eminent domain was clear abuse of discretion).

[169] See pp. 172–73 *infra.*

[170] If the agency acquires land at an early stage, tax revenues between the acquisition and resale will be lost, but the land may be retained without clearance and rents collected in the interim. In any event, however, the agency cannot acquire land before express federal authorization to do so. See 68 Stat. 647 (1954), 42 U.S.C. § 1455a (Supp. V, 1958).

[171] See RHYNE, MUNICIPAL LAW 405–06 (1957).

offers directed toward purchase or an option to purchase, or toward laying a basis for suit. Before approving a proposed purchase, federal officials often insist upon appraising de novo the amounts offered—which may delay the settlement or make it impossible.[172] Nevertheless, the vast majority of cases result in a negotiated purchase rather than in litigation.[173]

1. EVIDENCE OF ILLEGAL USE.—Market value is usually the standard for computing compensation in condemnation proceedings.[174] Since it is common for property in blighted areas to be exploited for an abnormally high return through maintenance in violation of municipal ordinances,[175] owners may demand of the agency a price inflated by an amount which reflects the earning potential of the illegal use. Exploitation may be accomplished through conversion of a single apartment into a number of smaller apartments so as to exceed maximum-density limitations and secure for the landlord a greater total rental. Similarly, he may increase his profit by failure to maintain and repair in accordance with housing-code standards.[176] Finally, revenues may be enhanced by the conduct of an enterprise which is made criminal by statutes other than housing codes. Although in some states the introduction of evidence of illegal use is permitted by statute or common law,[177] in others such

---

[172] Interview With Director of Chicago Housing Authority, in Chicago, Aug. 1958; Interview With Commissioner, Department of City Planning in Chicago, Aug. 1958. Presence of extensive federal supervision is seen by some as a guarantee against charges of improper action on the part of city officials. Interview With Executive Director of Citizens' Action Commission in New Haven, Aug. 1958.

[173] Interview With Director of Chicago Housing Authority, in Chicago, Aug. 1958.

[174] See 4 NICHOLS, EMINENT DOMAIN § 12.2 (3d ed. 1951). There are three systems used by the states for setting compensation: determinations by commissioners, subject to court review; determinations by commissioners subject to jury review de novo; and determinations by a jury. See Advisory Committee on Rules for Civil Procedure, Supplementary Report on Rule 71A, 28 U.S.C. following § 2072 (1952). See also Dillard, *Basic Problems in Eminent Domain*, 21 TEX. B.J. 297 (1958).

[175] See METROPOLITAN HOUSING AND PLANNING COUNCIL OF CHICAGO, THE ROAD BACK 16–17 (1954) (reprinted from the *Chicago Daily News*).

[176] Slum landlords may also fail to pay their real-estate taxes, since interest and penalties for nonpayment are less than interest on a loan secured by the slum property. Interview With Counsel to Redeveloper in Cleveland, Aug. 1958.

[177] For a collection of cases and statutes on the admissibility of evidence of illegal use, see HHFA, OFFICE OF THE ADMINISTRATOR, DIVISION OF LAW, ADMISSIBILITY OF EVIDENCE OF ILLEGAL USE OR CONDITION OF PROPERTY IN EMINENT DOMAIN PROCEEDINGS (1951). See also Winner, *The Rules of Evidence in Eminent Domain*, 32 DICTA 243 (1955); Note, 14 U. CHI. L. REV. 232 (1947).

evidence is excluded on the ground that its consideration might result in a collateral enforcement of the ordinance violated.[178] Even those states which prohibit the introduction of evidence of illegal use, however, may permit an appraiser to testify that in arriving at a valuation he took into account the existence of given conditions which constitute violations, as such conditions would be material to a potential buyer.[179] Furthermore, in most states, a party may request that the jury view the premises.[180] It is arguable that by these devices, compensation for the illegal use is effectively excluded from the award. On the other hand, it has been contended that, to the extent that evidence of income produced by the property is admissible, the fact finder may be influenced by such evidence despite a view of the premises or expert testimony that valuation is not accurately reflected by such income figures alone.[181]

Although the increment of value claimed by the owner which is attributable to illegal use might be eliminated by enforcement of the ordinance violated prior to institution of condemnation proceedings,[182] several problems common to code enforcement generally may be raised thereby. If enforcement requires a decrease in the density of occupancy, large numbers of families will be dislocated at a time when adequate relocation facilities may not yet have been made available under the plan.[183] Furthermore, such families may be unable to claim federal relocation payments, which are conditioned upon "displacement by an urban renewal project . . . respecting which a contract for capital grant has been executed. . . ."[184] Enforcement may also be impractical because of the lack

[178] *E.g.,* Freiberg v. South Side Elevated R.R., 221 Ill. 508, 77 N.E. 920 (1906); *cf.* Chicago Land Clearance Comm'n v. Darrow, 12 Ill. 2d 365, 146 N.E.2d 1 (1957). *But see* Department of Pub. Works v. Hubbard, 363 Ill. 99, 1 N.E.2d 383 (1936).

[179] Interview With Director of Chicago Public Housing Authority, in Chicago, Aug. 1958. On the role of the expert appraiser in the preparation of condemnation litigation for trial, see URA, TECH. MEM. No. 12 (1957). See also URA, ADVISORY BULLETIN NO. 6 (1958); Yates, *Testimony of the Expert Appraiser in Condemnation Proceedings,* 32 WASH. L. REV. 314 (1957).

[180] *E.g.,* ILL. REV. STAT. ch. 47, § 9 (1957).

[181] Interview With Director of Chicago Public Housing Authority, in Chicago, Aug. 1958.

[182] Interviews With Director of Metropolitan Housing and Planning Council of Chicago, in Chicago, July 1958. See Johnstone, *The Federal Urban Renewal Program,* 25 U. CHI. L. REV. 301, 344 (1958).

[183] Interview With Director of Cleveland Urban Renewal Agency, in Cleveland, Aug. 1958.

[184] 70 Stat. 1100 (1957), 42 U.S.C. § 1456(f)(2) (Supp. V, 1958); 24 C.F.R. §§ 3.100–.108 (Supp. 1958).

of necessary personnel and because of the resentment likely to be evoked by selective prosecution in a limited area.[185] Finally, if the violation consists of a failure to maintain and repair, forced compliance, although depressing the owner's profits, would increase the investment in the property and might have the effect of enhancing rather than diminishing the value of the property.[186]

If the only reason for the enforcement of municipal codes in renewal areas is to diminish the cost to the city of acquiring land, such enforcement might be open to attack as establishing an unreasonable classification in violation of the equal-protection clauses of the federal and state constitutions. It is arguable, however, that since codes may generally be enforced on an area basis,[187] the motive for selecting a particular area is not relevant. Furthermore, the selective enforcement of codes within the renewal area may reasonably be necessary to make the plan financially feasible.

2. LOSSES INCIDENT TO CONDEMNATION.—In contrast to inflation of prices by illegal use, owners and lessees may suffer certain losses which are not compensable.[188] The designation of an area or the announcement of a renewal plan usually causes an almost complete cessation of improvement and maintenance in the community, depreciating property values generally.[189] Because the area begins to lose residents, retailers who depend largely on neighborhood patronage and who usually are bound by long-term leases at fixed rentals, face a steady decline in revenues and profits.[190] If the tenant is able to vacate the premises, the landlord may suffer

[185] Interview With Director of Cleveland Urban Renewal Agency, in Cleveland, Aug. 1958.
[186] Interview With Official of ACTION in Cambridge, Mass., Oct. 1958.
[187] See p. 178 *infra*.
[188] See Cromwell, *Some Elements of Damage in Condemnation*, 43 Iowa L. Rev. 191 (1958); Hanify, *Elements of Damage in Eminent Domain—A New England View*, 34 B.U.L. Rev. 146, 148–54 (1954); Note, 27 U. Cinc. L. Rev. 119 (1958); Note, 43 Iowa L. Rev. 279 (1958); Comment, *Eminent Domain Valuations in an Age of Redevelopment: Incidental Losses*, 67 Yale L.J. 61 (1957).
[189] Interview With Director of Chicago Housing Authority, in Chicago, Aug. 1958. Such a collapse may be particularly undesirable in an area designated for conservation since accelerated deterioration of the area may render the program more costly and difficult. See URA, Advisory Bulletin No. 2 (1958). It has been suggested that in order to avoid many of the problems which follow the announcement of designation of the area, the agency ought to be given the right to take title to the land in advance of the final completion of the planning for the area. Interview With Attorney for Redeveloper in Washington, July 1958.
[190] Interview With Urban Renewal Consultant in Cambridge, Mass., Sept. 1958.

substantial loss, since it is likely to be impossible to lease the property to another. Because it is not uncommon for several years to elapse between the designation of an area and the acquisition of a particular piece of property, the loss to either landlord or tenant can be severe.[191] Moreover, dislocation caused by the ultimate taking may result in loss of goodwill[192] and substantial expenses of moving.[193] Compensation for such losses has traditionally been held unrecoverable either on the theory that they do not constitute "property" taken or that the measure of damages would be too speculative.[194] In one case, however, the court sustained a verdict based upon the value of the property to its owner, rather than upon its market value.[195] Since the value to the owner was greatly enhanced by prospective costs of moving heavy machinery utilized on the premises, recovery was three times the amount set by city appraisers.

In view of the increasing number of situations in which a public agency may take private property and of the very limited judicial scrutiny applied to such takings, the traditional measures of compensation paid and the policies underlying them require reappraisal.[196] To make renewal politically more palatable, compensation should be made for loss of profits, devaluation of property, and expenses of moving. Significantly, Congress has recognized certain of the hardships incident to traditional measures of compensation by providing relocation payments up to 100 dollars for individuals or families and up to 2500 dollars for businesses.[197] Many states have

[191] Interview With Assistant Executive Director of Boston Redevelopment Authority, in Boston, Aug. 1958. See Wilson v. City of Long Branch, 27 N.J. 360, 373–76, 142 A.2d 837, 844–46 (1958), *cert. denied*, 27 U.S.L. WEEK 3134 (U.S. Oct. 27, 1958).

[192] This is not necessarily true of wholesale and industrial concerns as contrasted with the small retailers who serve only local customers. Interview With Counsel to Redeveloper in Cleveland, Aug. 1958.

[193] See Calhoun, *Expenses of Moving in Eminent Domain Cases*, 30 DICTA 269 (1953).

[194] See Comment, 67 YALE L.J. 61, 74–81 (1957).

[195] City of Cleveland v. Arthur R. Mueller, No. 696928, Cuyahoga County, Ohio, C.P., May 24, 1957, *appeal dismissed*, No. 24492, Ct. App., April 19, 1958. See also Wolfson, New Pattern in Condemnation Compensation Set by Cleveland, Ohio Court Case (undated mimeograph).

[196] See Comment, 67 YALE L.J. 61, 89 (1957).

[197] 70 Stat. 1100 (1957), 42 U.S.C. § 1456(f) (Supp. V, 1958); 24 C.F.R. § 3.106 (Supp. 1958); see URA, ADVISORY BULLETIN No. 5 (1958). "At the end of 1957, there were 97 projects for which relocation grants [were] approved amount[ing] to more than $12,000,000 [and] . . . by the end of 1957, some

similar provisions.[198] An expansion of such legislation to permit compensation for other losses incident to a taking would be desirable, since the courts are not likely to adopt such a position in the foreseeable future. Moreover, despite the increasing availability of techniques for calculating such damages,[199] it would not be financially feasible for most private individuals and businesses to gather and present the elaborate proof necessary to make such a showing before a court. A statute might enable informal proof to be made before an administrator, who should have the power, pursuant to statutory standards, to limit the amount of recovery in cases in which damages would be highly speculative.

3. DELAY.—Postponement of a taking through protraction of condemnation proceedings may be advantageous to an owner or tenant. Business tenants in particular may require substantial time to find a suitable new location. Furthermore, they may seek to take advantage of an existing low rental as long as possible. Finally, delay may be an effective means of securing from the agency increased compensation and a commitment as to temporary relocation and ultimate opportunity to return to the redeveloped area.[200] Many of the incentives to delay might be eliminated by providing increased assistance and better facilities for relocation and a more liberal measure of compensation. Delay might further be discouraged by control of the burden of proof in condemnation suits in which the

---

42,998 families had been moved from project sites." Address by Commissioner Richard L. Steiner of the URA, International Seminar on Urban Renewal, The Hague, Aug. 1958.

[198] *E.g.*, CAL. HEALTH & SAFETY CODE § 33883. One city finds sixty dollars per family adequate for relocation. COMMUNITY REDEVELOPMENT AGENCY OF THE CITY OF LOS ANGELES, ANNUAL REDEVELOPMENT PLAN No. 1A, at 15 (1954). New York City, for example, offers a variety of relocation aids, including tenant information centers, cash bonuses for self-relocation, sponsor-paid expenses, cash payments to small businesses under state law, and special tenant-relocation committees. CITY OF NEW YORK, APPLICATION FOR RECERTIFICATION OF THE WORKABLE PROGRAM FOR URBAN RENEWAL OF THE CITY OF NEW YORK 1958–1959, at 36–38 (1958). However, area residents are often not properly informed of their rights in regard to relocation and many fail to secure maximum awards. Interview With Redevelopment Director of New Rochelle, N.Y., in New York City, Aug. 1958.

[199] See Kniskern, *Re-Use Land Utilization Studies and Advisory Consultation,* 25 APPRAISAL J. 325 (1957). See also Kratovil & Harrison, *Eminent Domain—Policy and Concept,* 42 CALIF. L. REV. 596, 611–20 (1954).

[200] Interview With Attorney in New Haven, Aug. 1958. In addition, the delay in the project and the uncertainties of title created by pending lawsuits tend to discourage the redeveloper. Interview With Redevelopment Project Sponsors in Boston, July 1958.

validity of official action is called in question. In some states, by the mere allegation of statutory or constitutional defects, a landowner may put the agency to the proof of each element ultimately necessary to support the taking. Public expense and delay could be mitigated if the agency were permitted to establish a prima facie case of validity by the introduction of the record of its own proceedings and those of the body granting approval to the plan.[201] The landowner would then be required to come forward with specific proof relating to particular objections in order to overcome the presumption of validity. Thus the city would be required to adduce detailed proof to sustain its burden of persuasion only on those issues to which meritorious objection had been raised, while no additional burden would be imposed upon the landowner with such an objection.[202]

A more direct approach to the problem of delay has been taken by those states which have enacted so-called "quick-take" statutes.[203] The agency acquires title to the property with little or no delay[204] after filing a proper petition and depositing in court an amount required by statute. The court may then proceed to determine the amount of compensation to which appropriate parties are entitled.[205] The amount deposited serves as security for ultimate payment and, in addition, may provide an available fund, to the

[201] Interview With Counsel to Chicago Land Clearance Commission, in Chicago, June 1958.

[202] Such a scheme is favored by many renewal officials. *Ibid.*

[203] See, *e.g.*, CONN. GEN. STAT. § 487d (Supp. 1955); N.J. REV. STAT. § 55:14 E–6 (Supp. 1950). See also RHYNE, MUNICIPAL LAW 407–08 (1957); Note, 27 NOTRE DAME LAW. 423 (1952); Dodge, *Land Acquisition for State Highways,* 1953 WIS. L. REV. 458, 460. Officials in states which have no quick-take provisions feel that this is a major cause of delay in projects. Interview With Executive Director of South East Chicago Commission, in Chicago, Aug. 1958.

[204] *E.g.*, N.J. STAT. ANN. § 20:1–12 (Supp. 1957). During the time period between the filing and the taking of possession, questions arise as to who is liable for taxes on the property, who has an insurable interest in it, and who can collect the rents upon it. Interview With Director of New Haven Redevelopment Agency, in New Haven, Aug. 1958.

[205] The court may have to determine the rights in the fund of owners of various limited interests in the land, notably long-term lessees and mortgagees, as well as their rights to ultimate compensation. See Kaplan, *Rights of Mortgagees in Condemnation Proceedings,* 12 BROOKLYN L. REV. 103 (1943); Stoyles, *Condemnation of Future Interests,* 43 IOWA L. REV. 241 (1958) (future interests); Note, 49 HARV. L. REV. 654 (1936) (dower); Note, 2 VILL. L. REV. 564 (1957) (covenant of quiet enjoyment).

extent of the uncontested portion of the award,[206] for use by affected parties in the interim. Such a statute brings into sharp conflict the public interest in speedy acquisition of land and the right of the individual to resist a taking which is not for a proper public purpose or not in accordance with statutory requirements.[207] In order to effectuate constitutional and statutory safeguards, the individual should be afforded an opportunity, subsequent to the filing of a petition by the agency, to contest the validity of the taking.[208] Although provisions for a speedy hearing on objections to the taking might be included in the eminent-domain statute itself, such objections are more likely to be raised in a plenary proceeding for declaratory judgment or injunction. Upon application for temporary relief, the court may exercise its discretion on the basis of the apparent merit of the claim and the relative hardship to the individual.

C. Relocation

1. STATUTORY REQUIREMENTS.—An element essential to the success of any renewal program involving demolition or strict code enforcement is the relocation of individuals and businesses displaced thereby.[209] Both state[210] and federal[211] statutes require adequate

---

[206] Agencies favor the payment of the part not in contest, since it saves the interest charge on that amount. Interview With Attorney in New York City, Aug. 1958; see Nashville Housing Authority v. Doyle, 197 Tenn. 555, 276 S.W.2d 722 (1955) (interest allowed from date of deposit with court).

[207] Interview With Attorney in New Haven, Aug. 1958.

[208] See Prunk v. Indianapolis Redevelopment Comm'n, 228 Ind. 579, 584–85, 93 N.E.2d 171, 173 (1950), *appeal dismissed*, 340 U.S. 950 (1951).

[209] "At present, the rate of relocation governs the rate of urban renewal. A continuing supply of subsidized low rent housing is essential for the rehousing of the low income group." Letter from Howard E. Green, President, Metropolitan Housing and Planning Council of Chicago to Hon. John A. Sparkman, May 7, 1958. See HHFA, OFFICE OF THE ADMINISTRATOR, DIVISION OF SLUM CLEARANCE AND URBAN REDEVELOPMENT, RELOCATION OF FAMILIES (1954). Other public-improvement projects also create the need for relocation facilities. See, *e.g.*, OFFICE OF CITY ADMINISTRATOR, CITY OF NEW YORK, TENANT RELOCATION AND THE HOUSING PROGRAM 4–6 (reprint 1954). See also Meltzer, *Relocation of Families Displaced in Urban Redevelopment: Experience in Chicago*, in URBAN REDEVELOPMENT: PROBLEMS AND PRACTICES 405–53 (Woodbury ed. 1953).

[210] See note 198 *supra*.

[211] 63 Stat. 417 (1949), as amended, 42 U.S.C. § 1455(c) (Supp. V, 1958); see Johnstone, *The Federal Urban Renewal Program*, 25 U. CHI. L. REV. 301, 337–41 (1958); HHFA, THE WORKABLE PROGRAM 4–5 (1957).

provision to be made for relocation. Some cities have attempted to place financial and administrative responsibility for relocation upon the redeveloper,[212] but this may prove to be unsatisfactory because such persons may not possess the requisite professional competence to deal with such a task.[213] Because of the numerous social and economic problems which must be solved in a relocation project, most cities have found that a separate agency must be created. A special agency may be established to handle the relocation incident to each renewal project,[214] or a permanent relocation agency may be established to find facilities for parties displaced by all projects of public improvement in the city.[215] Alternatively, some cities have employed a private firm to which all problems of relocation are referred.[216]

Failure of the plan to comply with applicable federal or state requirements regarding relocation may result in refusal of certification for federal aid or in an attack on the validity of the entire plan by those who will be displaced.[217] Furthermore, even though the plan on its face may comply with the applicable standards, if its administration proves inadequate or unworkable, federal certification may be withdrawn,[218] the Administrator of the HHFA may be able to enforce compliance with federal requirements,[219] or the action of the local administrative officials may be attacked as invalid.

2. FACILITIES FOR RELOCATION.—In the relocation of individuals and families displaced from a renewal area, it is crucial that the ultimate objectives of urban renewal be considered.[220] These per-

[212] See Mayor's Committee for Better Housing of the City of New York, Report of the Subcommittee on Urban Redevelopment, Including Slum Clearance, Neighborhood Conservation, and Rehabilitation 8, Aug. 1955.

[213] See, e.g., OFFICE OF CITY ADMINISTRATOR, CITY OF NEW YORK, TENANT RELOCATION AND THE HOUSING PROGRAM 11 (reprint 1954).

[214] Many agencies provide a relocation office on the site of each project to insure proper supervision. See, e.g., BOSTON REDEVELOPMENT AUTHORITY, FINAL RELOCATION REPORT, NEW YORK STREETS PROJECT (1958).

[215] See WASHINGTON HOUSING ASSOCIATION, REPORT ON RE-EXAMINATION OF THE NEED FOR A CENTRAL RELOCATION SERVICE (1958).

[216] See SLUM CLEARANCE AND REDEVELOPMENT AUTHORITY, VINE-DEER-CHATHAM PROJECT RELOCATION—A COMMUNITY EFFORT 1 (undated) (Portland, Me.).

[217] Such attacks are rarely successful. See pp. 140–41 supra.

[218] See Portland (Me.) Press Herald, Oct. 15, 1958, p. 1, col. 7.

[219] See 63 Stat. 418 (1949), 42 U.S.C. § 1456(c) (1) (1952).

[220] See DETROIT CITY PLANNING COMMISSION, PARKINS, NEIGHBORHOOD CONSERVATION 46 (1958).

sons must be relocated in such a way as to prevent the areas to which they move from becoming new slums. Their relocation must be supervised in order to act as an affirmative force in controlling the future development of the city.[221] Several means are employed to relocate those displaced. Such persons are generally given a priority in existing public housing.[222] The city may also erect new public-housing facilities off the site of the renewal project as part of the plan. Furthermore, the relocation agency may help parties to find vacancies in existing private facilities.[223] Finally, it may encourage private capital to construct new facilities to accommodate persons displaced from renewal areas.

Because the income level of a great number of those displaced from renewal areas is in excess of the maximum allowed to qualify for existing public-housing facilities, they are often precluded from obtaining such facilities. Although the city might take account of prevailing income levels in calculating the quality of new public housing to be constructed and the standards for admission thereto, it must as a practical matter keep such standards within the limits set by federal statutes granting aid to low-cost public housing.[224] Furthermore, it is often difficult to find a suitable location for new public housing. Although some cities have attempted to place such facilities on the renewal site or in already-existing sound areas so as

[221] The need for professional supervision is demonstrated by the fact that many who are self-relocated move to substandard housing. See CHICAGO PLAN COMMISSION, POPULATION AND HOUSING REPORT NO. 2, at 22 (1956). However, some administrative bodies urge self-help. See COMMUNITY REDEVELOPMENT AGENCY OF LOS ANGELES, BUNKER HILL URBAN RENEWAL PROJECT, RELOCATION PLAN 2 (1958). See also URA, TECH. MEM. NO. 10, at 6 (1957). It is claimed that forcing slum residents to find a new home may give some of them incentive to move to better housing. Interview With Director of Urban Renewal for the Department of City Planning in New York City, Aug. 1958. See also Banner, *Many People Will Move From Slums,* American City, June 1958, p. 111.

[222] HHFA, SLUM CLEARANCE AND REDEVELOPMENT PROGRAM, MANUAL OF POLICIES AND REQUIREMENTS FOR LOCAL PUBLIC AGENCIES pt. 2, ch. 6, § 4, at 2–3 (1955). In one city, out of 242 families relocated in one project, 48 were eligible for public housing and 23 were relocated there. HOUSING AUTHORITY OF LITTLE ROCK, FINAL RELOCATION REPORT, DUNBAR REDEVELOPMENT PROJECT (undated). In another project in the same city, out of a total of 60 families relocated, 47 were apparently eligible for public housing, but only 3 were relocated there. HOUSING AUTHORITY OF LITTLE ROCK, FINAL RELOCATION REPORT, PHILANDER SMITH PROJECT (1957).

[223] See NEW YORK COMMITTEE ON SLUM CLEARANCE, PENN STATION SOUTH 52 (1957).

[224] See 63 Stat. 422 (1949), 42 U.S.C. § 1415(8) (a) (1952).

to achieve "economic integration,"[225] such placement has been resisted by residents who fear that the presence of low-cost housing and low-income groups will depress property values in the neighborhood.[226] The courts, however, have upheld the taking of land to construct such housing against attacks that the taking was not for a public purpose within the meaning of the applicable constitutional provision and that it was an abuse of discretion conferred by the statute or the plan.[227] Absence of space within the city and the availability of relatively cheap land in the suburbs may make it desirable to construct new public-housing facilities outside the corporate limits of the city. Suburban areas, however, usually will not permit such housing to be constructed.[228]

Although many of those relocated secure privately owned facilities, the supply of private housing in the metropolitan area is often inadequate or its prices higher than those prevailing in blighted areas.[229] The federal government has sought to offer incentives to the construction of new privately owned facilities and the rehabilitation of existing facilities through mortgage insurance under section 221 of the Housing Act of 1954.[230] Private housing required by dislocation resulting from a certified renewal plan may qualify for this insurance, if requested by the community.[231] It has been suggested that the failure of section 221 to induce the construction

[225] See *Cleveland: City With a Deadline*, Architectural Forum, Aug. 1955, pp. 105, 135. See also Address by Ernest J. Bohn Before General Electric Meeting on "ACTION," Sept. 27, 1956, at 8; Mayor's Committee for Better Housing of the City of New York, Report of the Subcommittee on Urban Redevelopment, Including Slum Clearance, Neighborhood Conservation, and Rehabilitation 12–15, Aug. 1955.

[226] See, *e.g.*, Harper v. Trenton Housing Authority, 38 Tenn. App. 396, 274 S.W.2d 635 (1954).

[227] See St. Stephen's Club v. Youngstown Metropolitan Housing Authority, 160 Ohio St. 194, 115 N.E.2d 385 (1953); Harper v. Trenton Housing Authority, *supra* note 226.

[228] The state might remove this obstacle by conferring upon a municipality or local agency the power to acquire land outside its boundaries pursuant to an urban-renewal plan. See RHYNE, MUNICIPAL LAW 317–18 (1957); Note, 3 U.C.L.A.L. REV. 118 (1956).

[229] In one project, median site rental before demolition was $37 a month, while post-relocation median rental was $67. CHICAGO PLAN COMMISSION, POPULATION AND HOUSING REPORT NO. 2, at 18 (1956).

[230] 68 Stat. 599 (1954), as amended, 12 U.S.C. § 1715*l* (Supp. V, 1958). See HHFA, 221 Relocation Housing, 1957.

[231] 68 Stat. 599 (1954), as amended, 12 U.S.C. § 1715*l*(a) (Supp. V, 1958).

of an adequate supply of new private housing[232] is attributable to the low maximum amounts per unit set by the section,[233] which make it financially infeasible to construct adequate single-unit dwellings.[234]

Optimum relocation of those displaced from a renewal area is severely hampered by the restrictions imposed upon the movement of minority groups in most cities.[235] Members of these groups are likely to be present in substantial numbers in renewal areas.[236] Dispersion of a group throughout the city may be as unsatisfactory to the members of the group as to the residents in the neighborhoods in which they are relocated. Although the city might encourage minority groups to relocate themselves as a body,[237] it must be careful not to impose racial restrictions on their movement which might violate the equal-protection clauses of the federal and state constitutions or statutes prohibiting discrimination.[238] These problems of relocating minority groups have resulted in a further obstacle to the success of section 221. Resistance to the dispersion of minority groups throughout the city may either make it impossible to construct such housing or cause it to be placed in areas of the

[232] As of January 1958 there were 295 new homes built under § 221. See 15 J. HOUSING 123 (1958). Though Philadelphia actively looked for investors to build relocation housing under § 221, it was unable to elicit any interest in the program. See CITY OF PHILADELPHIA, WORKABLE PROGRAM FOR URBAN RENEWAL 1955, at 25 (1956).

[233] In order to meet this difficulty, the proposed 1958 Housing Act, S. 4035, 85th Cong., 2d Sess. § 111(a) (1958), would have increased the insurable limits, even at the risk of producing housing beyond the income range of displaced families. See S. REP. No. 1732, 85th Cong., 2d Sess. 9 (1958).

[234] Interview With Redevelopment Project Sponsor in Boston, July 1958; Interview With Counsel to Cleveland Development Foundation, in Cleveland, Aug. 1958. In addition, it is asserted that there is insufficient space in metropolitan areas for large numbers of single-family houses. Interview With Official, New York State Division of Housing, in New York City, Aug. 1958.

[235] Interview With Attorney in Baltimore, July 1958; see Wall Street Journal, April 7, 1958, p. 1, col. 1.

[236] See NEW YORK CITY PLANNING COMMISSION, URBAN RENEWAL 23–26; URBAN RENEWAL STUDY BOARD OF BALTIMORE, REPORT TO THE MAYOR 23 (1956).

[237] Many federal officials favor segregation in federally aided public housing. See MEYERSON & BANFIELD, POLITICS, PLANNING, AND THE PUBLIC INTEREST 20–21 (1955); N.Y. Times, Nov. 18, 1958, p. 63, cols. 1–4.

[238] See Detroit Housing Comm'n v. Lewis, 226 F.2d 180 (6th Cir. 1955); Kankakee County Housing Authority v. Spurlock, 3 Ill. 2d 277, 120 N.E.2d 561 (1954). See also HHFA, NONDISCRIMINATION CLAUSES IN REGARD TO PUBLIC HOUSING, PRIVATE HOUSING AND URBAN REDEVELOPMENT UNDERTAKINGS (rev. ed. 1957); 18 LAW. GUILD REV. 1–42 (1958); Business Week, July 19, 1958, p. 27.

city where land has remained vacant because it is economically undesirable, thus adding to the cost of the building and intensifying the problem of maximum-cost limitations under the section.[239]

Because of the obstacles to securing both public and private housing facilities off the redevelopment site, and because the new housing constructed on the redevelopment site generally must be designed for income groups higher than those displaced by the project,[240] many displaced individuals and families must accept substandard housing.[241] As a result, the complaint is made that redevelopment programs benefit one economic group at the expense of another.[242] Although the courts have refused to invalidate renewal programs on such grounds, [243] the existence of economic discrimination may impair public acceptance of such programs.[244]

IV. LAND DISPOSITION AND CONTROL OF RE-USE

A. *Inducements to Private Capital*

In order to dispose of large parcels of land cleared by renewal projects, the city must create a competitively attractive outlet for private investment dollars. The appeal of this type of investment is

[239] Interview With Counsel to Redeveloper in Cleveland, Aug. 1958.

[240] Interview With Director of Chicago Housing Authority, in Chicago, Aug. 1958; Interview With Counsel to Chicago Land Clearance Commission, in Chicago, Aug. 1958. See also *1958 S. Hearings* 296–97, 703.

[241] See, *e.g.*, 1956 HOUSING AUTHORITY OF LITTLE ROCK ANN. REP. 6, 10.

[242] Failure of the projects to provide adequate facilities for middle-income groups is the most common focus of such criticism. Interview With Eastern Representative of Council of State Governments in New York City, July 1958. See also Mitchell, *Middle-Income Housing: The New York Program*, 29 STATE GOV'T 127–30 (1956).

[243] See, *e.g.*, Foeller v. Housing Authority of Portland, 198 Ore. 205, 256 P.2d 752 (1953).

[244] Interview With Eastern Representative of Council of State Governments in New York City, July 1958.
In the relocation of businesses displaced from a renewal area, peculiar problems of preserving the going enterprise are presented. Although the problem is not acute with wholesale and industrial firms, the small business which caters primarily to residents in the area is of particular concern. Interview With Official of Cambridge Redevelopment Authority, in Boston, Aug. 1958; see *The Missing Link in City Redevelopment*, Architectural Forum, June 1956, pp. 132–33. The great harm caused to small businesses is a factor that might lead to repeal of redevelopment legislation. See *Editorial*, Architectural Forum, Sept. 1958, pp. 87, 89. Additional compensation paid to marginal retail operations, however, is open to the charge that it subsidizes what would otherwise be unprofitable operations.

limited by several factors. First, it is a relatively untried medium, and there are relatively few investors able to undertake the larger projects.[245] Furthermore, although construction costs tend to be uniform throughout the city, rent scales tend to be lower in the redeveloped area[246] because it is likely to be surrounded by blighted neighborhoods. Finally, investment appeal is limited by the extraordinary number of restrictions imposed by local, state, and federal laws. In small cities further limitations may be imposed by greater uncertainty of the demand for new housing, by reluctance of redevelopers to venture into new areas for a single project, by the strength of local opposition, and by the limited amount of knowledge about problems of renewing small towns.[247]

To overcome these limitations, cities have employed various means of making projects attractive to private investment. A redeveloper's return may be increased by a partial abatement of real-estate taxes or by assessing the value of the redeveloped property at a low figure.[248] Since redevelopment may increase the value of an area several fold,[249] a tax abatement or decrease in assessed valuation sufficient to increase the redeveloper's return by a significant

[245] See generally Remarks by Richard L. Steiner of the URA at the HHFA Region I Conference on Land Disposition and Redevelopment 5–6, New York City, Nov. 20, 1958.

[246] Interview With Redevelopment Project Sponsor in Cleveland, Aug. 1958. See also CHICAGO PLAN COMMISSION, PROGRAM OF REDEVELOPMENT 13 (1952).

[247] Letter from Community Planning and Urban Renewal Consultants in Newark to *Harvard Law Review*, Sept. 8, 1958. Under § 701 of the Housing Act of 1954, 68 Stat. 640, as amended, 40 U.S.C. § 461 (Supp. V, 1958), assistance is available to communities with populations under 25,000. See URA, A GUIDE TO URBAN PLANNING ASSISTANCE GRANTS (1955); Augur, *State Planning Assistance to Small Municipalities*, 28 STATE GOV'T 273–75 (1955). Small cities, however, may be able to plan more meaningfully for the entire community. Interview With Director of City Planning in New Haven, Aug. 1958. Further, they may be better able to offer assistance to a redeveloper. Interview With Redevelopment Project Sponsor in Cleveland, Aug. 1958.

[248] *E.g.*, Mo. REV. STAT. § 353.110 (1949). See DUGGAR & FORD, URBAN RENEWAL ADMINISTRATION 47 (1957). For example, if the annual rent derived from the redeveloped site is 10% of assessed value, abatement of the tax rate by .5% of that value will reduce expenses by 5% of the annual rental. Similarly, a reduction of 25% of the assessed value will effectively reduce a 2% tax rate by .5% and result in the same 5% of rental decrease in expenses. If the tax assessments are controlled by the county, there may be need for state approval for such abatement. *Compare* Opinion of the Justices, 334 Mass. 760, 135 N.E.2d 665 (1956), *with* Opinion of the Justices, 332 Mass. 769, 126 N.E.2d 795 (1955). See also Diehm v. City of New York, 208 Misc. 209, 143 N.Y.S.2d 298 (Sup. Ct. 1955).

[249] See NEW YORK CITY PLANNING COMMISSION, URBAN RENEWAL 92 (1958).

amount need not prevent a substantial increase in tax revenues.[250] Such assistance to redevelopers, however, may be forbidden by state constitutional or statutory provisions which prohibit public aid to private corporations[251] or the expenditure of public funds for other than public purposes.[252]

The provision by the city of certain community facilities within the renewal area may relieve the redeveloper of substantial costs and generally enhance the attractiveness of the area as an investment. By offering such inducements to redevelopers, however, officials are tempted to concentrate facilities in renewal areas, thus discriminating against the remainder of the city.[253]

It has been suggested that it would be impossible for a redeveloper to undertake a project without the increased availability of private capital brought about by section 220 Federal Housing Administration mortgage insurance.[254] Since real-estate investors desire recovery of their cash investment within a relatively short period of time,[255] it must be feasible to undertake the project with a very small amount of equity relative to debt capital.[256] Because rents in a redeveloped area tend to be lower than those of comparable buildings in other areas, the amount of equity relative to debt must be even lower than usual in order to provide a return satisfactory to the investor. Such a high ratio of debt to equity capital is generally far greater than that which most lending institutions are authorized to accept.[257] In order to make such a loan

---

[250] Moreover, taxes on property in the area are more likely to be paid promptly and service costs should decrease considerably. See ACTION, TIME FOR ACTION 7–8 (1955).

[251] E.g., ILL. CONST. separate § 2.

[252] See note 139 *supra*. See also Opinion of the Justices, 332 Mass. 769, 126 N.E.2d 795 (1955). However, informal agreements are often reached on methods of valuation. Interview With Redevelopment Project Sponsor in Boston, July 1958.

[253] Interview With Official of ACTION in Cambridge, Sept. 1958.

[254] See 68 Stat. 596 (1954), 12 U.S.C. § 1715k (Supp. V, 1958); Interview With a Redevelopment Project Sponsor in Cleveland, July 1958. See generally URA, Replacing Blight With Good Homes, Oct. 1955. See also 11 HHFA ANN. REP. 43–44 (1958).

[255] See *Hearings on Slum Clearance Before the Subcommittee on Housing of the House Committee on Banking and Currency*, 85th Cong., 2d Sess. 339 (1958).

[256] Interview With Counsel to Redeveloper in Cleveland, Aug. 1958.

[257] See, e.g., 38 Stat. 273 (1913), as amended, 12 U.S.C. § 371 (Supp. V, 1958). Banking laws in some states have been amended to permit 90% loans if they are federally insured. E.g., MASS. GEN. LAWS ANN. ch. 167, §§ 51, 51A (1958).

desirable as well as legally permissible, section 220 authorizes the FHA to insure loans secured by mortgages on property in certified renewal areas, up to ninety per cent of the estimated replacement cost[258] of the property and up to forty years maturity,[259] at a charge to the mortgagor of one-half per cent. Even with a ninety-per cent loan, however, many potential investors find that they cannot secure an adequate return on their investment.[260] Several devices may increase further the attractiveness of renewal projects. First, the FHA might reduce its charge from one-half to one-quarter per cent, in view of its profitable operations in the past.[261] Such a reduction would produce a considerable cost saving to redevelopers.[262] Because the profitability of mortgage insurance, however, depends heavily upon the business cycle, it is arguable that FHA rates must remain high enough to take account of possible future downturns.[263] Similarly, private insurers may be unwilling to assume risks dependent upon economic conditions.[264]

Second, in order to increase the effectiveness of FHA mortgage insurance in attracting private capital, the Federal National Mortgage Association is authorized to create a "secondary market" for such mortgages by purchasing them when investment funds are in

[258] The replacement cost includes a 10% allowance for "builder's and sponsor's profit and risk." See 68 Stat. 598 (1954), as amended, 12 U.S.C. § 1715k (d) (3) (B) (ii) (Supp. V, 1958). The amount of the allowance for the profit and risk of an investor-redeveloper, however, is calculated on a basis different from that of a builder-redeveloper. The proposed 1958 Housing Act, S. 4035, 85th Cong., 2d Sess. § 109(b) (1958), would have alleviated a difference between the amount of cash equity required to be invested by the two classes of sponsors. See S. REP. No. 1732, 85th Cong., 2d Sess. 6–8 (1958).

[259] A § 220 insured mortgage loan is made less attractive to lending institutions by the fact that upon default the bank receives 20-year debentures of the FHA rather than cash, under 48 Stat. 1249 (1934), as amended, 12 U.S.C. § 1710 (Supp. V, 1958). Interview With Assistant Director of New Haven Redevelopment Agency, in New Haven, Aug. 1958.

[260] Interview With Executive Director of Cleveland Development Foundation, in Cleveland, July 1958. Further, investors often complain about the delay entailed in procuring the insurance. See S. REP. No. 1732, 85th Cong., 2d Sess. 19 (1958). However, in one city in which there has been a great deal of activity under § 220, project sponsors attribute its success to the co-operative attitude of local FHA officials. Address by James H. Scheuer, International Seminar on Urban Renewal, The Hague, Aug. 1958.

[261] See 11 HHFA ANN. REP. 143 (1958).

[262] Cf. note 248 supra.

[263] Letter From Attorney in the HHFA, Office of the Administrator, to the Harvard Law Review, Dec. 5, 1958.

[264] Ibid. But see Interview With Counsel to Redeveloper in Cleveland, Aug. 1958.

short supply and by subsequently reselling them when such funds become available.[265] Of particular importance to urban renewal are the FNMA's "special assistance" activities,[266] which include the purchase of FHA-insured mortgages at interest rates below those prevailing generally. The anticipated effect of this activity, in conjunction with FHA mortgage insurance, is to enable investors to secure loans large enough in proportion to their equity at interest rates low enough to make the project feasible.

Third, private funds may be made available to help an investor raise the necessary equity in the project.[267] For example, the Cleveland Development Foundation, a private nonprofit corporation, will lend an investor seventy per cent of the equity required in conjunction with an FHA-insured mortgage, for a term of twenty years at four per cent interest payable only if earned.[268]

Finally, the FHA is authorized by section 213 to insure mortgages on co-operative apartments[269] subject to conditions similar to those imposed by sections 220 and 221. On the sale of each interest in the property, the redeveloper receives, in addition to periodic payments of the purchase price, a lump-sum down payment in the first year, which enables him to recover his investment more quickly.[270]

A project which does not produce a satisfactory cash return on the invested cash equity may nevertheless prove advantageous if the impact of its tax consequences on the taxpayer's business as a whole is considered. A project is desirable from an investment standpoint only if the annual "cash throw-off"[271] is such as to return the initial investment within a relatively short time.[272] To calculate the amount of cash throw-off before federal income tax, the amounts

[265] 67 Stat. 125 (1953), as amended, 12 U.S.C. § 1716 (Supp. V, 1958). For a discussion of FNMA activities, see generally 11 HHFA ANN. REP. 208–22 (1958). For a discussion of the nature of FNMA stock and its investment qualities, see Goodbody & Co., Research Study, Federal National Mortgage Association Corp., Feb. 26, 1958.

[266] See 24 C.F.R. §§ 400.21–.24 (Supp. 1958).

[267] See *Hearings on Slum Clearance Before the Subcommittee on Housing of the House Committee on Banking and Currency*, 85th Cong., 2d Sess. 34–41 (1958).

[268] For a discussion of the activities of this foundation, see Business Week, April 5, 1958, pp. 54–62.

[269] 64 Stat. 54 (1950), as amended, 12 U.S.C. § 1715e (Supp. V, 1958).

[270] Interview With Redevelopment Project Sponsor in Cleveland, July 1958.

[271] In real-estate terminology, "cash throw-off" is the return on invested capital after deduction of paid expenses and debt service from gross revenue.

[272] See *Hearings on Slum Clearance, supra* note 267.

needed to amortize the principal of the mortgage, rather than depreciation of the property, are deducted as current expenses. Although for tax purposes the amounts needed to amortize principal are not deductible, a deduction may be taken for the depreciation of the property.[273] For several reasons, the amount of depreciation so deducted may, in the early years, exceed the amount of principal amortized to calculate the cash throw-off. First, depreciation for tax purposes may be accelerated so as to exceed straight-line deductions in those years.[274] Second, even if straight-line depreciation is employed for tax purposes, the deductions taken may exceed amortization of principal because of the low ratio of principal to interest in the early years under a system of fixed-sum debt-service payments. Third, the useful life of the improvements for tax purposes may be less than the forty years needed for amortization of principal. Finally, the amount of the total investment upon which depreciation may be taken will exceed the amount of the total investment representing debt capital subject to amortization unless the amount represented by nondepreciable land exceeds the equity investment. Since a project which would produce little or no cash throw-off before federal income tax may thus produce a substantial loss for tax purposes in the early years, and since such loss may be deductible from other income of the taxpayer,[275] the tax savings produced thereby may make the project more desirable from an investment standpoint. Further, the property may be sold at a capital gain in a later year.

A further tax advantage may be gained by leasing rather than purchasing the land. While the owner of land may deduct neither depreciation nor the amount needed to amortize the principal of the mortgage on that land, a lessee may deduct the full amount of the rent.[276] Provided the annual rental exceeds what the lessee would have paid as owner for the sum of real-estate taxes attributable to the land and interest on the portion of the mortgage attributable to the land, the lessee will enjoy a greater tax deduction than if he owned the land. If the annual rental does not exceed the sum of the

[273] See INT. REV. CODE OF 1954 § 167(a).
[274] See INT. REV. CODE OF 1954 § 167(b). See also Miller, *The Rise in Apartments*, Architectural Forum, Sept. 1958, pp. 106–07.
[275] *But see* INT. REV. CODE OF 1954 § 269; Elko Realty Co. v. Commissioner, 29 T.C. No. 106 (Feb. 28, 1958).
[276] INT. REV. CODE OF 1954 § 162(a) (3).

debt service and real-estate taxes attributable to the land by so much as to offset the tax saving, the lessee will enjoy a greater cash throw-off on the entire project with less total investment. Although he may ultimately pay a greater sum for the use of land to which he never acquires title and will be less able to sell at a capital gain, preference for the lease method is based upon a willingness to forego possible future benefit in order to secure increased present income.[277]

B. *Selection of a Redeveloper*

In choosing the proper time at which to begin negotiations with prospective purchasers or lessees of the land, the agency must weigh several competing considerations. On the one hand, informal contact with an investor prior to actual disposition of the land may open the disposition to the attack that formal procedures required by statute in order to assure honest competition were shams.[278] Furthermore, it may be undesirable from a planning standpoint to permit the interests of a redeveloper, which might be adverse to those of the city, to influence the formulation of the plan. On the other hand, it may be risky for the agency to acquire land before being sure that there will be a market for it.[279] In addition, many officials feel that potential purchasers should be kept in mind when

[277] Interview With Counsel to Redeveloper in Cleveland, Aug. 1958.

[278] In Bleecker Luncheonette, Inc. v. Wagner, 141 N.Y.S.2d 293 (Sup. Ct.), *aff'd*, 286 App. Div. 828, 143 N.Y.S.2d 628 (1955), and 64th St. Residences, Inc. v. City of New York, 4 N.Y.2d 268, 150 N.E.2d 396, 174 N.Y.S.2d 1 (1958), the courts rejected the contentions that the statutorily required bidding procedure was a sham. In both cases, the ultimate purchasers, who were universities, had been in contact with the city during the formulation of the plan, and the parcel ultimately offered was suited only to their needs. Furthermore, participation of the redeveloper may also open the plan to the objection that the taking is for a private use.

[279] Interview With Redevelopment Director of New Rochelle in New York City, Aug. 1958; Interview With Redevelopment Official in St. Louis, Aug. 1958. For example, Portland, Me., acquired land under such circumstances, and has been unable for a considerable period to dispose of it. See Slum Clearance and Redevelopment Authority of Portland, Me., Vine-Deer-Chatham Sales Prospectus for 6 Acres of Land for Redevelopment in Portland, Me.; Interviews With Director of Slum Clearance and Redevelopment Authority, in Portland, Me., July & Aug. 1958. See also Mayor's Committee for Better Housing of the City of New York, Report of the Subcommittee on Problems of Relocation of Persons Displaced by New Housing and Other Public Improvements 4, June 1955:

It should be recognized that, at the beginning of a new program of this character, there is always considerable skepticism as to its efficacy. Sponsors willing and able to carry out projects did not storm the gates of the Committee on Slum Clearance, the Committee had to seek out potential

the planning is done, so as to render the parcel as marketable as possible.[280]

Although the federal statute does not require any particular method of disposition,[281] federal administrators, who are anxious that the city obtain as high a price as possible, prefer competitive bidding.[282] In the absence of a state statute requiring competitive bidding, local administrators are likely to differ as to the relative merits of particular techniques of disposition. To the extent that such officials are concerned with obtaining the highest possible price and with protecting themselves against charges of improper influence, competitive bidding is likely to be preferred. Many officials, however, feel that the inability to consider factors other than price and the financial responsibility of the bidder is highly undesirable.[283] As a result, some agencies have solicited bids based on the lowest rent to be charged and the space and facilities provided.[284] In other cities, the agency provides the plan and fixes the price, and awards the project to the sponsor bidding the lowest rent.[285] In Puerto Rico, an initial selection is made on the basis of price alone, but any unsuccessful bidder may subsequently raise his price offer to that of the successful bidder and then negotiate on the basis of facilities.[286]

---

sponsors and persuade them as to the feasibility of carrying out the initial projects.

But cf. URA, TECH. MEM. No. 14 (1958); URA, ADVISORY BULLETIN No. 7 (1958).

[280] Interview With City Planning and Urban Renewal Consultant in Cambridge, Sept. 1958.

[281] HHFA, Local Public Agency Letter No. 84, Land Disposition Methods and Policies 2, Dec. 21, 1956.

[282] Interview With Counsel to Redeveloper in Cleveland, Aug. 1958. The agency may divide the project among several redevelopers. CLEVELAND URBAN RENEWAL AGENCY, PRIVATE DEVELOPMENTS IN CLEVELAND URBAN RENEWAL AREAS (1957).

[283] Interview With Director of Cleveland Urban Renewal Agency, in Cleveland, July 1958. Even if the bid is formally on the basis of price alone, the agency can often restrict the terms and draw the specifications so as to limit the field to two or three bidders. Requiring from the bidder a deposit of from 30% to 40% of the expected price of the land further helps to limit the field.

[284] Although the agency may ask for bids of both the lowest projected rent and the most facilities, in an attempt to avoid difficult decisions, it may consider only the lowest rental bid. Interview With Redevelopment Project Sponsor in Cleveland, July 1958.

[285] Interview With Director of Cleveland Urban Renewal Agency, in Cleveland, July 1958.

[286] See Bid Form, Redevelopment Project in Puerto Rico, p. 3, para. 7.

If, subsequent to the formation of a contract for the disposition of the land, the FHA refuses to insure a mortgage on it, the redeveloper will generally be rendered financially incapable of undertaking the project. Some agencies have permitted the redeveloper's obligation to be conditioned upon the procurement of FHA insurance, but others have refused to agree to such a "walk-away" provision.[287] Although the redeveloper should be required to exercise reasonable diligence in obtaining the insurance, it would seem unwise to require him to undertake an economically burdensome project or to forfeit his deposit.

C. *Control of Re-use*

Not only the practical success of a project but also its ability to withstand legal attack may depend upon effective control over the use of the land subsequent to disposition. The most common method of control is the sale of the fee and the imposition of covenants running with the land which require it to be used in accordance with the area plan[288] and with the contract between the redeveloper and the agency.[289] To assure the effectiveness of the covenants, the agency, by the terms of the contract, may require all the documents to be recorded.[290]

The imposition of numerous and often vague restrictions on the use of the land, whether enforcible by injunction, by right of re-entry for condition broken, or by a possibility of reverter, may impede the procurement of a mortgage loan or of title insurance.[291] There has been as yet relatively little opportunity for enforcement problems to arise. Nevertheless, since such remedies are so drastic, it seems that the threat of enforcement will be sufficient to deter violations. Because of the complexities and uncertainties involved in

[287] Interview With Redevelopment Project Sponsor in Cleveland, Aug. 1958.
[288] See Slum Clearance and Redevelopment Authority of Portland, Me., Vine-Deer-Chatham Redevelopment Disposition Documents 15, March 27, 1958. In Los Angeles, the restrictions are to last for thirty years. COMMUNITY REDEVELOPMENT AGENCY OF LOS ANGELES, REDEVELOPMENT PLAN, BUNKER HILL URBAN RENEWAL PROJECT 23 (1958).
[289] See generally Ascher, *Private Covenants in Urban Redevelopment,* in URBAN REDEVELOPMENT: PROBLEMS AND PRACTICES 223–309 (Woodbury ed. 1953).
[290] See, *e.g.,* REDEVELOPMENT AGENCY OF SAN FRANCISCO, THE REDEVELOPMENT PLAN FOR THE WESTERN ADDITION APPROVED REDEVELOPMENT PROJECT AREA A–1, at 6 (1956). This practice creates difficulties when the plan is to be amended. Interview With Official of Title Insurance Company, in Cleveland, July 1958.
[291] *Ibid.*

the use of covenants, the leasing of land may increase in popularity.[292] However, the difficulty of obtaining a mortgage upon a leasehold and the desire of the agency to liquidate its investment in the land are likely to restrict the use of the leasing technique.

V. CONTROL OF EXISTING AREAS

It has become apparent that redevelopment or total clearance, although it has been effective in particular cases, cannot by itself arrest the decay of urban communities. The expense of totally clearing an area is too great for significant inroads to be made on urban deterioration through continued emphasis on the redevelopment technique.[293] Furthermore, because of the limited size of areas amenable to the total-clearance technique and the length of time required to carry out a redevelopment plan, other neighborhoods may deteriorate into slums while existing slums are being cleared.[294]

A program emphasizing conservation, on the other hand, can encompass areas of much greater size at far less public cost, because relatively little clearance is undertaken and because it is expected that a great deal of the impetus, financial and otherwise, should come from private parties, particularly from people located in the conservation area itself.[295] Since such a program stresses the preservation of existing neighborhoods, the problems of social and economic disruption incident to total-clearance plans are minimized. Problems of relocation are greatly reduced[296] and desirable social patterns can be retained.[297] Furthermore, conservation areas tend

[292] In one project in New Haven, a long-term lease has been used. Interview With Director of Department of City Planning in New Haven, Aug. 1958. The lease will have to contain restrictions similar to those used in the disposition of the fee. See City & County of San Francisco v. Ross, 44 Cal. 2d 52, 279 P.2d 529 (1955).

[293] Interview With Official of ACTION in New York, July 1958. It has been estimated that 85.5 billion dollars would be needed to redevelop the existing residential slums and blighted areas in the country. DEWHURST & ASSOCIATES, AMERICA'S NEEDS AND RESOURCES 511–12 (1955). See generally Office of the Development Co-ordinator, A New Approach to Urban Renewal for Philadelphia, March 1957.

[294] See id. at 1–2; Interview With City Planner in St. Louis, Aug. 1958.

[295] See pp. 172–76 infra.

[296] See URA TECH. MEM. No. 2, at 4 (1956). This is true only if rents do not substantially increase because of rehabilitation.

[297] Interview With Executive Director of Cambridge Redevelopment Authority, in Cambridge, July 1958.

to be strategically located for renewal purposes. Typically, total-clearance areas are surrounded by other bad neighborhoods, which exert an adverse influence on the redeveloped area.[298] Neighborhoods designated for conservation, on the other hand, usually lie adjacent to sound areas, which serve to anchor the renewed neighborhood.[299] Thus if a city is renewed from the outside in, the conservation areas may in turn serve to anchor the areas which need to be totally cleared.[300] For these reasons, the hopes of planners are turning increasingly to conservation of existing areas.[301] Although such programs raise many of the same problems as the redevelopment technique, they raise in addition certain problems which are unique and as yet relatively unexplored.

A. *Encouraging Participation*

It is generally acknowledged that the success of a conservation program depends largely on the co-operation and assistance of the area's owners and residents.[302] A greater degree of co-operation can be expected from an owner who resides in the area than from those absentee owners who regard the property simply as a wasting asset to be exploited for maximum revenues with minimum outlay for maintenance.[303] In either case, however, it is essential to carry out a concerted program, first, of encouraging owners of property in the area to rehabilitate it in conformity with standards set for the area, and second, of offering financial assistance to those who might

[298] See Office of the Development Co-ordinator, A New Approach to Urban Renewal for Philadelphia 1, 4, March 1957.

[299] Interview With Director of Cleveland Metropolitan Housing Authority, in Cleveland, July 1958; Office of the Development Co-ordinator, A New Approach to Urban Renewal for Philadelphia 4, March 1957.

[300] See URA Tech. Mem. No. 7, at 1 (1957).

[301] See Office of the Development Co-ordinator, A New Approach to Urban Renewal for Philadelphia, March 1957. Interview With City Planner in St. Louis, Aug. 1958.

[302] *E.g.*, New York City Planning Commission, Urban Renewal 5 (1958); National Association of Housing and Redevelopment Officials, Rehabilitation and Conservation, A Symposium, Washington, D.C. 9–10, Aug. 8–9, 1955; Interview With Counsel to Chicago Land Clearance Commission, in Chicago, July 1958.

[303] Interview With City Planner in New Haven, Aug. 1958. One city, however, interested landlords in rehabilitation by arranging for the rent-control board to allow increases in accordance with the improvements the landlord made. Moreover, owners found that tenants would pay as much as $3.50 to $5.00 a week more for improved dwellings. URA Tech. Mem. No. 8, at 2, 4 (1957). Of course if rent is raised too much, it may have the undesirable result of forcing present tenants out of the area.

otherwise be willing to rehabilitate but are financially unable to do so.

There are several means of enlisting the support of area owners and residents. One enabling act provides for the creation of community conservation councils, a majority of the council being legal or equitable owners of property in the area, which must approve a proposed plan of conservation before it may be carried out.[304] In some cities the establishment of neighborhood groups, having no official status, has been encouraged by the agency to act as a liaison between the agency and the area to be affected. These groups are designed to promote a co-operative attitude among area residents through education and persuasion and to help to assure that their wishes will be reflected in the final plan.[305] The agency itself commonly undertakes to inform area residents of the need for the plan, what it is intended to accomplish, and what their role will be.[306] In addition, groups formed on private initiative are often quite active in shaping community attitudes.

Programs of education and persuasion need to be supplemented by establishing visible evidence of physical improvement to act as an impetus to voluntary private rehabilitation.[307] The building of community facilities, such as parks, schools, and utilities, is aided by the Community Facilities Administration of the HHFA which offers loans, advances, and technical aid to cities to help provide such facilities.[308] Furthermore, the city can revise street patterns to

[304] Illinois Urban Community Conservation Act, ILL. REV. STAT. ch. 67½, § 91.12 (1957).

[305] St. Louis has promoted the establishment of neighborhood groups to insure co-operation and will not undertake a plan in an area without first getting some positive indication of community interest. Interview With City Planner in St. Louis, Aug. 1958. New Haven has established a city-wide group for similar purposes. Interview With Executive Director of Citizens Action Commission in New Haven, Aug. 1958. See also *Citizens Role in Planning for Urban Renewal Related*, 14 J. HOUSING 382–85 (1957).

[306] Cincinnati and Dayton have sent a trailer throughout the city. See 14 J. HOUSING 202–03 (1957). St. Louis has made use of educational television. Interview With City Planner in St. Louis, Aug. 1958. See generally NEW YORK PLANNING COMMISSION, URBAN RENEWAL 88–89 (1958); TENNESSEE STATE PLANNING COMMISSION, CITIZEN PARTICIPATION IN URBAN RENEWAL (1957).

[307] Interviews With Attorney in Newark, Aug. 1958, and City Planner in New Haven, Aug. 1958. See generally Baltimore Urban Renewal and Housing Agency, Report to Mayor Thomas D'Alesandro, Jr. on the Long-Term, Overall Effects on the Urban Renewal Program of School Sites To Serve the Harlem Park Neighborhood, Feb. 7, 1958.

[308] See HHFA, Programs of Community Facilities Administration, March 1958; 11 HHFA ANN. REP. 224–34 (1958).

reduce congestion and through traffic, and can provide additional off-street parking space.[309]

Owners may also be persuaded to contract with the city or with each other to carry on rehabilitation.[310] The greater the number willing to participate the greater is the public pressure exerted on nonparticipants. The contractual device is particularly valuable when major rehabilitation is to be undertaken.[311] Since such projects require the hiring of several types of craftsmen by a contractor, it may be uneconomical to rehabilitate only one structure at a time.[312] Moreover, an effective rehabilitation program contemplates that the increase in the property's value will be greater than the cost of the repairs undertaken.[313] Although rehabilitation of a particular structure is likely to increase its value to some extent, rehabilitation by a substantial number of owners will improve the neighborhood's appearance and thus enhance property values generally.[314]

A particularly troublesome problem is posed by the individual who is willing but financially unable to co-operate. It is usually desirable to avoid the application of coercive sanctions in such cases, both in order to preserve a co-operative neighborhood attitude and to prevent harshness to the individual. At least one city has established a fund for loans to such individuals at little or no interest.[315] It would be desirable to encourage the establishment of similar funds

[309] The major deficiencies in a Detroit conservation area were found to be the lack of parking facilities, heavy through traffic, and insufficient play area. URA TECH. MEM. No. 16, at 4 (1958). Since the taking of land for the creation of parking facilities has been upheld as being itself for a public purpose, e.g., Poole v. Kankakee, 406 Ill. 521, 94 N.E.2d 416 (1950); McSorley v. Fitzgerald, 359 Pa. 264, 59 A.2d 142 (1948), there should be little doubt of the public purpose when land is taken for such facilities as part of a conservation plan. It may be necessary, however, for the city to operate the facilities itself, or to exercise substantial control over private operators to whom the property is conveyed. See City & County of San Francisco v. Ross, 44 Cal. 2d 52, 279 P.2d 529 (1955).

[310] Interview With Assistant Executive Director of National Association of Housing and Redevelopment Officials in Washington, July 1958.

[311] See generally Zisook, *Rehabilitation—When Is It Economically Feasible in Renewal*, 15 J. HOUSING 157 (1958).

[312] Interview With Counsel to Redeveloper in Cleveland, July 1958.

[313] Interview With Counsel to Cleveland Development Foundation, in Cleveland, Aug. 1958.

[314] National Association of Housing and Redevelopment Officials, Rehabilitation and Conservation, A Symposium, Washington, D.C. 12, 18–19, Aug. 8–9, 1955.

[315] City of Toronto Act, By-Law No. 14466 (1936).

by local banks, merchants, and residents,[316] who stand to benefit from a rehabilitated neighborhood. Some municipalities in states where tax abatement is permitted have offered a tax credit related to increase in value of the property, or have frozen the assessment of the property for a number of years at its value before improvement.[317] The long-run advantages to the city from a successful conservation program[318] are generally expected to outweigh its immediate loss in revenue.[319] Finally, the Federal Housing Act of 1954 makes section 220 mortgage insurance available for rehabilitation of property in conservation areas.[320] This provision may make mortgage money available in areas where previously it was extremely difficult if not impossible to acquire such loans.[321] Although not all buildings in the area will be eligible for section 220 insurance, the FHA criteria for insurability stress potential value after accomplishment of the renewal plan rather than condition of the structures.[322] The usefulness of section 220 insurance in such

[316] See Urban Renewal Council, Legal Committee on Housing Code Enforcement in the District of Columbia, Report 5 (undated mimeograph); p. 166 *supra;* cf. Chicago Daily Tribune, Sept. 23, 1958, p. 1, col. 8; HHFA, APPROACHES TO URBAN RENEWAL IN SEVERAL CITIES, URBAN RENEWAL BULLETIN No. 1, at 30 (1954).

[317] *E.g.,* N.Y. TAX LAW § 5-h; see BOWERY SAVINGS BANK, SLUM CLEARANCE AND URBAN REDEVELOPMENT IN THE CITY OF NEW YORK 25 (1956); Guandolo, *Housing Codes in Urban Renewal,* 25 GEO. WASH. L. REV. 1, 47–48 (1956). Moreover, many types of repairs do not in any event increase tax assessments. See, *e.g.,* Detroit City Plan Commission, Neighborhood Conservation Information Bulletin, Taxes.

[318] Advantages contemplated are increased tax revenue, reduction of expenditures on services, and greater attractiveness of the city both to individuals and businesses. See LOS ANGELES DEPARTMENT OF BUILDING AND SAFETY, CONSERVATION 145–46 (1958).

[319] For an indication of anticipated increases in tax revenue, see NEW YORK CITY PLANNING COMMISSION, URBAN RENEWAL 92 (1958); Chicago Daily Tribune, Sept. 29, 1958, pt. 2, p. 2, cols. 3–5; *cf.* Mayor's Committee for Better Housing of the City of New York, Subcommittee on Middle-Income Housing With Proper Use of Tax Concessions and State or City Credit, Report 5, June 1955.

[320] 68 Stat. 596 (1954), 12 U.S.C. § 1715k (Supp. V, 1958).

[321] See New York State Division of Housing, The Housing and Neighborhood Renewal Tool Chest 26, Sept. 1957. Many feel that without widespread use of § 220 insurance, conservation programs will not be feasible. See NEW YORK CITY PLANNING COMMISSION, URBAN RENEWAL 5 (1958); Interview With City Planner in New Haven, Aug. 1958; Letter From Community Planning and Urban Renewal Consultants in Newark to *Harvard Law Review,* Sept. 8, 1958.

[322] See National Association of Housing and Redevelopment Officials, Rehabilitation and Conservation, A Symposium, Washington, D.C. 17, Aug. 8–9, 1955.

areas may depend to a large extent on making it relatively simple for the average owner to present an application.[323]

B. Coercive Techniques

1. ZONING.—Although zoning has been used primarily to prevent future deterioration of existing or newly developed neighborhoods, it may be of some effect in improving the character of conservation areas.[324] Though the courts have struck down retroactive application of zoning laws,[325] they have increasingly accepted the principle of gradual elimination, or amortization, of nonconforming uses, provided the amortization is over a reasonable period of time.[326] Such a period may be as great as twenty years or even longer depending on the use, but amortization within one year has been upheld.[327] The length of time generally needed to amortize, however, makes such a method of limited effectiveness. In addition, it may be politically impracticable.[328]

Some of the more noxious features of nonconforming uses may be eliminated by means of an ordinance which classifies uses not by the

[323] For a criticism of the red tape involved in acquiring § 220 insurance, see *1958 S. Hearings* 503.

[324] Since zoning ordinances, however, must take into account existing uses, they cannot substantially change the character of the neighborhood. Interview With Legal Specialist in Zoning, in Chicago, July 1958.

[325] *E.g.*, Jones v. City of Los Angeles, 211 Cal. 304, 295 Pac. 14 (1930); Des Jardin v. Greenfield, 262 Wis. 43, 53 N.W.2d 784 (1952). However, courts usually follow a strict policy against the extension or enlargement of nonconforming uses. See San Diego County v. McClurken, 37 Cal. 2d 683, 234 P.2d 972 (1951); State v. Cain, 40 Wash. 2d 216, 242 P.2d 505 (1952). Moreover, a community may agree to an enlargement of a nonconforming use for a limited period in exchange for a promise to terminate the use after this period. See Edmonds v. Los Angeles County, 40 Cal. 2d 642, 255 P.2d 772 (1953). See generally Comment, 1951 WIS. L. REV. 685. Whether a zoning statute will be given retroactive application depends at least in part on the value of the interest which is to be eliminated. See People v. Miller, 304 N.Y. 105, 106 N.E.2d 34 (1952). See also Harbison v. City of Buffalo, 4 N.Y.2d 553, 152 N.E.2d 42, 176 N.Y.S.2d 598 (1958).

[326] *E.g.*, Spurgeon v. Board of Comm'rs, 181 Kan. 1008, 317 P.2d 798 (1957) (court approved amortization after expressing disapproval of amortization in an earlier case). See Norton, *Elimination of Incompatible Uses and Structures,* 20 LAW & CONTEMP. PROB. 305, 308 (1955).

[327] State *ex rel.* Dema Realty Co. v. Jacoby, 168 La. 751, 123 So. 314 (1929); State *ex rel.* Dema Realty Co. v. McDonald, 168 La. 172, 121 So. 613 (1929). See also Spurgeon v. Board of Comm'rs, 181 Kan. 1008, 317 P.2d 798 (1957) (amortization within two years). *But see* Akron v. Chapman, 160 Ohio St. 382, 116 N.E.2d 697 (1953) (amortization within "a reasonable period" invalidated).

[328] Interview With Director of New Haven Redevelopment Agency, in New Haven, Aug. 1958.

type of activity carried on, but by the impact of that activity on the surrounding area, in regard to matters such as emission of smoke, noise, and odors.[329] The retroactive application of such an ordinance may be justified first, by a greater public interest in elimination of such features than in the elimination of nonconforming uses generally, and second, by the fact that the owner may not be required to discontinue the use entirely but only to remedy the objectionable manner in which it is carried on. If it is essential, however, that the use itself be discontinued, the agency may be able to take by eminent domain that portion of the value of the property attributable to the prohibited use, and to make compensation accordingly.[330]

2. HOUSING CODES.—(a) *Substantive Standards.* Although housing codes should ideally require maintenance of high standards of health and safety,[331] an enforcible code must set standards low enough so that it is generally feasible for owners of property even in the worst areas of the city to comply.[332] The existence of a housing code setting at least such minimal standards for the city is one of the seven elements of the federal workable program.[333] Some cities with standards lower than this minimum have thus been forced to raise them to qualify for federal aid.[334]

In order to maintain and upgrade the condition of a conservation

---

[329] See Northwestern Laundry v. City of Des Moines, 239 U.S. 486 (1916); People v. Consolidated Edison Co., 116 N.Y.S.2d 555 (Munic. Ct. 1952); cf. Reinman v. City of Little Rock, 237 U.S. 171 (1915).

[330] See State *ex rel.* Twin City Bldg. & Investment Co. v. Houghton, 144 Minn. 1, 176 N.W. 159 (1920); Slayton, *Conservation of Existing Housing*, 20 LAW & CONTEMP. PROB. 436, 448–49 (1955); cf. Linggi v. Garovotti, 45 Cal. 2d 20, 286 P.2d 15 (1955) (condemnation of an easement); Attorney General v. Williams, 174 Mass. 476, 55 N.E. 77 (1899) (regulating height of buildings and paying compensation therefor).

[331] For a list of model codes, see URA, ADVISORY BULLETIN No. 1, CODES AND ORDINANCES 10–11 (1958). See generally URA, BULLETIN No. 3, PROVISIONS OF HOUSING CODES (1956).

[332] See Note, 69 HARV. L. REV. 1115, 1117 (1956).

[333] See HHFA, THE WORKABLE PROGRAM 4 (1957). See also HHFA, LOCAL DEVELOPMENT AND ENFORCEMENT OF HOUSING CODES (1953); Urban Renewal Council, Legal Committee on Housing Code Enforcement in the District of Columbia, Report 1 (undated mimeograph); Letter From Frank P. Zeidler, Mayor of Milwaukee, reprinted in American City, June 1958, p. 185; Slayton, *Conservation of Existing Housing*, 20 LAW & CONTEMP. PROB. 436, 437–38 (1955).

[334] See American City, Dec. 1955, p. 161. The threat of the loss of federal aid also exerts effective pressure to enforce the codes. Interview With Director of New Haven Redevelopment Agency, in New Haven, Aug. 1958.

area, however, it may be necessary to set standards at a level higher
than that which it would be feasible to enforce in the worst
areas.[335] To accomplish this end, it has been suggested that the city
enact a "zoned housing code," which establishes different standards
for different areas.[336] Such classifications, however, may be held to
be a deprivation of equal protection under federal and state constitutions.[337] If an over-all plan of urban renewal is justified as a
device to accomplish at least traditional police-power objectives
through the elimination and prevention of slums, it would seem that
the accomplishment of such objectives requires the maintenance of
all areas in the city at least at such a level that the danger of their
becoming slums is remote.[338] It is generally not possible, however,
to achieve this result through the uniform application of a single
method to all areas of the city. On the one hand, the enforcement of
a housing code is not appropriate in areas already slums, because it is
not feasible to secure compliance with the high standards needed to
achieve the desired level,[339] and because even if enforcement were
possible, some objectionable features of structures in such areas can
often be eliminated only by demolition.[340] On the other hand,
enforcement of higher code standards in deteriorating areas not yet
slums is more likely to be feasible and to remove the causes and
symptoms of deterioration.[341] The application of higher standards
to the conservation area can thus be regarded as a step toward the
ultimate objective of a higher level for the city generally, the

[335] See Guandolo, *Housing Codes in Urban Renewal*, 25 GEO. WASH. L. REV.
1, 36, 37, 45 (1956); National Association of Housing and Redevelopment
Officials, Rehabilitation and Conservation, A Symposium, Washington, D.C.
12–13, Aug. 8–9, 1955.

[336] New Haven has adopted standards of maintenance for commercial and
industrial property applicable only to a particular conservation area. See
WOOSTER SQUARE REDEVELOPMENT AND RENEWAL PLAN, CITY OF NEW HAVEN
15–18 (rev. ed. 1958).

[337] See Brennan v. City of Milwaukee, 265 Wis. 52, 60 N.W.2d 704 (1953).

[338] Some planners, however, conceive of renewal as designed primarily as
a means of achieving economic improvement. Interview With Executive Director, South East Chicago Commission, in Chicago, Aug. 1958; see Sullivan,
*Administrative Procedure and the Advocatory Process in Urban Redevelop-
ment*, 45 CALIF. L. REV. 134, 138 (1957).

[339] See NEW YORK STATE DIVISION OF HOUSING, HOUSING LAW ENFORCEMENT
AND RELATED PROBLEMS 31 (1957).

[340] See METROPOLITAN HOUSING AND PLANNING COUNCIL OF CHICAGO, CON-
SERVATION 98 (1953).

[341] See NEW YORK STATE DIVISION OF HOUSING, HOUSING LAW ENFORCEMENT
AND RELATED PROBLEMS 35–36 (1957).

achievement of which requires the use of different methods in different areas.[342]

(b) *Inspections*. The enforcement of housing codes as well as the establishment of substantive standards has presented considerable difficulty.[343] Since cities have insufficient manpower to inspect all buildings at regular intervals,[344] their inspection staffs are generally restricted to occasional intensive coverage of small areas or to inspection after complaint. Enforcement only upon complaint is too haphazard a method to achieve significant results unless there is a concerted effort by residents to discover and report violations.[345] Although area enforcement has achieved more satisfactory results,[346] the total area which can be covered is relatively small. Furthermore, it is often difficult to determine in which area such enforcement will be most worthwhile.[347] Since the need for renewal short of total clearance is by hypothesis greatest in neighborhoods designated for conservation, area enforcement is likely to be most profitable in such neighborhoods.[348]

[342] See Wilson v. City of Long Branch, 27 N.J. 360, 377, 142 A.2d 837, 846 (1958), *cert. denied*, 27 U.S.L. WEEK 3134 (Oct. 27, 1958). See also Guandolo, *Housing Codes in Urban Renewal*, 25 GEO. WASH. L. REV. 1, 43–45 (1956); NEW YORK STATE DIVISION OF HOUSING, HOUSING LAW ENFORCEMENT AND RELATED PROBLEMS 30–32 (1957). The courts have not been troubled by the fact that housing codes are applied retroactively. See, *e.g.*, Health Dep't v. Rector of Trinity Church, 145 N.Y. 32, 39, 39 N.E. 833, 835 (1895); Richards v. City of Columbia, 227 S.C. 538, 88 S.E.2d 683 (1955). While enforcement of a zoned housing code in high-standard areas might result in greater expense to property owners than enforcement of present housing codes, the deprivation would undoubtedly be far less than that which would result from retroactive application of most zoning ordinances. Moreover, since housing codes appear to be more closely related to health and safety than zoning ordinances, retroactive application is more easily justified. See Queenside Hills Realty Co. v. Saxl, 328 U.S. 80 (1946) (court upheld regulation requiring fireproofing even though expense would be 30% of the building's value).

[343] See Guandolo, *Housing Codes in Urban Renewal*, 25 GEO. WASH. L. REV. 1, 12 (1956).

[344] See Note, 69 HARV. L. REV. 1115, 1123 (1956).

[345] It is expected that one phase of citizen participation in a conservation program will be reporting code violations and calling for code enforcement when needed. Interview With Attorney in Newark, Aug. 1958; see Office of the Development Co-ordinator (Philadelphia), Notes on Government's Role in a Conservation Area Program 5, Nov. 1956.

[346] See Note, 69 HARV. L. REV. 1115, 1125 (1956); Interview With Director of Urban Renewal Board in New York City, Aug. 1958.

[347] See NEW YORK STATE DIVISION OF HOUSING, HOUSING LAW ENFORCEMENT AND RELATED PROBLEMS 34, 36 (1957); *cf.* SIEGEL & BROOKS, SLUM PREVENTION THROUGH CONSERVATION AND REHABILITATION 1 (1953).

[348] See NEW YORK STATE DIVISION OF HOUSING, *op. cit. supra* note 347, at 35–36.

Effective code enforcement is hampered by a system which depends upon numerous inspections, each for a narrowly defined group of violations.[349] Some cities have evolved a system of inspection by teams composed of inspectors from appropriate departments[350] and, in at least one city, a member of the corporation counsel's office.[351] Such a team is less likely to be subject to improper influences than a single inspector.[352] Furthermore, the presence of a lawyer tends to assure that adequate evidence will be gathered to support a prosecution, and affords the prosecuting attorney a greater familiarity with the case.[353] Finally, the simultaneous presentation to the court of evidence of all violations charged in respect to a given building increases the likelihood of securing from it sympathetic enforcement and the imposition of effective penalties.[354] Although the team method may result in wasted time, since some members may be required to remain idle while others complete the inspection, officials in the largest cities favor it.[355] The wasted-time objection might be overcome by training a single man to make all types of inspections[356] and by assigning a member of the legal staff to work with him.

The authorization by municipal housing codes of entry upon property for inspection without a warrant may be open to question under the fourteenth amendment and state constitutional guarantees[357] against unreasonable search and seizure. Under such provisions, an individual may be deemed to have as great an interest in freedom from search by state officials for all purposes as in freedom from search for the purpose of securing evidence of criminal

[349] See Guandolo, *Housing Codes in Urban Renewal*, 25 GEO. WASH. L. REV. 1, 12–13 (1956).
[350] 1 NEW YORK STATE DIVISION OF HOUSING, HOUSING CODES 53 (1958); see, *e.g.*, SIEGEL & BROOKS, *op. cit. supra* note 347, at 110.
[351] Interview With an Assistant Corporation Counsel in Chicago, Aug. 1958.
[352] *Ibid.*
[353] These two problems have been major stumbling blocks to code enforcement. See NEW YORK STATE DIVISION OF HOUSING, HOUSING LAW ENFORCEMENT AND RELATED PROBLEMS 72 (1957). Assigning the same lawyers to these teams could result in the development of a body of corporation counsel expert in code enforcement.
[354] Interview With an Assistant Corporation Counsel in Chicago, Aug. 1958.
[355] Interview With Director of Cleveland Urban Renewal Agency, in Cleveland, Aug. 1958; Interview With an Assistant Corporation Counsel in Chicago, Aug. 1958.
[356] See 14 J. HOUSING 200–01 (1957).
[357] *E.g.*, OHIO CONST. art. 1, § 14.

guilt.[358] Since search of a dwelling without a warrant for the purpose of establishing guilt is unreasonable in the absence of an emergency,[359] it would be equally unreasonable to conduct an inspection of a dwelling without a warrant, especially since the state's interest in the apprehension of criminals is at least as great as in the enforcement of housing codes. It seems, however, that courts should uphold housing-code inspections without warrants on the ground that the applicable constitutional provision was intended to require a warrant—except in cases of overriding emergency—only when the search is conducted for the purpose of securing evidence of criminal guilt, and that although criminal convictions may ultimately result from inspections, the correction of conditions constituting a continuing violation of the code rather than the discovery of past guilt is the primary purpose of such inspections.[360] Moreover, to the extent that the requirement of a warrant is designed to prevent intrusion upon private property without probable cause to suspect guilt, there is less need for a warrant in cases involving housing-code inspections, the justification for which may be unrelated to suspicion of guilt.[361] It has also been argued that although the interest in privacy may be the same regardless of the purpose of a particular search, the need to conduct routine housing inspections, in regard to which probable cause for the issuance of a warrant could not ordinarily be established, outweighs the interest in privacy.[362] Under either theory, a search for inspection purposes should be deemed unreasonable only if conducted in an oppressive way.[363] Moreover, in most instances, individuals do not assert any right they may have to bar inspectors who have no warrant.[364] Tenants may welcome inspection as a step toward improving living conditions, and the absentee owner may lack standing to object to an intrusion upon the leased premises.[365]

[358] See District of Columbia v. Little, 178 F.2d 13 (D.C. Cir. 1949), aff'd, 339 U.S. 1 (1950) (constitutional question not considered in Supreme Court).
[359] See McDonald v. United States, 335 U.S. 451 (1948).
[360] See Givner v. State, 210 Md. 484, 124 A.2d 764 (1956); State ex rel. Eaton v. Price, 105 Ohio App. 376, aff'd, 168 Ohio St. 123, 151 N.E.2d 523 (1958).
[361] See District of Columbia v. Little, 178 F.2d 13, 23–24 (D.C. Cir. 1949) (dissenting opinion), aff'd, 339 U.S. 1 (1950) (constitutional question not considered in Supreme Court).
[362] E.g., Givner v. State, 210 Md. 484, 124 A.2d 764 (1956).
[363] See id. at 489, 124 A.2d at 774 (dictum).
[364] See NEW YORK STATE DIVISION OF HOUSING, HOUSING LAW ENFORCEMENT AND RELATED PROBLEMS 65 (1957).
[365] See United States v. Muscarelle, 63 F.2d 806 (2d Cir.), cert. denied, 290 U.S. 642 (1933).

(c) *Sanctions.* A more serious obstacle to effective code enforcement has been the lenient attitude frequently exhibited toward offenders by the courts, often because of unfamiliarity with the seriousness of the problem and the need for stringent enforcement.[366] The attitude may also be due to the reluctance of elected judges to deal harshly with their constituents as to offenses they may regard as involving relatively little moral culpability.[367] This suggests the desirability of establishing a court to handle only housing-code violations or of creating a special docket so that the same judges will try all such matters.[368] The development of a body of judges expert in code enforcement might tend to decrease judicial sympathy toward offenders.[369] It is arguable, however, that such a forum might come to act as an administrator concerned with effecting the objectives of the program rather than as an impartial tribunal.[370]

It is generally felt that more effective sanctions are needed to make code enforcement successful.[371] Although ordinances generally provide for jail sentences, as well as fines, in cases of repeated violation or disobedience of repair orders,[372] even the more flagrant violators usually receive at most a fine, which is often cheaper than making repairs and may be treated by landlords simply as a cost of doing business.[373] In addition to taking by eminent domain prop-

[366] See SIEGEL & BROOKS, *op. cit. supra* note 347, at 1; Interview With Eastern Representative of Council of State Governments in New York City, July 1958; *cf.* Note, 69 HARV. L. REV. 1115, 1126 (1956).

[367] Interview With Professor, Harvard Graduate School of Design, in Cambridge, Mass., Oct. 1958; Interview With Staff Member of New York State Division of Housing, in New York City, Aug. 1958; see SIEGEL & BROOKS, *op. cit. supra* note 347, at 1.

[368] See NEW YORK STATE DIVISION OF HOUSING, HOUSING LAW ENFORCEMENT AND RELATED PROBLEMS 72 (1957); Note, 69 HARV. L. REV. 1115, 1126 (1956); 3 NEW YORK STATE DIVISION OF HOUSING, HOUSING CODES 32 (1958).

[369] See 1 NEW YORK STATE DIVISION OF HOUSING, HOUSING CODES 57 (1958).

[370] Interview With Official of ACTION in Cambridge, Mass., Oct. 1958. It has been suggested that the use of administrative hearings might be an effective way of dealing with housing-code violations. See NEW YORK STATE DIVISION OF HOUSING, CODE ENFORCEMENT IN 53 NEW YORK COMMUNITIES 21 (1957). However, most cities appear reluctant to utilize such a system. NEW YORK STATE DIVISION OF HOUSING, HOUSING LAW ENFORCEMENT AND RELATED PROBLEMS 72 (1957).

[371] Interview With Housing Official in New York City, Aug. 1958; Interview With Chairman of Housing Subcommittee of American Bar Association in Washington, July 1958.

[372] *E.g.,* N.Y. MULT. DWELL. LAW § 304.

[373] See METROPOLITAN HOUSING AND PLANNING COUNCIL OF CHICAGO, CONSERVATION 58 (1953); N.Y. Times, Nov. 28, 1955, p. 33, cols. 3–4.

erty which is not maintained in accordance with standards set for the area,[374] a device relied upon heavily in most conservation plans,[375] civil sanctions offer a number of potentially effective possibilities. Even in the absence of a statutory provision permitting the granting of an injunction against violation, it is arguable that a court should be able to issue a mandatory injunction compelling the owner to repair, provided the city can demonstrate that the imposition of criminal penalties would be ineffective to deter continued violations.[376] In Chicago, under a state statute permitting a court to grant "an injunction . . . or . . . such other order as the Court may deem necessary,"[377] the city has secured the appointment of receivers to make necessary repairs and collect rent until their cost is recovered.[378] The threat of this remedy has frequently obviated the necessity of its employment.[379]

The city may act under a statute authorizing it to make repairs and place a lien on the property, subordinate to all existing liens, for the cost thereof.[380] However, this often results in the city bearing the cost of the repairs because the owner cannot be located or is judgment proof and the property is so heavily mortgaged that there is insufficient value left for the city to recover.[381] To be effective, such liens must have priority over pre-existing mortgages. Although the priority of a municipal repair lien is of no concern to an owner, against whom the imposition of such liens has been upheld,[382] a more serious problem is presented as to their validity against existing

[374] See p. 150 *supra*.

[375] See, *e.g.*, WOOSTER SQUARE REDEVELOPMENT AND RENEWAL PLAN, CITY OF NEW HAVEN 2, 12 (rev. ed. 1958).

[376] *Cf*. Galanty & Alper v. City of Maysville, 176 Ky. 523, 196 S.W. 169 (1917).

[377] ILL. REV. STAT. ch. 24, § 23–70.3 (1957).

[378] Interview With an Assistant Corporation Counsel in Chicago, Aug. 1958. There is indication that the power to appoint a receiver in cases of flagrant violation also exists in Los Angeles, Jackson, Miss., New Haven, and Syracuse, N.Y. Gazzolo, *Municipal Housing Codes*, 38 PUBLIC MANAGEMENT 105, 107 (1956); see Gray, Problems of Urban Redevelopment in a Declining Neighborhood 14–15, April 1, 1956 (unpublished thesis in Harvard Law School Library).

[379] Interview With an Assistant Corporation Counsel in Chicago, Aug. 1958.

[380] *E.g.*, ILL. REV. STAT. ch. 67½, § 91.14 (1957). A California statute permits a lessee to make repairs costing up to one month's rent and to deduct such cost from the rent. CAL. CIV. CODE § 1942.

[381] Interview With an Assistant Corporation Counsel in Chicago, Aug. 1958.

[382] *E.g.*, Adamec v. Post, 273 N.Y. 250, 7 N.E.2d 120 (1937); *cf*. City of Nashville v. Weakley, 170 Tenn. 278, 95 S.W.2d 37 (1936).

lienors. A statute authorizing a prior lien would seem more likely to be constitutional when applied so as to subordinate mortgages which, although attaching prior to the repair lien, were created subsequent to the enactment of the statute, since it can be presumed that the mortgage is entered into with knowledge that a subsequent repair lien, like a tax lien, may take precedence.[383] A New York statute granting to municipal repair liens priority over mortgages created before enactment of the statute was held to be unconstitutional in *Central Sav. Bank v. City of New York*.[384] The court stressed the fact that while the owner had the option to repair or vacate the building, the mortgagee had no such option by which he could protect his interests.[385] Possibly the court was also influenced by the fact that the mortgagee was a bank subject to a law which required that all its mortgage loans be secured by first liens.[386] In a later case,[387] a lower New York court upheld a lien for the cost of demolishing a building which had been found to be "unsafe,"[388] giving it priority over a mortgage entered into before the passage of the statute authorizing the imposition of the lien. Although the danger to the community of such a building may be more immediate than that of most buildings to which repair liens are applied, the fact that the existence of any code violations tends to promote the creation of slums indicates that the city may have as strong an interest in the elimination of such violations as in the demolition of structures presenting a more immediate threat. Even if the need for elimination of code violations generally is not as compelling, the imposition of a repair lien may be justified, since repair, unlike demolition, preserves and possibly increases the value of the mortgagee's interest. Moreover, since the imposition of prior liens has been upheld in analogous situations,[389] it would seem equally justifiable to sustain the use of such a lien to recover the cost of

[383] See, *e.g.*, Provident Institution for Sav. v. Mayor of Jersey City, 113 U.S. 506 (1885); *cf.* Home Bldg & Loan Ass'n v. Blaisdell, 290 U.S. 398, 435 (1934).
[384] 279 N.Y. 266, 18 N.E.2d 151 (1938), *cert. denied*, 306 U.S. 661 (1939).
[385] *Id.* at 277, 18 N.E.2d at 155.
[386] This case has been much criticized. See Note, 69 HARV. L. REV. 1115, 1124 (1956); 52 HARV. L. REV. 684 (1939); 33 ILL. L. REV. 726 (1939).
[387] Thornton v. Chase, 175 Misc. 748, 23 N.Y.S.2d 735 (Sup. Ct. 1940).
[388] *Id.* at 748, 23 N.Y.S.2d at 736.
[389] State courts have upheld such liens in drainage and street-repair cases. See, *e.g.*, Baldwin v. Moroney, 173 Ind. 574, 91 N.E. 3 (1910); Farmers' State Bank v. McReynolds, 1 S.W.2d 322 (Tex. Civ. App. 1927).

repairs, at least if mortgagees are given adequate opportunity to avert its imposition so as to protect their interests.[390]

Private groups are often quite active in bringing about compliance with housing codes. Neighborhood groups may be mobilized to report code violations.[391] Adverse newspaper publicity has been effective in bringing about the correction of certain undesirable conditions.[392] A private organization in one city has exerted pressure on slum landlords in various ways. It retains its own building inspector to investigate complaints from tenants and to assure that the violations are properly prosecuted. It maintains a file on each property owner in the area, the condition of his property, and the violations for which he has been prosecuted. When confronted with this information, lending agencies tend to refuse loans to the property owners involved and insurance companies often cancel fire insurance thereby defaulting any mortgages secured by the property.[393]

3. NUISANCE.—The power at common law[394] to abate a public nuisance provides another sanction which is potentially useful in a conservation program. In order to demolish a building as a nuisance, as opposed to merely causing it to be vacated, the courts have generally required a showing that the structure creates an immediate danger to the surrounding neighborhood and that it cannot feasibly be repaired.[395] The New York Model Housing Code would go farther by allowing demolition in the following cases: first, if a building is determined to be unfit for human habitation and the cost necessary to correct the violation is not reasonably related to the value of the building; second, if an order of the housing authority has not been complied with and if such a failure is deemed by the

[390] Giving the mortgagee notice of the proposed imposition of a prior lien may have the advantage of causing him to make the repairs. In one city, this has in fact occurred. Interview With Executive Director of South East Chicago Commission, in Chicago, Aug. 1958. The mortgage may give the mortgagee the right to make such repairs and add their cost to the debt.

[391] See note 345 *supra.*

[392] See METROPOLITAN HOUSING AND PLANNING COUNCIL OF CHICAGO, THE ROAD BACK (1954) (reprinted from the *Chicago Daily News*).

[393] Interview With Executive Director of South East Chicago Commission, in Chicago, Aug. 1958. See generally Dunham, *Private Enforcement of City Planning*, 20 LAW & CONTEMP. PROB. 463 (1955).

[394] *E.g.*, York v. Hargadine, 142 Minn. 219, 171 N.W. 773 (1919).

[395] *E.g.*, Crossman v. City of Galveston, 112 Tex. 303, 247 S.W. 810 (1923).

enforcement official to constitute a nuisance.[396] Demolition in the first situation might be justified on common-law nuisance principles, since a building which has been vacated, especially in a densely populated area, may constitute an immediate danger to the public.[397] Even if such a building would not be a nuisance at common law, it is arguable that the legislature may properly determine that such buildings contribute so directly to the deterioration of the community as to outweigh what is in most cases a relatively small loss to the owner caused by the demolition of an uninhabited structure which cannot be repaired.[398] Demolition in the second situation, however, seems indefensible, since if the structure can be repaired, its demolition without compensation is an unreasonably drastic means of securing compliance with a housing code.

VI. CONCLUSION

Perhaps the most impressive characteristics of the concept of urban renewal are its comparatively recent origin, its rapid and continued growth, and the variety of legal problems it has already posed or is likely to create in the near future. As such, it presents a challenge to the lawyer in recommending and drafting legislation; in advising public agencies in the interpretation of legislative and constitutional mandates; and in protecting private interests when they come into conflict with the objectives of public action.

An effective program of urban renewal must be based on long-range objectives and should bring to bear all available techniques, including city planning, public housing, total clearance, and conservation of existing areas. Such a program should be accompanied by a close co-ordination of all renewal activities and agencies under the direction of a strong executive authority. The implications of such a program for the planner and for the lawyer are numerous and far-reaching.

First, it is possible that renewal will become oriented more about metropolitan areas than cities or neighborhoods. As this occurs,

---

[396] See Minimum Housing Standards Ordinance §§ 320.7–.9, in 2 NEW YORK STATE DIVISION OF HOUSING, HOUSING CODES 46, 47 (1958).

[397] Interview With Director of New Haven Redevelopment Agency, in New Haven, Aug. 1958; Interview With Executive Director of Cambridge Redevelopment Authority, in Cambridge, Mass., July 1958; see Note, 69 HARV. L. REV. 1115, 1124 (1956).

[398] Cf. State v. Tower, 185 Mo. 79, 84 S.W. 10 (1904).

increased action by the states will be required, not only to provide the statutory authorization necessary to execute renewal programs and to relocate those displaced by the programs, but also to shoulder an increased share of the financial burden incident to expanded renewal activity. Although local renewal programs will undoubtedly continue to be heavily dependent upon a continuing supply of federal financial aid, it may be desirable to encourage more active participation by the states and to reappraise the need for federal controls which limit the discretion of local officials.

Second, renewal programs are likely to carry official action farther from traditional concepts of public use in the taking of land. Increasing emphasis has been laid on making urban areas economically attractive as well as assuring an adequate residential environment. Although there are indications that at least some courts, covertly if not avowedly, are willing to accept such objectives, it would seem wise to temper any such extension of public use with insistence upon a strong showing of relation between the particular taking and the over-all objectives of a plan and upon the use of the least harsh method necessary to accomplish the public objectives. To the extent that such objectives are closely related to the optimum re-use of the land as well as to eliminating existing slums, increased emphasis should be placed upon the utilization of methods of land disposition which make it possible to consider all the qualifications of a potential redeveloper and upon the imposition of meaningful obligations incident to re-use.

Third, so long as land acquisition forms a significant part of renewal, public agencies will need to find means of overcoming the delays incident to such acquisitions and to confront the problem of relocating those displaced. Since delay in a program increases the hardship to area owners and residents, tends to discourage redevelopers of the land, and results in adverse publicity, the agencies should both attempt to remove the incentives to delay and to utilize the more summary procedures for condemnation, provided that adequate opportunity for raising objections has been afforded. There is a need for more wisely supervised relocation not only of individuals but also of businesses and for increased compensation for losses incidental to business relocation. Furthermore, provision should be made for more housing for the so-called middle-income groups.

Fourth, as interest shifts from total clearance to the control of existing areas by a variety of conservation techniques, public agencies will undoubtedly be faced with the most severe test of their ability to secure public acceptance and support of renewal programs. Although programs of conservation are in strong need of new legal sanctions, their primary dependence is necessarily upon voluntary compliance, which appears to be encouraged most by the offering of economic incentives and assistance. At the same time, however, the effectiveness of housing codes must be considerably strengthened. Questions are likely to arise regarding the extent to which code standards can be raised or varied from one area of the city to another without running afoul of due-process and equal-protection limitations. Sanctions available for the enforcement of codes, short of taking by eminent domain, must be improved, and maximum use made of criminal penalties, injunctive relief, repair liens, demolition in extreme cases, and the co-ordination of enforcement activities with private groups.

Fifth, considerable effort needs to be made toward better protecting the interests of individuals while expediting public action. The effectiveness of judicial review is likely to remain severely limited as renewal plans become more complex, include wider areas, and involve greater investments of time and money. Therefore, hearings should provide meaningful opportunity for individuals to participate in and voice informal objections to renewal planning at an early stage when change is still practicable. Correspondingly, however, greater procedural formality might be demanded at the major decision-making stages in the formulation and execution of a plan, so as to lay a basis for more effective judicial review. Statutory procedures for securing such review should be provided so as to permit the consideration of as many issues as possible at a relatively early stage and to foreclose their consideration thereafter.

6 The Operation and Achievements of the Urban Renewal Program *

WILLIAM L. SLAYTON

I. THE BACKGROUND FOR URBAN RENEWAL

Urban Growth and Change

We are all familiar with the extraordinary rapidity of urban growth in all sections of our country, but I believe that it bears emphasis. This vast urban growth is being impelled by our continually increasing population, as well as by the basic shift in the distribution of our population toward urban and metropolitan centers. The urban population added since 1950 about equals the entire population of the Nation in 1870. The increase in our population from 151 million in 1950 to about 190 million in 1963 occurred almost entirely in our metropolitan and urban areas. During this same period, large numbers of our rural counties lost population, and our farm population declined.

Past urban growth will be dwarfed by that just ahead. During the next 20 years an increase of one-half to two-thirds in the population of our urban areas is expected. This increase will occur almost entirely on the fringe of our metropolitan areas, where the present

* Mr. Slayton is Commissioner of the Urban Renewal Administration in the U.S. Housing and Home Finance Agency. This article is an edited version of testimony he gave in November 1963 before the Subcommittee on Housing of the House Banking and Currency Committee in Washington, D.C. Some revisions have been made to reflect more current data and experience.

suburban population of 38 million will increase by another 65 to 80 million people.

The growing and shifting population, and the expanding urban development have created significant changes in the urban structure. This growth and change can create immense opportunities and benefits for all Americans. But it is important to understand its effects and costs, and to take intelligent measures to cope with the problems it creates.

A different character of change—and resulting problems—can be seen in each of the three major rings of a typical metropolitan area. In the center city, despite overall population losses, there is an increasing concentration of the poor and disadvantaged in deteriorating areas, unable to find shelter adequate for their needs elsewhere because of economic, racial, or other barriers. Also, the central business district, suffering from the loss or decline of certain of its functions, the presence of blighted structures and inadequate transportation facilities, is faced with being rebuilt or losing its vitality.

In the middle ring of the urban area, between the core and suburbia, large areas of aging housing are served by obsolete community facilities. Here, too, much of the industrial plant is outmoded and unable to compete with new plants on outlying suburban sites. This middle ring needs renewal, but renewal aimed primarily at conservation and rehabilitation rather than outright clearance.

In the outer ring, the suburban periphery, the growth pains of the metropolitan area are felt. The remarkable progress over the past decade in construction of new housing in the suburbs has too often been accompanied by a lack of planning for adequate community facilities and open space and a lack of sensible relationship to the central city.

This pattern of growth, changing and shifting functions, and decay is most dramatic in the large metropolitan areas. But smaller urban areas also are affected, either by similar patterns on a smaller scale, or by somewhat reverse situations—declining populations and economic activities that are accelerating the process of decay.

Problems of Eliminating Blight

The older, more intense problem of the city's deteriorating residential neighborhoods was the first to arouse the concern of the

Federal Government. This concern during the 1930's led to the program of federally assisted public housing. During World War II it led to a congressional study of housing problems and the related problems of slums and blighted areas. This study was carried out by a subcommittee, under Senator Robert A. Taft, of the Senate Special Committee on Post-War Economic Policy and Planning. After the war, further studies and investigations were made by both the Senate and House Committees on Banking and Currency.

As a result of these systematic investigations, the nature of the key problems and the necessary solutions became quite clearly understood. I would like to summarize these findings which, I believe, are still valid today.

In large measure, the growth and persistence of blight has its roots in the inability of private enterprise to rebuild without aid the deteriorating parts of the city's structure to meet changing needs and functions of urban areas. There are two basic obstacles. First, the entrepreneur faces the problem of assembling a number of parcels, under diverse ownerships, in order to create a tract large enough to support efficient, modern development and at the same time withstand the effects of adjacent blight. One or two "holdouts" can and sometimes do block his plans.

The second obstacle is the tremendously high cost. The acquisition costs to a private developer would often reflect inflated, speculative values. They would also include the costs of existing structures which, though deteriorating and obsolete, do have an economic value that becomes a significant item of cost when they are demolished to make way for new buildings.

History of Title I

Remedies for these two basic obstacles to the private redevelopment of slums became two of the principal concepts in title I of the Housing Act of 1949. Under the procedure established by title I, a community acquires and assembles properties in a blighted area, using its power of eminent domain where necessary. The procedure also requires the local and Federal governments to pay the net cost of urban renewal, which is the difference between the cost of acquiring and clearing slum properties and the income received when the land is sold or leased for public and private redevelopment. This difference, sometimes erroneously called a writedown, is not a subsidy to the private redeveloper, who must pay the fair value for the cleared land, but is a cost of achieving a public purpose—the elimination of slums.

In effect, by enacting title I, Congress clearly indicated that the clearance and redevelopment of blighted areas was a national objective, that private enterprise could not do it alone, that public power to assemble land was necessary, and that the public costs should be shared by Federal and local governments. In providing for a Federal sharing in the costs, the Congress recognized two hard facts. First, our cities were financially strapped—as they continue to be—by the squeeze between rising municipal expenditures and limited taxable resources. Secondly, and I think equally important, the Congress acknowledged that urban blight was a national problem and that the afflicted cities should not be expected to solve it alone. The human, social, and economic costs of slums spread far beyond municipal boundaries.

In enacting title I, the Congress recognized that slum clearance and redevelopment must involve more than assembling blighted parcels, demolishing the structures, and disposing of the land. It rightly insisted that it is a public responsibility to rehouse displaced families in decent, safe, and sanitary dwellings within their financial means. It also recognized that the eligible cost of a redevelopment project should include the costs of site improvements and supporting facilities provided by the locality—the public improvements necessary to create a stable neighborhood and support private reconstruction. Finally, it required the locality to prepare a plan for the area that would guide its redevelopment and be consistent with the general plan for the community as a whole.

I cite these additional elements of title I, not only because they are important in themselves, but because they necessarily increase the public cost of undertaking urban renewal.

The basic purposes and concepts embodied in title I of the 1949 act have not lost their validity. But a succession of amendments over the years has broadened the methods and objectives of the urban renewal program, for the most part reflecting both experience with the program and a better understanding of the needs of rapidly changing urban areas.

A number of the amendments in the Housing Act of 1954 were

aimed at the needs of the middle ring of an urban area, the vast "gray areas" of aging housing and inadequate urban facilities.The program concept was broadened from "slum clearance" to "urban renewal." Slum clearance and redevelopment was complemented by providing for rehabilitation and conservation of deteriorating areas not yet requiring demolition. This change recognized the need to conserve existing housing, and the impossible cost of eliminating all substandard conditions by acquisition and clearance alone.

The 1954 act provided new forms of FHA assistance for the rehabilitation and redevelopment of slums. A new program of FHA mortgage insurance (sec. 220) was authorized for use in rehabilitating existing dwellings and constructing new dwellings in urban renewal areas. A section 221 program was created to assist in the construction of low-cost housing for displaced families.

A 1954 amendment to title I provided for Federal demonstration grants to test and report on new or improved urban renewal techniques, particularly those related to the new rehabilitation approach. A new concept, the workable program for community improvement, was established, requiring that urban renewal, public housing, and urban renewal-oriented FHA mortgage insurance programs would be available only to those communities making satisfactory progress in developing their own communitywide programs of action to prevent as well as eliminate blight.

The Housing Act of 1954 also made the first of several exceptions to the strong housing orientation of title I as enacted in 1949. The original title I required that a slum clearance and redevelopment project be predominantly residential in character either before or after redevelopment. A 1954 amendment permitted 10 percent of the Federal grant funds to be used for projects not meeting this requirement.

In 1956, relocation payments were authorized to help displaced families and businesses meet the costs of moving. Also, the first broadening of the project concept of urban renewal took place with the authorization of advances for the preparation of general neighborhood renewal plans covering planning areas too large or complex to be executed as single projects.

In 1959, the concept was further expanded with the authorization of grants to assist communities in preparing community renewal programs under which the blight and deterioration of the entire locality are analyzed, resources to cope with the problem are identified, and an action program is formulated to rid the community of blighting conditions. The 1959 statute permitted 20 percent (instead of the former 10 percent) of Federal grant funds to be used for projects which were not predominantly residential either before or after renewal. It also added section 112 to title I in an effort to assist urban colleges and universities to achieve needed expansion and to cope with blight surrounding their campuses.

The Housing Act of 1961 further extended and liberalized the urban renewal legislation in several important respects, particularly with reference to special problem areas. In recognition of the need for and difficulty of obtaining housing for families of moderate income, provisions were adopted permitting sales of urban renewal sites at prices appropriate to the construction of such housing. These provisions were closely related to new FHA mortgage insurance authorized under section 221 (d) (3) of the National Housing Act. The challenge of stimulating and encouraging rehabilitation by private owners was recognized by a statutory provision permitting local public agencies themselves to rehabilitate a limited number of housing units as demonstrations for the benefit of project property owners and residents.

The 1961 act brought several other provisions of the urban renewal legislation to their current scope. Relocation payment provisions were liberalized; hospitals were added to section 112 in recognition that they, too, suffer from surrounding blight; and the percentage of grants available for nonresidential projects was raised again, this time from 20 to 30 percent. This increase in the authority to undertake nonresidential projects illustrates an important trend in the urban renewal process. It reflected a growing awareness of the importance of using renewal to revitalize the economic base and the taxable resources of cities, large and small. It recognized the contribution of urban renewal in creating better job opportunities as well as in improving housing conditions. These two objectives of renewal are interdependent.

Finally, the 1961 act, recognizing the magnitude of the scope and needs of the renewal program, doubled the previous authorization to a total of $4 billion. Another $725 million was authorized in 1964.

Largely under the stimulus of the Federal program, 50 States,[1] the District of Columbia, Puerto Rico, Guam, and the Virgin Islands now have urban renewal enabling legislation. Such legislation has been held constitutional in virtually all court tests, including at the present time the courts of last resort of 32 jurisdictions. Moreover, in 1954 the U.S. Supreme Court in *Berman* v. *Parker* strongly upheld the validity of urban renewal legislation.

II. HOW URBAN RENEWAL WORKS

The development of Federal urban renewal legislation in title I of the Housing Act of 1949, as amended, has determined the underlying concepts that have shaped the program. The legislation also has established both the roles of the public and private participants and the general nature of urban renewal operations.

Local Nature of Program Administration

A basic principle of title I is that urban renewal is a local program—locally conceived, locally planned, and locally carried out. This emphasis on local direction is one of the great strengths of urban renewal. Without this emphasis, it is doubtful whether any program could have been developed with sufficient flexibility to meet the myriad conditions faced by the hundreds of participating localities. The Federal role in urban renewal is primarily one of providing financial assistance, leadership, and general program direction.

Title I uses the simple generic term "local public agency" (LPA) in referring to the local body authorized to carry out urban renewal projects. However, under the various State enabling statutes, there is a wide variation in the nature of local public agencies. In some, a separate agency is authorized, usually with a governing board appointed by the mayor and subject to approval by the city council or other local governing body. In others, the powers of existing local housing authorities are extended to cover urban renewal. In still others, the city government itself is designated as the local public agency and the program is carried out through a department of city government.

[1] South Carolina communities, and New Orleans, La., have limited authority to undertake urban renewal projects. Land acquisition is limited to acquiring sites for public reuse.

While the administration of urban renewal activities resides in the local public agency, the ultimate responsibility for making the basic decisions in renewal rests in the elected governing body of the locality. In addition to the requirements of State law, the Federal law and policies establish several key checkpoints for action by the local governing body:

1. As a prerequisite to any Federal financing assistance, the local governing body must adopt a workable program for community improvement. While the workable program is concerned with communitywide rather than project activity, it does establish a framework for projects and assists in eliminating and preventing blight.

2. The application for Federal project planning funds must be accompanied by a resolution of the local governing body authorizing the application and designating the urban renewal area.

3. Before a project may be approved for execution, there must be a public hearing, and the local governing body must officially adopt the urban renewal plan, find that it conforms to the general plan for the locality as a whole, and determine that the proposed relocation of families and individuals to be displaced is feasible. In the resolution approving the plan, the local governing body also determines that the objectives of the urban renewal plan cannot be achieved through rehabilitation and must also recognize the city's responsibility to take certain actions, such as amending the zoning ordinance, vacating streets, and accepting new streets.

The necessity of providing the local share of project costs also creates a need for further local reviews. The local governing body must take the steps to provide the necessary funds, whether they are to be contributed as cash or used to finance public works provided as noncash local grants-in-aid. These obligations of the local government are generally set forth in a cooperation agreement entered into by it and by the local public agency, where the latter is a separate corporate body.

While the emphasis is on local initiative and action, the URA has a responsibility to insure that the purposes and methods of local renewal programs do conform with the intent of Congress, and that title I funds are used in the most effective and economical manner consistent with local objectives.

Planning Urban Renewal

In launching a renewal project, the first formal finding made by a local governing body is that the area selected is a slum, blighted, deteriorated, or deteriorating area. This finding is supported by data on buildings and environmental conditions. This and other information is included in a survey and planning application to the URA. Upon approval of this application, the community begins its project planning.

During the project planning stage the LPA conducts detailed surveys and studies and prepares the plans and estimates required to undertake the project. More intensive surveys are conducted as necessary to document in detail the uses and conditions of the structures in the area and the nature of the blighting influences. The data on the conditions in the project area are vital in determining the extent to which the project can be carried out by clearance or rehabilitation or a combination of both.

If families and individuals are to be displaced from the project area, the LPA must establish the feasibility of a relocation program. Surveys must be made of the number, size, and income of families to be displaced, and any other factors affecting their housing needs. Local relocation standards for decent, safe, and sanitary housing must be established, and the housing market must be surveyed to determine the availability of standard housing units to meet the anticipated relocation workload. If a shortage of such housing exists, actions must be initiated to produce the needed housing. Relocation planning is also carried out for anticipated displacement of business concerns.

If rehabilitation is involved, intensive surveys are made of the condition of the buildings to establish the structural and economic feasibility of rehabilitation. The financial conditions of the owners and residents must also be studied to determine their ability to make the necessary investments. To insure the success of any rehabilitation program, the LPA must develop a high degree of participation by owners and residents, as well as by public and private community organizations.

Appraisals must be made to set the cost of properties to be acquired, and title searches must be made of ownership. Land disposition and marketability surveys are also prepared as a guide to developing the new uses of the land.

Plans and cost estimates are prepared for all the other activities involved in carrying out the project, such as the provision of new streets and utilities, the demolition and grading of the area to be cleared, and the construction of necessary supporting facilities.

The major product of the planning period is the urban renewal plan—the formal statement of the goals and objectives of the project, the treatment to be utilized, and the controls over new uses. The plan must be studied by the local governing body in the approval of the project. It is also the basis upon which the Federal Government provides financial assistance. The courts have found the urban renewal plan to be essential to carry out the public purpose of urban renewal.

A typical urban renewal plan will identify the area covered and indicate in general terms the public actions to be taken to achieve the objectives of the project. It will establish land uses in the area; identify the changes to be made to the streets, other public rights-of-way, and utilities; and establish the controls to be applied to new development. These all play an important role in establishing the marketability and value of the land made available for redevelopment. Properties to be acquired will be identified or the conditions under which they may be acquired will be established. Rehabilitation standards will be established for those properties not to be acquired by the LPA. Before leaving the planning phase of a renewal project, I want to discuss very briefly two planning mechanisms—the community renewal program (CRP) and the general neighborhood renewal plan (GNRP)—both highly useful to a community in developing a sound basis for selecting and coordinating subsequent renewal projects.

Title I grants may pay two-thirds of the cost of preparing a CRP which embraces the renewal problems and needs of an entire city. The objective is a long range urban renewal program that is coordinated with all other renewal related local programs—with total needs in balance with total resources. Although local interest in community renewal programs was slow in developing, some 131 communities, as of May 1965, have now undertaken them.

Frequently, some urban renewal areas are quite large, and may exceed a reasonable and logical size for a single urban renewal project. In this instance, we may advance title I funds for the preparation of a general neighborhood renewal plan. This type of plan may cover, in a preliminary way, a large blighted area that will be renewed as a series of projects staged over a period of not more than 10 years. Since the enactment of the GNRP provision in 1956, some 225 plans of this type have been undertaken in 191 cities, as of May 1965.

Both the CRP and the GNRP help to create a much sounder basis for local urban renewal decisions and, therefore, help to make more effective use of Federal assistance for renewal projects.

The broadened planning base for local renewal programs, particularly under the community renewal program, permits a community to mesh its renewal planning with the planning of other programs, some of them involving Federal agencies. For example, it permits coordination with the highway planning assisted by the Federal Bureau of Public Roads. To aid in this planning coordination, the URA has established working relationships with several Federal departments and agencies, including the Bureau of Public Roads, the Area Redevelopment Administration, the General Services Administration, and divisions of the Department of Health, Education, and Welfare.

Renewal Action

After approval of the urban renewal plan by both the local governing body and the URA, Federal financial assistance for a renewal project is made available under a loan and grant contract. The locality then begins project execution activities—the work involved in translating the plans into renewal action.

Normally, the first phase of project operations is the acquisition of project properties, either through negotiation with the owners, or if necessary, by court condemnation proceedings. Acquisition is preceded by two independent appraisals. While the acquired properties are still occupied, the LPA must continue to manage and maintain the buildings and collect the rentals. A relocation service is established as speedily as possible, to provide displaced families with suitable housing within their means.

Where rehabilitation is involved, surveys are completed to determine needed improvements, and the LPA establishes an advisory service to help the residents with the architectural, financial, and construction problems involved in bringing their houses up to the standards established in the plan.

The removal of structures is normally done under a contract with a private contractor, as is the work involved in preparing the site and installing necessary streets and other site improvements. At the same time the city is engaged in providing the public facilities to support the new uses.

When the site is cleared, the land available for new development is publicly advertised to develop the market. Finally, as new private construction takes place, it must be inspected to assure that it is being carried out in accordance with the controls of the plan.

Financing Renewal

The basic Federal role in renewal planning and execution is to provide financial assistance which takes several forms:

Advances for the preparation of project plans. When the project goes into execution, the cost of planning becomes part of the overall cost of the project.

Temporary loans which serve as the working capital for the project. The LPA is authorized to obtain temporary loans either directly from the Federal Government or, with the benefit of a Federal guarantee of payment, from private lending institutions. Because of the more favorable interest rates available, most loans are obtained by the latter method.

Capital grants used to meet the Federal share of the net cost of the project.

Relocation grants borne entirely by the Federal Government, to cover: (1) payments for the costs of moving and losses of property, and (2) relocation adjustment payments, and small business displacement payments.

Definitive loans made available to localities where land is disposed of under long-term leases rather than by sale. The loans may run for as long as 40 years and are repaid from the income under the lease.

Determining Net Project Costs and Federal-Local Sharing

Determining the net cost and the method of sharing it involves these factors:

"Gross project cost" (line 1 of exhibit 1) is the total cost of carrying out all eligible operations in the urban renewal project or supporting it, except relocation payments. "Gross project cost" consists of two elements: (1) "Project expenditures" (line 2 of exhibit 1), those costs paid by the LPA out of money available to it; and (2) "Noncash local grants-in-aid" (line 5), those costs paid for directly by the locality. The latter may include costs of activities which might otherwise be paid out of "Project expenditures," such as: the donation of land, the demolition of structures, or the provision of site improvements such as streets and sidewalks. It may also include public facilities to support the new uses of the project area (such as schools, police stations, libraries, and parks) to the extent they serve and benefit the project, and certain statutory credits such as those relating to the acquisition of land by colleges, universities, and hospitals, or the provision of land for low-rent public housing projects.

Gross project cost is partially offset by income received from the disposition proceeds derived from the sale of project land for redevelopment (line 6 of exhibit 1). The difference between gross project cost and disposition proceeds is the net project cost (line

Exhibit 1

Example of the sharing of project costs (⅔ basis)

1. Gross project cost $1,500,000
    Total cost in carrying out project except relocation payments.
    Made up of 2 components:
2.　　　Project expenditures $1,300,000
        Direct expenditures by project, financed from—
3.　　　　　Maximum temporary loan (loan funds provided to the project either as direct Federal loan or by private loan under Federal guarantee) 1,150,000
4.　　　　　Local cash grant-in-aid (cash provided by locality) 150,000
5.　　　Noncash local grant-in-aid (land donations and public works provided by the locality) 200,000
6. Disposition proceeds (funds received from sale of project land for redevelopment) .... −450,000
7.　　　Net project cost (necessary public cost of undertaking the project) 1,050,000
        This is met by—
8.　　　　　Federal capital grant (⅔ of net project cost) 700,000
9.　　　　　Local grants-in-aid 350,000
        ⅓ of net project cost. The locality provides its share as—
10.　　Cash (line 4, above) 150,000
11.　　Noncash (line 5, above) 200,000

EXHIBIT 2

Example of calculating and repaying the Federal loan

1. Project expeditures (exhibit 1, line 2) $1,300,000
2. Local cash grant-in-aid (exhibit 1, line 4) .... −150,000
3.   Maximum temporary loan* (exhibit 1, line 3) 1,150,000
        Repaid from:
4.   Disposition proceeds (exhibit 1, line 6) 450,000
5.   Federal capital grant (exhibit 1, line 8) 700,000

* Actually, the amount of loan funds outstanding at any one time is considerably less. Funds are borrowed to meet cash requirements for periods ranging from 6 months to 1 year. Federal grant payments and disposition proceeds becoming available during the project may be applied directly to meeting project expenditures, thus reducing the need for borrowing.

7). Under the usual formula for the sharing of net project cost, the Federal contribution is a two-thirds capital grant (line 8). The local grant-in-aid is one-third of net project cost and is met through the local cash and noncash contributions to the project (lines 10 and 11). Where local grants-in-aid are in excess of project needs, the excess may be credited toward the locality's share of subsequent projects. This is called pooling credit.

In addition to the two-thirds sharing formula discussed above, there are two other formulas for the sharing of net project cost. For cities with a population of 50,000 or less (or of 150,000 or less in areas designated under the Area Redevelopment Act) the net project cost is shared on a three-fourths Federal, one-fourth local basis. An alternative three-fourths, one-fourth formula is provided for any locality which pays for administrative, overhead, and planning costs without charge to the project. It is interesting to note that approximately 85 percent of all projects include some cash contribution by the locality.

III. PROGRAM ACCOMPLISHMENTS AND DIRECTIONS

I think it is obvious from this rather brief summary that urban renewal is a difficult and complex task. While the expectations have been great, the tangible benefits sometimes seemed less apparent. Now the initial period of waiting is over, and the results of the program are becoming quite evident. I should now like to discuss the progress and accomplishments of the urban renewal program in the country as a whole, and where appropriate, indicate some of its current trends and directions.

Growth of the Urban Renewal Program

The steady growth in the number of localities participating in urban renewal shows the importance which the cities themselves place upon the program. There has been a steady increase from 31 localities at the end of our first fiscal year in 1950 to the 772 with urban renewal projects as of May 31, 1965.[2] Forty-four of the 50 States, the District of Columbia, the Commonwealth of Puerto Rico, Guam, and the Virgin Islands have undertaken urban renewal.

The interest in renewal has spread rapidly not only to all parts of the Nation but also to a variety of communities. Most of the larger cities undertook urban renewal quite early, but increasingly the smaller communities have become concerned with the need for eliminating blight, sustaining their economies and preserving their desirable residential qualities. At the end of fiscal year 1954, 44 percent of the communities in the program had populations of 100,000 or more; by 1964 this proportion had dropped to 14 percent, and more than half of the localities had populations of less than 25,000.

The proportions of the total Federal capital grants allocated to communities in various size groups are distributed quite evenly in relation to population. Although the capital grants received by the smaller cities tend to be somewhat larger relative to their populations, in absolute terms they are, of course, very much smaller.

By May 31, 1965, nearly 1600 urban renewal projects had been initiated. The progressive increase in the number of projects is evident in exhibit 3. For reasons which I will discuss later, there is necessarily a substantial leadtime between the initiation of planning for a project and its actual execution. Therefore, in the early years of this expanding program, the number of projects in planning exceeded those in execution. However, since 1958, the latter group has exceeded the number in planning and is presently increasing very rapidly. Now we are witnessing the same kind of sharp upward trend in project completions, and I expect the number and

---

[2] This does not include 25 communities which had not yet initiated actual projects but were preparing community renewal programs in preparation for project undertakings. The addition of these would bring the overall total to 797.

proportion of completions to rise rapidly from now on. At the end of calendar year 1964, in addition to the 174 closed out projects, there were 81 others with all land committed to a redeveloper.

EXHIBIT 3

Urban renewal projects by status, 1950–1965. URA–June 1965.

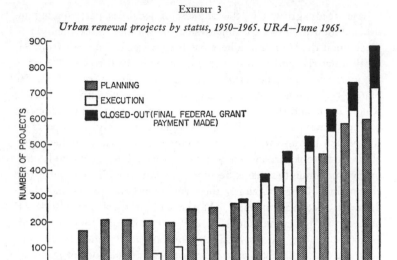

A substantial number of communities are now carrying out more than one project. This is particularly true of the larger communities and those which have been in the program for some time. Usually a community with several projects initiates them progressively so that at any single time they are at various stages of project activity. As a single project moves from one stage to another, it may first occupy primarily the time of the planners, then of the land acquisition people, then of the relocation specialists, and so on. However, as other projects follow, the workload of the entire local agency staff can remain relatively stable with substantial benefits for effectiveness and efficiency in operations.

The increasing number of communities now carrying out several projects suggests the desirability of finding additional ways of administering each local renewal program as an entity, rather than as individual projects. For example, we are now testing methods whereby local public agencies can budget administrative expenditures for all of their projects as a group, in order to eliminate unnecessary paper work and place greater emphasis on the effective administration of the program as a whole. We hope to find ways of extending this principle to other aspects of project operations.

Capital Grant Authorizations

Through a series of amendments to title I, new grant authorizations have supported the continued growth of the program. The Housing Act of 1961 brought the cumulative grant authorization for the urban renewal program to $3,975 million ($4 billion less $25 million for transportation demonstration grants). The 1964 Act raised the total authorization to $4,725 million.

Earlier in this statement I commented briefly on the successive acts of Congress which made title I funds available for projects which are not primarily residential in nature. Many of these projects, even though not predominantly residential either before or after redevelopment, do involve the elimination of significant areas of residential slums or the provision of sites for a sizable number of new housing units. The rate at which these applications are received reflects the increasing concern of many communities throughout the country for their downtown areas and other commercial and industrial sections which are so important to employment and the economic base of the communities, and upon which the provision of good housing and adequate community facilities and services is to a large extent dependent.

Evaluating Local Program Capacity

The rate of capital grant utilization reflects not only the desire of localities to carry out urban renewal but also their capacity to do so. The URA procedural requirements are designed to provide adequate assurance that such capacity exists before any community starts the actual execution of a specific project. For example, a land utilization and marketability study is required for each project at the outset of the planning stage so that the renewal plan can reflect realistically the market for land in the community. Before a capital grant contract is executed, numerous other studies must be completed to assure the feasibility of the project. The marketability of the particular project sites must be shown; there must be adequate evidence of the feasibility of any proposed rehabilitation; a detailed financing plan must be submitted, with firm commitments from the bodies which have agreed to contribute the local grant-in-aid; and a feasible and thoroughly documented relocation plan must be prepared.

In July of 1962, an additional major requirement was instituted to provide as much assurance as possible, even before the planning of an urban renewal project is initiated, that the performance of the local public agency on projects already underway evidences its capacity to undertake an additional project. Now, before the URA reserves capital grant funds for any additional project, it carefully evaluates the performance of the local public agency on its existing projects. The evaluation covers local performance in project planning, land acquisition, site clearance, relocation, project improvements, public facilities, local cash contributions, rehabilitation and conservation, land disposition, and any other actions prerequisite to project completion. This systematic review provides a necessary and important measure of assurance that communities applying for additional capital grant funds have the capacity to carry out the proposed additional projects effectively and within a reasonable time.

With this background on the growth and development of the program as a whole I should like to discuss accomplishments of the program in certain key phases of project operations.

Land Acquisition

In the actual execution of a project the first major step in many cases is the acquisition of the blighted area to be redeveloped. We think the record on land acquisition is a good one, partly because of the scale of the accomplishment but—even more importantly—because of the way in which it has been done.

In recent years the rate at which blighted areas have been purchased has risen very rapidly.

Through December 1964, there were 970 urban renewal projects on which planning had been completed and which had been approved for actual execution. These projects included 36,400 acres of land slated for acquisition and redevelopment.

Nearly 75 percent of this total area, or 27,026 acres, had been acquired by local public agencies and the balance was in process of acquisition. Perhaps it will help you to visualize this acquired area to think of it as more than 42 square miles.

Although there is necessarily some lag between the purchase of real estate in renewal areas and the actual demolition of the existing buildings, by December 1964 approximately 158,000 structures had been demolished.

In providing financial assistance for this large-scale acquisition of property, we have adopted strong measures to assure that the owners are treated fairly and impartially, and that the public interest is protected against the payment of excessive prices. Our procedures protect both interests.

The principal distinguishing features of property acquisition for urban renewal are: (1) the requirement of two independent appraisals of each parcel, and (2) the practice of making the Federal as well as the local determinations of appropriate acquisition prices before the LPA opens negotiations with property owners.

Obtaining two independent appraisals reduces the risk of error in determining the prices paid for properties. Discrepancies between appraisal reports, whether in the reporting of facts or in the analysis or judgments of the appraisers, highlight matters that otherwise could be easily overlooked.

The LPA initially determines the prices to be paid for properties on the basis of an on-site review of the appraisal reports. The appraisal reports and the LPA's proposed schedule of acquisition prices are then reviewed at the project by HHFA in order to establish the prices the LPA may pay for properties, either by direct purchase from the owners or by stipulations as to value in condemnation prodeedings.

We encourage LPA's to make every effort to reach an agreement with each owner on the acquisition price for his property. Condemnation proceedings on the issue of value are thus avoided except in cases where an owner will not accept a price which the LPA, with the concurrence of HHFA, believes to be the fair market value of the property. Condemnation proceedings are of course used where there is faulty title or where such action is a normal local practice.

Relocation

Title I of the Housing Act of 1949 has always required that there be a feasible method for the relocation of families displaced from urban renewal areas and that there must be enough decent, safe, and sanitary housing in existence or being provided to meet the needs of displaced families. The enactment of this provision by the Congress represented an extraordinary step in recognizing the public responsibility to assure adequate housing for families displaced by public action.

Through December 1964, more than 185,000 families had been relocated from urban renewal areas. A determined effort is made to keep track of all families and to see that each one has an opportunity to move into decent, safe, and sanitary housing. As a result, reports are available on the housing conditions of nearly 87 percent of all relocated families. The remaining 13 percent included 7 percent who moved out of the jurisdiction, 5 percent who were untraceable, and 1 percent who were otherwise removed from the workload. Over 92 percent of those whose rehousing conditions have been reported moved into decent, safe, and sanitary housing meeting the requirements of the approved relocation plans.[3]

Exhibit 4 shows the types of housing occupied by those relocated families whose housing conditions were known. As you will see, about 46 percent went into standard private rental housing, about 22 percent into standard sales housing, and about 24 percent into public housing. The remainder of less than 8 percent did not take full advantage of the relocation services offered to them, and relocated themselves into housing which did not meet the requirements of the locally approved relocation plan.

We are particularly pleased with the progress in the last year or two to improve even this high level of performance. The following table provides a basis for comparing the results of the relocation since January 1, 1962, with previous data. I am confident that even more progress in the quality of relocation will be made as a result of efforts now underway.

[3] In 1964, the U.S. Bureau of the Census conducted a nationwide survey of the housing of families displaced from urban renewal sites. Interviews conducted at 2,300 relocation housing units disclosed that 94 percent of the dwelling units were standard. [A report on this survey is included in Chapter 11 of this volume.—Ed.]

Family relocation—Program totals

	Cumulative to Dec. 31, 1961	Jan. 1, 1962 to Dec. 31, 1964	Cumulative to Dec. 31, 1964
All families relocated	127,136	58,045	185,181
Housing condition known (as percentage of all families)	86.1	87.6	86.6
Standard housing (as percentage of families whose housing condition is known)	91.8	94.6	92.7

The Relocation Requirement

Although the standards for relocation housing are locally determined, they are subject to Federal approval. In no case may the acceptable local standard be set below the level of the local housing code. Under URA regulations, these five types of standards must be met:

Physical standards (including the condition of the structure, bathroom facilities, kitchen facilities, sewage disposal, heating facilities, electrical power, and natural light and ventilation).

Occupancy standards (including the size and number of rooms in relationship to the family size and composition).

Health and safety standards (including the nature of egress and freedom from health hazards).

Ability-to-pay standards (expressed in terms of gross rent as a percentage of income, and criteria for determining a family's ability to purchase a house).

Location standards (accessibility to places of employment and desirability of the new location in terms of public utilities and commercial facilities).

Before a project may be approved for execution, the locality must submit evidence of the adequacy of the housing supply to meet anticipated relocation needs and the governing body of the locality must find that the proposed relocation program is feasible. The final authority for finding that the relocation requirements of section 105(c) of title I have been satisfied rests solely with the Housing Administrator and cannot be delegated.

Very early in the execution stage a relocation service is established, preferably at or near the project site. Each family, individual, and business in the project area is interviewed to explain the services available and to evaluate fully its needs and preferences. Appropriate referrals are made if the families or individuals require help from social welfare agencies.

Information on the current availability of private rental and sales units is developed by the project staff in cooperation with local real estate brokers, real estate boards, owners and operators of residential property, and others having a knowledge of the local market. Site individuals and families are referred to available units on the basis of their needs established by the relocation interview. Families interested in buying a home are given advice and guidance on how to proceed, including information on housing financed under the provisions of FHA's section 221. Families interested in and eligible for low-rent housing are given assistance in preparing their applications and advised as to their preference for admission.

EXHIBIT 4

Relocation of families from urban renewal projects, December 31, 1964. URA—June 1965.

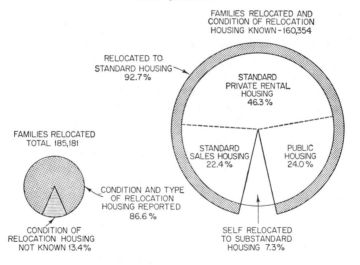

FAMILIES RELOCATED AND CONDITION OF RELOCATION HOUSING KNOWN - 160,354

RELOCATED TO STANDARD HOUSING 92.7%

STANDARD PRIVATE RENTAL HOUSING 46.3%

FAMILIES RELOCATED TOTAL 185,181

CONDITION AND TYPE OF RELOCATION HOUSING REPORTED 86.6%

STANDARD SALES HOUSING 22.4%

PUBLIC HOUSING 24.0%

CONDITION OF RELOCATION HOUSING NOT KNOWN 13.4%

SELF RELOCATED TO SUBSTANDARD HOUSING 7.3%

In spite of all efforts of the relocation advisory service, some families and individuals will move on their own initiative. An effort is made to trace the families so that their new quarters may be inspected. If the new quarters are found to be substandard, the families are offered further assistance in finding standard quarters.

Substandard units found in such followups are referred to the local code enforcement officials for further action.

EXHIBIT 5

Percent of families self-relocated into substandard housing, cumulative through 12/31/61 and semi-annual through December 1964

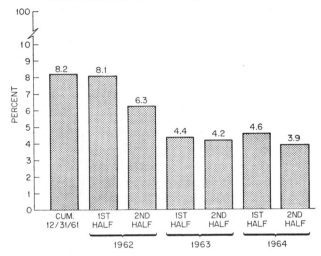

Relocation Payments

In addition to the requirement that adequate relocation facilities be available, the Congress provided in the Housing Act of 1956 for a system of relocation payments to cover the costs of moving and direct losses of property resulting from the move. These payments are covered by Federal grants and are administered by the local agencies under regulations established by the URA. The maximum payment for a family or individual is $200. For business concerns, payment may be as high as $25,000.

In 1964 Congress authorized the payment of up to $500 to families and elderly individuals to assist them in meeting the hardships of displacement. Also, a small business was made eligible for a small business displacement payment of $1,500, in addition to the normal relocation payment.

Current Trends in Relocation

On the whole, as the statistics show, the relocation aspects of urban renewal are being done well. Relocation performance has

Relocation payments—Program totals
(since authorized by Housing Act of 1956)

Families:	Cumulative to December, 1964
Number	112,540
Total payment	$8,238,553
Average payment	$73.20
Individuals:	
Number	42,734
Total payment	$1,974,463
Average payment	$46.20
Businesses:	
Number	28,526
Total payment	$45,947,431
Average payment	$1,610.72

shown steady improvement and every effort will be made to continue that trend.

The success of relocation is particularly noteworthy in view of the fact that the slums and deteriorating areas of the city hold the highest proportion of the poor and disadvantaged. The 1964 Census Bureau survey of families in urban renewal areas indicated that 40 percent had monthly incomes of less than $250. For such families the availability of an adequate supply of low-rent public housing units is an obvious necessity. But even this source will not meet all of the problems. Some family incomes are so low that they cannot afford the modest rents of low-rent public housing. Some families are so large that public housing cannot supply adequate sized units. The elderly, socially maladjusted families, and the homeless men of "skid row" cannot be easily rehoused. Although the relative number of these problem cases is low in most relocation workloads, they are a matter of acute concern.

We are now stressing, in many aspects of the urban renewal program, the importance of enlisting the full cooperation of the communities concerned in meeting these basic social problems. For example, many cities are now undertaking community renewal programs which include studies of the social problems and needs of people living in blighted areas. The CRP also offers an opportunity to develop better relocation plans—plans that account for the total demand for housing in the community and its urban area. In this respect it is worth noting that the displacement of families from urban renewal accounts for only a minute part of a city's housing needs. As a general illustration, renewal displacement amounts to only about 20,000 of the 12 million American families that move each year.

Similarly, improved relocation methods are being stressed in our regular project relocation activities and under the demonstration grant program authorized by section 314 of the Housing Act of 1954. These activities stress particularly the needs of the elderly and families with social problems, the relocation of homeless men from skid row areas, and the provision of specialized services to displaced business firms. The objective is to alleviate the impact of displacement and to help achieve, wherever possible, a positive gain through the relocation process.

The relocation of business establishments is a matter of growing concern, particularly as a result of the increasing proportion of projects involving nonresidential uses. While title I does not include all of the same stringent requirements for displaced businesses as it does for families, local agencies do provide businesses with a similar high standard of relocation assistance. In many instances, highly specialized help has been given to analyze the needs of the business and to find appropriate facilities for its continued operations. Referral is made to the Small Business Administration which, under its displaced business disaster loan program, has provided low-interest rate financing to facilitate the transition from old to new quarters.

As might be expected, satisfactory data on the success of business relocation are difficult to develop. In a considerable number of cases, the change required by relocation and the availability of new facilities have brought an expansion and improvement of operations. Of the businesses which have failed to reestablish themselves a large proportion were in the retail and service categories. Unquestionably a number of these have been extremely marginal enterprises that would have experienced difficulty remaining in business even without moving.

The Expanding Conservation Program

The 1954 act added a most important tool—conservation and rehabilitation—to the urban renewal kit. Vast areas of cities are marked by blight and deterioration that is still susceptible to corrective action short of wholesale clearance. Our success in meeting the challenge offered by these areas while there is still time will determine not only the quality of our communities but also the ultimate extent and cost of slum clearance.

There exist in every city opportunities for the rehabilitation of older and deteriorating homes which are still basically sound in structure and which with proper treatment can have their economic life extended for many years. These homes form one of the best and largest resources for standard housing for lower middle- and middle-income families. The increasing interest of cities throughout the country in this aspect of the urban renewal program has been demonstrated by a steady expansion in the number of projects involving rehabilitation. By the end of calendar year 1964, there were 229 projects in execution which included a significant amount of rehabilitation, often in conjunction with some clearance and redevelopment activity.

In a sense, rehabilitation is even more difficult and complex than clearance and redevelopment, primarily because accomplishment depends so much upon the decisions and voluntary actions of many individual owners of a great variety of separate properties. Each individual situation involves its own distinctive. combination of owner motivations, physical and financial characteristics of the property, and environmental factors. The process requires a high degree of participation by the local citizenry; skilled guidance for small property owners with respect to design, finance, construction, and other factors; extensive coordination with many city departments; and full participation by local financing institutions.

Lack of experience in this field, on the part of the local and Federal agencies and the construction industry in general, resulted in a slow start. However, in recent years great emphasis has been placed on solving these problems with the result that substantial achievements are beginning to be evident as shown in the following table. By December 31, 1964, over 52,000 structures and 120,510 dwelling units had been identified as requiring rehabilitation in projects which had reached the execution stage. Rehabilitation had been completed or was in process on over 62 percent of the structures in this workload and nearly 55 percent of the dwelling units. Work had been completed on over 23,000 structures, including a total of more than 43,000 dwelling units. Especially gratifying is the fact that the number of dwelling units on which rehabilitation had been completed rose nearly 53 percent during the fiscal year 1964.

Status of rehabilitation, December 31, 1964

	CURRENT WORKLOAD		COMPLETED OR IN PROCESS		COMPLETED	
	Number	Per-cent	Number	Per-cent	Number	Per-cent
Structures	52,601	100	32,663	62.1	23,822	45.3
Residential	46,814	100	30,046	64.2	22,205	47.4
Other	5,787	100	2,617	45.2	1,617	27.9
Dwelling units	120,510	100	65,765	54.6	43,699	36.3

Our experience has shown that even when essential neighborhood improvements are provided, there are still two principal problems which face the typical propertyowner in raising the standards of his own property. One is the difficulty of securing long-term mortgage funds for rehabilitation through conventional financing sources; the other typically is the owner's lack of knowledge of what is needed, of the sources of assistance, and simply of how to go about getting the job done.

We believe that a major breakthrough has been achieved in the rehabilitation program by our agreement with the Federal Housing Administration on new minimum property standards for rehabilitation in urban renewal areas.[4] With these standards in effect, the way is now open for FHA to play its essential part in financing residential rehabilitation which meets desirable but practical standards. Experience had indicated that FHA regular minimum property standards for new construction could not be applied successfully to rehabilitation. These standards would have required rehabilitation so extensive that the occupants in many cases could not afford the necessary expenditures even with the liberal financing terms provided by FHA mortgage insurance. Moreover, it was physically impossible to alter some of the older buildings enough to conform to the standards. As a result, the FHA mortgage insurance programs have received only limited use in urban renewal projects involving rehabilitation.

The new standards are designed to correct this situation and to provide a basis for a desirable level for rehabilitation with considerable flexibility to meet local situations and needs. They recognize the vast differences that exist among urban renewal areas and the variations in the quality and condition of houses in different loca-

[4] The Housing Act of 1964 established a program of 3 percent, direct loans for rehabilitation.

tions. Additionally, the standards reflect the fact that the amount of physical improvement that can be achieved in urban renewal conservation areas is limited by the incomes of the persons in these areas and by the fact that the properties to be rehabilitated, although basically sound, generally were built several decades ago.

It would be difficult to overemphasize the importance of adequate long-term financing for the rehabilitation program. The remaining periods on many mortgages, particularly in the older sections of our cities, are relatively short. The same level of periodic payments called for under these existing mortgages often could repay an appreciably larger loan if the period were substantially extended. Therefore, in many cases the availability of long-term credit through FHA mortgage insurance can enable an owner of his own home or of rental property to refinance existing loans and pay for substantial property improvements without increasing his mortgage payments. We are already finding that this is one of the most important inducements to property rehabilitation, once adequate neighborhood improvements and services are assured.

A fine example of the effect of refinancing can be seen from a specific case of a three-family house rehabilitated in New Haven, Conn. Prior to rehabilitation, the house carried two conventional mortgages and attachments worth approximately $15,000, requiring monthly payments of about $225. Approximately $2,500 was borrowed to rehabilitate the structure. The new FHA section 220 mortgage covering both the refinancing and the cost of rehabilitation required monthly payments of only $102 due to a lower interest rate and a longer repayment term. This example is by no means an isolated one although the reduction in monthly payments usually will not be as dramatic.

Since the adoption of the new FHA rehabilitation standards, a series of very useful regional training conferences has been held with participation by the Federal Housing Administration, the Urban Renewal Administration, and local public agencies. Our objective has been to accelerate the field implementation of the standards and encourage fuller FHA–URA–LPA coordination in rehabilitation activities. Priority attention is also being given in these workshop sessions to the pressing need for local public agencies to employ staff or consulting services adequate in numbers and skills to provide effective home improvement advice to property owners.

One major goal of this cooperative local-Federal effort is to give owners in rehabilitation areas the "one stop" service under the urban renewal property rehabilitation program that new-home buyers receive from lending institutions in applying for FHA mortgage insurance.

The fine potential of the conservation and rehabilitation phase of the urban renewal program is visibly demonstrated in an increasing number of communities. For example, in Grand Prairie, Tex., a community of 30,000 people, rehabilitation and conservation have been combined with clearance and redevelopment in the South Dalworth project area. To November 1963 the owners had spent more than $200,000 on the rehabilitation of 148 properties. This upgrading of existing properties, coupled with clearance of dilapidated buildings and the provision of public improvements, has stimulated the expenditure of more than $1,600,000 for new homes. Financing of rehabilitation and new construction is now readily available. When the project began in 1958, very few of the homes had any kind of mortgage financing.

In Little Rock, that community used the rehabilitation and conservation program in combination with clearance and redevelopment to renew the 80-acre livestock show project area. New streets, playgrounds and other improvements have been provided. Owners have spent over $204,000 on property improvements—not including expenditures on lawns, shrubbery, and other items for which no building permit is required. New homes built in the area cost about $900,000. FHA-insured mortgages under section 220, as well as conventional loans, were used to finance the private improvements. The tax yield for this area before renewal was $3,161; the estimated future tax yield will be $18,611, an increase of nearly 500 percent. Even more important is the very substantial improvement in living conditions that has been achieved.

A great many other rehabilitation success stories already exist or are rapidly in the making.

Historic Preservation

There is another very important aspect of conservation and rehabilitation which I would like to touch upon briefly. Through this aspect of the program, urban renewal—rather than being a destroyer of our architectural and historical heritage—is a means of restoring and enhancing it. Among the many cities with urban renewal projects involving the preservation of historic sites are: Mobile, Ala.; Philadelphia, Pa.; York, Pa.; Monterey, Calif.; Portsmouth, N.H.; Providence, R.I.; New Haven, Conn.; and Norfolk, Va.

Much of the stimulation and guidance for historic preservation in urban renewal can be traced to the publication of a report on an urban renewal demonstration grant project for the College Hill area in Providence, R. I. This document, which has become a classic in its field since its release in 1959, contains graphic and narrative proposals to restore buildings in the historic College Hill area, to institute zoning, planning, and urban renewal measures to preserve its character, and to attract private investment to the rehabilitation and modernization of the area for present-day use. As a followup to this report, in January 1963, the URA published a guide, Historic Preservation Through Urban Renewal, which explains how title I assistance can be used in rehabilitating and conserving structures and neighborhoods of historic significance, and describes how this was done in 14 communities.

The URA also has cooperated with the National Park Service in developing ways of coordinating our historic preservation efforts. We encourage local renewal agencies to tap the wealth of information in Park Service regional offices and to work with local historical societies and organizations.

Land Disposition and New Development

For those interested in the future of America's cities there are few experiences more dramatic and exciting than to revisit a city after an extended absence and suddenly come upon fresh and striking new homes, apartments, offices, shops, or cultural institutions rising where a few years before there was only disorder and decay. This drama can be experienced today in any number of cities throughout the country—for the vision of the Congress in 1949 is now being strikingly fulfilled.

Well planned and well located urban renewal sites are very much in demand, and the pace of land disposition is rapidly increasing as shown in exhibit 6. In fact, the total area which local public agencies conveyed to redevelopers in the 2 fiscal years 1962 and 1963 exceeded

EXHIBIT 6

Land conveyed for redevelopment, fiscal years 1957–1964. URA–June 1965.

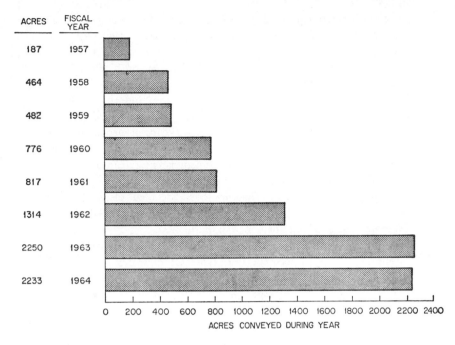

ACRES CONVEYED DURING YEAR

EXHIBIT 7

Ratio of private redevelopers' investment to federal capital grant. Coverage: 588 projects in which some or all land was disposed of as of June 1964. URA– June 1965.

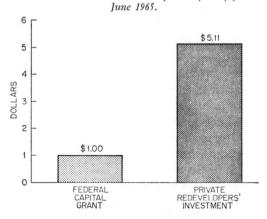

the entire area which had been transferred to redevelopers in the whole of the preceding period from the beginning of the program in 1949.

The rapid progress in disposition and redevelopment is the fruit of a sometimes long but necessary period of preparation that must take place before land in urban renewal areas can actually be redeveloped. After a project is planned, sufficient property must be acquired so that full disposition parcels are assembled; families must be relocated and buildings demolished. Often old site improvements must be removed and new ones installed. Land is then marketed and redevelopers selected under careful procedures involving public scrutiny. Contract terms must be worked out and agreed upon. Even after a sales agreement is entered into with the selected redeveloper, the local public agency usually does not convey possession until it has approved detailed plans that the redeveloper and his architect have worked out, and until the redeveloper has obtained financing commitments.

As I have said, about 27,026 acres had been acquired by local public agencies by December 31, 1964. Of course a considerable part of this area was still going through the necessary demolition, relocation, and other preparatory stages which I have already described. But it is interesting to see that redevelopers had been selected for more than 60 percent of all of the land that had been acquired. Only a relatively small proportion of the acquired area— about 12 percent—was ready for redevelopment but without a redeveloper on December 31, 1964. Undoubtedly redevelopers have been selected for additional land since that date.

The following table shows in some detail the status of the 16,318 acres, or nearly 26 square miles, for which redevelopers had been selected. Redevelopment had been completed or was actually under construction on more than one-half. Most of the balance had been placed under contract, and plans, financing arrangements, and other preparations for actual construction were being completed. The total area for which redevelopers had been selected increased by more than 6,700 acres—or about 71 percent in the last 2½ years.

The land area on which construction had been completed or was actually underway increased even more sharply—by 124 percent. The rapid progress reflects the successful maturing of the urban renewal program, the strong demand for good sites, and the constant effort by local public agencies and by ourselves to speed up the rate of disposition and redevelopment.

Exhibit 7 shows the relationship of the Federal capital grant to the total private investment in urban renewal. Overall, it appears that approximately $5 of private funds are invested for each dollar of Federal capital grant. Of course, as more projects involving sizable rehabilitation areas come into being and as less intensive development, such as garden type apartments, occurs, this ratio may change.

Status of land acquisition, disposition, and redevelopment—All projects approved for execution through June 30, 1962 and Dec. 31, 1964

	JUNE 30, 1962		DEC. 31, 1964	
	Acres	*Percent*	*Acres*	*Percent*
Total land for acquisition	25,610	100.0	36,400	100.0
Acquired	18,733	73.1	27,026	74.2
Not acquired	6,877	26.9	9,374	25.8
Total land acquired	18,733	100.0	27,026	100.0
Redeveloper selected	9,555	51.0	16,318	60.4
Ready for disposition	3,171	16.9	3,308	12.2
Not ready for disposition	6,007	32.1	7,400	27.4
Land with redevelopers selected	9,555	100.0	16,318	100.0
Redevelopment completed	2,785	29.2	6,724	41.2
Redevelopment underway	1,198	12.5	2,629	16.1
Under contract, redevelopment not started	3,313	34.7	5,234	32.1
Not under contract	2,259	23.6	1,731	10.6

Almost three-fourths of all land disposed of, exclusive of streets and alleys, had been purchased by private persons or organizations. Most of this will be used for residential purposes; the remainder will be devoted to commercial, industrial, or institutional uses. Over 67,000 dwelling units of all kinds had been completed, and nearly 20,000 more were under construction.

The Future Market for Urban Renewal Land

In order to evaluate factors affecting the long-term trends in urban renewal, the URA recently employed the services of a private professional group of experts in market analysis and marketing methods to report on the factors involved in the demand for redevelopment sites over the next 12 to 15 years. Their report is most encouraging. Whereas the demand for space resulting from postwar shortages appears to be declining, there is an increasing pressure for the upgrading of both residential and nonresidential accommodations. This demand will be highly particularized, placing a premium on good site selection, quality planning, and careful marketing. We expect to be placing increasing stress on these factors to assure that future urban renewal projects are realistically related to the potentials of the market.

Construction and Taxable Values

Because one of the objectives of urban renewal has always been to sustain and increase the capacity of cities to meet rising needs for essential public facilities and services, the impact of urban renewal upon taxable values is particularly important. Significant increases are already evident. From estimates prepared by local public agencies throughout the country, it appears that after redevelopment assessed values are averaging between four to five times the values prior to slum clearance. To the extent that localities use decreased assessments on new construction to foster certain social objectives such as the provision of moderate income housing, this ratio may decline (exhibit 8).

There is a great deal of variation in the degree of tax benefit from

EXHIBIT 8

Comparison of assessed valuations before and after urban renewal. Coverage: Based on information for 518 projects in which redevelopment was started or completed. URA–June 1965.

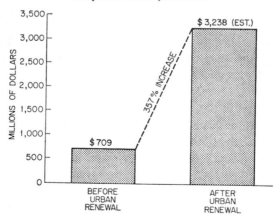

city to city, depending upon the types of urban renewal projects undertaken. The following examples include several which illustrate the full potential:

The redevelopment of Southwest Washington, D.C., is expected to produce about $4,846,221 annually in taxes after the completion of redevelopment, as compared to about $592,016 previously. This is an increase of about eight times in the yearly tax revenue.

The Gratiot project in Detroit resulted in taxes increasing from $70,000 before redevelopment to $512,000 after, and this occurred despite a 31-percent decrease in the taxable land area.

Mayor Richard J. Daley, of Chicago, has stated that the annual tax revenues from 27 redevelopment projects in his city are expected to increase from $2,321,442 to $4,794,368.

Calexico, Calif., was the first city in that State to complete an urban renewal project (project 1). Before redevelopment, the 21-acre project paid $4,400 annually in property taxes. According to our latest information, the same area is now paying approximately $16,400.

Prior to redevelopment, annual taxes on the properties in the Norfolk, Va., downtown project were $165,650. It is estimated that when redevelopment is completed, the annual taxes will amount to $375,000.

The Clinton Park project in Oakland, Calif., a rehabilitation and conservation project, resulted in nearly $7 million worth of new construction, and tax revenues from the project area rose from $49,000 to $195,000 upon completion.

These tax revenue increases were obtained directly from land and improvements within the urban renewal project areas. It is our experience that urban renewal also generates new investment outside the project area—particularly the fringes—and that this, too, results in higher assessed valuations and tax levies. However, as yet we have no way of measuring this increase. It is also significant that the tax revenue increases occurred despite the fact that in most of these projects urban renewal resulted in an increase in the proportion of tax-exempt land—parks, playgrounds, and so on—in the redeveloped areas.

Disposition Price and Methods

When urban renewal project land is made available to redevelopers, it must be sold at a price comparable to that which similar land elsewhere in the community would bring if subject to the controls and benefits of the urban renewal plan. To establish a base for that price, Federal policy requires that two independent appraisals be made of the land in relationship to existing land prices in the community. Before HHFA will concur in a disposition price, a further review is made by a staff real estate specialist. For the program as a whole, disposition prices for cleared land have averaged out at about $1 per square foot. This may be compared with an acquisition cost for land and improvements of approximately $2.05 per square foot.

The marketing of any large amount of land is always a complex process, and one that becomes more so when it is vitally related to achieving the urban renewal objectives warranting the public investment involved. Given the variety of local objectives and circumstances, no single disposition method would suffice. URA policy therefore permits the use of a variety of methods, including:

Price competition, including public auctions or the use of competitive sealed bids.

Nonprice competition, the establishment of a fixed publicly announced price with competition between developers on the basis of other factors, such as design criteria or moderate rentals. Sometimes the land is simply made available to the first taker at the fixed price, such as for lots to individuals for single-family homes.

Negotiated agreements, in which price and moderate rentals, design, or other criteria are negotiated, subject to public disclosure before ultimate disposal.

In addition to the above methods, special criteria as to disposition prices are established in title I for land which will be utilized for public low-rent housing and for moderate-income housing provided by various kinds of nonprofit and limited dividend groups. Localities are also permitted to give priorities to former owners or occupants of property in the project area to purchase sites.

The FHA mortgage insurance programs play an active and important role in urban renewal residential redevelopment. Cooperative actions have been developed whereby the staffs of LPA's, FHA, and URA work on specific aspects of projects in the planning, execution, and redevelopment stages.

In projects involving residential reuse, it is customary for the LPA to confer extensively with FHA insuring offices on market conditions, market absorption, and land values. The purpose is to determine a fair value for the land which is also an amount which FHA will recognize for mortgage insurance. Prospective redevelopers are thus informed of the amount before submitting an offer to buy or lease.

Subsequent to disposition of the land, URA involvement in actual redevelopment and new construction is held to the minimum necessary to assure achievement of the urban renewal objectives and to protect the Federal interests. URA concurs in the disposition contract between the local agency and the redeveloper which requires—

1. The use of the land for only the purposes permitted by the plan. The LPA is required to review and concur in construction plans before title to the land is conveyed.

2. The prompt carrying out of redevelopment, including assurances of the availability of adequate financing prior to conveyance of title.

3. Concurrence by the LPA in any substantial change of interest in the property by the buyer before construction is completed. This is to assure that the land is purchased for redevelopment rather than for speculation and resale.

Since November of 1962, when the President issued E.O. 11067 relating to Equal Opportunity in Housing, we have had an affirmative obligation in our disposition program, that there be no discrimination on the basis of race, color, creed, or national origin. It was limited in application to the sale, lease, rental or other disposition of residential property and related facilities.

With the enactment of the Civil Rights Act in July of 1964 and the promulgation of regulations pursuant to title VI, discrimination was prohibited under any program or activity receiving Federal financial assistance. The obligation to avoid discimination now extends to the disposition of all project land as well as to public facilities and the expenditures of educational institutions or hospitals for which the locality receives noncash local grant-in-aid credit.

Every redeveloper of urban renewal land now covenants for himself, his successors and assigns, that there will be no discrimination in the sale, lease, rental, use, or occupancy of the land or any improvements erected on the property. The covenant is contained in the deed, which also makes the United States a beneficiary of the covenant, entitled to enforce it. In the case of public facilities, hospitals and educational institutions, the obligation is made binding through a statement of assurances or a cooperation agreement with the providing entity.

Disposition for Low- and Middle-Income Housing

Under section 107(a) of title I, a special method is provided for the disposition of project land for low-rent public housing. Such land may be sold under a special definition of value based on the prices which would be paid for land for private rental housing having physical characteristics similar to the proposed low-rent housing. In addition, a special grant-in-aid credit is available to the project so that the locality does not make local contributions which would not be necessary if the public housing were built outside the renewal area.

From the beginning of the Federal urban renewal program in 1949 to December 31, 1964, about 27,000 units of federally assisted low-rent housing had been developed or were being developed within urban renewal areas. As of December 31, 1964, the plans for some 104 renewal projects in advanced planning or execution indicated an intent to dispose of land for low-rent housing under the favorable terms, permitted since 1959, of section 107(a).

The Housing Act of 1961 provided substantial additional incentives for the use of urban renewal land for moderate-income housing. Partly this was through the addition of section 107(b) which authorized a special disposition price for such land where the housing would be provided by a limited dividend or nonprofit organization. Partly this was through the authorization of FHA below-market interest loans under section 221(d)(3). As of March 31, 1965, 126 section 221(d)(3) housing projects had reached the FHA allocation stage in urban renewal projects. These will include over 17,000 dwelling units. As more experience is gained in the use and possibilities of these mechanisms, we can anticipate a substantial increase in the development of moderate-income housing in urban renewal projects.

I would like to cite a few interesting examples of moderate-income housing in urban renewal areas that are using the benefits of section 221(d)(3). The Communications Workers of America, Local 3808, is the sponsor of a 178-unit project in the East Nashville urban renewal area in Nashville, Tenn. Rents are $68.50 for two-bedroom units and $78.50 for three-bedroom apartments. In Atlanta, Ga., a total of 520 apartments are being built in the Butler Street urban renewal project with rentals at $75.50 monthly. A church nonprofit corporation is the sponsor. As a final illustration, a non-profit corporation in Greensboro, N.C., has sponsored an apartment development in the Cumberland urban renewal project. Rents for the apartments already built and underway range from $60 for one-bedroom units to $77.50 for three bedrooms.

The Urban Renewal Administration has recently encouraged and authorized local public agencies to prepare illustrative plans for moderate-income housing projects. These plans will provide a much better basis for attracting potential sponsors into the moderate-income housing field.

In pointing out that many redevelopment sites are being used for low- and moderate-cost housing, I do not want to minimize the role of rehabilitation. The rehabilitation and conservation of basically sound housing offers perhaps the greatest potential resource for expanding the supply of good middle-income housing—and low-income housing too.

Universities and Hospitals as Redevelopers

For the past several years there has been a remarkable growth in the interest and participation of universities in urban renewal. Part of this interest is an outgrowth of the great pressure on universities to expand their physical facilities to meet rising enrollments. During the past 30 years enrollments in colleges and universities have more than tripled, and are expected to double or triple again during the next 20 years. The task of preparing for this growth is overwhelming, and must fall largely upon existing institutions. But new facilities cannot be created unless there is land available, and most of our urban universities are landlocked. While they have been making major efforts to acquire land on the open market, this has proven very difficult. The universities have come to realize that urban renewal can assemble land needed for expansion, when the land is blighted. Accordingly they have become active redevelopers.

In addition to the need for expansion space, universities have begun to recognize a need to create a desirable neighborhood environment compatible with their functions. Many urban universities have found that they are surrounded by blight and deterioration which, in some cases, is detrimental to the safety of their students and faculty. Furthermore, these blighted areas do not provide decent residential areas for the faculties close to the universities.

The university interest in urban renewal is matched by that of municipal officials who understand the important role that universities play in the economic and cultural life of the community. The universities make a significant contribution to the local economy with their large payrolls and the substantial expenditures by their students. But even beyond these direct expenditures, the presence of a university and its technological and research resources serves as a major factor in attracting industry to the community.

The Congress recognized the importance of the university-municipality relationship and the role urban renewal could play in enhancing this relationship when it added section 112 to title I in the Housing Act of 1959. Section 112 offers two advantages to renewal projects which provide space for university expansion or create a more compatible environment for university functions: (1) such projects are exempt from the residential requirements of title I and (2) certain expenditures by the university in acquiring land near urban renewal projects may be credited toward the local share of carrying out the project.

In the Housing Act of 1961, the Congress recognized that urban hospitals have many of the same problems faced by colleges and universities; accordingly section 112 was extended to include hospitals.

Design and Redevelopment

The redevelopment taking place in urban renewal projects is setting the standards for our cities for many decades. If we fail to create a long-term satisfying urban environment, we will be derelict in our responsibility. Because of this we are strongly encouraging localities to make good urban design a basic renewal objective.

As one step in this direction, we have encouraged local agencies to employ the services of professional design specialists from the outset of project planning through the review of redevelopers' plans. We also have supported the inclusion of design objectives among the criteria to be considered in the disposition of project land, and we have been very much heartened by the success of design competitions used to select redevelopers. However, as much as we are concerned with good design, we have no intention of subordinating the equally vital concern of assuring that the land be sold at its fair value.

In the short span of 16 years urban renewal has become accepted as a major responsibility of government—Federal, State, and local. Hundreds of communities of all sizes have shown that renewal is a necessary and desirable means of eliminating blight, aiding those people afflicted by it, and rebuilding the physical, economic, and social vitality of urban areas on a scale consistent with the demands of a growing urban Nation. The record fully justifies the judgment of the Congress in creating the Federal program which provides the aid that these and other cities must have if they are to continue their efforts.

The program has done much to revitalize our urban areas and is increasingly emphasizing the human aspects of renewal. While much remains to be accomplished, I am confident of the outcome if we maintain the present momentum and aims of the program.

PART III

URBAN RENEWAL IN PRACTICE:

THREE CASES

7 Urban Renewal in Newark *

HAROLD KAPLAN

Newark was the first city in New Jersey and among the earliest in the nation to begin an urban renewal program.[1] Less than eighteen months intervened between the passage of the 1949 Housing Act and the announcement of Newark's first slum clearance project.[2] Many in the Housing Authority now cite this "jump" as an important contribution to their subsequent success. By submitting a concrete clearance proposal earlier than most other cities in the United

* Reprinted from *Urban Renewal Politics: Slum Clearance in Newark*, New York, Columbia University Press, 1963, pp. 10–38. Figures 1 and 2 have been eliminated from this edition.

[1] The following account relies heavily on personal interviews and Newark Housing Authority documents. NHA officials kindly permitted the author free access to their files. They also proved most generous with their time. It should not be concluded, however, that they agree with the final product.

The best written sources on NHA are its own documents: NHA Minutes; NHA-Redevel. Minutes; *From the Ground Up* (1958); *Redevelopment Sites in Downtown Newark* (1959); *Construction Report* (1956); *Rebuilding Newark* (1952); *Public Housing in Newark* (1944). In addition: *New Jersey Revised Statutes*, Cum. Supp., 55:14A-3, 4, 6; New Jersey Department of Conservation and Economic Development, Division of Planning and Development, *Directory of Local Housing Authorities and Redevelopment Agencies* (Trenton, N.J., 1959); New Jersey Legislature, *Report of the Legislative Middle Income Housing Study Commission* (Trenton, N.J., 1956).

[2] "*Getting the Jump*": NHA-Redevel. Minutes, April 12, June 14, Oct. 11, 1950; Newark *News*, Feb. 1, 4, April 27, 1950; City Commissioners' Minutes, July 27, Aug. 10, 24, Sept. 7, 21, 1949, Jan. 11, April 4, May 3, Nov. 8, 1950.

States, Newark was able to secure a prior claim to federal funds and to acquire a reputation for competence among federal officials.

Newark could move swiftly in the field of redevelopment because a large municipal organization, the Newark Housing Authority, led by an aggressive Executive Director, Louis Danzig, was poised to act immediately after passage of the 1949 Act. The Housing Authority of the City of Newark had been created in 1938 under the terms of the U.S. Housing Act of 1937 and the New Jersey Local Housing Authorities Act of 1938. Like housing authorities throughout the country, it was an independent public corporation responsible for the construction and management of low-rent housing projects. It was managed by a locally appointed board of six housing authority commissioners and was sustained by federal subsidy, the rent from its projects, and federally guaranteed housing authority bonds. By 1949 NHA was, with the exception of the Board of Education, the largest spender of funds and the largest dispenser of contracts in the city government.

Danzig and his staff had recognized the shortcomings of public housing for some time and had lobbied for legislation on urban redevelopment. Even before Congress and the New Jersey Legislature took final action in 1949, Danzig had his legal staff prepare an ordinance making NHA the city's official redevelopment agency. Immediately after passage of the federal and state legislation, Danzig submitted this ordinance to the city commissioners. The good relations that he had established with the commissioners during the public housing years facilitated rapid approval of the ordinance.

This quick start not only gave NHA the jump on most other cities; it also provided the Authority with a strategic edge over most local interests. These local groups failed to recognize the significance of the new program until several clearance projects were under way. By the time these groups were mobilized and prepared to make demands on the Authority, NHA had already established good working relations with the key federal and local officials.

Danzig did not wait for the federal Division of Slum Clearance and Urban Redevelopment to get organized before launching his own survey of potential sites. When federal officials indicated that funds for preliminary surveys would not be available until spring, 1950, Danzig went ahead with staff and funds borrowed from NHA's public housing accounts. Here, once again, Danzig could utilize the resources and organization that NHA had amassed in the 1940s to get a quick start on the new program.

It was during one of his frequent trips to Washington, and one of his frequent attempts to prod federal officials into faster action, that Danzig met Joseph Nevin. Nevin had been an initiator of public housing in New Jersey and had over twenty years of public housing experience behind him. He was recognized as one of the leading housing officials in the nation. Danzig did not succeed in getting federal officials to move faster on the new program, but he did persuade Nevin to leave the Public Housing Administration in order to serve as NHA's Director of Redevelopment. By the close of 1949 NHA had the jump in another sense. It had acquired and retained a staff of housing officials, lawyers, and administrators—a staff which combined experience in housing, sound political instincts, and a strong loyalty to the clearance program.

THE DECISION-MAKING PROCESS

Newark's urban redevelopment policies are products of the interaction of two elements: the goals of NHA's professional staff and the demands of certain nonlocal participants, like the Urban Renewal Administration, the Federal Housing Administration, and the private redevelopers.

NHA officials often say that their clearance decisions are made on the basis of "technical" rather than "political" criteria and that projects are planned in a "nonpolitical" environment. In one sense, those statements are true. NHA's clearance policies have not been the result of open conflict among local interest groups. Such conflict over slum clearance has been rare and has not affected the substance of NHA's decisions. NHA has provided the initiative for all clearance projects. The work of its expert staff has been shielded from random interference by local interests. Though the demands of such interests are often anticipated and taken into account by NHA's staff, decisions on projects are made in a low-temperature atmosphere and are often delegated to middle-rank staff men.

By a nonpolitical environment, Authority officials also mean that the cues of redevelopers and federal officials, rather than those of local interests, necessarily govern NHA's clearance decisions. Negotiations with nonlocal actors are conducted by Nevin and his immediate subordinates; dealing with local interests is deemed political, and this is handled by Danzig. Both are bargaining relations. Since the nonlocal participants largely determine the success or failure of local redevelopment, NHA's negotiations with them have a greater impact on the substance of clearance policy.

The initial goals of NHA's redevelopment officials were derived from their own experiences in public housing, from the values of the housing profession, and from the wording of the 1949 Act. These officials defined Newark's redevelopment problem as a lack of standard housing for middle-income families and an excess of substandard or slum housing. The purpose of the new program was to find the most dilapidated areas in the city, to clear them, and then to sell the areas to private redevelopers who would build moderately priced housing. NHA summed up its goals in one phrase: "Middle-income housing on cleared slum sites."

During Newark's first decade in urban redevelopment NHA discovered that these goals were only partially attainable within the Title I program as it was then defined. From 1949 to 1959 NHA had to learn which portions of its initial program were acceptable to private redevelopers, FHA, and URA, and which parts were not. This, briefly, was the course of redevelopment policy making during the first ten years.

NHA officials also learned that a rigid commitment to the initial goals and a refusal to accept half-victories would foreclose all clearance action. They eventually came to place greater emphasis on winning some kind of clearance than on obtaining clearance strictly in accordance with their initial purpose. As far as NHA officials were concerned, it had to be either pragmatism and flexibility in the planning of projects or no projects at all.

THE NORTH WARD: ADJUSTMENTS IN PURPOSE

In beginning the search for an initial redevelopment site, NHA was guided by its original definition of the program's purpose.[3] In the

[3] *The North Ward: Adjustments in Purpose:* NHA-Redevel. Minutes, Dec. 13, 1950, May 16, Sept. 19, Nov. 14, Dec. 12, 1951, Jan. 19, March 14, 1952; NHA Minutes, Jan. 7, 16, Feb. 7, Sept. 19, Nov. 14, 1951; NHA, Redevelopment Plan for the Branch Brook Park and Broad Street Redevelopment Projects (NJ UR 3–1, 3–2), approved Feb., 1953; other NHA publications cited in Note 1. See also: Newark *News*, Jan. 20, 1952; CC, The Practical Aspects of Middle Income Housing, 1959.

early part of 1950 Nevin and his staff identified the sixteen most blighted areas in the city, ranked these sixteen according to degree of blight, and assigned top priority to four of the worst areas. Discussions were then held among NHA's top men to determine which of the four sites should be selected for immediate action. During these discussions, however, Danzig and Nevin soon realized that an extrapolation of their experiences in public housing would not guarantee success in urban redevelopment. They realized that there were two new actors to contend with. The participation of FHA and the private redevelopers was not required in the earlier program; it was essential in urban redevelopment.

The key question about any redevelopment site was whether a private firm could make a profit on middle-income housing in that area. If the answer was negative, no redeveloper would buy the site, and no FHA official would agree to insure mortgages for construction there. In public housing NHA could afford to select sites according to the degree of blight present. In urban redevelopment the acceptability of a site to the two new participants had to take precedence in site selection, or NHA would later be stuck with unmarketable vacant land.

There seemed, in fact, to be an inverse correlation between the degree of blight in an area and its acceptability to FHA and the redevelopers. Middle-income housing probably wasn't feasible in the midst of a hard-core slum or a Negro ghetto. At least, FHA and most developers believed it was so, and that was the important thing. They argued that no market for middle-income housing existed in these areas and that few people could be induced to move there. Moreover, projects in the midst of slum areas, as public housing experience showed, tended to be rapidly inundated by the surrounding blight.

The ideal solution, from NHA's point of view, was to tear down the entire ghetto and build a "city within a city." But the federal Division of Slum Clearance would not finance such massive operations, and NHA didn't know where it could get the redevelopers to buy all that land. The more NHA officials pondered this problem, the more convinced they became that the Title I program contained an internal contradiction. Newark probably could not have the construction of middle-income housing in addition to the clearance of its worst slums until some changes were made in federal legislation or policies.

The result of this soul searching was a fresh start in site selection. In its second effort NHA sought areas that were in need of clearance but that also were acceptable to FHA and redevelopers. This subordination of slum clearance to site feasibility forced NHA to bypass the hard-core slums of the Central Ward and to select instead a site in the North Ward. This site was within the area marked for clearance by the Central Planning Board's Master Plan and, thus, was a defensible choice for NHA's initial effort in redevelopment. It was also on the outer edges of the slum belt and in better condition than most parts of the Central Ward. The North Ward site, in short, was not sufficiently blighted or interracial to repel redevelopers or FHA.

In setting the boundaries and format of this project, NHA sought to protect redevelopment from the encroachment of the surrounding slum areas. NHA's decision to draft an ambitious proposal covering about fifteen blocks and to think in terms of area redevelopment rather than a redevelopment project was motivated by its earlier experience with the "disappearance" of public housing projects. The locus and contours of this site were dictated by a search for natural boundaries (a railroad, a park, and a major thoroughfare) to contain the project as a community within itself and protect it from its immediate environment. NHA officials were so strongly committed to the clearance of a large area surrounded by natural boundaries that, when federal officials cut back the area slated for redevelopment, they refused either to reduce the size of the clearance area or to sacrifice one of the natural boundaries. Instead, they proposed to retain redevelopment along the outer boundaries of the site and to fill in the middle spaces with public housing. This, then, was the final format of NHA's first effort in urban redevelopment: a 1,550-unit public housing project bordered on both sides by privately redeveloped housing.

NHA officials knew they were acting cautiously, but they were very eager to make their first effort a success. They were prepared to gamble on redevelopment in a hard-core slum, but not on the first project. Indeed, no one at that time knew whether redevelopment was feasible on any site in Newark. Perhaps Newark's high wage rates, high taxes, and high costs of construction would prevent the building of true middle-income housing anywhere in the city. Perhaps there was no market for middle-income housing in Newark or its environs. NHA officials realized that, if the first project did not answer these questions in Newark's favor, there would be no second project. For this reason, they saw the North Ward as a pilot project which would demonstrate the viability of redevelopment in Newark to FHA and the redevelopers. For the same reason, they were taking no risks in site selection at this initial stage.

But NHA officials had not weakened their commitment to slum clearance. Despite the problems of site feasibility in the Central Ward, they knew that they could not continue to ignore that area. In 1952, after the announcement of the North Ward project, they began reconsidering sites in the Central Ward.

THE CENTRAL WARD: REDEVELOPMENT IN THE GHETTO

The expansion of the urban redevelopment concept by Congress in 1954 encouraged NHA to try redevelopment in the Negro ghetto.[4] Since early 1950 NHA officials had been convinced that no mere project, not even one as large as the North Ward project, would be safe from slum encroachment in the Central Ward. Only a full-scale demolition of the ghetto, or total neighborhood redevelopment, would succeed in that area. The 1954 Federal Housing Act renewed the slum clearance provisions of the 1949 Act and added a program of federal aid for local renewal activities other than clearance. This legislation permitted local agencies to designate an entire neighborhood as an Urban Renewal Area. Within this area the local agency would be empowered to conserve all sound structures, rehabilitate the sound but deteriorating structures, and clear the structures that were beyond saving. Under the terms of this Act NHA could launch a varied and comprehensive attack on the Central Ward.

NHA officials began with the hard core of Newark's slum belt, a section known at that time as the Third Ward. They then expanded their proposed renewal area, first to establish natural boundaries for the site in the form of major commercial thoroughfares, and then to include some fringe areas suitable for private redevelopment. The

[4] *The Central Ward: Redevelopment in the Ghetto:* NHA, Urban Renewal Plan: Old Third Ward Urban Renewal Project, tentative version, Jan., 1960; NHA publications cited in Note 1; NHA-Redevel. Minutes, April 13, June 1, 1955, Jan. 14, April 18, 1959, Jan. 13, 1960; Newark *News*, Dec. 19, 1954, March 13, 18, April 6, 10, 14, May 27, June 5, 19, 1955, Jan. 19, 27, 1956, Jan. 31, March 6, Aug. 16, 1957, Jan. 30, 1958.

Housing Authority's plan was to concentrate public housing construction in the Negro area, with private redevelopment in the less
dilapidated areas to the west. Tearing down the entire ghetto was
not feasible; area-wide renewal seemed to be the best alternative.

These plans were dashed when URA concluded that the 100-
block area was too large and eliminated forty blocks on the west.
NHA decided to proceed with the renewal of this sixty-block area
and made its formal announcement in April, 1955. Renewal would
begin with a public housing project, NHA said, to help relocate
those who would subsequently be displaced by clearance for redevelopment.

But URA had eliminated all those blocks suitable for private
redevelopment and had left NHA with nothing but public housing
sites. In addition, by cutting down the area and restricting the
amount of funds available for clearance in the reduced area, URA
made it impossible for the Authority to leave any major imprint on
the ghetto. Central Ward renewal, then, would amount to the clearance of a few sites in a hard-core slum, without any attempt to alter
the basic character of the slum.

NHA officials realized that home builders would not participate
in Central Ward redevelopment under these terms. The fear of
being left with vacant sites led NHA to reduce the area slated for
clearance even below the federal limit. The Authority's staff knew
that most buildings in the Central Ward should be torn down, not
dressed up. "The real question," as one official put it, "was what we
were going to do with all that cleared land."

Yet, NHA was dubious about the chances of private redevelopment even in this diminished clearance area. Eventually, Housing
Authority officials decided to build their own public housing projects on two of these cleared sites and to sell the rest to the City, the
Board of Education, and the Boys' Club of Newark. Redevelopment
by public or quasi-public institutions helped NHA avoid some of
the problems involved in attracting private builders to a Negro
ghetto, but it did not eliminate the problem of site feasibility. Such
institutions had their own special needs and usually did not want to
build on the sites NHA most desired to clear. For its own public
housing projects, however, NHA could select two of the most
blighted areas in the Central Ward.

NHA's inability to achieve either private redevelopment or "a city within a city" was demonstrated in the Central Ward Urban Renewal Plan, completed early in 1960. It revealed that thirty-two blocks in the renewal area would be either rehabilitated or left untouched. Fifteen blocks would be cleared for two public housing projects; ten for redevelopment by public institutions. Three blocks would be cleared for private redevelopment, including the construction of a new supermarket. Thus, of the sixty blocks in the renewal area, only two would be redeveloped for middle-income housing. This, moreover, was to come in the last stage of the project.

NHA officials view this plan as a major achievement, no less significant because it falls short of the Authority's initial goal. To them, it is something of a miracle that any Title I activity proved feasible in the Central Ward.

INDUSTRIAL REDEVELOPMENT: ALL RULES HAVE EXCEPTIONS

The initiation of light industrial redevelopment on Jeliffe Avenue was a departure from the way in which most clearance projects in Newark were begun.[5] Only here can one say without question that a local group significantly affected NHA's initial planning or that a project hinged on NHA's negotiations with a local interest.

In 1955 NHA drafted a proposal asking URA either to restore the forty blocks it had lopped off the Central Ward renewal area or to designate these forty blocks as another renewal area. At the same time NHA learned that a subcommittee of realtors from the Newark Economic Development Committee (NEDC) had selected four tentative sites for a privately financed industrial redevelopment project. One of the sites was a fifteen-block zone within the forty-block area NHA had resubmitted to URA. . . . Danzig was eager to involve local corporations in the redevelopment program. He was willing to accommodate them with concessions even on matters of substantive policy. He tried to convince NEDC members that they would be unable to clear the area without federal aid. He then offered to incorporate their plans for industrial redevelopment into his forty-block proposal.

[5] *Industrial Redevelopment: All Rules Have Exceptions:* NEDC Minutes, March 23, May 4, June 1, 29, Sept. 28, Oct. 19, Dec. 21, 1955, Feb. 8, March 14, April 11, Oct. 10, Nov. 14, Dec. 12, 1956, March 13, June 12, Sept. 11, 1957; Newark *News*, March 21, Sept. 20, 1956, Nov. 13, 14, 19, Dec. 19, 1957, July 8, 13, Aug. 24, 1958.

The businessmen were difficult to sell on Title I, but they finally agreed. Shortly afterwards URA officials cut back the area to twenty-five blocks, though retaining the entire industrial zone. Jeliffe Avenue, then, turned out to be more of an industrial redevelopment project than NHA had originally planned.

The extent of NHA's concessions, however, should not be overestimated. To begin with, the Authority had applied for this forty-block area before it began its campaign to sell Title I to NEDC. Secondly, since light industry was the only usage suitable to the Jeliffe Avenue area, NHA probably would have proceeded in that direction in any event. What NEDC apparently viewed as a concession was simply NHA's next logical step. Thirdly, local businessmen did not actively seek a role in planning this project; they were persuaded by NHA officials to become a part of the planning process. Finally, after the formal announcement in November, 1957, NHA's control of project planning on this site was absolute.

RUTGERS AND SETON HALL: REDEVELOPMENT
FOR INSTITUTIONAL USE

Housing Authority officials see themselves operating in a tightly confined box created by the terms of the 1949 Act, by the needs of private redevelopers, and by the policies of federal housing agencies.[6] One way out, as they learned in the North Ward, is to find a site where middle-income housing might prove possible. Another is to modify the Authority's emphasis on housing and to have institutions redevelop the land for their own use. Colleges building new facilities or corporations building new home offices need not worry about finding middle-income housing markets or making a profit. They presumably find enough benefit in central city location, moreover, to absorb the high costs of construction. NHA learned another lesson from the Central Ward project: that it is often more efficient to secure redevelopers first and then to negotiate the appropriate site with them.

In 1955 and 1956 NHA's program moved toward such redevelopment for institutional use. A major effort was made to have local

[6] *Rutgers and Seton Hall: Redevelopment for Institutional Use:* NHA-Redevel. Minutes, Oct. 8, 1958, April 8, July 8, Nov. 11, 1959; Newark *News,* Sept. 28, Oct. 9, 16, Nov. 16, 1958, Jan. 26, March 10, June 19, 23, July 2, 8, 9, 19, Sept. 28, 1959, Jan. 10, 1960.

corporations, colleges, labor unions, and hospitals consider building under Title I. A plan for the expansion of Rutgers University in Newark, under the 1949 Act, had been drafted by NHA's staff as early as 1950 but had been laid aside. For the reasons stated earlier, Danzig had preferred that NHA's first project demonstrate the viability of middle-income housing in Newark. Furthermore, the various branches of Rutgers had been unable to agree on a concerted effort, and Governor Alfred Driscoll had been opposed to any expansion of Rutgers at state expense.

In 1955 Danzig renewed the idea of a college expansion project and began an intensive selling campaign that went on for two years. Seldom have NHA officials worked harder to arrange a project.

First, Danzig brought the various branches of Rutgers University together and led them to agreement on a common expansion plan. He also worked through the New Jersey Association of Housing and Redevelopment Officials (NJAHRO) to sell the idea of a school construction bond issue to Governor Robert Meyner and the New Jersey Legislature. As NHA also persuaded the Newark Museum, the Newark Public Library, and the Newark College of Engineering to join in constructing new facilities on the site, the project gradually grew into a "cultural center." In September, 1958, the Authority announced the designation of a fifteen-block renewal area, just south of the North Ward project, for the expansion of local educational and cultural facilities.

Danzig also sought the participation of the local Catholic university, Seton Hall. A proposal for the construction of new educational and religious facilities under Title I had been broached much earlier to Seton Hall officials, but now NHA stepped up its efforts. Since all other local colleges were involved in Title I, it was both fair practice and good policy to include Newark's Catholic college. While Seton Hall was eventually drawn into the program for entirely different reasons, its inclusion probably served to neutralize the Catholic Church as a source of potential opposition to the college expansion project and to the state bond issue.

Seton Hall officials also had to be sold on the idea of Title I. After long negotiations they agreed to participate, but only if their project would be kept separate from the other college project. Thus, in April, 1959, NHA announced the clearance and rehabilitation of two blocks surrounding Seton Hall's downtown campus. It was to be a second college expansion project, one mile away from the proposed cultural center.

Redevelopment by public institutions may have helped NHA avoid some of the problems involved in redevelopment for middle-income housing, but it did not give NHA any greater flexibility in site selection. The colleges generally insisted on redeveloping areas adjacent to their present campuses. In order to protect its separate identity, Seton Hall insisted on a site removed from that of the other college project. None of the institutions was any more willing to redevelop sites in the hard-core slums than private home builders would have been. Once again, NHA found itself unable to select sites solely on the basis of the degree of blight, the presence of natural boundaries, or the absence of mixed land uses and other persistent blighting factors.

REAPPRAISAL AND DEPARTURE

Many of NHA's practical rules of thumb became definite policies in 1958.[7] During that year a crisis in the North Ward project led NHA officials to reappraise their entire program. In the course of this reappraisal NHA officials made explicit the lessons of their first eight years in redevelopment and systematized the day-by-day tactics they had been pursuing. They now see this new awareness and strategy as the key to their remarkable success in 1959.

By spring, 1956, NHA had not received any expressions of interest in the North Ward site from either local or nonlocal redevelopers. Authority officials realized that, unless they immediately started an intensive search for redevelopers, any attempt to dispose of the land by competitive bidding would be a fiasco. After an anxious and busy year Danzig and Nevin stimulated several respectable bids. In May, 1957, bids were received, and the land was sold.

The site lay vacant for six months, however, while NHA, the redeveloper, and FHA argued on the terms of mortgage insurance. In November the redeveloper announced that he could not come to

---

[7] *Reappraisal and Departure:* For the North Ward crisis see: NHA-Redevel. Minutes, May 16, Sept. 12, 1956, May 15, July 10, Oct. 16, 1957, Feb. 26, May 14, Oct. 31, 1958; Newark *News,* Nov. 16, 1958, Aug. 23, Oct. 11, 1959. The new strategy is described in: Louis Danzig, Housing and Urban Renewal Guides in the Development of Our City, June, 1959; Newark *News,* Oct. 5, 1959.

terms with FHA and that he was withdrawing from the project. The site lay vacant for another few months before NHA convinced the Metropolitan Corporation of America to assume responsibility for the project. In order to salvage the project and to meet FHA's requirements, NHA permitted this company to raise the rentals and to revise the redevelopment plan. The Metropolitan Corporation also wanted a guarantee that their redevelopment proposal would be accepted by NHA and that the competitive bidding procedure would be a formality.

NHA officials regard their difficulty in disposing of the North Ward site as the worst crisis of their redevelopment program. The lessons contained in the loss of one redeveloper and the securing of a second were not lost on them. They were determined not to begin another project without first having secured a redeveloper and tailoring the project to his needs. "We took an awful chance in the North Ward," one official said, "by guessing at what redevelopers wanted. Then we had to go around peddling vacant land. Now we let the redevelopers *tell* us where they want to build." What was the point of having the staff prepare a redevelopment plan, if the redevelopers later found it unworkable? The new rule was: "Find a redeveloper first, and then see what interests him."

NHA became convinced that the redevelopers want to negotiate agreements at the outset of a project and that they will shy away from cities trying to dispose of already cleared sites by competitive bidding. NHA also came to realize that the competitive bidding requirements need not be unduly constricting. Without prior arrangement, bids for a site are not forthcoming. The Authority found it necessary to make arrangements with a redeveloper, then advertise for bids, and, finally, sell the site to the only bidder.

The North Ward crisis and several other events also convinced the Authority's staff that local business corporations would never participate in redevelopment to the extent that NHA had originally expected. Despite years of campaigning, Danzig could not persuade even one local corporation to redevelop a site in Newark or to finance redevelopment by others. When local interests, like Rutgers and Seton Hall, agreed to participate, NHA discovered problems that were not present in its dealings with outside redevelopers. In dealing with Seton Hall, NHA was bargaining not merely with a redeveloper but with a religious institution. In dealing with Rutgers,

NHA found itself bargaining with the city's leading corporation executives who sat on the colleges' boards of trustees. In short, redevelopment by local interests increased both NHA's negotiating problems and its involvement in local politics. Apparently for these reasons, Danzig and Nevin decided to focus their attention on attracting nonlocal, nationally known home builders like Zeckendorf, Turner, and Parker.

If the important men in home building were to be drawn to Newark, NHA realized that it would have to make the lure attractive. In talking to redevelopers, Authority officials discovered that they had to make choice sites available and let the builders suggest the appropriate rentals. It is not surprising, then, that NHA's efforts led to projects involving high-priced apartments on sites immediately surrounding the central business district. Insistence on slum sites or moderate rents would have destroyed the venture before it began. NHA once again discovered that if the city's worst slums were to be cleared, it would have to be for public housing.

THE DOWNTOWN PROGRAM

NHA's new efforts were prefaced by a small, locally sponsored project.[8] After years of intensive effort by NHA, Jack Lehman, president of the United States Realty and Investment Company, agreed to sponsor a middle-income housing project. In so doing, however, he rejected all of NHA's site suggestions in order to build on South Broad Street, perhaps because United States Realty owned a good deal of property there. He cautiously insisted on a two-block project, moreover, even though NHA argued that projects of this size were not feasible. As one informant phrased it: "The Lehman proposal wasn't a project, it was part of a project." Other redevelopers would have to be drawn into that area to support United States Realty's plans. This project only heightened NHA's interest in attracting outside redevelopers.

The crisis in New York City's Title I program, which broke in spring, 1959, was a windfall for NHA's new venture. A number of prominent home builders, including Jack Parker of Long Island,

[8] *The Downtown Program:* NHA-Redevel. Minutes, April 8, May 21, June 10, July 8, Oct. 14, Nov. 11, 1959; Newark *News*, Dec. 23, 1958, Jan. 9, March 8, May 23, June 14, 24, July 2, 8, 9, 10, 19, Oct. 4, 8, 15, 16, Nov. 5, Dec. 12, 17, 20, 1959, Jan. 10, 14, 1960.

were told by Robert Moses, head of New York's clearance program, that there would be little clearance activity in New York for a while. Allegedly, Moses referred them to Newark for the interim. They quickly found that Danzig—like Moses—was both flexible and autonomous as a negotiator.

Parker, the first builder to be rerouted to Newark, insisted on the clearance of a massive area which would give him room enough to build luxury apartments over the next ten years. Parker and NHA officials negotiated for several months before agreeing on a vast 125-block site in the South Broad area. Parker was interested in some choice downtown sites and in some sound residential areas. NHA drew the boundary lines to include these, as well as certain hard-core slum areas. The final site was suitable to NHA because it bordered on the Central Ward project and might entice Parker into some further redevelopment in the ghetto. The site also bordered on, and served to buttress, the two-block Lehman project.

After reaching a detailed agreement with Parker, but prior to a formal announcement of their plans, NHA officials sounded out URA on this procedure. The Washington office could not publicly condone the selection of redevelopers before the selection of a site. The Philadelphia office, however, embarrassed by the large number of vacant sites in the region, gave NHA its informal blessing.

With the announcement of Parker's proposal NHA discovered that the nation's largest redevelopers tended to follow each other. As soon as NHA had captured one "big name," Newark became known among that small clique of home builders as a good place to build in. Now that the program had caught on and Newark was "hot," NHA's long months of pressure on these redevelopers began to pay dividends. Within a few months of the Parker project NHA was ready to announce two more ambitious proposals.

The Penn Plaza proposal involved the clearance of fifteen blocks in a run-down commercial area near Pennsylvania Station for the construction of luxury apartments, stores, and office buildings. Since plans to clear "Skid Row" had been circulating for at least fifteen years, the site and boundaries of this project were set largely by tradition. Oscar Stonorov, an architect hired by the City to supervise a study of the central business district, helped NHA persuade the Gilbane Construction Company of Providence, Rhode Island, to undertake redevelopment in this area.

The Essex Heights proposal, announced in December, 1959, was the result of a long campaign by NHA to bring the Turner Construction Company to Newark. Prolonged negotiations had yielded agreement on a twenty-five-block site straddling a good part of the downtown area but also extending west into the hard-core slum. By adding some slum areas to a downtown redevelopment project, NHA had once again encouraged home builders to risk limited activity in the ghetto.

By January, 1960, the total number of renewal projects in Newark for which federal commitments had been received involved clearance or rehabilitation of well over 300 blocks. Over $700 million in local and federal funds was required for the completion of these projects. Although URA committed funds for the completion of all NHA projects then current, it insisted that such funds be spread out over a ten-year period. In January, 1960, URA gave NHA $26 million in a lump sum as the first annual installment of this plan.

Although Housing Authority officials realize that the downtown projects will be the focus of their attention for the next decade, they have not shut the door on negotiations for additional projects. NHA has conceded that the local demand for new housing will be met by these downtown proposals, but it has continued to consider new proposals for nonresidential redevelopment or for redevelopment by public institutions. Early in 1960 it seemed likely that NHA's next proposal would be an expansion in medical facilities by the United Hospital Foundation of Newark. Preliminary discussions were also being held on a light industrial project to be sponsored by William Zeckendorf and on a central office building for local organized labor. All three projects would be in the downtown area.

THE MEANING OF SUCCESS

High quantitative achievements in project building have been attained through a highly flexible application of NHA's initial values. Thus, the Authority has not always been able to obtain the construction of moderately priced apartments or to clear as much of the hard-core slums as they would like. Some local observers who say that NHA has been overly accommodating to the redevelopers would quarrel with a characterization of the program as successful.

It also is said that no one really knows whether the current middle-income housing projects will ultimately prove successful for the redevelopers.

The term "success" is used to indicate effective action or project building within the limits of the present Title I program. Most of the modifications in purpose that NHA has made are prerequisites to achievement, given the current status of federal legislation, re-developer demands, and URA and FHA policies. Success is also defined in relation to the limitations set by the locale. Many of NHA's actions have been dictated by the problems of attaining middle-income housing in a city like Newark. Within these limitations NHA has managed to tear down a great deal of substandard housing and to initiate a great deal of new construction. Few agencies in a similar situation could have done more.

One may quarrel with this interpretation of the program and still concede that NHA as an agency has been successful. NHA has been less interested in executing particular redevelopment policies than in taking significant steps to reverse Newark's decline. In 1949 NHA officials set out to improve the local housing situation and to achieve whatever redevelopment action was possible under the circumstances. Those goals have, for the most part, been attained.

STAGING A PROJECT

The nonpolitical context of NHA's decision making does not insure that agency officials can afford to be oblivious to the problem of securing local acceptance.[9] The Authority's staff, in fact, has developed a conscious strategy for facilitating such acceptance, at the same time protecting its flexibility in dealing with outside parties. This strategy centers around the staging of projects or the sequential order of negotiations. To an extent, the procedures described below have been forced upon NHA by the exigencies of dealing with redevelopers and federal officials. But NHA officials are fully aware of the strategic uses of this procedure.

The keys to NHA's staging process are the elaborate, preliminary

---

[9] *Staging a Project:* Since the statements in this and the following subsections are the author's own synthesis of personal interviews and of a large body of written data, the sources of these statements cannot be precisely pinpointed. The generalizations are, to a large extent, documented and illustrated throughout the remainder of the study.

negotiations involving NHA, redevelopers, and federal officials, and the low visibility of this preparatory stage. The result of these informal, unpublicized negotiations is a detailed project package. The necessary political support for this package is negotiated in advance in order to avoid public defeats or open skirmishes. Local officials generally must accept the package as is or risk jeopardizing the entire proposal.

NHA's first step in its recent projects has been to find a redeveloper interested in Newark. It is self-evident to NHA officials that decisions on sites and their uses must be adapted to the demands of the investor if projects are to be successful. Such demands, moreover, can best be met if NHA remains the City's sole spokesman in these dealings. No one outside NHA has direct dealings with the redevelopers. Most local participants first learn of a new clearance project when they read the formal announcement by NHA in the newspapers.

It also is self-evident to Authority officials that the formative stages of a project must be protected from excessive public interference. The redevelopers themselves demand secrecy so that they can either back out gracefully or make a dramatic announcement of their plans. In addition, NHA officials feel that the announcement of tentative or alternative plans serves to excite opposition in several neighborhoods, whereas only one area will eventually be cleared. Such a preliminary announcement also gives various local interests the idea that the situation is still fluid and, hence, still amenable to their influence. NHA seldom makes a public announcement until it knows exactly what the project is to be.

NHA's next step, after finding a redeveloper, is to begin discussions with URA in order to secure federal planning funds and a capital grant reservation. Some indication of FHA's willingness to insure a mortgage on the site is also sought. For as long as a year the Director of Redevelopment will shuttle back and forth between the Philadelphia office of URA, the New York office of FHA, and the redeveloper's staff, in search of a plan agreeable to all. From NHA's point of view this is the most crucial stage of a project; it also is the most difficult hurdle to overcome. Once a plan suitable to all interests has been found, the acquiescence of local officials is assured. As one Authority official put it: "There's no point in even talking about a project with the people down at City Hall until Philadelphia

[URA] gives the go-ahead." To NHA officials the amazing thing is not that the City backs them fully, but that they ever get URA, FHA, and the redeveloper to agree.

This procedure also has its strategic value. Federal approval of a project makes subsequent local approval extremely likely. If City officials were to try to amend the project, they would disrupt the balanced network of negotiations and probably stop the flow of capital into Newark. When NHA proposals are submitted on the eve of a federal deadline, as they often must be, the pressure on City officials to approve without amendment or delay is even greater.

NHA officials have had good working relations with URA's Philadelphia office from the beginning. The Regional Office has occasionally intervened in local disputes to support NHA's position. When other renewal groups or agencies have tried to deal with URA, they have found that only Danzig and Nevin have good access to the Regional Office. This access has also permitted NHA officials to become the interpreters of federal housing legislation and policies for all others in Newark.

SECURING CITY HALL SUPPORT

NHA's next and final step before a formal announcement is to clear the project with the mayor or, before 1954, with the majority bloc of city commissioners. Even at this early stage the mayor is under pressure to ratify NHA's arrangements with Philadelphia and the redevelopers. If there were any serious political objections to the project, NHA presumably would take them into account. Exactly how far NHA would go in accommodating the mayor is a moot point, for neither Ralph Villani, Mayor from 1949 to 1953, nor Leo Carlin, Mayor after 1953, ever raised any major objections.

The support of municipal agencies involved in public construction related to slum clearance is often as important as the support of the mayor. Any clearance project, but particularly area-wide renewal, requires the widening and repaving of streets, the construction of schools, the relocation of sewers and underground utilities, and other supportive actions by local agencies. To avoid embarrassment after the formal announcement of a project, NHA attempts to extract beforehand a tentative promise of cooperation from the appropriate agencies. Since renewal projects are more palatable to local officials if a large part of the City's one-third share can be defrayed by local construction, NHA has had added incentive for involving public works agencies in its projects.

These agencies have their own good reasons for negotiating with NHA. Most of them find that they can increase their share of the municipal budget and facilitate approval of their projects by linking their activities to an expanding, federally aided program. The Superintendent of Schools, for example, backed NHA's first two projects with public school construction. With URA paying part of the cost of these new schools, approval by the Board of Education was virtually assured, even if it meant slightly increasing the capital budget for those years. This coordination of programs has served, though unintentionally, to weaken whatever control City Hall has over NHA through the City's one-third contribution. The major part of that contribution has been imbedded in the Board of Education's capital budget, where it is less available to manipulation by the mayor or the City Council.

The problem that confronts NHA is how to gain the support of relevant agencies without exposing the project to wholesale intervention by City Hall. How can certain agencies be lined up in advance without accumulating additions or amendments that eventually would make the project unworkable? If the project is ever to get started, the line of participation must be drawn somewhere.

NHA has responded to this problem by distinguishing between those agencies which must be consulted in advance and those agencies whose concurrence usually can be counted upon once the formal announcement has been made. Construction agencies generally fall into the first category; service and regulatory agencies into the second. In the pre-announcement consultations, moreover, NHA tries to extract a pledge of cooperation by outlining the probable effect of the project on the agency concerned and indicating the supportive action required from the agency. Although all questions of the agency will be answered by NHA, the project plans are not made available for general inspection. To minimize potential political interference, NHA's staff members also try, wherever possible, to deal with the corresponding staff official in the agency, not with the top man. Thus, Nevin deals exclusively with the Superintendent of Schools, Edward Kennelly, and lets Kennelly make all presentations to the Board of Education.

The successful nature of these operations was demonstrated in March, 1953, when relevant agency heads were brought together to testify on the proposed redevelopment plan for the North Ward. Commissioner Leo Carlin, who probably expected this meeting to point up NHA's lack of communication with City Hall, found that most of his subordinates in the Department of Public Works already had discussed the project with Nevin and had pledged their support. The agencies indicated that they had been briefed on their role, but they revealed no extensive familiarity with the details of the plan. The agency heads who had not been briefed proved unwilling to stand in the way of the project.

Later, Carlin, as mayor, altered his former position and encouraged negotiations between Nevin and the administrative agencies. Only in those rare cases when NHA and an agency are deadlocked do the negotiations rise to the mayor's office and become visible to the newspaper-reading public. The 1954 City Charter's attempt to centralize authority at City Hall apparently did nothing to disrupt NHA's relations with the administrative agencies. In April, 1955, a meeting of agency heads to discuss the Central Ward project showed the same pattern of support for NHA that had emerged in the 1953 meeting.

THE FORMAL ANNOUNCEMENT

About two years generally intervene between the initial selection of a site and the formal announcement of a project. The proposal is not publicized during this time, in part to protect NHA's negotiations with URA, redevelopers, and City Hall, and in part to secure a maximum impact for the formal announcement. By agreement with the local reporters covering urban renewal, a few discreet hints about a project may be periodically released, but the major announcement is saved for a big spread in the Sunday editions.

Outside of its attempt to stage the announcement of a project, however, NHA does not devote any substantial resources to publicity or public relations. Authority officials have said that too much publicity often stimulates organized interests that otherwise would have remained inert. The public relations staff of the business bloc developed an over-all rationale of the renewal program, which NHA officials have been inclined to let stand. Outside of this,

NHA's sole public relations efforts have centered on maintaining good relations with the press.

The Newark *News* has been a major spokesman for the conservative, reform-minded civic leaders and a leading supporter of charter revision, the Carlin administration, and slum clearance. Because of this concern with good government, critics of NHA generally receive short shrift in the editorials of the *News*. In addition, neither the *News* nor Newark's other important daily, the *Star Ledger*, gives significant attention to NHA's negotiations with local parties. These dailies, like many other newspapers, define "news" as dramatic action or conflict. Since overt conflict among the renewal participants is infrequent, press treatment of local renewal is limited largely to formal announcements by NHA.

Reporters covering local renewal often are baffled by the technical questions involved. By seeking clarification of these questions from Authority officials, the reporters help reinforce NHA's position as interpreter of federal policies. Through this symbiotic relationship, moreover, NHA has inadvertently gained considerable influence over the treatment of its activities by the local press. It has had no reason to fear newspaper attacks or attempted exposés.

THE ACCUMULATION OF COMMITMENTS

After the Authority announces a project and the mayor approves an application to URA for survey and planning funds, the pressure on the City Council to add its assent is overwhelming. By this time, to quote one informant, the project is "frozen." The councilmen must consider the proposal on a "take it or leave it" basis; rarely have they seriously considered "leaving" a proposal approved by NHA and the mayor.

As the project progresses and the amount of funds and energy expended by NHA, URA, the redevelopers, and City Hall agencies accumulates, the commitment of these participants to the project increases proportionately. NHA may begin a project despite some major problem or disagreement among the participants, confident that the accumulation of commitments will eventually lead to an agreement or solution.

Such an accumulation of commitments also makes effective intervention by local interests increasingly difficult. The City Council must eventually approve an urban renewal plan and a relocation plan, and the Central Planning Board (CPB) must declare the entire area blighted, but such action normally has been routine. As members of the Council and CPB have said, effective local review of clearance proposals can occur only at the very outset of a proposal.

At the later stages NHA follows the same procedure used in launching a proposal. The urban renewal plan, for example, is discussed with the redevelopers, then with URA and FHA, and finally with the administrative agencies at City Hall. After further discussion with the mayor it is presented to the City Council and CPB. At this point the time, energy, and money already expended preclude serious local review.

MAINTAINING THE PACE

In the post-announcement stage NHA, the redeveloper, and URA continue to negotiate in order to determine what specific uses are appropriate to the site.[10] In this way it is not basically different from the pre-announcement stage, although the bargaining becomes more and more specific. The initial plan of a project or the public image presented in the formal announcement may have to be altered substantially as new problems emerge and the demands of participants change. A rigid commitment by NHA officials to the initial plan would strain, if not break, the commitment of other parties to the project. From NHA's point of view the major problem of the post-announcment stage is not to execute the initial plan without alteration but to keep the commitments of outside parties "warm."

One way to maintain such commitments is to maintain a rapid pace throughout the project. Redevelopers and federal officials quickly lose interest in projects that drag on interminably. For this reason, prolonged consideration by the City Council or CPB can prove highly damaging. For the same reason, NHA will hasten to break deadlocks in negotiations, even if it means a further departure from the initial plan.

[10] *Maintaining the Pace:* For the pyramiding of resources see Robert A. Dahl, *Who Governs? Democracy and Power in an American City* (New Haven, Yale University Press, 1961), Chapter 19; for the strategy of activism as practiced by independent authorities see Wallace S. Sayre and Herbert Kaufman, *Governing New York City: Politics in the Metropolis* (New York, Russell Sage Foundation, 1960), pp. 337–43.

In October, 1959, when URA told Authority officials that funds for the downtown program would have to be spread over a ten-year period, Danzig and Nevin devised a plan to proceed simultaneously with all projects. Rather than handle each project serially and risk losing some redevelopers who were awaiting their turn, NHA divided the larger projects into stages and sought immediate action on the first stage of all projects. In this way all of the commitments to all of the projects were maintained.

This emphasis on rapid and sustained activity applies not only to particular projects but to the entire program. Since the early 1940s NHA officials have emphasized the importance of keeping active and of always having a few proposals under consideration. Activism draws redevelopers to the city, impresses federal officials, stimulates the morale of the agency's staff, and gives the agency an edge in its negotiations with local interests. In the world of urban renewal, project building seems to yield more project building, and clearance activity seems to acquire a momentum of its own. After a certain point successful agencies can do nothing wrong. They are rarely involved in political skirmishes because they are rarely challenged.

There also seems to be a cycle of failure. Inactivity, a loss of status among redevelopers and federal officials, and increasing vulnerability to local political interference seem to reinforce each other. As some NHA officials see it: "a program either catches fire or it doesn't."

One further comment about NHA's strategies should be made. It may be said that the Authority's rules of thumb provide no help in securing local approval of a ten-year redevelopment plan or a long-range scheme of interrelated projects. In fact, NHA's emphasis on gaining approval of the particular project at hand and on avoiding general policy statements is deliberate. NHA believes that ten-year redevelopment plans are impractical, cannot be realized, and only serve to impede the Authority's negotiations with outside parties. It is also convinced that the difficulty experienced in securing local approval of a proposal increases in direct proportion to the all-encompassing character of that proposal. Agencies should not submit a proposal until they know exactly what they want. Proposals should be worded in the most specific terms possible, and more general questions on "where the program is going" should be avoided. Publicizing long-range policy statements or seeking local approval of a ten-year plan is unnecessary to renewal achievement. More than that, it invites disaster.

THE "CLEAN DEAL"

Ask most Housing Authority officials to explain the success of their redevelopment program, and they will reply that private redevelopers and federal officials know they can get a "clean deal" in Newark. When taking part in a slum clearance project in Newark, these outside participants do not have to make separate arrangements with a variety of local officials, yielding concessions at each step in the negotiations and often getting embroiled in local politics. Instead they conduct all their business with a few men in the Housing Authority. These men have the freedom from local interference to bargain flexibly and are sufficiently confident of their control of local renewal processes to make broad commitments. Having once reached a settlement with Danzig, private redevelopers need not concern themselves with having to amend the agreement or with making political payoffs in order to facilitate its local acceptance. The officials of URA, moreover, need not worry that the project will become a local political football once federal funds have been committed. NHA not only has the autonomy to deal freely with these participants, it also has the capacity to deliver on all its promises in record time.

One observer may have exaggerated NHA's importance, but not by very much, when he said: "They [NHA] own the slums. They can sell any piece of real estate in that area to a redeveloper before it's even acquired. And they don't have to check with anyone [in Newark] before they do it. City Hall has got to back them up." This is another way of saying that the Authority has attained its major goals: a free hand to deal with outside participants and a guarantee of unqualified local acceptance of the resulting clearance proposal. To NHA officials a local redevelopment program stands or falls on whether it attracts the necessary outside commitments. A redevelopment agency that has transformed local renewal processes into a routine operation will have little difficulty in attracting these commitments.

This, in summary, is the pattern of policy formation in Newark's urban redevelopment program. The pattern depends upon the existence of a stable and permissive local environment where organized responses to the agency's decisions can be predicted—and often discounted—in advance. NHA's aggressive procedures would probably backfire if used in a less firmly structured political situation.

At the same time, it would be unwise to overemphasize environmental factors and to underestimate the importance of NHA's personnel and their strategies. The formal organization of urban renewal in all cities tends to be more or less dispersive. Before a project can be launched, a large number of independent actors must be persuaded to participate. Some person or agency must bring all the parties together, negotiate support for the project, and quiet or mediate opposition. Someone must build an organization to provide the dispersed renewal structure with an informal peak. An acquiescent local environment may make the job of the renewal entrepreneur easier, but an acquiescent environment alone is insufficient. There must also exist in the same person or agency both the awareness of the need for this entrepreneurial function and the political skill to carry it out.

In Newark NHA's top staff have the necessary entrepreneurial abilities. In this group (Louis Danzig, Joseph Nevin, Samuel Warrence, Augustine Kelly, and Joseph Reilly) are combined the skills of the housing official, the administrator, the lawyer, and the politician. These men share a strong loyalty to the program and to Newark, a willingness to put in long hours, and an instinctive feeling for the politics of administration. It is true that their task as renewal entrepreneurs has been facilitated by the permissiveness of the local political environment, but it is also true that they had the insight to recognize this permissiveness and to adopt procedures to exploit it. They also had a hand in shaping that environment. . . . NHA's responses to the political environment and its efforts to shape that environment are basic concomitants of Newark's success in urban renewal. One member of the business bloc grudgingly admitted: "Without Lou Danzig and Joe Nevin, there'd be nothing in the city—no clearance, no Jack Parker, no Turner-Galbreath—nothing—just a lot of talk and plans."

8   Urban Renewal in Boston *

WALTER McQUADE

The stately hallways of Boston's City Hall and its annex are painted two shades of the oily eye-ease green associated with run-down optometrists' shops; the wood trim is chocolate brown. The paint is chipped, the floors cracked. There are bare electric bulbs. The old building, put up by Boston Brahmins in the elegant Empire style about the time of the Civil War, has been dingily treated by newer tenants, Boston Irish politicians.

But enter the elevator and rise ten floors in City Hall Annex, and suddenly the wall colors change to such vivid tones as mustard. Office doors are painted in bright primaries; lowered ceilings accommodate new lighting fixtures and acoustical surfaces, and even the grin of air-conditioning grilles. The general atmosphere, however, is not cool in any season. People walk swiftly in the halls. For jammed into the top two floors of City Hall Annex is the main office of the Boston Redevelopment Authority, a zealous young multitude of no fewer than 480 city planners and promoters of city plans who have been brought in to push a massive urban-renewal effort in Boston, of all places.

Urban renewal is an issue in most of America's cities; the nation

* Reprinted from *Fortune* Magazine (June 1964), where it appeared under the title "Boston: What Can a Sick City Do?" by special permission. Copyright © 1964 by Time Inc.

has been working at it for fifteen years with little more than mediocre success. But in Boston big things have begun that may well hold important lessons for businessmen in the rest of the U.S. who are concerned about their environments. Boston is being turned into a laboratory demonstration of renewal techniques, which are being applied to its waterfront, to its central business district, and to eight of the city's ancient neighborhoods. All told, this effort may affect 25 percent of Boston's area and 50 percent of its population.

In making these big plans Boston has shrewdly tapped Washington's deep money well. So far some $120 million of federal funds have been committed to the Boston experiment, with $33 million more pending in Washington. But the animating idea for Boston's redevelopment came out of the city itself, which is really two cities in one. The first is the Boston of a cultivated Yankee minority symbolized by such elders as banker Ralph Lowell, seventy-three, trustee Henry L. Shattuck, eighty-four, and Charles A. Coolidge, sixty-nine, of the venerable law firm, Ropes & Gray. The other Boston lies on the far side of a deep, cold sea of historic hatred and is Irish Boston, which is today led by a forceful mayor named John F. Collins.

Collins, at forty-four, is a big man, who surprised everybody but himself by getting elected mayor in 1959. He exudes the carefree, sunny charm of a curly-headed parochial choir boy grown slightly older. He is all warmth and innocence, however, only until you get closer, within range of his Univac mind. Part of the story behind Boston's renewal effort is that Coolidge, Lowell, Shattuck, and their influential friends did come within range and willingly have stayed there, galvanized by the wild hope, the flickering faith, that, after a half century of sliding, they may have found an effective leader.

Collins is an unusually solvent politician. He owes almost nothing to anyone, the Kennedys, the McCormacks, or even Richard Cardinal Cushing. Guarding this independence is his quality of keeping most people at arm's length. His brusque decisiveness does not encourage lengthy exchanges, political palship. Crippled by polio nine years ago, he uses his wheelchair as a cordial but commanding excuse to avoid the nightly round of routine political appearances that has riddled some mayors' stomachs and rattled their governing resolve. Instead, Collins stays home evenings and rolls himself down a ramp into his garage, converted into an office. Says he: "I was cast perfectly for this job. I'm not the kind of man who goes out chasing parties at night, and I don't sleep much, so I work. A mayor, if he chooses to, can sit behind his desk an hour and a half a day, total, dealing only with emergencies as they come up. We've had that type on occasion. But that's old-fashioned."

A BOSTON BALANCE SHEET

Boston, however, was intensely old-fashioned, if not outworn, when he took over. If the new mayor had drawn a balance sheet for Boston in early 1960, the list of debits would have been long. Perhaps the most obvious minus was Boston's waterfront, the original manufacturer of so many of its fortunes in the rum trade, silk trade, tea trade, and the export of ice to the tropics. It was dead. Business had moved out; the big ships were no longer putting in. Boston was now considered an edge of a market, not a center; goods came in by truck from the ports of New York and Baltimore. A few people had moved into the old granite waterfront warehouses and made magnificent apartments out of them, but the owners of the historic old India Wharf were planning to rip its superstructure down and turn the pier into a parking lot, to the anguish of architectural antiquarians.

Also facing the new mayor in 1960 was the fact that the central retail district of Boston looked to be on its last legs. Ancient in its buildings, in its growth lagging sadly behind the suburbs, downtown boasted only two notably smug department stores. These were the massive Jordan Marsh, biggest store in New England, and Filene's seven stories of medium high-style merchandise poised aloof over a grabbingly successful bargain basement, rumored to do nearly half of Filene's downtown gross. In ten years 14,000 downtown jobs had disappeared, and $78 million of taxable assessments had evaporated just in the central business district.

Meanwhile most of the city's residential neighborhoods had gone downhill and have remained sharply stratified in Irish and Italian enclaves. One reason: the median family income in Boston is the lowest of the seven major U.S. metropolitan areas. Population of the city was headed down, business activity was, too; since the 1930's, $500 million of Boston's business had fled beyond the tight borders of the city, followed in the 1940's and 1950's by a tenth of the prewar population. Today the Boston region has a population exceeding two million, but the city itself has shrunk to fewer than 700,000. The suburbs are both close and rampantly independent; Boston is hemmed in by a Balkanized set of seventy-eight uncooperative municipalities.

Leaders of the exodus were most of the old Boston families and prominent business proprietors of the city, who simply withdrew from civic responsibility, leaving dear Boston to the devices of the Boston Irish politicians and their Italian immigrant allies. The anciently rich and their trustees stored their stocks and bonds in safe deposit in Providence. Nothing appeared possible; little seemed imperative. The Boston Symphony was still supreme; the public gardens beautiful; none of the swan boats in the park were sinking; the Ritz continued to serve just about the best martinis in the world. But the city continued to languish.

A TOP IN TAXATION

The specific infection for all this decay was Boston's traditionally obscene politics and staggering real-estate tax, far and away the highest of any major city in the U.S.—$101.20 per $1,000 of assessed valuation in 1959, more than twice as high as in New York or Chicago. The tax rate had poisoned the well for real-estate investors, keeping the postwar U.S. building boom at bay. Commercial valuations in Boston also were very high, frequently above market value. In the 1950's building investments in this city appeared so perilous that no big insurance company, even Boston's own, would pick up more than token mortgages. In this matter an ominous example existed in the Back Bay area.

Shortly after World War II, John Hancock Mutual Life Insurance Co. decided to put up the first major postwar office building in Boston, a tower connected to a property it already owned. The building, which was constructed largely during the last mayoralty reign of James Michael Curley, the man with the golden voice and brass touch, was undertaken with the expectation that it would result in a realistic assessment. But when it was finished, the assessment of the old building plus new wing had been upped from $6,500,000 to a total of $24 million. Hancock went to court and has since been partially unburdened—the appraisal is back to $21,900,-000. But the tax load on that office building is still almost $2 per square foot per year. In Curley's time the knocking down of assessments, or granting of abatements, flourished—infamously and secretively. In his last year in office in 1949, abatements ran to $10,247,765, or 11.6 percent of the total tax levy that year. But nobody knew who got abatements or precisely why, although there was much speculation on the subject. Another characteristic was that the abatements were almost never permanent, but had to be argued, or otherwise arranged, year after year. Until 1952 the Boston abatement records were kept in City Hall, reportedly in pencil.

Mayor John Hynes, Curley's successor, had made a hopeful beginning in the 1950's to getting some building going in Boston with a plan to replace the infamous old Scollay Square with a group of city, state, and federal office buildings, but in 1960 this was still a paper plan. Also on paper was proposed legislation to encourage Prudential Insurance Co. of America to build a towering office building *cum* hotel *cum* apartment houses on the site of the old Boston & Maine track yard in the Back Bay section. Instead of assessing the Pru development and taxing it in the crippling conventional manner, the proposal was to cut the city in for 20 percent of the gross rental income with a guarantee from Pru of $3 million a year. Influential people such as Coolidge and powerful ones such as Cardinal Cushing were strongly behind it, although some of the local bankers and businessmen were quietly bucking this concession to an out-of-town enterprise.

END OF THE WEST END

But the large essay of the Hynes administration into actual renewal had been a disaster. The West End, an entire neighborhood, thirty-eight blocks, forty-one acres, and 9,000 residents in the middle of the city, was wiped out—a low-rent, low-rise Italian tenement section. With federal help, the land was condemned and bought for $7.40 per square foot, revalued at $1.40 per square foot, and leased for a yearly rental approximating 6 percent of the lower value to a syndicate headed by a political supporter of the Mayor. The area was ruthlessly cleared to make way for a cluster of high-rise, high-rent apartment houses, a banal grouping of blunt, balconied towers on a treeless plain—and a bitter warning to all of the timeworn Boston neighborhoods of what renewal might mean to them, too. Skirting this area was another of the typical urban scars of the 1950's in America, the John F. Fitzgerald Expressway, an eight-lane strand of concrete slashed through the ancient fabric of the city like a trail of lava on legs. This state-built road was the most expensive in the U.S., costing more than $28,940,000 per mile.

There were some entries on the plus side of Collins' ledger—but even some of these were smudged. Boston had a widespread rapid-transit system, the first subway built in the U.S. (One of the kiosks was even declared a national historic landmark last year.) But the mass-transit system carried fewer passengers in 1960 than sixty years earlier. What it lacked was links with the new suburbs, which fought them off in fear rather than taking the risk of sharing in the transit deficit, which in 1960 was $22,500,000. Boston's interior network of new roads was also, in theory, one of the nation's most extensive, but it also lacked links, because the state legislature—regarded by proper Bostonians as a malicious group of scoundrels—had given the many municipalities that crowd in around Boston the right to refuse passage to roads. Boston's commuter railroads were plainly, if slowly, perishing, although here something might be salvaged. The Massachusetts Turnpike Authority had been able to pick up one ready-made route right into the Back Bay on the old Boston & Maine roadbed, and there were other railroad rights-of-way in virtually perfect locations for expanding the mass-transit system. But in Boston a mayor can only hope and argue for such events. The roads, as well as the rapid transit and numerous other normal city prerogatives, are run by the state legislature. And who dominated the state legislature? It was the man Collins had demolished in the mayoralty race two months earlier, Senator John E. Powers of South Boston, who is not known as a quick forgiver.

Thus Collins started with the odds against him, and little wonder that even the hopeful thought he would quickly run out of steam. Instead, he moved rapidly to swing important elements in the situation to his side. In Boston there is no Richard Mellon to help get things going as in the case of Pittsburgh. But in 1959 some of the leaders of the city had formed what they called a coordinating committee, sixteen men who met monthly in the boardroom of

Ralph Lowell's bank. Most of the members of this agony society had backed Collins' opponent in the 1959 mayoralty race (explaining today, with exquisite Puritan honesty, that they simply had thought Powers was going to win)—a fact well known to Collins when he took office. But shortly after election day Collins challenged this committee to help him, and, startled by his lack of rancor, Boston's Brahmins began working with a will, bringing in consultants to assist in reorganizing the city's tax-assessing office, the building department, and the city's personnel practices. The committee men also paid the consultants' fees.

AN IRISH LA GUARDIA

More important, Collins quickly got to the question of how Boston could tap more federal funds, which since the Housing Act of 1949 have been made available to help renew run-down cities. Here he needed expert advice and shortly picked Edward J. Logue, who, next to Collins himself, deserves credit for putting Boston's present ambitious plans on the road. Logue is one of those appointees who seem to draw the political spotlight more steadily than even the showiest elected officials. He is often compared with Robert Moses —perhaps because they both have disarming humor worn casually over very fast tempers—but he actually is made a lot more like the late Fiorello La Guardia—a truculent liberal. He began his career as a Philadelphia labor lawyer in 1948, but soon took a job with Governor Chester Bowles in Connecticut, and there studied action politics under Democratic boss John Bailey in the state legislature, eventually leaving that academy of the practical to accompany Bowles to India as ambassador's assistant. It was in 1954, after he came back from India, that he went to work for ebullient Mayor Richard Lee in New Haven, and between them the two wrote renewal history by accomplishing more with less cash than was done in almost any other U.S. city. Lee and Logue also wrote the urban-renewal plank at the Democratic Convention in Los Angeles in 1960.

By that time Logue had been lured to Boston. Part of the attraction was salary; his starting wage was more than that of any other redevelopment executive in the nation or the mayor of Boston or the governor of Massachusetts—$30,000 per year plus fringe benefits. But the real lure was the decrepitude of Boston itself. Logue believes in the necessity for renewal czars, and Boston rewrote laws to make him one.

Logue has one official title, Development Administrator for the Boston Redevelopment Authority but, in effect, it covers two jobs combined for him. First, he is the boss of a semi-autonomous agency set up by the Commonwealth of Massachusetts to carry out federally assisted renewal projects in Boston. But he is also head of the office of development for the mayor, and thus is in direct charge of all city planning as well. In most other cities one agency cooks up a plan and several other agencies serve it—and frequently it gets cold in the handling. But Logue both cooks and serves. This is a fine strategic situation: renewal thus becomes city planning's chief instrument. The eyes of planners all over the country are on this administrative setup, covetously, although the very broadness of the approach is strenuous.

The first thing Logue did in Boston—after buying a house on Beacon Hill and getting to be a member of the·old Tavern Club— was diagram just how cheap renewal could be, if managed right, and how a great building boom, involving both public and private capital, could be engineered. Mayor Collins' first major civic proclamation reflected the recommendations, outlining ten areas to work on, including Hynes's government-center proposal for Scollay Square, the business district, the waterfront, plus renovation of the most run-down residential neighborhoods. Collins and Logue then went to work on the Eisenhower housing administrators in Washington, and within weeks they persuaded these men, whom Logue calls "the Feds," to approve and finance the ten simultaneous renewal areas in Boston under various programs. They raised Boston from seventeenth ranking in the list of cities with federal commitments to fourth place—behind only New York, Philadelphia, and Chicago. Considering Boston's relative size, and late start, it is by far the busiest of all the big cities. Federal regulations now discourage cities from undertaking more than one redevelopment project at a time, restraining them from biting off more than they can chew, but in Boston, Logue says, "We have got to wholesale renewal. The trouble with this town in the past has been that there has been too much retailing—doing things for individuals, sometimes as political favors and sometimes just because that's the way they do things here."

THE PAYOFF

Logue's exhaustive knowledge of the federal renewal directives and his inventiveness have had large results. In effect, he and Collins are getting a huge multiproject program under way at relatively little cash cost to the city. Their chosen instrument, as noted, has been the Housing Act of 1949, which as amended gives cities a powerful method for buying up and clearing land and then selling it to private developers at an attractive price. The public cost of the Boston program is now budgeted at about $180 million, of which the federal government will put up two-thirds or about $120 million, leaving Boston to cover the rest. But in Massachusetts the state matches city appropriations for urban renewal, and so the cost to Boston is reduced to some $30 million.

In fact, however, Boston's actual cash outlay will be much less than that, running to only about $7,850,000, and most of this was committed for early renewal projects before Logue's arrival. Since his arrival he has committed only $72,500 in cash while securing some $105 million of promises from Washington, with an additional $33 million now pending. How has he done it? The answer lies in the fine print of the law, which allows cities to reduce out-of-pocket expenses while still enjoying the federal-government subsidy, and Logue and Collins have made full use of these provisions.

For instance, the law provides that instead of putting up cash a city may meet its obligations for a project area by building new schools, parks, playgrounds, and other improvements which will serve the area. Boston desperately needs such improvements and has a considerable capital-building program under way, which is largely financed by issuing new municipal bonds. Collins has cleverly plugged this capital program into the urban-renewal program over the next dozen years. In doing so he reduces the cash he would otherwise have to put up for clearing the renewal sites and, in effect, makes the federal and state governments meet most if not all of the immediate expense.

There are still further ways to shrink the city's actual cash commitment, and they have not been overlooked by Collins and Logue. It often happens that institutions such as hospitals, universities, or churches own land in a renewal area. This land has gone off the city tax rolls. Under Section 112 of the Housing Act of 1961, the city can apply to Washington for compensation and in effect can get $2 of federal credits for every $1 worth of land that such institutions have bought. Logue engaged the expert who worked out the details of this device, Julian Levi of the University of Chicago, to analyze the land buying of Boston's widespread institutions (42 percent of all Boston real estate is tax exempt, more by far than in any other major city), and Levi came up with the figure of $30 million, which signifies $60 million for Boston in the Treasury in Washington.

All cities engaged in renewal are familiar with Section 112—they cannot afford not to be. But it is Logue's further day-by-day manipulations of the money side of renewal that is getting him the reputation of a genius in his trade. These are brilliantly demonstrated in the government-center project, contents of which will include, besides City Hall, state buildings, federal buildings, and private-rental office buildings. Boston's contribution to the project cost in the sixty-acre tract in theory would be about $6,400,000 (one-sixth of total cost). But the city will actually contribute no cash, only site improvements. The largest will be in the form of a 2,000-car parking garage, the construction cost of which Boston can finance outside its debt limit. Then the garage could be leased to a commercial operator, presumably at rentals sufficient to make it self-liquidating. In the same project, the government center, the subway under Scollay Square had a famous screeching curve, which has been straightened partly with federal money, as an essential design change acceptable to the urban-renewal executives in Washington. It made Boston the first city to spend this kind of federal renewal money on its rapid-transit system, a very significant development to all cities with transportation problems.

UPROAR OVER ARCHITECTURE

So Logue is obviously a bright man with the balance sheet. But urban renewal involves far more than dollars and cents. It is a grinding political process in which the best of plans, and cheapest of plans, have to be sold to all sorts of people. As noted above, the government center in Boston is being very skillfully financed. But Logue's plans for its design have kicked up a municipal row of the first order. It all began in 1961, when Logue engaged the New York architect, I. M. Pei, to shape the proposed project very carefully so that it would be a total essay in civic architecture, not just a miscellaneous collection of ambitious buildings. Among other details, the plans called for blocking off a city street, demolishing two elderly office buildings, and replacing them with a plaza and a lean new office tower thirty-five stories high, to be built by a private developer for rental. In 1963, Logue announced that Gerald Blakeley of Cabot Cabot & Forbes had agreed to put up the speculative building. The principal tenant was to be the New England Merchants National Bank, owner of one of the buildings that had to come down.

But this did not suit William J. Foley Jr., member of the nine-man Boston City Council, who sometimes refers to Logue as "that Washington influence peddler." Foley immediately branded the whole arrangement a "sweetheart deal" and opposed it. The timing could hardly have been worse for Logue; last year's mayoralty primaries were coming up, and two of the councilors, Patrick F. McDonough and Gabriel F. Piemonte, wanted to be mayor. The council voted the Cabot Cabot & Forbes building down after bitter wrangling, and it became a nagging issue in the campaign. At present the proposal is before the council once more, with sponsorship of the building open to any developer who wants to compete for it; but meanwhile a $2,500,000 conspiracy suit has been filed against Cabot Cabot & Forbes, the New England Merchants National Bank, Logue, Blakeley, and Richard Chapman, president of the bank, by the owners of the other old on-site building scheduled for demolition.

This is probably only a temporary setback, but criticism of Logue is a constant. He is referred to by some of the Celtic members of the City Council as "a gray-flannel Irishman," a snarl in Boston. Foley says sweepingly, "He's crazy. He's a megalomaniac. The truth is not in him. The outline of Logue's program is to go from the harbor to the South End, across Boston's taxable breadbasket, expend astronomical sums of money, and wind up with little if any net increase in taxable property." Logue by now ruefully accepts the fact that nothing comes easily in Boston, but he battles on, saying, "In this town, to prove you're serious, you've almost got to be an exhibitionist. Periodically you've got to show your guts, and give them a chance at you with those sharp knives of theirs. This is a town where they keep score every day, like Washington. But what other city has all of Boston's problems? It's stimulating."

Despite many an alarum and excursion, Logue and Collins seem to be getting ahead. Collins was returned to office last fall with one of the greatest pluralities ever rendered a Boston mayor. His stock with the business community has steadily risen as the result of his courageous action in paring some 1,200 jobs from the city payroll and lowering Boston's notorious tax rate four years in a row. As a result, the business contribution to Boston's renewal has been specific and tangible. As far back as 1961, Collins got the Greater Boston Chamber of Commerce, then led by Charles Coolidge, to take over the task of replanning the city's waterfront and promoting its development. The chamber's plan, which cost $200,000 to complete, calls for utilizing derelict wharf areas as sites for marinas, an aquarium, and for new apartment houses that will accommodate some 2,200 families. The chamber will move parts of Boston's decrepit vegetable and fish markets to more efficient quarters, as has been done in Philadelphia.

Collins has also enlisted other businessmen to help bring some order and new vitality to Boston's crumbling traffic-jammed downtown retailing district, which lies on the other side of the government center from the waterfront project. In this task he again relied heavily on Coolidge, who has become chairman of the central-business-district committee, with the backing of Edward Mitton, the portly president of Jordan Marsh, and Harold Hodgkinson, chairman of Filene's. These two mighty merchants put their renowned rivalry aside temporarily and together made the rounds of the stores, the banks, the newspapers, and other businesses in the area "hat in hand"—as Mitton puts it—and came back with a good hatful of funds—$250,000—for replanning the whole district. Designed by Victor Gruen, the plan calls for 6,000 new parking spaces in garages above and below ground, with some midtown streets closed off to create pedestrian islands. It also calls for eliminating some of the older buildings of the area.

THE NEIGHBORHOODS

Meanwhile Collins and Logue are deeply committed to improving various run-down residential neighborhoods, under the slogan

"Planning with People." In this complex task their aim is not to rip down whole areas but rather to work selectively, replacing only the worst. Of the eight neighborhoods slated for such treatment, the one furthest along is the Washington Park section of Roxbury, the city's Negro ghetto, which lies only a twenty-minute taxi ride away from the center of Boston.

Roxbury was once one of the better middle-class sections of town, a prosperous Jewish enclave in an overwhelming Catholic community. But in the 1940's the middle-class Jewish families had begun to move away to suburbs such as Newton and Brookline, and more Negroes—both the prosperous and the poor—moved in. The big houses were split into small apartments and ran down. By the 1950's two financial signals of blight were flying: insurance companies would not renew fire coverage, and banks would not buy mortgages. Negro leaders, and white residents, began beating on Mayor Hynes's door for help. When Collins came into office, he opened the door wide.

The first of the renewal techniques applied to Roxbury involves the rehabilitation of old residences without any bullldozing at all. To spur this job along, Logue took over a house in Washington Park and moved in a team of technicians to help people figure out the physical side of the job, and to bring in contractors to bid on the work, ranging from new roofs to new wiring. Collins also enlisted the help of Boston's banks, which have pledged some $20 million toward new mortgages to finance the rehabilitation. Some of the financing feats are startling; even after the cost of the rehabilitation is added to old mortgages, it is frequently possible to shrink the monthly debt service charges. A B.R.A. survey of Washington Park indicated that, of 570 mortgaged properties judged practical for rehabilitation, 40 percent would have their monthly mortgage payments lowered. Another 24 percent would remain level in monthly charges, while only 36 percent would go up. Refinancing was figured on the basis of FHA Section 200 mortgages at $5\frac{1}{4}$ percent.

But the big trouble with rehabilitation as a renewal technique is that it is achingly slow, and essentially undramatic. Most of the improvement goes on indoors and so is not visible enough to inspire the neighbors to keep up. Too many people simply refuse to rehabilitate. In a renewal area the city can force the issue by resorting to condemnation, but this is a dangerous weapon politically—especially used against owner-occupants. In any case, only 150 acres of the 502-acre Washington Park renewal project is slated for the bulldozer, complete clearance.

WHAT KIND OF NEW HOUSING?

When parts of a neighborhood do have to be cleared, the decision remains: what to build on the land. Currently Boston favors putting up garden apartments financed under Section 221(d)(3) of the 1961 Housing Act. This program makes available very low-cost financing for nonprofit sponsors of housing developments (usually churches or unions), which can obtain 100 percent mortgages. Similarly, limited-dividend corporations can obtain 90 percent mortgage financing in return for restricting annual income on investment to 6 percent. The current mortgage rate is only 3⅜ percent, made possible by the fact that these mortgages are bought by the Federal National Mortgage Association, which is nicknamed Fanny May in the financial trade.

The 221(d)(3) approach is manna to mayors who have been much criticized of late for tearing down areas without taking care of the inhabitants. The program is also endorsed by the National Association of Home Builders, for practical reasons. A builder who organizes a limited-dividend corporation and builds a 221(d)(3) project can penetrate the lower-cost housing market with a virtually guaranteed profit, a 6 percent annual return, plus a builder's profit of up to 10 percent on construction. His annual management fee usually adds to profits, and finally, there is a rapid-depreciation tax advantage. As an added teaser, Collins has limited the local real-estate tax to 15 percent of gross rentals.

Rentals in 221(d)(3) garden apartments are often in the range of $75 per month for one-bedroom apartments to $105 for four-bedroom apartments—and the early Boston projects will hit this range. But even these rents are still too high for most of the displaced slum families. Says Mayor Collins, "What we need is housing for the family with children that is now paying $50 a month for a substandard apartment. It can afford to pay $75 a month—but not $95." So Collins and Logue are feeling their way toward new techniques, and Logue may have found one. He is currently dickering with the Boston Housing Authority to sign leases on a tenth of the apartments in the early 221(d)(3) projects, offering the agency all three- and four-bedroom units. The Housing Authority would then subsidize the rents of these apartments down to about $70 per month for the really poor families that are legally eligible for such aid.

HUMANITY—AN ENDLESS PROBLEM

In addition to trying to untie financial knots of this kind, Collins and Logue have to cope with all kinds of human complexities. There are neighborhoods in Boston that are militantly unwilling to let the Redevelopment Authority come near them—remembering with bitter clarity what happened in the West End. One such district is Charlestown, which sits across the lower Charles River behind the Navy Yard. Except for the monument up top, Bunker Hill, and a few good residential blocks around it, Charlestown today is decaying. Because Boston's trash collectors have seldom been zealous, empty lots became car parks or dumps. There is a rat problem. The people who remain, however, are tough, determined, and insular—only a few Negro families have dared move in, for example. When, after almost two years of work within Charlestown, including 135 neighborhood meetings, the Boston Redevelopment Authority advertised a community-wide hearing, Logue and his staff walked into a near riot. The fact that the head of the appointed B.R.A. board is a popular Catholic priest, Monsignor Francis Lally—one of Cardinal Cushing's closest aides—restrained the crowd but slightly. Even he was booed, and it was necessary to clear the aisles a number of times.

A FURTHER KIND OF FRUSTRATION

And even where communities welcome renewal, all kinds of frustrations arise in holding sponsors in line. For example, in 1963, Logue lined up a double-barreled backing for a 221(d)(3) garden apartment to be called Academy Homes. The official nonprofit sponsor was a strong Boston union—the local of the Building Service Employees International—and Logue paired it with the experienced First Realty Co. of Boston as the operating developer, with the understanding that the apartments would be completed for occupancy by the fall of 1963. However, squabbles between the sponsor and the developer kept delaying construction, and Logue finally decided to lop the developer off, even though Max Kargman, president of First Realty Co., is reported to be close to Mayor Collins. At the showdown meeting of the Boston redevelopment board, chaired by Monsignor Lally, Kargman, backed up by a knot of lawyers, fought hard to stay in the deal, complaining that it was the complicated experimental design of the proposed apartments that had caused the delays. James Colbert, another of the five-man B.R.A. board and a salty Boston political writer, at length interrupted Kargman in the recital of complaints: "But, Mr. Kargman, if there are so many problems, wouldn't you just as soon bow out of the renewal?" Kargman shot back, "No, problems is our business!" Whereupon the deft Monsignor Lally inserted quietly, "*No*, Mr. Kargman, *solving* problems is your business." And Logue had won one.

But at the next weekly meeting of the board, the business agent of the sponsoring union, Edward T. Sullivan, was present and plainly angry. After twenty-five stalwart years in the labor movement, Sullivan, a bull-like man, had himself been accused in a newspaper of contemplating the construction of Academy Homes with non-union labor—and this knife had been inserted in his back by none other than the secretary-treasurer of the local building-trades council, John Deady. Sullivan roared defiance. "Deady wakes up in the morning and lights a cigar," he shouted. "If the ash falls off his cigar on his stomach, you're union. If it doesn't, you're not!" But Deady was probably correct. The Massachusetts building trades have 10,000 members, of whom a token total of only eighty-one journeymen and seven apprentices are Negroes—and half the trades have excluded Negroes entirely. How could the job be both union and—as federal regulations demand—integrated? So Academy Homes—which, at that, is located in the Negro district, Washington Park—is still lagging.

So renewal comes down to a delicate political art as well as dollars and cents. Fortunately, Logue's personal dash and unquenchable élan have attracted talented and zealous young people from all over the country to work for him. Like their boss, many of them work hours that proper Bostonians find quite incredible. Logue pounds his people hard, but he pays them well, particularly by comparison to the main body of Boston city employees. For example, a week before last Christmas, the Boston radiobroadcasters broke the news that B.R.A. people were getting raises ranging from $250 to $2,000 per year, and an envious shudder seemed to run through the other nine floors of City Hall Annex. The other city employees were getting no Christmas raises; was Santa trapped on the top floors?

The explanation was simple enough: the city of Boston wasn't providing the cash; Washington was. A full 90 percent of Logue's large payroll is paid by normal advances made by the federal Urban Renewal Administration on projects in the planning stages. The city, at that, pays only $5,000 of the administrator's own cash salary. Federal advances take care of other parts of the process, too, including 80 percent of the cost of remodeling the B.R.A. offices, which totaled more than $450,000 with air conditioning.

Whether Washington should be so generously subsidizing urban renewal in Boston and in other cities across the nation is a question that goes beyond the scope of this article. The more practical question is whether the taxpayer's money is going to succeed in bringing New England's most eminent city back to sound health and productivity, and here everything depends on how fast private investment comes in behind government outlays.

On this point some Bostonians are still pessimistic. It is true, they grant, that Prudential is spending $200 million on its Back Bay complex, but they point out that the rehabilitation program out in the neighborhoods is dragging—and it is. The government center, fastest moving of all the projects, is dismissed as mostly government building (although it will also include a pair of large private-rental buildings). The critics also fear its effect on the general office-rental picture in Boston. What will happen, they ask, when the present government space, rented all over the city, totaling something like 1,100,000 square feet, is dumped on the rental market?

THE BRIGHTER VIEW

On the other hand, the Redevelopment Authority last year commissioned an independent market analysis of the long-range need for new office space, apartments and hotel accommodations in the city, and some impressive figures were arrived at by consultant Robert Gladstone, of Washington, D.C. He is confident that the downtown

Boston market alone can soak up by 1975 6,000 to 9,000 new apartments, 5,500,000 square feet of new offices, 3,500 to 3,750 new hotel rooms, and a million square feet of new retail space—if mass transit is improved.

Most local experts accept Gladstone's apartment prognostication. So far as office space is concerned, optimists and pessimists alike agree that the impending NASA installation in Massachusetts, if located within the city, would presumably fill all the office vacancies. Even without NASA, a new office block now being put up, which is backed by British capital, recently leased 85 percent of its floor space before its steel frame was begun. One thing is certain: a real building boom finally is on in Boston. The Federal Reserve Bank predicts well over a billion dollars in new construction.

So the shrewdness and the brass of the old seaport seems to be paying off again. M. Fred Smith, who got the Pru Building under way in Boston, and now heads the Oakland Corp. in Pittsburgh, thinks he knows why: "Boston has lost its mills and other low-skill manufacturers, but this is something every other major U.S. city is going to have to go through soon. But you've got to realize that Boston is loaded with brains and people with technical talent. Why, in Pittsburgh, we're spending $600 million just to attract people with talent; it's that simple."

Logue muses: "Urban renewal is not perfect, but it's adequate. Yup, it's tedious—some of the developers' slogan is, 'In real estate, anyone with money can make money. Without money, it takes talent.'" He sighs. "And that talent takes too much time. Right now we're going through the same tough period we went through in New Haven." Then his voice gets younger again, "But come around in the fall. By September there will be so much steel going up in government center that we'll be able to hang the doubters from it."

Says Mayor Collins, his alert, flesh-sheathed Roman face studying the interviewer imperatively: "The toughest part of the renewal program is behind us. This summer it begins to show. The danger is in moving too slowly, in letting it languish. You cannot just sit there and wait for something to happen—you have to make it happen."

Charles Coolidge leans back in his wooden chair in the book-stacked old Yankee law office over Federal Street: "We're in some things here in Boston that have never been attempted before. We're not sure we can pull it off, but we'll try." Coolidge's Bostonian ancestors very possibly expressed the same cautious optimism about the tea trade, and the silk trade, and the exporting of ice to the tropics.

9 The Industrial Corporation in Urban Renewal*

Hubert Kay

The rebuilding—and, one may hope, the beautifying—of American cities is now recognized as one of the major challenges to American civilization. But who is to do the job? During most of the last quarter century the task of adapting the cities to great population shifts has been left almost wholly to professional real-estate developers and various government agencies. The results in many cases are hardly edifying. But of late a "third force" has been entering the urban picture—the country's industrial corporations, which are, increasingly, transacting "public" business that cannot be done by individuals and should not in a free society be handed over to government.

Real-estate development, indeed, is rapidly becoming a major sideline of industrial firms, which have abundant cash and credit at their disposal. Some, notably such oil companies as Humble and Sunset International, are building entire new planned communities from scratch. Others, with results both bad and good, are adding various edifices to established cities. The Pennsylvania Railroad's share in razing its grand old New York City terminal to make way for an office building cum sports arena has won it no plaudits from

* Reprinted from *Fortune* Magazine (October 1964), where it appeared under the title "The Third Force in Urban Renewal," by special permission. Copyright © 1964 by Time Inc.

people concerned with aesthetics. Over the New York Central's forty-five-acre freight yards along the Hudson River in Manhattan's West Thirties, U.S. Steel may erect a $100-million development of office buildings and industrial plants, plus apartments for 12,000 families, in order to demonstrate to builders that steel is superior to prestressed concrete. A development of this size could be another human-filing-case monstrosity or—not impossibly—an inspiring contribution to the amenities of city life.

To date, however, by far the most interesting and significant leaders of the new movement are the big aluminum companies, Alcoa and Reynolds. In part, like ordinary developers, they are building or planning to build on choice sites in good neighborhoods. But most of their projects are in what have been or still are the worst of neighborhoods. Both companies are neck-deep in the lagging and bitterly criticized urban-renewal program. Their experiences provide new insights into what can be done to help rid cities of those laboratory cultures of human decay, the slums.

Both companies were originally moved by desire to increase their sales of architectural aluminum and to make a reasonable profit in real estate itself. But with the same commendable self-interest, both also sought a larger goal. Says Leon E. Hickman, Alcoa executive vice president and finance-committee chairman who is in charge of his company's real-estate ventures: "Of course we're in business to make money, and our stockholders should fire us if we don't. But if we want our company to survive as a private enterprise, we can't stop there. We must do things which the average American, who fears Big Business, will consider a service to him and to our country."

ZECKENDORF'S "SOFT SELL"

For Hickman and Alcoa big real-estate operations are by now a matter of course. In the early Fifties, Alcoa reared its aluminum-sheathed headquarters in Pittsburgh's Golden Triangle as part of a movement led by banker Richard K. Mellon, an Alcoa director, and Democratic boss David L. Lawrence to regenerate a "tired, worn-out mill town." Today, from their offices, Alcoa executives can see two of their great urban-renewal projects taking shape: Washington Plaza and Allegheny Center. All told, the company now controls well over $300 million worth of residential and commercial properties. If the present plans are carried out, it may end up with a billion dollars worth.

The seeds of this tremendous involvement were planted back in the late Thirties when Alcoa—for years the only great aluminum producer in America—was attacked by the Antitrust Division for monopoly. In the end Alcoa was convicted of no wrongdoing, and its near monopoly was broken less by court decision than by the sale to Reynolds and Kaiser of the government-owned aluminum plants built by Alcoa for World War II. After peak profits in 1956, a glut of productive capacity in the industry began to hurt. Alcoa's net profit as a percentage of sales and the price of its stock began to decline. Clearly, the old giant was going to have to get out with the rest and scramble for new business.

One obvious realm for generating new business lay in the multi-billion-dollar construction industry; and here Reynolds was already preparing to break new ground. In 1959 it hired Albert M. Cole to head a subsidiary specializing in housing. As a Congressman from Kansas, Cole had helped to write the Housing Act of 1949, which launched the urban-renewal program, and as head of the Housing and Home Finance Agency under Eisenhower he had administered the federal housing program, including urban renewal. Under his guidance, Reynolds has shrewdly specialized in low-rise and moderate-cost housing, in which it could try out its new architectural products. With eleven projects in as many cities in being or prospect, it has by now sold three projects and parts of three others—at a profit.

Initially nudged by Reynolds, Alcoa took the plunge in 1960. "Our venture," recalls Leon Hickman, "started modestly enough with a decision to seek two dramatic locations, preferably one on each coast, on which we might construct high-rise buildings designed to demonstrate what we considered to be the proper uses of architectural aluminum—curtain walls, doors and door frames, windows, awnings, balconies, acoustical ceilings, canopies, column coverings, façades, foil insulations, mullions, partitions, railings, siding, stair rails, Venetian blinds, weather stripping, conduit, ducts, wiring, and a host of other items. In the aggregate these account for at least 25 percent of the entire aluminum market."

Though Alcoa knew all that was worth knowing about building

aluminum plants, it had—except for its headquarters building and some employee housing at out-of-the-way plants—little experience in other real-estate development. Looking for a partner who knew the business, it encountered the ebullient William Zeckendorf of New York's Webb & Knapp—and its fate was sealed. Hickman's soft-spoken tribute to Zeckendorf is that of one master salesman to another: "He was the one who persuaded us that real estate is a good investment in itself, not just a way of selling more aluminum. He's a brilliant and surprising fellow. He doesn't raise his voice even as loud as mine. You expect bombast, and he gives you a soft sell. We were oversold at times, but we don't blame him for anything. We think very highly of Bill around here."

Zeckendorf already had his fingers on the two "dramatic locations" that Alcoa wanted for its aluminum showcases. One, at the north end of the six-block stretch of Manhattan's First Avenue that has been renamed United Nations Plaza, was a full city block facing the U.N. buildings in their spacious setting to the south. There Zeckendorf and his British associates had planned—in the main for U.N. delegates now scattered in homes and offices throughout the city—a wide six-story office building topped by twin thirty-two-story towers of cooperative luxury apartments. The other site was the 260-acre Twentieth Century-Fox movie lot, which, if Los Angeles had a heart, would be in it. It lies just west of Beverly Hills and a few blocks from Wilshire Boulevard. On this onetime Tom Mix horse ranch Zeckendorf envisioned Century City, a gleaming miniature metropolis of towering apartment houses and office buildings.

Bill Zeckendorf's dreams, however, have always outrun his means. Glittering real-estate deals (the more complex the better) are so irresistible to him that he is chronically short of cash and in the toils of what he calls "my Shylock friends," who charge him up to 24 percent interest. Alcoa gladly put up $5 million for the future Century City site, and pledged its virtually unlimited credit for the balance of the $43-million price. (Eighty acres were leased back to Twentieth Century–Fox for ninety-nine years, at $1,500,000 per year.) It invested similarly in the U.N. Plaza site. But it was resolved to acquire no more than a 40 percent equity in either project along with responsibility for 60 percent of the financing, leaving development and management to its partners.

In so resolving, the officers and directors of the sedate old industrial giant underestimated both (1) Zeckendorf's optimism and persuasiveness, and (2) their own growing fascination with real estate. Gradually, as Zeckendorf failed to come up with his share of the necessary millions, Alcoa found itself bailing him out and thus coming to own a larger and larger share not only of the two original projects but also of several other Zeckendorf developments. With growing ownership, it found itself moving from the role of financial angel to that of active real-estate developer and manager.

The decisive break came in June, 1963. Amicably and reluctantly, Alcoa and Zeckendorf dissolved their partnership. All Webb & Knapp interests in five large highrise apartment developments—three in New York City, one in Philadelphia, and one in Pittsburgh—were acquired by Alcoa and Zeckendorf's British partner, Covent America Corp. Alcoa got majority control and full managerial responsibility. The Webb & Knapp interests in the Century City and U.N. Plaza projects were also divided between Alcoa and British investors.

By mid-1964, having acquired majority interests in another Pittsburgh project and one in Indianapolis and a minority interest in a San Francisco development, Alcoa had invested $50 million of its own cash, plus mortgage borrowings, in real estate with a book value of more than $300 million. Of the ten major developments listed in the box below, six are federally assisted urban-renewal projects with the usual FHA-insured financing, and a seventh (Allegheny Center) differs from them only in its private financing. At mid-1964 these seven represented about 60 percent of the cost of Alcoa projects to date.

"HIROSHIMA FLATS"

This big involvement by Alcoa, no less than the pioneering done by Reynolds, promises well for urban redevelopment. It also, however, highlights a number of problems that other industrial companies contemplating ventures in this field would do well to understand. Some of these problems are more or less inherent in the urban-renewal program itself. Under this program the federal and city governments share the cost of buying and clearing slum areas, and thereafter the land is sold to private developers. All too often the sites chosen are too small or otherwise unsuitable for development purposes; and no sensible developer will build in a location where he thinks people will not want to work and live.

"Something is plainly wrong," says Alcoa's Hickman, noting that while cities by mid-1963 had acquired 21,970 acres for renewal, redevelopment was completed or in process on only 6,130 acres. It is true that developers had been "selected" for nearly 58 percent of the acquired acreage. But the selection of a developer for a renewal site, even when it is accompanied by his deposit of a few thousand dollars of "earnest money," does not necessarily guarantee that he will ever actually buy the land, let alone build on it.

The hostility of slum neighbors to renewal projects is heightened by the sight of acres of bulldozed rubble, bearing such local nicknames as Hiroshima Flats, lying idle for years while they await redevelopment. People who have been ousted from their homes and businesses in such areas are not necessarily appeased by the fact that, according to URA, 80 percent of the 160,000 families thus far displaced by urban renewal have been relocated in "standard" ("decent, safe, and sanitary") housing, while only 6 percent have refused assistance and settled again in "substandard" (i.e., slum) housing. (The rest have moved to other cities or otherwise disappeared from official view.) Even slum dwellers may grow fond of their homes and neighborhoods, and businessmen who are compensated only for their fixtures and moving expenses may be wiped out.

TAXES VS. PROFITS

As corporate citizens, Alcoa and Reynolds are deeply concerned about all this. But as developers investing millions of their stockholders' dollars, their primary concern must necessarily be with their long-term financial return. Some critics hold that urban renewal is a monstrous political device for enriching some citizens at the expense of others. But when the Association of Reserve City Bankers investigated the program in 1962, its Committee on Urban Renewal—headed by First Pennsylvania's William L. Day with Chase Manhattan's David Rockefeller as vice chairman—reported this finding: "The difficulty of obtaining redevelopers who are willing and qualified to undertake renewal projects . . . is one of the major problems facing the effort. Far from being a 'gold mine' to redevelopers, few projects have yielded even reasonable profits to the redeveloper."

As Alcoa sees it, a major burden of the redeveloper—and a major deterrent to potential redevelopers of urban-renewal land—is the insatiable municipal appetite for taxes. For an example, consider one of the three Manhattan urban-renewal developments that Alcoa took over from Zeckendorf, Kips Bay Plaza. The slum tenements on the three middle East Side blocks it occupies once paid the city (when it could be collected) $205,000 a year in taxes. Against this trickle, the city paid high for the deteriorated area's many police, fire, and maintenance problems. Now the three blocks, joined into one superblock, contain two high-rise towers with 1,118 apartments renting from $141 to $435 per month, plus a small shopping center. In addition to eliminating the costs of maintaining streets, many sewers, and much police and fire protection, the development pays $775,000 a year in taxes—nearly four times the previous amount. The tax increase alone represents a 30 percent annual return on the city's investment in acquiring the land. This is fine for the city. But the fact is that Kips Bay and the two other Alcoa renewal projects in New York are still running in the red largely because of excessive taxes.

But it is not just the size of the taxes levied that hurts; it is also the timing. It takes a minimum of two years to fill up a renewal apartment house to a satisfactory 90 to 95 percent of capacity, since the project is usually close to existing slums. These are years of heavy losses and the losses are painfully increased by the fact that, once the developer has put up new buildings, many cities tax them at the productive value they would have if fully rented. Here big industrial companies like Alcoa have an advantage, of course, over ordinary developers—an advantage that is one reason the urban-renewal program urgently needs their participation. The full-time developer, traditionally short of cash and harassed by debt, may well decide that prospective losses during the fill-up period leave him no alternative but to (1) stay out, (2) go broke, or (3) put up shoddy buildings that will soon begin to lose both their rental and tax productivity. Corporations with the financial strength of Alcoa or Reynolds, on the other hand, can erect substantial buildings without worry about foreclosure or distress sale of their properties.

Furthermore, for income-tax purposes Alcoa and Reynolds can deduct their real-estate losses (created in part by high depreciation charges) from their profits on aluminum. As a result, Alcoa figures that the cash drain on a company in its position is about half what it would be for a developer with no other business.

Alcoa's Major Real-Estate Projects		
Project	Location	Alcoa Owner-ship
Group I United Nations Plaza	New York	70%
Century City	Los Angeles	67
Group II James Whitcomb Riley Center	Indianapolis	61
Group III Allegheny Center	Pittsburgh	80
Group IV Kips Bay Plaza	New York	90
Lincoln Towers	New York	88
Park West Village	New York	82
Society Hill	Philadelphia	90
Washington Plaza	Pittsburgh	85
Golden Gateway	San Francisco	25

I *Building developments conceived independently of an urban-renewal program and financed through banking and insurance sources.*

II *A locally sponsored redevelopment project financed through banking and insurance sources.*

III *An urban-redevelopment project financed through banking and insurance sources.*

IV *Urban-redevelopment projects financed by conventional methods with FHA insurance.*

Nevertheless, the cash drain is there, and unless cities begin to assess urban-renewal developments realistically during the fill-up period even an Alcoa or a Reynolds may feel impelled to cut its commitments in the renewal field and concentrate on commercial projects. Says Hickman: "We have to ask ourselves each day whether our shareholders would not be better served if we devoted our real-estate efforts to properties in favorable neighborhoods such as Century City and U.N. Plaza, rather than participation in the redevelopment of slum areas. The latter is the more challenging, probably the more worth while to the community, but private capital is only justified in participating if there is reasonable prospect that the battle can be won."

THE "MADDENING" DELAYS OF FHA

In addition to taxes Hickman is worried by the "maddening" delays and restrictions of the Federal Housing Administration, which insures mortgage loans up to 90 percent of a developer's costs in building on renewal land. Hickman objects first to FHA's $20-million limit on a project loan. "More and more excellent redevelopment programs," he observes, "are for several times this maximum figure, and this is highly desirable, for programs ought to be aimed at removing blight from an entire neighborhood. But this low ceiling leads to artificial division of many renewal projects into a series of $20-million packages for FHA purposes. Reflect for a moment on how you would refinance one of those redevelopments if you wanted to sell one of the properties. It ain't easy!"

Though conceding that a governmental body authorized to risk public monies must exercise due care, Hickman thinks that FHA overdoes it. The delays resulting from its snail-paced feasibility studies, approvals of plans, and inspections of construction are, he declares, "maddening in all instances and financially expensive in most. The fact that the developer so largely loses control of his own property, and the timing of its development, is a deterrent to attracting private enterprises such as Alcoa into FHA-insured projects."

Reynolds' Cole regretfully agrees, not only about FHA procedures and practices but about those of the Urban Renewal Administration itself. "They're too cumbersome, time-consuming, and restrictive," he declares. "They should be simplified. Where we failed during my administration of HHFA was in not organizing and coordinating the various housing agencies to accomplish our objectives. They're still not coordinated, still not accomplishing the objectives of urban renewal; an administrator just can't penetrate all the way through the bureaucracy. One specific trouble with FHA is that its people as a whole are grounded in single-family housing. The agency needs more people who understand the special problems of renewal."

Reynolds, specializing in single-family housing to date, is sticking to FHA-insured financing on residential projects, but Alcoa's patience has worn thin, and it is trying out other techniques. In the case of Allegheny Center in Pittsburgh, Alcoa and its partners have relied on private financing. Says Hickman: "The great beauty of bank and insurance loans is that once the ability and integrity of the borrower are established, the lender takes whatever security is agreed upon but keeps his hands off the management of the business. If ways could be found whereby banks, insurance companies, and pension trusts could raise their lending limits in qualified situations, I think redevelopers in Alcoa's position would be favorably disposed to financing most redevelopment projects through such private channels."

Alcoa has pushed this philosophy one step further in the case of the James Whitcomb Riley Center in Indianapolis. This project, involving both slum clearance and redevelopment, was locally sponsored and has involved no federal money at all. Alcoa liked this idea so well that it bought what developed into a majority interest in the project. "We think there should be more of this kind of thing," says Hickman, "and so we got in to applaud and to lend a hand."

Both Alcoa and Reynolds have found that broad community support from business and political leaders is crucial to success. The function of such a group is aptly defined by Cincinnati's Citizens Development Committee, which calls itself "prodder, opener of doors, and remover of obstacles in finance, legislation, education, promotion, etc." Pittsburgh's Allegheny Conference on Community Development, which antedates the urban-renewal program, has probably achieved more than any other such group in the nation. It is closely followed by Philadelphia's Old Philadelphia Development Corporation. Other cities in which Alcoa or Reynolds has found notably effective civic groups include Washington, Providence, Syracuse, and San Francisco. Group enthusiasm is the more necessary because renewal, to be fully successful, must involve entire slum neighborhoods as part of an over-all city plan. To do less, notes Hickman, is "like removing part of a cancer. Eventually, the surrounding slums will reclaim the island of redevelopment as surely as some airstrips of New Guinea went back to the jungle."

HOMEY—LIKE YANKEE STADIUM

It is tardily being recognized that good architecture is essential to urban renewal if the program is to fulfill its grand objective of making American city life more livable. The worst faults of renewal design appear in New York City, where high building costs and clumsy zoning regulations have dictated the postwar pattern of huge, identical apartment slabs separated by wide malls of grass upon which tenants and their children are forbidden to trespass. The effect is about as homey as Yankee Stadium on a Monday morning. In odd corners of each development are tiny playgrounds —called "tot lots"—in which old-fashioned swings, slides, and seesaws have been abandoned in favor of strange devices that suggest pop-art sculpture and defy the visitor's attempt to imagine a child using them.

All three of Alcoa's Manhattan renewal developments, which were inherited from Zeckendorf, share these defects to a great degree, though they have some redeeming features. The Kips Bay Plaza buildings are gracefully proportioned and diminish slab monotony through I. M. Pei's artfully designed recessed windows. Park West Village, which offers superb views of Central Park from thousands of its windows, provides about half of its tenants with a bit of private outdoor living space in the form of a terrace balcony. Lincoln Towers has bigger (though fewer) terraces, and some good views. In all three, the provision of abundant open space between buildings is admirable.

But the waste of that space for living purposes in these and other renewal developments is inexcusable—especially in a city where handsomely iron-fenced Gramercy Park, with its well-placed trees, shrubs, flower beds, gravel paths, and numerous benches, has been demonstrating for more than a century how a small private park can not only add to the joy of living for tenants of its surrounding brownstones and apartment houses but also upgrade a sizable neighborhood, sustaining and raising both the quality and value of real estate for blocks around.

Elsewhere, urban-renewal projects, including those of the aluminum companies, tend to be more fortunately designed. Moreover, cities as well as the federal government are recognizing that bulldozing down whole areas and building from the ground up is not the only way to refurbish the American city. The Housing Act of 1964 contains a new provision authorizing loans at rates not to exceed 3 percent for restoring and rehabilitating old buildings that are not beyond repair. Philadelphia offers a striking example of how new and old renewal techniques may be combined, with Alcoa and other industrial companies playing a leading part in the renovation.

The critical battle is being fought out in the Society Hill area, which got its name from the fact that in the seventeenth century William Penn sold the land to the Free Society of Traders. Lying near the Delaware River only three blocks from Independence Hall, this area fell into complete decay, with the old Graff House, in which Jefferson drafted the Declaration, being replaced by a hot-dog stand. In 1956, Philadelphia's leading citizens joined to rescue Society Hill from its ignominy. Their Old Philadelphia Development Corporation, which has since extended its interest and potent influence to other renewal projects, has been headed from the start by William L. Day, chairman of the First Pennsylvania Banking & Trust Co. Now the old Philadelphia food market and most of the slums along the waterfront are gone, cleared by urban renewal.

Among the slum buildings were some 500 fine old houses in which once lived such elegant families as the Girards, Powels, Shippens, and Wistars. These have been certified and marked by the Philadelphia Historical Commission. The city has given their owners a choice between selling and restoring at least their façades. Meanwhile, on land cleared of nonhistoric slums, Alcoa is completing three graceful thirty-one-story apartment towers designed by I. M. Pei, plus a facing block-long row of modern town houses, which Pei skillfully designed to blend with both his modern apartments and the historic colonials across the street. On adjoining blocks of cleared land Alcoa has built an additional fourteen town houses, of a possible 200, on the traditional model, and meanwhile the restoration of the genuine colonials proceeds. Leon Hickman believes that all this will eventually "put Williamsburg in the shade," though he concedes that "you have to be something of a Daniel Boone to move there now."[1]

A few miles away in southwest Philadelphia, Reynolds is helping to make life more livable for the city's less prosperous citizens. Most

[1] Among the Daniel Boones who have bought and restored historic Society Hill mansions at reported costs of $100,000 to $200,000 each are former Mayor Richardson Dilworth, the chief leader of the Philadelphia renaissance; C. Jared Ingersoll, director of U.S. Steel and other corporations; and Henry M. Watts Jr., who commutes to his job as board chairman of the New York Stock Exchange. Many of the old houses can be bought and restored for much less. (Alcoa's new ones are in the $35,000 to $47,000 range.)

of the 2,500 acres in its New Eastwick, the nation's biggest urban-renewal project, were formerly swampland, reclaimed in part with fill from the dredging of a Delaware ship channel. On grassy cul-de-sacs Reynolds is building attractive and roomy row houses, which, at $12,250 to $14,900, sell for an initial $1,000 plus about $115 per month. Eastwick's old reputation as a swampy slum and graveyard of prohibition-era gangsters has slowed sales. So, too, has the development's integration, though New Eastwick's present white and Negro tenants live amicably together. "We expected to sell a thousand houses there by now," Albert Cole told FORTUNE recently, "but we've sold only 253." But Reynolds, moving ahead with plans for a shopping center, is confident of the project's eventual success —and of its own ability to hold out during the waiting period.

HOPE FOR HARLEM?

All this is encouraging and indicates that that flexible instrument, the U.S. industrial corporation, has a large part to play in eradicating "the shame of the cities." Indeed, the possibilities of redevelopment are endless. So far government and private effort have concentrated solely on building and renovation. But why not go further? As an extreme example, why not a project in Harlem that would combine slum clearance with corporate investment in fabricating plants, which would help provide jobs as well as roofs for those who need them? This kind of thing would be quite impossible for government alone to pull off, but is not impossible once corporations are brought into the process. And as new and imaginative projects are put in motion, Alcoa's Hickman will be able to say with even more conviction than he does today: "Urban redevelopment is good for Alcoa, and Alcoa is good for urban redevelopment."

PART IV

RELOCATION AND

COMMUNITY LIFE

10 The Housing of Relocated Families*†

Chester Hartman

Large-scale relocation of families and individuals, such as that occasioned by highway construction and urban renewal, necessarily raises basic questions of social welfare and public policy. Among the more important issues are: how relocation affects the family's ability to meet the society's minimum standards for quality and quantity of living space; the extent to which the family can fulfill its needs and desires in terms of housing and neighborhood characteristics and convenience to employment, community facilities, family, and friends; the costs—financial, social, and emotional—involved in experiencing forced change, and the unintended consequences of such changes; the differential incidence of benefits and costs on various subgroups within the relocation population; the effect of population

* Reprinted from the *Journal of the American Institute of Planners*, Vol. 30, No. 4 (November 1964), pp. 266–286.

† This report is part of a study entitled "Relocation and Mental Health: Adaptation Under Stress," conducted by the Center for Community Studies in the Department of Psychiatry of the Massachusetts General Hospital and the Harvard Medical School. The research is supported by the National Institute of Mental Health, Grant # 3M 9137–C3. I would like to acknowledge the intelligent and sensitive commentary on earlier drafts of this paper offered by Marc Fried, Herbert Gans, and Melvin Webber. Jack Meltzer, Director of the Center for Urban Studies at the University of Chicago, has indicated to me that over a year ago he undertook a study of relocation for HHFA, which reviews many of the same reports referred to in this paper and arrives at remarkably similar conclusions about the impact of relocation.

redistribution on the city's ecological patterns, particularly with respect to racial segregation, and how these more general effects influence the individual family's housing experience.

Obviously, questions such as these can be answered only by a comprehensive investigation of the impact of relocation. A follow-up study of the population dislocated from Boston's West End urban renewal area—a centrally located, 48-acre neighborhood of some 7,500 persons that was demolished in 1958–1959 to make way for a luxury apartment-house complex—provides one of the few sources of comprehensive, independently gathered and analyzed data on the effects of slum clearance and relocation on housing welfare. This research has already produced findings which throw light on the psycho-social effects of dislocation and the subsequent adaptation experience.[1] The present paper will be concerned primarily with housing changes and the financial costs involved for a random sample of more than 500 displaced West End households (approximately 20 percent of the households living in the area at the time of land-taking) who were first interviewed just prior to dislocation and reinterviewed approximately two years thereafter. The central focus will be on changes in several features of housing status: location, housing type and tenure, living space (outdoor and indoor), housing quality, and rent levels.[2] In order to place the West End findings in a broader context and to gain greater perspective on the problem of relocation, some 30 studies which report follow-up assessments of one or more aspects of housing conditions among relocated families are also reviewed here.[3] The overall results of

[1] See Marc Fried, "Grieving for a Lost Home," *The Urban Condition,* ed. Leonard J. Duhl (New York: Basic Books, 1963) [reprinted in Chapter 13 of this volume.—Ed.]; Marc Fried, "Social Change and Working Class Orientations: The Case of Forced Relocation," to be published in *Mobility and Mental Health,* ed. Mildred Kantor (New York: D. Van Nostrand, 1964).

[2] Data on location, apartment size, rents, and tenure were gathered in the course of the two interviews. Additional data derive from housing and neighborhood surveys that were undertaken for pre-relocation dwellings by the interviewers, and for post-relocation dwellings by a specially trained crew of housing surveyors. A total of 540 respondents (female household heads between the ages of 20 and 65) answered at least one interview: 432 responded to both interviews, 41 to the pre-relocation interview alone, 67 to the post-relocation interview alone. Through surveys and outside sources, some data are available for the entire sample of 540.

[3] The comparative studies are those located in the libraries of the Harvard Graduate School of Design, the City Planning Departments of the Massachusetts Institute of Technology and the University of Pennsylvania, and the Philadelphia Housing Association. Miss Linda Greenberg of the Philadelphia Housing Association kindly assisted in making available to me materials from the Philadelphia libraries.

these rehousing studies will be compared with the West End findings; the studies are cited by number according to the list of references at the end of this article, and Chart I (p. 316) contains the results of the studies in capsular form.

The studies reviewed, which include several reports from the 1930's and 1940's, as well as some more recent reports dealing with relocation caused by programs other than urban renewal, indicate that relocation results vary markedly for different projects and at different points in time. Sufficient information is not available to determine the reasons for these variations, but clearly where there are a great many sound low-rent vacancies available, and where relocation planning and services are competently provided, more satisfactory results are to be expected than under opposite conditions. Despite differences of this kind, inclusion of a range of studies may help to indicate common and persistent features of the relocation process.

WHERE DID THEY GO?

Figure 1 and Table I show the residential relocation of the West End sample.[4] The most striking feature of the redistribution is its "shotgun" pattern—the absence of large-scale clustering in the vicinity of the project area, the relatively weak centripetal pull within roughly a six-mile radius of the West End, and the spread of large numbers of families into virtually every section of Boston and every one of the inner-core suburbs. Approximately the same number of relocated families are found in each of the first five one-mile rings surrounding the West End. Thirty-eight percent re-

---

[4] At the time of the post-relocation interview, roughly one-fourth of the sample was no longer living at the address to which they had moved directly after leaving the West End (and of this group, slightly less than one-third had moved more than once). The post-relocation address has been defined as the dwelling at which the post-relocation interview was held (for those persons to whom no post-relocation interview was administered, the address at which they were living at the time the majority of post-relocation interviews were held). This formulation for multiple movers was used in part because the most detailed data from the interviews refer to current residence, in part because this address in a sense is more realistically the chosen rehousing, as it usually represents adjustment from an initially unsatisfactory choice.

The multiple movers will be the subject of a later paper dealing with variations in the process of housing adjustment. For purpose of the present paper, however, it should be noted that in terms of the variables discussed here, no major differences have been found for these multiple movers between the initial relocation dwelling and the dwelling at which the follow-up interview was held.

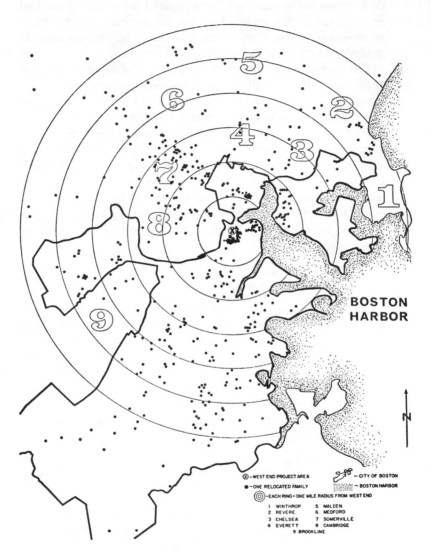

BOSTON
HARBOR

⊗ — WEST END PROJECT AREA   — CITY OF BOSTON

● — ONE RELOCATED FAMILY   — BOSTON HARBOR

◎ — EACH RING · ONE MILE RADIUS FROM WEST END

1 WINTHROP   5 MALDEN
2 REVERE   6 MEDFORD
3 CHELSEA   7 SOMERVILLE
4 EVERETT   8 CAMBRIDGE
        9 BROOKLINE

FIGURE 1

Relocation of West End Sample

located outside Boston in other parts of the metropolitan area, and another 6 percent left the metropolitan area entirely.[5]

This dispersion is in sharp contrast with the findings reported in most other studies of the redistribution of relocated families. These

TABLE I   *Relocation destinations of West End sample*

Distance from West End in miles	(1) Num- ber	(2) Per- cent	(3) Number dwelling units in each 1-mile ring (%)	(4) Expected number of re- locatees within 6-mile radius B	(5) Index of Disper- sion (1)÷(4)
0–1	91	17	21,000 (5)	23	3.96
1–2	89	17	61,000 (16)	73	1.22
2–3	86	16	73,000 (19)	87	0.99
3–4	78	15	87,000 (23)	106	0.74
4–5	76	14	87,000 (23)	106	0.73
5–6	39	7	55,000 (14)	64	0.61
	(459)		384,000 (100%)	459	
Boston SMSA, 6+ miles	45	8			
Massachusetts, Outside Boston SMSA	12	2			
New England, Outside Massa- chusetts	5	1			
U.S., Outside New England	8	2			
Outside United States	3	1			
	532 A	100%			

A Eight households from the original sample could not be traced to a relocation address.

B This is the expected distribution under the assumption that those who relocated within a 6-mile radius distributed themselves proportionate to the existing population of each 1-mile ring (as represented by the total number of dwelling units).

5 Extrapolation from sample data to the entire West End population indicates that 3,300 persons left the city of Boston as a result of the West End renewal project; of these, roughly 2,800 settled in other parts of the metropolitan area, and 500 left the Boston metropolitan area entirely. Population shifts of this scale may precipitously place major rehousing and welfare burdens on smaller cities and towns, and represent one aspect of the broader implications of renewal policy that should be studied more carefully.

studies indicate that most families clustered in the immediate vicinity of the area from which they were dislocated. For example, a survey of relocation in New York's Lower East Side [26] reported that 86 percent of the families which were dislocated to make way for the construction of Knickerbocker Village resettled in "the adjoining blocks" (see Chart I). Fifty-five percent of the families relocated from a Baltimore urban renewal area [2] resettled within one-half mile of their former homes, 96 percent within two miles. And Reynolds, in his survey of urban renewal and public housing relocation in 41 U.S. cities [33], reported that "a majority of all families . . . took up new addresses not further than about one mile and a half, or 12 city blocks, from their old addresses." With respect to individual cities, Reynolds reports that two-thirds of all families displaced by public housing and urban renewal programs in Chicago, and three-fourths of those in Philadelphia, relocated less than two miles from their former homes; in nine smaller communities, the proportion of families that relocated within two miles ranged from 80 to 95 percent. The only exceptions to this extreme concentration were found in some areas of New York and Chicago. In these very large cities, a combination of the transportation system (with rapid, cheap, and single-fare transit) and the complex workings of racial ecology frequently resulted in a more widespread distribution of relocatees (although the pattern is polynuclear rather than randomly scattered).

Evidence from these studies and from the West End suggests that a number of factors produced the atypical pattern of wide dispersion from the West End. First, the population was almost entirely white, which meant that families were not subject to the exclusionary pressures that so severely limit the rehousing choices of nonwhite families.[6] Family incomes were relatively high, providing for a fairly wide area of choice and possibility.[7] In addition within a five- to six-mile radius of the West End, residential areas are primarily working-class or lower middle-class. And finally, there was an extremely low rate of sound vacancies throughout this area,

[6] As indicated in Chart I, most follow-up studies deal with nonwhite populations. The significance of racial factors will be discussed in greater detail below.

[7] Twenty percent of the pre-relocation sample had weekly family income in excess of $100, 43 percent in excess of $75.

so that concentrated relocation would have been difficult, and opportunities for rehousing were especially limited in the area immediately adjacent to the West End.

WHAT KIND OF HOUSING DID THEY MOVE INTO?

Type

Housing in the West End was relatively homogeneous: almost all the buildings were small, attached brick tenements, four or five stories high, with one or two apartments per floor. From this common starting point, West Enders chose a wide variety of housing types (Table II). The largest group moved into multifamily housing: 35 percent into private apartments, plus an additional 11 percent into public housing. Forty-three percent moved into two- or three-family homes, the dominant building types in most sections of Boston and in the inner-core suburbs. Only 11 percent moved into single-family homes.

In the few other studies which report on housing type [8, 9, 26, 36, 37], a wider variety of pre-relocation housing situations usually existed, and little change in the aggregate distribution occurred after relocation.

TABLE II   *Housing types of relocation dwellings, West End sample*

	Number	Percent
Single-family house	56	11
Two-family house	107	21
Three-family house	112	22
Apartment house, tenement	173	35
Public housing	53	11
	501	100%

Tenure

Ten percent of the sample owned their homes in the West End (a surprisingly high proportion, considering that almost all buildings were small tenements). Following relocation, 21 percent were home-owners. Table III, which compares pre- and post-relocation housing tenure, indicates that although the overwhelming majority (74 percent) were renters before and after relocation, a modest proportion (16 percent) took the opportunity to buy homes upon relocating, while 5 percent forsook ownership status after leaving the West

End. The remaining 5 percent were owners in the West End who subsequently purchased homes.

Interestingly, only 43 percent of those buying homes upon relocation purchased single-family homes; the remainder bought larger buildings (29 percent bought two-family homes, 18 percent three-family homes, and 10 percent tenements) for use as income-producing property, in some cases for use by kin.[8] (Purchase of income-producing property was far more frequent among those who were owners in the West End than among those buying for the first time.) With the exception of two studies [18, 35] that report on relocation from government-owned temporary wartime housing in which all the families were renters, no significant or consistent changes in tenure following relocation are reported.

TABLE III   *Housing tenure, pre- and post-relocation, West End sample*

West End Tenure	Post-Relocation Tenure	
	Owner	Renter
Owner	22	26
	(5%)	(5%)
Renter	80	359
	(16%)	(74%)

HOW MUCH SPACE DID THEY SECURE?

Indoor Space

The average number of rooms per household was 4.35 in the West End, and rose to 4.94 in the relocation dwellings. Forty-six percent of the families moved into dwellings containing more rooms than their West End apartment, while 54 percent did not gain space (35 percent moved into dwellings with the same number of rooms, 19 percent moved into apartments with fewer rooms). Gain and loss of household space was closely related to housing type. The greatest gains were secured by those who moved to single-family houses. Substantial, although smaller, gains were achieved by those who moved into two- and three-family houses. Only a minority of those who moved into apartment houses and public housing gained apart-

---

[8] Two studies from Chicago and one from Portland, Maine [8, 9, 36], also report a high incidence of purchase of multifamily buildings among post-relocation owners. In each of these three surveys, approximately 85 percent of the homes purchased were classified as "income properties" (buildings containing more than one unit).

ment space. If net changes in household space are calculated, taking into account post-relocation changes in household size,[9] 41 percent of all households showed an increase in space, while 59 percent did not (of these, 32 percent maintained the same amount of space and 27 percent experienced a decrease).

Although overcrowding was not a major problem in the West End, overall apartment densities decreased as a result of relocation, and there was a slight drop in the proportion of households living at densities higher than 1.00 persons per room (see Table IV). Nine percent of the families moved from overcrowded conditions into an apartment where household density was 1.00 or less, while 4 percent moved from a previously adequate situation into overcrowded conditions.

TABLE IV   *Household densities, pre- and post-relocation, West End sample*

West End Density (*persons per room*)	Post-Relocation Density (*persons per room*)			
	Less than 1.00	1.00	*More than* 1.00	*TOTAL*
Less than 1.00	234	16	6	256 (62%)
1.00	63	24	12	99 (24%)
More than 1.00	25	13	21	59 (14%)
TOTAL	322 (78%)	53 (13%)	39 (9%)	414 (100%)

A review of household space changes brought about in other rehousing efforts indicates that there has been a general failure to ameliorate overcrowded conditions in the course of relocation. In only 6 of the 18 studies reporting such information was there any significant gain in aggregate living space following relocation, and even in these instances the degree of overcrowding following relocation remained extremely high for the most part. In Philadelphia, for example, the Housing Association reported an 18 percent drop in the proportion of families living at densities of 1.01

[9] That is, change in number of persons subtracted from change in number of rooms: addition of one room and one person is considered no change; the same number of rooms but loss of a household member is considered a net gain of space.

Forty-one percent of all families responding to both interviews reported a change in household size between the first and second interviews, due to births, departure of grown children, marriage, divorce, and separation, and combining households with friends or relatives. The majority of these changes (59 percent) were increases, rather than decreases, in family size.

persons per room or higher, but nonetheless fully two-fifths of the families still were overcrowded after slum clearance [30]. The majority of rehousing studies, however, report no important changes in household densities following relocation and a few even report a considerable *increase* in overcrowding. The report on relocation from the site of Norris Homes in Philadelphia [31] shows that 37 percent of the families were living at densities of 1.01 or more persons per room, both before and after relocation. The average number of rooms per household rose from 3.7 to 4.0 for families displaced from public housing sites in Chicago during 1952–1954 [8], but the proportion of families living at densities of 1.01 or more rose from 31 percent to 33 percent, and 36 percent of all households were "doubled up" following relocation. Baltimore reports an increase in families living at densities of 1.01 or more from 19 percent to 21 percent following relocation [2], and reloca-tion from the Michael Reese Hospital site in Chicago [29] resulted in an increase from 24 percent to 27 percent in the proportion of families living in conditions of extreme overcrowding (densities of 1.51 persons per room or higher). It seems clear that relocation generally does little to improve the overcrowded conditions that existed in the original clearance area.

Outdoor Space

The West End was a densely populated neighborhood with narrow streets, no building setbacks, and virtually no private or public open space within it. In contrast, a great many relocatees moved into homes which provided them with varying amounts of private or semi-private outdoor space: 6 percent of the relocation sample had extensive yards, 32 percent had small yards, and 26 percent had token yards. While it is clear that relocation resulted in an increase in private open space for many West Enders and more of the amenities of light and air generally considered desirable by planning criteria, at the same time most of the relocated households lost proximity to (and hence use of) major public recreational areas within easy walking distance of the West End. City- and even metropolitan-wide recreational resources such as the Boston Com-mon, the Public Garden, and the Charles River parks were utilized intensively by a great many West Enders. Additionally, as other papers on the West End have shown, a considerable portion of

West End life took place in the streets, which were very much a part of the personal living space of most residents.[10] The question of whether small private yards are more valuable and desirable than communal and large public spaces is a matter that must be investigated more carefully, for it raises problems of considerable importance in evaluating and planning the urban environment.

WHAT WAS THE QUALITY OF THE HOUSING THEY MOVED INTO?

In the aggregate, the physical quality[11] of relocation housing represented an improvement over West End housing conditions, as is clear from Table V. These figures, however, reflect the physical deterioration of housing in the West End during the six-year period between the time that redevelopment plans were first announced and the time of our interviews, shortly after the city took title to the land.[12] Hence the data exaggerate somewhat the positive effects of relocation. However, some aggregate improvement in housing quality seems almost certain to have occurred.

[10] See Marc Fried and Peggy Gleicher, "Some Sources of Residential Satisfaction in an Urban 'Slum'," *Journal of the American Institute of Planners*, XXVII (November, 1961), 305–315; Chester Hartman, "Social Values and Housing Orientations," *Journal of Social Issues*, XIX (April 1963), 113–131.

[11] Data on pre-relocation housing include ratings of condition and appearance of both building and dwelling unit. These ratings are available for only 307 of the 473 persons interviewed, since about one-third of the initial interviews were held after the family had moved from the West End.

The rating of relocation housing was made as part of a special survey of the residence and neighborhood for every address at which persons in the sample had lived from the time of dislocation to the time of the second interview. Post-relocation housing conditions were judged by structural condition and maintenance of the respondent's building, plus interview questions about plumbing facilities. Addresses outside the Boston metropolitan area were not rated, nor were ratings possible for buildings demolished since the time of the respondent's residence there.

[12] There were wide reports of accelerated deterioration in the West End as a direct result of the uncertainty and disruption caused by the rumors and changing plans regarding the fate of the neighborhood: some families moved out prematurely and few families chose to move into the area, thereby sharply increasing the vacancy rate and reducing the normal maintenance which accompanies occupancy; stores lost patronage and owners were forced to abandon their businesses. By the time of land-taking, only 2,555 of the 3,671 units in the project area were occupied, a vacancy rate of over 30 percent. In comparison, the vacancy rate in the project area was only 3.1 percent in 1950, as reported in Housing Census block statistics. For a more comprehensive picture of the effects of redevelopment on the West End community, prior to actual land-taking, see Herbert Gans, *The Urban Villagers* (New York: The Free Press of Glencoe, 1962), pp. 281–335.

TABLE V   *Structural condition of housing, pre- and post-relocation, West End sample*

West End Condition		Good	Fair	Poor	TOTAL	
			Post Relocation Condition (Substandard)			
Good		87	13	9	109	(41%)
Fair	(Substandard)	46	9	6	61	(23%)
Poor		63	13	22	98	(37%)
TOTAL		196	35	37	268	
		(73%)	(13%)	(14%)		(100%)

The degree of improvement in the quality of the housing may be considered from several vantage points. Two-fifths of the families in the sample were living in sound housing in the West End; after relocation, nearly three-fourths were in sound housing. At the other extreme, more than one-third were in dilapidated housing in the West End, but less than one-fifth were living in such poor housing after relocation. Another way of viewing these data is to compare the pre-relocation and post-relocation housing for each household. Thirty-two percent of the West End population lived in standard housing both before and after relocation; 19 percent lived in substandard housing both before and after. On the other hand, 41 percent moved from substandard pre-relocation housing to standard post-relocation housing; and 8 percent moved from standard pre-relocation to substandard post-relocation housing.

Further improvement in facilities and amenities is indicated by the fact that the proportion of families with central heating rose from 41 percent to 72 percent following relocation.[13] Virtually all families (97 percent) had a private bathroom before and after relocation.

A review of the findings from other studies indicates that in most cases housing quality, measured in terms of structural condition and facilities, improved considerably after relocation.[14] Thus, for

[13] Central heating does not necessarily mean more and better heat, however; particularly in working-class areas, it may frequently be (in Herbert Gans' phrase) "central non-heating."

[14] The question of change in housing quality is extremely difficult to assess, for no consistent or standard system of measurement is used by local authorities. Moreover, most reports fail to clarify what standards are used in judging housing condition—census categories, local codes, or special criteria established by the local authority. The limitations of even the most widely accepted single standard for judging housing quality in this country were recently noted by the former Assistant Chief of the Census Bureau's Housing Division, who wrote regarding preparations for the 1960 Housing Census: ". . . All persons

families displaced from Chicago public housing sites during 1957–1958 [9], 83 percent of the families were living in substandard housing before relocation, 42 percent afterwards. In Philadelphia, prior to relocation 83 percent of the households dislocated from the Norris Housing site [31] were living in structures in poor condition, compared with 35 percent following relocation. And the number of families from New York's Manhattantown site [4] living in buildings in poor condition dropped from 39 percent to 18 percent following relocation. While most studies report considerable improvement, significant numbers—in some cases, the majority of families—still live in substandard housing following relocation. The Philadelphia Housing Association reports [30] that 72 percent of the relocated families it studied continued living in substandard housing, and Reynolds' data [33] indicate that for the 41 cities surveyed, roughly 60 percent of the relocated families were still living in substandard conditions.

The few studies that treat separately the housing conditions of those who relocated into public and private housing indicate that families who relocated in private housing as a whole fared considerably worse than those in public projects. The lethargic rate of new public housing construction in recent years and the scant increase in authorizations requested under the Administration's 1964 housing legislation, together with the reluctance of many displaced families to move into public projects, may mean that the growing relocation loads of the next few years will be increasingly dependent on the private stock—a situation which bodes further difficulties for successful relocation.[15]

---

familiar with data on the condition of housing recognized that the subjective elements entailed in this classification rendered it one of the weakest among all the housing statistics collected." See Frank Kristof, "The Increased Utility of the 1960 Housing Census for Planning," *Journal of the American Institute of Planners,* XXIX (February, 1963), 40–47.

Data on housing condition reported in this section and in Chart I may therefore vary considerably in definition and significance. Questions of standards and reliability of local reports are discussed below in the Postscript.

[15] See Chester Hartman, "The Limitations of Public Housing: Relocation Choices in a Working-class Community," *Journal of the American Institute of Planners,* XXIX (November, 1963), 283–96.

Preferential treatment for displaced families in public housing may offset these trends, but whether public housing will in fact be able to accommodate significant numbers of displaced families will in part depend on the economic and social characteristics of the displaced families themselves. This type of preferential treatment, however, provides little net gain to the community, as priority treatment for displaced families serves to deprive other low-income families of needed housing.

WHAT RENTS ARE THEY PAYING?

It is clear from Tables VI and VII that relocation resulted in a marked increase in housing costs. In the West End, 88 percent of all households were paying less than $55 per month for their apartments, while only 30 percent were paying similarly low rents[16] after relocation. Conversely, only 2 percent were paying $75 per month or more in the West End, while after relocation 45 percent were paying at least $75 per month, and 20 percent were paying over $95 per month. Median rent rose from $41 to $71, a 73 percent increase. In terms of the incidence of rent change, 86 percent were paying higher rents after relocation, while relocation resulted in decreased rents for only 4 percent. Individual rent increases varied widely, but over half the households were paying at least $30 per month more after relocation, and two-fifths were paying at least $40 more.

TABLE VI   *Monthly rents, pre- and post-relocation, West End sample*

Rent	West End	Post-relocation
$0–34	24%	5%
35–54	64	25
55–74	9	25
75–94	2	25
95+	—	20
	99%	100%
Median rent	$41	$ 71

TABLE VII   *Changes in monthly rent, West End sample*

Amount by which present rent differs from West End rent	Number	Percent
$20 + less	11	2
$10 less	11	2
Same as W. E. rent	43	9
$10 more	74	16
$20 more	81	18
$30 more	58	13
$40 more	70	15
$50 more	61	13
$60 + more	50	11
	459	99%

[16] Unless otherwise indicated, the term "rents" will be used throughout to mean "housing costs," whether for owners or renters.

Although absolute change in rent level is an important index, perhaps a more relevant consideration for housing welfare is the change in rent level relative to family income. The general effect of relocation was to increase markedly the proportion of income being spent for housing.[17] Expressed as a median, the rent/income ratio rose from 13.6 percent in the West End to 18.6 percent following relocation. To analyze this increase more closely, rent/income ratios were calculated for each household; the aggregate distribution for both pre- and post-relocation samples is presented in Table VIII.[18] These data bring out dramatically the impact of increased expenditures for housing following relocation. The proportion of households paying less than 15 percent of their income for housing declined sharply from 64 percent in the West End to only 30 percent after relocation. At the other end of the scale, only 20 percent of the families paid 20 percent or more of their income for rent in the West End, but 43 percent paid this much after relocation.

Table IX indicates the direction and magnitude of individual

TABLE VIII   *Distribution of pre- and post-relocation rent/income ratios, West End sample*

Rent/Income ratio	West End	Post-Relocation
Less than 5.0%	3%	0%
5.0–9.9%	18	7
10.0–14.9%	42	23
15.0–19.9%	17	28
20.0–24.9%	10	19
25.0–29.9%	1	9
30.0–39.9%	6	8
40% or more	3	6
	100%	100%
Median rent/income ratio	13.6%	18.6%

[17] This increase occurred despite a fairly widespread incidence of higher reported incomes in the post-relocation interviews. Forty-five percent of the families reported post-relocation income in a higher category—and 12 percent in a lower category—than that reported in the West End interview (weekly family income was reported and tabulated in $25 ranges: $0–24, $25–49, and so on). While detailed evaluation and analysis of the implications of these changes is beyond the scope of this article, some evidence from the interviews suggests that the increases are in large part attributable to the addition of secondary income sources as a direct response to increased housing costs. A study of relocation in Indianapolis [15] also reports this phenomenon.

[18] Since rent as well as income was reported and tabulated in terms of ranges ($10 groupings for monthly rent, $25 groupings for weekly income), for purposes of computation the midpoint of each range was used.

household changes in rent/income ratio for the 360 households for whom both pre- and post-relocation data on rent and income are available. These data indicate that 74 percent of the population were paying a higher proportion of their income for housing after relocation, 11 percent were paying approximately the same proportion, and only 15 percent were paying a smaller proportion. The magnitude of these changes was frequently quite large: following relocation, substantial numbers of households were paying proportions of their income that exceeded by 10, 15, and even 20 percent the proportion they were paying in the West End.[19]

TABLE IX   *Changes in rent/income ratio, pre- and post-relocation, West End sample*

	Number	Percent
Present rent/income ratio less *than West End ratio by:*		
more than 15%	5	1
11–15%	9	3
6–10%	12	3
5% or less	29	8
Present rent/income ratio same *as West End*	40	11
Present rent/income ratio more *than West End ratio by:*		
5% or less	92	26
6–10%	91	25
11–15%	47	13
more than 15%	35	10
	360	100%

Table X relates rent changes to housing changes and indicates, as expected, that the greater the increase in rent, the better the relocation housing. Among those whose rent increased, the greater the amount of the increase, the lower the proportion of people living in substandard housing.[20] The overall index of housing change also shows that the greater the rent increase, the greater the

---

[19] To make completely clear a point which may be obscured by the limitations of syntax, I am speaking here of absolute changes over time in data which express the relation of two items of information at a given point in time. We are interested in the absolute rent/income ratio before and after relocation, not in the change relative to the original ratio. Changes from 6 percent to 16 percent, 10 percent to 20 percent, 14 percent to 24 percent, are all grouped together as increases by 10 percent, even though these are quite different degrees of change in relative terms.

[20] Paradoxically, the results appear to be inconsistent with regard to the condition of the apartments of the few families whose rents decreased. This is no doubt attributable to the fact that this group contains many persons who, upon relocation, combined households with a related individual or family.

overall housing improvement. What is perhaps most noteworthy about these data, however, is that a relatively large number of families moved into substandard housing or failed to improve their overall residential status despite increased rents. Recalculating the data in Table X, we find that, among all the families whose rent increased following relocation, fully 27 percent moved into unsound housing and an equal percentage showed no overall improvement on the index of residential change.

TABLE X   *Change in monthly rent and housing quality, West End sample*

Difference between Present Rent and West End Rent	Good	Condition of Relocation Apt. (Substandard)		Housing Change Index[A]		
		Fair	Poor	Better	Same	Worse
less	75%	19	6	36%	36	29
same	65%	12	23	47%	25	28
$0–19 more	62%	21	17	63%	22	15
$20–39 more	77%	11	12	72%	22	6
$40 + more	84%	7	9	87%	11	2

[A] This is an index of relative residential change in neighborhood quality, housing condition, and amount of interior space, weighing the three components equally. Any improvement or worsening is treated equally, regardless of the degree of change or the level at which it takes place. "Better" means that there has been an improvement in at least two of the three items, or in only one if the other two have remained constant. "Same" means that all three items have remained at the same level, or that one has improved, the other deteriorated, and the third remained constant. "Worse" means that at least two items have deteriorated, or that only one has, with the other two remaining constant.

The phenomenon of increased housing costs following relocation is characteristic of virtually all the rehousing efforts reviewed. With only one exception,[21] every relocation study, from the early 1930's until the present, reports increased rents, in some cases relatively small, but in most instances quite substantial. Thus, among the families forced to move from seven public housing sites in Chicago in 1952–1954 [8], 85 percent of all the renters experienced rent increases, with one-fourth paying at least $50 more per month

[21] The exception is the relocation of a (primarily white) group of elderly individuals and couples in Providence [19]. Sixty-three percent of this group reported lower rents, and only 6 percent reported higher rents. The reason for this is probably the very high vacancy rate in Providence during the 1950's, caused by rapid population loss (Providence lost over 16 percent of its population during the period 1950–1960, the largest population decline of any U.S. city with over 200,000 population), which led to a weakened rental market and lower rents.

following relocation. In San Francisco, the median monthly rent of families displaced from the Western Addition Area [27] rose from $39 to $58 following relocation. The Philadelphia Housing Association report [30] indicated that 79 percent of the group they studied experienced rent increases upon relocating and 19 percent experienced decreases, with the median rent $33 before relocation, $46 after relocation.

The sudden and large-scale increase in demand for low-rent housing caused by major renewal projects clearly is a key factor in causing higher rents, particularly in areas of housing shortage. In the words of a Chicago Housing Authority report [9], "city-wide trends in the housing market also contributed to higher rentals, and in a period of rising rents increases were frequently instituted when an apartment is rented to a new tenant." Data from the West End, from Buffalo, and from New York City [4, 6, 26] indicate further that low rents are frequently associated with length of residence, and that upon moving from clearance sites many families are deprived of special advantages which accrue from extended residence (for example, performance of janitorial duties in exchange for reduced rent, and acquaintanceship with the landlord), and which permit these families to pay lower rents.

The increased burden of these higher rents is revealed in the several studies which report rent/income ratios. For example, the San Francisco study [27] indicated that the median rent/income ratio rose from 17 percent to 23 percent following relocation. The 1957–1958 Chicago study of families displaced from public housing sites [9] reported an increase in the median rent/income ratio following relocation from 16.6 percent to 26.3 percent. Breaking down changes in rent/income ratio by income level, this same study indicates the degree to which poorer families suffer most from these increases: among those earning less than $3000 per year (35 percent of all households) median rent/income ratio rose from 35.3 percent before relocation to 45.9 percent after relocation; among those in the $3000 to $3999 bracket, the median ratio increased from 18.3 percent to 25.4 percent; and among those earning over $5000, the median ratio increased from 9.1 percent to 17.4 percent.[22]

22 In his testimony before Congress on February 17, 1964, HHFA Administrator Robert Weaver referred to "a recent survey of 789 families relocated to private housing from urban renewal projects in 9 cities." Forty-three

Finally, several other reports indicate the extent to which families must pay increased rents for substandard housing. A 1939 report on the results of relocation from a public housing site in Boston [23] indicated that 23 percent of those paying higher rents relocated in housing inferior to their previous homes. The 1952–1954 Chicago Housing Authority report [8] indicated that families who relocated in substandard housing experienced a median monthly rent increase of $27. And the 1957–1958 Chicago Housing Authority report [9] indicated that 41 percent of those in substandard housing were paying $80 or more per month gross rent, 19 percent were paying over $90 and 8 percent were paying over $100 per month.

RACIAL FACTORS

Since Negroes constituted only about 1 percent of the West End population, the special relocation difficulties faced by nonwhites are not revealed in our interviews. The majority of other studies deal with totally or predominantly nonwhite populations and provide some indication of the special significance of racial factors in relocation.

Every study of racially mixed relocation areas in which the effects of relocation are analyzed separately for white and nonwhite households indicates that the effects of discrimination make decent relocation housing more difficult and expensive to obtain for nonwhites and force them to pay high rents, even for poor housing. Examination of Chart I indicates further that the most unsatisfactory relocation results reported, in terms of increased rents and the high percentages of families who relocated into substandard housing, were in predominantly- or all-Negro areas [4, 8, 9, 10, 15, 27, 29, 30, 31, 33, 37].

Reports from Buffalo, San Francisco, and Seattle [6, 27, 35]

---

percent of the families interviewed experienced an increase in rent-to-income ratio of more than 5 percentage points. In Baltimore, the median ratio rose from 23 percent to 29 percent following relocation, in Louisville from 28 percent to 31 percent. Fifteen percent of all relocated families in the nine cities had to pay 40 percent or more of their reported income for rent after relocation. (See *Hearings on H.R. 9751, Housing and Community Development Legislation, before the Subcommittee on Housing of the Committee on Banking and Currency*, House of Representatives, 88th Congress, 2nd Session, pp. 41–42.)

indicate that the geographical dispersion of displaced nonwhite families was far more limited than that of white families. Chicago experience [8] indicates that for nonwhites, "contrary to the general market, rents did not follow housing quality with any clear consistency" and that "demand held prices generally within the middle range of rents regardless of deficiencies." The report of the Connecticut Civil Rights Advisory Commission [16], while presenting no data on pre-relocation rents or post-relocation housing conditions, indicates that Negroes and Puerto Ricans were paying considerably higher rents following relocation than were white families. Experience in Chicago and Akron [8, 9, 18] illustrates the severe difficulties faced by Negro home-buyers. The studies indicate minimal use of government-insured loans, a high incidence of purchase through installment contracts (leaving the home-owner without the usual equity protection of a title deed and mortgage loan), and short amortization periods (usually under fifteen years) which, combined with high prices, result in exceedingly high monthly payments. These reports also indicate the difficulties Negro families faced in finding new places to live. In Akron, the time required to find a new home was seven weeks for the average white family, and more than 20 weeks for the average Negro family. In both Chicago and Akron, Negro families were forced to rely primarily on informal sources, such as friends and relatives, in locating a new apartment; in contrast, white families were able to rely on newspaper ads and real estate agencies. The Akron study also reports that the new apartments of Negro families contained fewer and smaller rooms and fewer amenities (private kitchen, private bathroom, hot running water) than did the new apartments of white families. Buffalo's experience [6] likewise documents a significantly higher incidence of overcrowding and doubling-up among nonwhite relocatees.

Relocation may also have an important effect on the overall residential patterns in the city, particularly since the majority of people displaced by renewal have been Negroes. Depending on the goals of the relocation plan and the nature of relocation services offered to displaced families, the process can be one that fosters dissolution of the racial ghetto or one that perpetuates residential segregation and creates further tensions by rapid population shifts. From the few studies in which these broader questions are discussed, it would appear that relocation efforts have gone no further than dealing with the individual family and its housing problems, with the result that existing patterns of racial segregation have either continued or have become intensified. Census tract data from two Chicago studies [8, 9] indicate that that city's huge displacement program during the early 1950's at first sent large numbers of Negro families into predominantly white areas, which shortly thereafter "tipped"; by the late 1950's most of the displaced families were filling vacancies in the predominantly nonwhite neighborhoods. Figures on Buffalo's Ellicott relocation project (an area 80 percent nonwhite) show that 69 percent of the relocated families (and an even higher percentage of nonwhite families) moved into the seven census tracts directly north of the redevelopment area, tracts from which 12,000 white families had departed and into which 9,000 nonwhite families had moved during the 1950–60 decade [6]. The report of the Connecticut Advisory Committee to the U.S. Commission on Civil Rights [16] indicates that although neighborhood racial composition was relatively unchanged for nonwhite families before and after relocation, "there seems to be little doubt about the flight of white families into all-white neighborhoods after relocation."[23]

RELOCATION AID

Nearly all the studies which examine the quality of assistance in finding housing and the general role of official agencies in the relocation process emerge with rather negative conclusions. In most instances, the number of families who eventually relocate into housing which they found with agency aid (other than referrals to public housing) is strikingly small. Our data indicate that only 15 percent of West End families (including those who moved into public housing) found their new apartments with the help of

[23] For a fuller discussion of some of the more general issues concerning the racial aspects of relocation, see George B. Nesbitt, "Relocating Negroes From Urban Slum Clearance Sites," *Land Economics,* XXV (August, 1949), 275-88; John B. Collins, "Relocation of Negroes Displaced by Urban Renewal, with Emphasis on the Philadelphia Experience" (unpublished Master's thesis, Wharton School, University of Pennsylvania, 1961); Wolf Von Eckardt, "Bulldozers and Bureaucrats," "Black Neck in a White Noose" (Parts I and V of the series "Urban Renewal and the City"), *New Republic,* September 14, 1963, October 19, 1963.

relocation officials.[24] In Philadelphia, a city with one of the more responsible and effective renewal programs and one of the first to have a centralized relocation service, only 0.5 percent of all families displaced during the first two years of this service went into private rental housing on referral from the Rehousing Bureau [30]. In Providence [19], only 15 percent of the families reported using the Family Relocation Service, and only 6 percent reported that they had found their new apartment through this Service. The Chicago Housing Authority studies [8, 9] and the reports on New York City's Manhattantown and West Side Renewal areas [4, 14] indicate similar findings. And in Reynolds' survey [33], local authorities reported that less than one-third of the displaced families relocated into apartments offered by the official agencies, and that "the bulk of the cooperatively relocated clientele consisted of small-sized families . . ."

What is perhaps most disturbing about reports on relocation aid is the high percentage of original site families who are "lost." For example, the New York City Planning Commission [12] reported that 43 percent of the tenants displaced from 39 public housing sites during the 1946–1952 period moved to unknown addresses, and in San Francisco [27] approximately 1,600 of the 3,700 households who were enumerated in the original site survey "left the area without seeking the aid of or providing rehousing data to the relocation office." Whether this represents lack of assiduous follow-up techniques on the part of relocation officials, ignorance of available services, or hostility on the part of displaced residents, so high a rate of disappearance would seem to be unacceptable as a by-product of public improvement projects.[25]

24 West End data on attitudes toward relocation officials further indicate that only 13 percent of the families interviewed had positive feelings about the persons whose job it was to help them find housing. In response to a question asked in the post-relocation interview ("What kind of contact did you have with the relocation people?") it was not unusual to receive responses (two years after the time of contact) such as the following: "They didn't do a damn thing for us"; "They treat people terribly"; "They didn't even try."
One of the few detailed interview studies of the relocation process [4] notes that nearly half the tenants interviewed reported receiving absolutely no help from the site office in locating new quarters and that (again, two years after relocation) "on balance, feeling among tenants can conservatively be described as resentful and distrustful."
25 A further group of "lost" families, usually completely overlooked in the relocation operation, are those families who move out of a clearance area between the time of site census and actual land-taking. In the West End, our

Scattered evidence seems to suggest that the quality of relocation help offered by public agencies may be a significant factor in determining the quality and costs of relocation housing. Evidence from several studies [14, 16, 30, 33] indicates that where the relocation staff is competent and sensitive in providing lists of available vacancies and in counseling families in need of help, a higher proportion of families relocate in standard and satisfactory housing, at lower rents; more areas of the city are seen as possible relocation destinations, thus widening the family's area of choice; and the tendency to relocate along racial lines into sharply segregated areas is reduced.[26] However, the limited overall benefits reported even in those places where superior relocation services are offered suggest that the problems involved in relocating families require far more fundamental solutions than can be brought about by improvement of relocation services.

CONCLUSION

Although the results of forced relocation appear to vary widely from project to project, on the whole relocation has made a disappointingly small contribution to the attainment of "a decent home in a suitable living environment for every American family." Given the premise that one of the cardinal aims of renewal and rehousing should be the improved housing welfare of those living in substandard conditions, it is questionable whether the limited and inconsistent gains reported in most studies represent an acceptable level of achievement. Not only have the gains been limited, but they have been accompanied by widespread increases in housing costs,

---

data show that approximately 8 percent of the population surveyed during the period December, 1957 to January, 1958 were no longer living in the neighborhood by the time of land-taking in April, 1958. A Minneapolis study of a skid-row population [22] showed that 24 percent of the population in the original survey had moved by the time of land-taking. These early movers are not the official responsibility of the public authority and in most cases are not offered the home-seeking services or relocation payments available to those who remain until actual land-taking. Yet their dislocation is clearly caused by the renewal process and their subsequent housing conditions ought to be considered part of the public responsibility.

[26] A major survey research project is currently underway in Topeka, partly under the auspices of the Menninger Foundation, to determine, through use of experimental and control groups, the effects of intensive social and psychological services on the dislocation and adaptation experience.

CHART 1 Selected Findings from 33 U.S. Relocation Studies

The chart on the following pages shows these findings in a simple, comparable form. Some data have been recalculated and reformulated from the published figures, and in a few cases outside sources (maps, correspondence) have been used to supplement the information given.

The studies are presented in chronological sequence, together with the name of the author or sponsoring organization. Numbers in brackets refer to the references at the end of this article. Racial composition of the population, where known, is also given in brackets (a question mark indicates that information on race was not given directly, but was either inferred from other materials in the study or from outside sources).

STUDY	DESTINATION	TYPE, TENURE	DWELLING SPACE	CONDITION	RENTS
NEW YORK, 1933, Lavanburg Foundation [white] [26]	86 percent relocated in the "adjoining blocks"	Tenements: 100 percent pre; 99 percent post	Density 1.01+: 50 percent pre; 47 percent post	Living in Old Law Tenements: 96 percent pre; 83 percent post	Average monthly rent: $16 pre; $18 post
ATLANTIC CITY, 1936, New Jersey State Housing Authority [97 percent nonwhite] [37]	39 percent within ¼ mile; 83 percent within ½ mile; 96 percent within ¾ mile	1-family/row house: 70 percent pre; 62 percent post. 2-family: 15 percent pre; 18 percent post	Average number of rooms: 6.2 pre, 5.1 post; Density 1.01+: 10 percent pre, 23 percent post	Units unfit for use: 83 percent pre, 34 percent post; Major repairs needed: 99 percent pre, 86 percent post	Median monthly rent: $12 pre; $15 post. 34 percent paying higher rents; 48 percent paying higher rents; 29 percent paying lower rents
MINNEAPOLIS, 1938, Chapin [racially mixed] [7]	84 percent within ¾ mile	N.A.	Little overcrowding pre- or post-relocation	N.A.	Average monthly rent: $16 pre; $18 post
BOSTON, 1939, Housing Association of Metropolitan Boston [primarily nonwhite] [23]	N.A.	N.A.	12 percent more space: 34 percent no change; 54 percent less space	78 percent living in "better" apartments	67 percent paying higher rents: (23 percent of those paying higher rents in worse housing)
PHILADELPHIA, 1940, Philadelphia Housing Authority [88 percent nonwhite] [32]	N.A.	6 percent owners pre; 6 percent owners post	N.A.	Needing major repairs or unfit for use: 90 percent pre, 37 percent post; Good condition: 1 percent pre, 20 percent post	Median monthly rent: $18 pre; $19 post
DETROIT, 1950, Detroit Housing Commission [17]	N.A.	N.A.	Post-relocation: 27 percent doubled-up (no pre-relocation data available)	12 percent moved to sub-standard housing (no pre-relocation data available)	N.A.
CHICAGO, 1952, Pendleton, Heller [90 percent nonwhite] [29]	36 percent within 1 mile; 59 percent within 2 miles	12 percent owners pre; 9 percent owners post	Density 1.51+: 24 percent pre; 27 percent post	Private bath: 45 percent pre, 53 percent post; Central heat: 83 percent pre, 92 percent post	$50 or less/month: 94 percent pre; 62 percent post. 46 percent paying at least $16/month more post

Study				
NEW YORK CITY, 1953, City Planning Commission [12]	N.A.	N.A.	N.A.	"73 percent . . . exclusive of those who doubled up or moved into furnished rooms or rooming-houses obtained apartments which appeared to be standard."	N.A.
CHICAGO, 1952–1954, Chicago Housing Authority [primarily nonwhite] [8]	29 percent within 1 mile; 66 percent within 3 miles; 10 percent within 5 miles or more	*1-family:* 2 percent pre; 4 percent post; *5+ dwelling units:* 48 percent pre; 46 percent post	*Median number of rooms:* 3.7 pre, 4.0 post; *Density 1.01+:* 31 percent pre, 33 percent post; *Doubled-up households:* 39 percent pre, 36 percent post	*Standard:* 18 percent pre, 53 percent post; *Bldg. 60+ years old:* 89 percent pre, 68 percent post	(Renters only) 85 percent paying higher rents: average increase "about twice" previous rent. *Median monthly rent:* $37 pre; $67 post
SEATTLE, 1954, Seattle Housing Authority [83 percent white] [35]	(Private housing only) 43 percent within 1–1½ miles	0 percent owners pre; 19 percent owners post	N.A.	N.A.	N.A.
AKRON, 1955?, East Akron Community House [52 percent nonwhite] [18]	N.A.	0 percent owners pre; 38 percent owners post	*Average number of rooms:* 4.0 pre; 4.7 post	(Renters only) *Private bath:* 100 percent pre; 62 percent post	*Pre:* $33 (all families paying same rent). *Post:* 70 percent paying over $50 per month; 18 percent over $75
INDIANAPOLIS, 1956, Community Surveys, Inc. [primarily nonwhite] [15]	N.A.	N.A.	N.A.	Generally improved conditions	(Renters only) ". . . nearly all are paying rents . . . 100 percent—250 percent more than . . . in Area 'A'."
NEW YORK CITY, 1956, Women's City Club [4]	59 percent in Manhattan (23 percent within Manhattantown area)	N.A.	*Density 1.01+:* 26 percent pre; 10 percent post	*Poor condition:* 39 percent pre, 18 percent post; *Central heating:* 70 percent pre, 97 percent post	*Average monthly rent:* $41 pre; $56 post; 53 percent paying higher rents. (Private housing only). 51 percent paying one-fifth or more of income for rent; 32 percent one-fourth or more.

CHART 1 (Continued)

STUDY	DESTINATION	TYPE, TENURE	DWELLING SPACE	CONDITION	RENTS
NEW YORK CITY, 1957, Morningside Heights Association [Primarily nonwhite, Puerto Rican?] [28]	57 percent within Manhattan (19 percent Harlem, 13 percent Washington Heights, 10 percent Upper West Side, 15 percent other); 33 percent other New York City.	N.A.	*Average number of rooms:* 4.3 pre, 4.0 post; 5+ *rooms:* 43 percent pre, 29 percent post	N.A.	*Average monthly rent:* $51 pre; $61 post (relocated by management)
CHICAGO, 1957–1958, Chicago Housing Authority [nonwhite] [19]	"About a third of the households moved to other private dwellings within the vicinity of the clearance site."	19 percent owners pre; 18 percent owners post *1–2 family house:* 16 percent pre; 21 percent post	*Median number of rooms:* 4.1 pre, 4.6 post; *Density 1.01+:* 34 percent pre, 30 percent post; *Doubled-up:* 33 percent pre, 34 percent post	*Substandard:* 83 percent pre, 42 percent post; *Central heating:* 56 percent pre, 75 percent post	*Median monthly rent:* $57 pre; $85 post $100+/*month:* 2 percent pre; 27 percent post *Median rent/income ratio:* 16.6 percent pre; 26.3 percent post
BOSTON, 1958, Boston Redevelopment Authority [primarily nonwhite?] [5]	29 percent within ½ mile; 45 percent within 1 mile; 73 percent within 3 miles; 16 percent 5+ miles	13 percent owners pre; 9 percent owners post	N.A.	*Post-relocation:* 77 percent standard, 14 percent substandard, 9 percent unreported (no pre-relocation data available)	N.A.
PORTLAND, 1958?, Slum Clearance and Redevelopment Authority [93 percent white] [36]	74 percent within ½ mile; 86 percent within 1 mile	22 percent owners pre; 21 percent owners post	N.A.	N.A.	*Under* $20/*month:* 50 percent pre; 17 percent post; *under* $30/*month:* 90 percent pre; 63 percent post
PHILADELPHIA, 1958, Philadelphia Housing Authority [primarily nonwhite?] [31]	37 percent within 2 blocks; 56 percent within 4 blocks	N.A.	". . . Extent of overcrowding . . . just about as great," 37 percent living at densities 1.01+ post.	*Poor condition:* 83 percent pre, 35 percent post; *Good condition:* 4 percent pre, 17 percent post	Average monthly rent post-relocation 37 percent higher than pre-relocation average. $30+/*month:* 23 percent pre; 69 percent post
PHILADELPHIA, 1958, Philadelphia Housing Association [95 percent nonwhite] [30]	50 percent within ½ mile; 88 percent within 2 miles; 2 percent 4+ miles	N.A.	*Density 1.01+:* 59 percent pre; 41 percent post	*Unsatisfactory housing:* 100 percent pre; 72 percent post	*Median monthly rent:* $33 pre; $46 post 72 percent paying higher rents; 19 percent paying lower rents.
CHICAGO, 1958, Land Clearance Commission [43 percent nonwhite] [10]	N.A.	N.A.	N.A.	92 percent relocated into decent, safe housing (no pre-relocation data available)	*Average monthly rent:* $25 pre, $51 post; $50+/*month:* 5 percent pre, 54 percent post
U.S. Sample, 1955–1959, Reynolds [55 percent nonwhite] [33]	". . . Majority of all families relocated . . . not further than about 1½ miles from their old addresses."	N.A.	N.A.	Ca. 60 percent relocated in substandard housing (no pre-relocation data available)	". . . Relocatees most often paid more in rents for off-site shelter than they were paying before displacement."

318

NEW YORK CITY, 1959, Braislin, Porter and Wheelock [34]	56 percent within Manhattan (33 percent within neighborhood immediately adjacent to site)	N.A.	N.A.	N.A.	N.A.
MORRISTOWN, 1959, Housing Authority of the Town of Morristown [25]	74 percent within 6 blocks	N.A.	N.A.	100 percent substandard pre; 0 percent substandard post	N.A.
BALTIMORE, 1951-1960, Baltimore Urban Renewal and Housing Authority [91 percent nonwhite?] [3]	50-82 percent moved within same area *Mount Royal Plaza site*: 43 percent within ½ mile; 68 percent within 1 mile; 89 percent within 2 miles	N.A.	N.A.	N.A.	N.A.
LITTLE ROCK, 1953-1960, Housing Authority of the City of Little Rock [primarily nonwhite] [24]	N.A.	48 percent owners pre; 53 percent owners post	N.A.	86 percent substandard pre; 10 percent substandard post	N.A.
PROVIDENCE, 1960, Rhode Island Division of Aging [primarily white?] [19]	65 percent within 4 Census tracts bordering site; of these, most within several blocks of original residence	N.A.	Ca. one-fourth moved to larger units; 7 percent to smaller units	Ca. one-third of the units deteriorated, pre- and post-relocation	6 percent paying higher rents; 63 percent paying lower rents *Less than $45/month*: 15 percent pre; 63 percent post
SAN FRANCISCO, 1960, Lichfield, Smith [66 percent nonwhite] [27]	51 percent remained in W. Addition Area (ca. 1 mile radius surrounding site)	9 percent owners pre; 17 percent owners post	*Density 1.00+*: 50 percent pre; 36 percent post	74 percent moved to better area; 23 percent to worse area	*Median monthly rent:* $39 pre; $58 post 83 percent paying higher rents; 12 percent paying lower rents. *Median rent/income ratio:* 17 percent pre; 23 percent post
PORTLAND, 1961, Citizens Urban Renewal Effort [97 percent white] [11]	N.A.	N.A.	N.A.	N.A.	61 percent paying higher rents

CHART 1 (Continued)

STUDY	DESTINATION	TYPE, TENURE	DWELLING SPACE	CONDITION	RENTS
BALTIMORE, 1961, Baltimore Urban Renewal and Housing Authority [2]	(Private housing) 55 percent within ½ mile; 79 percent within 1 mile; 96 percent within 2 miles	11 percent owners pre; 14 percent owners post	*Average number of rooms:* 5.4 pre, 5.1 post; *Density 1.01+:* 19 percent pre, 21 percent post	*Dilapidated structure:* 86 percent pre, 11 percent post; *Central heating:* 22 percent pre, 58 percent post	(Private renters only) *Median monthly rent:* $43 pre, $53 post; *$60+/month:* 13 percent pre, 39 percent post
BUFFALO, 1961, Buffalo Municipal Housing Authority [6] [80 percent nonwhite]	40 percent within 1 mile, 70 percent within 2 miles	26 percent owners pre; 29 percent owners post	*Median number of rooms:* 6.15 pre, 6.19 post; *Density 1.01+:* 13 percent pre, 8 percent post; *Doubled-up:* 18 percent pre, 13 percent post	99+ percent moved to homes in "substantial compliance" with Minimum Standards Housing Ordinance (no pre-relocation data available)	Pre (average): $63 per month, Post (median): $65
DALLAS, 1961, Texas Transportation Institute [1] [white]	58 percent within 1 mile	100 percent owners pre; 93 percent owners post	*Average number of rooms:* 5.54 pre; 5.55 post	*Average age:* 29 years pre, 19 years post; *Brick or masonry construction:* 16 percent pre, 51 percent post	*Mortgaged homes:* 29 percent pre, 29 percent post; *Average mortgage:* $3061 pre, $7215 post
NEW YORK CITY, 1962, Community Service Society [85 percent nonwhite, Puerto Rican] [14]	17 percent within renewal area; 63 percent within Manhattan	N.A.	N.A.	93 percent moved to standard housing (no pre-relocation data available)	*Average monthly rent (estimate):* $63 pre, $72 post; *$101+/month:* 7 percent pre, 19 percent post
MINNEAPOLIS, 1963, Housing and Redevelopment Authority [22] [96 percent white]	70–80 percent within 1 mile	N.A.	N.A.	*Standard housing:* 17 percent pre; 83 percent post	*Under $20/month:* 44 percent pre, 3 percent post; *$35+/month:* 14 percent pre, 38 percent post

often incurred irrespective of an improvement in housing or the ability or desire to absorb these costs. In most clearance areas, some degree of improvement is inevitable, since people are being moved out of marginal or substandard sections.[27] (As the Chicago Housing Authority observed [8], "It would have been difficult for families leaving the sites to have found a worse segment of the city's housing than the one they had occupied.") The real questions for public policy have to do with the degree of improvement the community should demand from rehousing operations and the nature of the costs imposed.[28]

It is an inescapable conclusion that relocation has been only an ancillary component of the renewal process; were this not the case, the community would find totally unacceptable "slum clearance" projects which leave as many as two-thirds of the displaced families still living in substandard conditions, or which actually increase the incidence of overcrowding. With few exceptions, relocation in this country has not truly been a rehousing effort (in the British sense of the word), a plan which focuses primary attention on the problem of how to insure that people living in substandard housing are resettled into decent homes. In city after city, one sees that the great amount of time and effort spent in investigating and condemning housing conditions in the slums that local authorities wish to tear down is in no sense matched by corresponding public and professional interest in the fate of displaced families once they have been dislodged. It is perhaps revealing to note that only one-half of one

[27] Many clearance sites (such as the West End), however, contain a considerable amount of decent housing. In all probability, this is true primarily of large sites and of projects where the dominant renewal goals relate to the proposed re-use of the site—such as, civic centers, downtown renewal, and upper-income housing—rather than to efforts at eliminating blighted, unsalvageable structures. In these areas, the number of families living in standard housing prior to relocation should be noted carefully, since ostensibly satisfactory aggregate post-relocation housing conditions may in fact represent only a minor gain.

[28] Clearly, these questions must be placed in the context of housing changes among the population as a whole. A recent HHFA report shows that in the 1950–60 decade the proportion of occupied substandard units fell from 72 percent to 44 percent among the nation's nonwhite population, and from 32 percent to 13 percent among the white population. (See *Our Nonwhite Population and Its Housing*. Washington: Housing and Home Finance Agency, Office of Program Policy, July, 1963.) Since the major portion of this improvement occurred without resort to forced displacement from substandard housing, conclusions about the benefits that flow from relocation must incorporate assumptions about what would have happened to the same population in the absence of forced change.

percent of the $2.2 billion of gross project costs for all federally-aided urban renewal projects (through 1960) was spent on relocation.[29]

Review of reports and procedures relating to relocation reveals further that environmental considerations are virtually absent in the assignment and evaluation of relocation dwellings. This is in part understandable, since, despite the wording of the 1949 Housing Act, no meaningful criteria have yet been established as to what constitutes a "suitable living environment." But at a minimum the local authority should insure that displaced families do not relocate in areas slated for clearance or rehabilitation in the near future, and thereby become part of a population of repeatedly displaced persons. Yet consideration of this factor, which will undoubtedly make the already difficult job of finding decent relocation housing for low-income families even more complex, has rarely been incorporated in the plans and reports of local authorities. (In one of the few reports to consider this factor, the New York City Planning Commission [12] in a sample survey found that of the 709 tenants moving from public housing sites into private housing who reported new addresses, 49 percent moved into housing in areas mapped for future redevelopment.) Given the realities of the low-income housing market and the impact of public programs, it is likely that, for many families, relocation may mean no more than keeping one step ahead of the bulldozer.

It is clear, too, that relocation results in a somewhat selective incidence of benefits in terms of housing welfare, but imposes a quite unselective incidence of costs, personal as well as financial. These results suggest that far greater attention must be paid to the impact and dynamics of the dislocation and relocation experience on various subgroups within the affected population. Review of the literature on mobility, preparedness for change, and modes of adaptation, as well as preliminary analysis of West End data,[30] suggests that families who relocate satisfactorily are by and large those with adequate financial, personal, and social resources, those who are prepared for upward mobility and who (despite frequent initial resentment about having to leave a satisfying environment)

[29] See Martin C. Anderson, "The Federal Urban Renewal Program: A Financial and Economic Analysis" (unpublished Doctoral dissertation, M.I.T., 1962).
[30] Fried in Kantor, *op. cit.*

view forced relocation as an opportunity to obtain the kind of housing that they have long desired. On the other hand, those who are least prepared and able to effect a positive change, because of inadequacies in income and personal or social resources, appear to incur heavy costs in terms of severe personal and social disruption, failure to improve housing conditions, and increased housing expenses that are difficult to absorb or unrelated to housing improvement. To a considerable extent, then, the various reports on rehousing suggest that relocation may be resulting in a "rich get richer, poor get poorer" effect. Present renewal operations are, however, highly unselective and do not permit discrimination between families most and least able to profit by the experience. Nor do they provide a variety of aids and programs designed to fit the needs of the different types of families contained in a relocation population. With a greater understanding of the effects of relocation and of the various subgroups within a relocation population, it may be possible to devise more sophisticated programs which will, through incentives, hasten the mobility of those prepared to make changes, and will at the same time be sensitive to the special needs of those who cannot cope with forced change, by providing new services and benefits for them or by obviating the necessity to relocate.

It is of course appropriate to question whether the results of the studies reported here and the conclusions that flow from these findings are applicable to the current housing picture. Over two-thirds of the studies reviewed in this paper report on relocation activities that occurred during the 1950's; only one study is dated as recently as 1963. Thus the data cited here do not permit any definite statements about the results of relocation activity in recent years—more specifically, since 1961 and the change in Administrations. Clearly, there have been new emphases in the federal government's housing policies: the President's executive order on equal opportunity in housing, the moderate-income (Sec. 221(d)(3)) housing program, pilot projects in new ways to house low-income families, a shift away from the bulldozer approach to urban renewal, and increased concern for the problems of relocated families. Nonetheless, it remains unclear whether the shortcomings described in this paper are entirely things of the past. In the first place, reliable data on current relocation experience are not yet available (see the

Postscript to this article). Second, it is only through local operating agencies that actual changes will come about, and there still exist wide differences in local conditions and in the aims and personnel of these agencies; these differences make it extremely difficult to translate changes in federal policies and procedures uniformly and rapidly to the local level. Third, the limited supply of low-cost housing continues to make relocation a difficult task. The housing shortage of the early 1950's has been eased considerably, but we do not know whether it has eased sufficiently to provide for current high rates of displacement resulting from urban highway construction, redevelopment projects, and the "financial bulldozer" of rehabilitation. The filtering of housing undoubtedly has helped to create additional vacancies in urban areas, but it is doubtful whether a sufficient number of vacant units are: *one*, in sound condition; *two*, available at prices the poor can afford; *three*, open to nonwhite occupancy; and *four*, suitably located for the social and economic needs of displaced people. The volume of new public housing—another potential resource for relocation—has been small, and the program has been beset by a great many other difficulties. In short, changes have doubtless taken place, and what is happening in 1964 is quite different from what went on in 1954. The question is how much have things changed and how far are we still from acceptable levels of achievement. In view of past experience, the burden of proof must be on the public agencies to produce valid answers to these questions and to demonstrate that satisfactory relocation is now being achieved.

Finally, we must consider how issues of housing welfare relate to the context provided by analysis of the human costs and benefits of relocation. Our findings from the West End, supported by similar studies from other cities, suggest that the deleterious effects of the uprooting experience, the loss of familiar places and persons, and the difficulties of adjusting to and accepting new living environments may be far more serious issues than are changes in housing status.[31]

[31] See Fried in Duhl, *op. cit;* Fried in Kantor, *op. cit;* Marc Fried, "Effects of Social Change on Mental Health," *American Journal of Orthopsychiatry,* XXXIV (January, 1964), 3–28; Herbert Gans, "The Human Implications of Current Redevelopment and Relocation Planning," *Journal of the American Institute of Planners,* XXV (February, 1959), 15–25; Chester Hartman, "The Limitations of Public Housing: Relocation Choices in a Working-Class Community," *op. cit.;* Vere Hole, "Social Effects of Planned Rehousing," *Town Planning Review,* XXX (July, 1959), 161–173; Peter Marris, *Family and Social*

If we are to undertake valid cost-benefit analyses of the impact of relocation, it is essential that the investigation of housing change be placed in the larger context of residential change, the various social and psychological aspects of community life, and how they vary among different population groups. During the coming years, thousands of American families will be forcibly dislocated through the workings of governmental programs such as urban renewal, highway construction, and public housing, as well as by the workings of private market mechanisms. It is a serious challenge to the housing and planning professions, as well as to the society as a whole, to clarify and comprehend the effects of relocation and to improve these programs in the light of our increased knowledge.

A POSTSCRIPT

It is evident that relocation presents a serious problem for local public agencies. On the one hand, they have a statutory obligation to relocate all families who so desire in decent, safe, and sanitary housing, convenient to their place of work and at rents they can afford; on the other hand, the agency's rebuilding operations do not provide suitable housing for those displaced. The conflict between demands and resources becomes evident when one considers the magnitude of family displacement, the fact that displaced families for the most part have the double disadvantage of being both poor and nonwhite, the shortage of low-rent standard vacancies in most cities, the limited usefulness of public housing as a relocation resource, and the competition for relocation housing from families displaced by the highway program and other forms of public and private construction. The nature of this conflict was eloquently described more than a decade ago by Jack Meltzer, who wrote: ". . . In the final analysis any relocation plan is dependent on an available supply of housing, both public and private. To recognize the fact that relocation must inevitably accelerate competition for

Change in an African City (London: Routledge and Kegan, Paul, 1961); Peter Marris, "The Social Implications of Urban Redevelopment," *Journal of the American Institute of Planners*, XXVIII (August, 1962), 180–86; J. M. Mogey, *Family and Neighbourhood* (London: Oxford University Press, 1956); Charles Vereker and John B. Mays, *Urban Redevelopment and Social Change* (Liverpool: Liverpool University Press, 1961); Michael Young and Peter Willmott, *Family and Kinship in East London* (Glencoe, Ill.: The Free Press, 1957).

an already inadequate supply of housing, particularly for housing at levels that the bulk of relocatees can afford, and then to proceed with the relocation of families without providing for meeting this need is to fly in the face of reason and reality. This becomes doubly serious when Negroes are being relocated, since the competition for housing is most serious for the Negro, and further, a situation is created largely by public action that results in pressures upon the social fabric without an assumption of responsibility for coping with the effects of these pressures."[32]

Given these conflicts, there are bound to be inherent defects in a system that requires the agency executing these programs to evaluate relocation results. Accordingly, one must question whether local authorities are free to judge and report on the results of their relocation operations in an objective and impartial manner. In effect, the local agency may have no choice but to issue extremely positive relocation reports: anything less than this might produce legal, political, and ethical conflicts and could slow up or curtail the entire rebuilding effort, which is the principal goal of the authority and its programs.

Official relocation figures, as reported by local renewal authorities and compiled by the Urban Renewal Administration, indicate that relocation has consistently resulted in an extremely high percentage of families living in standard housing. URA data indicate that through September, 1963, only 7.7 percent of the 141,210 families displaced from urban renewal sites for whom post-relocation information is available (87 percent of the total number of families displaced) moved into substandard housing.[33] These reports are widely used by federal and local officials and in planning literature to describe the results of urban renewal, and they contribute significantly to the public's image of the program.[34] Recently, however, responsible persons in the housing and planning field have

[32] Jack Meltzer, "Relocation of Families Displaced in Urban Redevelopment: Experience in Chicago," *Urban Redevelopment: Problems and Practices,* ed. Coleman Woodbury (Chicago: Univ. of Chicago Press, 1953), p. 452.

[33] Letter from Peter P. Riemer, Director, Program Data and Evaluation Branch, Urban Renewal Administration, May 21, 1964.

[34] See, for example, President Johnson's Message to Congress on Housing and Community Development (*New York Times,* January 28, 1964, p. 16); *Urban Renewal Notes,* March–April, 1964; Robert C. Weaver, "Current Trends in Urban Renewal," *Land Economics,* XXXIX (November, 1963), 325–41; Martin Meyerson, *et al., Housing, People, and Cities* (New York: McGraw-Hill, 1962), p. 311.

been questioning the reliability of official figures.[35] Careful study of local housing conditions has led many observers to conclude that in view of the extent of displacement and the income and demographic characteristics of relocation caseloads, it is highly improbable that relocation could have had such consistently beneficial results.

Data collected by the Center for Community Studies on the West End relocation operation—probably the first large-scale, independently-gathered data on the results of relocation—show some marked discrepancies with official Boston Redevelopment Authority data on the West End and furnish support for the prevailing skepticism about official findings. The comparative data, presented in Table XI, indicate extremely large differences in findings with respect to both condition and tenure (although the proportion going into public housing and the geographical distribution of displaced families—the latter not shown in this presentation—are almost identical in both sets of figures). According to the official data, less than 2 percent of the West End families moved into

TABLE XI *Post-relocation housing conditions of West End population, Boston Redevelopment Authority data and Center for Community Studies data*[A]

	B.R.A. Data (1506 families)	C.C.S. Data (433 families)
Standard private rental	81.3%	45.5%
Standard private sales	6.9	19.0
Public housing	10.1	10.2
Substandard private rental	1.7	23.0
Substandard private sales	—	2.4
TOTAL	100.0	100.1

[A] Official B.R.A. data are taken from the Report on Relocation of Families and Individuals (Form H–666) for the West End Project Area, submitted to the Urban Renewal Administration, dated October 31, 1963. Housing condition is reported for 1506, or 87 percent, of the 1731 families displaced, but is not reported for the 824 dislocated individual householders.

To increase comparability of data, all one-person households have been removed from the C.C.S. sample, and for those families who moved from their initial relocation address before the follow-up interview, we have used the rating of the dwelling the dislocated family moved to directly after leaving the project area (as noted in footnote 4, the data presented in previous sections refer to the dwelling in which the respondent was living at the time of the follow-up interview, regardless of how many times the family had moved since leaving the West End).

[35] See, for example, William G. Grigsby, *Housing Markets and Public Policy* (Philadelphia: Univ. of Pennsylvania Press, 1963), p. 286n. [Reprinted in Chapter 25 of this volume.—Ed.]

structurally substandard housing; according to the independently-gathered data, over 25 percent relocated into structurally substandard housing. Whereas the official data indicate that less than 7 percent of West End families bought homes upon leaving the neighborhood, interview data collected by the Center for Community Studies indicate that three times as many families—over 21 percent—moved into their own homes.

Without more detailed investigation, it is impossible to trace the source of these discrepancies with any precision.[36] It should be noted, however, that the Center for Community Studies housing surveyors were all well-trained college graduates and made use of criteria approximating those of the U.S. Housing Census. A recent detailed study of the relocation process by Gordon N. Gottsche (coincidentally, also with reference to Boston's West End) offers a critique of the evaluation and data-gathering systems employed by the local authority and suggests one possible source for discrepancies of this sort [20]. Gottsche's principal conclusions are that with respect to post-relocation housing evaluations, "there is no systematic method for the relocation fieldworker to use in the evaluation process" and that a system of "compromised standards" was used in the evaluation process, whereby standards employed in the pre-relocation housing surveys were far more inclusive and detailed than the standards used in evaluating post-relocation housing. Gottsche details and documents these conclusions: lack of recorded inspection specifications, complete freedom of the local authority to establish its own standards and inspection procedures, wholesale but undocumented condemnation of the environment of

---

[36] The Center for Community Studies housing surveys were made approximately two years after relocation, whereas Boston Redevelopment Authority surveys of these same addresses were made at the time of relocation. It is unlikely, however, that this time lag could introduce differences of the magnitude indicated in Table XI. (Furthermore, Gottsche's survey [20], which indicates similar discrepancies, was made at roughly the same time as the B.R.A. surveys.) However, this does raise the issue of "housekeeping," which seems to have attained some prevalence in official circles. Several renewal officials have claimed in conversation that displaced families are relocated into standard homes, but because of poor housekeeping habits and inadequate training turn decent homes into slums within a very short time. Clearly, this argument is applicable only to some aspects of substandard housing: inadequate plumbing or absence of dual egress is not a situation created by a family's behavior. Further, to my knowledge no evidence has ever been offered to support this contention. The matter should be studied, however, since this reasoning appears to have some currency.

the renewal site as "uniformly bad," but failure to consider physical or social features of the environment at all in the post-relocation evaluation, and the generally poor level of data recording. Inspection of a (non-random) sample of some 80 relocation dwellings led Gottsche to state that ". . . the governmental standard was compromised in about one-half of the cases, with the structure requiring either demolition or major rehabilitation."

It is not clear whether these critical findings, based on observations of a single operation, can be generalized to other cities and to more recent procedures. It is difficult and expensive to obtain independent data, local authorities are frequently reluctant to allow inspection of their records and operating procedures, and until recently few responsible persons have dared express skepticism about the operations of public bodies undertaking renewal. Only a few reports in the above review make reference to this issue. Hollman, in his Philadelphia study [30], reported that the sample he took from Rehousing Bureau files showed results different from the Philadelphia reports to the URA, differences which for the categories "self-relocated to standard private rental housing" and "substandard housing" were statistically significant, although the universe was not entirely the same. In 1962, the U.S. Comptroller General began a series of spot-checks of local renewal operations and reported that federal government inspection of the buildings in Cleveland's Erieview renewal project showed only 20 percent of the buildings to be substandard, although reports of the local authority submitted to the HHFA regional office in Chicago classified 71 percent of the buildings as substandard.[37] This report goes on to recommend that local authorities be more closely supervised by the federal agencies with respect to the standards they employ and the accuracy of data they submit. A great deal of further investigation is needed in order to clarify these matters, but it is clear that as long as relocation remains a secondary interest in the renewal process and the primary impetus for renewal is to replace low-income housing with "higher" uses, there will be strong pressures to use compromised standards and to understate any adverse impact of the relocation process on displaced families.

[37] Comptroller General of the U.S., *Report to the Congress of the U.S.: Premature Approval of Large-Scale Demolition for Erieview Urban Renewal Project 1, Cleveland, Ohio, by the Urban Renewal Administration. Housing and Home Finance Agency* (Washington, D.C., June, 1963).

As a final note, it is difficult to refrain from commenting on the overall quality of relocation reports, as evidenced by the studies reviewed in this article. The most serious shortcoming is the inadequate quantity of relevant post-relocation data. In order to assess the impact of relocation, one must at a minimum have data on geographic dispersion, changes in living space, housing conditions before and after relocation, and changes in housing costs. Yet only 8 of the 33 studies reviewed contained information on all four of these factors in sufficient quantity to permit the reader to evaluate the impact of relocation. Most studies pay little attention to that part of the relocated population which has "disappeared," and conclusions are made solely on the basis of data on those families for whom information is available. Yet the "lost" families are generally the least stable, most transient group in the area, with fewest resources, and probably fare far worse than those families who receive help and whose post-relocation whereabouts are known. Rarely are conclusions qualified or offered as tentative in view of this unknown factor.[38]

[38] It should be noted that the West End study minimized this skewing tendency markedly. The original sample was drawn randomly from relocation office site occupancy cards. The resultant sample of 585 represented approximately one-fifth of all project area households meeting our sample criteria (the household had to contain a female between the ages of 20–65). Detailed follow-up interview data are available for 499, or 85 percent of the original sample, and some data on housing (including housing type, location, condition of neighborhood and building) are available for 540, or 92 percent of the original sample. This combination of random sampling technique and assiduous follow-up procedure to ensure a high rate of response is virtually unique among studies of this kind and makes the West End data probably the most reliable of all studies reported here.

Of the studies compiled for this article, only one posited various assumptions about the "lost" families and used these assumptions as part of the total analysis and overall findings. (It is perhaps significant to note that this report was done by a private organization rather than a public agency.) In the Philadelphia Housing Association's report on relocation in Philadelphia in 1955–1957 [30] nearly half the total caseload was found to have disappeared or refused to cooperate with relocation officials. Of those reporting, 45 percent went into satisfactory housing. However, the Association presents its findings for the entire sample in terms of three assumptions about the unreported group: that the distribution of the unreported sample is identical to the reported sample; that the proportion of the unreported sample relocating into substandard housing is the same as the proportion among the reported sample who relocated into private rental housing without official aid; that the condition of the unreported families is identical to their condition prior to relocation. Under these various assumptions, the proportions of the total caseload relocating in satisfactory housing are, respectively, 45 percent, 28 percent and 21 percent. The report then goes on to explain why it considers the intermediate assumption the most probable of the three and says (realistically) that even this assumption is probably somewhat more positive than the real case; it then makes this preferred assumption the basis for reporting and discussion.

Further, most reports, as evidenced by their style and manner of presentation, apparently are written in order to "sell" relocation, to prove a case; texts are frequently characterized by a roseate tone, stressing achievements and either minimizing or ignoring negative consequences.[39] Even in cases where the tabulated data are comprehensive and objective, texts of official reports are frequently deceptive. Thus, a Chicago Housing Authority report [9] contains the following sentence: "The median rent/income ratio for all households in site dwellings was 16.6%; after relocation this median ratio increased to 26.3%, but was still less than 20% for households with income of $5000 or more"; and the generalization that "all income groups shared in better housing after relocation" (this latter interpretation is based on a table of post-relocation housing condition by income levels, which indicates that among families earning $3000 a year—35% of the population—only 33% relocated into standard housing). Another Chicago Housing Authority study [8] presents detailed data on increases in rent and rent/income ratios following relocation (among the highest reported in any relocation study), which are then described in the following manner: "After moving, most families in each income group still paid less than ¼ of their income for rent, except for those with income under $3000 [over one-third of the population!]. Although the remaining ⅓ paid 25% or more, rents for families in this group usually did not exceed 30% of income." A more objective observer would probably be far less sanguine in describing these findings.[40]

We are still a long way from knowing all that needs to be known about the effects of relocation.[41] Without more detailed knowledge

[39] Consider, for example, the concluding remarks of the Chicago Land Clearance Commission's *Final Relocation Report, Project No. UR Ill. 6–3* [10]: "Some of the individual householders in the project area required a great deal of help and furnished some of the more complex relocation problems. . . . In each case the relocation staff did wonders through sympathetic, patient and helpful attitudes. . . . The relocation job in project UR Ill. 6–3 proved . . . that redevelopment of a slum and blighted area is advantageous in all its aspects." It would seem that rhapsodic prose of this sort is out of place in any official evaluation report, particularly in one which offers as little information as this one does, and in which average monthly rent for the displaced families is shown to have more than doubled following relocation (see the summary of findings in Chart I).

[40] It is interesting to note that the best relocation reports—in terms of clarity, comprehensiveness, and objectivity—are those written by private, rather than public, agencies [see 4, 26, 27, 29, 30].

[41] The introductory words to two of the earliest relocation studies are as applicable today as they were three decades ago. The Lavanburg Foundation's 1933 study of New York's Lower East Side [26] noted: "Housing experts

of these effects—in terms of housing, community life and psycho-
social reactions—it is impossible to know the ultimate results of
our present actions: whether we are improving the living conditions
of slum families or merely shifting the slum to another section of
the city; whether relocation aids the slum family or whether
renewal is merely a device to use urban land for more favored
groups in the society. These are questions of vital importance, and
there is strong evidence to support a conclusion that the executors
of these acts cannot at the same time impartially judge what they
have done. In terms of funds, time, and manpower, we allocate far
too few resources to feedback analysis of social welfare programs.
Not only must we elevate this function to a higher priority, but it
must be structured in such a way as to eliminate the possibility of a
built-in bias in our evaluations. Given the factors outlined above,
one must conclude that this phase of the renewal operation should
be placed outside the local renewal authority, either with another
government agency or with a non-governmental research group.
Only in this way can we be sure that the objective tools and
methods of the social scientist will be brought to bear on the reporting and analysis of these critical issues.

REFERENCES

1. Adkins, William G. and Eichman, Frank F. Jr. *Consequences of Displacement by Right of Way to 100 Home Owners, Dallas, Texas.* Bulletin No. 16. College Station, Texas: Texas Transportation Institute, A & M College of Texas, September, 1961.
2. Baltimore Urban Renewal and Housing Agency, Research Division. *The New Locations and Housing Characteristics of Families Displaced from Area 3-C.* Baltimore: Urban Renewal and Housing Agency, March, 1961.
3. Baltimore Urban Renewal and Housing Agency, Research Division. *Ten Years of Relocation Experience in Baltimore, Maryland.* Baltimore: Urban Renewal and Housing Agency, June, 1961.
4. Black, Elinor G. *Manhattantown Two Years Later: A Second Look at Tenant Relocation.* New York: Women's City Club of New York, April, 1956.

frequently ponder over specific questions in connection with slum clearance without arriving at definite conclusions, because of the lack of explicit factual information." Chapin's 1936 study of Minneapolis [7] begins with these words: "When a slum is cleared of insanitary dwellings, what becomes of the people who lived in the slum? . . . Answers to these questions have long been sought, but often met in terms of opinion rather than facts. Especially neglected have been the psychological and social aspects of the problem."

5. Boston Redevelopment Authority. *Final Relocation Report, New York Streets Project—UR Mass. 2–1.* March, 1958. (Mimeographed.)
6. Buffalo Municipal Housing Authority. *Ellicott Relocation: Objectives, Experience, and Appraisal.* Buffalo, N.Y.: Municipal Housing Authority, November, 1961.
7. Chapin, F. Stuart. "The Effects of Slum Clearance and Rehousing on Family and Community Relationships in Minneapolis," *American Journal of Sociology,* XLIII (March, 1938), 744–63.
8. Chicago Housing Authority. *Relocation of Site Residents to Private Housing: The Characteristics and Quality of Dwellings Obtained in the Movement from Chicago Housing Authority Slum Clearance Sites, 1952–1954.* Chicago: Housing Authority, November, 1955.
9. Chicago Housing Authority. *Rehousing Residents Displaced from Public Housing Clearance Sites in Chicago, 1957–1958.* Chicago: Chicago Housing Authority, October, 1960.
10. Chicago Land Clearance Commission. *Final Relocation Report, Project No. UR Ill. 6–3 (W. Central Industrial District).* Chicago: Chicago Land Clearance Commission, April, 1958.
11. Citizens Urban Renewal Effort (CURE). *Report of Survey on Relocation of Families in Connection with the Bayside Park Urban Renewal Project.* Memorandum to the Portland, Maine City Council, April, 1961.
12. City Planning Commission, City of New York. *Tenant Relocation Report.* New York: City Planning Commission, January 20, 1954.
13. Cohn, Samuel M. *Report of the Site Survey and Description of the Work of Relocation PA–2–3.* Philadelphia Housing Authority, Department of Research and Information, September, 1940. (Typewritten.)
14. Community Service Society of New York. *A Demonstration Project in Relocation.* New York: Community Service Society, April, 1962.
15. Community Surveys, Inc. *Redevelopment: Some Human Gains and Losses.* Indianapolis, 1956.
16. Connecticut Advisory Committee to the United States Commission on Civil Rights. *Report on Connecticut: Family Relocation under Urban Renewal.* Washington, July, 1963.
17. Detroit Housing Commission. *Monthly Report.* November–December, 1950, pp. 4–9.
18. East Akron Community House. *Where Will They Go?: A Study of 77 Families Forced to Move from the "Mobile Houses,"* East Akron, Ohio, 1955 (?).
19. Goldstein, Sidney and Zimmer, Basil. *Residential Displacement and Resettlement of the Aged: A Study of the Problems of Rehousing Aged Residents Displaced by Freeway Construction in Downtown Providence.* Providence: Rhode Island Division on Aging, 1960.
20. Gottsche, Gordon N. "Relocation: Goals, Implementation and Evaluation of the Process, with Reference to the West End Redevelopment Project in Boston, Mass." Unpublished Master's thesis, M.I.T., 1960.
21. Housing and Home Finance Agency. Urban Renewal Administration. *Relocation from Urban Renewal Areas Through December, 1961.* Washington, 1962(?).

22. The Housing and Redevelopment Authority in and for the City of Minneapolis. *Report on the Relocation of Residents, Businesses and Institutions from the Gateway Center Project Area.* Minneapolis: Housing and Redevelopment Authority, November, 1963.
23. Housing Association of Metropolitan Boston. *Comparative Survey of Present and Former Dwellings of Families Displaced by the Development of a Public Housing Project in Boston.* Boston: Housing Association, October, 1939.
24. Housing Authority of the City of Little Rock, Ark. *Final Relocation Report, Dunbar Redevelopment Project.* 1953(?).
——. *Final Relocation Report, Philander Smith Project Ark. R–1.* January, 1957.
——. *Relocation in the Livestock Show Area of Little Rock, Arkansas.* May, 1960.
——. *Relocation in the Westrock Urban Renewal Project Area.* September, 1960.
25. Housing Authority of the Town of Morristown, New Jersey. *The First Fifty Families: An Analysis of the Relocation Program.* June, 1959. (Mimeographed.)
26. Lavanburg Foundation. *What Happened to 386 Families Who Were Compelled to Vacate Their Slum Dwellings to Make Way for a Large Housing Project.* New York: Lavanburg Foundation, 1933.
27. Lichfield, Nathaniel. "Relocation: The Impact on Housing Welfare," *Journal of the American Institute of Planners,* XXVII (August, 1961), 199–203. See also, Smith, Wallace. "Relocation in San Francisco," *Bay Area Real Estate Report.* 4th quarter, 1960.
28. Morningside Heights, Inc. *Relocation: Critical Phase of Redevelopment: The Experience of Morningside Gardens.* New York, 1957.
29. Pendleton, P. Kathryn and Heller, Howard U. "The Relocation of Families Displaced by an Urban Renewal Project," Master's thesis, Department of Sociology, University of Chicago, 1952.
30. Philadelphia Housing Association. *Relocation in Philadelphia.* Philadelphia: Housing Association, November, 1958.
31. Philadelphia Housing Authority. *Relocation of Families: A Report on the Relocation Operation for the Norris Low-rent Housing Development.* Philadelphia: Housing Authority, 1952.
32. *Report to the Philadelphia Redevelopment Authority on Completion of Morton Relocation Contract by the Germantown Settlement.* Philadelphia, 1961(?). (Mimeographed.)
33. Reynolds, Harry W. Jr. "The Human Element in Urban Renewal," *Public Welfare,* XIX (April, 1961), 71–3, 82.
——. "Population Displacement in Urban Renewal," *American Journal of Economics and Sociology,* XXII (January, 1963), 113–28.
34. Schorr, Philip. *Final Report on Relocation Operations from Fordham University and Lincoln Center Sites.* New York: Braislin, Porter and Wheelock, Inc., November, 1959.
35. Seattle Housing Authority. *Locations and Ownership of Housing Obtained by 1093 Families Moving From Seattle Temporary Public Housing Units—March, 1953 through September, 1954.* 1956(?). (Mimeographed.)

36. Slum Clearance and Redevelopment Authority, and Child and Family Services. *Vine-Deer-Chatham Project Relocation: A Community Effort.* Portland, Maine, 1958(?).
37. State Housing Authority. *Present Dwellings of Former Residents of the Site of Stanley S. Holmes Village, Atlantic City, New Jersey.* Trenton, N.J., June, 1936. (Mimeographed.)
38. Warrence, Samuel. "A Report on Relocation of the Elderly," *Essays on the Problems Faced in the Relocation of Elderly Persons.* Prepared by the Institute for Urban Studies, University of Pennsylvania, and National Association of Housing and Redevelopment Officials, Philadelphia, June, 1963.

11 The Housing of Relocated Families: Summary of a Census Bureau Survey

U.S. HOUSING AND HOME FINANCE AGENCY

ABOUT THE SURVEY

The primary purpose of the survey was to ascertain the adequacy of the housing units to which families displaced from urban renewal sites are relocated. This being the objective, it was important to be able to interview families as soon after relocation as possible in order to minimize the attrition which would otherwise develop as a result of the normal mobility of the population. To secure a sample of recent displacees, therefore, the 163 local public agencies in the United States, except Alaska and Hawaii, which had placed Title I Urban Renewal projects into execution during calendar years 1962 and 1963, were asked to supply lists of all families relocated during the three-month period June 1 through August 31, 1964. Of the 163 LPAs selected, 132 had families who were relocated during the three-month period in question. Certified lists of the names and addresses of 2,842 families displaced during the June-August period were turned over to the United States Bureau of the Census.

Between Thanksgiving 1964 and early January 1965, Census interviewers undertook to locate as many as possible of the housing units for which the relocation address of the family was within the same metropolitan area as the LPA which supplied the information.

For 2,300 of the 2,842 families the housing unit to which they moved was located by the Census interviewer. The remaining 542 families consist of those families for whom an interview was not conducted. Addresses for 278 of these were faulty or inadequate, 138 families had moved outside the metropolitan area, and 126 families were not at home or refused to be interviewed.

| | | Housing Units for Which Census Interviews Were Completed | | | | | |
| | | White | | | Nonwhite | | |
	Total	Total	Self-Relocated	LPA Aided	Total	Self-Relocated	LPA Aided
Interview completed	2300	1090	883	207	1210	717	493
Percent	100	47	38	9	53	31	22
Occupied by relocated household	2146	1017	823	194	1129	663	466
Percent	100	47	38	9	53	31	22

In line with the objective of the survey of obtaining the character of the housing into which displaced families were relocated, Census enumerators were instructed to obtain data on housing condition and plumbing facilities of all 2,300 units regardless of whether the relocated families still occupied them. Information with respect to household characteristics, satisfaction with location, etc., were, however, obtained only from the 2,146 displaced households still occupying sample units. The actual number of households responding to individual questions is given in the text table accompanying the discussion of each question.

HOUSEHOLD INCOME

Poverty was common among the families covered by the survey. Thus, the Census found that 40 percent reported income of less than $3,000 in 1964 and nearly 80 percent had incomes of less than $6,000. The income of half the nonwhites was below the $3,000 level compared with only about one-quarter of the white families.

Reflecting the high proportion of families at the lower end of the income scale, the median income for all reporting was only $3,814 compared with $5,631 for all nonfarm families as reported by the Bureau of the Census for 1963.

		White			Nonwhite		
Family Income in 1964	*Total*	*Total*	*Self-Relocated*	*LPA Aided*	*Total*	*Self-Relocated*	*LPA Aided*
Number reporting	1973	908	724	184	1065	624	441
Percent, total	100%	100%	100%	100%	100%	100%	100%
Less than $2000	22	16	13	27	26	23	30
$2000–$2999	18	13	11	19	22	20	25
$3000–$3999	13	11	11	12	16	15	16
$4000–$4999	12	13	13	14	11	12	9
$5000–$5999	12	14	14	16	10	12	8
$6000–$6999	9	12	14	4	7	7	6
$7000–$7999	6	8	9	3	4	5	3
$8000–$9999	5	8	9	2	2	3	2
$10,000 or more	3	5	6	3	2	3	1
Median	$3,814	$4,797	$5,158	$3,318	$3,139	$3,497	$2,798

HOUSEHOLD SIZE AND COMPOSITION

Of the families interviewed in the survey, 47 percent were white, 53 percent nonwhite. The median sized household contained three persons, with the nonwhite households tending to run somewhat larger than their white counterparts, 3.2 vs. 2.9.

The most predominant sized families contained only two persons. These accounted for 32 percent of the white group, 26 percent of the nonwhite.

There were, however, slightly more than one-third of the households which contained 5 or more persons with nearly 8 or more

Size of Household			
Number of persons	*Total*	*White*	*Nonwhite*
Number reporting	2146	1017	1129
Percent, total	*100%*	*100%*	*100%*
1	2	2	3
2	28	32	26
3	19	19	18
4	17	18	16
5 or more	34	29	37
Median	3.0	2.9	3.2

persons. The typical households, both white and nonwhite, were made up only of related persons. Only 4 percent of the white families, 8 percent of the nonwhite families, contained any nonrelatives.

LENGTH OF TIME AT PREVIOUS ADDRESS

A major portion of those interviewed—59 percent—had lived 5 or more years at their previous address, while an additional 32 percent had been on the urban renewal site for between one and five years. Only a handful—2½ percent—had lived less than 6 months at their pre-relocation address. In other words, the group interviewed had their roots well established in the neighborhood from which they were displaced.

The nonwhite families showed a tendency to have lived a slightly shorter time in their previous neighborhood than whites, with roughly 55 percent of them having been five years or more in their

Length of Time at Previous Address			
	Total	White	Nonwhite
Number reporting	2145	1016	1129
Percent, total	100%	100%	100%
Less than 3 months	*	1	*
3 to 6 months	2	2	2
6 months to 1 year	7	6	8
1 to 5 years	32	28	35
5 years or more	59	63	55

*Less than ½ of 1 percent.

previous quarters. Some 63 percent of the whites had lived in their quarters that long.

TYPE OF UNIT

More than half of the families were relocated into one-family dwellings. Most of the balance went into apartments in apartment buildings. Only 3 households, all of whom were self-relocated, moved into trailers.

Type of Unit			
	Total	Self-Relocated	LPA Aided
Number reporting	2281	1589	692
Percent, total	100%	100%	100%
1-family house	53	55	48
Apartment in apartment house	36	32	44
Part of house as apartment	9	10	6
Other—trailers, flats above stores, etc.	2	3	2

The greater use of public housing by the LPAs is reflected in the fact that 44 percent of the families aided by them in finding housing were placed in apartments in regular apartment buildings. Among the self-relocated, slightly less than one-third went into apartment houses but a higher proportion moved into single family dwellings.

HOUSING QUALITY

With respect to the quality of the housing in which relocated families were found by the Bureau of the Census, the figures show that the vast majority of the displaced families were relocated in standard housing, units which were not dilapidated and which had private bath and toilet facilities. Thus, 94 percent of the relocated families—97 percent of the whites and 91 percent of the nonwhites —were living in standard housing at the time of the survey.

All of these standard units had toilet and bathing facilities for the exclusive use of the families which lived there. Moreover, a very substantial proportion of them were reported by Census as being in sound structures, ones which were well maintained and had few, if any, observable defects. In 9 percent of the cases, however, the houses were regarded as deteriorating. This means that the units, while still providing adequate shelter for their occupants, were under maintained with the result that there were observable defects, the continued neglect of which could ultimately make the units substandard. Somewhat more of the nonwhites—10 percent—were found to be living in standard, though deteriorating, units than was true of white households, where only 8 percent were so housed.

Significantly, 70 percent of the displaced families found their own housing accommodations.[1] In the case of white families, 19 percent used LPA help. Among nonwhite families, the proportion who used assistance in finding housing was over 40 percent. White families did about as well for themselves in finding good housing—96.6 percent— as when they turned to the local public agency for aid—97.1 percent. Nonwhites, in contrast, had less success in finding standard housing than did the LPA. Nearly 95 percent of the nonwhites relocated by the local agencies were found by Census to be in standard housing. Only 89 percent of those who relocated themselves were as well housed.

TYPE OF HOUSING

While the use of public housing was not a major factor in accounting for the high proportion of standard housing into which displaced families as a group were relocated, 13 percent of the group surveyed were rehoused in public housing. Three-fourths of these were nonwhites.

[1] While only 30 percent of the households were relocated in housing units to which they were referred by an LPA, 89 percent of all the displaced families reported that they received some type of assistance in the relocation process. This assistance in most instances took the form of financial aid. In addition, some families received counseling and actual assistance in locating suitable housing units.

Housing Quality

		White			Nonwhite	
	Total	Total	Self-Re-located	LPA Aided	Total	Self-Re-located	LPA Aided
Number reporting	2277	1081	876	205	1196	711	485
Percent, total	100%	100%	100%	100%	100%	100%	100%
Standard	94.0	96.7	96.6	97.1	91.4	89.1	94.9
Sound, with all plumbing facilities	84.8	88.5	88.4	88.8	81.4	76.2	89.1
Deteriorating, with all plumbing facilities	9.2	8.2	9.2	8.3	10.0	12.9	5.8
Substandard	6.0	3.3	3.4	2.9	8.6	10.9	5.1
Sound, lacking or sharing facilities	2.3	1.3	1.3	1.4	3.2	3.5	2.7
Deteriorating, lacking or sharing facilities	1.6	1.1	1.1	1.0	2.1	2.8	1.0
Dilapidated	2.1	0.9	1.0	0.5	3.3	4.6	1.4

Type of Housing

	Total	White			Nonwhite		
		Total	Self-Relocated	LPA Aided	Total	Self-Relocated	LPA Aided
Number reporting	2178	993	791	202	1185	694	491
Percent, total	100%	100%	100%	100%	100%	100%	100%
Public housing	13	7	1	30	18	2	41
Private housing	87	93	99	70	82	98	59

Of the public housing used for displaced families, 90 percent was made available through the relocation efforts of local public agencies. Only 10 percent—6 percent nonwhite, 4 percent white—of the public units went to families who undertook to find housing for themselves.

RENTS OF RELOCATED HOUSEHOLDS

The process of relocation has led to increases in the rent bill for some of the families moved out of renewal areas, with the median gross rent going from $66 to $74. Contributing to this rise in the median was the increase in the proportion of families paying more than $100 a month. Thus, the Census Bureau found that among present renters, for whom gross rents were reported, 20 percent were now paying that much compared with only 9 percent prior to relocation. The biggest increase came among white families, where the percentage paying more than $100 rose from 9 to 24. Among nonwhites the rise was less pronounced, going only from 9 to 17 percent. At the same time that the proportion of families paying over $100 increased, the portion paying $50 to $75 dropped sharply, from 45 percent to 29 percent. It was only at the bottom of the rent scale that no significant changes occurred. The percent of families paying less than $50 a month remained virtually unchanged—21 percent prior to relocation, 22 percent after.

It would appear that the efforts of local public agencies in finding quarters for displaced families played an important role in holding down rent increases. Thus, among families aided by LPAs, there was a rise from 17 to 29 percent among white families and from 26 to 39 percent among nonwhite families paying less than $50 a month for rent. In contrast, among self-relocated families the proportion paying less than $50 dropped from 14 to 7 percent for whites and from 23 to 14 percent for nonwhites.

The higher proportion of self-relocated families paying over $100 a month for rent is a reflection, in part at least, of the generally higher income of this group.

RENT-INCOME RATIOS

Since there was no significant change in the levels of income of relocated households during the period under study, the rise in rent

Gross Rents

	Pre-Relocation Rent			Post-Relocation Rent		
	Total	White	Nonwhite	Total	White	Nonwhite
Number reporting	1299	536	763	898	369	529
Percent, total	100%	100%	100%	100%	100%	100%
Less than $30	4	2	5	6	3	7
$30–$49	17	13	20	16	10	21
$50–$74	45	50	41	29	25	32
$75–$99	25	26	25	29	38	23
$100–$124	7	7	7	14	14	14
$125–$149	1	1	1	4	6	2
$150 and over	1	1	1	2	4	1
Median rents	$66	$68	$65	$74	$83	$67

Gross Rents

| | Self-Relocated | | | | LPA Aided | | | |
| | White | | Nonwhite | | White | | Nonwhite | |
	Before	After	Before	After	Before	After	Before	After
Number reporting	414	273	427	245	122	96	366	284
Percent, total	100%	100%	100%	100%	100%	100%	100%	100%
Less than $50	14	7	23	14	17	29	26	39
$50–$74	52	24	43	34	42	27	40	32
$75–$99	25	41	25	32	30	30	24	16
$100 or more	9	28	9	20	11	14	10	13

levels led to some increase in the proportion of income being spent for rent. Among a group of identical families who were renters before and after relocation and for whom gross rent information was reported the median proportion of income paid for rent rose from 25 percent to nearly 28 percent.

| | Gross Rent as a Percentage of Income | | | | | |
| | Before Relocation | | | After Relocation | | |
	Total	White	Nonwhite	Total	White	Nonwhite
Number reporting	716	284	432	716	284	432
Percent, total	100%	100%	100%	100%	100%	100%
Less than 10%	3	4	2	1	1	1
10–14	14	20	10	8	9	7
15–19	16	18	14	15	18	13
less than 20%	*33*	*42*	*26*	*24*	*28*	*21*
20–24	17	19	16	19	19	19
25–34	19	15	22	25	27	24
20–34%	*36*	*34*	*38*	*44*	*46*	*43*
35–64	24	19	28	26	22	29
65 or more	7	5	8	6	4	7
35% or more	*31*	*24*	*36*	*32*	*26*	*36*
Median	25.1	22.2	28.4	27.7	26.1	28.9

The most drastic shift which took place was in the proportion of families where rent accounted for less than 20 percent of their income. Here the ratio dropped from 33 to 24. At the other end of the scale there was no significant change in the percentage of families paying 35 percent or more of their income for rent. Here the proportion rose only fractionally, from 31.3 to 31.8 percent.

It was among white families that the biggest decline occurred in the proportion whose gross rent was less than 20 percent of their income. There the ratio dropped from 42 to 28. Among nonwhites, in contrast, the decrease was only from 26 to 21 percent. At the upper end of the scale—those whose rents were 35 percent or more of income—the proportion of white families rose fractionally from 24 percent to slightly over 26 percent while the proportion of nonwhites remained virtually unchanged at just under 36 percent.

SIZE OF UNITS

The increase in rents experienced by relocated families is attributable in part at least to the fact that, when they relocated, some households, particularly nonwhites, moved into larger quarters.

Number of Rooms	Size of Units					
	Total		White		Nonwhite	
	Previous	Present	Previous	Present	Previous	Present
Number reporting	2141	2288	1013	1082	1128	1206
Percent, total	100%	100%	100%	100%	100%	100%
1	1	*	1	*	1	*
2	4	2	2	1	5	2
3	13	10	9	7	17	11
4	24	26	23	25	25	27
5	25	29	27	30	24	28
6	17	20	19	22	15	19
7	7	7	9	8	6	7
8 or more	9	6	10	7	7	6
Median	4.3	4.4	4.6	4.5	4.1	4.3

* Less than ½ of 1 percent.

For both white and nonwhite families, the use of one- and two-room units was virtually eliminated, and the proportion of three-room units was noticeably decreased, particularly among nonwhites.

Because of some decrease in the use of large units—7 or more rooms—the median room count for white occupied units dropped fractionally from 4.6 to 4.5. For nonwhites in contrast the median sized unit increased from 4.1 to 4.3. As a result the median sized units for all families relocated inched up from 4.3 to 4.4 rooms.

TENURE

The relocation process has resulted in an increase in home ownership. Prior to relocation, 67 percent of those surveyed were renters, 33 percent owners. After relocation the percentage of renters had decreased to 63, while the proportion of owners had risen to 37. Since the survey did not probe into motivations, it is impossible to say to what extent the increase of home ownership was voluntary, to what extent it may have reflected an inadequate supply of satisfactory rental housing in some cases.

While home ownership increased among both white and nonwhite families, it was among the whites that the gains were greatest, the percentage going to 46 percent compared with 32 percent for the nonwhites.

| | Tenure | | | | | |
| | Previous Home | | | Present Home | | |
	Total	White	Non-white	Total	White	Non-white
Number reporting	2145	1017	1028	2146	1017	1029
Percent, total	100%	100%	100%	100%	100%	100%
Owned	33	40	29	37	46	32
Rented	67	60	71	63	54	68

PLACE OF EMPLOYMENT

The Census survey turned up a significant proportion of household heads—36 percent—who had no fixed place of employment. These were people like laborers, mechanics, and charwomen who customarily shift from job to job or site to site as employment opportunities arise, together with the unemployed and the retired. For this group, it is not possible to gauge the impact of relocation upon their jobs even if they were in the labor force. Among the large group—nearly two-thirds of the household heads in the sample—who did have a fixed place of work at the time of the survey, the Census found that there were only 10 percent who had changed their jobs after their families had been relocated. This would suggest that relocation was not a seriously disruptive factor as far as place of employment was concerned.

| Employment Status | | | |
	Total	White	Nonwhite
Number of household heads in labor force and with fixed place of employment	1363	662	701
Percent, total	100%	100%	100%
Same place of employment after relocation	90.2	89.7	90.6
Different place of employment after relocation	9.8	10.3	9.4

Among nonwhite workers there was a slightly lesser incidence of job change after relocation—9.4 percent—than among white household heads—10.3 percent.

JOURNEY TO WORK

Of those workers with a fixed place of employment, more than one-third—37 percent—reported a significant change in their journey to work. On the other hand, 13 percent find that it now takes them less time to get to work. The remaining 50 percent, moreover, believe that there has been no significant increase in travel time to and from their jobs.

Journey to Work

	Total	White	Nonwhite
Number reporting	1336	648	688
Percent, total	100%	100%	100%
Much more time	37	35	38
About the same	50	51	50
Much less	13	14	12

Partially, at least, because of their greater tendency to remain in their pre-relocation jobs, somewhat more of the nonwhite workers —38 percent—found it now takes them longer to get to work. Among white workers, only 35 percent found this situation to prevail.

NEIGHBORHOOD SHOPPING

Two-thirds of the relocated families found neighborhood shopping at their new location at least as convenient, if not more so, than at their previous address. There was very little difference in opinion between white and nonwhite households on this count. Forty-three percent of each race found the stores as conveniently located. Twenty-five percent of the white families and 22 percent of the nonwhites even considered their new shopping facilities more convenient.

Convenience of Neighborhood Shopping

	Total	White	Nonwhite
Number reporting	2144	1016	1128
Percent, total	100%	100%	100%
Much more convenient	23	25	22
About the same	43	43	43
Much less convenient	34	32	35

There were, however, one-third of the families who found present shopping much less convenient than before they moved. Among white families, 32 percent regarded the situation as such. A slightly larger proportion—35 percent—of nonwhite households shared this view.

LOCAL PUBLIC TRANSPORTATION

Better than 70 percent of the families studied by the Bureau of the Census regarded the local public transportation serving their new home to be either as satisfactory or more satisfactory than what they had had previously.

As a group, nonwhite households appeared to be more satisfied with their present public transportation facilities than whites. Thus, 73 percent regarded the service to their new address as satisfactory if not better than what was available in their old neighborhood. For white households the proportion of this mind was 67 percent.

Satisfaction with Local Public Transportation			
	Total	*White*	*Nonwhite*
Number reporting	2136	1012	1124
Percent, total	*100%*	*100%*	*100%*
Much more satisfactory	18	16	19
About the same	53	51	54
Much less satisfactory	29	33	27

Among the households who felt that public transportation was much less satisfactory after they relocated, the proportion of dissatisfied households was much higher among the whites—33 percent —than among the nonwhites—27 percent.

DISTANCE TO CHURCH

Not all the families surveyed had any religious affiliation or attended a place of worship frequently enough to have any views upon the effect of their move upon the distance to church. Among those to whom it did matter, something over half—55 percent— reported that their place of worship was either closer or no farther away than before they moved. Far more white families found this to be true than did nonwhites. For whites the proportion was 59 percent, for nonwhites it was only 51 percent.

Distance to Church			
	Total	*White*	*Nonwhite*
Number reporting	2055	961	1094
Percent, total	*100%*	*100%*	*100%*
Closer	21	20	22
About the same distance	34	39	29
Farther away	45	41	49

Of the families who found their church farther away than previously, the proportion was considerably higher—49 percent— among the nonwhites than it was among the whites, where only 41 percent felt the distance was greater.

12 A Comment on the HHFA Study of Relocation*

CHESTER HARTMAN

Although widely hailed by national and local renewal officials as the refutation of recent criticism, the recent study made for the Housing and Home Finance Agency by the Census Bureau, *The Housing of Relocated Families,* has by no means definitively resolved the relocation issue and in many respects is characterized by the same biases and lack of candor criticized in other official reports. Briefly, I have the following comments and questions about the HHFA study:

1. The study refers only to households that have entered the relocation agency's caseload—that is, only to those families living on the site at the time of land-taking. But a large number of families move out of renewal areas prior to actual land-taking, although nonetheless as a result of the impending forced displacement (this is a factor of increasing importance as the period of project planning lengthens). In an earlier article[1] I cited attrition rates of 8 percent and 24 percent in two projects just between the time of site census

* This is an edited version of part of a comment by Mr. Hartman which is scheduled to appear in the November 1965 issue of the *Journal of the American Institute of Planners.*

[1] Chester Hartman, "The Housing of Relocated Families," *Journal of the American Institute of Planners,* Vol. 30, No. 4 (November 1964), footnote 25. [Reprinted in Chapter 10 of this volume.—Ed.]

and actual land-taking; many others had doubtless seen the hand-writing on the wall and had left even before this census was taken. While this may be an inevitable byproduct of planned change, it should also be acknowledged as one of the important factors in assessing renewal efforts. We should endeavor to learn as much as possible about these families, rather than offering our knowledge about the official caseload as the sole data upon which to judge the impact of relocation.

2. The study omits individual householders entirely, because (according to Robert Weaver, in a letter dated April 29, 1965) "the LPA reports on one-person households were not sufficiently detailed at the time of survey to enable the Census to include them." Yet nearly 30 percent of all displaced households fall into this category, and individuals usually fare much worse than families in the relocation process. This is an important fact, which greatly limits the meaning of the report, and should have been openly acknowledged.

3. The study group was drawn from 132 cities of varying size, from Somersworth, New Hampshire, and Russellville, Arkansas, to New York and Chicago. It is at the least a plausible assumption that relocation problems and results are entirely different in small cities and towns than in large metropolitan centers. Yet nowhere does one find a breakdown of housing conditions, costs, and so forth, by city size and geographical area. It may well be that relocation problems in fact are negligible in small areas and exist primarily in large cities. If so we should know this, and our policies and programs should be guided by this knowledge. I submit that if the intent of the HHFA study had been more professional and less political—that is, had tried to learn more about relocation rather than refute and discredit the critics—such breakdowns would have been made and reported. (The figures reporting housing type of relocation dwellings, indicating that 53 percent of the relocated families moved into single-family homes, suggest that the data had a strong bias toward small cities and towns.)

4. Rents paid following relocation expressed as a percentage of income are disturbingly high, and we must question the impact of these excessive housing costs on the total family budget (although the increase in this burden as a result of relocation appears to be slight). The median rent/income ratio following relocation was 27.7 percent for the sample (28.9 percent for the nonwhite families

as a group). Thirty-two percent of the sample were paying more than 35 percent of their income for rent after relocation (36 percent of the nonwhite sample). There is, however, no breakdown of rent change or changes in rent/income ratio by income group; no way of knowing if the burden was greatest on those least able to bear the high costs of housing, as was suggested by data in at least one of the studies I cited. No information at all is given on the post-relocation housing costs of nonrenters (nearly two-fifths of the sample), who presumably are paying more than the renters. (Incidentally, the effect of relocation in increasing rents appears to be significantly less burdensome in this study than in the other recent HHFA survey of 789 families which Administrator Weaver cited during the Congressional hearings on the 1964 Housing Act,[2] a study undertaken to buttress the Agency's pleas for Congressional approval of the Relocation Adjustment Payment provision of the 1964 Act.) I am also confused by the small rent increases experienced by nonwhite families—only a 2 dollar increase in median monthly rent, compared with a 15 dollar median increase for white families—which would seem to require some explanation, in view of what is known about the housing problems and costs of low-income nonwhite families. In response to my inquiries, Dr. Weaver cites the larger proportion of nonwhites than whites relocating into public housing as the principal reason for the difference in median rents. Yet the difference in use of public housing by race is not that great (11 percent), and the total proportion of nonwhites who relocated into public housing was only 18 percent anyway. Some further explanation, not clear from the printed report, would seem to be involved.

5. There are no data on pre- and post-relocation overcrowding (the figures given on median apartment size for the sample as a whole pre- and post-relocation are not useful for evaluating changes in overcrowding).

6. Of the original 2842 households in the sample, 542 were not reached, primarily due to inability to find the family. The classification "standard housing," as used in the HHFA report, includes units in deteriorating condition, if they have all plumbing facilities (only 84.8 percent of the sample relocated into sound units with all plumbing facilities). At another extreme, using this stricter (and more usual) definition of standard housing and dealing with the

[2] *Ibid.*, footnote 22.

entire original sample of 2842, it could be said, with no greater bias than is contained in the official statement that 94 percent of all displaced families relocate in standard housing, that we know of no more than 69 percent of the original sample who relocated into decent housing $\left(\frac{.848(2842-542)}{2842}\right)$. Further, there is nothing in the HHFA study which tells of the housing conditions of relocated families prior to displacement—what proportion were forced to move from standard units. And of course we are still left with that ever present question of standards: How do the standards used in evaluating pre-relocation conditions compare with those used in judging post-relocation housing, and how do post-relocation results obtained by Census criteria compare with results obtained by applying the usually more stringent requirements of local housing codes? Until we have information of this sort we have very little that permits a reliable statement of how relocation has improved housing standards.

7. No figures are given on the proportion of families who relocated into areas slated for future clearance or rehabilitation, a key, but frequently neglected, aspect of the long-range results of relocation (although HHFA's instruction form to the local agencies called for this information, and it presumably has been collected).

8. Finally, my confidence in the credibility of the report is diminished by the fact that it was done by one federal agency at the request of another federal agency—the operating agency in the field of renewal—which is in full control of the data, its release, and its reporting, and by the fact that it was apparently done in order to refute the critics rather than as a piece of objective research in evaluating current programs. The report would have been much more convincing had it come from a body (such as a university research center) whose freedom to design and carry out the study, analyze and question the data, and report results was in no way restrained and whose motivation in undertaking the research was to learn and not to defend. (The recent study of business relocation in Providence by Professor Basil Zimmer, under a grant by the Small Business Administration, is an example of the kind of thoroughness and objectivity to be sought; here a government agency whose concern was to learn more about and to uphold the interests of the group it was established to serve supplied the funds

for an independent study.[3]) Some rather frustrating experiences over the last three months in trying to obtain further information from HHFA about the survey data have not increased my confidence in the ostensible findings of the report.

Let me also mention in this context two other recent studies by federal agencies, which have received far less publicity than the HHFA study. First, the Advisory Commission on Intergovernmental Relations has issued a comprehensive report on the role of various government agencies in the relocation process which would seem to support many of my findings and offer some important recommendations in the field of relocation.[4] The ACIR report lays particular stress on the continuing shortage of decent, low-rent housing as the major obstacle to adequate relocation, with the clear implication that despite changes in attitude, techniques, and services the relocation problem will persist until the basic underlying housing problem is faced.

Second, the General Accounting Office has been undertaking a series of investigations into relocation practices of local renewal agencies. These investigations, nine in number, cover the period 1955–1964 and were centered in Puerto Rico, the District of Columbia, San Francisco, and the Fort Worth region of HHFA. All nine investigations uncovered major deficiencies in the relocation process, including inadequate supervision of local agencies by URA, prolonged relocation periods, lack of inspection of relocation dwellings, lack of follow-up of "lost" families, relocation into substandard housing (although local agencies reported these same families as having moved into standard housing), and URA approval of local relocation plans despite lack of evidence as to the availability of suitable relocation housing. The more recent of the GAO reports are of particular interest. A 1962 GAO review of workable programs administered by the Fort Worth regional office of the HHFA states: "We found that, in certain cities whose workable programs had been certified and recertified, families displaced by slum clearance projects were relocated permanently into substandard hous-

---

[3] Basil Zimmer, *Rebuilding Cities*, Chicago, Quadrangle Books, 1964. [Pages 324–348 of this book are reprinted in Chapter 14 of this volume.—Ed.]

[4] Advisory Commission on Intergovernmental Relations, *Relocation: Unequal Treatment of People and Businesses Displaced by Government*, Washington, D.C., the Commission, January 1965.

ing." A 1964 GAO report on renewal projects in Missouri and Kansas states "that a significant number of the families displaced from urban renewal projects in St. Louis, Missouri, and Kansas City, Kansas, were relocated into substandard housing and that a substantial number of the families displaced in these cities and in Columbia, Missouri, were not afforded relocation assistance." And a 1964 report on the District of Columbia concludes that the Redevelopment Land Agency: "(1) used standards for determining the acceptability of dwellings for relocating families displaced from urban renewal areas which were less stringent than the standards used for evaluating the physical condition of dwellings in determining the eligibility of an area for urban renewal, (2) made inadequate inspections of housing for displaced families, (3) prepared incomplete inspection reports, and (4) referred some displaced families to substandard or uninspected housing." (A summary of all 23 GAO reports on urban renewal during the 1955–1964 period, prepared by the Legislative Reference Service of the Library of Congress, is included on pp. 715–23 of Part 2 of the House Subcommittee on Housing hearings on the Housing and Urban Redevelopment Act of 1965.)

In sum, I feel that the findings and contentions of my original study have not been refuted and that many of its important points have been ignored, such as the questions of different standards in evaluating pre- and post-relocation housing, the social and psychological impact of displacement and adjustment to relocation, and the differential impact of costs and benefits on various socio-economic groups. It is my belief that we will not have a satisfactory answer to the problem of relocation until improvement of housing conditions for low- and moderate-income families is seen as paramount, and the monies, energies, and professional talents currently available under the urban renewal program are redirected toward a different set of priorities. Until that time I still call for more and better independent evaluations of the results of our current efforts.

13 Grieving for a Lost Home: Psychological Costs of Relocation*

MARC FRIED

INTRODUCTION

For some time we have known that the forced dislocation from an urban slum is a highly disruptive and disturbing experience. This is implicit in the strong, positive attachments to the former slum residential area—in the case of this study the West End of Boston—and in the continued attachment to the area among those who left before any imminent danger of eviction. Since we were observing people in the midst of a crisis, we were all too ready to modify our impressions and to conclude that these were likely to be transitory reactions. But the post-relocation experiences of a great many people have borne out their most pessimistic pre-relocation expectations. There are wide variations in the success of post-relocation adjustment and considerable variability in the depth and quality of the loss experience. But for the majority it seems quite precise to speak of their reactions as expressions of *grief*. These are manifest in the feelings of painful loss, the continued longing, the general depressive tone, frequent symptoms of psychological or social or somatic distress, the active work required in adapting to the altered situation, the sense of helplessness, the occasional expressions of both

* Reprinted from *The Urban Condition,* edited by Leonard J. Duhl, New York, Basic Books, Inc., 1963, Chapter 12. Copyright © 1963 by Basic Books, Inc., Publishers.

direct and displaced anger, and tendencies to idealize the lost place.[1]

At their most extreme, these reactions of grief are intense, deeply felt, and, at times, overwhelming. In response to a series of questions concerning the feelings of sadness and depression which people experienced *after* moving, many replies were unambiguous: "I felt as though I had lost everything," "I felt like my heart was taken out of me," "I felt like taking the gaspipe," "I lost all the friends I knew," "I always felt I had to go home to the West End and even now I feel like crying when I pass by," "Something of me went with the West End," "I felt cheated," "What's the use of thinking about it," "I threw up a lot," "I had a nervous breakdown." Certainly, some people were overjoyed with the change and many felt no sense of loss. Among 250 women, however, 26 percent report that they still feel sad or depressed two years later, and another 20 percent report a long period (six months to two years) of sadness or depression. Altogether, therefore, at least 46 percent give evidence of a fairly severe grief reaction or worse. And among 316 men, the data show only a slightly smaller percentage (38 percent) with long-term grief reactions. The true proportion of depressive reactions is undoubtedly higher since many women and men who report no feelings of sadness or depression indicate clearly depressive responses to other questions.

In answer to another question, "How did you feel when you saw or heard that the building you had lived in was torn down?" a similar finding emerges. As in the previous instance, the responses are often quite extreme and most frequently quite pathetic. They

[1] See Abraham, K., "Notes on the Psycho-analytical Investigation and Treatment of Manic-Depressive Insanity and Allied Conditions" (1911), and "A Short Study of the Development of the Libido, Viewed in the Light of Mental Disorders" (1924), in *Selected Papers of Karl Abraham*, Vol. I, New York: Basic Books, 1953; Bibring, E., "The Mechanisms of Depression," in *Affective Disorders*, P. Greenacre, ed., New York: International Univ. Press, 1953; Bowlby, J., "Processes of Mourning," *Int. J. Psychoanal.*, 42:317–340, 1961; Freud, S., "Mourning and Melancholia" (1917), in *Collected Papers*, Vol. III, New York: Basic Books, 1959; Hoggart, R., *The Uses of Literacy: Changing Patterns in English Mass Culture*, New York: Oxford Univ. Press, 1957; Klein, M., "Mourning and Its Relations to Manic-Depressive States," *Int. J. Psychoanal.*, 21:125–153, 1940; Lindemann, E., "Symptomatology and Management of Acute Grief," *Am. J. Psychiat.*, 101:141–148, 1944; Marris, P., *Widows and Their Families*, London: Routledge and Kegan Paul, 1958; Rochlin, G., "The Dread of Abandonment," in *The Psychoanalytic Study of the Child*, Vol. XVI, New York: International Univ. Press, 1961; Volkart, E. H., with S. T. Michael, "Bereavement and Mental Health," in *Explorations in Social Psychiatry*, A. H. Leighton, J. A. Clausen, and R. N. Wilson, eds., New York: Basic Books, 1957.

range from those who replied: "I was glad because the building had rats," to moderate responses such as "the building was bad but I felt sorry," and "I didn't want to see it go," to the most frequent group comprising such reactions as "it was like a piece being taken from me," "I felt terrible," "I used to stare at the spot where the building stood," "I was sick to my stomach." This question in particular, by its evocative quality, seemed to stir up sad memories even among many people who denied any feeling of sadness or depression. The difference from the previous result is indicated by the fact that 54 percent of the women and 46 percent of the men report severely depressed or disturbed reactions; 19 percent of the women and about 31 percent of the men report satisfaction or indifference; and 27 percent of the women and 23 percent of the men report moderately depressed or ambivalent feelings. Thus it is clear that, for the majority of those who were displaced from the West End, leaving their residential area involved a moderate or extreme sense of loss and an accompanying affective reaction of grief.

While these figures go beyond any expectation which we had or which is clearly implied in other studies, the realization that relocation was a crisis with potential danger to mental health for many people was one of the motivating factors for this investigation.[2] In studying the impact of relocation on the lives of a working-class population through a comparison of pre-relocation and post-relocation interview data, a number of issues arise concerning the psychology of urban living which have received little systematic attention. Yet, if we are to understand the effects of relocation and the significance of the loss of a residential environment, it is essential that we have a deeper appreciation of the psychological implications of both physical and social aspects of residential experience. Thus we are led to formulations which deal with the functions and meanings of the residential area in the lives of working class people.

THE NATURE OF THE LOSS IN RELOCATION:
THE SPATIAL FACTOR

Any severe loss may represent a disruption in one's relationship to the past, to the present, and to the future. Losses generally bring

[2] This is implicit in the prior work on "crisis" and situational predicaments by Dr. Erich Lindemann under whose initiative the current work was undertaken and carried out.

about fragmentation of routines, of relationships, and of expectations, and frequently imply an alteration in the world of physically available objects and spatially oriented action. It is a disruption in that sense of continuity which is ordinarily a taken-for-granted framework for functioning in a universe which has temporal, social, and spatial dimensions. From this point of view, the loss of an important place represents a change in a potentially significant component of the experience of continuity.

But why should the loss of a place, even a very important place, be so critical for the individual's sense of continuity; and why should grief at such loss be so widespread a phenomenon? In order to clarify this, it is necessary to consider the meaning which this area, the West End of Boston, had for the lives of its inhabitants. In an earlier paper we tried to assess this, and came to conclusions which corroborate, although they go further, the results from the few related studies.

In studying the reasons for satisfaction that the majority of slum residents experience, two major components have emerged. On the one hand, the residential area is the region in which a vast and interlocking set of social networks is localized. And, on the other, the physical area has considerable meaning as an extension of home, in which various parts are delineated and structured on the basis of a sense of belonging. These two components provide the context in which the residential area may so easily be invested with considerable, multiply-determined meaning. . . . the greatest proportion of this working-class group . . . shows a fairly common experience and usage of the residential area . . . dominated by a conception of the local area beyond the dwelling unit as an integral part of home. This view of an area as home and the significance of local people and local places are so profoundly at variance with typical middle-class orientations that it is difficult to appreciate the intensity of meaning, the basic sense of identity involved in living in the particular area.[3]

Nor is the intense investment of a residential area, both as an important physical space and as the locus for meaningful interpersonal ties, limited to the West End.[4] What is common to a host

[3] Fried, M., and Gleicher, P., "Some Sources of Residential Satisfaction in an Urban Slum," *J. Amer. Inst. Planners,* 27:305–315, 1961.

[4] See Gans, H., *The Urban Villagers,* New York: The Free Press of Glencoe, 1963; Gans, H., "The Human Implications of Current Redevelopment and Relocation Planning," *J. Amer. Inst. Planners,* 25:15–25, 1959; Hoggart, R., *op. cit.;* Hole, V., "Social Effects of Planned Rehousing," *Town Planning Rev.,* 30:161–173, 1959; Marris, P., *Family and Social Change in an African City,*

of studies is the evidence for the integrity of the urban, working-class, slum community as a social and spatial unit. It is the sense of belonging someplace, in a particular place which is quite familiar and easily delineated, in a wide area in which one feels "at home." This is the core of meaning of the local area. And this applies for many people who have few close relationships within the area. Even familiar and expectable streets and houses, faces at the window and people walking by, personal greetings and impersonal sounds may serve to designate the concrete foci of a sense of belonging somewhere and may provide special kinds of interpersonal and social meaning to a region one defines as "home."

It would be impossible to understand the reactions both to dislocation and to relocation and, particularly, the depth and frequency of grief responses without taking account of working-class orientations to residential areas. One of our primary theses is that the strength of the grief reaction to the loss of the West End is largely a function of prior orientations to the area. Thus, we certainly expect to find that the greater a person's pre-relocation commitment to the area, the more likely he is to react with marked grief. This prediction is confirmed again and again by the data.[5] For

Evanston, Ill.: Northwestern Univ. Press, 1962; Mogey, J. M., *Family and Neighbourhood*, New York: Oxford Univ. Press, 1956; Seeley, J., "The Slum: Its Nature, Use, and Users," *J. Amer. Inst. Planners*, 25:7–14, 1959; Vereker, C., and Mays, J. B., *Urban Redevelopment and Social Change*, New York: Lounz, 1960; Young, M., and Willmott, P., *Family and Kinship in East London*, Glencoe, Ill.: The Free Press, 1957.

[5] The analysis involves a comparison of information from interviews administered *before* relocation with a depth of grief index derived from follow-up interviews approximately two years *after* relocation. The pre-relocation interviews were administered to a randomly selected sample of 473 women from households in this area at the time the land was taken by the city. The post-relocation interviews were completed with 92 percent of the women who had given pre-relocation interviews and with 87 percent of the men from those households in which there was a husband in the household. Primary emphasis will be given to the results with the women since we do not have as full a range of pre-relocation information for the men. However, since a split schedule was used for the post-relocation interviews, the depth of grief index is available for only 259 women.

Dr. Jason Aronson was largely responsible for developing the series of questions on grief. The opening question of the series was: Many people have told us that just after they moved they felt sad or depressed. Did you feel this way? This was followed by the three specific questions on which the index was based: (1) Would you describe how you felt? (2) How long did these feelings last? (3) How did you feel when you saw or heard that the building you had lived in was torn down? Each person was given a score from 1 to 4 on the basis of the coded responses to these questions and the scores were sum-

the women, among those who had said they liked living in the West End *very much* during the pre-relocation interviews, 73 percent evidence a severe post-relocation grief reaction; among those who had less extreme but positive feelings about living in the West End, 53 percent show a similar order of grief; and among those who were ambivalent or negative about the West End, only 34 percent show a severe grief reaction. Or, considering a more specific feature of our formulation, the pre-relocation view of the West End as "home" shows an even stronger relationship to the depth of post-relocation grief. Among those women who said they had no real home, only 20 percent give evidence of severe grief; among those who claimed some other area as their real home, 34 percent fall into the severe grief category; but among the women for whom the *West End* was the real home, 68 percent report severe grief reactions. Although the data for the men are less complete, the results are substantially similar. It is also quite understandable that the length of West End residence should bear a strong relationship to the loss reaction, although it is less powerful than some of the other findings and almost certainly it is not the critical component.

More directly relevant to our emphasis on the importance of places, it is quite striking that the greater the area of the West End which was known, the more likely there is to be a severe grief response. Among the women who said they knew only their own block during the pre-relocation interview, only 13 percent report marked grief; at the other extreme, among those who knew most of the West End, 64 percent have a marked grief reaction. This relationship is maintained when a wide range of interrelated variables is held constant. Only in one instance, when there is a generally negative orientation to the West End, does more extensive

---

mated. For purposes of analysis, we divided the final scores into three groups: minimal grief, moderate grief, and severe or marked grief. The phrasing of these questions appears to dispose the respondent to give a "grief" response. In fact, however, there is a tendency to reject the idea of "sadness" among many people who show other evidence of a grief response. In cross-tabulating the "grief" scores with a series of questions in which there is no suggestion of sadness, unhappiness, or dissatisfaction, it is clear that the grief index is the more severe criterion. Those who are classified in the severe grief category almost invariably show severe grief reactions by any of the other criteria; but many who are categorized as "minimal grief" on the index fall into the extremes of unhappiness or dissatisfaction on the other items.

knowledge of the area lead to a somewhat smaller proportion of severe grief responses. Thus, the wider an individual's familiarity with the local area, the greater his commitment to the locality. This wider familiarity evidently signifies a greater sense of the wholeness and integrity of the entire West End and, we would suggest, a more expanded sense of being "at home" throughout the entire local region. It is striking, too, that while familiarity with, use of, and comfort in the spatial regions of the residential area are closely related to extensiveness of personal contact, the spatial patterns have independent significance and represent an additional basis for a feeling of commitment to that larger, local region which is "home."

THE SENSE OF SPATIAL IDENTITY

In stressing the importance of places and access to local facilities, we wish only to redress the almost total neglect of spatial dimensions in dealing with human behavior. We certainly do not mean thereby to give too little emphasis to the fundamental importance of inter-personal relationships and social organization in defining the mean-ing of the area. Nor do we wish to underestimate the significance of cultural orientations and social organization in defining the charac-ter and importance of spatial dimensions. However, the crisis of loss of a residential area brings to the fore the importance of the local spatial region and alerts us to the greater generality of spatial conceptions as determinants of behavior. In fact, we might say that a *sense of spatial identity* is fundamental to human functioning. It represents a phenomenal or ideational integration of important experiences concerning environmental arrangements and contacts in relation to the individual's conception of his own body in space.[6] It is based on spatial memories, spatial imagery, the spatial framework of current activity, and the implicit spatial components of ideals and aspirations.

It appears to us also that these feelings of being at home and of

[6] Erik Erikson includes spatial components in discussing the sense of ego identity and his work has influenced the discussion of spatial variables. In distinguishing the sense of spatial identity from the sense of ego identity, I am suggesting that variations in spatial identity do not correspond exactly to variations in ego identity. By separating these concepts, it becomes possible to study their interrelationships empirically.

belonging are, in the working class, integrally tied to a *specific* place. We would not expect similar effects or, at least, effects of similar proportion in a middle-class area. Generally speaking, an integrated sense of spatial identity in the middle class is not as contingent on the external stability of place or as dependent on the localization of social patterns, interpersonal relationships, and daily routines. In these data, in fact, there is a marked relationship between class status and depth of grief; the higher the status, by any of several indices, the smaller the proportions of severe grief. It is primarily in the working class, and largely because of the importance of external stability, that dislocation from a familiar residential area has so great an effect on fragmenting the sense of spatial identity.

External stability is also extremely important in interpersonal patterns within the working class. And dislocation and relocation involve a fragmentation of the external bases for interpersonal relationships and group networks. Thus, relocation undermines the established interpersonal relationships and group ties of the people involved and, in effect, destroys the sense of group identity of a great many individuals. "Group identity," a concept originally formulated by Erik Erikson, refers to the individual's sense of belonging, of being a part of larger human and social entities. It may include belonging to organizations or interpersonal networks with which a person is directly involved; and it may refer to "membership" in social groups with whom an individual has little overt contact, whether it be a family, a social class, an ethnic collectivity, a profession, or a group of people sharing a common ideology. What is common to these various patterns of group identity is that they represent an integrated sense of shared human qualities, of some sense of communality with other people which is essential for meaningful social functioning. Since, most notably in the working class, effective relationships with others are dependent upon a continuing sense of common group identity, the experience of loss and disruption of these affiliations is intense and frequently irrevocable. On the grounds, therefore, of both spatial and interpersonal orientations and commitments, dislocation from the residential area represents a particularly marked disruption in the sense of continuity for the majority of this group.

THE NATURE OF THE LOSS IN RELOCATION:
SOCIAL AND PERSONAL FACTORS

Previously we said that by emphasizing the spatial dimension of the orientation to the West End, we did not mean to diminish the importance of social patterns in the experience of the local area and their effects on post-relocation loss reactions. Nor do we wish to neglect personality factors involved in the widespread grief reactions. It is quite clear that pre-relocation social relationships and intrapsychic dispositions *do* affect the depth of grief in response to leaving the West End. The strongest of these patterns is based on the association between depth of grief and pre-relocation feelings about neighbors. Among those women who had very positive feelings about their neighbors, 76 percent show severe grief reactions; among those who were positive but less extreme, 56 percent show severe grief; and among those who were relatively negative, 38 percent have marked grief responses. Similarly, among the women whose five closest friends lived in the West End, 67 percent show marked grief; among those whose friends were mostly in the West End or equally distributed inside and outside the area, 55 percent have severe grief reactions; and among those whose friends were mostly or all outside, 44 percent show severe grief.

The fact that these differences, although great, are not as consistently powerful as the differences relating to spatial use patterns does not necessarily imply the *greater* importance of spatial factors. If we hold the effect of spatial variables constant and examine the relationship between depth of grief and the interpersonal variables, it becomes apparent that the effect of interpersonal contacts on depth of grief is consistent regardless of differences in spatial orientation; and, likewise, the effect of spatial orientations on depth of grief is consistent regardless of differences in interpersonal relationships. Thus, each set of factors contributes independently to the depth of grief in spite of some degree of internal relationship. In short, we suggest that *either* spatial identity or group identity may be a critical focus of loss of continuity and thereby lead to severe grief; but if *both* bases for the sense of continuity are localized *within the residential area* the disruption of continuity is greater, and the proportions of marked grief correspondingly higher.

It is noteworthy that, apart from local interpersonal and social relationships and local spatial orientations and use (and variables which are closely related to these), there are few other social or personal factors in the pre-relocation situation which are related to depth of grief. These negative findings are of particular importance in emphasizing that not all the variables which influence the grief reaction to dislocation are of equal importance. It should be added that a predisposition to depression markedly accentuates the depth of grief in response to the loss of one's residential area. But it is also clear that prior depressive orientations do not account for the entire relationship. The effects of the general depressive orientation and of the social, interpersonal, and spatial relationships within the West End are essentially additive; both sets of factors contribute markedly to the final result. Thus, among the women with a severe depressive orientation, an extremely large proportion (81 percent) of those who regarded the West End as their real home show marked grief. But among the women without a depressive orientation, only a moderate proportion (58 percent) of those who similarly viewed the West End as home show severe grief. On the other hand, when the West End is not seen as the person's real home, an increasing severity of general depressive orientation does *not* lead to an increased proportion of severe grief reactions.

THE NATURE OF THE LOSS IN RELOCATION: CASE ANALYSES

The dependence of the sense of continuity on external resources in the working class, particularly on the availability and local presence of familiar places which have the character of "home," and of familiar people whose patterns of behavior and response are relatively predictable, does not account for all of the reaction of grief to dislocation. In addition to these factors, which may be accentuated by depressive predispositions, it is quite evident that the realities of *post*-relocation experience are bound to affect the perpetuation, quality, and depth of grief. And, in fact, our data show that there is a strong association between positive or negative experiences in the post-relocation situation and the proportions who show severe grief. But this issue is complicated by two factors: (1) the extent to which potentially meaningful post-relocation circumstances can be a satisfying experience is *affected* by the degree and tenaciousness of previous commitments to the West End, and (2) the post-relocation "reality" is, in part, *selected* by the people who move and thus is a function of many personality factors, including the ability to anticipate needs, demands, and environmental opportunities.

In trying to understand the effects of pre-relocation orientations and post-relocation experiences of grief, we must bear in mind that the grief reactions we have described and analyzed are based on responses given approximately two years after relocation. Most people manage to achieve some adaptation to their experiences of loss and grief, and learn to deal with new situations and new experiences on their own terms. A wide variety of adaptive methods can be employed to salvage fragments of the sense of continuity, or to try to re-establish it on new grounds. Nonetheless, it is the tenaciousness of the imagery and affect of grief, despite these efforts at dealing with the altered reality, which is so strikingly similar to mourning for a lost person.

In coping with the sense of loss, some families tried to remain physically close to the area they knew, even though most of their close interpersonal relationships remain disrupted; and by this method, they appear often to have modified their feelings of grief. Other families try to move among relatives and maintain a sense of continuity through some degree of constancy in the external bases for their group identity. Yet others respond to the loss of place and people by accentuating the importance of those role relationships which remain. Thus, a number of women report increased closeness to their husbands, which they often explicitly relate to the decrease in the availability of other social relationships for both partners and which, in turn, modifies the severity of grief. In order to clarify some of the complexities of pre-relocation orientations and of post-relocation adjustments most concretely, a review of several cases may prove to be instructive.

It is evident that a very strong positive pre-relocation orientation to the West End is relatively infrequently associated with a complete absence of grief; and that, likewise, a negative pre-relocation orientation to the area is infrequently associated with a strong grief response. The two types which are numerically dominant are, in terms of rational expectations, consistent: those with strong positive feelings about the West End and severe grief; and those with negative feelings about the West End and minimal or moderate grief. The two "deviant" types, by the same token, are both numerically smaller and inconsistent: those with strong positive pre-relocation orientations and little grief; and those with negative pre-relocation orientations and severe grief. A closer examination of those "deviant" cases with strong pre-relocation commitment to the West End and minimal post-relocation grief often reveals either important reservations in their prior involvement with the West End or, more frequently, the denial or rejection of feelings of grief rather than their total absence. And the association of minimal pre-relocation commitment to the West End with a severe grief response often proves on closer examination to be a function of a deep involvement in the West End which is modified by markedly ambivalent statements; or, more generally, the grief reaction itself is quite modest and tenuous or is even a pseudo-grief which masks the primacy of dissatisfaction with the current area.

GRIEF PATTERNS: CASE EXAMPLES

In turning to case analysis, we shall concentrate on the specific factors which operate in families of all four types, those representing the two dominant and those representing the two deviant patterns.

1. The Figella family exemplifies the association of strong positive pre-relocation attachments to the West End and a severe grief reaction. This is the most frequent of all the patterns and, although the Figella family is only one "type" among those who show this pattern, they are prototypical of a familiar West End constellation.

Both Mr. and Mrs. Figella are second-generation Americans who were born and brought up in the West End. In her pre-relocation interview, Mrs. Figella described her feelings about living in the West End unambiguously: "It's a wonderful place, the people are friendly." She "loves everything about it" and anticipates missing her relatives above all. She is satisfied with her dwelling: "It's comfortable, clean and warm." And the marriage appears to be deeply satisfying for both husband and wife. They share many household activities and have a warm family life with their three children.

Both Mr. and Mrs. Figella feel that their lives have changed a great deal since relocation. They are clearly referring, however, to the pattern and conditions of their relationships with other people. Their home life has changed little except that Mr. Figella is home more. He continues to work at the same job as a manual laborer with a modest but sufficient income. While they have many economic insecurities, the relocation has not produced any serious financial difficulty for them.

In relocating, the Figella family bought a house. Both husband and wife are quite satisfied with the physical arrangements but, all in all, they are dissatisfied with the move. When asked what she dislikes about her present dwelling, Mrs. Figella replied simply and pathetically: "It's in Arlington and I want to be in the West End." Both Mr. and Mrs. Figella are outgoing, friendly people with a very wide circle of social contacts. Although they still see their relatives often, they both feel isolated from them and they regret the loss of their friends. As Mr. Figella puts it: "I come home from work and that's it. I just plant myself in the house."

The Figella family is, in many respects, typical of a well-adjusted working-class family. They have relatively few ambitions for themselves or for their children. They continue in close contact with many people; but they no longer have the same extensiveness of mutual cooperation in household activities, they cannot "drop in" as casually as before, they do not have the sense of being surrounded by a familiar area and familiar people. Thus, while their objective situation is not dramatically altered, the changes do involve important elements of stability and continuity in their lives. They manifest the importance of externally available resources for an integral sense of spatial and group identity. However, they have always maintained a very close marital relationship, and their family provides a substantial basis for a sense of continuity. They can evidently cope with difficulties on the strength of their many internal and external resources. Nonetheless, they have suffered from the move, and find it extremely difficult to reorganize their lives completely in adapting to a new geographical situation and new patterns of social affiliation. Their grief for a lost home seems to be one form of maintaining continuity on the basis of memories. While it prevents a more wholehearted adjustment to their altered lives, such adjustments would imply forsaking the remaining fragments of a continuity which was central to their conceptions of themselves and of the world.

2. There are many similarities between the Figella family and the Giuliano family. But Mrs. Giuliano shows relatively little pre-relocation commitment to the West End and little post-relocation grief. Mr. Giuliano was somewhat more deeply involved in the West End and, although satisfied with the change, feels that relocation was "like having the rug pulled out from under you." Mr. and Mrs. Giuliano are also second-generation Americans, of similar background to the Figellas'. But Mrs. Giuliano only moved to the West End at her marriage. Mrs. Giuliano had many objections to the area: "For me it is too congested. I never did care for it . . . too many barrooms, on every corner, too many families in one building. . . . The sidewalks are too narrow and the kids can't play outside." But she does expect to miss the stores and many favorite places. Her housing ambitions go beyond West End standards and she wants more space inside and outside. She had no blood relatives in the West End but was close to her husband's family and had friends nearby.

Mr. Giuliano was born in the West End and he had many relatives in the area. He has a relatively high status manual job but only a modest income. His wife does not complain about this although she is only moderately satisfied with the marriage. In part she objected to the fact that they went out so little and that he spent too much time on the corner with his friends. His social networks in the West End were more extensive and involved than were Mrs. Giuliano's. And he missed the West End more than she did after the relocation. But even Mr. Giuliano says that, all in all, he is satisfied with the change.

Mrs. Giuliano feels the change is "wonderful." She missed her friends but got over it. And a few of Mr. Giuliano's hanging group live close by so they can continue to hang together. Both are satisfied with the house they bought although Mrs. Giuliano's ambitions have now gone beyond this. The post-relocation situation has led to an improved marital relationship: Mr. Giuliano is home more and they go out more together.

Mr. and Mrs. Giuliano exemplify a pattern which seems most likely to be associated with a beneficial experience from relocation.

Unlike Mr. and Mrs. Figella, who completely accept their working-class status and are embedded in the social and cultural patterns of the working class, Mr. and Mrs. Giuliano show many evidences of social mobility. Mr. Giuliano's present job is, properly speaking, outside the working-class category because of its relatively high status and he himself does not "work with his hands." And Mrs. Giuliano's housing ambitions, preferences in social relationships, orientation to the class structure, and attitudes toward a variety of matters from shopping to child rearing are indications of a readiness to achieve middle-class status. Mr. Giuliano is prepared for and Mrs. Giuliano clearly desires "discontinuity" with some of the central bases for their former identity. Their present situation is, in fact, a transitional one which allows them to reintegrate their lives at a new and higher status level without too precipitate a change. And their marital relationship seems sufficiently meaningful to provide a significant core of continuity in the process of change in their patterns of social and cultural experience. The lack of grief in this case is quite understandable and appropriate to their patterns of social orientation and expectation.

3. Yet another pattern is introduced by the Borowski family, who had an intense pre-relocation commitment to the West End and relatively little post-relocation grief. The Borowskis are both second-generation and have four children.

Mrs. Borowski was brought up in the West End but her husband has lived there only since the marriage (fifteen years before). Her feelings about living in the West End were clear: "I love it—it's the only home I've ever known." She had reservations about the dirt in the area but loved the people, the places, and the convenience and maintained an extremely wide circle of friends. They had some relatives nearby but were primarily oriented towards friends, both within and outside the West End. Mr. Borowski, a highly skilled manual worker with a moderately high income, was as deeply attached to the West End as his wife.

Mr. Borowski missed the West End very much but was quite satisfied with their new situation and could anticipate feeling thoroughly at home in the new neighborhood. Mrs. Borowski proclaims that "home is where you hang your hat; it's up to you to make the adjustments." But she also says, "If I knew the people were coming back to the West End, I would pick up this little house and put it back on my corner." She claims she was not sad after relocation but, when asked how she felt when the building she lived in was torn down, a strangely morbid association is aroused: "It's just like a plant . . . when you tear up its roots, it dies! I didn't die but I felt kind of bad. It was home. . . . Don't look back, try to go ahead."

Despite evidences of underlying grief, both Mr. and Mrs. Borowski have already adjusted to the change with remarkable alacrity. They bought a one-family house and have many friends in the new area. They do not feel as close to their new neighbors as they did to their West End friends, and they still maintain extensive contact with the latter. They are comfortable and happy in their new surroundings and maintain the close, warm, and mutually appreciative marital relationship they formerly had.

Mr. and Mrs. Borowski, and particularly Mrs. Borowski, reveal a sense of loss which is largely submerged beneath active efforts to deal with the present. It was possible for them to do this both because of personality factors (that is, the ability to deny the intense affective meaning of the change and to detach themselves from highly "cathected" objects with relative ease) and because of prior social patterns and orientations. Not only is Mr. Borowski, by occupation, among the highest group of working-class status, but this family has been "transitional" for some time. Remaining in the West End was clearly a matter of preference for them. They could have moved out quite easily on the basis of income; and many of their friends were scattered throughout metropolitan Boston. But while they are less self-consciously mobile than the Giulianos, they had already shifted to many patterns more typical of the middle class before leaving the West End. These ranged from their joint weekly shopping expeditions to their recreational patterns, which included such sports as boating and such regular plans as yearly vacations. They experienced a disruption in continuity by virtue of their former spatial and group identity. But the bases for maintaining this identity had undergone many changes over the years; and they had already established a feeling for places and people, for a potential redefinition of "home" which was less contingent on the immediate and local availability of familiar spaces and familiar friends. Despite their preparedness for the move by virtue of cultural orientation, social experience, and personal disposition, the change was a considerable wrench for them. But, to the extent that they can be categorized as "over-adjusters," the residue of their lives in the West End is primarily a matter of painful memories which are only occasionally reawakened.

4. The alternate deviant pattern, minimal pre-relocation commitment associated with severe post-relocation grief, is manifested by Mr. and Mrs. Pagliuca. As in the previous case, this classification applies more fully to Mrs. Pagliuca, since Mr. Pagliuca appears to have had stronger ties to the West End. Mr. Pagliuca is a second-generation American but Mrs. Pagliuca is first-generation from an urban European background. For both of them, however, there is some evidence that the sadness and regret about the loss of the West End should perhaps be designated as pseudo-grief.

Mrs. Pagliuca had a difficult time in the West End. But she also had a difficult time before that. She moved into the West End when she got married. And she complains bitterly about her marriage, her husband's relatives, West Enders in general. She says of the West End: "I don't like it. The people . . . the buildings are full of rats. There are no places to play for the children." She liked the apartment but complained about the lady downstairs, the dirt, the repairs required, and the coldness during the winter. She also complains a great deal about lack of money. Her husband's wages are not too low but he seems to have periods of unemployment and often drinks his money away.

Mr. Pagliuca was attached to some of his friends and the bars in the West End. But he didn't like his housing situation there. And his reaction tends to be one of bitterness ("a rotten deal") rather than of sadness. Both Mr. and Mrs. Pagliuca are quite satisfied with their post-relocation apartment but are thoroughly dissatisfied with the area. They have had considerable difficulty with neighbors: ". . . I don't like this; people are mean here; my children get blamed for anything and everything; and there's no transportation near here." She now idealizes the West End and claims that she misses everything about it.

Mr. Pagliuca is an unskilled manual laborer. Financial problems create a constant focus for difficulty and arguments. But both Mr. and Mrs. Pagliuca appear more satisfied with one another than before relocation. They have four children, some of whom are in legal difficulty. There is also some evidence of past cruelty toward the children, at least on Mrs. Pagliuca's part.

It is evident from this summary that the Pagliuca family is deviant in a social as well as in a statistical sense. They show few signs of adjusting to the move or, for that matter, of any basic potential for successful adjustment to further moves (which they are now planning). It may be that families with such initial difficulties, with such a tenuous basis for maintaining a sense of continuity under any circumstances, suffer most acutely from disruption of these minimal ties. The Pagliuca family has few inner resources and, having lost the minimal external resources signified by a gross sense of belonging, of being tolerated if not accepted, they appear to be hopelessly at sea. Although we refer to their grief as "pseudo-grief" on the basis of the shift from pre-relocation to post-relocation statements, there is a sense in which it is quite real. Within the post-relocation interviews their responses are quite consistent; and a review of all the data suggests that, although their ties were quite modest, their current difficulties have revealed the importance of these meager involvements and the problems of re-establishing anew an equivalent basis for identity formation. Thus, even for Mr. and Mrs. Pagliuca, we can speak of the disruption in the sense of continuity, although this continuity was based on a very fragile experience of minimal comfort, with familiar places and relatively tolerant people. Their grief reaction, pseudo or real, may further influence (and be influenced by) dissatisfactions with any new residential situation. The fact that it is based on an idealized past accentuates rather than minimizes its effect on current expectations and behavior.

CONCLUSIONS

Grieving for a lost home is evidently a widespread and serious social phenomenon following in the wake of urban dislocation. It is likely to increase social and psychological "pathology" in a limited number of instances; and it is also likely to create new opportunities for some, and to increase the rate of social mobility for others. For the greatest number, dislocation is unlikely to have either effect but does lead to intense personal suffering despite moderately successful adaptation to the total situation of relocation. Under these circumstances, it becomes most critical that we face the realities of the effects of relocation on working-class residents of slums and, on the basis of knowledge and understanding, that we learn to deal more effectively with the problems engendered.

In evaluating these data on the effect of pre-relocation experiences on post-relocation reactions of grief, we have arrived at a number of conclusions:

1. The affective reaction to the loss of the West End can be quite precisely described as a grief response showing most of the characteristics of grief and mourning for a lost person.

2. One of the important components of the grief reaction is the fragmentation of the sense of spatial identity. This is manifest, not only in the pre-relocation experience of the spatial area as an expanded "home," but in the varying degrees of grief following relocation, arising from variations in the pre-relocation orientation to and use of local spatial regions.

3. Another component, of equal importance, is the dependence of the sense of group identity on stable, social networks. Dislocation necessarily led to the fragmentation of this group identity which was based, to such a large extent, on the external availability and overt contact with familiar groups of people.

4. Associated with these "cognitive" components, described as the sense of spatial identity and the sense of group identity, are strong affective qualities. We have not tried to delineate them but they appear to fall into the realm of a feeling of security in and commitment to the external spatial and group patterns which are the tangible, visible aspects of these identity components. However, a predisposition to depressive reactions also markedly affects the depth of grief reaction.

5. Theoretically, we can speak of spatial and group identity as critical foci of the sense of continuity. This sense of continuity is not *necessarily* contingent on the external stability of place, people, and security or support. But for the working class these concrete, external resources and the experience of stability, availability, and familiarity which they provide are essential for a meaningful sense of continuity. Thus, dislocation and the loss of the residential area represent a fragmentation of some of the essential components of the sense of continuity in the working class.

It is in the light of these observations and conclusions that we must consider problems of social planning which are associated with the changes induced by physical planning for relocation. Urban planning cannot be limited to "bricks and mortar." While these data tell us little about the importance of housing or the aspects of housing which are important, they indicate that considerations of a non-housing nature are critical. There is evidence, for example, that the frequency of the grief response is not affected by such housing factors as increase or decrease in apartment size or home ownership. But physical factors may be of great importance when related to the subjective significance of different spatial and physical arrangements, or to their capacity for gratifying different socio-cultural groups. For the present, we can only stress the importance of local areas as *spatial and social* arrangements which are central to the lives of working-class people. And, in view of the enormous importance of such local areas, we are led to consider the convergence of familiar people and familiar places as a focal consideration in formulating planning decisions.

We can learn to deal with these problems only through research, through exploratory and imaginative service programs, and through a more careful consideration of the place of residential stability in salvaging the precarious thread of continuity. The outcomes of crises are always manifold and, just as there is an increase in strain and difficulty, so also there is an increase in opportunities for adapting at a more satisfying level of functioning. The judicious use of minimal resources of counseling and assistance may permit many working-class people to reorganize and integrate a meaningful sense of spatial and group identity under the challenge of social change. Only a relatively small group of those whose functioning has always been marginal and who cannot cope with the added strain of adjusting to wholly new problems are likely to require major forms of intervention.

In general, our results would imply the necessity for providing increased opportunities for maintaining a sense of continuity for those people, mainly from the working class, whose residential areas are being renewed. This may involve several factors: (1) diminishing the amount of drastic redevelopment and the consequent mass demolition of property and mass dislocation from homes; (2) providing more frequently for people to move within their former residential areas during and after the renewal; and (3) when dislocation and relocation are unavoidable, planning the relocation possibilities in order to provide new areas which can be assimilated to old objectives. A closer examination of slum areas may even provide some concrete information regarding specific physical variables, the physical and spatial arrangements typical of slum areas and slum housing, which offer considerable gratification to the residents. These may often be translated into effective modern architectural and areal design. And, in conjunction with planning decisions which take more careful account of the human consequences of urban physical change, it is possible to utilize social, psychological, and psychiatric services. The use of highly skilled resources, including opportunities for the education of professional and even lay personnel in largely unfamiliar problems and methods, can minimize some of the more destructive and widespread effects of relocation; and, for some families, can offer constructive experiences in dealing with new adaptational possibilities. The problem is large. But only by assuring the integrity of some of the external bases for the sense of continuity in the working class, and by maximizing the opportunities for meaningful adaptation, can we accomplish planned urban change without serious hazard to human welfare.

14 The Small Businessman and Relocation*

BASIL ZIMMER

The present analysis was based on the experiences of approximately 300 businesses that had been displaced through governmental action [in Providence, Rhode Island] during the five-year period 1954 through 1959. The data were obtained through personal interviews. Completed interviews were obtained from 292 of the 311 establishments contacted. This represents a response rate of 94 percent. Approximately one-third of the units had been displaced by urban renewal projects and the remaining two-thirds were from highway project areas. The general analysis did not distinguish the problems of displacement and relocation by type of project. But when attention was focused on aspects where the particular type of project was important, data were presented separately. However, the major focus throughout has been on the consequences of displacement and relocation, regardless of the specific type of public improvement program involved.

The displaced businesses in the present study were predominantly small establishments. Nearly one-fifth were owner-operated with no employees. Eight units out of ten employed fewer than ten workers. While the median for all of the displaced establishments was only 3.2 employees, this ranged from a low of only 1.4 for service estab-

* Reprinted from *Rebuilding Cities*, Chicago, Quadrangle Books, 1964, pp. 324–348.

lishments to 9.2 for manufacturing, wholesale, and construction units. Less than 9 percent employed twenty or more workers. These businesses were apparently firmly established, in that more than 90 percent had been in business for more than five years, and three-fourths for more than ten years. We also found that two-thirds of the establishments had been in operation in the same neighborhood for ten years or more. Further, it was observed that the owners were long-time residents of the Providence area. Less than 10 percent had lived in the area less than 25 years, whereas half had lived in the area for 45 years or more. Thus it is evident that these are not fly-by-night or even temporary businesses. Rather, the establishments affected were units of long standing.

While the study was limited only to those businesses displaced within the central city, it is of particular interest to note that more than half of the owners did not live in the city. Thus it is apparent that the consequences of public improvement programs within the city reach beyond the corporate limits. In passing, it is noted that place of residence showed considerable selectivity. The owners who lived in the suburbs tended to be younger and better educated than those living in the city. They also owned the larger businesses, and they were more likely to own the non-food-related retail as well as manufacturing, wholesale, and construction establishments.

Urban renewal programs tended to displace different types of businesses than were displaced by highway projects. In the former, we found a disproportionately large number of food-related retail and service establishments. Renewal projects also contained smaller businesses than were displaced by the highway construction program. Among renewal projects, nearly seven units out of ten employed fewer than three workers, as compared with four out of ten in highway project areas. Owners of businesses in renewal areas tended to be older and less well educated. In these areas, businesses disproportionately catered to a neighborhood-type market and served a particular ethnic or racial group. Such businesses tended to be less well-to-do than the units displaced by the highway program.

Monthly rentals in renewal projects were found to be substantially lower than in highway project areas, as were sales also. Many of the businesses in renewal areas were small, marginal, neighborhood-type units, whereas those displaced by the highway were larger and were more firmly established economically. This explains in part why units from renewal areas responded more negatively to the move than businesses displaced by the highway. The latter were in a better financial position to absorb the disruptive effects of the move, whereas the former were less able to tolerate the costs and the temporary losses resulting from such a change. This observation finds support in the differences in the proportion of establishments that successfully relocated from each type of project.

Since it was not possible to locate all of the displaced establishments, we have expressed business losses to the community in two ways, that is, as "known" losses and as "probable" losses. The known losses were computed on the basis of actual data gathered through interviews with the owners, whereas the probable losses were inferred from the best available evidence. In the latter instances, we could find no evidence that would even suggest to us that the business was still in operation. Actually when all efforts failed to find any trace of these units it seemed safe to conclude that they were probably no longer in business in the area. On this assumption, an analysis of our data showed that the loss rate was slightly higher among units displaced from urban renewal areas. Approximately 40 percent of these establishments discontinued in business, as compared with 30 percent of those displaced from highway project areas. Thus the loss rate is one-third higher in renewal areas. Without regard to type of project, the loss rate was highest among food-related retail units and lowest among the establishments in the manufacturing, wholesale, and construction category. In short, the types of units least likely to survive displacement were predominantly those businesses that had a close and frequent relationship with their customers. Such units largely served a neighborhood-type market. The owners tended to know most of their customers who came disproportionately from a particular ethnic or racial group. Because of this closer and apparently more recurrent relationship with their customers, who tended to live in close proximity, these establishments were much more sensitive to the disruptive effects of the move. Such customer relationships were most likely to obtain in renewal areas.

As expected, the smaller establishments had the lowest survival rate. One-third of the non-survivors had no employees and more than three out of four had less than three workers. But among the survivors, only four out of ten were in this size class. Viewed differently, the proportion that did not survive the move ranged from a low of 10 percent among those with ten or more workers to a high of 40 percent among those with no employees. Thus it is evident that displacement worked a particular hardship on the smaller establishments. Such units were likely marginal even prior to the move. Displacement jeopardized this minimal balance. These businesses could not survive the change. Although the loss of such units actually means little to the commercial and industrial structure of the city, the losses, nonetheless, are of crucial consequence to the owners of individual business establishments.

The relationship between average monthly sales and rate of survival was found to be a marked one, but further analysis proved it to be much more involved than appeared at first blush. Median monthly sales of the survivors prior to the move were 3.5 times higher than sales of the non-survivors. This ratio obtained within each type of project. Although median sales varied markedly by type of project, there was a comparable relative difference between survivors and non-survivors within each type of project. Urban renewal businesses while at the original location clearly operated at a much lower level than those displaced by the highway. Of particular interest, however, is that the median monthly sales of the survivors in renewal areas were lower than the sales of the non-survivors from highway projects. Also the median sales of the non-survivors from highway project areas were 2.5 times larger than the sales reported by the non-survivors from renewal areas. The apparent inconsistencies here are due largely to differences in rent levels. The rent-to-sales ratio in both types of projects is much higher among the non-survivors. The lower sales in renewal areas were more than compensated for by much lower rentals. Thus the median monthly sales of the survivors from renewal areas were slightly lower than the sales of the non-survivors displaced by highway projects, but rents varied markedly. Consequently the rent burden at the original location among the latter units was nearly double that of the former. The proportions of sales devoted to rents were 4.3 percent and 2.4 percent respectively. Apparently the lower operating costs in the renewal areas made these businesses less marginal, and placed them in a better position financially to survive the disruptive effects of the move.[1] Not to be overlooked here also is that different types of businesses were displaced from the renewal areas; thus the absolute dollar value of sales may have a different meaning than for the types of businesses in highway project areas that did not survive the move. It may be that the "break point" varies according to the quality of the area from which the businesses are moved, as well as by the type and size of business displaced.

As we pursued our analysis further, we found that even though many of the non-survivors were operating close to a subsistence level prior to displacement, nearly all expressed the opinion that they would have continued in business indefinitely had they not been forced to move out of the area. It may well be that they could have done so, since many had no employees and either owned the building occupied or paid low rentals. Operating costs were apparently minimal. It is worthy of note that 94 percent of the non-survivors had been in business for more than five years, and 91 percent had occupied the same location for five years or more. Actually one unit in three that did not survive the move had been at the same location for more than fifteen years. Of particular interest is the very low proportion of non-survivors that had entered business during the war years, and the very high proportion that entered business during the early postwar period.

It should be noted that not all non-survivals were business failures in the traditional sense. Some used displacement as an opportunity to discontinue in business, which they had vague plans to do anyway. The move provided the external stimulus which was needed in order to reach a definite decision. In other instances, the business was discontinued because the owner had a "more attractive" job offer. However, a majority of the owners would have preferred to remain in business, but did not do so for a variety of reasons.

Following displacement, approximately one-fifth of the non-survivors entered the ranks of the unemployed, but this probably represented a temporary condition. Although a majority of the non-survivors reported that they were through with business, some still

[1] Part of the differential ability to survive displacement may have been due to different policies and practices concerning compensation for the cost of the move. In highway project areas, the cost of the move was the responsibility of the owner—which may well have been too much of a burden for businesses operating at this level. A comparable burden was not faced by such businesses in renewal areas.

hoped to re-enter business at some future but largely unspecified date. At any rate, for a substantial minority unemployment was at least a temporary condition in the transition from business to some other position in the labor force. A similar proportion went into retirement after closing down their business. However, this was not always voluntary nor was it without problems, in that many were probably not covered by any formal retirement system. Accordingly, their present and future income would be severely limited. The fact that many resented retirement and sought in vain for "something to do with their time," was probably not peculiar to this group, in that it frequently occurs at this stage of the life cycle. Many went into retirement because they felt that they were too old to start over. Also they were too old to find other employment. Thus, in effect, when they closed down their business they were forced out of the labor market. The harmful effects for the unemployed and, to a lesser extent, the retired, are readily apparent.

But a majority of the non-survivors entered the labor market in different functional positions. More than half of those employed entered white collar occupations, while one-fourth hold jobs at the craftsman level. About one in five was engaged at the semi-skilled operative level. In general the level at which the former business owners entered the labor market was closely related to the size of their business prior to displacement. Thus those who employed three or more workers were nearly five times as likely to enter white collar occupations as those who had no employees. Conversely, the latter disproportionately entered manual-type jobs or retired. The owners of the smaller establishments were also more likely to enter the ranks of the unemployed.

It is of particular interest to note that a substantial majority of those who are currently working entered the same line of work as they were engaged in while in business. We also found that the business experience apparently prepared the former owners for better jobs than they had held prior to entering business. At least they had higher status positions in the labor force at the time of the study than the positions from which they had originally entered business. Our data showed that while none had entered business from the professional-managerial level, nearly one-fifth of those who are currently working moved into such positions after closing down their businesses. On the other hand, approximately three out of five entered business from blue collar work, but we found only one in five engaged in work at this level. To what extent this upward mobility was due to the business experience as such, and how much was due merely to the passing of time, cannot be determined.

The present income of the non-survivors is in the aggregate substantially lower than that reported by those who continued in business. This, of course, is to be expected because of the large number of unemployed and retired. However, the point of particular interest is that nearly nine out of ten of the non-survivors experienced a decrease in income. Although changes in income vary by type of activity entered, in no occupational category was a decline reported by less than seven former owners out of ten.

There was general agreement among the non-survivors that they would have been better off if they had not been displaced. They also felt that if the government is going to force businesses to move, owners who do not relocate should be compensated not only for their property but also should be compensated for the "worth of the business" as well. The general feeling among the non-survivors was that displacement had deprived them of their source of livelihood, and they should have been compensated accordingly.

In addition to the losses due to the non-survivors, there were also losses to the central city (but not to the community) resulting from some of the establishments moving beyond the corporate limits of the city. From the point of view of the city, this type of movement has practically the same effect as "going out of business," for the economic contribution of such establishments is lost to the city. Not only are the jobs lost, but the tax base is accordingly decreased. This type of movement represented less of a numerical loss of establishments but more of an absolute loss to the city than did the non-survivors, for the suburban movement was selective of different-type establishments.

In the process of displacement and relocation, the central city tended to retain a high disproportionate number of the smaller establishments, whereas the larger units were more likely to move to the suburbs. The latter areas seemed to attract the businesses that wanted to own the building they occupied. The types of business that were overrepresented in the suburbanization movement were those in non-food-related retail and those in the manufacturing, wholesale, and construction category. The latter, more so than any other type of business, tended to move to the suburbs. The city, however, retained the food-related retail and service establishments. Jewelry manufacturing firms also relocated in the city. This they did because of the advantages of being in the jewelry district. There seems to be general agreement among owners of jewelry manufacturing firms that the suburbs would not offer any advantages for these units. On the contrary, the suburbs were thought to be too inaccessible, especially for buyers when they come to the area to place their orders. Also such a location would cut the units off from other jewelry establishments with whom they were likely to be functionally related.

In general the proportion of units moving to the suburbs varied directly and consistently by size of business. The median-sized business that relocated in the city employed 3.8 workers at the time of displacement, while those moving to the suburbs averaged 7.2 workers. This, of course, means that the suburbanization of "jobs" far exceeded the suburbanization of establishments. Of particular interest is the fact that the losses to the city through businesses moving to the suburbs following displacement far exceeded the losses due to units going out of business, even though the number of establishments that did not survive the move nearly doubled the number of units that relocated in the suburbs. A comparison of the losses showed that the median-size units that moved to the suburbs were more than four times larger than the units that went out of business. The aggregate job opportunities lost through the suburbanization of businesses were more than double the number of jobs lost, including the positions of the owners themselves, through units closing down their business operations. It is noted further that while the non-survivors were largely small food-related retail, neighborhood-type businesses, the units that moved to the suburbs were predominantly those in the manufacturing, wholesale, and construction category.

Unquestionably units going out of business cause serious losses for the individual owners, but from the point of view of the city, as far as the tax base is concerned, the losses due to businesses moving out of the city are of more importance. This was abundantly evident from a comparison of rental and sales prior to displacement. The median monthly rent paid by the non-survivors at the old location was $80, whereas those that continued in business and moved to the suburbs paid more than $200. Differences in median monthly sales were even more marked. While the non-survivors reported median sales of less than $1,700 per month prior to displacement, the businesses that moved to the suburbs had median sales in excess of $8,200. This represents nearly a five-fold difference in average monthly sales. Although less than one unit in five relocated in the suburbs, the movement out was such that the loss to the city of jobs and volume of business far exceeded the proportionate movement of establishments. The significance of this type of loss to the city needs no elaboration.

Movement to the suburbs seems to have been influenced by the place of residence of the owner. Our data showed that a substantial number of those who moved to the suburbs moved closer to home than they were prior to displacement. Persons who lived in the suburbs were more than five times as likely to move their business to the suburbs as were those who lived in the city. When viewed from a different perspective, we found that nearly nine out of ten owners who moved their business to the suburbs lived in the suburbs, as compared with less than half of those who relocated in the city. Thus not only does the influence of public improvement programs extend beyond the corporate limits of the city, but the changing distribution of population from city to suburbs portends a change in the distribution of commercial and industrial functions also.

It may be that we have observed the early stages of a new rationale for an even more widespread settlement pattern in urban centers than has developed to date. Owners of businesses apparently now have a greater amount of freedom and wider range of choice in the selection of a site because of the marked improvements in transportation and the general reliance on the private automobile as the predominant mode of travel. The problem of space in the traditional sense seems to have lost much of its meaning in the local community setting, even though owners continue to report accessibility as a very important factor in selecting a site. Because of the higher incomes and higher levels of living in general, workers and customers alike appear to be willing and able to overcome the costs of distance. Thus, in the modern context, with the widespread ownership of private automobiles and adequate highways, nearly any location is readily accessible. Employers seem to be no longer dependent on workers living in close proximity. Also businesses can more effectively attract customers from greater distances. Consequently business owners in relocation have been able to select sites largely in relation to their own place of residence. Under present conditions, it is possible for owners to live and have their place of business away from the densely settled areas of the city. Many businesses seem no longer to be as dependent upon a specific location. This suggests that the time-cost variable may have lost much of its original significance as a limiting factor influencing either residential locations, places of employment, or the sites for many commercial establishments. At any rate, our data indicate that many owners located their businesses for their own convenience, with little or no regard for the time-cost factor for either their workers or their customers. We would infer from this that, as transportation facilities are improved, this more widespread pattern of settlement of commercial and industrial establishments is likely to develop further. This obviously works to the disadvantage of the city.

Businesses moving to the suburbs seem to occupy more attractive sites than businesses that relocated in the city. At least a larger proportion of the units that relocated in the suburbs moved to newer, better buildings with more space than they had previously occupied. As compared with those that remained in the city, businesses in the suburbs occupied much larger buildings. Also they were more likely to occupy newly constructed structures. Improvements in parking facilities were observed in both areas, but such improvements were more marked among the units that moved to the suburbs.

Following relocation the units that moved to the suburbs seemed to have made a more favorable adjustment than the businesses that remained in the city. This is reflected not only in respect to the economic variables considered, but also in general reaction to the new location. Suburban businesses had a larger proportion who were satisfied with the progress they had made at the new site, and they were more certain they would not have done any better had they remained at the original site. Suburban units also had a larger proportion who stated a preference for doing business at the present location.

The more favorable reaction among the businesses in the suburbs was to be expected, in the light of the selective movement originally, and in terms of what happened to these units economically since the move. While the units that remained in the city experienced an increase in rent and a substantial decline in sales after the move, the opposite was found in the suburbs. Rentals declined slightly, but sales increased by approximately the same proportion that they had declined in the city. Consequently the rent-to-sales ratio in the suburbs declined by 20 percent following the move, but increased by 49 percent among the businesses that remained in the city. In short, the suburbs not only attracted the bigger and better establishments but also proved to be an attractive location for such businesses.

There was a marked improvement in parking facilities following the move. Less than half reported off-street parking at the original site, but this increased to two-thirds at the new location. Prior to the move, less than 40 percent of the businesses reported parking to be adequate, but after the move this increased to more than 70 percent. All types of businesses reported more adequate parking at the new location, but it was the non-food-related retail, manufacturing, wholesale, and construction establishments that were most likely to report adequate facilities at the new site. This was due in large part to the larger proportion of units that moved to the suburbs. Jewelry firms, service establishments, and food-related retail firms, other than those that relocated in a new shopping center, had the largest proportions reporting that parking was inadequate at the new site. This, of course, was due to the type of areas into which these businesses moved. They tended to remain in, or at least near to, the original location. Thus they relocated in the old built-up part of the city where space for parking was more limited. But even among these units, there was a substantial improvement in parking accommodations following relocation.

The changes observed by size of business were even more marked. Prior to the move it was the large units that had the largest proportion with inadequate facilities, but after the move these units were the most likely to report facilities to be adequate. While the proportion of small units reporting adequate parking increased by only 25 percent, the increase among the large units exceeded 200 percent. Thus one of the apparent consequences of the move was that parking facilities were much improved. This improvement, however, was not shared equally by all types of businesses. Nonetheless the ever-present problem of providing adequate parking facilities was apparently successfully resolved by a majority of the businesses.

For the individual business establishment, the cost of the move is of crucial significance. Particularly is this the case in highway project areas where no compensation is available. However, it is important also in renewal areas, for frequently the amount paid by the government is insufficient to cover the full costs. The median cost of the move for all of the units that relocated was approximately $1,000. This ranged only slightly by type of project. However, on closer inspection we found the median to be somewhat deceptive, since the businesses displaced by highway projects tended to be concentrated disproportionately in the top costs category. The modal costs for renewal projects were between $1,000 and $3,000, but were more than $3,000 for the units displaced by the highway. This difference takes on added significance when we note that only in renewal areas were any legislative provisions made for covering the costs of the move. But even in these projects, there were instances where costs would not be covered through some technicality. Also, compensation could not exceed a specified upper limit. At any rate, less than half of the units from renewal areas, and none of those from highway project areas, report that all of the costs of the move were covered. Thus while a heavy financial burden for moving was placed on many businesses, the full impact of the burden fell on those units displaced by the highway program.[2]

Costs of the move were found to vary by type and size of business. This was to be expected; thus the question on which attention was focused pertained to the relative costs of the move for selected subgroups. When costs were computed in terms of per-employee costs or as a ratio to median monthly sales, significant differences were found by a number of important subgroups. Although service units showed the lowest median costs, they had the largest relative costs by both measures. Jewelry manufacturing units also had a disproportionately high relative burden. These units also

[2] Under more recent legislation, states may adopt legislation which would provide compensation for covering the costs of the move up to a maximum of $3,000, when displaced by highway construction projects.

had the largest median costs. The relative burden was least for the non-food-related retail and those in the manufacturing, wholesale and construction category. The median costs of the move ranged from only $300 for small establishments (those with less than two employees) to more than $3,800 among the large units (eight or more workers). However, the relative costs varied inversely with size. The burden of the small units exceeds the large ones two-fold. However, the smaller units (in renewal areas) were more likely to have the costs of the move covered, since the costs would not exceed the upper limits, but in highway project areas this was not the case, in that the full burden fell on the individual business concern. While the absolute costs of the move varied directly by size, the relative burden, in terms of ability to absorb such costs, was inversely related to size of business. Service units and, to a lesser extent, jewelry firms carried a disproportionate burden also. The latter units, in particular, were displaced by the highway program. Thus among these businesses the unit costs were high and there were no provisions for covering the costs of the move.

We found that in some instances procedures were followed which indirectly helped to ease the burden relative to the costs of the move. That is, some owners seem to feel that at least part of the cost of the move was covered indirectly through the price received for their property. This practice was reflected in the proportion of owners who reported that they had been treated fairly as far as the cost of the move was concerned. Owners, particularly of the larger businesses, were much more likely to report fair treatment than renters of equal-size establishments. The larger owners seemed to have been in a better position to negotiate a more favorable price for their building. This apparently served to absorb at least part of the expense of moving. Even though the law technically did not make any provisions for covering any part of the costs of the move, we found that nearly one-fifth of the owners reported that they have received some compensation, and even in renewal areas where provisions were made to cover the costs of the move, owners were more likely than renters to report that the full costs had been covered, whereas renters disproportionately reported only partial coverage. Apparently when the costs exceeded the upper limits for renters, no adjustments were possible, but for owners a higher price could be agreed on for the property involved. At any rate, in both types of projects, owners who reported that they had received a "fair price" for their property were the ones most likely to report that they had been treated fairly in respect to the costs of the move.

It is particularly noteworthy that nearly half of the owners displaced by highway projects who reported that they had received a fair price for their building reported that they had been treated fairly as far as the cost of the move is concerned. This seems to be a very high proportion of such responses when we recall that no direct compensations were made to defray the costs of moving. That nearly half would respond thusly under the circumstances, when technically the whole burden of the move had to be absorbed by the individual business, is strong presumptive evidence, at least to the writer, that some indirect help had been provided through some adjustment in the price received for their property. The possible abuses arising out of such practices are as obvious as they are dangerous. Also, such practices do not provide any adjustments that can be offered to renters, and thus place a differential burden on tenants. That this was a rather common practice was evident from reading over the case materials. It was explicitly stated by many. Although more prevalent in highway project settlements, it was also evident in renewal projects, especially when the costs of the move exceeded the legislative upper limits. But here too the practice discriminated against tenants. Failures to pay the costs of moving directly, or even to cover the costs indirectly, were aspects of the displacement process which were frequently and bitterly criticized particularly by tenants and by owners of small establishments.

There was a considerable amount of change in tenure following the move. One-fourth of those who owned prior to displacement moved to rented quarters, while one-fifth of the renters became owners. The net result was a slight increase in the proportion of businesses that owned the building they occupied. However, a majority of the establishments continued to be tenants at the new location. Thus an analysis of rentals served as a rough index of the relative costs of doing business for a majority of the businesses following the move, as compared with the original location.

Rentals increased substantially at the new locations. The increases, however, were more marked among the units displaced from renewal areas than from highway project areas. Rentals in the latter area were nearly double those in the former area prior to the move, but after the move the rent excess was only slightly more than 50 percent. The major shifts in rentals occurred in the extremes, particularly among the businesses displaced from renewal areas. The proportion paying less than $50 declined from 47 percent to only 27 percent. Among the highway units, the major shift occurred in the top rental category. Whereas only 12 percent had paid $300 or more per month prior to the move, this increased to 27 percent after relocation. The proportionate increase in rentals among units displaced from renewal areas was three times the increase among units from highway project areas. The rent increases were 45 percent and 15 percent respectively. This, of course, was due to the fact that in the deteriorated areas needing renewal the original rent levels were much lower. Our data clearly showed that one of the consequences of displacement was that rental costs increased for a majority of the units. Nearly six units out of ten reported present rents to be higher than rents paid prior to the move.

A point particularly worthy of note is that the relative rent burden exceeded the absolute increase, since sales declined after the move. Rent, as a percent of sales, increased by 24 percent. The increased burden varied markedly by a number of subgroups. Service units in particular carried a heavy rent burden in relation to sales even prior to the move, but at the new location the burden increased and the differential was more marked. Similarly, the small units and those serving predominantly neighborhood markets carried a disproportionately heavy rent burden at both locations. These units also showed above-average percent increases following the move. Again this was due in large part to the type of areas from which they had been displaced. At both locations, their median rent levels were much lower than for businesses in other subgroups, but the proportionate increase in rentals following the move exceeded the other sub-categories. While rents increased, median sales declined at the new location, thus placing an increased rent burden on these units. In most other sub-categories, rents also increased and sales declined, but the proportionate changes were less marked. Thus while the large units experienced a larger absolute and percent increase in rents following the move than smaller units, sales declined less. Consequently the rent burden did not increase proportionately.

It is to be expected that rents and even the rent burden would increase following the move, for most of the businesses are in a much more favorable environment, that is, a majority moved to newer, better buildings in better areas. These improvements were reported with approximately equal frequency by businesses displaced by the highway as well as those from renewal areas. In only a minority of the cases did the quality of the site decline. And this occurred predominantly when the business relocated in close proximity to the original location. The smaller establishments, and those serving a neighborhood area, were most likely to show a decline, since they tended to remain in the same general area, whereas the large businesses were most likely to move to more distant zones and more attractive areas. Rent differentials changed accordingly.

Displacement and relocation create special problems for businesses that depend primarily on a neighborhood market. Yet these are the types of businesses that are most likely to be located in areas in need of renewal. In the present study approximately one-third of the displaced businesses served a local neighborhood market area. This varied markedly by type of project, however, ranging from more than half of the businesses from renewal areas to less than one-fifth of those displaced by highway construction programs. But, regardless of the cause of displacement, the disruptive effects were similar. A major difference by type of project pertained to the type of customer ordinarily served prior to the move. Businesses in renewal areas were four times as likely to serve a particular ethnic or racial group. This is to be expected since it is in such areas that minority groups live. It is this dependence on a particular type of customer and on a recurrent type of relationship that makes the small businesses and those serving a small geographical area distinct from other-type businesses in the problems encountered in relocation.

The non-survival rates were found to be substantially higher for neighborhood-type businesses than for those serving a larger area. Since such units were dependent on a small local population, displacement was particularly disruptive. To remain in the same general neighborhood was not a solution, since many of their former customers had also been displaced from the area. Nonetheless this was the type of move made by many such businesses. More than one-third of the neighborhood-type businesses moved one-tenth mile or less, and three-fourths moved within a radius of one-half mile of the original site. The median distance moved was only one-fourth mile. While the median costs of the move were less than for other types of businesses, the relative costs in relation to sales exceed those of businesses that served a larger market area. This is particularly meaningful in highway project areas where none of the costs were covered. In such cases, the brunt of the burden fell on the small neighborhood businesses which were likely to be marginal units at best and least likely to be able to afford such a burden. Also these units, more so than other-type businesses, experienced declines in sales following relocation. At the same time, rents increased. The net result was that they experienced more of a relative increase in rent burden than any other subgroup. The rent burden as a proportion of sales increased 80 percent following the move. While median rents increased by more than one-fifth, median monthly sales declined by nearly one-third. The consequences of these changes need no further elaboration.

The negative consequences of relocation were most severe for neighborhood-type businesses. More than half of these units reported a decline in sales. This was approximately double the proportion found among businesses that served a larger market area. Thus it is not surprising that owners of neighborhood-type establishments were much less satisfied with the progress made since the move. They stated a distinct preference for the former location as a place to do business, and a substantial majority reported that they would have done better had they not moved. The proportion of such responses exceeded by two and one-half times comparable responses found in any other market area category. Among the businesses that served a larger market area, a majority reported that they would not have been any better off if they had not moved. The latter, quite generally, responded favorably to the move. The rather negative evaluation of the neighborhood-type businesses which are predominantly food-related retail and service establishments is understandable, in view of the changes in income following relocation. A substantial majority reported a decrease.

Considering all of the relocated businesses, the adjustment following the move was predominantly favorable, even though selected subgroups experienced substantial losses. In our analysis we focused on two dimensions of adjustment; the one pertained to the objective changes measured economically, while the second was expressed psychologically in attitudinal evaluations regarding the new location. In respect to both dimensions a majority of the relocated businesses appeared to have responded favorably to the move. This, however, varied significantly by a number of subgroups, as was clearly shown in our discussion of neighborhood-type businesses where we observed significant economic losses. Consistent with this was a marked negative reaction on the part of these businesses to the whole relocation process. This, of course, suggests that in order to properly assess the consequences of relocation, attention must be focused on specific sub-categories. Thus our analysis proceeded accordingly.

When our attention was focused on economic variables, we found that the relocated businesses fell evenly into three groups as far as changes in volume of business are concerned. Approximately one-third reported more business than prior to the move. An equal proportion reported no change, while the remaining one-third experienced a decline. More favorable responses were found in their evaluations regarding changes in the value of their businesses following the move. The most frequent response was that the business had increased in value. Only a small minority reported a decline. A less favorable response was reported with respect to changes in income. However, even here a substantial minority (nearly one unit in four) reported an increase, while one-third reported no change. This, of course, means that a majority either held their own or improved their income following the move. But for a substantial number (43 percent), income declined at the new location. This decline, however, was largely due to small neighborhood-type businesses. Declines were reported disproportionately by food-related retail and service establishments. These businesses, as we have noted several times, were predominantly dependent on a recurrent relationship with customers living in close proximity. Movement out of an established area proved to be particularly disruptive for such businesses. Many were unable to survive displacement and, of those that did relocate, many experienced rather severe economic losses. Food-related retail and service establishments were the types of businesses that had the largest proportion that reported a decline in sales following the move. Jewelry manufacturing firms also had an above-average proportion reporting a decline, but it was generally agreed that this change was quite independent of the move. Rather, the owners attributed the decline to the overall depressed condition of the jewelry market at the time of the study.

Small businesses encountered much more difficulty in moving to a new location than did the larger establishments. Nearly half experienced a decline in volume of business and a substantial majority (60 percent) reported a decline in income. This is nearly 50 percent higher than the proportion for all businesses. Small units could ill afford such a decline, in that their median income at the new location was less than $4,000. However, a distinct majority of the businesses in the median and large-size categories made a favorable economic adjustment. They were able to either maintain the same business volume or to show an improvement. Similarly, for a majority, income remained the same or increased. Approximately one-third of the median and large units were better off after the move than prior to displacement. In many instances, the move gave them an opportunity to expand their business which was not possible at the old location. This was evident from remarks such as: "We were slowly strangling down in that area—that place was too small—the area was too congested for our business—we have been able to expand here because of more space but we couldn't have expanded at the old location—we were glad to leave—we wanted to expand and the move gave us the push forward we needed—we were blocked at the old location because of the poor condition of the building—we were growing and sooner or later would have to find a larger place—it was a good thing that it happened to us—moving shook the businesses up and in five years they will be in much better shape than if they hadn't moved." In these instances the consequences of displacement were to their advantage.

At the time of displacement, the reaction seemed to have been predominantly negative. Highly emotional and angry responses were frequent. Much of the unfavorable reaction, however, was found to be due to uncertainty as to what would happen to their businesses. Owners were suspicious that the move would be harmful, and thus the change was viewed with considerable apprehension. This view proved to be justified, at least in part, for approximately one-third of the establishments went out of business. There was general consensus among these owners that they had been badly handled. The reaction of the non-survivors to the whole displacement program was distinctly negative. A substantial majority expressed the opinion that they would be better off if they had not been forced to move. The owners of nearly all of these establishments reported that they would have continued in business indefinitely at the old site if they had not been displaced. With few exceptions, the non-survivors experienced a decline in income, even though a majority entered the labor force in some other capacity. Clearly displacement worked a real hardship for this group.

Later developments also showed that many of those that relocated were also justified in being apprehensive concerning the consequences of displacement, for many experienced economic losses as a result of the move. But such losses were reported by less than a majority. If we focus on the non-survivors and on those who experienced economic losses, the reaction to the move would, of course, be negative, but when attention is focused only on the establishments that continued in business, we find the appraisal of the move to be favorable. However, it is not overwhelmingly so. Nonetheless we found that only one-third of the units reported that they would have done better if they had not moved, and an equally small proportion stated a preference for the old location as a place to do business. Less than one-fourth expressed dissatisfaction with the progress made at the new site. Thus in respect to all three questions a majority either made no evaluative distinction between the old and new location or responded more favorably toward the new site. It is noteworthy that nearly half of the owners who relocated reported that they would not have done any better if they had not moved. A similar high proportion preferred the present location as a place to do business. A nearly equal number were found in the top satisfaction category when asked to evaluate the progress they had made at the new site. These reactions, however, varied markedly by a number of selected subgroups.

A favorable reaction to the move was reported by a majority of the owners of non-food-related retail establishments and those in the manufacturing, wholesale and construction category. Similarly favorable responses were reported by the owners of the larger businesses and those serving a non-local market area. Businesses that moved to the suburbs responded much more favorably to the move than those that remained in the city. This was not unrelated, however, to the type of selectivity that occurred in this movement.

Also it was due in part to differences in site characteristics in the two areas. The suburbs attracted the kinds of establishments the owners of which responded most favorably to the move, that is, the younger, better educated owners who were concentrated in the higher income categories. Owners possessing these characteristics accounted for a disproportionately large part of the favorable reactions to the new locations.

On the negative side, it was the food-related retail and service units and the small neighborhood-type establishments that responded least favorably to displacement and relocation. Their more negative reaction was due to their greater dependence on a recurrent relationship with customers living in close proximity, many of whom came from a particular ethnic or racial group. Consequently such units were very sensitive to a change in location. For the most part, these units were not satisfied with the progress they had made since the move, and disproportionately they reported that they would have done better had they remained at the old location. They also stated a preference for the original location as a place to do business. In short, our analysis has shown that the reaction to the new location varies consistently and significantly by a number of important variables. Accordingly, to understand the consequences of displacement and relocation, as already noted, full attention must be focused on subgroupings.

As far as the city is concerned, the displacement of commercial and industrial establishments results in considerable losses.[3] Part of the loss to the city is due to a changing distribution of these functions in the community, resulting from public improvement programs which disrupt established patterns. Not only do many of the displaced establishments go out of business, but other establishments move out of the city to the nearby suburban areas. This movement was found to be of more significance than would be implied from the relative number of units that leave the city, since from the point of view of volume of business and jobs the suburban

---

[3] This is not a net loss, however, since no account has been taken of any gains that may have been realized in rebuilding the cleared areas. Nor has any attempt been made to measure what effect the new highways have on attracting new businesses to specific areas. This is only an account of what happens to the existing establishments at the time of displacement. Also we have not assessed what the long-range costs would be to the city if these public improvement programs had not been undertaken.

movement was more costly to the city than losses experienced through establishments going out of business. We would expect that, as programs resulting in displacements become more extensive as well as accumulative, as they will in the future, the suburban movement is likely to increase, since fewer sites may be available in the city. It is readily apparent that the pressure for sites is certain to increase as more and more commercial structures are demolished. To lose such businesses to the suburbs is to decrease the number of jobs in the city and to detract accordingly from the tax base. This, cities can ill afford.

It would seem that, from the point of view of the welfare of the city, public improvement programs should be phased in such a way as to minimize the opportunities for such losses. This could be done, for example, by scheduling improvement projects in such a way as to provide space and accommodations for the establishments that are to be forced to move prior to their displacement. This suggests that clearance should be used to provide industrial and commercial spaces not only to attract new businesses and industry and thus add to the employment and tax base of the city, but also to house displaced establishments from other project areas in order to keep them in the city. The carrying out of such programs would represent gains for the city insofar as they would successfully prevent units moving from the city in order to find adequate sites. The present system is driving many of the more attractive businesses out of the city; thus, from the point of view of the city, the current programs are realizing less than their full potential.[4]

The programs for rebuilding cities are effectively eliminating the small marginal businesses. For such units, relocation is frequently not feasible. These businesses tend to be owned by older persons and those with very limited financial resources. Displacement in such cases has the effect of depriving the owners of their usual livelihood, meager as it may have been prior to the disruption. For the most part, the owner received no compensation for his loss, even though he had been forced to vacate his site. In some instances where they happened to own the building that they occupied, some minor adjustments may have been made in the price paid for the

---

[4] It is noted, however, that such phasing of public improvement programs would likely not effectively resolve the typical relocation problems faced by small neighborhood-type businesses.

property which would make the loss less severe. But no such even token adjustments were possible in the case of renters. However, regardless of tenure, the move was most costly for the particular types of businesses that could least afford the loss.

To date, renewal and other public improvement programs, including highway construction, are efficient in the physical clearance of built-up areas, but they have not been able to accommodate the very small businesses that traditionally have been dependent upon sites in deteriorated areas where rents are low. These businesses are at best marginal. They operate at minimal levels; nonetheless, in their operations they provide at least a very small return to the owner. The business provides him with a job as well as an income. The owners of such units, however, are unable to absorb the disruptive effects of the move, and thus close down their business. Although the loss of such units means little, if anything, to the city, the consequences represent real hardships for the individual owners. Perhaps it is incumbent upon the responsible governmental agencies to make equitable adjustments when public improvement programs are such as to make continuance in business economically unfeasible for individual owners. Such cases are limited, for, as we have found, only certain kinds of businesses are particularly sensitive to the disruptive effects of dislocation. However, these units account for a disproportionate number that suffer economic losses as a result of the move, and they also account for a disproportionate amount of the negative reactions that are expressed concerning the forced moves.

Neighborhood-type businesses constitute one type that pays a heavy price when displaced. Not only do they lose their business site but they are largely deprived of their market area as well. Consequently business failures and other economic losses are frequent. Closely related to this are the similar heavy costs that must be borne by food-related retail and service establishments. Few of these units gained from the move and, when they did, it was found to be due to a combination of atypical circumstances. Among such units that relocated, a substantial number experienced declines in sales while at the same time they experienced increases in rents. As a consequence of these changes, they were in a less favorable position after the move.

If we are to continue to rebuild our cities through extensive urban renewal programs and through the construction of modern highways, it is evident that we need to know more about the consequences of that expense and effort. The really basic question seems to be whether the aggregate gains are worth not only the aggregate social and economic costs, but worth the individual costs as well. This study has attempted to assess some of these costs.

In our analysis of the experiences of approximately 300 business establishments, we have presented ample evidence to show that, in many instances, the individual costs were high. The costs to the city were also substantial. Losses resulted either from the discontinuance of the business or through movement of the business to the suburbs. However, at the same time we found that there were real gains realized by many of the displaced businesses. Thus to emphasize only the negative effects and reactions to the move would be to give a false impression of the consequences of displacement. For instance, only a few of the larger businesses (those employing eight or more workers) were hurt by displacement. A much larger proportion was better off after the move than while at the original location.

Our findings are abundantly clear. One of the apparent changes wrought by these programs is the changing distribution of these functions. Displacements are hastening the suburbanization movement of commercial and industrial establishments. Also the problems resulting from displacements tend to be most severe among small business establishments and those largely dependent on a particular neighborhood market area, as well as on those units owned by persons who are perhaps too old to start over again. Many of these businesses may well be marginal in the larger economic system, but to the owners their business operation is a way of life as well as a means of making a living. Neither dimension can be easily ignored when individual costs are measured.

PART V

GOVERNMENT AND CITIZEN
PARTICIPATION IN
URBAN RENEWAL

15 Planning and Politics: Citizen Participation in Urban Renewal*

JAMES Q. WILSON

Few national programs affecting our cities have begun under such favorable auspices as urban renewal. Although public housing was from the very first a bitterly controversial policy, redevelopment and renewal by contrast were widely accepted by both Democratic and Republican administrations and had the backing of both liberals and conservatives, labor and business, planners and mayors. Yet today, almost fourteen years after urban redevelopment was inaugurated as Title I of the Housing Act of 1949, the program is beset with controversy and, what is even more dismaying to its supporters, lagging far behind its construction goals.

Although there are nearly 944 federally-approved slum clearance and urban renewal projects scheduled for over 520 different communities, only a little more than half have proceeded to the point where the cities are authorized to begin assembling and clearing land. And most important, of all the projects authorized, only 65 have been completed.[1] In New York, the city which has been the most active in renewal programs of all kinds, all the publicly-supported projects undertaken over the last quarter century cover

* A slightly revised version of an article which first appeared in the *Journal of the American Institute of Planners*, Vol. 29, No. 4 (November 1963), pp. 242–249.
[1] Housing and Home Finance Agency, *Housing Statistics: Annual Data*, April, 1962, p. 76.

408 / JAMES Q. WILSON

less than one per cent of the city's surface.[2] Further, most of the projects completed can be found in or near the central business districts of cities rather than in residential areas, and they have often involved clearing, not slums, but deteriorating commercial and industrial structures.

Some of the reasons for the relatively slight accomplishments of urban renewal are not hard to find. Federally-sponsored projects such as renewal require dealing successfully with almost endless amounts of red tape; it has taken a long time for city governments and private developers to acquire the knowledge and experience required for this. Furthermore, even though the federal government pays most of the cost of assembling and clearing the land on which a project is planned, it is not always easy to find a private developer to whom the land can be sold.

An additional reason for slow progress in urban renewal is racial. Blighted areas are often Negro areas. The political and social problems involved in relocating Negroes in other areas of the city are often sufficiently formidable to make opposition to the renewal program as a whole very powerful.

But the most important reason for controversy and slow progress is the mounting disagreement over the methods and even the objectives of urban renewal. The coalition among liberals, planners, mayors, businessmen, and real estate interests which originally made renewal politically so irresistible has begun to fall apart. Liberals, who still see the rehabilitation of the central city as a prime goal for government, have begun to have doubts, particularly about redevelopment that involves wholesale clearance by bulldozers. They are disturbed by charges from many Negro leaders—whom liberals are accustomed to regarding as their natural allies—that liberals have aided and abetted a program which under the guise of slum clearance is really a program of Negro clearance. They have been disturbed and even angered by the elimination of whole neighborhoods, like the Italian West End of Boston; by the reduction in the supply of low-cost housing to make way for high-cost housing built with federal subsidies; and by what they take to be the inhuman, insensitive, and unrealistic designs of some city planners. Jane

[2] See Raymond Vernon, *The Myth and Reality of Our Urban Problems* (Cambridge, Mass.: Joint Center for Urban Studies of MIT and Harvard, 1962), p. 40.

Jacob's book, *The Death and Life of Great American Cities,* is expressive of one powerful segment of opinion in this regard.[3] The liberals are everywhere demanding that redevelopment (that is, wholesale clearance) be abandoned in favor of rehabilitation— conserving as many existing structures as possible.

Mayors and other city officials in some cities (although not yet in all) have seen in these debates a sign that a program which began as "good politics" has turned into something which at best is difficult politics. When it seemed possible that a vigorous and ambitious mayor could place himself at the head of an alliance of liberals, planners, businessmen, and newspapers on behalf of restoring the central city, urban renewal became a top priority civic objective. An initial burst of enthusiasm greeted renewal in almost every city where the idea was broached. But after the first few projects were undertaken, the hidden political costs began to become evident. Voters who did not like being called slum-dwellers and who liked even less being forced out of their old neighborhoods began to complain. As the enthusiasm of the civic boosters began to wane, many mayors began to wonder whether they were going to be left alone on the firing line to answer for projects which the boosters had pushed them into in the first place.

What in many ways is the most interesting aspect of the controversy surrounding urban renewal is not the breakup of this coalition, however, but the growing resistance of neighborhoods to clearance and renewal programs. The growth of neighborhood resistance to urban renewal has been gradual and cumulative. Many of the earliest redevelopment projects were completed with little organized opposition. Somehow, however, people have learned from the experience of others, and today, in cities which have been engaged in renewal for several years, the planners often find prospective renewal areas ready and waiting for them, organized to the teeth. In Chicago, for example, the Lake Meadows redevelopment project met with relatively little organized indigenous opposition (although considerable opposition from forces outside the area). The Hyde Park-Kenwood project, undertaken a few years later,

---

[3] See also, as an example of liberal objections to renewal, Staughton Lynd, "Urban Renewal—for Whom?" *Commentary,* January, 1961, pp. 34–45. The consequences of urban renewal for the underprivileged in American cities are discussed in Peter Marris, "The Social Implications of Urban Redevelopment," *Journal of the American Institute of Planners,* XXVIII (August, 1962), 180–186.

was greeted with considerably more opposition. Today, plans for the Woodlawn and Near West Side areas have been met with impassioned opposition from many of the residents of the neighborhoods involved. Similarly, the West End project in Boston had relatively little difficulty in dealing with people in the area; the project planned for Charlestown, begun some time later, has been —at least for the time being—stopped dead in its tracks by organized neighborhood opposition. Today, according to Robert C. Weaver, Administrator of the Housing and Home Finance Agency, "in nearly every major city in the country and many small cities there are heated debates over urban renewal projects that are underway or under consideration."[4]

Mr. Weaver might well be concerned over these debates, for federal policy requires local citizen participation in the formulation of local renewal plans before federal money can be spent on them. As he himself stressed on another occasion, "We mean [by citizen participation] not just a passive acceptance of what is being done, but the active utilization of local leadership and organization which can profitably assist in the community's efforts."[5]

Local citizen participation on a city-wide basis is usually not difficult to obtain. "Civic leaders" representing various groups and interests in the community can always be assembled for such purposes. But getting the participation, much less the acquiescence, of citizens in the renewal neighborhood is something else again. Although federal law does not require participation at this level, the increased vigor of neighborhood opposition has made such participation expedient if not essential—particularly with the new emphasis on rehabilitation and self-help.

THE HYDE PARK-KENWOOD EXPERIENCE

The fullest account we have of such participation is that found in the book, *The Politics of Urban Renewal*, by Peter H. Rossi and Robert A. Dentler. This study dealt with one neighborhood—Hyde Park-Kenwood in Chicago—which in many ways is remarkable if not unique. The site of the University of Chicago, it is heavily

---

[4] Quoted in *St. Louis Post-Dispatch*, February 27, 1963.
[5] From an address to the 50th Anniversary of the Family Service Association of America, New York City, November 13, 1961.

populated with University professors and business and professional people, all possessing an inordinate amount of education, experience, and skills, and all having a strong commitment to the community. From 1949 on, these people were organized into the Hyde Park-Kenwood Community Conference, a neighborhood group with a professional staff, dedicated to conserving the area against blight. Actual planning for the area was not, of course, done by this organization—that was beyond its resources—but by the planning staff of the University of Chicago and by various city agencies.

The Community Conference took a deep and continuing interest in the $30,000,000 urban renewal plan for the area and meticulously examined and discussed every part of it. Local and federal authorities judged the Conference to be an excellent example of genuine grass-roots participation in a major renewal effort. After the plan was finally approved by the Chicago City Council, it commanded widespread (although not unanimous) citizen acceptance, even though about 20 per cent of the buildings in the community were to be torn down.

In evaluating the work of this local citizens group, Rossi and Dentler conclude that the Hyde Park-Kenwood Community Conference played two important roles. First, it stimulated public awareness of the necessity and practicability of change and gave people confidence that something could be done to save their neighborhood. Second, the Conference managed to create a climate of opinion in which the actual planning was done, and, although it is impossible to tell exactly what impact this climate had on the planners, it is likely that the general mood of the community as articulated by the neighborhood organization influenced at least the most general goals that were embodied in the final plan.

But it is also important to note what the Conference did not do. According to this study, the organization did not play a crucial part in influencing the specific details of the plan. Instead, it created broad popular acceptance for a plan which was not entirely in keeping with its own objectives. Rossi and Dentler conclude that the "maximum role to be played by a citizen-participation movement in urban renewal is primarily a passive one."[6]

Considering what I have said about the rising opposition of local

[6] Peter H. Rossi and Robert A. Dentler, *The Politics of Urban Renewal—The Chicago Findings* (New York: Free Press of Glencoe, 1961), p. 287.

neighborhoods to urban renewal, the acquiescence of this grass-roots organization seems to require explanation. In the narrowest terms, this support was due to the fact that the Hyde Park-Kenwood Community Conference represented that part of a very heterogeneous community which would ultimately benefit from renewal. The upper-middle-class professors, housewives, and business and professional men (both white and Negro) who made up the bulk of the Conference were mostly people who were going to remain in the community and whose peace, security, cultural life, and property values would probably be enhanced by a successful renewal plan. The persons who were to be moved out of the community and whose apartments and homes were to be torn down were usually lower-income Negroes who, with very few exceptions, were not part of the Community Conference.

But this narrow explanation in terms of self-interest is only partly true, for if low-income Negroes were not directly represented on the Conference they were often represented vicariously—at least in the eyes of the Conference members. Time and again the Conference, or leading members of it, pressed the city to provide middle- and low-income public housing in the renewal area in part to accommodate persons who would be displaced by demolition. The Conference was firmly committed to the idea of a multiracial community; some of its members were committed in addition to the idea of a multiclass community.

I would argue that this broader consideration was equally as important as the narrower one in explaining the positive and constructive role of the Conference. The organization was made up to a large degree of persons who attached a high value to community-wide and neighborhood-wide goals, even (in some cases) when attaining those goals entailed a sacrifice in personal, material satisfactions. They are people who partake to an extraordinary extent of what Edward C. Banfield and I have called in a forthcoming book the "community-regarding" or "public-regarding" political ethos.[7] This ethos, which is most likely to be found among citizens who rank high in income, education, or both, is based on an enlarged view of the community and a sense of obligation toward it. People who display it are likely to have a propensity for looking at and making

[7] Edward C. Banfield and James Q. Wilson, *City Politics* (Cambridge, Mass.: Harvard University Press, 1963), esp. chap. xvi.

policy for the community "as a whole" and to have a high sense of personal efficacy, a long time-perspective, a general familiarity with and confidence in city-wide institutions, and a cosmopolitan orientation toward life. In addition, they are likely to possess a disproportionate share of organizational skills and resources.

It is just these attributes, of course, which make such people most likely to participate effectively in organizations whose function—whatever their ostensible purpose—is to create a sense of community and of community confidence and to win consent for community-wide plans. They are, in short, precisely those attributes which are likely to produce "citizen participation in urban renewal" that planners and community organizers will consider "positive and constructive"—this is, participation which will influence some of the general goals of renewal and modify a few of its details, but allow renewal to proceed.

SOCIAL DIFFERENCES IN CITIZEN PARTICIPATION

Most neighborhoods which planners consider in need of renewal are not, however, like Hyde Park-Kenwood in Chicago and are not heavily populated with citizens like the ones who organized the Hyde Park-Kenwood Community Conference. Most renewal areas are likely to be low-income, often Negro sections, many of whose inhabitants are the opposite in almost every respect from the cosmopolitan elite of Hyde Park-Kenwood. Such people are more likely to have a limited time-perspective, a greater difficulty in abstracting from concrete experience, an unfamiliarity with and lack of confidence in city-wide institutions, a preoccupation with the personal and the immediate, and few (if any) attachments to organizations of any kind, with the possible exception of churches.[8] Lacking experience in and the skills for participation in organized endeavors, they are likely to have a low sense of personal efficacy in organizational situations. By necessity as well as by inclination, such people are likely to have what one might call a "private-regarding" rather than a "public-regarding" political ethos. They are intimately

[8] Cf. Seymour Martin Lipset, *Political Man* (Garden City, N.Y.: Doubleday & Co., 1960), chap. iv, and Robert Agger, *et al.*, "Political Cynicism: Measurement and Meaning," *Journal of Politics*, XXIII (August, 1961), 477–506. See also the vivid account of the culture of a lower-income Italian section of Boston in Herbert J. Gans, *The Urban Villagers* (New York: Free Press of Glencoe, 1963).

414 / JAMES Q. WILSON

bound up in the day-to-day struggle to sustain themselves and their families.

Such people are usually the objects rather than the subjects of civic action: they are acted upon by others, but rarely do they themselves initiate action. As a result, they often develop a keen sense of the difference between "we" and "they"—"they" being outside, city-wide civic and political forces which seek to police them, vote them, and redevelop them. It is quite natural that the "they" are often regarded with suspicion.

Although such people are not likely spontaneously to form organizations to define and carry out long-range very general civic tasks, it is wrong to assume that they are not likely to organize—or to allow themselves to be organized—for any purpose. The important thing is not that they are unorganizable, but that they can be organized only under special circumstances and for special purposes. Except for organizations which are in some sense extensions of the family and the church, lower-income neighborhoods are more likely to produce collective action in response to threats (real or imagined) than to create opportunities. Because of the private-regarding nature of their attachment to the community, they are likely to collaborate when each person can see a danger to him or to his family in some proposed change; collective action is a way, not of defining and implementing some broad program for the benefit of all, but of giving force to individual objections by adding them together in a collective protest.

The view which a neighborhood is likely to take of urban renewal, then, is in great part a product of its class composition. Upper- and upper-middle-class people are more likely to think in terms of general plans, the neighborhood or community as a whole, and long-term benefits (even when they might involve immediate costs to themselves); lower- and lower-middle-class people are more likely to see such matters in terms of specific threats and short-term costs. These differences account in great measure for some of the frustrations of the planners, redevelopers, and community organizers who are involved in urban renewal. Whereas it is relatively easy to obtain consent to renewal plans when people are thinking in terms of general goals and community-wide benefits, it is much harder—often impossible—when people see the same set of facts in terms of possible threats and costs.

This interpretation of lower-class behavior applies in its full force only in the extreme case, of course. There are many stable working class neighborhoods where indigenous leadership can be developed and involved in urban renewal programs on a "constructive" basis. The Back of the Yards area of Chicago is an example of one neighborhood of blue-collar families with strong local leadership. But many potential renewal areas, particularly in Negro sections, do not even qualify as "stable working class." Half of all urban Negro families had an income of less than $3,000 a year in 1960. Thus, although the contrast I draw between middle-class and lower-class with respect to their attachment to neighborhood and community is deliberately extreme, it must be remembered that urban renewal is a policy intended in great part to apply to "extreme" areas.

COMMUNITY ORGANIZATION STRATEGIES

Among community organizers, two radically different strategies have been evolved to produce citizen participation under such circumstances. One recognizes the special character of depressed lower-income neighborhoods and seeks to capitalize on it. The most prominent and controversial exponent of this approach is Saul D. Alinsky, executive director of the Industrial Areas Foundation of Chicago. He has created in a lower-income, heavily Negro area near the University of Chicago an organization ("The Woodlawn Organization") built in large part upon the residents' fears of urban renewal. According to a recent account, "Alinsky eschews the usual appeals to homeowners' interests in conserving property values or to a general neighborhood spirit or civic pride—appeals, in his view, that apply only to middle-class neighborhoods." Instead, he "appeals to the self-interest of the local residents and to their resentment and distrust of the outside world."[9] If residents do not have what I have called a "public-regarding" ethos, Alinsky is perfectly willing to appeal to their "private-regarding" ethos and to capitalize on the fact that collective action among such people is possible only when each person fears some threat to his own interests.

[9] Charles E. Silberman, "The City and the Negro," *Fortune*, LXV (March, 1962), 88–91. See also Saul D. Alinsky, "Citizen Participation and Community Organization in Planning and Urban Renewal," address before the Chicago chapter of the National Association of Housing and Redevelopment Officials, January 29, 1962.

By stimulating and focussing such fears, an organization is created which can then compel other organizations—such as the sponsors of an urban renewal project—to bargain with it. Often the only terms on which such negotiations are acceptable to the neighborhood organization are terms unacceptable to the sponsors of renewal, for they require the drastic modification or even abandonment of the renewal plan. When an organization is built out of accumulated fears and grievances rather than out of community attachments, the cost is usually the tearing up of any plans that call for really fundamental changes in the landscape. On the other hand, such an organization may be very effective in winning special concessions from city hall to remedy specific neighborhood problems.

Many, probably most, planners and community organization specialists reject Alinsky's tactics. To them, his methods produce and even exacerbate conflict rather than prevent it, alienate the neighborhood from the city as a whole rather than bring it into the normal pattern of civic action, and place a premium on power rather than on a co-operative search for the common good.

The alternative strategy of most community organizers is to stimulate the creation of neighborhood organizations which will define "positive" goals for their areas in collaboration with the relevant city agencies and in accord with the time schedule which binds most renewal efforts. In Boston, for example, efforts have been made to stimulate the formation of neighborhood associations which will provide citizen participation in (and citizen consent to) the plans of the Boston Redevelopment Authority (BRA). So far this strategy has had some success, but only in those areas where rehabilitation rather than clearance is to be the principal renewal tactic. In one Negro area, Washington Park-Roxbury, a middle-class Negro organization was given a BRA contract to help organize the neighborhood to discuss renewal plans calling for rehabilitation, spot clearance, and the construction of some lower-middle-income housing. The plans were approved. In Charlestown, an old Irish neighborhood, the original proposals of the BRA were rejected by a citizens' organization created by Action for Boston Community Development (ABCD), a city-wide welfare agency financed in part by the Ford Foundation. The BRA decided to modify the plans and dispense with the services of ABCD; the final plan, developed after protracted discussions between BRA planners and

Charlestown residents, emphasized rehabilitation and was approved. In a third area, North Harvard–Allston, the BRA decided to rely on wholesale clearance and redevelopment; there, no effort was made to obtain citizen participation and the plan was approved by the city council without the consent of the neighborhood.

IMPLICATIONS FOR RENEWAL PROGRAMS

If one's goal is urban renewal on any really large scale in our cities, the implications of these observations are disturbing. The higher the level of indigenous organization in a lower-class neighborhood, the poorer the prospects for renewal in that area.

To say that the prospects are poorer does not, of course, mean that renewal will never occur with the consent of strong indigenous organizations in lower-class areas. But the difficulty is substantially increased, and a protracted, subtle, and assiduous wooing of neighborhood sentiment must first take place.[10] Perhaps this explains why, at least until very recently, most local urban renewal directors made no effort to encourage citizen participation except on a city-wide basis—with little or no representation from the affected neighborhood.[11]

In short, while the devotion of some planners today to the concept of "planning with people"—that is, citizen participation in neighborhood rehabilitation—may be an improvement over old-style urban redevelopment which ignored or took little account of neighborhood interests, the enthusiasm with which the new doctrine is being advocated blurs many important problems. The most important of these is that "planning with people" assumes on the part of the people involved a willingness and a capacity to engage in a collaborative search for the common good. The willingness is

[10] See the account in Alfred G. Rosenberg, "Baltimore's Harlem Park Finds 'Self-Help' Citizen Participation Is Successful," *Journal of Housing*, XVIII (May, 1961), 204–209. The initial reaction in the neighborhood to a renewal plan was bitter and got worse for three years. Patient community organization managed to overcome some of this resistance after much effort.

[11] See the survey reported in Gerda Lewis, "Citizen Participation in Urban Renewal Surveyed," *Journal of Housing*, XVI (March, 1959), 80–87. Questionnaires returned by about half the local renewal directors in the 91 cities which had approved "workable programs" as of July 31, 1956, showed that "the residents of project areas . . . seem to be relatively uninvolved in urban renewal"; representation from these areas on citizens' committees dealing with renewal was "almost totally absent."

obviously almost never present when the persons involved will be severely penalized by having their homes and neighborhoods destroyed through wholesale clearance. Nor will that willingness be present when "rehabilitation" means, as it sometimes does, that the residents must at their own expense bring their homes up to standards deemed satisfactory to the renewal agency or have their homes taken from them. But what is less obvious is that it may not be present, even when such clearance is not envisaged, because of important class differences in the capacity to organize for community-wide goals. This means that middle-class persons who are beneficiaries of rehabilitation will be planned with; lower-class persons who are disadvantaged by rehabilitation are likely to be planned *without*.

The fact that some people will be hurt by renewal does not, of course, mean that there should be no renewal. There are scarcely any public policies which do not impose costs on someone. What it does mean is that planners might more frankly take such costs into account, weighing them against the benefits renewal may confer on individuals and the community. There is little except obfuscation to be gained from attempting to maintain, as the slogan "planning with people" implies, that urban renewal and perfect democracy are and always should be compatible; that not only can the city be revitalized, it can be revitalized with the consent of all concerned.

If we decide to try to obtain the consent of those neighborhoods selected for renewal, we had better prepare ourselves for a drastic reevaluation of the potential impact of that program. Adjusting the goals of renewal to the demands of the lower classes means, among other things, substantially reducing the prospects for assembling sufficiently large tracts of cleared land to make feasible the construction of dwelling units attractive to the middle-class suburbanite whom the city is anxious to woo back into its taxing jurisdiction. This, in turn, means that the central city may have to abandon the goal of recolonizing itself with a tax-paying, culture-loving, free-spending middle class and be content instead with serving as a slightly dilapidated way-station in which lower-income and minority groups find shelter and a minimal level of public services while working toward the day when they, too, can move out to a better life. That, of course, is in great part the function that at least the older central cities of this country have always performed, and until we run out of lower classes (a day unfortunately far in the future), that may be the function they must continue to perform.

POLITICAL EFFECTS

Not only does the question of citizen participation in urban renewal have important implications for the goals of planning and even for one's conception of the function of the central city; it also goes to the heart of a fundamental problem in the urban political process. Resolving this issue is not simply a problem in planning priorities, but in addition a problem in electoral politics.

American mayors today are faced with the problem of governing cities in which to a great extent the traditional sources of political power have been dispersed or eliminated. The old-style political machine is gone except in a very few big cities. Party organization generally is weak. Mayors must still assemble the power to govern but they can rarely do so today by relying on loyal party lieutenants who occupy the lesser city offices and who sit on the council. Instead, the mayor must try to piece together that power out of the support he can receive from city-wide interests, such as newspapers, civic associations, business organizations, and labor unions. Support from such sources, valuable as it is, does not always carry with it the assurance that the support of the rank-and-file voter will also be forthcoming. Average citizens have a way of not sharing (or sometimes not even knowing about) the enthusiasms of the top civic leadership.

To insure against this possibility, many "new-style" mayors are trying to build up new neighborhood associations and enter into relationships with old ones in order to provide themselves with a way of reaching the average voter and of commanding his support. In Boston, for example, it is an open secret that Mayor John Collins is hoping that the support and attention he has given various neighborhood associations will be reciprocated, on election day, by the support of their members for him.

To the extent that these neighborhood associations are courted by mayors, they attempt to extract in return concessions on matters of city policy (such as street sweeping, garbage collection, or playground maintenance) which affect their areas. They see themselves as instruments for adapting the programs of an impersonal city bureaucracy to the various and often conflicting needs of neighbor-hoods. In a sense, they perform (for entirely different reasons, of course) the same function which the political machine once per-formed.

The neighborhood civic association is widely regarded as not only a new mechanism for representing citizen wants to the city bureau-cracy, but a means of ending the political "alienation" of those citizens. Much has been written of late to suggest that a large and perhaps growing number of people are "alienated" from the Ameri-can political process, but particularly from the political process in their communities. In Boston,[12] Cambridge,[13] Detroit,[14] Nash-ville,[15] upstate New York,[16] and various other places where studies have been made, the voters—usually (though not always) those with little income or education—feel, we are told, estranged from and even threatened by the political life of their cities. To the extent that this alienation exists (and the studies are not very precise on this), the neighborhood civic association is seen as an important way of giving the citizen a meaningful and satisfactory relationship with his community—a way, in short, of ending his "alienation."[17]

It is not yet clear, however, whether such neighborhood groups will provide a means whereby citizens overcome their "alienation" or whether they will simply provide a forum in which citizens can give expression to it. These groups, after all, are usually concerned about neighborhood, not city-wide, problems, and the member's

[12] Murray B. Levin, *The Alienated Voter* (New York: Holt, Rinehart & Winston, 1960), pp. 58–75. See also Murray B. Levin and Murray Eden, "Political Strategy for the Alienated Voter," *Public Opinion Quarterly,* XXVI (Spring, 1962), 47–63.

[13] See William A. Gamson, "The Fluoridation Dialogue: Is It An Ideological Conflict?" *Public Opinion Quarterly,* XXV (Winter, 1961), 526–37, and Arnold Simmel, "A Signpost for Research on Fluoridation Conflicts: The Concept of Relative Deprivation," *Journal of Social Issues,* XVII (1961), 26–36.

[14] Arthur Kornhauser, *Attitudes of People Toward Detroit* (Detroit: Wayne University Press, 1952), p. 28.

[15] E. L. McDill and J. C. Ridley, "Status, Anomia, Political Alienation and Political Participation," *American Journal of Sociology,* LXVIII (September, 1962), 205–213.

[16] Wayne E. Thompson and John E. Horton, "Political Alienation as a Force in Political Action," *Social Forces,* XXXVIII (March, 1960), 190–5 and Horton and Thompson, "Powerlessness and Political Negativism: A Study of Defeated Local Referendums," *American Journal of Sociology,* LXVII (March, 1962), 485–93.

[17] Cf. William C. Loring, Jr., Frank L. Sweetser, and Charles F. Ernst, *Community Organization for Citizen Participation in Urban Renewal* (Bos-ton: Massachusetts Department of Commerce, 1957), pp. 232–238.

attachment is often at most only to his immediate family and neighbors, not to the community as a whole. Neighborhood associations seek many goals in their dealings with city hall. Generally speaking, however, they want higher levels of community services but they oppose extensive physical changes in their areas, as would be caused by highway construction or urban renewal programs.

For city-wide officials, such as mayors and planners, the crucial problem is how to make attention to these neighborhood demands compatible with city-wide programs, almost all of which will, to some extent, impose hardships on some neighborhoods. The old-style political leaders who were bosses of city machines were not faced to the same degree with this problem. Whenever they could, they avoided the conflict between neighborhood and city by not proposing any extensive programs designed to appeal to city-wide interests. When such programs were politically unavoidable, they resolved the inevitable conflict by "buying off" their neighborhood opponents. The bosses used the jobs, favors, and patronage which they controlled to enforce their wills on neighborhood political leaders and to compensate the neighborhood voters for their distress.

Today's mayor can neither avoid proposing large programs to satisfy city-wide interests nor can he buy off the neighborhood opponents of such projects. Under these circumstances, the mayor must move cautiously between the twin evils of doing so little as to disappoint community-regarding voters and doing so much as to antagonize private-regarding voters.

Citizen participation in urban renewal, then, is not simply (or even most importantly) a way of winning popular consent for controversial programs. It is part and parcel of a more fundamental reorganization of American local politics. It is another illustration—if one more is needed—of how deeply embedded in politics the planning process is.

16 Local Government
and Renewal Policies

NORTON E. LONG

Mounting concern is expressed by public officials, publicists and an odd assortment of businessmen, liberals and others over the alleged decay and decline of the central city and the older suburb. Causes of alarm are as varied as fear for the decline of our culture if central cities cease to provide propitious locations for museums, universities, symphonies and operas, and anxiety over the social consequences of the central city's becoming the segregated container of poverty and color increasingly alienated from the affluent white suburbs that surround it.

Clear thinking about the congeries of problems that are bundled together is made difficult by propagandist hysteria and muddled metaphors that raise emotions but fail to enlighten. Thus the core city is treated as a heart of a metropolitan area that may become diseased and thus suffer dire ill not only to itself but extending to the whole metropolitan body. No vital statistics on central city heart attacks are offered, however, nor any evidence on metropolitan bodies suffering from central city heart disease. The metaphor sometimes presents itself as the central city in the role of a tree and the suburbs as clinging parasitic vines who are destined to fall with the tree in a common fate. Again the metaphor is not designed to lead to factual translation but to poetic and evocative conviction.

The rhetoric of political persuasion and nostalgic sentimental mysticism is designed to avoid both facts and rational analysis.

The assumed healthy state of the city is never spelled out. Unlike humans, cities rarely die, though they do decline and some fail to grow. The vital statistics of cities are as yet undeveloped. Accordingly it is difficult to make meaningful comparisons with past states in their history. In terms of what dimensions can we say they are getting better or worse? Impressionism is rife, and the literary imagination has free rein. Since those who view with alarm the present trends are short on reliable statistics or documentation, the debate takes on a character that defies decision by reference to objectively verifiable facts. A melange of fact, fancy and ideology creates conditions in which the putative virtue of intentions counts for more than reasoned argument and evidence.

What has clearly happened to many central cities is that they have built up the greatest part of their available land and have been prevented from expanding by the resistance of other local government units. As a result the ecology of growth and decay which used to coexist in the growing city tends to become more and more divided between city and suburbs with the city as the oldest, most built-up area, usually accounting for far more of the decay than the growth. However, the condition of the central city may be duplicated in an even more aggravated form in older declining suburbs.

The imbalance between growth and decay in the territorially constricted city has serious consequences for the city and perhaps for the society generally. Aging city real estate has rising maintenance costs with declining revenues. Residential and other demand turns toward the more modern and attractive structures built beyond central city borders. The attractiveness of these newer structures economically and otherwise produces a selective migration of population and industry from the central city. The net result of this is to increase central city costs while at the same time reducing central city resources. To the extent this becomes significantly the case, the process might be expected to feed on itself. Those who can move out, escaping the rising taxes the declining base necessitates, and those seeking a high level of public goods transfer their residence from the central city, whose financial squeeze must result in service deficiencies.

Looking at this process one may distinguish between what happens as a result of the earliest settlement's being largely populated with the oldest and most obsolescent structures and what happens because the earliest settlement is largely built up and tightly hemmed in by political boundaries. Conceivably local government might have been so designed that it would have contained all or most metropolitan growth within it, as was the case at one time with the early central city. In such a case the local fiscal disparities and population segregations that now confront us could not have taken their present form. Differences between growth and decay, suburb and slum, would have been the differences in neighborhoods observable in all cities. If growth and decay were balanced off, they might indeed be regarded as complementary and the panic over the decline of the central city seen in a perspective of regional change and development.

But the political isolation of the central city and the older suburb from the rest of the metropolitan area represents more than a mere line on a map. It represents significant differences in available resources for the provision of public goods. It represents likely frictions and rigidities in the labor and housing markets. It represents a structuring of identifications and values that have major consequences for the political decision-making process. Each corporate community develops its own political and economic nationalism, and its public officials and leadership tend to score success and failure in terms of narrowly selfish particularistic and parochial concerns. It is a race for corporate survival and a place in the sun in which "every man for himself and devil take the hindermost" is a maxim built into the system.

Public urban renewal policy has been built on an acceptance of the jurisdictional divisions of the urban status quo. It has sought remedies for urban blight and decay in terms of measures designed piecemeal for each segmented urban jurisdiction. This policy was initially based on the supposition that relatively minor hindrances stood in the way of a natural process of renewal by which a city, like a forest, would replace its decay with new growth covering the same territory. The failure of this beneficent process to take place was ascribed to difficulties in land assemblage requiring powers of eminent domain not possessed by private developers. However, despite the supposed economics of natural renewal, public policy went beyond the use of eminent domain for land assemblage to the use of subsidy for land write-down. It was thus clearly recognized that natural renewal with eminent domain would not work. Had genuine concern with economics been a major criterion of decision, the necessity of subsidy would have forced rethinking of the argument. However, claims were made that the renewed area would, like a beneficent cancer in reverse, uplift surrounding land values and, like some Keynesian multiplier, permit the natural renewal to proceed elsewhere once the locational pump had been primed. That landowners should demand prices comparable to those paid by renewal authorities and that these prices without write-down subsidies should inhibit new construction outside the renewal area seems economic logic.

Nonetheless the theory of urban renewal has historic warrant. Neighborhoods and cities have in fact renewed themselves and are now, in the vast majority of cases where renewal is going on, doing so without subsidy under private auspices and the profit motive. Bernard Frieden's *The Future of Old Neighborhoods* gives eloquent testimony to the vitality of the renewal process. But as Frieden's study abundantly shows, there is an economics to the natural renewal process. It doesn't occur everywhere, equally, at all times and under all circumstances.

In a sense the official theory of urban renewal refused to admit the possibility of permanent locational obsolescence. Agricultural land, mines, even whole states, may fall victim to technological change and population movements, but not central business districts. Ponce de Leon's fountain of eternal youth was supposed to apply to them even though the fountain had to be found in the federal treasury.

The history of many cities had made the theory of natural renewal highly plausible. The deficiency of the theory was its failure to recognize the dependence of locational values on the effects of transport technology. The dynamism of this technology, opening up a wide range of competing locational choices, has upset the stable pattern of the city of the pedestrian and the horse, and even that of the age of steam and the trolley. The motor car and the truck have invaded the locational Garden of Eden, and the world will never be the same. To change the figure, one may suspect that not all urban renewal's horses nor all its men will ever restore the central city to what it was again.

As Herbert Gans has pointed out, our public policy has been much as if we regarded our aging motor cars as a mobile slum and thus a public eyesore and perhaps, to use the ubiquitous figure applied to slums of blight and disease, a health hazard on the highways. Thus public policy would be to subsidize the destruction of these vehicles and reduce the mobile slums. General Motors, Ford, and Chrysler might find much to applaud in such a policy if the used car market gets inconvenient. Absurd as it might seem to subsidize the destruction of aging motor cars and thereby deprive people of their means of transport, it has not seemed absurd to subsidize the destruction of much-needed scarce low-rental housing.

The metaphors that have substituted for facts and theory in dealing with slums, housing occupied by the poor, have made it possible to follow a policy with houses that would have been readily seen to be absurd with respect to motor cars.

Absurd as the policy has been, looked at from a public, federal objective which was initially concerned with housing low-income groups, it has not been absurd from the point of view of central city mayors, the Housing and Home Finance Agency, or the constellation of interests that have found urban renewal useful or profitable. The tragedy of the nation's housing program was that its support was always more as public works for countercyclical purposes than as a broadly accepted program of redistribution to the poor. When after World War II the New Deal coalition broke up, public housing became less and less politically viable. Given the income limitations on public housing residence and the position of the Negro in the economy, it was inevitable that public housing should emerge as Negro housing, with all the consequent hostility that fact was bound to engender.

The late Senator Taft feared that the urban renewal program would mean that instead of subsidizing the housing of those who could not afford it we would end up by subsidizing housing for those who could. In this he has proved prophetic.

Central city mayors strapped for funds have found a public relations gold mine in renewing central city business districts, providing luxury apartments and new capital investment with federal subsidy. Harassed federal housing officials have found new and heretofore unlooked for allies in downtown businessmen, banks, the real estate industry, and the metropolitan press. To this new-found business respectability they could add the continuing ideological support of liberals and labor. While some years ago a symposium in *Law and Contemporary Problems* in which federal officials themselves took part sounded a warning note, it is only now that a swelling chorus of critics as various as Michael Harrington and Martin Anderson point to the program's devastating impact on the supply of housing for the poor. The bureaucracy reacts with outraged protestations of its good intentions and cries of foul.

It is grossly unfair to point the finger of moral blame at bureaucracies because they respond to the survival interests of their agencies, which are to please the customers who can generate effective political demand for their wares. A major misfortune of our federal system is that the national government, because of its constitutional limitations, intervenes in local affairs through single-purpose agencies. While it can spend for the general welfare, it spends through a housing agency or through a bureau of public roads. As a result its single-purpose impacts are uncoordinated by any effective or well thought out concern for the local community as a whole. "My job is housing, not education or employment. My job is to build roads, not to plan for social welfare." This seems to be the no-nonsense philosophy of the single-purpose agency. The result is an unplanned, unforeseen impact. Frequently, in the case of the housing agency, it amounts to a subsidizing of the internecine warfare that fragments a metropolitan housing and labor market.

Mayors, like bureaucracies, respond to the forces that seem likely to elect and re-elect them. It is not surprising that beefing up the central city business district, attracting middle-class luxury apartment dwellers, and reducing the numbers of the poor and Negroes should have its appeal. This is the more the case since the federal government picks up a large share of the tab. Democratic Mayor Richard Lee of New Haven became a folk hero by persuading the Eisenhower Administration to subsidize Republican businessmen to remain in New Haven rather than relocate outside the city. Mayor Lee's exploit has set a fashion. Unfortunately, the arithmetic of the sums spent in New Haven makes the generalization of its experience astronomically costly and hence unlikely. However, far lesser sums can keep an urban lottery going in which any mayor with the right political arithmetic may win.

What has happened with federal subsidies in urban renewal

appears likely to be extended to the field of transport. Mass transit, in its extended form at least, is sick and getting sicker. Fare box revenues have to be supplemented with tax dollars. The federal government is being asked as that jurisdiction most capable of raising revenue to pick up part and perhaps down the road a very large share of the bill. Again the justification of this proposal largely depends on the supposed ill effects on downtown and the central city of the failure or lack of rail mass transit. Despite the unpromising experience of the Long Island Railroad in what would appear to be the classically favorable high-density to high-density situation, the San Francisco Bay area has embarked on a new rail mass transit program with only an ultimate hope of federal aid.

Concern with urban change has led to the typical political response, an attempt to halt the threat to vested values by untoward market forces through government subsidy of those values. With billions invested in central city real estate and rich legacies of attached sentiment, it would be idle to expect anything but an attempt to offset the operation of the economy by political means. The farm program is the model of governmental intervention to impede market reallocation of resources. At this point, however, federal intervention in cities more resembles a rivers and harbors grab bag than a policy as developed as the farm program.

From the foregoing it should appear that there are two main competing methods of resource allocation with their variants at work. On the one hand there is the market, in its varied forms with their limitations; on the other there is the political decision-making process. Both decision-making processes need to be considered on their merits as they produce socially desirable results. The merit of the market is the likelihood that competing possibilities will be considered. That is, in the process of market allocation alternatives in terms of profitability, market demand and opportunity costs are built into the decision-making process. For a variety of purposes market determinations are inadequate to achieve the appropriate ends of public policy. The range of values represented by market forces may not include or at least adequately weight those considered important by public policy. Education and welfare are clearly of this sort, though a mixture of market and public forces might need considering rather than exclusive reliance on one or the other. What is crucial about the decision-making process, public or market, is the policy outcome it produces. Here one of the major differences between market and political decision-making is that we have a theory of the coordinative operation of the market, whereas in political decision-making we know that purposive, planned coordination to secure a general intended result is rare and difficult. In political decision-making we are likely to have the unintended piecemeal cumulation of the impacts of single-purpose agencies. This latter is especially true of federal impacts, since there is no local budgetary process or planning process to harmonize them in terms of any conception of the local community as a whole.

The lack of any structure in the federal government to consider, at the very least, the likely but unintended cumulative effect of federal programs on cities has been pointed out by Robert Connery and Richard Leach. Given the structure of interests and power, it is unlikely that even a cabinet office of urban affairs would achieve coordination in the present system. However, there is at least a chance that we might develop a theory of what we were about in the large as opposed to the present unthought-out historical accumulation of piecemeal vested interventions. This to be sure would amount to the federal government's having a theory of the desirable structure of local government. To be fair, the Housing and Home Finance Agency has had its doubts about the present lack of coordination and has been moving gingerly towards the encouragement of metropolitan planning.

An adequate theory of the political decision-making system needs to examine the kind, range and weight of the values that are built into the relevant governmental centers of decision that determine the production and allocation of public goods and burdens as they affect cities and suburbs. The Housing and Home Finance Agency, the Bureau of Public Roads, the Department of Health, Education and Welfare, and the Pentagon, to name but four, all have major effects on local governments. The structure of powers and the controlling definitions insure that quite different values and obviously uncoordinated ones will govern their impact. What is true at the federal level is reproduced at the state. But the higher levels of government are less important in many ways in their value fragmentation than the local.

At one time the size and compositions of an ecology of local governments such as eighteenth-century Boston were probably of little importance except for religious divergences. The mix of classes was roughly the same. The difference in fiscal capability, given the modest scale of public goods, was probably of limited significance. This has radically changed. Public goods, especially for the lower income groups, are of major importance. The fragmentation and segregation of the metropolitan area have created a situation where each separate political community is in no sense a sample of people roughly similar to its neighbor. It differs in resources, in class, in ethnic and frequently in religious make-up. Thus the constituency to which each separate set of officials and civic leaders must look has built-in differences. The population mix of the metropolitan area as a whole has no political or civic leadership that must look to its total characteristics. Equally there is no way of mobilizing total metropolitan fiscal or human resources.

Two conflicting purposes are at war in American local government. First, we are more and more concerned with the consumption of public goods. This has a number of consequences. As the poor of the central city become politically aroused and competent, the old neighborhood differences in the provision of public services come under attack, and in any event more is demanded in the way of public services, with consequent increasing municipal costs. The provision of public goods becomes a municipal avenue for the redistribution of income. To escape this redistribution and to secure segregated quality public goods are major appeals of the suburb. In fact the growth of the importance of public goods in our consumption raises the serious problem of how we are to give effect to the inequality of incomes in their consumption. A range of suburbs provides a ready answer. If rents and housing costs segregate by income, it becomes possible to consume differentially public goods in accordance with one's income. The older system of neighborhood differentiation in the central city had always been vulnerable to the egalitarian norm among fellow citizens, to say nothing of legal requirements. But beyond this the higher income groups were subject to the political power to tax of their more numerous fellows.

The market array of differentiated public goods presented by central city and suburbs with their varying population mixes has seemed to some an admirable means of providing freedom and diversity in the consumption of public goods and to others a superior mode of managing conflict.

It has, however, major limitations for realizing the second great purpose that is at war with this first in American local government. If the first purpose in American local government is to promote the possibility of segregation and differentiation in the consumption of public goods, the second and contradictory purpose that is emerging is redistribution. We normally think of the federal government as the major and all-important instrument for the redistribution of wealth because of the income tax and the New Deal welfare programs. We are now beginning to appreciate the significance of education and the housing and labor market for the redistribution of roles, which is what is fundamental. Here local government and local leaderships are of enormous significance, as the civil rights struggle makes abundantly clear.

Metropolitan Toronto has been an enormous success as a public works agency to meet physical needs of near disaster proportions, acting through the common consent of the representatives of its corporate constituents. Now that it has moved from physical public works to a consideration of redistribution, the matching of human needs with unequally distributed fiscal resources, its success is less impressive.

One should not minimize the value of Toronto's public works accomplishment and its relevance to the American metropolitan area. But when that is recognized, it must be faced that the really critical task is that of redistribution. For this task the fragmented metropolitan area has neither tools nor will. It is organized to frustrate the emergence of any sense of territorial community. It provides no means to institutionalize an effective leadership or to mobilize the ample human and fiscal resources it contains. The problems of today's cities can scarcely be dealt with seriously in areas less inclusive than the metropolitan housing market and the metropolitan labor market. Housing, jobs and education are the critical items on the municipal agenda of redistribution.

Local governments that do not embrace the resources, human and material, to handle these problems and represent the full range of the population involved with them will prove fatally anemic. The problems will not disappear. Their solution will pass to central levels of government. Centralization must make up for local incapacity. The costs in loss of local self-government and their consequences for democracy nationally will be serious.

Our present piecemeal intervention in local governments is largely designed to make viable the status quo. If a paramount need is local government capable of mobilizing the leadership, popular support and fiscal resources necessary to meet redistributive tasks that face us, then present federal policy or lack of policy toward urban change is an expensive luxury.

We must get to the serious task of examining how we can go about building local governments seriously capable of meeting our redistributory needs with as much freedom for differentiation in life styles and public goods consumption as may be compatible with meeting those needs. To do this we require some kind of minimal agreement on what we think the role of local government should be. Given our commitment to federalism and the decentralization of power, that role has to be considerable if the critical demands of present-day society are to be met. Where local leaderships are inadequate to the task of managing conflict and dealing with change, the federal government may be compelled to intervene. Where its intervention is through the blunt instrument of force, only time is bought. We are increasingly aware of the prime importance of indigenous leadership.

As presently constituted, our metropolitan areas fragment and dissipate human and material resources. The pattern of local governments implicitly and explicitly emphasizes the pursuit of certain values and the neglect or rejection of others. Specifically, no government is concerned with optimizing the use of the area-wide resources of the housing market or the labor market. This has led in the case of urban renewal to the destruction of scarce low-rent housing in the central city and its replacement with relatively abundant high-rent luxury housing. Given the powerlessness of the poor and the definition of the situation by central city officials, such a policy has seemed to make sense. Commitment to the local government status quo has made federal housing officials the abettors of policies that are designed to accentuate intermunicipal competition for scarce tax assets rather than an area-wide rational allocation of housing supply to meet the range of human needs and incomes. The pattern has built into it a balkanized competitive nationalism. Federal policy, following the lines of least resistance, tends to accept and accentuate it. Thus the poverty program conceives of poverty as being meaningfully attacked by disparate and competitive cities and towns with little or no over-all common action, and this in the face of the reality of the metropolitan housing and labor market.

In the case of the metropolitan area, the whole is considerably less than the sum of its parts. Or, more accurately, there is no whole. Yet the alternative to the creation of some meaningful, governmentally effective whole is the festering of unsolved problems and the transfer of power to those levels of government that are adequate in resources and decision-making capacity. The metropolitan area is for most people the lowest level at which an adequate sample of people and problems can be given a territorially structured government. To deal with the problems a government needs to have to deal with them in terms of its constituency and to be able to deal with them in terms of its resources. The two hundred-odd metropolitan areas that contain the bulk of us have the resources, human and material, to take on major tasks, but their lack of effective organization for these tasks paralyzes capabilities, vision and will. We are organized to avoid major local efforts rather than to undertake them. The philosophy is one of escape from rather than acceptance of governmental challenge.

The gerrymandering of the poor, the Negro, and even the rich that occurs in our metropolitan areas creates a condition of powerlessness and irresponsibility. It has been viewed by many with satisfaction as a kind of metropolitan public goods shopping center where one votes with one's feet and one's pocketbook. Consumership becomes the synonym for citizenship and all problems are solved by the workings of the political analogue of the market. This reduction of politics to economics has an escapist attraction. But it won't work. Even the democracy of the buck requires political action to insure the freedom of the market from noneconomic discrimination.

If the burden of government is not to mount inexorably to the federal level, strong local governments, strong in human and material resources with territories and constituencies embracing the full range of major problems and population resources, need to be grown. The federal government must substitute for its policy of piecemeal intervention and shoring up of the local status quo a positive, well-thought-out concern for the kind of local government that can and will bear the burdens that now concern us. Creativity was not done with once and for all with the Philadelphia Convention.

The other side of the coin of creating strong adequate local areal governments is the maintenance of variety, diversity and local creativity. While lack of human and material resources creates the apathy of powerlessness, inadequately structured size may forbid participation and engender a monotonously mediocre bureaucratized uniformity. Dean Rose of the University of Toronto School of Social Work, in his case against the total amalgamation of the corporate units of Toronto Metro into the City of Toronto, makes much of New York's inability to create meaningful civic participation at the neighborhood level. Giantism creates serious problems, especially if it destroys spontaneity, involvement and creative diversity. We need to think carefully of the structure of government that can insure the essentials of redistribution, serve as an adequate protagonist for areal planning and the metropolitan housing and labor market, and still permit room enough for a vital and even competitive diversity among its municipal components. Municipalities which seek to renew themselves do so most effectively through the maintenance of their public goods: education, police and the services. Private parties will spend large sums to renew aging structures where these services excel. The most powerful antidote to locational obsolescence in the hands of a municipality is not in the brick and mortar cosmetics of urban renewal but in the continued human renewal of the quality of its public service. Encouragement of this competitive vitality is needed to avoid the bureaucratic lethargy of giantism.

In a society devoted to the conflicting goals of freedom and equality we have to strike an uneasy and constantly shifting balance. Committed to equality of opportunity, we are equally committed to the recognition of unequal achievement. As public goods become an ever greater part of our consumption, we must re-examine the structure of their production and distribution for its consequences, intended and unintended, on the implementation of our ideals.

PART VI

PLANNING AND DESIGN

17 Cities, Planners, and Urban Renewal*

WILLIAM ALONSO

The city planning profession, like most adolescents, is self-conscious. It worries about its appearance, it strikes poses, it adopts and discards heroes, it revolts against its parents while depending on them. It tries, in short, to establish its own identity. This identity is the product of its intellectual ancestry and of its early development, of its current situation and, perhaps to a greater extent than other professions, of the appearances and realities of the object of its concern, which is the city. It is a profession in rapid change, full of contradictions and given to excesses. Such a subject cannot be portrayed at rest and separately from its object, and so we will consider some of the forces that have made it what it is, but principally we will consider some of the issues that confront it and how it is coping with them, for it is in action that the importance and the weaknesses of the profession can be seen.

City planning in the United States stems from several roots, of which the earliest is architectural. The 1893 Columbian Exposition in Chicago dazzled Americans with the classic magnificence of the fairgrounds, and many visitors returned to their communities eager

* Reprinted by permission from *Daedalus*, published by the American Academy of Arts and Sciences, Brookline, Massachusetts, Vol. 92, No. 4 (Fall 1963), *The Professions*, pp. 824–839, where it appeared under the title "Cities and City Planners."

to ennoble their appearance in a movement called City Beautiful. The common manifestation of this movement was a superficial playing with boulevards, waterfronts and neoclassical architecture, but some of the writings of the period show a sensitive awareness of the society and the economy to be housed in this splendid container. The City Beautiful faded gradually out of American planning. Aesthetic concern for three-dimensional design returned with vigor only after World War II, and then largely as a result of European influences such as the Congrès International de l'Architecture Moderne (CIAM), of which Le Corbusier was the principal figure. However, those who now practice in this vein owe their first allegiance to architecture rather than to city planning, and they often call themselves urban designers.

Other seminal influences are harder to differentiate from one another. The muckrakers and other early reformers focused interest on the housing of workers, considering finances, family life and social organization as well as design. The development of urban sociology, mostly in Chicago in the 1920's and 1930's, served to document the conditions of urban living and shifted attention from the aesthetic of urban form to an analytic geography concerned with the social and economic landscape of the city. The New Deal provided funds and a national program for reform, emphasizing slum clearance and public housing. The naive social darwinism popularized by Herbert Spencer had held that poverty and slum conditions were the just deserts of the inferior and necessary conditions for social progress. It now became an article of faith that slums and bad housing were the cause of ill health, criminality, illegitimacy and other social evils. Consequently there was as much effort directed to tearing down slums as to providing new housing for those displaced. Today this seems a gallant charge against windmills. We have learned, for instance, that the slum is often a tightly knit social fabric that provides security and gradual acculturation to urban life, and that moving its inhabitants to antiseptic piles of brick can be cruel. We have learned that slums are often manifestations of racial as well as of class inequality, but we have not learned much about solving this thornier problem. This does not mean that nothing need be done about slums, but that the brave solutions that had seemed so evident have proved inadequate, and that learning advances slowly and painfully.

Advocates of city planning, as most urban reformers, were deeply suspicious of corrupt municipal governments, and they advocated the use of appointed commissions that could keep their hands clean of the filth of politics. From the 1920's to World War II untold planning commissions were organized, and each would hire a planner to produce a Master Plan. This consisted of proposals for parkways, a waterfront improvement, a new city hall and other items, and, always, a zoning ordinance. Public works, for obvious reasons, could often be sold by the commission to the city government. The zoning ordinance, stating what land could be used for what purposes, was often adopted, but it tended to degenerate. Seldom prepared with sufficient understanding of structural relationships, its administration consisted of a joyful or reluctant granting of variances and exceptions, so that it soon became riddled with holes. The planning commission in a social sense, and the zoning ordinance in a real estate sense, represented middle and upper class values and were too often holding operations against the forces of change. Since zoning combined conservatism with the planning advocated by the progressives, it often enjoyed considerable support together with indifferent success.

Faith that technical analysis is superior to the political process as a means of arriving at decisions has been another fountainhead of planning, at least since Hoover's 1920's. Techniques have improved by leaps and bounds in recent years in such areas as the estimation of the demand for housing, offices and highways and the calculation of the impact of particular measures. Many questions have thus been validly removed from the politician to the analyst, and this has given strength to the apolitical view of planning.

But there is a strong counter-current, and in many cases planning is moving closer to politics with the realization that what is needed is not so much a plan as a planning process. That is to say, the Master Plan, reflecting its architectural ancestry, presented a picture of an ideal final stage, much as the plans for a building represent the completed building, and the only question was how to carry it out. Today it is clear that in the nature of things every plan is tentative, both because information is imperfect and because there is no final stage: there is always a future beyond the stage projected. What is needed is continuing planning, which produces every year a plan for the next few years, and every few years a plan for the next two or three decades, so that the next steps and the distant goals are known at all times. With this concept, plans have become the companions of policy and the planner has moved inside government into a position similar to that of a general staff in an army. When plans are statements of policies the emphasis shifts from the solution of particular problems through particular projects to a view of the city as a complicated system to be guided as well as corrected.

These are the architectural, the reformist and the technocratic roots of planning. Other influences might be mentioned, such as the utopian movements with their long and colorful history, or the paradoxical importance of the romantic anti-urban attitudes in England and America, of which Lewis Mumford is a representative. There is also the British version of city planning, which is called town planning, and the continental versions, which are often called urbanism. Suffice it to say that they are closer to physical design and further from the social sciences than is American city planning.

Training for the profession is offered in the United States and Canada at some three dozen accredited schools of planning, almost all offering postgraduate programs only, two to three years long and leading to the degree of Master of City Planning. People are attracted into the profession from many fields. Students from an architectural background are now only a modest plurality. Most of the others come from liberal arts and the social sciences, some from law and the natural sciences. Their motives for entering planning are mixed. Because of the great shortage of planners, good wages and rapid promotion are certain to attract people. But altruistic motives are also important: a desire to improve our environment, to help make the good life possible in cities. Some people, although very few now, are dedicated to particular ideologies, from New Deal liberalism to several forms of socialism. The majority are apparently not interested in political ideas. Rather they feel good will toward their fellow man and, in a general way, they wish to improve his lot.

In recent years doctoral programs have gained in importance. These are offered by half a dozen universities, and they direct their training to research and teaching rather than to professional practice. Their development has raised again the question of whether the field has a valid body of knowledge or of expertness. No clear answer emerges. Certain topics interest planners principally, and others fall within traditional academic disciplines. Perhaps the answer is that the planner brings a point of view, an area of concern or a set of questions that he must answer as best he can because of the urgent problems of cities. The approach is eclectic in that it takes much from others, but the pressure of responsibility for action rather than of knowledge for its own sake forces a shifting synthesis which, whatever its intellectual inadequacies, goes to the issues and does not trouble itself with the territorial rights that tradition has established between, let us say, economics and geography. Had city planning the self-confidence, it might paraphrase the well-known definition that mathematics is what mathematicians do.

The situation of planners in this respect is very similar to that of medicine some time ago. Medicine is also a goal-oriented activity that makes use of other academic fields such as chemistry and biology. It uses their tools and findings and raises questions which may be explored by people in the field itself or in related fields. In the same way, in recent years, planning has produced a great deal of research activity under a variety of labels, including that of planning. There has resulted an explosion of knowledge and, unfortunately, a greater flood of literature with which no one person can hope to keep up, leading to the paradox of specialization in a profession that a decade ago prided itself in producing generalists in an age of specialists.

The naming of the planning association, which was founded in 1917, stimulated a revealing debate in choosing between American Institute of Planners or American Institute of Planning. The issue at stake was whether the organization should represent the activity of planning, in which anyone can participate by thinking intelligently about the future, or whether it should represent a particular body of men who labeled themselves city planners. The second alternative was chosen, and today the American Institute of Planners follows a policy of professional closure. It has persuaded agencies to write into their job specifications educational and experience requirements, and it has been discussing the establishment of registration examinations. The British Town Planning Institute, unconcerned with the semantics of its name, has had such examinations for years.

This is the profession that is trying to meet the challenge of urban change. By and large, it is right and sensible to train people to deal with urban problems and to permit them to advise the public and the authorities on these matters. It is true that our knowledge of urban phenomena is rudimentary, comparable perhaps to the knowledge of the human body at the time of Harvey's discovery of the circulation of blood. That is to say, we know a great deal, not nearly enough and much of it wrong. Still, the problems are there and decisions must be made. The advice of a good planner is probably the best available, but it is likely that in ten or fifteen years our understanding will have advanced through research and experience to where the advice of the average planner will be better than that of the best today, just as today's planners are better than those of one or two decades ago.

Knowledge is inadequate and solutions shallow, and to improve this situation it is right to be impatient with the profession. It has attracted as yet relatively few first-rate minds, and these must be prodded to produce their best. The apostolic zeal of the aesthetic and reformist heritages and many years of frustration still manifest themselves in a crusading attitude of yea-saying and a distrust of criticism. City planners are more influential than ever before, and there is a danger that power may corrupt, that mistakes will be repeated and justified rather than teach how things may be better done. Success can too easily be measured by activity and expenditure.

Perhaps these dangers to the profession can best be made clear by considering the urban situation today and by showing the inadequacy of the more popular solutions. A modern city is the most complex social and economic system that has ever existed, and, to keep from getting lost, we will focus on the interplay between size and structure of cities as the background for current planning practice.

When things change in size, they tend to change in structure. A grown man is not, at least physically, merely a very large baby. Science fiction to the contrary, being a fly implies being neither bigger nor smaller than the usual size of flies. A mutant the size of a freight car is impossible: it could not fly, its legs would buckle if it tried to walk, and, anyway, it would die of asphyxiation, since its breathing mechanism can serve only bodies a fraction of an inch in diameter. Size and structure depend upon each other. The critical relation between size and structure applies as well to social organisms such as nations and cities. But while the relation is easily accepted by most people in the biological realm, for some reason we seem to have difficulty in understanding it in the social realm, and this often leads to trouble. The fact is that, with economic development, cities and countries tend to grow, and as their size increases, their structure changes.

Looking at it from the other side, a change in structure tends to demand a change in size. Economic development is a continuing change in the structure of a society. With economic development the size of cities has changed. In the eighteenth century, a city of a few tens of thousands was a large and important city, and a few hundred thousands made a very large city in the nineteenth. In the twentieth century we have seen the city of a few millions emerge as the dominant form. Of course, this many people simply do not fit into the municipal boundaries which had been established for the earlier, smaller cities. The population has spilled over, and the urban mass covers a number of municipal units, in many cases in the United States straddling two and even three states. This urban mass, which we call by the awkward names of metropolitan area or metropolis, is the true city of today. We still refer to parts of the metropolis as "cities" or "towns," and these parts maintain their existence as municipal corporations, but they are no longer true cities in the sense of a geographic community of work and home. The facts have changed, but our thinking—much less our system of government—has not kept up with them.

But the metropolis is no mere large-scale model of the older city any more than the *Queen Mary* is a large-scale model of the *Santa María*. It is well known that economic development has brought specialization to the work of men. It has also brought about the specialization of space for men's activities. Work, home, shopping and recreation are more separated than they have ever been. Vast areas of homes specialize by race, income, family, size, age and tastes of residents. Shops cluster and separate according to price, style, variety and type of goods offered, and according to whether they are reached on foot, by car or by mass transit. Factories and offices gather and separate in complicated rhythms of their own. The great variety of indoor and outdoor amusements distribute themselves in this space according to the markets they serve.

Those who disparage the monotony of our metropolitan areas see only half the picture. There are in fact more things under the sun than there used to be, but these things are usually grouped together rather than mixed. There is therefore little variety in any one place, although there is more variety to the whole. Curiously, those who complain of monotony often also complain of the chaos of our urban areas. This apparent contradiction disappears if we think of these critics as on foot in the first instance and in a car in the second. If one is walking, the immediate area seems large and unchanging. But if one is in a car, one travels much faster and sees more things in a short time, and then the great variety of the city may become bewildering.

Bewildering, yes; but is it chaos? Chaos is only the absence of order, and order is nothing but the understanding of structure. There can be no question that our metropolitan areas have a structure, and that serious students of cities understand it fairly well, know how it got to be that way, and how it is likely to develop. The chaos of which the critics complain, then, refers not to the lack of structure but to the difficulty of perceiving it; and the problem is not one of restructuring but one of making understanding easier. A person moving through a city must be given visual clues and explanations of where he is and where he is going, of what these places are and of how they are related to each other. Many suburban residential areas should be given a more intense focus and clearer edges. Adjacent areas, such as the financial and the commercial in most downtowns, should be differentiated and articulated. People must be given a clearer image of the structure of urban areas while preserving variety and surprise within the elements of that structure. This is a very recent way of looking at urban design, but it should have considerable impact, taking the aesthetics of city planning beyond the architectural consideration of groups of buildings to the treatment of urban form as such.

The bigger pieces making up the mosaic of the metropolitan structure have also been criticized on grounds other than aesthetic. That side of sociology that used to be called social philosophy has attacked the social monotony of the suburbs, and most planners have concurred. The organization man, the member of the lonely crowd, seeks status in the endless urban sprawl by living in a house with a picture window which is usually cracked. These critics deplore the anonymity, the dullness, the conformism and the shallowness of suburban living, and they point out how short the suburbs fall of that pastoral ideal which they question in the first instance. Children brought up in this synthetic environment know nothing of the real world outside, meet only children of families exactly like their own, and grow up to be intolerant, uninteresting, ignorant conformists. The meeting place for men is the town dump, which is lacking in dignity. The women lead lives of intolerable loneliness and boredom or of frantic activity as charwomen, chairwomen, nursemaids, or hostesses, according to whom one reads.

These portraits or caricatures have proliferated recently. Some of the strokes in these portraits may be questioned, such as the relative ranges of experience of central city and suburban children, but the distaste of the authors for this suburban way of life is what is important. These critics are not just reporting on a way of life: they are judging it. By the skillful use of language they are criticizing and trying to change the tastes of their readers to have them see the suburban way of life in a new and most unflattering light. The fact, the evidence shows, is that this way of life is what most Americans want, that they are getting it and that they feel, and are supported by any reasonable comparison, that they never had it so good. Whether these people are instances of ensnared *Boobus americanus* or latter-day Candides happily tending their gardens depends on one's viewpoint. In my opinion, they are achieving their ideal, however imperfectly. Various city planners have proposed alternative modes of considerable merit and ingenuity, but their schemes have had only local and partial success. If there is to be any fundamental change, it will have to be by an extraordinary innovation in the field of taste, offering an alternative type of housing and manner of living which is as deeply rooted in the traditions and feelings of our society as is the present suburban house. What this alternative may be, if there is one, we will not know until it succeeds.

The changes in size, and therefore in structure, of cities have affected their centers as well as their edges. While the suburbs have continued to grow very fast, virtually every central city has lost population in the last decade. This has brought about a strange alliance between the intellectual—usually liberal—critics of the suburbs and those businessmen—usually conservative—with an interest in central city real estate. Their combined argument runs: the city (the central city is meant) is dying; the city is the focus of our economy and the center of our culture; therefore, unless something is done, our economy is endangered and our culture is weakened. This, of course, is nonsense. The city today is the metropolitan area, and it is growing lustily. As it grows it is developing and changing in structure, redistributing people and activities. What is in fact happening is that, as a result of this redistribution, businesses and people are shifting out from the center. This hurts some downtown businesses, though it benefits business at other locations, where new centers are forming. Like all transitions, it has its costs and dangers, but to argue that it imperils the economy as a whole would be like arguing that the development of the automobile hurt the horseshoe and buggywhip industries, and that therefore it imperiled the economy. On the cultural side as well, the argument is weak. People can move about very rapidly (this is what has made the suburbs possible), and can attend lectures, concerts, museums or the theater regardless of where they live. It may be that the suburbanite prefers to watch television, but that is a fundamental problem of our culture's tastes and attitudes, not of geographic location. If he were somehow dragged back, kicking and screaming, to the central city, once he quieted down a bit he would presumably turn on his television set.

In the past few years there has been a great deal of effort to put new life into the central cities, spearheaded by the federal Urban Renewal Program and generally endorsed by city planners. This program has much good in it, but the obsolete fractioning of our metropolitan areas into many different tax units has perverted local motives and has resulted in many futile and very expensive projects. Suppose, for instance, that a central city has a slum area. It is a well-documented fact that slum areas cost a city, in terms of police and fire protection, welfare payments, schools and other expenses, much more than they pay in taxes. On the other hand, an area of wealthy residents in apartments pays into the city much more than it takes out in municipal services. A city is, in legal terms, a municipal corporation, and like any other corporation it will be anxious to exchange a losing line for a profitable one. In other words, any municipality will gladly trade its poor for some other municipality's rich.

Under the Urban Renewal Program, a city may do just that. It may acquire a slum area under eminent domain, clear it of its buildings and sell it to a developer. No one today can afford to build for the poor without subsidy. On expensive central land it is nearly impossible to build at all except for the rich, and even that must be done at high density by means of apartment towers. On central land, the city can be quite certain that it is exchanging the poor slum-dwellers for wealthy apartment-dwellers. The cost of this operation to the city is one third of the difference between what it paid for the area to its previous owners and what the developer pays the city for it. The federal government pays the other two thirds. The profits to the city will be the increased tax revenue resulting from newer and more expensive property plus the savings in city services. This is likely to prove profitable to the municipal corporation. For instance, one large recent project cleared an area where the average income of families was $234 per month and built there apartments with an average rent of $200 per month. Only families with a monthly income of $1000 or more would normally pay such rents.

But if this type of renewal eliminates slums in an area and improves municipal finances, what is wrong with it? The answer is simple. One must look not at areas but at people; not at the finances of one tax unit but at the finances of the metropolitan area. The poor who lived in the slum have simply moved elsewhere, and the municipality hopes that they have moved to some nearby municipality, which will then be obliged to contend with their money-losing presence. Usually, the poor not only receive no direct benefit, but the clearing of the slum may reduce the housing supply for their income group, making higher rents and more crowding likely in the low-rent housing market. The high-income groups could have had housing, new or old, elsewhere, probably in the suburbs. What has happened is that the various tax units in the metropolitan area are playing an expensive game of musical chairs with the poor and the rich for tax dollars. The poor that one city has got rid of go to another city; the expensive housing that one city has gained has been gained at the expense of another city, and there is no net gain for the metropolitan area.

The federal government is playing an equivocal role with respect to metropolitan structure. With its right hand, the Urban Renewal Program, it is trying to breathe new life into the centers of metropolitan areas, counter to the ongoing structural trends. With its left, however, it is reinforcing these trends and weakening the center. It does this with its F.H.A. mortgage insurance policies and its income tax policies, which permit the homeowner to deduct the interest on his mortgage and the property tax on his home, while the renter can deduct no part of his rent. This makes owning much more attractive financially than renting and provides a powerful extra push to the suburbs. Suburbanization is the basic trend of large cities, deeply rooted in taste and the economics of land. It would take government intervention and controls of a different order of magnitude than the current Urban Renewal Program to reverse these trends, even without contradictory policies.

Meanwhile, preserving the fiction that the metropolis is composed of independent parts makes the process of growth more painful for the suburbs as well as for the center. While central cities worry because they are losing the middle and upper classes and are left only with the poor, who tend to be minorities such as Negroes, Puerto Ricans, or Mexicans, the suburbs pretend that these poor are not *their* poor, and that the suburban population is not made up of stockbrokers, professionals and insurance men but rather of homesteaders and Jeffersonian farmers conducting their affairs in a small, self-contained community not affected by the problems in the central cities. But the suburbs have their problems too, both social and financial. Because they are composed of families with children, one third to one half of their population is in the public schools; because they are absorbing most of the population growth of the nation, they need new streets, sewers and other facilities; and much of their energy is spent in anxious battle to keep out people with incomes lower than their own as well as others who would not "fit." Every part of the metropolis is encouraged to beggar its neighbor, and the egoism and short-sightedness of fictional independence serve only to create new problems.

Business and industry as well as population are also being redistributed, and Urban Renewal is also trying to preserve these activities in the central city. But again, the geographic fragmentation of an obsolete governmental structure tends to distort and pervert the renewal decisions. A recent federal publication, trying to show that the renewal of commercial and industrial areas makes economic sense, presented approvingly the case of a central city in which renewal had resulted in $180,000,000 of new construction and an increase of $200,000 in yearly property taxes to the city. This makes no economic sense to me: the increased tax revenue is only about one tenth of 1 per cent of the total investment, not big enough to be a justifying factor. Furthermore, from the point of view of the private investor, taxes are an expense, not a profit. When we look at the public share of the investment we can understand what has happened. The federal government contributed $8,000,000 and the city, $4,000,000. The new taxes represent 5 per cent on the city's investment. This is a reasonable return on the city's investment of $4,000,000; but to base the economic sense of an investment forty-five times as big on a reasonable return to the city is akin to basing the decision to have a major operation on the attractiveness of his fees to the surgeon. Such things happen, but they are not often considered desirable. They are, in fact, unethical and immoral.

The important questions are whether the total private and public investments are an efficient use of capital, profitable by ordinary business standards; and whether the total public investment to have the development take place in the central city is productive when compared with the efficiency of development elsewhere or of no development at all. This is a difficult question, but it is seldom asked by city planners, let alone answered. It may be that such an investment is wise, but we do not know that it is.

The ordinary investment criteria are not the only ones that apply in such cases. There are important qualitative changes which do not appear in any balance sheet, but which nonetheless may benefit every inhabitant of the metropolis. Without positive action the urban center may wither, and the metropolis may become a vast, amorphous, headless amoeba. A strong center is needed socially, economically and psychologically, for it is here that urban life is lived in full, and virtually all activities in the metropolitan area focus towards it. Here is the center of power, where a new enterprise may be conceived over lunch; here a woman may shop at a department store, look at expensive merchandise in exclusive shops, have dinner in a fine restaurant, and then go to the theater; here one may find a shop that specializes in stringed instruments or clothing for six-foot women, a man who can repair jade or ivory, someone who is an expert in importing from Hong Kong, an agency that can supply the names and addresses of a few thousand street railway enthusiasts or likely opponents of the death penalty. But this variety and richness is possible only because there are enough things and enough people downtown to attract more things and more people. Let the size of the downtown area drop below the necessary critical mass, and dissolution will follow. There will not be enough six-foot girls coming downtown for there to be a shop especially for them. There will not be enough lunch-time demand to keep a fine restaurant going, and if there are no restaurants, the theaters will suffer. Unless downtown is big enough, there will be no downtown. Some activities will move to the suburbs, but many will die or will never come into existence. Life will become much duller and more homogenized.

But why, if metropolitan areas are getting bigger, should the downtown area be in any danger? Once again, it is a matter of critical size. The suburbs have grown enough, and are far enough away from the old center, for there to be enough local demand to justify local department stores, lawyers and architects, fashion and furniture stores, and other services. Of course, these do not have the variety and size of their downtown equivalents, but they have grown largely at the expense of the downtown area. Industry has been shifting from railroads to trucks, and increasingly it prefers one-story buildings with ample parking, leading, of course, to suburban locations; and industry pulls related activities along with it. Even some large offices have tried moving to the suburbs, but with indifferent success.

These changes in metropolitan structure have indeed placed the downtown area in danger, for each move reduces its size and its attractiveness. But is this a short-run danger or a long-run destiny? Consider the trends that favor downtown. The employment composition of every country, as it develops, shifts increasingly to white collar jobs, and these are typically downtown jobs. Automation and rapid communication not only increase the proportion of "head" over "hand" workers; they permit their spatial separation. As physical production is automated and depersonalized, and as communications improve, managers and supervisors can send impersonal orders to a more distant production line and still be downtown for the advantages of personal contact with other decision-makers. Therefore, although the physical production part of industry may continue to become suburban, the management of that production may become more centralized. And as our population becomes richer and better educated, it seeks the luxurious, the sophisticated and the specialized, which are the major attractions of downtown. In short, then, there are very powerful forces which in the long run will mean a resurgence of the downtown area. It will be a different downtown in that it will be a more purely distilled essence of what we have today; but it will be all the better for that.

Is Urban Renewal in the downtown area a holding operation to counteract the short-run forces which are endangering the urban center until these long-run trends establish themselves? The answer is yes and no. Urban Renewal is for the preservation of the downtown area, but it uses short-run arguments and short-run thinking. It uses subsidies to create new and glamorous buildings without asking how these buildings will be used in thirty years. For instance, most of our important metropolitan areas were founded next to water, and downtown was based on proximity to the port on the edge of the urban area. But, as the port decreases in relative importance (which it almost universally has), and the urban area increases in size, downtown tends to seek the center of the urban mass. It creeps away from the water, at a rate of perhaps one-half mile every twenty years. Are not many of today's projects in the older parts of downtown trying to recreate a center on land that is fated to be an edge? Are they not trying to bring an old center back to life, rather than being midwives to the birth of a new and more viable center?

It makes excellent sense to subsidize the center if the danger to its critical size is a temporary one and a return to health is likely in the long run. But it is less than wise to pour money into glamorous architectural groupings looking with admiration and civic pride only to the size of the capital investment, the increased tax base and the added floor space. If the urban centers are shrinking, their immediate problem is overcapacity, and adding floor space will not solve it; if rents at the center are too high, so that suburban locations are more attractive by comparison, expensive buildings, strongly assessed and paying high taxes, are unlikely to be the solution. It cannot be denied that new and well-designed buildings have a glamor that attracts businesses and customers, and that they may give the downtown area a feeling of effervescence and restore confidence. But new buildings get old very quickly.

To save the downtown area, what is needed is a downtown that works well. Many of the new downtown projects are composed mostly of free-standing buildings, handsomely set about in open space, designed as sculpture on a grandiose scale. The emphasis is put on the project as such, not on the downtown area as a part of the urban system. Not enough attention is paid to the way one element relates to another. For instance, most downtowns have evolved with buildings standing side by side, filling up the blocks, with the streets as channels between them. According to their economic strength and ability to pay rent, activities take locations on the main street, on the side streets, or on the back streets, all close to each other and dependent on each other. Most of the new developments place their buildings standing free *within* the block, and little or no provision is made for those businesses that would go on side and back streets because they cannot pay prime rents. Yet many of these smaller businesses are the lubrication and the ball bearings needed for the smooth operation of the larger businesses, and many of them, such as restaurants, bars and book and specialty stores, make downtown interesting and human. The downtown area is the brain tissue of the metropolis, a complex, evolving, and little understood organ. If it is sick, it may require surgery, but this surgery should be done with sensitive fingers, with the finest surgical instruments, and with the closest attention to what is in fact being done.

In the past half-century our cities have outgrown our concepts and our tools, and I have tried to show how the lagging understanding of the changes in kind that go with changes in size has led us to try remedies which are unsuited to the ills of our urban areas. In this sense, I have been writing mostly about the past and present. What about the future? For the past few years there has been growing professional and popular interest in the step beyond the metropolis, even though we have yet to digest the present reality. The words *megapolis* and *megalopolis* are being heard with increasing frequency, usually applied to an almost continuous string of cities running from Washington, D.C. to Boston. And once this idea is launched, similar patterns are seen emerging on the West and Gulf Coasts, in Argentina and Venezuela, in Indonesia and in Europe.

The pattern does not consist of a string of metropolitan areas standing shoulder to shoulder, fighting for space like a crowd in a subway, but of metropolitan areas in a functioning group, interacting with each other. In the same manner that economic development has made the size of the typical nation inadequate and has called for super-nations, it seems that soon—at least in historical time—urban units will go beyond the scale of the metropolis to the scale of the megapolis. And just as the metropolitan area is not made up of an accumulation of little cities complete in themselves but on a system of specialized and therefore dissimilar areas, the various metropolitan units of megapolis will specialize and become more different from each other than they are today. No one knows with any certainty what the fields of economic specialization will be, or how the social specialization which occurs in metropolitan areas will reappear at the megapolitan scale, though comparisons between Washington, New York, Boston, and other cities are quite suggestive. It does seem likely that history may continue to outpace our ability to grasp and deal with our urban problems, and that, like generals, city planners may be fated always to fight the day's battles with the outworn ideas of their last war.

But even today, at the level of metropolitan development, perhaps the ultimate question is who is to be the planner's client. Is it the commission, the mayor, the council or the voters? Is it only the residents of the city, or future residents, or those who work there but live elsewhere? Should consideration be given to the interests of the region and the nation when they run counter to the city's? When we say a plan is good and desirable, who will benefit and who wants it? I have emphasized the effects of the municipal fragmentation of urban areas. Most city planners are in favor of metropolitan government but work for a particular municipality. What is their responsibility and who is their public? Questions of goals and clients are particularly difficult for city planners, but ultimately it is these questions of ethics and responsibility that distinguish a profession from other occupations.

18 Improving the Design Process in Urban Renewal*†

ROGER MONTGOMERY

Hundreds of urban renewal projects are under way all over the country, each built according to a plan. A look at the results shakes our faith in the efficacy of plans.

Can plans influence design? What kinds make good designs? Renewal planners examine their work, sense its frequent impotence, and look for new, foolproof types of plans. Recently this search has assumed new dimensions as experience with both renewal and design have led us to see these not as static objects but as processes.[1]

In the beginning, city planners recommended that renewal take place only in a well orchestrated relation to "the master plan of the whole urban territory."[2] Congress decided against such compre-

* Reprinted from the *Journal of the American Institute of Planners*, Vol. 31, No. 1 (February 1965), pp. 7–20.

† The author wishes to acknowledge the support of the Rockefeller Foundation and Washington University for making possible the field studies on which this paper is based, the help of the Urban Renewal Administration in making data available, and the help of Michael Lowe in researching and redrawing plans.

[1] G. Thomas Kingsley has stated the case for studying the process rather than the product of urban renewal design in his "The Design Process in Urban Renewal: An Analysis of the San Francisco Experience" (unpublished M.C.P. thesis, University of California, 1963).

[2] "Report of the Committee on Urban Redevelopment," Alfred Bettman, chairman, in American Society of Planning Officials, *Planning 1943: Proceedings of the Annual Meeting* (Chicago: the Society, 1943), p. 94. American Institute of Planners, "A Statement of Policy on Urban Renewal," adopted July 1959, brings this view nearly up to date.

hensiveness in passing the Housing Act of 1949, which called for project plans only. The statutory requirement that each of these "indicate its relationship to definite local objectives"[3] operationally meant little in achieving comprehensive planning frameworks. Planners responded by making project plans into miniature city plans complete with land use and circulation maps, zoning ordinances, and the rest of the familiar apparatus of the comprehensive plan.

There are alternative approaches. Urban renewal plans need not be miniature city plans. Pittsburgh proved otherwise with the redevelopment plan for the Gateway project, written by a lawyer in 1950.[4] It contains no maps or zoning ordinances. It reads like a contract and declaration of principle, not a planning report or blueprint. Such plans are rare. Most efforts and most innovations aim to build in more comprehensiveness. Many have succeeded. Federal policies added the "workable program" and the General Neighborhood Renewal Plan in 1954, the Community Renewal Program in 1959, and the progressive relaxation of limitations on nonresidential renewal.

How does design fare in this drive for comprehensiveness? Directly the impact seems small, but indirectly this focus probably has had large effects. It means city planning becomes less and less concerned with the day-to-day processes of design. Yet planners cannot give up their grip on initiating layouts. Architect Theo Crosby writes: "The usual planning method using block models is very much open to question, for the planner fixes the position and form of the building without being in any way responsible for the architecture. The architect fills in the pattern the way a child colors a drawing book. In this discrepancy the quality of wholeness is lost."[5]

Urban renewal superimposes this split between planner and architect on the dichotomy between public control and private initiative which, for example, divides land use determinations from invest-

---

[3] Housing Act of 1949, Public Law 171, 81st Congress, Title I—Slum Clearance and Community Development and Redevelopment, section 110 (b) (1).

[4] No plan in the *Urban Renewal Manual* sense existed for the Gateway project. Its place was taken by the *Redevelopment Contract* between the Urban Redevelopment Authority of Pittsburgh and the Equitable Life Assurance Society of the United States, February 14, 1950.

[5] Theo Crosby, "Contributions to CIAM 10," *Architects Yearbook* 7, ed. Trevor Dannatt (New York: Philosophical Library, 1956), p. 39.

ment decisions. Nowhere is this split more damaging than in the urban design process. When "wholeness" is lost, only partial solutions are possible. This is not to say a single hand must shape everything; on the contrary, many hands are always needed. But when they work at cross purposes, results are inevitably diminished. Urban renewal shows this over and over: improved neighborhood street layouts get built in the most banal municipal vernacular, and the streets get lined with bizarre bits of get-rich-quick building. A redeveloper and his designer may come up with a brilliant solution to high-density housing only to have it buried by the mindless repetition of ancient planning errors.

These, and problems like them, have been the everyday experience of renewal managers. Of more than 1400 projects on the books, some 400 have been completed or are in an advanced stage of development.[6] Most of these have been executed with slight concern for design; a few have sought to achieve something more. This experience has led to new insights into the connections between project plans and project design. Recent cases suggest that a sophisticated "process comprehensiveness" may hold the key to improved results. This paper will examine some of this experience.

EARLY EXPERIENCE IN DETROIT

Detroit stands among the first American cities to attempt urban renewal. Before World War II, the city began slum clearance and redevelopment through public housing under PWA and the Housing Act of 1937. During and immediately after World War II, faced with the overpowering extent of slums and blight, and stymied by ideological reservations about government-subsidized housing, the city, in concert with private homebuilding leaders, formulated the "Detroit Plan." This plan provided for municipal slum clearance, using eminent domain if necessary, with private redevelopment on land purchased at a write-down from the city.[7]

Although the Gratiot area had been marked for clearance in the late 1930's, nothing happened for ten years until planning began in

---

[6] Housing and Home Finance Agency, Urban Renewal Administration, *Report of Urban Renewal Operations*, July, 1964. Data on project status from URA redevelopment data files.

[7] The Detroit Plan is described in Charles F. Edgecomb, "Detroit," *Planning 1947: Proceedings of the Annual Meeting, American Society of Planning Officials* (Chicago: A.S.P.O., 1947), pp. 152–57.

1947 within the framework of the Detroit Plan.[8] The first tentative scheme resembled the preliminary design stage or "development plan" of a public housing project (Figure 1). In this totally unprecedented situation, tentativeness can be easily understood. The uncertainties of planning are illustrated by the variety of viewpoints on the controls to be placed on private development. Detroit Housing Director Charles F. Edgecomb described the alternatives to ASPO:

For instance, there is one school of thought that says the city should make the site and building plans and keep complete control of the home development. I would think that this would be about as much private enterprise as the welfare or the fire departments.

There is the middle of the road group which believes that the city should prepare the site plans and make available to interested capital basic drawings of utilities, streets, etc., and then set up a committee composed of representatives of the building department, city plan commission and the housing commission to check the proposals of potential builders in the area to see that they conform with broad specifications as to density, architecture and land coverage. I, personally, go along with this group.

The other extremists in the picture believe that the city should take out the property needed for its municipal improvements and auction off the rest of the property to the highest bidder. This would leave the area wide open to exploitation by speculators.[9]

Before Detroit could resolve its dilemma among these approaches, the United States Housing Act of 1949 was passed. Detroit converted Gratiot to a federally aided effort, and Congress and the Housing and Home Finance Agency settled the issue. Federal urban redevelopment statutes permitted no construction with renewal money other than site improvements and streets, and required renewal to give maximum opportunity to private enterprise. HHFA held that these provisions prohibited architectural and site designs in project plans. Plans would state "proposed land uses and building requirements" to control private development.[10]

[8] Detroit City Plan Commission, "Revised Narrative Report on Redevelopment Plan: Gratiot Redevelopment Project," D.M.-I (mimeographed, the Commission, December 1951), pp. 30–31. An account of the Gratiot Project from 1946 through 1958 can be found in Robert J. Mowitz and Dell S. Wright, *Profile of a Metropolis* (Detroit: Wayne State University Press, 1962), pp. 1–79. Design aspects of the Detroit Plan proposals for Gratiot are illustrated in Detroit Housing Commission, *Detroit Plan* (Detroit: the Commission, 1950).

[9] Edgecomb, *op. cit.*, p. 157.

[10] Housing Act of 1949, *op. cit.*, sections 105 (a) ii, 110 (c), and 110 (b) (2).

FIGURE 1

"Detroit Plan," Gratiot Area, Detroit City Plan Commission, ca. 1949
(redrawn from City Plan Commission data)

458

For two years after the Housing Act of 1949 became law, Detroit's planners, housing officials (the Detroit Housing Commission was designated as the official renewal agency in 1950), city council, mayor, HHFA staff, and local homebuilders debated the pros and cons of various land use, street, and density patterns. A plan jelled in the spring of 1952 (Figure 2). It followed neighborhood unit-superblock theory and aimed at housing former slum dwellers in the project area. The scheme set forth a land use map and a zoning-like declaration of restrictions covering use, density, and building layout. These, backed up by City Planning Commission reviews of site plans and architecture, would, it was hoped, insure an adequate redevelopment design.

In the summer of 1952, an auction was held to select redevelopers. Not a single bidder came forth. After nearly a decade of working with residential developers, the city faced a staggering fact: cleared land in Gratiot was unmarketable. Despite the incentive of land cost write-down, other factors including "gray area" location, Negro clientele, and forbidding housing costs formed obstacles which defeated the planners' heroic labors.

Since costs were presumed a major factor, the planners responded to the impasse by amending the plan to permit higher densities and other concessions to reduce the builder's unit costs and improve marketability. This effort to attract private redevelopers was tested the following year in another auction. Two bids were received. Six months later, when the high bidder revealed his construction plans, the planners were stunned. He proposed a scheme drawn for a project "in the East" crudely superimposed on the Gratiot tract.[11] Attempts to achieve a better design were fruitless. The plan commission would not approve the plans offered. After more than a year, in the early summer of 1954, the city council, stimulated by the bidder's implication in recent FHA scandals, cancelled the sale contract.

In the meantime land acquisition had been completed; as in most early renewal projects, this was delayed by years of litigation required to establish public purpose for the takings. Clearance, too, was complete. By then Gratiot was known as "ragweed acres" (its twin in St. Louis was "Hiroshima flats"). Relocation, prior to

[11] Interview report. This interpretation conflicts with the Mowitz-Wright account, but the meaning is not changed.

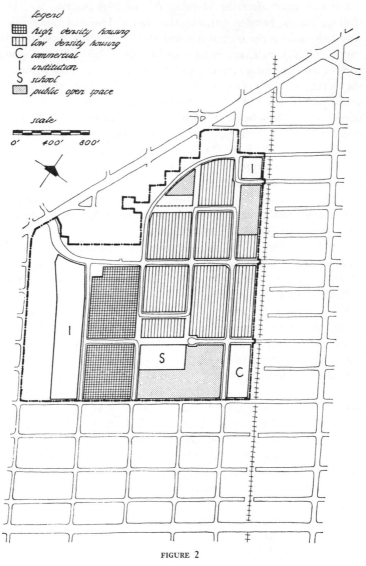

FIGURE 2

Land-Use Plan from Approved Urban Renewal Plan for Gratiot, 1951
(redrawn from City Plan Commission data)

clearance, produced characteristically violent upheavals. Evidence suggests that administrative brutality characterized relocation in Gratiot as it did elsewhere through the early fifties. Except for the Wayne University Medical School building, completed in 1953, and the Lafayette Neuropsychiatric Center, completed a little later, nothing had been built in the seven years the project had been actively underway. Pressures built up to move at any cost to get something—anything—built. Ironically, an intensive planning effort, marked by continuous debate over the most abstruse points of neighborhood design, *produced no buildable result*. Planning hopes were stalled by investor disinterest.

GAPS IN DESIGN PROCESS

"The urban renewal program," Scott Greer and David W. Minar have observed, "is completely dependent upon the private market for its 'renewal' effects." They find the renewal program limited by "(1) the dichotomy of public versus private control, (2) the tension between federal and municipal agencies, (3) the division of power among different federal agencies, and (4) the fragmentation of power at the local community level. Each is not so much a problem to solve as a powerful constraint to be 'lived with'; one that can distort the program beyond recognition in terms of its stated aims."[12] These constraints separate plans from the process of their realization. They shatter design responsibility into bits and pieces.

Case study evidence can be understood by using a "gap" hypothesis. This idea derives from the seamlessness of urban design processes. Design decisions flow in an uninterrupted stream from the earliest ones about programming and goals to final details of construction and use. One decision builds on the next; all are interrelated. To cut the stream dismembers the design process and cuts off one participant from the others. Each designer's world becomes limited to his separate pool of responsibility. The planner becomes cut off from the social analyst, the street-lights man, the redeveloper's banker and architect.[13]

[12] Scott Greer and David W. Minar, "The Political Side of Urban Development and Redevelopment," *The Annals of the American Academy of Political and Social Science*, vol. 352 (March, 1964), 66.

[13] The interdependence of design decisions, from programming to construction, is recognized in the formation of the Development Groups re-

A fragmented design process is built into urban renewal. Of the many gaps, the most important divides the design continuum into zones of public control at one end and private control at the other (Figure 8). At the public end of the spectrum lies the realm of the comprehensive plan. This is cast in terms of design goals such as "balanced community" and pressures for economic development and tax base increase. On the private side, design responds to different goals. Here individuals and firms seek to maximize income, personal comfort, and status aspirations. They frame these in limited terms bounded by the lot line of a particular redevelopment transaction. Little positive influence flows across the gap from comprehensive plans which outline public hopes for neighborhood units, superblocks, industrial parks, shopping centers, and civic centers.[14]

The "gap" hypothesis suggests that successful accomplishment in urban renewal design results from building bridges across public-private, federal-local, federal interagency, and local interagency splits. It sets a theoretical framework for understanding attempts to improve renewal design by viewing them as gap-closing or bridge-building efforts.

Planning and design efforts at Gratiot after the 1954 collapse can be seen in this light. Within the month, a public-spirited pair of businessmen unveiled a new plan. While couched in rudimentary design terms, it clearly aimed at building a bridge between public plans and private investors. This proposal stimulated the creation of a new vehicle which could both plan and redevelop: the Citizens Redevelopment Committee, which was a "power structure group" charged by the city council with getting Gratiot moving. CRC began simultaneous planning, design, and marketing efforts.

This time there was a functional connection between redevelopment investor, building designer (and cost calculator), and planner.

---

sponsible for much large-scale planning and building in Britain. These units bring together in a single team the planners, administrators, fiscal experts, engineers, social scientists, architects, and builders charged with making the project. A seamless responsibility corresponds to a seamless task. Intention at Harlow and Cumbernauld finds precise realization in brick and mortar. See Roger Walters, "Purpose and Organization of Development Groups," *Royal Institute of British Architects Journal*, LXVIII (May, 1961), 273–79.

14 The gap hypothesis corresponds to ideas advanced in more general form by Meyerson and Banfield to explain the failure of planning in Chicago housing site selection. See Martin Meyerson and Edward C. Banfield, *Politics, Planning and the Public Interest* (Glencoe, Ill.: The Free Press, 1955), pp. 274–75.

Changes occurred at all levels, new social goals were adopted, and with them, higher potential rent schedules. A distinguished team of designers was enlisted to plan and design the project. In late 1954, Oscar Stonorov, Minoru Yamasaki, and Victor Gruen (through his associate Carl Van Leuven) unveiled the new scheme for Gratiot. It was neither a public housing site plan, nor a land use diagram, but an architectural layout for a quilt-like pattern of various residential buildings, supported by detailed architectural study of prototypes[15] (Figure 3).

An intensive marketing campaign began. Meanwhile the renewal agency, plan commission, and HHFA made the necessary amendments and approved the new plan. This process drew a sharp issue between the city planning people and the Citizens Redevelopment Committee designers. Neighborhood unit-superblock ideas dominated the thinking of the planning staff. The new CRC group sought to form a grand central avenue along which housing clusters were fastened. The outcome would not be determined by debate of planning theories, however, though much of this went on. Ironically, the success of CRC's marketing campaign led to a neighborhood unit-superblock victory. CRC wanted to find a single developer for the project.[16] At least one committee member predicted that any developer of the requisite size would insist on building his own design, using his own architect, and would show little interest in a ready-made CRC scheme. This was exactly what happened. In the summer of 1955, just a few months after the CRC plan was unveiled, it was abandoned when the committee joined forces with Herbert Greenwald of Chicago to purchase the Gratiot land.

Greenwald had distinguished himself internationally as the patron of the famous German-born, Chicago architect, Ludwig Mies van der Rohe. Mies set to work on Gratiot. By the fall of 1955 he had produced a new plan in association with his long time collaborator, town-planner Ludwig Hilberseimer (Figure 4).[17] This plan was a

[15] "Redevelopment f.o.b. Detroit," *Architectural Forum*, CII (March, 1955), 116–25.

[16] My interview data disagree in some details with the account by Mowitz and Wright, *op. cit.*, pp. 66–72.

[17] "Detroit Redevelopment," *Architectural Forum*, CIV (April, 1956), 122–23, compares the Mies plan with the Stonorov-Yamasaki-Gruen plan. "The Miesian Superblock," *Architectural Forum*, CVI (March, 1957), 128–33, and "A Tower Plus Row Houses in Detroit," *Architectural Forum*, CXII (May, 1960), 104–13, are representative of the many articles dealing with the architecture of Mies' plan as proposed and as built.

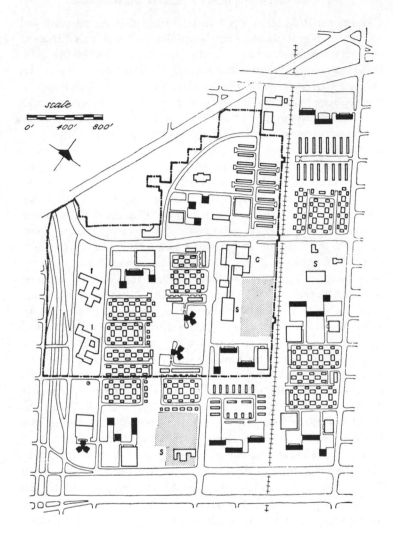

FIGURE 3

Site Plan for Gratiot by Citizens Redevelopment Committee; Stonorov, Yamasaki and Gruen, Architects and Planners, 1954 (redrawn from Citizens Redevelopment Corporation data)

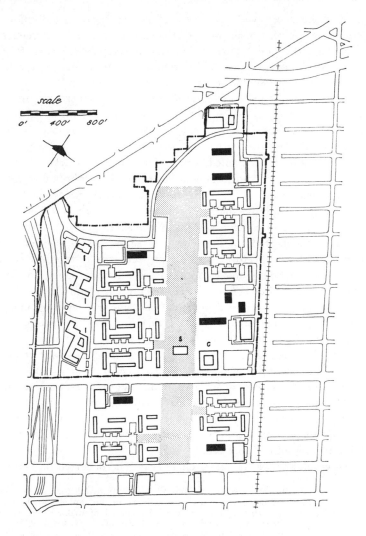

FIGURE 4

Site Plan for Gratiot by Greenwald, Redeveloper, van der Rohe, Architect, and Hilberseimer, Planner, 1955 (redrawn from *Architectural Forum* and City Plan Commission data)

detailed site design with some generalized architectural indications. Following the settlement unit-superblock precepts of Hilberseimer, it rejected the grand avenue. The design received approval from CRC and the city planners: CRC reluctant to scrap its costly plan, the city planners delighted to return to earlier principles.[18]

Aside from the design and layout of buildings, there was much similarity between the Mies and S-Y-G proposals. Both accepted a changed social and economic program. While CRC member Walter Reuther talked of these plans as "integrated communities," actually they were aimed at a limited, upper middle-income market—Negro and white, of course, but economic facts would sharply limit Negro demand. Presumably none of the displaced former residents of the Gratiot area would be able to scrape up the new rents.[19] The two plans also shared a concern with a larger planning universe than the Gratiot area itself. Both included in a single layout coordinated plans for the Lafayette Extension project area contiguous with Gratiot to the South, and Elmwood Park, a former public housing site, across the railroad cut to the East (Figures 3, 4, and 5).

It took about a year to complete Mies' plans and get work under way. In the fall of 1958, for the first time in 11 or 12 years, people began moving in, rather than out, of Gratiot. They could choose to live in a high-rise slab, two-story row houses, or one-story atrium houses. Initially there was resistance to paying $100 to $300 per month for downtown apartments. This sluggish response to the apartments, coupled with objections to some disagreeable functional features of the two-story buildings, led to a new wave of pessimism. In 1960 there were scores of vacancies. By 1964, none were left: there was a waiting list instead.

However, a tragic and far-reaching event had occurred: in Febru-

[18] On practically the same day as Mies' plan was approved, the S-Y-G plan received national recognition for design excellence in the annual awards program of *Progressive Architecture*. Such is the hazard of making awards to unbuilt projects. *Progressive Architecture*, XXXVII (January, 1956), 76.

[19] The "gap" problem seems just as damaging to social and economic intentions as to design. The public-private split is particularly crippling. Greer and Minar write that "the local public authority must either gamble on its knowledge of the private land market or prenegotiate sales. In either event, renewal occurs not where it might benefit the community directly but where it must do so *indirectly through benefiting the private investors.*" Greer and Minar, *op. cit.*, p. 66 (italics added). The heavy criticism renewal has received for building luxury apartments on the ruins of slums seems pointless as long as ideological considerations place renewal at the mercy of the private market. Rehousing slum dwellers requires socialist solutions.

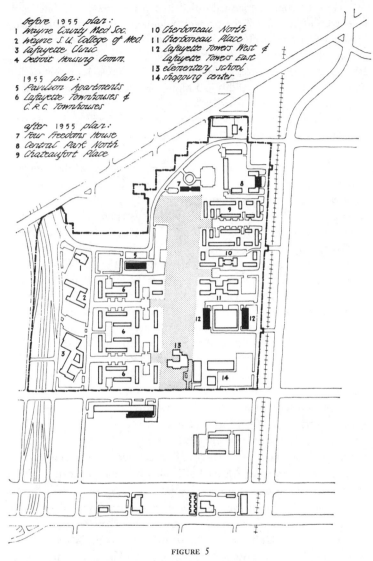

before 1955 plan:
1 Wayne County Med Soc.
2 Wayne S.U. College of Med
3 Lafayette Clinic
4 Detroit Housing Comm.

1955 plan:
5 Pavilion Apartments
6 Lafayette Townhouses &
C.R.C. Townhouses

after 1955 plan:
7 Four Freedoms House
8 Central Park North
9 Chateaufort Place

10 Cherboneau North
11 Cherboneau Place
12 Lafayette Towers West &
Lafayette Towers East
13 elementary school
14 shopping center

FIGURE 5

Plan of Gratiot as Built Including Adjoining Lafayette Extension Project and
Part of Elmwood Park Project, 1964 (redrawn from City Plan Commission
and Detroit Housing Commission data)

467

ary, 1959, Herbert Greenwald died in a plane crash. No one could take over and complete the project, which was less than half finished (500 units of a projected 1800). The rest of the project fell back in the lap of the Detroit Housing Commission. Bit by bit they sold it off: a public school site, 60 one-story row houses, 3 groups of low apartment buildings, 2 additional high-rise slabs, designed by Mies, a shopping center, and one other high apartment building (Figure 5). During this time the market improved steadily. Particularly, the one-story row houses or atrium houses seem to have tapped an inexhaustible demand.

But what happened to the Mies design? With eight different developers (plus the park and street departments), each with his own architect and landscape architect, the result was about what might be expected. Plan Commission review, assisted by a voluntary architectural advisory board, prevented absolute chaos. The result is no disaster, but it is less attractive and it functions more awkwardly than the completed part of the earlier scheme (Figure 7). Measuring design quality at Gratiot or anywhere else raises extraordinary difficulties. Objectivity comes hard, and in the minds of some is irrelevant to the subject. Peter Smithson, the British architect and critic, finds "the essence of what one is searching for is missing from all large-scale developments all over the world, but it can be smelt at Lafayette Park (Mies' part of Gratiot)." Yet the American critic Sybil Moholy-Nagy has damned it mercilessly.[20] While such conflicting judgments may never be resolved, time and less iconoclastic norms make useful evaluation possible. Now that people have lived in Mies' settlement for more than five years, their behavior and the waiting lists demonstrate their affection for it. To the outsider, the design is consistent, powerful, and memorable. Its architectonic austerity is softened by Albert Caldwell's verdant landscape. Where else in America can a school without a parking lot hold a happy PTA meeting? Gratiot joins Radburn, that other incomplete monument, as one of the few triumphs of American urban design.

City planning, DHC, and HHFA approval of the Mies design in 1956 necessitated amending the Gratiot Urban Renewal Plan to incorporate the changes in density, street pattern, open space, and

---

[20] A. and P. Smithson, "Postcript: Philadelphia and the London Roads," *Architectural Design*, XXXII (August, 1962), 401. Sybil Moholy-Nagy, "Villas in the Slums," *Canadian Architect*, September, 1960, 39–46.

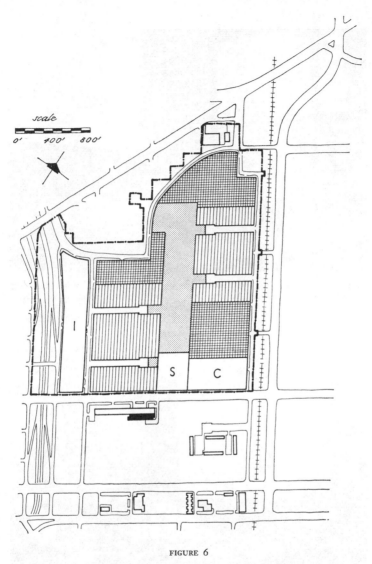

scale

0' 400' 800'

FIGURE 6

Land-Use Plan from Final Approved Urban Renewal Plan for the Gratiot
Project, 1960 (redrawn from City Plan Commission data)

(a) Part of Gratiot Completed According to van der Rohe's Design; Lafayette Townhouses and Pavilion Apartments, Owners (photo courtesy of Detroit Housing Commission)

(b) Part of Gratiot Completed after van der Rohe's Design Was Abandoned; Cherboneau Place, Owner; Clifford N. Wright and Associates, Architects (photo courtesy of Detroit Housing Commission)

FIGURE 7

parceling of the land. These changes were embodied in a new land use map and set of controls and restrictions patterned along zoning lines (Figure 6). The death of Greenwald, subsequent abandoning of the Mies scheme, and the arrival of a heterogeneous group of redevelopers to finish up Gratiot provided a fine test of the efficacy of the conventional tools of American city planning in "implementing" design. The evidence suggests that they were of little value. The one tool that seemed to have any effect was design review. On one parcel, the review forced a modified version of the original Mies site plan in place of a mindless bit of suburbia; on another it scotched an equally mindless attempt at "Georgian" exterior decor.

The failure of the Gratiot urban renewal plan to guide project design after the patron had died, confirms the general failure of "comprehensive plan implementation tools" to bridge the design gap and positively influence the environmental order of cities. This is no surprise to American planners. What is surprising is the failure of many to recognize that, in urban renewal, the constraints of police power regulation do not obtain. Instead, there are unprecedented opportunities for innovation.

While the Gratiot renewal image petered out in piecemeal constructions, in other cities renewal design accomplishments were even more disappointing.[21] Shaken by this dismal experience, agencies in a number of localities began to experiment with new kinds of plans and processes in the early 1960's. These efforts struck out in two directions. One aimed at using the opportunities for tight control implicit in the urban renewal plan. The other took advantage of renewal's possibilities for control through process. A third effort married aspects of both streams. The innovations which came out of this ferment formed the background for further developments in Detroit. Today, next to Gratiot, the Elmwood Park project is using many of these ideas.

Police power land use controls in city planning are founded on the twin principles of *one*, uniformity of application, and *two*, withholding development rights—and thus influencing land value—only where public health, safety, morals, or general welfare are threatened. Land use controls in urban renewal stem from sharply

[21] Results of the author's field surveys of more than 200 projects will be published. They substantiate the dismal general level of design accomplishment.

different premises. The requirement that land be valued for its planned uses automatically recognizes the impact of controls on potential development rights. The appraisal and disposition processes take into account land value effects of controls since disposition is at "fair value for uses in accordance with the urban renewal plan."[22] Thus, the nature and intensity of controls need not be limited by a concern which restricts the exercise of the police power in zoning and subdivision regulation. For the same reason, there is no need for uniform application of controls in renewal. Each parcel may be controlled independently and its value determined accordingly.

These essential differences have gone largely unnoticed.[23] A few planners, particularly those with an interest in architectural form, have sensed the special power of renewal plan land use controls. In an attempt to close the design gap, they have literally written a complete and detailed design into the controls. Setback lines can be made mandatory building lines; height limits can be made to work as both minima and maxima; entrances and even fenestration patterns can be written into controls. Functional layout may be made completely specific; that is, a drug store here, restaurant there, rather than necessarily broad listings of permitted or prohibited uses. The imagination of the planner—and the market place—are practically the only limits. "Tight" plans emerge. Compared with the typical urban renewal plan based on the usual implementation tools, "tight" plans greatly enlarge the extent of public control over the design continuum (Figure 8). Such plans seek comprehensive regulation of renewal processes.

At Erieview in Cleveland, I. M. Pei fashioned such a tight plan based on an elaborate, highly refined overall design for the project area.[24] In a redevelopment situation where he was backed by a downtown power structure group similar to Detroit's CRC, Pei produced a plan stated in specific architectural terms (Figure 9). Around it he framed the formal controls of the urban renewal plan

[22] Housing Act of 1949, *op. cit.*, section 110 (c) (4).
[23] John Delafons notes the differences between zoning and renewal plan controls in *Land-Use Controls in the United States* (Cambridge, Mass.: Joint Center for Urban Studies of M.I.T. and Harvard University, 1962), pp. 71–77.
[24] I. M. Pei and Associates, *Erieview Cleveland Ohio: An Urban Renewal Plan for Downtown Cleveland* (New York: I. M. Pei and Associates, October, 1961).

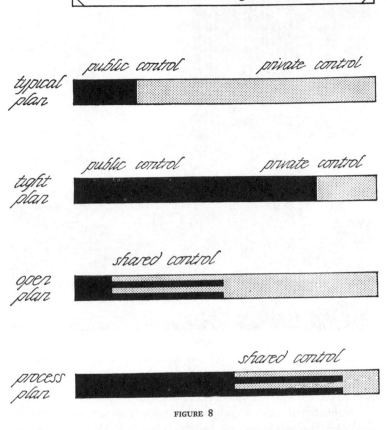

FIGURE 8

Division of the Design Continuum into Zones of Public (Governmental) and Private (Entrepreneurial) Responsibilities in Four Approaches to Urban Renewal Planning

(Figure 10). The land purchaser or redeveloper and his architect were expected to fill in the pattern, and they are doing so: Erieview is being built as designed (Figure 11).

The Cleveland Development Foundation and its group of downtown business leaders marketed the plan for Erieview very much the way CRC marketed its plan for Gratiot. If their customer in Cleveland had been the patron of Mies van der Rohe, would the Pei

FIGURE 9

Rendering of Erieview; I. M. Pei and Associates, Architects and Planners, 1961 (courtesy of I. M. Pei and Associates)

plan have held up? Erieview redevelopment designs were subject to an architectural review procedure, with Pei serving as review advisor to the public agency. Imagine Gratiot if Mies had exercised design review authority over the parcels remaining unbuilt at Greenwald's death!

Erieview's tight plan received such powerful, sympathetic support during its execution that it is difficult to determine whether the tight controls or the marketing and review procedures were the more responsible for its success. What if no investor were willing to risk adding several hundred thousand square feet of rental space to Cleveland's central area? What if the more creative architects were in the service of the private developer, not the public agency? These questions suggest defects in the tight plan approach.

When specific building form and site layouts get built into an

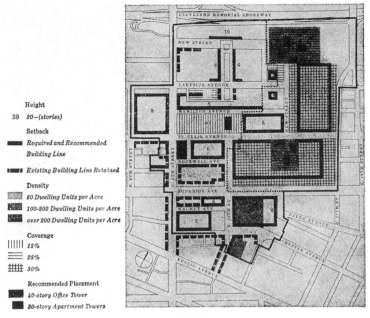

Height

30 *30–(stories)*

Setback

■■■ *Required and Recommended Building Line*

■■■ *Existing Building Line Retained*

Density

▨ *60 Dwelling Units per Acre*

▩ *100-200 Dwelling Units per Acre*

▨ *over 200 Dwelling Units per Acre*

Coverage

|||||| *15%*

≡ *25%*

▦ *30%*

Recommended Placement

■ *40-story Office Tower*

■ *30-story Apartment Towers*

FIGURE 10

Control Diagram for Erieview; I. M. Pei and Associates, Architects and Planners (courtesy of I. M. Pei and Associates)

urban renewal plan, it takes formal action by both local legislature and the federal agency to make any significant change. Plan amendments prove costly in time, energy, and money, and often generate pointless conflicts.

Renewal projects typically take about seven years to move from legislative approval of the urban renewal plan to an advanced stage of redevelopment and rehabilitation. The best market research is shaky under these conditions: over periods of three to ten years, it must predict specific uses at specific intensities on specific sites at the scale of individual buildings and parcels. Theoretical and practical difficulties argue powerfully for deferring detailed design decisions until a time much nearer actual redevelopment.[25] Since

[25] Land market prediction difficulties and their impact on renewal programs need careful examination. David A. Wallace's "Renaissancemanship," *Journal of the American Institute of Planners*, XXVI (August, 1960), 157–76, suggests this problem may justify a return from "comprehensive" urban renewal planning to "projectitis."

FIGURE 11
Erieview under Construction; Galbraith, Developer; Harrison and
Abramovitz, Architects (photo by author)

tight plans risk swimming against the current of investment decision, they may be risky and hard to execute. Does a local renewal
administrator have the political power to enforce a tight plan in the
absence of market support? To what extent should an architectural
image be subjected to such pressures?

An equally problematical objection to tight plans derives from
functionalist architectural theory, which holds that design is a
response to real conditions. Can good urban renewal design emerge
from a make-believe world based on chancy predictions about land
markets in place of informed builder-clients? In the absence of more
pressing determinants architectural form and site layout may tend
toward empty formalism.

"OPEN" PLANS

An alternative to both tight plans and conventional ones emerged in
Hartford, Connecticut's Bushnell Plaza project. Here an "open"
plan put the emphasis on *process.* Its land use controls did not locate
uses on a map. Spatial arrangement of the required high-density

housing, public park, parking, and landscaped areas, and the inclusion and arrangement of the permitted theater, office, and commercial space were left to the redeveloper and his site planners[26] (Figures 12 and 13). To assure a well designed result, the urban renewal plan set forth a design process. This included a procedure for the design of public spaces (site improvements) which insured that they would dovetail with the private redevelopment design. Most important, it established a process for land disposition which made design quality a principal factor. It required active, formal collaboration between public planner and private architect during design development. Land disposition was handled in two stages: first, a prequalification of prospective redevelopers on the basis of business and financial criteria; second, a design competition. The plan provided that the chosen redeveloper would be given a year in which to complete "the final design plans"—their scope was defined—during which time "he will be required to work in close cooperation and coordination with the staff of the agency. . . ."

In support of its "open" controls and its carefully defined design process, the Bushnell Plaza plan contained a formal statement of renewal objectives. Federal regulations require no such statement. Since it is rare for a locality to see beyond bureaucratic requirements, it is rare to find a renewal plan with a stated purpose. It is rarer still to find any indication of design goals. In an open plan such statements of purpose are crucial. Hopes for realizing fine project design depend on the design process as set forth in the plan. To guide this process, to meet requirements for adequate public notice of public action, to avoid arbitrary action, the goals toward which action and process are directed must be spelled out. The open plan is not a miniature comprehensive city plan; it is a miniature "constitution" which guides and legitimatizes public actions.[27]

Seen in terms of the gap hypothesis and the public-private control

[26] Hartford Redevelopment Agency, "Redevelopment Plan for Bushnell-Plaza Project, Conn. R-51" (mimeographed, the Agency, September, 1961); and interview data.

The Bushnell Plaza plan exhibits a particularly clear understanding of the special nature of urban renewal plan controls. Residential density was controlled simply by stating, "the residential structure or structures shall contain not less than 275 units nor more than 325 units . . ."; the public park was required to be "not less than 40,000 square feet nor more than 60,000 . . ."; the controls on the park precisely stated the function it was to serve.

[27] This view of the urban renewal plan is to be articulated in a forthcoming article by Herbert M. Franklin.

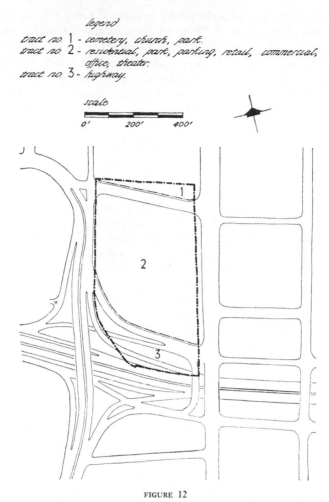

legend

tract no. 1 - cemetery, church, park.
tract no. 2 - residential, park, parking, retail, commercial, office, theater.
tract no. 3 - highway.

scale

0'   200'   400'

FIGURE 12

"Land-Use Map" for Bushnell Plaza (note that it does not show land uses); Hartford Redevelopment Agency, 1961 (redrawn from Hartford Redevelopment Agency data)

dichotomy, the open plan establishes a zone of shared control within the design continuum (Figure 8). Public interest in good design gets more effective representation than in the land use map—zoning controls of the typical urban renewal plan. In contrast to the tight plan, the open approach accepts the primary role of private entre-

FIGURE 13

Model of Final Design of Bushnell Plaza; Bushnell Plaza Associates, Developers; I. M. Pei and Associates, Architects and Planners; 1963 (courtesy of Hartford Redevelopment Agency and I. M. Pei and Associates)

preneur in redevelopment investment decisions. The seven-year interval between plan approval and active redevelopment cannot cripple open plans to the same extent that it injures tight ones. Not the least of their virtues, open plans provide room for architectural —and entrepreneurial—creativity at points where tight plans shut it out.

With all their advantages, such plans have defects. For instance, trouble arises from the limited American experience with procedural or administrative land use control in place of statutory standards. At Bushnell Plaza, this kind of difficulty occurred when the agency became stalled during the second stage of land disposition and was unable to act swiftly in selecting a redeveloper.

One of the points that held up this disposition reveals another aspect of land use control having a special relevance to urban renewal planning. The plan contained a height limit which served no purpose because there were no issues of shading adjoining properties, or need for an indirect control of the intensity of use, or threat to an esthetically pleasing skyline. It probably appeared because a strictly bureaucratic reading of HHFA's *Urban Renewal Manual* seemed to require it. Its effect was also to limit architectural opportunity. Its arbitrariness was confirmed when the redevelopment proposal which was judged best on many criteria violated the height limit. There was no reason for keeping the height limit except that the proposal had to conform to the controls of the plan. And in terms of planning goals, the control was meaningless; yet it inhibited selection of the best design.

This experience indicates the importance of distinguishing planning controls from design or development controls. Because planning concerns, such as overall land use intensity or residential density, have so long been controlled indirectly through restrictions on lot size, building height, or yard sizes, confusing the two has become a conditioned response. *Planning controls* deal with those factors of community interest affecting the world outside the tract in question. *Development controls* are concerned with the specific layout and organization of an actual development design. Development controls are relevant only in terms of a real design. When development controls are based on "standards" and irresponsible "illustrative designs"—irresponsible because not really to be financed and built—they only inhibit urban design.

Another defect of open plans lies in their tendency to circumscribe public initiative. A considerable body of design theory recommends use of public works as catalytic agents to stimulate and direct private actions.[28] In Bushnell Plaza, the delegation of responsibility for public works design to the redeveloper left little room for appropriate public leadership. In other situations, experience shows that functional complexity or market softness may be overcome by public leadership in preparing detailed overall designs. Edmund Bacon has described this process at Penn Center, where governmental initiative crystallized a design concept to be taken up by the private investors. Charles Center in Baltimore exhibits this situation in a recent renewal project where the functional and market situations were inappropriate for an open plan.

---

[28] Among the theories propounding a network of catalytic public works in urban renewal design are the "design structure" concepts put forth by Edmund N. Bacon in "Architecture and Planning," *Journal of the American Institute of Architects,* XXV (June, 1961), 68–90; and "capital design" or "capital web" by David A. Crane, in "The City Symbolic," *Journal of the American Institute of Planners,* XXVI (November, 1960), 280–92.

DESIGN PROCESS CONTROLS

The most recent wave of innovation in relating renewal planning to design has sought to draw on the advantages of tight and open plans while avoiding the defects of both approaches. A series of projects on the West Coast articulated these ideas, beginning with an experiment in land disposition methods in San Francisco's Diamond Heights project. To overcome the inadequate and uncertain effect of a routine land use map and zoning ordinance plan, the redevelopment agency commissioned a special study of the neighborhood shopping center in this project. A preliminary design plan was prepared by architect Lawrence Lackey in collaboration with the landscape architects, Royston, Hanamato and Mays.[29] This plan was embodied in the invitation for redevelopment proposals, which stated that the winning bidders would be expected to follow the plan, or they might submit an alternative design of their own which would be gauged by the agency against the yardstick of the Lackey-Royston scheme.[30]

In this modest event lay the seeds of an approach holding the advantages of flexible, open project plans, yet retaining every opportunity for appropriate public leadership in design decisions. In quick succession Sacramento, Fresno, Vallejo, and Oakland, California, picked up the idea and elaborated it. These cities worked out a "comprehensive process" method with three main components:

1. PRELIMINARY WORK AND THE URBAN RENEWAL PLAN Studies are undertaken to explore design potentials and to establish a strategy for design actions. From these studies come the *design objectives and controls* set forth in the urban renewal plan and the

---

[29] Lawrence Lackey, Royston, Hanamoto and Mays, "Diamond Heights Neighborhood Center: An Urban Design Report to the San Francisco Redevelopment Agency," December, 1961. San Francisco Redevelopment Agency, *Two Commercial Sites: Diamond Heights, San Francisco* (San Francisco: the Agency, March 19, 1962).

[30] Design plans used in land disposition must be viewed as an articulation of the approved urban renewal plan if this process is to meet the test that land must be sold for fair value for the uses according to the urban renewal plan. This point was clarified by URA in *Local Public Agency Letter No. 267,* "Design in Urban Renewal: Supplement No. 1 to *LPA Letter No. 249,*" May 23, 1963. Design plans move in the direction of increased governmental involvement in design details. This move by URA indicates a partial reversal of early interpretations of statutory requirements limiting construction and providing maximum opportunity for private enterprise.

actions and procedures devised to accomplish the objectives. The plan follows the open or flexible mode rather than building in a tight design. (Note that this is just the beginning of project planning work, not the end. Conventional planning—and urban design—have ended in the survey and planning phase before renewal action gets under way.)

2. DESIGN PLAN At the beginning of renewal operations, the public agency prepared design plans in incremental but continuous fashion. These plans may become detailed: they may include the actual design of the site improvements and other public construction, advisory material and designs for owners who are rehabilitating their properties, and design plans to serve as a basis for land disposition and redevelopment. The degree of detail and refinement will vary from time to time during the years of project execution, and from place to place within the project, in order to meet real situations as they occur. In terms of modern planning theory, this permits *loss cutting* as well as *goal seeking* behavior on the part of the planners and designers.[31]

3. DESIGN ACTION Each renewal action—site improvement, rehabilitation, land disposition, redevelopment—either follows the design plans or the design plans are used as yardsticks against which alternatives are measured. Processes for reviewing redevelopment proposals, effecting design coordination, organizing land disposition, and so on, are detailed, enunciated, and put into operation.

In this approach, the public agency works with reliable market information, since it need not freeze designs years in advance of renewal action. An unpredictable new development need not force a long bureaucratic hassle over amending the official urban renewal plan. This approach permits powerful public leadership in design without sacrificing flexibility.

In the Gratiot case, imagine the ease with which the Mies design could have been completed had it been an agency design plan rather than a private one dependent upon a patron, and had the public agency more powerful tools in its hands than land use maps and zoning regulations. Imagine, too, the reduction in costly, repeated, and overly detailed site layouts and building type studies initiated

---

[31] See Albert O. Hirschman and Charles E. Lindblom, "Economic Development, Research and Development, Policy Making: Some Convergent Views," *Behavioral Science*, VII (April, 1962), 215–16.

too far ahead of actual investment decision. Think of the reduction in pointless bureaucratic infighting if amendment of the official plan were not needed each time a Stonorov or Mies appeared.

Some comprehensive process planning components appear in most renewal projects where distinguished design occurs. Edmund Bacon, for instance, has made the role of process explicit in achieving the elegant architecture and articulate overall structure of Washington Square East in Philadelphia.[32] New Haven uses a ramified, comprehensive process approach: in Wooster Square and Dixwell it intentionally stretched out design and planning over all the years of project operation. David Crane has also emphasized the importance of process; his influence evidently appears in the Boston Redevelopment Authority's sophisticated set of procedures for insuring high quality design.[33]

Federal policy has been slow to catch up. No significant changes in the *Urban Renewal Manual* and federal review criteria reflect the importance of process over plan. However, a change may be on the way since a series of recent advisory statements have emphasized new ideas in renewal design and planning.[34]

At Elmwood Park, Detroit has turned to a comprehensive process to overcome some of the problems which caused so much trouble at Gratiot. The urban renewal plan for this project was completed in 1961[35] (Figure 14). It is no model of totally open planning, but neither is it a tightly constructed attempt to build in a design. Various factors held up action until 1963, when the housing commission engaged a team to prepare a design plan. Crane and Gorwic,

[32] Edmund N. Bacon provides a convincing account of the use of design in this yardstick role in "A Case Study in Urban Design," *Journal of the American Institute of Planners*, XXVI (August, 1960), 224–35.

[33] David Crane, "The Public Art of City Building," *The Annals of the American Academy of Political and Social Science*, vol. 332 (March, 1964), 84–94. He recommends a six-step process ranging from design consideration in the master plan to design review of private building.
Boston Redevelopment Authority, *Design and Urban Renewal* (Boston: The Authority, 1964?).

[34] Housing and Home Finance Agency, Urban Renewal Administration, *Local Public Agency Letter No. 249*, "Design in Urban Renewal," August 20, 1962. Urban Renewal Administration, *Urban Renewal Notes: Design in Urban Renewal*, July-August, 1963. William L. Slayton, Urban Renewal Administration Commissioner from 1961 to the present, has made numerous speeches and published various articles on behalf of increased attention to renewal design processes. See, for instance, "Design Goals for Urban Renewal," *Architectural Record*, CXXXIV (November, 1963), 149–52.

[35] Detroit City Plan Commission, "Elmwood Park Rehabilitation Project No. 1, Urban Renewal Plan" (mimeographed, January, 1961).

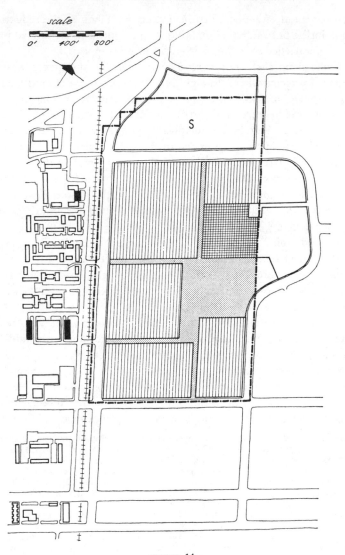

FIGURE 14

Land-Use Plan for Elmwood Park Project No. 1, Including Parts of Adjoining
Gratiot and Lafayette Extension Projects; Detroit City Plan Commission;
1961 (redrawn from City Plan Commission data)

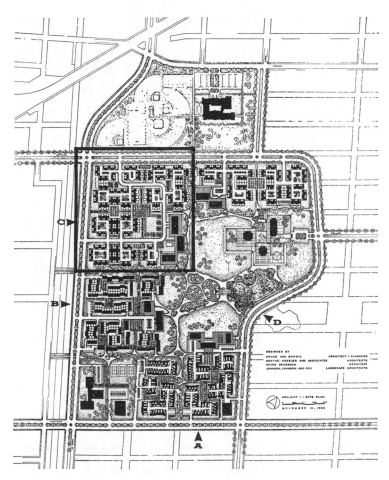

FIGURE 15

Design Plan for Elmwood Park Project No. 1, Detroit Housing Commission; Crane and Gorwic, Architects and Planners; Meathe and Kessler, Architects; 1963 (courtesy of Detroit Housing Authority and Crane and Gorwic). Area marked "C" shown in Figure 16.

architect-planners; Meathe and Kessler, architects; Irving Grossman, architect; and Johnson, Johnson, Roy, landscape architects made up the group. Their plan provided a variety of different owner-occupied house types and elevator apartments, plus a system of public spaces and land parceling geared to the design (Figure 15). In

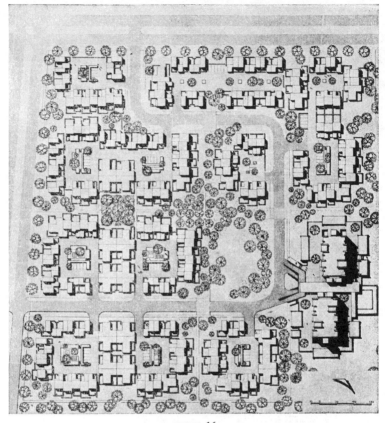

FIGURE 16

Final Site Plan for Parcel No. C of Elmwood Park Project No. 1; Aberdeen Gardens Redevelopment Co., Redeveloper; Eberle M. Smith Associates, Architects (courtesy of Eberle M. Smith Associates)

1964 DHC began work using the design plan as a basis for site improvements, and as the yardstick for a fixed-price, competitive land disposition covering the first six of eleven parcels. Sixteen prospective redevelopers submitted proposals. Four were selected: one to develop three parcels. Of the successful bidders, one elected to follow exactly the design plan, and the others submitted alternatives judged equal to or better than the yardstick design (Figure 16). The four developers, with their architects and site planners, are now collaborating with the plan commission group on design. Every indication on the Detroit scene, and from precedent elsewhere, suggests that the outcome will be a stunning demonstration of fine urban renewal design.

In comparison with the land use map-zoning plan and open-plan approaches, Elmwood Park and the other process approaches to renewal designs register clear benefits in relevant public control and in decisive public leadership. These benefits rest in part on the value of the design plan in making procedural controls work smoothly. Contrasted with tight plans, design plans and process controls cope with the unpredictability of market and talent. They help, too, by forcing planning out of its fixation on plans and into an active, continuous participation in the process of renewal. The new comprehensiveness can bridge the gap between public renewal intentions and the private entrepreneurs through whom these hopes must be realized.

PART VII

CHALLENGES AND RESPONSES

19 The Federal Bulldozer*

Martin Anderson

Business leaders have heard many times in recent years that our housing and our cities are decaying, that private enterprise cannot save them, that the government must step in and "help" private enterprise with urban renewal, and that they—as responsible citizens and businessmen—should collaborate with the government in this effort.[1] In my judgment, none of these statements is true.

The purpose of this article is to evaluate the federal urban renewal program—its goals, its methods, its accomplishments—and to compare them with those of the free marketplace. A comparison of the results that these two forces—the federal urban renewal program and private enterprise—have produced since 1949 brings out some fundamental issues and questions that have been obscured in a fog of good intentions and platitudes. The basic question is this: Should the federal urban renewal program be continued and expanded, or should it be stopped? I shall argue that it should be stopped.

* Reprinted from the *Harvard Business Review*, Vol. 43, No. 1 (January–February 1965), pp. 6–21, where it appeared under the title "Fiasco of Urban Renewal."
[1] See, for example, Leland Hazard, "Are We Committing Urban Suicide?" Thinking Ahead, HBR July–August 1964, p. 152.

GOALS OF RENEWAL

In response to continual exhortation and pressure to do something to "save" the cities and improve housing, Congress enacted the federal urban renewal program in 1949, proceeding on the conviction that a program of this type would help to—

. . . eliminate substandard and other inadequate housing through clearance of slums and blighted areas;

. . . stimulate sufficient housing production and community development to remedy the housing shortage;

. . . realize the goal of a decent home and a suitable living environment for every American family.

I doubt that anyone can argue with these goals. Better homes, improved neighborhoods, and the elimination of slums—all are desirable. The difficulty is not with the goals, but with the means of accomplishing them and with the consequences that result.

HOW PROGRAM WORKS

In essence the federal urban renewal program attempts to rebuild rundown areas of cities by feeding large amounts of public money and government power into the normal operations of the private marketplace. It does not complement the private market; it short-circuits it.

This is how the program works. First, a section of a city is designated as an urban renewal area, and plans are drawn up and approved by the local renewal agency, the local governing body, and the federal authorities in Washington. A public hearing is then held at which local renewal officials document their case for urban renewal. At this time other persons interested in the project have the opportunity to speak for or against it.

Once the planning is complete, execution starts. Though some execution activities may be carried on simultaneously, there are six basic steps:

(1) *Land acquisition.* The land and the buildings are usually acquired by negotiation with the owners, but if this fails, the renewal authorities will use the power of eminent domain to force

the recalcitrant owners to sell; in cases like this, the purchase price is determined by independent appraisers.

(2) *Displacement and relocation.* Individuals, families, and businesses located in the area are forced to move and find homes or establish businesses elsewhere. The law provides for some compensation and requires renewal authorities to relocate them satisfactorily, although in practice this does not always happen.

(3) *Site clearance.* The wrecking cranes and the bulldozers demolish any buildings not considered useful by the renewal authorities.

(4) *Site improvements and supporting facilities.* The cleared land is usually improved by the construction of streets, sewers, water mains, lighting systems, schools, libraries, and parks.

(5) *Disposition of improved land.* The cleared and improved land can be sold, leased, donated, or retained by the renewal agency. Usually the land is sold to private persons either by competitive bidding or by negotiation between renewal officials and the private buyer.

(6) *New construction.* The new construction may be residential, industrial, commercial, or public; so far it has been predominantly private residential. The private developer is usually obliged to build according to a general plan approved by the renewal authorities.

This, then, is urban renewal—damned by some, praised by many, and understood by very few. At first glance, urban renewal would seem to be a most desirable program, both plausible and appealing. The picture is often painted like this: *before*—dirty, dark, ugly slums; *after*—clean, bright, beautiful buildings. The contrast is clear, the appeal seductive, but this picture shows only the hopes and wishes of urban renewal. The realities of its costs and consequences are drastically different.

EVERYBODY PAYS

Urban renewal is, of course, expensive. The gross project cost of urban renewal includes all expenses incurred by a local renewal authority—planning costs, land, buildings, overhead, interest, relocation, site improvements, and supporting facilities.

Assume that all this costs $9 million for a good-sized project. Where does the money come from?

Some of it comes from private developers who buy the cleared and improved land. On the average, private developers have been buying urban renewal land for about 30% of the gross cost of the project—say, $3 million for our $9 million project. This leaves the city with a net cost of $6 million. The federal government will pay two-thirds of this net cost, or, in this case, $4 million.

Thus, for our $9 million project, we get $3 million from the private developer who becomes the new owner, $4 million from taxpayers all over the United States, and $2 million from taxpayers living in the community with the urban renewal project. Additional features, called noncash grants-in-aid, can reduce the net cost to the city still further.

Because the federal government subsidizes two-thirds of the net cost to the city, some people feel that urban renewal is a bonanza that cannot be passed up. This might be true if only one city were engaged in urban renewal; but there are over 1,500 projects in about 750 cities throughout the country. Through federal taxes, the residents of any one of these cities are helping to pay for all the other projects. As more and more cities attempt to "get their share" and the over-all cost of the program rises, the cost to all necessarily increases.

BETTER HOUSING?

One of the most serious consequences of the federal urban renewal program is the effect that it has had on the supply of housing, especially low-rent housing. This is ironic because one of the goals of the program is to improve living conditions. Why has this goal not been realized?

The typical urban renewal project destroys a great many homes. Between 1950 and 1960, the program was responsible for the destruction of approximately 126,000 housing units. Of these homes, 101,000 had been classified as substandard by the local renewal authorities, while 25,000 were in good condition. The good ones were destroyed because they were judged to be incompatible with the proposed plan for the area.

I have estimated that in this same decade approximately 28,000 new housing units were completed within urban renewal areas.[2] About 25,000 of these were privately owned homes; 3,000 or so were public housing units. Score: 126,000 down, about 28,000 up. This means that almost four times as many homes were destroyed as were built.

The total effect on housing conditions was even worse. All the 126,000 homes that were destroyed were located in older sections of cities, and almost all were low-rent units. It is doubtful whether the average rent paid exceeded $50 or $60 a month. On the other hand, the rents of the new privately owned homes were very high. For example, those homes built in 1962 in urban renewal areas had rents averaging $195 a month. (A small percentage rented for over $360 a month!) Hence it was virtually impossible for any person displaced from an urban renewal area to move back in; he could afford it only if he moved into public housing. And only 3,000 units of public housing were built—an insignificant number in comparison to the number of units destroyed.

Thus the net effect of the federal urban renewal program in the field of housing for the period I have studied can be summed up in this way:

- More homes were destroyed than were built.
- Those destroyed were predominantly low-rent homes.
- Those built were predominantly high-rent homes.
- Housing conditions were made worse for those whose housing conditions were least good.
- Housing conditions were improved for those whose housing conditions were best.

IMPROVED LIVING CONDITIONS?

Private studies indicate that the people displaced by urban renewal usually move into housing of approximately the same quality as the housing they were forced out of—but they often pay more for it. Their predicament is compounded, not alleviated, by urban renewal. Government studies, on the other hand, indicate that about 80% of the displaced people move into standard housing. Obviously,

[2] *The Federal Bulldozer: A Critical Analysis of Urban Renewal, 1949–1962* (Cambridge, The M.I.T. Press, 1964), pp. 65–67.

both the private studies and the government studies cannot be correct.

I suspect the reason for the discrepancy between them is that local government officials decide whether or not a dwelling unit in an urban renewal area is standard or substandard, and their estimates are therefore subject to bias. An official interested in speeding up the process of an urban renewal project may be tempted to apply high housing standards to justify the taking of the property, and then, when it comes to relocating the people displaced, he may be tempted to use quite low housing standards to justify the quick relocation of these people.

The notion that over 80% of the displaced people move into good housing is difficult to reconcile with other relevant facts. The people living in these areas are relatively poor. A great many of them come from minority groups; approximately two-thirds of all those forced to move are Negroes and Puerto Ricans. Good-quality, conveniently located housing costs so much more than poor housing that it is difficult to conceive of hundreds of thousands of low-income people, many of them subject to racial discrimination, suddenly moving from low-quality housing into higher-quality housing at rents they can afford.

And then one might ask the following question: If it is true that all this good-quality, conveniently located, low-rent housing is available, why then is it necessary to force these people out of their homes with a bulldozer? Would it not be far simpler, more just, and much cheaper just to *tell* them about the better homes available elsewhere?

ONE MILLION EVICTIONS

The number of people affected by the program was small during its first few years of operation. But I have estimated that as of December 31, 1962, approximately 1,665,000 persons were living or had lived in urban renewal areas. This is about the same number of people that live in Detroit, Michigan—the fifth largest city in the United States. Some of these people have already been forced out; the rest will be on their way eventually.

The number of people actually evicted so far is very large. By March 31, 1963, about 609,000 persons had been forced to move, and the number has, of course, continued to go up. I estimate that at least 1,000,000 people will be evicted by the end of 1965. And this is by no means the end; in fact, it is probably just a small start. In 1962, William Slayton, the Commissioner of the Urban Renewal Administration, stated that approximately 1,000,000 families would be displaced during the next decade. This means that somewhere around 4,000,000 persons will be actually displaced by 1972—or about one person out of every 50 living in the United States.

GOOD FOR BUSINESS?

Although most urban renewal areas are predominantly residential, they often contain a number of businesses. These businesses range from one-man offices to industrial concerns with several hundred employees. According to a 1960 report financed by the Small Business Administration:

It is estimated that there are over 100,000 business firms in all 650 project areas. . . . The approximately 100,000 firms scheduled for dislocation from project areas on December 31, 1959, represent a beginning only. . . . New projects have been started at an increasing rate. Although no precise forecasts have been made, it is expected that the volume of business dislocations from renewal areas over the 1960–1970 decade will be at least twice the 100,000 already underway or planned.[3]

What happens to a business when it is forced to move? Does it stay in business? Where does it move to?

According to the study quoted above, many firms never relocate at all. This study covered 14 cities with 21 urban renewal projects containing a total of 2,946 displaced firms. The finding: 756 of them either went out of business or disappeared. Similar findings have been made by others:

• A study conducted by Brown University in the city of Providence, Rhode Island, found that 40% of the businesses displaced went out of business.[4]

• A study prepared by the Library of Congress concluded that

[3] William N. Kinnard, Jr., and Zenon S. Malinowski, *The Impact of Dislocation from Urban Renewal Areas on Small Business*, prepared by the University of Connecticut under a grant from the Small Business Administration, July 1960, pp. 2–3.
[4] Chamber of Commerce of the United States, *Washington Report*, December 20, 1963.

urban renewal projects "are destroying small businesses and jobs and contributing to the unemployment problem."[5]

What about rents for firms forced to relocate? In the study prepared for the Small Business Administration, a sample was taken of four cities that contained 1,142 displaced firms. Only 41, or 3.1%, actually moved back into the urban renewal area. The researchers observed:

. . . Approximately 75 percent of those who do relocate find quarters within one mile of their former location; and nearly 40 percent within one-quarter mile. They generally occupy about the same floor area they did before (which is less than they claimed to want or need), at a square foot rental at least double what they were paying (which is much more than they claimed to be able to afford or to be willing to pay).[6]

THE TAX MYTH

One of the most valued arguments presented by those who favor expansion of the urban renewal program is that it will strengthen and increase the tax base and thus increase tax revenues to the city. Unfortunately, this has not happened, and the chances of urban renewal producing a significant tax revenue increase in the future are small.

The latest data I have on new construction actually started in urban renewal areas goes through March 31, 1961. It shows that the urban renewal programs actually *decreased* the tax revenues flowing into the cities' tax coffers. By the end of 1960, approximately $735 million of real estate had been destroyed in urban renewal project areas. About $824 million of real estate construction had been started, $577 million of which was privately owned and thus taxable. If we optimistically assume that 70% of this total amount privately started was ever finished, the net result is about $400 million worth of taxable property—$335 million *less* than we had before urban renewal!

Is this a temporary situation, or is an adverse tax effect a fundamental quality of urban renewal? Several factors militate against net tax increases:

(1) Interim tax losses from real estate destroyed are often overlooked. Once buildings are down, no taxes are paid on them. Nor

5 *Ibid.*
6 W. N. Kinnard, Jr., and Z. S. Malinowski, *op. cit.,* p. 75.

are any taxes paid until new buildings have been put up. The new buildings will probably be worth much more than the old ones. But the length of time between the destruction of the old buildings and the construction of the new ones can easily be five years or more. During this time the city is losing tax revenue.

(2) Tax revenue increases that would have occurred in the absence of urban renewal must be considered. In most cases, a certain amount of new construction and rehabilitation would probably have been accomplished with private funds, thereby increasing the tax base with no cost to the city.

(3) Much of the new construction in the urban renewal area would have been built elsewhere in the city anyway. Some experts in the field estimate that from 50% to 75% of this construction would have been accomplished by private enterprise.[7]

(4) Many of the new tenants in an urban renewal area will come from other parts of the city. What happens to the value of the buildings they vacate?

(5) Some cities have had to give special tax abatements to induce private developers to come in. This, of course, will further reduce any net gain in tax revenues that might materialize.

To be sure, *some* of the factors operating may tend to increase the tax revenues. If an urban renewal project is successful, it is possible that the value of the surrounding buildings may increase. But before this is translated into increased taxes, the assessment on the buildings must be raised.

The whole issue of tax revenue changes is still a cloudy one and will probably remain so. It should be kept in mind that the net change will be the result of many complex factors. It is not enough just to compare the value of the old real estate with the proposed value of the new real estate. Timing of payments, effect on the rest of the city, what would have happened without urban renewal— these must all be considered, along with the fact that the process of urban renewal itself costs the city a considerable amount of money.

CONSTITUTIONAL?

Under the Constitution of the United States, it is understood that a man is free to use his property as he desires as long as he does not

[7] See *The Federal Bulldozer,* pp. 180, 181.

500 / Martin Anderson

interfere with the rights of others. Traditionally, public use is the *only* reason for which the government may seize private property. The Supreme Court changed this in 1954, and today, under the federal urban renewal program, it is possible for the government to seize the property of one man, destroy it, and then sell the cleared land to some other man at a negotiated price.

The Constitution clearly states that the power of eminent domain may be used only to seize private property for public use. Approximately 70% of the new construction in urban renewal areas is privately owned. By no distortion of the thinking process can this be construed to be a public use; it is clearly a private use.

The Supreme Court essentially justified this procedure on the grounds that it was in the public interest. They neatly sidestepped the problem of clearly defining the public interest. The use of the public interest to justify a government program often means that one group of people will gain at the expense of some other group. Those who do not mind sacrificing the rights of a few persons in the name of the public interest eventually may end up sacrificing the rights of the public in the name of the public interest.

The equation of public interest with public use is a dangerous principle to accept. It means that the government theoretically could seize anyone's property for any reason that an official claimed was in the public interest if he could justify it to the satisfaction of the court. Every citizen has the responsibility of questioning the decisions of the Supreme Court. The Court is not infallible in its interpretation of the law; and its decisions can be reversed.

POWER OF FREE ENTERPRISE

According to certain experts, things are getting worse in urban housing. In a report of the President's Commission on National Goals in 1960, Catherine Bauer Wurster stated:

There is a great deal of seriously substandard housing in American communities, and spreading "gray areas" in various stages of actual or potential decay, plus commercial and industrial blight. It is quite evident that economic progress alone does not cure these evils, and that local governments cannot do the necessary job alone. . . .[8]

[8] "Framework for an Urban Society," *Goals for Americans—The Report of the President's Commission on National Goals* (Englewood Cliffs, New Jersey, Prentice-Hall, Inc., 1960), p. 229.

Others have made similar statements. If they are correct, it seems that we are in for serious trouble. Fortunately, the actual developments of recent years contradict these pessimistic opinions.

Impressive progress has been made toward achieving the objectives set forth by Congress in 1949. Over-all housing conditions have improved dramatically, in cities and outside of cities, for the poor and for the rich, and for the nonwhites as well as the whites. This progress has been furthered by businessmen operating in the free marketplace. The improvements in housing quality and the increase in the housing supply accomplished through private enterprise are shown in Exhibit 1. To summarize some of the more important aspects of the record:

• Both the relative and absolute changes in housing quality between 1940 and 1960 were striking. In 1940, 51% of all housing in the United States was considered standard or sound; in 1950 the proportion had moved up to 63%; and in 1960, fully 81% was classified as standard. If this trend continues, it is likely that the Census of 1970 will reveal that 90% to 95% of all our housing is standard.

• From 1950 to 1960 alone the total number of standard homes increased from 29.1 million to 47.4 million, a 63% increase in just ten years. This increase of over 18 million standard homes was the result of both new construction and rehabilitation. Over 12 million new units were built, and the number of substandard units declined from 17 million to under 11 million. Virtually all of this was accomplished by private construction, rehabilitation, and demolition efforts; massive amounts of private funds were invested in housing. These investments were in no way connected with the federal urban renewal program.

• From 1945 to 1960, private mortgage debt outstanding increased by almost $170 billion. Although approximately 40% of this total was insured by the federal government through the Federal Housing Administration and the Veterans Administration, this does not mean that the government was responsible for the increase in housing quality. The underlying demand for housing and the growing income of those who desired better housing were clearly the predominating factors. The effect of government insurance pro-

EXHIBIT 1
The housing story

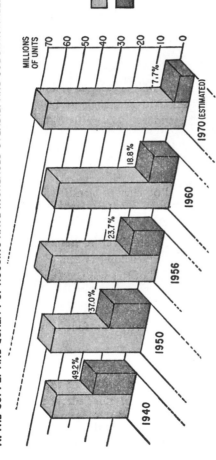

A. THE SUPPLY AND QUALITY OF HOUSING HAVE INCREASED STEADILY AND SUBSTANTIALLY SINCE 1940.

MILLIONS OF UNITS

70
60
50
40
30
20
10
0

49.2%
1940

37.0%
1950

23.7%
1956

18.8%
1960

7.7%
1970 (ESTIMATED)

KEYS

TOTAL U.S. HOUSING INVENTORY

SUBSTANDARD HOUSING

B. THE QUALITY OF HOUSING IN LARGE CITIES IS STEADILY IMPROVING.

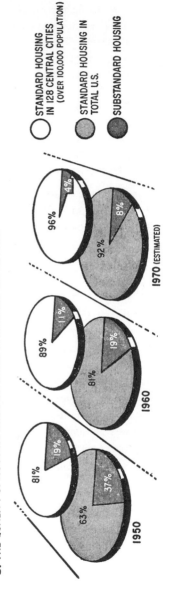

81%
19%
63%
37%
1950

89%
11%
81%
19%
1960

96%
4%
92%
8%
1970 (ESTIMATED)

STANDARD HOUSING IN 128 CENTRAL CITIES (OVER 100,000 POPULATION)

STANDARD HOUSING IN TOTAL U.S.

SUBSTANDARD HOUSING

C. IN ALL REGIONS THE PROPORTION OF SUBSTANDARD HOUSING IS BEING REDUCED.

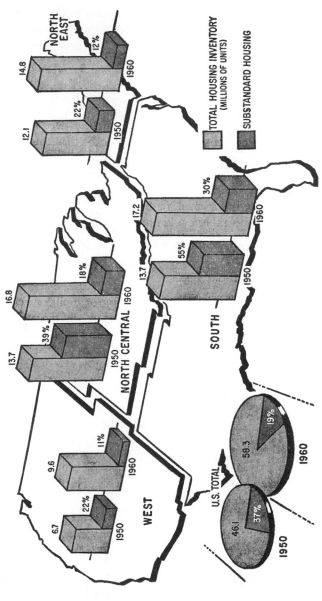

NORTH EAST
12.1 — 1950 — 22%
14.8 — 1960 — 12%

NORTH CENTRAL
13.7 — 1950 — 39%
16.8 — 1960 — 18%

WEST
6.7 — 1950 — 22%
9.6 — 1960 — 11%

SOUTH
13.7 — 1950 — 55%
17.2 — 1960 — 30%

U.S. TOTAL
46.1 — 1950 — 37%
58.3 — 1960 — 19%

TOTAL HOUSING INVENTORY
(MILLIONS OF UNITS)

SUBSTANDARD HOUSING

SOURCES: A.—*Hearing Before a Subcommittee of the Committee on Banking and Currency*, U.S. Senate, 87th Congress, Housing Legislation of 1961, p. 463; B. and C.—U.S. Bureau of the Census, 1950 and 1960.

grams was probably to produce a slight increase in the amount of housing starts; but it should be kept in mind that if these government insurance programs had not existed, private insurance companies, such as the Mortgage Guaranty Insurance Corporation, would have surely developed at a much faster rate than they did.

• The amount of really bad housing—that classified as dilapidated by the Bureau of the Census—declined from 9.8% in 1950 to 5.2% in 1960. The 1960 over-all vacancy rate was slightly over 9%. The number of dilapidated homes was actually smaller than the number of vacant homes. Vacancy rates were much higher for poor housing than for good housing. In 1960, 6.8% of the standard housing was vacant, whereas the vacancy rate was 20% for dilapidated housing. Then, as now, the fact seemed to be that there were a certain number of people who either could not or would not spend enough money to rent or to buy the available standard housing.

HOUSING FOR MINORITIES

It is sometimes charged that the free working of capitalism cannot produce gains for some groups of people, particularly the nonwhite population. Many are convinced that the only answer must lie in the direction of greater government intervention and higher public subsidies.

In fact, the nonwhite population of the United States has enjoyed a very substantial increase in the quality of its housing. From 1950 to 1960 there was an over-all net increase of 1,813,000 standard units and a decrease of 537,000 substandard units. Between 1950 and 1960, the percent of standard housing occupied by nonwhites doubled—going from 28% to 56%. Most of the bad housing is now located in the South, where only 38% is standard. In the Northeast, 77% is standard; in the North Central, 73%; in the West, 79%. In comparisons like this it should be remembered that the rents paid by whites are about 29% higher than those paid by nonwhites, and that the values of the homes owned by whites are over 82% higher.

The housing conditions of nonwhites have improved substantially, and although the quality of their housing does not yet equal that of the whites, it is rapidly approaching it, particularly in areas outside the South. Compared to the federal urban renewal program, the private marketplace is making swift, substantial progress.

MARCHING METROPOLISES

The same type of improvement in housing quality that has taken place throughout the country has taken place in our cities. In 1960, fully 88.6% of the housing located in central cities of over 100,000 population was classified as standard. In these same 128 central cities, the dilapidated housing had declined to slightly over 3% of the total. In our 13 largest cities, taken as a group, 90.1% of all housing was standard in 1960; only 2.6% was dilapidated.

Housing quality in cities has been continually improving, and now, as in the past, housing in cities is substantially better than in the country taken as a whole. Today the bulk of the relatively small amount of bad housing that still exists lies outside of our cities, particularly in the rural areas. Only 18% of the substandard housing lies within cities having populations of more than 100,000. There appears to be a definite correlation between the degree of urbanization and the amount of good housing.

Since the war, construction activity has been booming all over the United States and its cities. From 1950 to 1960, approximately $52.6 billion of new building construction went up in cities with populations over 100,000. Only a little over 1% of this was urban renewal construction. If our cities are "declining," as is often claimed, how does one account for the steady increase in building activity?

What about the worrisome claim that the middle-income group is disappearing from the city? The city of the future is prophesied by some as the city of the very rich and the very poor. The facts indicate that this has not happened and probably will not happen. If we define "middle-income" as $4,000 to $10,000 a year, we find that almost 57% of all people living in large cities fall within this range. In fact, the income distribution in large cities is roughly the same as that for the country as a whole. Today's city is not the city of the very rich and the very poor; it is predominantly the city of the middle-income group.

By any objective measure, the indications are clear that our cities—in over-all terms—are continually improving and that today they are better than they ever were before.

Validity of Data

The foregoing facts were taken from the data on housing quality collected every ten years by the Bureau of the Census. These Census data were the result of observations made by 150,000 enumerators, all of whom were given careful instructions on how to classify housing.

The three categories used in 1960 were "sound," "deteriorating," and "dilapidated." Categories or definitions of categories vary slightly from decade to decade, but adjustments were made to make the data comparable in time, and the effect of the slightly changed definitions was negligible. Generally speaking, "sound" housing has no defects or has slight defects that would normally be corrected during regular maintenance (lack of paint, for example). "Deteriorating" housing needs more repair than that required by normal maintenance (a shaky porch or broken plaster, for example). "Dilapidated" housing does not provide safe and adequate shelter.

Although the Bureau of the Census data can be criticized, they are by far the best available today—most accurate, broadest in scope, and most consistent over time. I emphasize this because a considerable number of self-styled experts consider their lone opinions superior to those of 150,000 trained enumerators. They would justify their conclusion that the city or housing is deteriorating solely on the basis of their visual impressions. This is not a valid way to measure changes in housing quality. The amateur's experience is very limited, his standards cannot be identified, and there is no way of knowing whether his standards change from year to year.

The next time you hear that the city is deteriorating, ask: "In what way? By whose standard?"

CONCLUSION

Since 1949 two different methods have been used to grapple with the "problems" of housing and cities. One of these is basically the system of free enterprise, guided by the complex interplay of the marketplace. The other force is the federal urban renewal program, guided by over-all plans prepared by city planning experts and backed up with the taxpayers' money and the police power of the government.

The facts tell us that private enterprise has made enormous gains, while the federal program has not. Contrast, for example, the fantastic increase of 18 million homes in areas outside urban renewal projects with the net decrease of homes within urban renewal projects. Consider also the decrease in low-rent housing and the increase in high-rent housing in the urban renewal areas; urban renewal actually subsidizes high-income groups and hurts low-income groups. Add to this the destruction of businesses and the forcible displacement of people from their homes. The program endangers the right of private property—commercial and residential —in its equating of public interest with public use.

The over-all results of the government program, when compared to the results of private forces, are negligible. Its over-all costs, when compared with its results, are high. On balance, the federal urban renewal program has accomplished little of benefit in the past, and it appears doubtful that it will do better in the future.

However, there are times when participating in a federal urban renewal project—as a contractor, a banker, or a businessman—may be attractive if only short-run gains or profits are considered. Participation may make it possible for a businessman to get that location he wants from an owner who has been unwilling to sell; it may renovate an adjacent area and thus increase the value of his property; it may eliminate buildings that are visually offensive to him; and he may even make some money out of it.

But in supporting the program for these or other reasons, the businessman should be aware that he is supporting a government program that, in the long run, is detrimental to his own interests. It uses the concept of eminent domain in such a way that private property—business as well as residential—can be taken and resold by the government to other private persons for their own use simply because it is supposed to be in the public interest. It implies acceptance of the idea that private enterprise cannot work effectively in the field of housing and that government must intervene, when, in fact, this is not true. It subsidizes some businesses and construction interests that are in direct competition with those of other private businessmen. During execution it lowers the tax base of the city—in some cases perhaps permanently—and thus increases the tax burden for the rest of the city.

And, finally, the businessman may be hurt directly when the local renewal authorities decide that the area in which *he* is located is blighted! The irony of Washington's urban renewal program is that without the enthusiastic collaboration of many businessmen it would come to a grinding halt.

In my judgment, the program should be repealed now. This could be accomplished simply by not authorizing any new projects. All projects currently under contract could be carried through to completion if the individual cities desired to do so.

As the Greek philosopher Aristotle stated more than 2,200 years ago: "Even when laws have been written down, they ought not always to remain unaltered."

What would be the results of such clear-cut, positive action? Would slums proliferate? Would housing get worse? Would cities die? Clearly, *no*. The record of what has been achieved outside of the federal urban renewal program by private forces is concrete evidence of what can be done by an essentially free-enterprise economic system. If this is what can be accomplished by free enterprise, the rational course of action is to encourage it to function, not to attack it or to sabotage it.

20 Urban Renewal Realistically Reappraised*

ROBERT P. GROBERG

Recent—and often misguided—critical outpourings against urban renewal justify an effort to determine realistically the actual and potential contribution of government to the solution of urban problems. Broadly defined, urban renewal can encompass all public and private efforts to improve city form and life. Realism requires recognition at the outset that there are no panaceas for every problem a city may possess and that some "solutions" create or emphasize other problems. Equally, realism requires careful consideration of the genesis and purposes of government programs with limited objectives so that criticism of them relates to their efforts and not to the broader notion of urban renewal goals. One recent attempt at major analysis[1] has gone astray partly because its author failed to see clearly the historical perspective and the limits of federal aid for slum clearance and redevelopment authorized by Congress under the Housing Act of 1949 and its amendments.[2]

* Reprinted with permission from a symposium, *Urban Problems and Prospects,* appearing in *Law and Contemporary Problems,* Vol. 30, No. 1 (Winter 1965), published by the Duke University School of Law, Durham, North Carolina. Copyright © 1965 by Duke University.

[1] MARTIN ANDERSON, THE FEDERAL BULLDOZER (1964) [hereinafter cited as ANDERSON]. [An article by Anderson summarizing his findings is included in Chapter 19 of this volume.—Ed.]

[2] Note that the 1949 Act authorized federal loans and grants for what was defined as "slum clearance and redevelopment" and is now often cited as "urban redevelopment." The term "urban renewal" did not come into use until the Housing Act of 1954 amended and broadened the 1949 program to encompass

509

The author of *The Federal Bulldozer* views this urban redevelopment assistance as though it had been expected by the Congress to solve *all* national housing problems. He cites the 1949 Declaration of National Housing Policy, preface to a comprehensive housing act with six separate titles, as though that declaration pertained only to title I. He then proceeds to condemn urban renewal for not achieving the aims of titles II, III, IV, V, VI, and other national housing efforts. *The Federal Bulldozer* is based on the assumption that federal assistance for local slum clearance and redevelopment projects was meant to achieve the housing aims of such other programs as low-rent public housing and FHA mortgage insurance. By incorporating these and other myths in his analysis, he began with unrealistic expectations for urban renewal efforts undertaken with federal assistance.

I. URBAN RENEWAL IS A LOCAL PROGRAM

Another myth incorporated into *The Federal Bulldozer* is that there is a separate, monolithic "federal urban renewal program" run from Washington by decree. The author completely misunderstands that urban renewal is a local program. He makes it appear that the power to plan, acquire, and prepare project sites for redevelopment or rehabilitation is vested in the federal government and based on an opinion of the United States Supreme Court. He does not recognize that the federal government cannot initiate any project. He does not mention that there can be no urban renewal project anywhere unless:

—a state legislature has first adopted an enabling law to give cities the governmental power for urban renewal, and some forty-eight states have;

—an elected city council has first organized an operating local renewal agency, and some 800 cities have;

—the same city council has first approved the project, and some 1600 projects have been so approved;

—the local government has first authorized local public expenditures

---

a city-wide program—including renewal of commercial and industrial areas—rather than individual projects. With new emphasis on code enforcement, structural rehabilitation and neighborhood conservation, the objectives were extended to slum prevention as well as slum clearance. Amendments since then have sought to improve the assistance and provide better tools to achieve the program's goals.

to supplement federal funds, and more than one billion dollars in local public funds have been so approved to back the program;
—local citizens are participating in the urban renewal process, as required by law, and citizens everywhere are so doing.

By ignoring these facts, he never explains that the program depends completely on active local political support, given through the established system of representative government. The author does not state that the federal government neither operates any bulldozer, nor acquires any property for any urban renewal project. Instead, he alleges that "the federal urban renewal program is a firmly entrenched giant, reaching into virtually every important city in the United States . . ."[3] and falsely claims that "the federal government . . . will forcibly displace . . . American citizens . . ."[4] and that "the Urban Renewal Administration reported . . . that . . . businesses had already been acquired by them [*i.e.*, the URA] in urban renewal projects throughout the United States. . . ."[5] The federal government cannot select a project area, cannot prepare a plan, cannot acquire property, cannot demolish dilapidated structures, cannot sell the land or install the public improvements. Yet these are the critical steps in urban renewal projects. This misleading emphasis on the "federal" role in urban renewal programs all but obscures the fact that the powers to carry out urban renewal derive from state enabling legislation.[6]

In fact, some twenty-five states had slum clearance and redevelopment legislation of some kind prior to the Housing Act of 1949. New York state, for example, passed a constitutional amendment in 1938 and enacted legislation in 1942 authorizing slum clearance and redevelopment projects. State enabling acts have withstood constitutional attacks based on state and federal constitutional provisions beginning in 1947 in Pennsylvania.[7] By 1954 (when the U.S. Supreme Court upheld redevelopment legislation for the District of Columbia),[8] the courts in twenty-one states had reviewed such

---

[3] ANDERSON 33.
[4] *Id.* at 55.
[5] *Id.* at 68.
[6] For a summary and citations to state enabling acts, see HOUSING AND HOME FINANCE AGENCY, LIST OF CITATIONS TO STATUTES, CONSTITUTIONAL PROVISIONS, AND COURT DECISIONS (1962).
[7] Belovsky v. Redevelopment Authority of the City of Philadelphia, 357 Pa. 329, 54 A.2d 277 (1947).
[8] Berman v. Parker, 358 U.S. 269 (1954).

legislation, and in all but two states had upheld the constitutionality of urban redevelopment. At present urban renewal legislation has been tested and upheld in the highest courts of thirty-three states. Only in South Carolina, Georgia, and Florida has such legislation successfully been assailed. In Georgia a later constitutional amendment authorized the undertaking of urban renewal, while in Florida the position originally taken has been modified substantially by the state's highest court. In short, the author of *The Federal Bulldozer* seems to have been quite unaware, as are many opponents of urban renewal, that if his suggestion for "repeal" of the "federal" urban renewal program were adopted (cf. chapter fourteen), the program's authority would not be impaired at all because, with constitutional powers derived from the states, it is locally run.

II. THE USE OF THE POWER OF EMINENT DOMAIN IN URBAN RENEWAL RESTS ON A LONG TRADITION OF STATE COURT DECISIONS

At this late date complaints concerning the constitutional basis of urban renewal would seem ill-timed.[9] They may arise from those who ignore or misread the historical basis for government action to solve the problems of society. Foes of urban renewal have attempted to create a mythology with respect to the "inviolate" right of private property in support of their contention that government should not have the power to act in removing slums, and they have focused their attacks on the Supreme Court of the United States: "The federal urban renewal program has drastically altered the traditional concept of eminent domain; it is doubtful if any of the founding fathers could recognize it in its present form."[10] Instead of citing "the founding fathers," they cite Pitt and Blackstone, the latter in a classic example of tearing statements from context: "Regard of the law for private property is so great that it will not authorize the least violation of it, not even for the general good of the whole community; for it would be dangerous to allow any private man, or even any public tribunal, to be the judge of this

---

[9] For a well-reasoned discussion of these issues, see COLEMAN WOODBURY (ED.), URBAN REDEVELOPMENT: PROBLEMS AND PRACTICES, pt. IV, "Eminent Domain in Acquiring Subdivision and Open Land in Redevelopment Programs: A Question of Public Use" (1953).

[10] ANDERSON 188.

common good. . . ." The preceding lines are the full text of a quote from *The Federal Bulldozer*.[11] The identical passage is also cited in a book published in 1962.[12] Both books ignored what came before and what followed in Blackstone's *Commentaries*. The quoted passage is preceded in Blackstone by the phrase "save only by the laws of the land" and is followed by: "In this and similar cases the legislature alone can, and indeed frequently does, interpose, and compel the individual to acquiesce . . . by giving him a full indemnification and equivalent for the injury thereby sustained."[13] Thus, while Blackstone recognized the importance of private property, he also acknowledged that the legislature could authorize the taking of property for proper purposes upon payment of just compensation to the owner. This view was incorporated in the fifth amendment to the United States Constitution: ". . . nor shall private property be taken for public use without just compensation." It was written into some, but not all state constitutions.[14] But its incorporation in the federal and state constitutions still left to the legislatures the determination of what were proper purposes for the use of eminent domain.

In some states from the very start it was clear that private uses served public purposes. For instance, Idaho's constitution of 1890, cited by Professor Haar:[15]

The necessary use of lands for the construction of reservoirs or storage basins, for the purpose of irrigation, or for rights of way for the construction of canals, ditches . . . or for the drainage of mines . . . or any other use necessary to the complete development of the material resources of the state, or the preservation of the health of its inhabitants, is hereby declared to be a public use and subject to the regulation and control of the state.

Such state constitutional provisions or amendments were adopted over a period from 1780 (Massachusetts) to 1938 (New York).

11 *Id.* at 185.
12 THOMAS F. JOHNSON, JAMES R. MORRIS & JOSEPH G. BUTTS, RENEWING AMERICA'S CITIES ch. III, at 46 (The Institute for Social Science Research, 1962).
13 I WILLIAM BLACKSTONE, COMMENTARIES ON THE LAWS OF ENGLAND 138 (Sharswood ed. 1895).
14 Professor Charles M. Haar of the Harvard Law School observes that: "The constitutions of most of the thirteen original states did not require compensation upon the condemnation of land. . . . But with the establishment of roads, limitations began to appear. . . ." CHARLES M. HAAR, LAND USE PLANNING 470 (1959).
15 *Id.* at 411.

The courts of most states have ruled that "public use," as it appears in state constitutional provisions authorizing takings of private property by eminent domain, is equivalent to "public benefit." As one leading text puts it:[16]

Anything that tends to enlarge the resources, increase the industrial advantages and promote the productive power of any considerable number of the inhabitants of a section of a state, or which leads to the growth of towns and the creation of new resources for the employment of capital prosperity of the whole community and, giving the constitution a broad and comprehensive interpretation, constitutes a public use. Under this view it has been held that the scope of eminent domain has been made as broad as the powers under the police and tax provisions of the constitution.

In accord with this view innumerable state legislatures and courts have authorized eminent domain proceedings in behalf of mills, railroads, power companies, private universities, and for other private concerns whose operations were considered to involve "public benefit." In these instances the property was taken by a *private* enterprise through a judicial proceeding which assured the payment of just compensation to the property owner; the title was not acquired by a public body or agency.

On the other hand, in urban renewal programs the property is acquired by a local *public* agency pursuant to the provisions and safeguards of an urban renewal plan adopted by a city council or other local governing body, after public hearings. Although most courts consider the elimination of the slum to be the public purpose for which the power of eminent domain may be employed, they also recognize that the prevention of future slums is a related public purpose. The existence of an official urban renewal plan is considered by these courts to be necessary to assure that this public purpose is served.

Thus, there is a tradition of broad interpretation of the term "public use" which would justify the use of eminent domain for urban redevelopment despite the fact that the property might eventually end up in private ownership. But in line with the finding that slum clearance and prevention are the public purposes which justify the employment of eminent domain in urban renewal, most courts have held that the disposition of the land is *incidental*, and

[16] PHILIP NICHOLS, THE LAW OF EMINENT DOMAIN § 7.2 (Sackman & Van Brunt, 3d ed. rev., 1963).

the fact that it may be sold to private parties for private use does not vitiate the public purpose of slum clearance.

There is a minority view which holds in South Carolina where the sale of such land must be to public bodies. The foes of urban renewal hold fast to this narrow position, and they interpret the language of the fifth amendment of the United States Constitution literally. Not only does this fly in the face of the tradition described above, it flies in the face of what is now thoroughly understood to constitute the general well-being of society in the twentieth century. The following quote from a California court opinion which upheld an urban renewal project on predominantly vacant land sums it up:[17]

> It might be pointed out that as our community life becomes more complex, our cities grow and become overcrowded, and the need to use for the benefit of the public areas which are not adapted to the pressing needs of the public becomes more imperative, a broader concept of what is a public use is necessitated. Fifty years ago no court would have interpreted, under the eminent domain statutes, slum clearance even for public housing as a public use, and yet, it is now so recognized. To hold that clearance of blighted areas as characterized by the [California] act and as shown in this case and the redevelopment of such areas as contemplated here are not public uses, is to view present day conditions under the myopic eyes of years now gone.

III. HOW CRITICS MEASURE URBAN RENEWAL RESULTS

With a mistaken view of its purposes and of how it works, *The Federal Bulldozer* proceeds to measure the accomplishments of federally-aided urban renewal in a unique and misleading way. By measuring aggregate national figures with a premature cut-off date the book reveals little more about urban renewal than that the process takes time, a fact that urban renewal officials had long before conceded.[18]

The unfortunate consequence of the "aggregate" view is that it focuses:

[17] Redevelopment Agency of City and County of San Francisco et al. v. Hayes et al., 122 Cal. A.2d 777, 802–03, 266 P.2d 105, 122 (1954).

[18] Perhaps this confirmation that it takes time to renew cities is useful. The old image of urban renewal—as a type of public works operation that can be planned, scheduled and executed with precision and dispatch—dies hard. The old view has led congressmen and others to emphasize the number of projects completed—a matter of federal bookkeeping—rather than real accomplishments.

—on the value of slum areas eliminated;

—on "low rent" dwellings (a euphemism for slums) demolished;

—on tax revenues lost (rather than decline stopped);

—on vacant land (rather than potential redevelopment).

A. *Real Estate Tax Increases Overlooked*

By considering all projects together, those just beginning demolition as well as those with new construction completed, it is possible to show—with an expanding program—that more buildings have been eliminated than have been constructed. Take, for example, the treatment of real estate taxes in *The Federal Bulldozer.*

The author alleges that tax increases in urban renewal are a "myth." He sets up sharply contrasting facts, based on "admittedly rough" estimates, employed because he believed "the federal government does not publish figures" on taxes. By estimating the total value of real estate "destroyed" up to 1961 and comparing it to his estimate of the "total amount of private construction started" he derived the conclusion: ". . . if you destroy $650–$700 million of real estate and construct about $400 million, it is apparent that tax revenues must decrease."[19] Aside from ignoring the declining tax revenues and the increasing cost of municipal services in slum areas, the author overlooked published government figures which showed that taxes had, in fact, increased.

Published testimony of Urban Renewal Commissioner William L. Slayton,[20] cited on page fourteen of *The Federal Bulldozer* for a different point, showed that by 1963 actual assessed valuation had increased from $168 million to $694 million for 185 project areas with land disposition completed. This indicated a 312 percent increase, notwithstanding the fact that about one-fourth the taxable property before redevelopment was converted to public and other nontaxable uses. Why the dramatic difference between the author's estimates and the Commissioner's testimony? URA figures compare taxes before and after redevelopment in the *same* projects. The author compares his estimate of the assessed value of slum structures demolished to his estimate of the value of new construction. Thus, he compares demolition in 485 projects with construction on 191

---

[19] ANDERSON 166.

[20] *Hearings on Urban Renewal Before the Subcomm. on Housing of the House Comm. on Banking and Currency,* 88th Cong., 1st Sess. 472 (1963).

projects. Without explaining the significance of this comparison he simply shows a tax loss with which he supports his "myth" claim. Such a showing is not hard to make. Stated another way, it means that when the first slum building was demolished in the first urban renewal project, the taxes on it, indeed, were reduced.

URA's figures for all projects in which land disposition is complete provide a more accurate and meaningful picture, since they relate demolition to *its* replacement construction. For the individual city, of course, these figures must be examined further. The local share of project cost and the period during which land is vacant and no taxes are earned are commonly offset against increased taxes from new construction. Although impressive increases have been frequently reported, not all projects are undertaken for their tax benefits. Public, civic or institutional redevelopment, while taking land off the tax rolls, benefit immediately surrounding areas and cities as a whole, as demonstrated by the Lincoln Square project in New York City with its Center for the Performing Arts. Even tax-producing projects are redeveloped under plans which limit the intensity of use and thus do not necessarily return as much as a prior, overintensive use. Furthermore, there are other considerations that in an economic sense must be weighed against the numerical increase in taxes, a few of which are cited in *The Federal Bulldozer*. One important one, ignored in the book, is the significance to a city of securing new construction within the city boundaries, such as new apartments or the Macy department store which located in downtown New Haven, rather than in the suburbs. Although the market which Macy's has tapped could perhaps have been reached from a suburban location, the tax and other economic consequences for New Haven are quite different with the downtown location.

Finally, the author's "myth" regarding taxes in urban renewal projects seems to cut no ice with the banking firms that have purchased municipal bonds authorized in the state of California and elsewhere to finance urban redevelopment projects. The bonds are pledged against and are repaid out of the actual increased taxes from project areas.

Thus, the effects of urban renewal projects on city finances must be measured in various ways to derive valid conclusions about the economic value of urban renewal for an individual community. A large tax gain from a single project does not solve a city's financial problems, nor does a decrease from a single project necessarily aggravate them.

B. *Family Relocation Achievements Discounted*

The most common charge of urban renewal critics is that the program is creating new slums by displacing families from old ones. These critics discount the facts stated in official reports and ignore the positive contribution which urban renewal has made by setting a new standard of public responsibility for those displaced by government activity. They emphasize such factors as neighborhood "disruption," increased rents and the small percentage of families whose housing conditions are not improved. While these are admittedly important problems which receive priority attention from urban renewal practitioners, they should be kept in proper perspective.

Among the provisions of title I of the Housing Act of 1949, local government for the first time was given responsibility for helping people who are about to be displaced by slum clearance activities to find and move into decent housing—before displacement can take place. No other public program ever had assumed such responsibility. The original legal requirement ("that there be a feasible method" for relocating displaced families from the project area) has been extended since 1949 to include individuals and businesses. The record now stands for urban renewal at eighty percent of all displaced families rehoused into standard accommodations.

In addition to relocation planning and services, in 1956 urban renewal provided, for the first time, government payments for moving expenses and loss of property, and, beginning in 1964, special federal rent supplements for displaced low-income families and for single aged people, as well as extra adjustment payments for displaced small businesses.

Since this assumption of public responsibility by urban renewal, other public programs—highway construction in 1962, public housing in 1964—have begun providing assistance and payments. The U.S. Advisory Commission on Intergovernmental Relations has recommended that the urban renewal relocation requirements for helping those displaced be adopted by all federal grant-in-aid programs. The Select Subcommittee on Real Property Acquisition, U.S. House of Representatives, under the chairmanship of Representative Clifford Davis of Tennessee, made similar recommendations.

Critics take different views of these accomplishments. By assuming that urban renewal is *the* nation's housing program, they find it possible to claim relocation failure when displaced families are not rehoused in project areas, when new housing built on project land is not for low-income families, or when no housing at all is constructed in project areas. They also cite statistics for support: 126,000 "low income" units demolished, against only 28,000 constructed, only 3,000 of which were for low-income families. Furthermore, they discount the reports of local public agencies, assembled by the Urban Renewal Administration, which have consistently shown that overall, about eighty percent of all families displaced have relocated into decent housing. For families whose whereabouts are definitely known, the figure now stands at over ninety percent relocated in standard housing, as recently confirmed by a study of 2,300 such families in 132 cities, undertaken by the Bureau of the Census in 1964.

What evidence is there for doubting the validity of these figures? *The Federal Bulldozer* alludes to a single source in support of the claim that families relocated from urban renewal have not found better housing:[21] "In 1961 the School of Public Administration of the University of Southern California concluded a four-year inquiry into urban renewal relocation programs in 41 cities throughout the United States."

The Federal Bulldozer does not cite the report of this inquiry; it cites only one article describing it.[22] The book's repeated references to this article do not mention that Professor Reynolds describes families displaced *both* by public housing construction and urban renewal, nor do they mention that the article refers only to the mid-1950s. In at least ten of the forty-one cities surveyed, urban renewal relocation did not start until 1958 or later. The book does not mention that this article, indicating poor relocation results wherever local agencies did not (or could not) provide relocation

[21] ANDERSON 60. *The Federal Bulldozer's* repeated use of the term "evicted" for "displaced" or "relocated" belies the fact that a cumulative total of less than 1.1%, or 1,902, of all 175,644 families who had moved from urban renewal projects by mid-1964 had been evicted.
[22] Reynolds, *What Do We Know About Our Experience With Relocation?*, J. INTERGROUP RELATIONS 342 (1961).

services, singles out the relative success of urban renewal relocation services:[23]

> The high correlation existing between proffered thorough-going
> counseling services for relocatees in at least fifteen municipalities and
> the great number of satisfactory relocations therein, especially in regard
> to the minimization of substandardness and transiency in the off-site
> dwellings, is noteworthy.

The author of *The Federal Bulldozer* and others who cite Mr.
Reynolds' article seem to have been unaware that, as a former staff
member of the Philadelphia Housing Authority, he was particularly
interested in stimulating planned relocation efforts and counseling
services in displacement caused by public housing construction. Mr.
Reynolds already had published another article about this same
study[24] which concluded that "city-aided families paid lower rent
increases and now have better housing than their self-relocated
counterparts. Clearly the counseling–advisory service has been well
worth the effort."

Good housing, important for improving social conditions, is not
alone sufficient to solve the problems of disadvantaged families.
Rehousing "services," sometimes limited in the earliest years of the
program to the mere provision of lists of vacancies, have been
expanded in many cities to include a full range of social counseling
and services, with such aids as auto transportation to inspect relocation housing, referrals to health and welfare agencies, advice on
financing, assistance in packing, and help in furnishing the new
home. The new poverty program promises still more assistance for
those least able to cope with the consequences of relocation and
should provide more of the tools needed to improve city life as well
as city environment.

C. *Private Investment Magnitude Mistaken*

A unique feature of the Housing Act of 1949 was that private
enterprise was expected to undertake most of the redevelopment,
thus making possible a large scale program with limited public
expenditures. At least one critic contests this:[25]

[23] *Id.* at 345.
[24] Reynolds, *Family Relocation Can Succeed in Urban Renewal Work,* The
U.S. Municipal News, April 15, 1960.
[25] See ANDERSON 142.

The view that the public will finance and pay for most of the cost of urban renewal differs significantly from the current views by most of the people associated with the program. This is possibly the most significant conclusion coming out of this study.

But the author's "most significant conclusion" is based on a confusion of cost and expense (compounded by a half-billion-dollar misunderstanding) and a unique interpretation of "finance" (carried further by a mistaken assumption and an erroneous prediction).

The experience of local public agencies, as reported by the Urban Renewal Administration from time to time, indicates that for each dollar of *federal grant*, from four to six dollars of private construction has occurred. These figures compare federal grants to actual construction costs reported for projects in execution with land sold and rebuilding under way. By extending this ratio to the total of federal grants authorized up to 1964 ($4.7 billion) it is possible to estimate a private investment potential of from $18.8 to $28.2 billion.

The author of *The Federal Bulldozer* was attracted to study urban renewal by reports of this investment potential. Unfortunately, his analysis went astray. He substituted his approximation of project *expenditures* for capital *grants* and derived a different ratio which, he claims, disproves the government's four- or six-to-one experience. His findings, thus, disprove nothing with respect to the government's reported ratio. They do prove, however, that he was not fully aware of the meaning of the government's comparison.

In addition to mixing cost and expenditures, he committed a significant definitional error which led to a half-billion dollar misunderstanding. In discussing project expenditures he stated that "refunded" loans amounted to $554 million and are essentially the same as outstanding loans. But refunded loans, having been paid off, are *not* the same as "outstanding loans." If they were, a homeowner's $20,000 mortgage debt, when refinanced at a lower interest rate, would be counted as a $40,000 debt. The author misunderstood the nature of a refunded loan and defined it as "one that has come due and has been refinanced or extended past its original due date." But refunded loans, having been refinanced from a different source, are *not* extended. His half-billion dollar misunderstanding is taken as of 1962. For his analysis of project expenditures, he took 1960 figures, and thus reduced the error to $347 million.

The author's substitute ratio comes to $1,430 million "public money spent" (including the extra $347 million of refunded money and an additional $17 million in planning advances that are counted twice) which he compares to $460 million in private investment. His expressed interest in the public money figure is to suggest that the large amount of cash needed for urban renewal project operations as the program grows "might put significant demands on the financial markets in the near future, as well as affect the government's credit or interest rate position."[25a] He does not explain why this might be so. Considering that only a portion is outstanding at any one time, and that approximately ninety percent of temporary loans are privately held, there is no evidence that the effect will be adverse.[26]

In discussing his estimated $460 million private investment figure the author reflects his unique interpretation of the role of the Federal National Mortgage Association (FNMA) in financing urban renewal construction. He considers FNMA to be a long term direct investor, rather than a temporary lender.

FNMA helps to support, under a congressional charter, special housing programs for which private market financial investment may be inadequate from time to time. FNMA purchases FHA-insured mortgages for urban renewal residential construction, but it also sells them—to the private market. This sales activity, which has significantly increased in recent years, has reflected not only the greater volume of funds that was made available for mortgage financing, but also the general recognition accorded by the private mortgage lending industry to the soundness and credit-worthiness of the mortgages purchased by FNMA under its special support programs such as the one for urban renewal housing.

The author of *The Federal Bulldozer* mistakenly assumed that

[25a] *Id.* at 28.

[26] Another important urban renewal role for private enterprise, not often considered in evaluating the program, has been the provision of working capital for project execution activities. Temporary loan notes, backed by the government, have been purchased by banking institutions at interest rates below the rate charged for direct federal loans. When the program began most loans were direct federal, but gradually private lenders have increased their participation until they account for approximately 90% of the funds borrowed by local public agencies to finance urban renewal project operations. These loans are repaid out of federal grants, the proceeds from land sales, and local cash contributions.

"most commitments made by FNMA are exercised by the lenders" and he estimated the degree of FNMA involvement by calculating the percentage of mortgages insured by FHA that were either purchased *or* under commitment to be purchased by FNMA. He provided the following example for the year 1960, based on his mistaken assumption:[27]

As of December 31, 1960, FHA had insured about $296 million of mortgages in urban renewal areas. At that time FNMA had purchased or issued commitments to purchase $274 million or 92.5 percent of these mortgages.

But, in fact, lenders had not exercised "most" of their commitments. In attempting to trace the $274 million figure, the National Association of Housing and Redevelopment Officials obtained the following information from FNMA officials: FNMA purchased $102 million of the $277.6 million commitments made by 1960, for a thirty-seven percent "involvement," rather than the 92.5 percent cited by the author. As of December 31, 1964, FNMA's cumulative purchases were $209 million of its total $434 million commitments for FHA section 220 mortgages, or forty-eight percent involvement. FNMA's cumulative purchases up to 1962, the author's cut-off period, never exceeded forty-seven percent of commitments.

Until 1962, FHA-insured urban renewal mortgages depended almost exclusively on FNMA assistance. But housing financing conditions have changed dramatically since then, and FNMA has changed its regulations to encourage more private financing. As a result, and with a significant drop in mortgage interest rates nationally, private lending institutions have purchased so many FNMA-held mortgages and cancelled so many commitments that FNMA's share of FHA-insured urban renewal residential mortgages had dropped to an annual commitment rate of approximately four percent (or a cumulative rate of about twenty percent) in 1964. The trend that has resulted in this drop, although noted and discussed at length by the author, was completely misunderstood by him. The author erroneously predicted that FNMA's share of urban renewal mortgages would level off at somewhere over fifty percent. With the continued sharp decline in FNMA participation, the author's conclusions about the long-term public and private sources

[27] ANDERSON 133.

of funds for urban renewal residential construction, based on this prediction, are therefore discredited.

In addition to overstating the federal government's share of residential redevelopment financing efforts, through FNMA, *The Federal Bulldozer* claims that private funds for urban renewal commercial and industrial construction will not be forthcoming. The author based this claim on cumulative figures up to 1961 of $115 million in private nonresidential construction, but by the end of 1964, the figure for this category had grown to more than $1 billion. Together, the sharply-reduced FNMA participation, and the nine-fold increase (from $115 to $1,089 million) in private investment in commercial and industrial and institutional urban renewal construction have lowered the total share of "federal" money for "financing" private urban renewal construction from *The Federal Bulldozer's* alleged thirty-five percent to about five percent.[28] The book's conclusion about the significant federal share of the early 1961 total of $824 million redevelopment financing is based on an array of figures from the past that can no longer be used to interpret the nature of the program. By December 1964, the total construction in urban renewal areas had increased to $3,274 million and of that, private construction amounted to $2,258 million.[29]

D. *Private Redevelopers' Attitudes Misrepresented*

In addition to mistaking the amount of private investment in urban renewal, *The Federal Bulldozer* misrepresents the attitudes of private redevelopers. The author suggests that urban renewal was intended to provide quick and "lucrative" profits to redevelopers,

---

[28] Greater availability of private banking resources for construction in urban renewal areas was made possible by changes in regulations governing the nearly 2,000 members of the Federal Home Loan Bank system. The Housing Act of 1964 eased investment limitations so that members of the system may now invest up to 5% (or $3 billion) of their total assets in urban renewal construction. Furthermore, members are now, for the first time, authorized to become active redevelopers in their own right.

[29] It should be noted that the author does not discuss the new moderate-income housing program, § 221(d)(3), authorized by the Housing Act of 1961, which is entirely supported by FNMA. An updated review of the extent of FNMA involvement in all urban renewal residential development, however, would have to include § 221(d)(3) housing. It is reasonable to assume that most program analysts would place redevelopment expenditures for this housing in the public sector because of the below-market interest rate, which under § 221(d)(3) makes FNMA purchase of the mortgage inevitable, and, in effect, provides privately-built housing financing with what amounts to an indirect federal loan.

while an examination of the law and other public documents shows that the price redevelopers have to pay for the land is fair value for the uses specified for the project. The federal law and the contract between the local renewal agency—documents not cited in the book—require continued redeveloper participation until construction has been completed according to the specifications of the publicly-approved urban renewal plan. This required long-term approach is part and parcel of the public-private relationship and the application of various governmental mechanisms to achieve the objective of the Declaration of National Housing Policy that "private enterprise shall be encouraged to serve as large a part of the total need as it can" and that "governmental assistance shall be utilized where feasible to enable private enterprise to serve more of the total need."

The principal governmental financing mechanism for this purpose is the special FHA federal mortgage insurance for residential reconstruction in urban renewal areas.

The Federal Bulldozer's discussion of the role of the private redeveloper in urban renewal focuses on the point that[30]

Events are developing which seem to indicate that even some of the largest and most sophisticated private urban renewal redevelopers are becoming seriously disenchanted with the program.

To support this statement, the book cites the experiences of two well-known developers.[31] One of them, Marvin Gilman, was quoted to the effect:[32] "Yet, if we, as redevelopers, are to continue to sow, soon we shall have to reap, or one must be off to greener fields." When asked by the National Association of Housing and Redevelopment Officials to comment on this quotation, Mr. Gilman explained that it was taken out of context, and that he had been

[30] ANDERSON 121.
[31] Redeveloper William Zeckendorf is also cited in *The Federal Bulldozer* as having lost interest in urban renewal, with the observation that "For example, in recent years, Mr. Zeckendorf has sold off most of his urban renewal interests to other investors." ANDERSON 108. But, as has been widely reported in the press, Mr. Zeckendorf's sale of his urban renewal interests had little to do with his attitudes on urban renewal; instead, it was the result of pressures on his financial holdings, recently reviewed in considerable detail in Life, Feb. 12, 1965, p. 74. Another carefully researched article, Kay, *The Third Force in Urban Renewal*, Fortune, Oct. 1964, p. 130, covers the role of large private redevelopers' attitudes and includes an account of Zeckendorf's sale of his urban renewal interests. [The Kay article is included in Chapter 9 of this volume.—Ed.]
[32] ANDERSON 108.

talking about his impatience at the groundbreaking delays in one particular project. He added:

Martin Anderson has misused what I said in 1961 . . . when I was criticizing the delays caused by the lack of experience of all of us—in the private sector as well as the public sector.

Since 1961, the experience of developers has grown geometrically, and we have done much of the needed streamlining. This is exemplified by the fact that almost every developer I know is still interested in the program. I personally am anxious to expand my Baltimore project, and I have just broken ground on a new project in Wilmington.

Those of us who understand how urban renewal works, know that it was never meant to provide "tantalizing high profits," nor was it designed to provide a quick return for speculation. Redevelopment is a long-term investment that promises a fair return on dollar and labor invested.

The words of Leon Hickman, executive vice-president of the Aluminum Company of America (ALCOA) are used in *The Federal Bulldozer* as the author's final citation in chapter seven, italicized by him to emphasize the disenchantment of private redevelopers with urban renewal: [33] "Our experience as a seed money angel was early in the game and relatively painless. *But we have seen enough to know that we have had it.*" This citation was taken by the author from a July 1964 magazine article, "Urban Renewal Stands Condemned as a Costly Failure," which quoted a small part from a February 1964 speech by Mr. Hickman.

Had the author checked Mr. Hickman's speech[34] he would have found an eloquent exposition of the government's concept of partnership with private enterprise, and an explanation of how private investors have gradually been led into urban redevelopment. By only seeking the words he needed, the author was kept unaware of this passage in Mr. Hickman's speech, immediately preceding the citation quoted above from *The Federal Bulldozer:*

Having mentioned three things that we have learned, namely that urban redevelopment is a good business for ALCOA, that a company like ALCOA is good for the urban redevelopment program, and that we ought to assume direct responsibility for the management of our projects, let me next mention three things that we have unlearned: First, we have

[33] *Id.* at 122.
[34] Hickman, *Alcoa's Renewal Role Explained,* 21 J. HOUSING 190, 195 (1964).

unlearned any faith in the seed money concept of financing a redevelopment.

Thus, in the words cited by the author of *The Federal Bulldozer*, Mr. Hickman was merely indicating that ALCOA was adding to its "seed money" investment activity the direct responsibility for the planning, construction and management of its investments in urban renewal projects, and that ALCOA had "had it" as only a seed money angel.

When Mr. Hickman finished his exposition, he made this concluding summary statement at the end of the same speech:

> There you have it. ALCOA is in urban redevelopment up to its neck. Like most people, we're learning the hard way. We have the conviction that urban renewal is essential if our cities are to survive, and that ALCOA can play a constructive role in that battle and, at the same time, bring home to its shareholders a reasonable return on their investment.

E. *Census Data Distorted*

Perhaps the most serious "myth" cited by critics of urban renewal has been the one that goes to the very need for the program—the quality of housing in the United States. Until information on this subject is seen clearly, and understood thoroughly, no realistic appraisal can be made of the need for urban renewal or the magnitude of the efforts necessary to accomplish its goals.

The author of *The Federal Bulldozer* tried to substantiate a decline in the number of "substandard" housing units in the United States to support his argument that unaided private enterprise could successfully eliminate our housing problems and that there was no need for urban renewal. In support of his argument, he cited various national reports measuring the quality of individual dwelling units—which by themselves do not relate to the focus of urban renewal on the urban *environment*. A careful re-examination of the same figures he has studied, as well as pertinent others he has ignored, indicates that the actual deterioration of housing in this country has exceeded combined public and private efforts to stem urban blight and decay. His case rests largely on the use of percentages which obscure the real number of poor housing units that have remained in the United States for decades. Unfortunately, other critics of urban renewal have accepted his case uncritically, and have incorporated his distortions into their discussions.[35]

The 1950 Census data on condition of housing showed 4.3 million dilapidated units[36] while the 1960 Census showed 2.9 million. However, after each of these censuses, the Bureau conducted a post-enumeration survey on a sample basis to obtain an evaluation of the differences that may have resulted from definitional changes or by enumerator error.[37] The results of these samples, weighted to produce national totals, revealed that there was no significant change in the number of dilapidated housing units over the decade. There were 4.1 million dilapidated units in 1950 and the same number in 1960! This finding is consistent with the results of the Components of Inventory Change Survey—taken by the Census Bureau in 1959—which reported 4.0 million dilapidated units.

The author of *The Federal Bulldozer* reported only the larger decrease in dilapidated housing units, without reference to the post-enumeration surveys or the Components of Inventory Change Survey. He reported it as a drop from 9.9 percent in 1950 to 5.2 percent in 1960.[38]

There is no question, of course, about the overall increase in good housing in the United States since World War II. But the author's reported decrease in bad housing reflects only the addition of some 16 million new units during the decade. Thus, the core of his alleged findings—that dilapidated housing declined substantially—which forms the basis for his recommendation for the repeal of urban

[35] See Wilson, *Urban Renewal Does Not Always Renew*, Harvard Today, Jan. 1965, p. 2; Gans, *The Failure of Urban Renewal*, Commentary, April 1965, p. 29. [The Gans article is included in Chapter 22 of this volume.—Ed.]

[36] The Census definition of "dilapidated" is a unit which "does not provide safe and adequate shelter and in its present condition endangers the health, safety, or well-being of the occupants."

[37] The Census Bureau employed a three-way classification (sound, deteriorating, dilapidated) in 1960 to measure condition, compared with a two-way classification (not dilapidated, dilapidated) in 1950. Although the 1950 concept of "dilapidated" was retained for 1960, the Bureau acknowledges that the change introduced "an element of difference" in the statistics. This "element of difference" was noted by others, who are cited in *The Federal Bulldozer*, but the author's effort to compensate for it failed. For the post-enumeration figures, compare U.S. Dep't of Commerce, Bureau of the Census, *The Post Enumeration Survey: 1950*, table 14, with *Accuracy of Data on Housing Characteristics*, table 2A, Evaluation and Research Program of the United States Censuses of Population and Housing, 1960.

[38] Anderson 198–200.

renewal, has been discounted and disproved by data in the Census itself. Based merely on percentages, the improvement is illusory.

The author also attempted to identify a substantial decline in the amount of "substandard" housing between 1940 and 1960.[39] But the definition of "substandard" rests mainly on the use of the Census term "dilapidated." The concept of "dilapidated" replaced the concept of "needing major repairs" which was used in the 1940 Census. The Census Bureau reports that the two terms differ significantly, and that the 1940 results are not comparable with either 1950 or 1960 results on condition. Yet the author fashions— from these "not comparable" terms—a line graph[40] which is described in his text as follows:[41] "If we project the trends indicated in figure 13.1 it is entirely possible that the Census of 1970 may reveal that 90 to 95 percent of the total amount of housing will be classified standard." But the same projection, as the author does not point out, could be realized without the elimination of a single "substandard unit." As with the percentage of dilapidated units discussed above, it depends on the pace of new construction.

In another attempt to identify a substantial decline in the amount of "substandard" housing by 1970, in order to demonstrate *no need* for urban renewal, the author cited a report prepared for the National Association of Home Builders[42] which was based on quite the opposite assumption—that urban renewal will continue at an *active level:*

The 1960–1970 data are extrapolations of these data assuming a reasonably high level of economic activity during the 1960's, as well as an active housing program by local and Federal governments assisting private enterprise in eliminating poor housing and constructing an adequate supply to meet the demand as it develops.

Other distortions in the author's discussion of housing quality can only be summarized here. He has attributed the increase of good

[39] The term "substandard" is not employed in the Census. It was developed by users of the Census reports—including the Public Housing Administration and the National Association of Home Builders—to combine Census data on housing condition with that on plumbing facilities, for a more comprehensive index of the quality of housing.

[40] ANDERSON 198 (figure 13.1).

[41] *Id.* at 197.

[42] Reprinted in *Hearings on Housing Legislation of 1961 Before a Subcommittee of the Senate Committee on Banking and Currency,* 87th Cong., 1st Sess. 428 (1961).

housing for Negroes during the 1950s by falsely citing a figure of all newly-available standard public *and* private housing as though it did not include public housing. He has alleged that middle-class families are still in the majority in central cities by conveniently assigning to them a minimum annual income level of $4,000 (thereby including families eligible for public housing in most large cities and many smaller ones), and by equating the term "central cities" with "all cities in the United States with populations over 100,000" (thereby including those with city limits ten miles removed from the core). And he has estimated the size of the rehabilitation need in the United States by the number of "substandard" housing units (thereby omitting approximately five million units classified by the Census as deteriorating in condition but including all dilapidated units).

CONCLUSION

It is unfortunate that urban renewal, so sorely in need of careful study, has become clouded with myth and misunderstanding. Much otherwise productive time must be spent dispelling the haze cast by its critics. This article has discussed only a few of the faults in a book which, more than any other work, has collected and compounded the errors and distortions recited by critics of urban renewal. Although critics usually approach their topics with special interests, the author of *The Federal Bulldozer* labored under an unusual handicap. He set out to evaluate a government program which is based on cooperation with private enterprise, with the preconceived notion that the two are in competition:[43] "In 1949 . . . two forces set to grapple with the problems of housing and cities. One of these forces was private enterprise . . . and the other was the federal urban renewal program. . . ." Furthermore, he approached this program—which requires the taking of private property for the benefit of the public—with the conviction that private property is paramount to the public interest:[44]

The attitude of the government of the United States toward the concept of private property rights has been slowly changing. The right to own private property is synonymous with freedom, and in the earlier

[43] ANDERSON 228.
[44] *Id.* at 184.

years of this country was treated with the utmost respect. . . . [B]ut we are now at the point where many people will argue that the traditional rights of property must not stand in the way of broader social objectives or "human rights." The concept of broader social objectives has never been clearly defined, but it usually means that the rights of some will be sacrificed to the advantage of others. As for "human rights," it need only be noted that the right of property is probably the most important of all human rights.

As discussed earlier, the author failed to see what is the traditional concept of private property in the United States. But, given the prejudices cited above, it is not likely that knowing the truth would have freed him to make an objective study.

Other specialists approaching urban renewal critically—as "housers," "planners," "sociologists," or from other disciplines—bring with them a tendency to see the program in their own terms. But urban renewal is a comprehensive approach to a many faceted problem. What is needed for a realistic evaluation is a specialist who can rise above his field, or a generalist well acquainted with the program and its origins.

Certainly, a city with one or two projects in planning or in execution cannot be said to have "an urban renewal program," if a "program" implies broad scope and continuity. Only in such cities as New Haven, Pittsburgh, or Philadelphia can we see the potential of a comprehensive program. Unfortunately, those who know from first hand what this potential is are often too busy working to achieve it to be able to write about it. Since the Congress has not seen fit to provide adequate funds for research on urban renewal, an extra responsibility rests on those private institutions that finance research in this field to make sure it will be better spent.

21 *The Federal Bulldozer:* A Review*

WALLACE F. SMITH

The burden of this book[1] is perhaps best summed up in a statement which the author makes in his closing chapter. "The federal urban renewal program attempted to run counter to the tide of the private market—the results have been dismal." This points to the value of Anderson's book and at the same time to its basic inadequacy. It may not be much of a trick to find melancholy statistics of urban renewal performance—lagging land sales, the scale and impact of relocation, and some financial absurdities—but he has done an energetic job in pulling them together.

Yet Dr. Anderson is not up to showing that there is any basic incompatibility between the private urban land market, which he defends, and the urban renewal program, which he recommends be discontinued. When he takes the "classic" position that the private market will do a better job of slum removal than government agencies can, he is creating a false dichotomy and is detracting in an important way from the force of his statistical criticisms. If the private market actually can clear the slums—and Anderson offers some challenging evidence that it could—people would be relocated

* Reprinted from the *Journal of the American Institute of Planners,* Vol. 31, No. 2 (May 1965), pp. 179–180.
[1] Martin Anderson, *The Federal Bulldozer,* Cambridge, M.I.T. Press, 1964.

in the process and large sums of money would be spent. Whether this is to be done by a public or a private agency is, per se, immaterial. If we take the view that the basic aim of urban renewal is to accelerate a private market process, then the appearance of conflict disappears and the problem becomes one of seeing that the public programs are rational, efficient adjuncts to the community of private interests and decision-makers. The design of an optimum program to pursue this aim would be a challenge to the intellectual talents which Dr. Anderson clearly possesses, and it is unfortunate that he overlooked it.

Some unfriendly reviews of this book have appeared, based on the assumption that the book is a calculated diatribe against welfare programs in general. Essentially, however, the book is a technical study with things of interest and value to both the friends and the foes of urban renewal. The author's field is finance, and as his Preface indicates, he undertook the study out of interest in the sources of finance for urban renewal and in the financial decision-making process. His discussion of the effectiveness of urban renewal is rather obviously a by-product which may perhaps have gotten out of hand. This fact explains much of the unevenness of the book. For example, his discussion of the planning phase of redevelopment projects is concerned only with the length of time involved, with its consequences for the present value of costs and benefits. He exhibits no curiosity about how the planning is done. The cavalier and occasionally shallow tone of the book may appeal to those who enjoy a good scrap.

The technical contributions of the book are five:

1. A summary of statistics for the program through 1962, drawn largely from federal agency sources, with some intelligent interpretations. Anderson supplies estimates where actual data are not available. It might be supposed that an author's strong biases would enter into such estimates, but for the most part they seem reasonable and perceptive. An imaginative method of estimating the length of project execution phases is a case in point.

2. An investment model which might be useful to developers contemplating the acquisition of land in a redevelopment area. Though it neglects the construction period, it provides estimates of

annual cash flow before and after taxes, and rates of return. One chapter of the book traces the steps usually followed in financing a project on agency-cleared land.

3. A less elaborate model, or formula, for minimizing the local share of project costs.

4. A less persuasive, largely verbal analysis of the economic non-feasibility of rehabilitation. Here Anderson's absorption with mortgage financing seems particularly appropriate.

5. A review of the evolution of the courts' attitudes on condemnation for redevelopment. Anderson's differences with court rulings will probably not be very influential, and he risks appearing ridiculous in questioning them. This seems a shame, for the wordings of critical decisions show the courts to be gloriously innocent of urban realities, confusing noble intentions with sufficient ability and understanding to carry them out.

These substantive elements play a distinctly subordinate role to four principal themes around which the attack on urban renewal is really centered. These four issues are not new with Anderson, but he develops them with such force that renewal's friends may in the future find themselves offering defenses against them instead of just ignoring or scoffing at them.

One of these is the charge that renewal projects alter principally the location of construction activities in a city rather than the volume of such activity. Such shifting weakens two of the principal arguments for urban renewal, the "employment stimulus" effect and the "increased tax base" effect. Of all the building which took place in cities of 100,000 or over during the period of his study, only 1.3 percent was on urban renewal sites, and of this a major portion, he contends, would have been constructed anyway. The doubt thus cast on increases in the tax base is intensified by an imaginative analysis of the time lag involved between demolition and the occupancy of new taxable improvements. Depending on one's discount factors, the losses incurred during this period may outweigh the ultimate putative gain.

Another issue concerns the effect of renewal upon the welfare of the original inhabitants of the area. Relocation payments were actually made to just over half the families and individuals who moved from project areas through 1961, and the average payments were well under the $200 maximum. These predominantly low-income relocatees find themselves paying substantially more for housing after their move, and Anderson questions that the quality of their housing has improved. Thus, "their predicament is compounded, not alleviated, by urban renewal." This will be disputed by many people closer to the administration of the program than Anderson, but he provides that ultimate rebuttal, ". . . why, if all this good housing at low rents is available, didn't they move before urban renewal nudged them along?" The answer, if there is one, lies in complexities of situation and of purpose which he does not discuss, but which, in fact, the proponents of urban renewal have not expounded too clearly either.

A third theme of the book is an effort to discredit the "seed money" concept of the federal role in renewal, by tracking down the sources of financing employed in reconstruction of renewal areas. Anderson finds that the bulk of it is public rather than private. The Federal National Mortgage Association is the pivotal area. He estimates that through March, 1961, $1,430 million of public money had been spent to stimulate $460 million in strictly private construction, much of which would have been spent anyway. His conclusion is that urban renewal is essentially a public program rather than a device for attracting private funds into the rebuilding of our cities. As an aside he notes that delinquencies in F.N.M.A.'s portfolio of Section 220 loans have been at phenomenal levels.

The fourth identifiable theme is to the effect that the private market has meanwhile been making vastly greater progress in solving the slum problem. The author compares the characteristics of the housing inventory in 1950 and in 1960, and forecasts a stock 90 to 95 percent "standard" by 1970, irrespective of the pace of renewal. He points to marked improvements in the housing of nonwhites during the decade, and he strives to disprove the notion that central cities have become disproportionately low-income areas.

Putting these points together, Anderson feels that the nation's housing goals can only be reached through free enterprise; urban renewal should cease.

None of these contentions is immune to serious criticism. The data are not ideal, and the analytical structure is often loose. The major points may not logically imply the dramatic conclusion. Even where the analysis seems particularly effective a little reflection will reveal serious flaws. For example, Anderson argues that the tax base is diminished rather than increased by renewal simply because demolition—the scale of the entire program—is increasing at an increasing rate; the lagged construction activity is thus unable to catch up with demolition. While this is plausible for the aggregate of all urban renewal programs, it is not necessarily valid for a particular city. The accelerating pace of the program may be primarily extensive, involving more and more cities; but an individual city will find its tax base reconstructed within a measurable span of time.

It would be unfortunate, however, if the only thinking which this book stimulates among advocates of renewal is of this nit-picking nature. There is interminable opportunity for heaving statistical brickbats into the fragile structure of Anderson's anti-renewal argument, and some may be tempted to do this in the hope that by discrediting any little point the ultimate usefulness of renewal as currently practiced will be vindicated. This book may not be the most sophisticated guide to soul-searching on the subject of renewal, but one could hope that it would at least be seized upon as an occasion for soul-searching. Some of the points in the book are carping and weak, but if they are shot down others will take wing because the program is in fact a mass of conundrums. It is not self-evident that accelerated slum-clearance or revival of the central city is in the public interest. If this ever seemed self-evident it is less so day by day. Anderson's book is a major, though not overwhelmingly skillful, heresy. It joins a library of anti-renewal literature, the composite of which is more effective than any single piece.

Some careful reformulation of urban goals is long overdue. Is the problem of the slum best handled by the wondrous mechanics of the market (which are evidently a mystery to many planners), by the cerebrations of the planner (which are surely unsuspected by the mere property owner), or by the earthy realism of politics? Do we think the troubles of our cities stem from their real estate? What is the task which has really been assigned to local redevelopment directors?

If there were good answers to these questions there would be no alarm at the appearance of such a book as Anderson's.

22 The Failure of Urban Renewal*

HERBERT J. GANS

Suppose that the government decided that jalopies were a menace to public safety and a blight on the beauty of our highways, and therefore took them away from their drivers. Suppose, then, that to replenish the supply of automobiles, it gave these drivers a hundred dollars each to buy a good used car and also made special grants to General Motors, Ford, and Chrysler to lower the cost—although not necessarily the price—of Cadillacs, Lincolns, and Imperials by a few hundred dollars. Absurd as this may sound, change the jalopies to slum housing, and I have described, with only slight poetic license, the first fifteen years of a federal program called urban renewal.

Since 1949, this program has provided local renewal agencies with federal funds and the power of eminent domain to condemn slum neighborhoods, tear down the buildings, and resell the cleared land to private developers at a reduced price. In addition to relocating the slum dwellers in "decent, safe, and sanitary" housing, the program was intended to stimulate large-scale private rebuilding, add new tax revenues to the dwindling coffers of the cities, revitalize their downtown areas, and halt the exodus of middle-class whites to the suburbs.

* Reprinted from *Commentary* (April 1965), pp. 29–37, by permission. Copyright © 1965 by the American Jewish Committee.

For some time now, a few city planners and housing experts have been pointing out that urban renewal was not achieving its general aims, and social scientists have produced a number of critical studies of individual renewal projects. These critiques, however, have mostly appeared in academic books and journals; otherwise there has been remarkably little public discussion of the federal program. Slum-dwellers whose homes were to be torn down have indeed protested bitterly, but their outcries have been limited to particular projects; and because such outcries have rarely been supported by the local press, they have been easily brushed aside by the political power of the supporters of the projects in question. In the last few years, the civil rights movement has backed protesting slum-dwellers, though again only at the local level, while rightists have opposed the use of eminent domain to take private property from one owner in order to give it to another (especially when the new one is likely to be from out-of-town and financed by New York capital).

Slum clearance has also come under fire from several prominent architectural and social critics, led by Jane Jacobs, who have been struggling to preserve neighborhoods like Greenwich Village, with their brownstones, lofts, and small apartment houses, against the encroachment of the large, high-rise projects built for the luxury market and the poor alike. But these efforts have been directed mainly at private clearance outside the federal program, and their intent has been to save the city for people (intellectuals and artists, for example) who, like tourists, want jumbled diversity, antique "charm," and narrow streets for visual adventure and aesthetic pleasure. (Norman Mailer carried such thinking to its farthest point in his recent attack in the *New York Times Magazine* on the physical and social sterility of high-rise housing; Mailer's attack was also accompanied by an entirely reasonable suggestion—in fact the only viable one that could be made in this context—that the advantages of brownstone living be incorporated into skyscraper projects.)

But if criticism of the urban renewal program has in the past been spotty and sporadic, there are signs that the program as a whole is now beginning to be seriously and tellingly evaluated. At least two comprehensive studies, by Charles Abrams and Scott Greer, are nearing publication, and one highly negative analysis—by an ultra-conservative economist and often irresponsible polemicist—has al-

THE FAILURE OF URBAN RENEWAL / 539

ready appeared: Martin Anderson's *The Federal Bulldozer*.[1] Ironically enough, Anderson's data are based largely on statistics collected by the Urban Renewal Administration. What, according to these and other data, has the program accomplished? It has cleared slums to make room for many luxury-housing and a few middle-income projects, and it has also provided inexpensive land for the expansion of colleges, hospitals, libraries, shopping areas, and other such institutions located in slum areas. As of March 1961, 126,000 dwelling units had been demolished and about 28,000 new ones built. The median monthly rental of all those erected during 1960 came to $158, and in 1962, to $192—a staggering figure for any area outside of Manhattan.

Needless to say, none of the slum-dwellers who were dispossessed in the process could afford to move into these new apartments. Local renewal agencies were supposed to relocate the dispossessed tenants in "standard" housing within their means before demolition began, but such vacant housing is scarce in most cities, and altogether unavailable in some. And since the agencies were under strong pressure to clear the land and get renewal projects going, the relocation of the tenants was impatiently, if not ruthlessly, handled. Thus, a 1961 study of renewal projects in 41 cities showed that 60 percent of the dispossessed tenants were merely relocated in other slums; and in big cities, the proportion was even higher (over 70 percent in Philadelphia, according to a 1958 study). Renewal sometimes even created new slums by pushing relocatees into areas and buildings which then became overcrowded and deteriorated rapidly. This has principally been the case with Negroes who, both for economic and racial reasons, have been forced to double up in other ghettos. Indeed, because almost two-thirds of the cleared slum units have been occupied by Negroes, the urban renewal program has often been characterized as Negro clearance, and in too many cities, this has been its intent.

Moreover, those dispossessed tenants who found better housing usually had to pay more rent than they could afford. In his careful study of relocation in Boston's heavily Italian West End,[2] Chester

[1] M.I.T. Press, 272 pp.
[2] See the November 1964 issue of the *Journal of the American Institute of Planners*. The article also reviews all other relocation research and is a more reliable study of the consequences of renewal than Anderson's. [The Hartman article is included in Chapter 10 of this volume.—Ed.]

Hartman shows that 41 percent of the West Enders lived in good housing in this so-called slum (thus suggesting that much of it should not have been torn down) and that 73 percent were relocated in good housing—thanks in part to the fact that the West Enders were white. This improvement was achieved at a heavy price, however, for median rents rose from $41 to $71 per month after the move.

According to renewal officials, 80 percent of all persons relocated now live in good housing, and rent increases were justified because many had been paying unduly low rent before. Hartman's study was the first to compare these official statistics with housing realities, and his figure of 73 percent challenges the official claim that 97 percent of the Boston West Enders were properly rehoused. This discrepancy may arise from the fact that renewal officials collected their data after the poorest of the uprooted tenants had fled in panic to other slums, and that officials also tended toward a rather lenient evaluation of the relocation housing of those actually studied in order to make a good record for their agency. (On the other hand, when they were certifying areas for clearance, these officials often exaggerated the degree of "blight" in order to prove their case.)

As for the substandard rents paid by slum-dwellers, this is true in only a small proportion of cases, and then mostly among whites. Real-estate economists argue that families should pay at least 20 percent of their income for housing, but what is manageable for middle-income people is a burden to those with low incomes who pay a higher share of their earnings for food and other necessities. Yet even so, low-income Negroes generally have to devote about 30 percent of their income to housing, and a Chicago study cited by Hartman reports that among non-white families earning less than $3,000 a year, median rent rose from 35 percent of income before relocation to 46 percent afterward.

To compound the failure of urban renewal to help the poor, many clearance areas (Boston's West End is an example) were chosen, as Anderson points out, not because they had the worst slums, but because they offered the best sites for luxury housing— housing which would have been built whether the urban renewal program existed or not. Since public funds were used to clear the slums and to make the land available to private builders at reduced costs, the low-income population was in effect subsidizing its own removal for the benefit of the wealthy. What was done for the slum-dwellers in return is starkly suggested by the following statistic: *only one-half of one percent* of all federal expenditures for urban renewal between 1949 and 1964 was spent on relocation of families and individuals; and 2 percent if payments to businesses are included.

Finally, because the policy has been to clear a district of all slums at once in order to assemble large sites to attract private developers, entire neighborhoods have frequently been destroyed, uprooting people who had lived there for decades, closing down their institutions, ruining small businesses by the hundreds, and scattering families and friends all over the city. By removing the structure of social and emotional support provided by the neighborhood, and by forcing people to rebuild their lives separately and amid strangers elsewhere, slum clearance has often come at a serious psychological as well as financial cost to its supposed beneficiaries. Marc Fried, a clinical psychologist who studied the West Enders after relocation, reported that 46 percent of the women and 38 percent of the men "give evidence of a fairly severe grief reaction or worse" in response to questions about leaving their tight-knit community. Far from "adjusting" eventually to this trauma, 26 percent of the women remained sad or depressed even two years after they had been pushed out of the West End.[3]

People like the Italians or the Puerto Ricans who live in an intensely group-centered way among three-generation "extended families" and ethnic peers have naturally suffered greatly from the clearance of entire neighborhoods. It may well be, however, that slum clearance has inflicted yet graver emotional burdens on Negroes, despite the fact that they generally live in less cohesive and often disorganized neighborhoods. In fact, I suspect that Negroes who lack a stable family life and have trouble finding neighbors, shopkeepers, and institutions they can trust may have been hurt even more by forcible removal to new areas. This suspicion is supported by another of Fried's findings—that the socially marginal

[3] See "Grieving for a Lost Home," in *The Urban Condition*, edited by Leonard Duhl. [This article is included in Chapter 13 of this volume.—Ed.]

West Enders were more injured by relocation than those who had been integral members of the old neighborhood. Admittedly, some Negroes move very often on their own, but then they at least do so voluntarily, and not in consequence of a public policy which is supposed to help them in the first place. Admittedly also, relocation has made it possible for social workers to help slum-dwellers whom they could not reach until renewal brought them out in the open, so to speak. But then only a few cities have so far used social workers to make relocation a more humane process.

These high financial, social, and emotional costs paid by the slum-dwellers have generally been written off as an unavoidable by-product of "progress," the price of helping cities to collect more taxes, bring back the middle class, make better use of downtown land, stimulate private investment, and restore civic pride. But as Anderson shows, urban renewal has hardly justified these claims either. For one thing, urban renewal is a slow process: the average project has taken twelve years to complete. Moreover, while the few areas suitable for luxury housing were quickly rebuilt, less desirable cleared land might lie vacant for many years because developers were—and are—unwilling to risk putting up high- and middle-income housing in areas still surrounded by slums. Frequently, they can be attracted only by promises of tax write-offs, which absorb the increased revenues that renewal is supposed to create for the city. Anderson reports that, instead of the anticipated four dollars for every public dollar, private investments have only just matched the public subsidies, and even the money for luxury housing has come forth largely because of federal subsidies. Thus, all too few of the new projects have produced tax gains and returned suburbanites, or generated the magic rebuilding boom.

Anderson goes on to argue that during the fifteen years of the federal urban renewal program, the private housing market has achieved what urban renewal has failed to do. Between 1950 and 1960, twelve million new dwelling units were built, and fully six million substandard ones disappeared—all without government action. The proportion of substandard housing in the total housing supply was reduced from 37 to 19 percent, and even among the dwelling units occupied by non-whites, the proportion of substandard units has dropped from 72 to 44 percent. This comparison leads Anderson to the conclusion that the private market is much more effective than government action in removing slums and supplying new housing, and that the urban renewal program ought to be repealed.

It would appear that Anderson's findings and those of the other studies I have cited make an excellent case for doing so. However, a less biased analysis of the figures and a less tendentious mode of evaluating them than Anderson's leads to a different conclusion. To begin with, Anderson's use of nationwide statistics misses the few good renewal projects, those which have helped both the slum-dwellers and the cities, or those which brought in enough new taxes to finance other city services for the poor. Such projects can be found in small cities and especially in those where high vacancy rates assured sufficient relocation housing of standard quality. More important, all the studies I have mentioned deal with projects carried out during the 1950's, and fail to take account of the improvements in urban renewal practice under the Kennedy and Johnson administrations. Although Anderson's study supposedly covers the period up to 1963, many of his data go no further than 1960. Since then, the federal bulldozer has moved into fewer neighborhoods, and the concept of rehabilitating rather than clearing blighted neighborhoods is more and more being underwritten by subsidized loans. A new housing subsidy program—known as 221(d)(3)—for families above the income ceiling for public housing has also been launched, and in 1964, Congress passed legislation for assistance to relocatees who cannot afford their new rents.

None of this is to say that Anderson would have had to revise his findings drastically if he had taken the pains to update them. These recent innovations have so far been small in scope—only 13,000 units were financed under 221(d)(3) in the first two years—and they still do not provide subsidies sufficient to bring better housing within the price range of the slum residents. In addition, rehabilitation unaccompanied by new construction is nearly useless because it does not eliminate overcrowding. And finally, some cities are still scheduling projects to clear away the non-white poor who stand in the path of the progress of private enterprise. Unfortunately, many cities pay little attention to federal pleas to improve the program, using the local initiative granted them by urban renewal legislation to perpetuate the practices of the 1950's. Yet even with the legislation of the 1960's, the basic error in the original design of urban renewal remains: it is still a method for eliminating the slums in order to "renew" the city, rather than a program for properly rehousing slum-dwellers.

Before going into this crucial distinction, we first need to be clear that private housing is not going to solve our slum problems. In the first place, Anderson conveniently ignores the fact that if urban renewal has benefited anyone, it is private enterprise. Bending to the pressure of the real-estate lobby, the legislation that launched urban renewal in effect required that private developers do the rebuilding, and most projects could therefore get off the drawing board only if they appeared to be financially attractive to a developer. Thus, his choice of a site and his rebuilding plans inevitably took priority over the needs of the slum-dwellers.

It is true that Anderson is not defending private enterprise *per se* but the free market, although he forgets that it only exists today as a concept in reactionary minds and dated economics texts. The costs of land, capital, and construction have long since made it impossible for private developers to build for anyone but the rich, and some form of subsidy is needed to house everyone else. The building boom of the 1950's which Anderson credits to the free market was subsidized by income-tax deductions to homeowners and by F.H.A. and V.A. mortgage insurance, not to mention the federal highway programs that have made the suburbs possible.

To be sure, these supports enabled private builders to put up a great deal of housing for middle-class whites. This in turn permitted well-employed workers, including some non-whites, to improve their own situation by moving into the vacated neighborhoods. Anderson is quite right in arguing that if people earn good wages, they can obtain better housing more easily and cheaply in the not-quite-private market than through urban renewal. But this market is of little help to those employed at low or even factory wages, or the unemployed, or most Negroes who, whatever their earnings, cannot live in the suburbs. In consequence, 44 percent of all housing occupied by non-whites in 1960 was still substandard, and even with present subsidies, private enterprise can do nothing for these people. As for laissez faire, it played a major role in creating the slums in the first place.

The solution, then, is not to repeal urban renewal, but to transform it from a program of slum clearance and rehabilitation into a program of urban rehousing. This means, first, building low- and moderate-cost housing on vacant land in cities, suburbs, and new towns beyond the suburbs, and also helping slum-dwellers to move into existing housing outside the slums; and then, *after* a portion of the urban low-income population has left the slums, clearing and rehabilitating them through urban renewal. This approach is commonplace in many European countries, which have long since realized that private enterprise can no more house the population and eliminate slums than it can run the post office.

Of course, governments in Europe have a much easier task than ours in developing decent low-income projects. Because they take it for granted that housing is a national rather than a local responsibility, the government agencies are not hampered by the kind of real-estate and construction lobbies which can defeat or subvert American programs by charges of socialism. Moreover, their municipalities own a great deal of the vacant land, and have greater control over the use of private land than do American cities. But perhaps their main advantage is the lack of popular opposition to moving the poor out of the slums and into the midst of the more affluent residents. Not only is housing desperately short for all income groups, but the European class structure, even in Western socialist countries, is still rigid enough so that low- and middle-income groups can live near each other if not next to each other, and still "know their place."

In America, on the other hand, one's house and address are major signs of social status, and no one who has any say in the matter wants people of lower income or status in his neighborhood. Middle-class homeowners use zoning as a way of keeping out cheaper or less prestigious housing, while working-class communities employ less subtle forms of exclusion. Consequently, low-income groups, whatever their creed or color, have been forced to live in slums or near-slums, and to wait until they could acquire the means to move as a group, taking over better neighborhoods when the older occupants were ready to move on themselves.

For many years now, the only source of new housing for such people, and their only hope of escaping the worst slums, has been public housing. But this is no longer a practical alternative. Initiated during the Depression, public housing has always been a politically embattled program; its opponents, among whom the real-estate lobby looms large, first saddled it with restrictions and then effectively crippled it. Congress now permits only 35,000 units a year to be built in the entire country.

The irony is that public housing has declined because, intended only for the poor, it faithfully carried out its mandate. Originally, sites were obtained by slum clearance; after the war, however, in order to increase the supply of low-cost housing, cities sought to build public housing on vacant land. But limited as it was to low-income tenants and thus labeled and stigmatized as an institution of the dependent poor, public housing was kept out of vacant land in the better neighborhoods. This, plus the high cost of land and construction, left housing officials with no other choice but to build high-rise projects on whatever vacant land they could obtain, often next to factories or along railroad yards. Because tenants of public housing are ruled by a set of strict regulations—sometimes necessary, sometimes politically inspired, but always degrading—anyone who could afford housing in the private market shunned the public projects. During the early years of the program, when fewer citizens had that choice, public housing became respectable shelter for the working class and even for the unemployed middle class. After the war, federal officials decided, and rightly so, that public housing ought to be reserved for those who had no other alternative, and therefore set income limits that admitted only the really poor. Today, public housing is home for the underclass—families who earn less than $3000–$4000 annually, many with unstable jobs or none at all, and most of them non-white.

Meanwhile the enthusiasm for public housing has been steadily dwindling and with it, badly needed political support. Newspaper reports reinforce the popular image of public-housing projects as huge nests of crime and delinquency—despite clear evidence to the contrary—and as the domicile of unregenerate and undeserving families whose children urinate only in the elevators. The position of public housing, particularly among liberal intellectuals, has also been weakened by the slurs of the social and architectural aesthetes who condemn the projects' poor exterior designs as "sterile," "monotonous," and "dehumanizing," often in ignorance of the fact that the tightly restricted funds have been allocated mainly to make the apartments themselves as spacious and livable as possible, and that the waiting lists among slum-dwellers who want these apartments remain long. Be that as it may, suburban communities and urban neighborhoods with vacant land are as hostile to public housing as ever, and their opposition is partly responsible for the program's having been cut down to its present minuscule size.

The net result is that low-income people today cannot get out of the slums, either because they cannot afford the subsidized private market, or because the project they could afford cannot be built on vacant land. There is only one way to break through this impasse, and that is to permit them equal access to new subsidized, privately built housing by adding another subsidy to make up the difference between the actual rent and what they can reasonably be expected to pay. Such a plan, giving them a chance to choose housing like all other citizens, would help to remove the stigma of poverty and inferiority placed on them by public housing. Many forms of rent subsidy have been proposed, but the best one, now being tried in New York, is to put low- and middle-income people in the same middle-income project with the former getting the same apartments at smaller rentals.

Admittedly, this approach assumes that the poor can live with the middle class and that their presence and behavior will not threaten their neighbors' security or status. No one knows whether this is really possible, but experiments in education, job training, and social-welfare programs do show that many low-income people, when once offered *genuine* opportunities to improve their lives and given help in making use of them, are able to shake off the hold of the culture of poverty. Despite the popular stereotype, the proportion of those whom Hylan Lewis calls the clinical poor, too ravaged emotionally by poverty and deprivation to adapt to new opportunities, seems to be small. As for the rest, they only reject programs offering spurious opportunities, like job-training schemes for non-existent jobs. Further, anyone who has lived in a slum neighborhood can testify that whatever the condition of the building, most women keep their apartments clean by expenditures of time and effort inconceivable to the middle-class housewife. Moving to a better apartment would require little basic cultural change from these women, and rehousing is thus a type of new opportunity that stands a better chance of succeeding than, say, a program to inculcate new child-rearing techniques.

We have no way of telling how many slum-dwellers would be willing to participate in such a plan. However poor the condition of the flat, the slum is home, and for many it provides the support of neighboring relatives and friends, and a cultural milieu in which everyone has the same problems and is therefore willing to overlook occasional disreputable behavior. A middle-income project cannot help but have a middle-class ethos, and some lower-class people may be fearful of risking what little stability they have achieved where they are now in exchange for something new, strange, demanding, and potentially hostile. It would be hard to imagine an unwed Negro mother moving her household to a middle-income project full of married couples and far removed from the mother, sisters, and aunts who play such an important role in the female-centered life of lower-class Negroes. However, there are today a large number of stable two-parent families who live in the slums only because income and race exclude them from the better housing that is available. Families like these would surely be only too willing to leave the Harlems and Black Belts. They would have to be helped with loans to make the move, and perhaps even with grants to buy new furniture so as not to feel ashamed in their new surroundings. They might be further encouraged by being offered income-tax relief for giving up the slums, just as we now offer such relief to people who give up being renters to become homeowners.

Undoubtedly there would be friction between the classes, and the more affluent residents would likely want to segregate themselves and their children from neighbors who did not toe the middle-class line, especially with respect to child-rearing. The new housing would therefore have to be planned to allow some voluntary social segregation for both groups, if only to make sure that enough middle-income families would move in (especially in cities where there was no shortage of housing for them). The proportion of middle- and low-income tenants would have to be regulated not only to minimize the status fears of the former, but also to give the latter enough peers to keep them from feeling socially isolated and without emotional support when problems arise. Fortunately, non-profit and limited dividend institutions, which do not have to worry about showing an immediate profit, are now being encouraged to build moderate-income housing; they can do a more careful job of planning the physical and social details of this approach than speculative private builders.

If the slums are really to be emptied and their residents properly housed elsewhere, the rehousing program will have to be extended beyond the city limits, for the simple reason that that is where most of the vacant land is located. This means admitting the low-income population to the suburbs; it also means creating new towns—self-contained communities with their own industry which would not, like the suburbs, be dependent on the city for employment opportunities, and could therefore be situated in presently rural areas. Federal support for the construction of new towns was requested as part of the 1964 Housing Act, and although Congress refused to pass it, the legislation will come up again in 1965.[4]

To be sure, white middle-class surburbanites and rural residents are not likely to welcome non-white low-income people into their communities even if the latter are no longer clearly labeled as poor. The opposition to be expected in city neighborhoods chosen for mixed-income projects would be multiplied a hundredfold in outlying areas. Being politically autonomous, and having constituencies who are not about to support measures that will threaten their security or status in the slightest, the suburbs possess the political power to keep the rehousing program out of their own vacant lots, even if they cannot stop the federal legislation that would initiate it. On the other hand, experience with the federal highway program and with urban renewal itself has demonstrated that few communities can afford to turn down large amounts of federal money. For instance, New York City is likely to build a Lower Manhattan Expressway in the teeth of considerable local opposition, if only because the federal government will pay 90 percent of the cost and thus bring a huge sum into the city coffers. If the rehousing program were sufficiently large to put a sizable mixed-income project in every community, and if the federal government were to pick up at least 90 percent of the tab, while also strengthening the

---

[4] Meanwhile, several private developers are planning new towns (for example, James Rouse who is building Columbia near Baltimore, and Robert Simon who has already begun Reston, outside Washington) in which they propose to house some low-income people.

appeal of the program by helping to solve present transportation, school, and tax problems in the suburbs, enough political support might be generated to overcome the objections of segregationists and class-conscious whites.

Yet even if the outlying areas could be persuaded to cooperate, it is not at all certain that slum-dwellers would leave the city. Urban renewal experience has shown that for many slum-dwellers, there are more urgent needs than good housing. One is employment, and most of the opportunities for unskilled or semi-skilled work are in the city. Another is money, and some New York City slum residents recently refused to let the government inspect—much less repair their buildings because they would lose the rent reductions they had received previously. If leaving the city meant higher rents, more limited access to job possibilities, and also separation from people and institutions which gave them stability, some slum residents might very well choose overcrowding and dilapidation as the lesser of two evils.

These problems would have to be considered in planning a rehousing program beyond the city limits. The current exodus of industry from the city would of course make jobs available to the new suburbanites. The trouble is that the industries now going into the suburbs, or those that would probably be attracted to the new towns, are often precisely the ones which use the most modern machinery and the fewest unskilled workers. Thus, our rehousing plan comes up against the same obstacle—the shortage of jobs—that has frustrated other programs to help the low-income population and that will surely defeat the War on Poverty in its present form. Like so many other programs, rehousing is finally seen to depend on a step that American society is as yet unwilling to take: the deliberate creation of new jobs by government action. The building of new towns especially would have to be coordinated with measures aimed at attracting private industry to employ the prospective residents, at creating other job opportunities, and at offering intensive training for the unskilled after they have been hired. If they are not sure of a job before they leave the city, they simply will not leave.

The same social and cultural inhibitions that make slum residents hesitant to move into a mixed-income project in the city would, of course, be even stronger when it came to moving out of the city. These inhibitions might be relaxed by moving small groups of slum residents en masse, or by getting those who move first to encourage their neighbors to follow. In any case, new social institutions and community facilities would have to be developed to help the erstwhile slum-dweller feel comfortable in his new community, yet without labeling him as poor.

Despite its many virtues, a rehousing program based on the use of vacant land on either side of the city limits would not immediately clear the slums. Given suburban opposition and the occupational and social restraints on the slum-dwellers themselves, it can be predicted that if such a program were set into motion it would be small in size, and that it would pull out only the upwardly mobile— particularly the young people with stable families and incomes— who are at best a sizable minority among the poor. What can be done now to help the rest leave the slums?

The best solution is a public effort to encourage their moving into existing neighborhoods within the city and in older suburbs just beyond the city limits. Indeed, a direct rent subsidy like that now given to relocatees could enable people to obtain decent housing in these areas. This approach has several advantages. It would allow low-income people to be close to jobs and to move in groups, and it would probably attract the unwed mother who wanted to give her children a better chance in life. It would also be cheaper than building new housing, although the subsidies would have to be large enough to discourage low-income families from overcrowding—and thus deteriorating—the units in order to save on rent.

There are, however, some obvious disadvantages as well. For one thing, because non-white low-income people would be moving into presently white or partially integrated areas, the government would in effect be encouraging racial invasion. This approach would thus have the effect of pushing the white and middle-income people further toward the outer edge of the city or into the suburbs. Although some whites might decide to stay, many would surely want to move, and not all would be able to afford to do so. It would be necessary to help them with rent subsidies as well; indeed, they might become prospective middle-income tenants for rehousing projects on vacant land.

Undoubtedly, all this would bring us closer to the all-black city that has already been predicted. For this reason alone, a scheme that pushes the whites further out can only be justified when combined with a rehousing program on vacant land that would begin to integrate the suburbs. But even that could not prevent a further racial imbalance between cities and suburbs.

Yet would the predominantly non-white city really be so bad? It might be for the middle class which needs the jobs, shops, and culture that the city provides. Of course, the greater the suburban exodus, the more likely it would become that middle-class culture would also move to the suburbs. This is already happening in most American cities—obvious testimony to the fact that culture (at least of the middlebrow kind represented by tent theaters and art movie-houses) does not need the city in order to flourish; and the artists who create high culture seem not to mind living among the poor even now.

Non-white low-income people might feel more positive about a city in which they were the majority, for if they had the votes, municipal services would be more attuned to their priorities than is now the case. To be sure, if poor people (of any color) were to dominate the city, its tax revenues would decrease even further, and cities would be less able than ever to supply the high quality public services that the low-income population needs so much more urgently than the middle class. Consequently, new sources of municipal income not dependent on the property tax would have to be found; federal and state grants to cities (like those already paying half the public-school costs in several states) would probably be the principal form. Even under present conditions, in fact, new sources of municipal income must soon be located if the cities are not to collapse financially.

If non-whites were to leave the slums en masse, new ghettos would eventually form in the areas to which they would move. Although this is undesirable by conventional liberal standards, the fact is that many low-income Negroes are not yet very enthusiastic about living among white neighbors. They do not favor segregation, of course; what they want is a free choice and then the ability to select predominantly non-white areas that are in better shape than the ones they live in now. If the suburbs were opened to non-whites—to the upwardly mobile ones who want integration now—

free choice would become available. If the new ghettos were decent neighborhoods with good schools, and if their occupants had jobs and other opportunities to bring stability into their lives, they would be training their children to want integration a generation hence.

In short, then, a workable rehousing scheme must provide new housing on both sides of the city limits for the upwardly mobile minority, and encouragement to move into older areas for the remainder. If, in these ways, enough slum-dwellers could be enabled and induced to leave the slums, it would then be possible to clear or rehabilitate the remaining slums. Once slum areas were less crowded, and empty apartments were going begging, their profitability and market value would be reduced, and urban renewal could take place far more cheaply, and far more quickly. Relocation would be less of a problem, and with land values down, rebuilding and rehabilitation could be carried out to fit the resources of the low-income people who needed or wanted to remain in the city. A semi-suburban style of living that would be attractive to the upper-middle class could also be provided.

At this point, it would be possible to begin to remake the inner city into what it must eventually become—the hub of a vast metropolitan complex of urban neighborhoods, suburbs, and new towns, in which those institutions and functions that have to be at the center—the specialized business districts, the civil and cultural facilities, and the great hospital complexes and university campuses —would be located.

Even in such a city, there would be slums—for people who wanted to live in them, for the clinical poor who would be unable to make it elsewhere, and for rural newcomers who would become urbanized in them before moving on. But it might also be possible to relocate many of these in a new kind of public housing in which quasi-communities would be established to help those whose problems were soluble and to provide at least decent shelter for those who cannot be helped except by letting them live without harassment until we learn how to cure mental illness, addiction, and other forms of self-destructive behavior.

This massive program has much to recommend it, but we must clearly understand that moving the low-income population out of the slums would not eliminate poverty or the other problems that stem from it. A standard dwelling unit can make life more comfortable, and a decent neighborhood can discourage some anti-social behavior, but by themselves, neither can effect radical transformations. What poor people need most are decent incomes, proper jobs, better schools, and freedom from racial and class discrimination. Indeed, if the choice were between a program solely dedicated to rehousing, and a program that kept the low-income population in the city slums for another generation but provided for these needs, the latter would be preferable, for it would produce people who were able to leave the slums under their own steam. Obviously, the ideal approach is one that coordinates the elimination of slums with the reduction of poverty.

As I have been indicating, an adequate rehousing program would be extremely costly and very difficult to carry out. Both its complexity and expense can be justified, however, on several grounds. Morally, it can be argued that no one in the Great Society should have to live in a slum, at least not involuntarily.

From a political point of view, it is urgently necessary to begin integrating the suburbs and to improve housing conditions in the city before the latter becomes an ominous ghetto of poor and increasingly angry Negroes and Puerto Ricans, and the suburbs become enclaves of affluent whites who commute fearfully to a downtown bastion of stores and offices. If the visible group tensions of recent years are allowed to expand and sharpen, another decade may very well see the beginning of open and often violent class and race warfare.

But the most persuasive argument for a rehousing program is economic. Between 50 and 60 percent of building costs go into wages and create work for the unskilled who are now increasingly unemployable elsewhere. A dwelling unit that costs $15,000 would thus provide as much as $9000 in wages—one-and-a-half years of respectably paid employment for a single worker. Adding four-and-a-half million new low-cost housing units to rehouse half of those in substandard units in 1960 would provide almost seven million man-years of work, and the subsequent renewal of these and other substandard units yet more. Many additional jobs would also be created by the construction and operation of new shopping centers, schools, and other community facilities, as well as the highways and public transit systems that would be needed to serve the new suburbs and towns. If precedent must be cited for using a housing program to create jobs, it should be recalled that public housing was started in the Depression for precisely this reason.

The residential building industry (and the real-estate lobby) would have to be persuaded to give up their stubborn resistance to government housing programs, but the danger of future under-employment, and the opportunity of participating profitably in the rehousing scheme, should either convert present builders or attract new ones into the industry. As for the building trades unions, they have always supported government housing programs, but they have been unwilling to admit non-whites to membership. If, however, the rehousing effort were sizable enough to require many more workers than are now in the unions, the sheer demand for labor—and the enforcement of federal non-discriminatory hiring policies for public works—would probably break down the color barriers without much difficulty.

While the federal government is tooling up to change the urban renewal program into a rehousing scheme, it should also make immediate changes in current renewal practices to remove their economic and social cost from the shoulders of the slum-dwellers. Future projects should be directed at the clearance of *really harmful* slums, instead of taking units that are *run down but not demonstrably harmful* out of the supply of low-cost housing, especially for downtown revitalization and other less pressing community improvement schemes. Occupants of harmful slums, moreover, ought to be rehoused in decent units they can afford. For this purpose, more public housing and 221(d)(3) projects must be built, and relocation and rent assistance payments should be increased to eliminate the expense of moving for the slum-dweller. Indeed, the simplest way out of the relocation impasse is to give every relocatee a sizable grant, like the five hundred dollars to one thousand dollars paid by private builders in New York City to get tenants out of existing structures quickly and painlessly. Such a grant is not only a real incentive to relocatees but a means of reducing opposition to urban renewal. By itself, however, it cannot reduce the shortage of relocation housing. Where such housing now exists in plentiful supply, renewal ought to move ahead more quickly, but where there is a shortage that cannot be appreciably reduced, it would be wise to eliminate or postpone clearance and rehabilitation projects that require a large amount of relocation.

Nothing is easier than to suggest radical new programs to the overworked and relatively powerless officials of federal and local renewal agencies who must carry out the present law, badly written or not, and who are constantly pressured by influential private interests to make decisions in their favor. Many of these officials are as unhappy with what urban renewal has wrought as their armchair critics and would change the program if they could—that is, if they received encouragement from the White House, effective support in getting new legislation through Congress, and, equally important, political help at city halls to incorporate these innovations into local programs. But it should be noted that little of what I have suggested is very radical, for none of the proposals involves conflict with the entrenched American practice of subsidizing private enterprise to carry out public works at a reasonable profit. The proposals are radical only in demanding an end to our no less entrenched practice of punishing the poor. Yet they also make sure that middle-class communities are rewarded financially for whatever discomfort they may have to endure.

Nor are these suggestions very new. Indeed, only last month President Johnson sent a housing message to Congress which proposes the payment of rent subsidies as the principal method for improving housing conditions. It also requests federal financing of municipal services for tax-starved communities, and aid toward the building of new towns. These represent bold and desirable steps toward the evolution of a federal rehousing program. Unfortunately, however, the message offers little help to those who need it most. Slum-dwellers may be pleased that there will be no increase in urban renewal activity, and that relocation housing subsidies and other grants are being stepped up. But no expansion of public housing is being requested, and to make matters worse, the new rent subsidies will be available only to households above the income limits for public housing. Thus, the President's message offers no escape for the mass of the non-white low-income population from the ghetto slums; in fact it threatens to widen the gap between such people and the lower-middle-income population which will be eligible for rent subsidies.

On the other hand, as in the case of the War on Poverty, a new principle of government responsibility in housing is being established, and evidently the President's strategy is to obtain legislative approval for the principle by combining it with a minimal and a minimally controversial program for the first year. Once the principle has been accepted, however, the program must change quickly. It may have taken fifteen years for urban renewal even to begin providing some relief to the mass of slum-dwellers, but it cannot take that long again to become a rehousing scheme that will give them significant help. The evolution of federal policies can no longer proceed in the leisurely fashion to which politicians, bureaucrats, and middle-class voters have become accustomed, for unemployment, racial discrimination, and the condition of our cities are becoming ever more critical problems, and those who suffer from them are now considerably less patient than they have been in the past.

23 Some Blessings of Urban Renewal*

CHARLES ABRAMS

The mass displacements of the renewal program have led to an increasing barrage of criticism that could be satisfied by nothing short of the program's repeal. These critics are as naive as those who unconditionally defend the program in its every aspect.[1] A program which siphons federal money into our languishing cities would be a legislative curiosity if it did no good at all. If it did no more than incite some eight hundred cities (not to mention the thousands of other communities receiving planning grants) to take a constructive look at their environments and replan them, it could not be rated a total loss.

The renewal law has virtues as well as vices, and the vices exist largely because the measure is actually a half-measure. What the program needs is amplification, not abolition, a complementary housing program to make it workable, and an enlargement of its basic concept to do what its name implies. In a nation whose

* Reprinted by permission of the author and publishers from *The City Is the Frontier*, New York, Harper and Row, 1965, Chapter 9. Copyright © 1965 by Charles Abrams.

[1] See, for example, Martin Anderson, *The Federal Bulldozer*, M.I.T. Press, 1964, in which the author makes some good criticisms of the program, makes no mention of its virtues, and then bluntly asks for its repeal. If the same technique were applied to foreign aid, relief, old age assistance, Medicare, public housing, or, for that matter, any federal program, no federal program would deserve continuance.

affection for its cities is inconspicuous, it makes no sense to scuttle any program, however imperfect, that aims to help them. In politics, it is always easier to amend than to win something new, and harder to regain what has been lost than to supplement what exists. In criticizing the deficiencies of the performance, moreover, the critic is obliged not only to assess the past experience but also to envisage the program's potentials under an administration that has learned from its mistakes. With this in view, some of the accomplishments of the program are summarized in the following sections.

RATIONALIZATION OF DISPARATE PLOTS AND
TRAFFIC PROBLEMS

American cities were built mostly in spurts and grew in metastasis. While grace may show itself in a period piece here or there, or in a surviving "money no object" opus by a Stanford White or lesser genius, the general imprint has been that of the jackpot, not the temple. Careful planning of a city or a subdivision was the exception, for the spur was land speculation and turnover, not long-term utility. The spark given to city planning by the building of the nation's capital was extinguished in the subsequent rush for gain. The development of the railroad, machine, and industry smothered whatever interest existed in the better city environment. The grid-iron plan of the East moved on to the West. Laid out by land companies, a site could be sold without the buyer or seller ever seeing it. Cities grew thereafter in fitful response to the needs of the incoming poor, and no city was ever built well during a mass migration of poor people.

The New England town and its common survived in places. But American cities mostly reflect the odds and ends of slapdash—the minimum flat or bandbox erected on small lots quickly to house immigrants—and when a town was planned, it was often of the sordid company town variety.

Happily our engineering knowledge was limited in the nineteenth century; much of what was built facing the streets was dispensable without excessive loss. Unhappily, what we are putting up today will be lasting and much of it will not be much better. We are more competent engineers, but design is still shaped by the quick buck.

Urban renewal has the potentials for correcting past errors. Its most important asset is the power of land assemblage, the proper use of which can rectify obsolete street patterns and help create more wholesome environments planned as workable units. New Haven is a good example, Boston's old waterfront promises another. Neither would have been possible without the right to assemble plots and rebuild according to plan.

The power of land assemblage makes possible the establishment of contiguity between plots and the bringing into use of land with unmarketable titles that have held up development of whole sections; it facilitates the synchronization of public and private improvements as well as the planning of cohesive shopping centers. It allows room for more squares and parking spaces and is a useful tool for a long overdue rebuilding of cities enslaved to the 20- to 25-foot lot, the traffic-laden street, and the gridiron pattern. It provides the opportunity for enlarging the street system surrounding the new projects, the closing of streets where necessary, the diversion of traffic, the addition of streets or widening of intersections. It makes possible the creation of footways separating pedestrian traffic from the automobile, and two-level or double-decked streets which have been talked about ever since Leonardo da Vinci put forth his plan for a model city. It facilitates running the new highways into the central city's shopping centers and the creation of off-street parking and enclosed parking spaces. In short, the renewal project supplies a multipurpose opportunity in place of the piecemeal efforts to correct traffic problems, provide playgrounds and open spaces, provide neighborhood amenities, and new housing, public and private.

ENCOURAGEMENT TO AESTHETICS

The exercise of public power to enforce aesthetics as well as safety, comfort, health, morale, and welfare had long been restricted by the courts.[2] Now, since the Supreme Court's decision in *Berman* v. *Parker* (1954), official agencies no longer need show that a slum is a slum with all the abominations ascribed to it by criminologists and slumsisters. In this respect, it may ultimately induce fewer projects that displace the poor. Like patriotism, however, which George

[2] *Haller Sign Works* v. *Physical Culture Training School*, 249 Ill. 436 (1911): "The courts of this country have with great unanimity held that the police power cannot interfere with private property rights for purely aesthetic purposes."

Jean Nathan once described as the arbitrary veneration of real estate over principles, the aesthetics of some renewal operations venerate profit above honor.[3] Under a system in which every investment dollar over the 90 percent mortgage is held to a minimum, a renewer may see beauty as costing too much and yielding too little. So too, some officials with the new power over beauty may in beauty's name condemn a Negro settlement for a park or a project.

Yet not all officialdom is devoid of moral and aesthetic sensibilities, and some have given their architects and planners the latitude to design something seemly. Others have become concerned about losing their old architectural landmarks and have called upon urban renewal to preserve them. With more than 1,500 projects approved for more than 740 communities and only 118 completed by 1964, an over-all appraisal is premature. But if there are projects that are not much better than the run-of-the-mill speculation, there are also those with merit. When profit is the motive, the influence of better design may be subordinated, for it is not easy to effect a good compromise between design and dollars. But since William Slayton took over the Urban Renewal Administration, a serious effort has at last been made to make design a major factor.

One now sees plazas and pedestrian malls, underground parking, and a better relationship between buildings. The manufacturers who were to build plants in New Haven had always relied on stock plans pulled out of a file by an industrial engineer—today they have been induced to employ architects. Elsewhere builders have been shown preliminary models of new designs which had never been within their contemplations and they have begun to accept them. The combination of rehabilitation and new building as part of a single project now makes for a project unity which could never have been achieved before. The use of landscaping interspersed in a project (as in Hartford Plaza), more spacing between buildings, and the placing of schools as part of the project (as in New Haven) are other gains.

Thus there are bright spots in the total picture as well as dismal

[3] Alexis de Tocqueville reflected that the people of a democratic nation "will habitually prefer the useful to the beautiful, and they will require that the beautiful be useful" (*Democracy in America*, Century, 1898, II, 56). After de Tocqueville, however, America became more interested in what was salable or rentable, rather than beautiful. The architect who can produce something that is profitable as well as beautiful is the still-undiscovered genius.

ones, but without the pressure for something better, all or most would have been the routine speculation or stock plan. Washington, D.C.'s Southwest project, New Haven's contributions, Philadelphia's Society Hill, San Francisco's Western Addition, and Detroit's Lafayette Square are among the program's better contributions. There will doubtless be others and one of the most hopeful signs is that the more prominent architects have been brought into the picture—I. M. Pei in Pittsburgh, New York, Boston, and Philadelphia; Mies van der Rohe in Detroit and Baltimore; Paul Rudolph in Boston and New Haven; William W. Wurster in San Francisco; Minoru Yamasaki in Honolulu—while others are being given the chance for the first time to add design to profit criteria. "By slow degrees, we are learning a new technique," says the architectural critic, Douglas Haskell, and urban renewal is supplying the occasion. How much of the product will be better in the end will depend not only on the architects but on a more enlightened federal policy, on whether the market in a city justifies the additional investment, and on whether more cities will subordinate their yearning for higher tax receipts to better architecture and planning.

SPUR TO CIVIC INTEREST

If the patterns of cities are chaotic, the interest of citizens has been inert. If the slumberers have been occasionally aroused to protest, it has usually been because of the threatened destruction of a landmark they were accustomed to pass but never look at. Rarely has civic exertion been expressed in a passion for the creative.

Recently, however, the central city's loss of population and the departure of chain stores has brought out a kind of last ditch, never-say-die gallantry among the good-citizen residuum. They have been joined by the real estate men and department store owners as well as by leaders of the threatened institutions. The Charles Street Center in Baltimore was initiated and planned largely by a group of downtown businessmen who saw both the handwriting on the wall and the figures on their balance sheets. In Washington, D.C., and Providence, Rhode Island, similar groups helped with the new plans for the downtown area. In Boston, the Chamber of Commerce put up the initial planning funds for studying the city's waterfront area, and businessmen have also sparked interest in New Haven, Hartford, Philadelphia, Cincinnati, Norfolk, St. Louis, Denver, Pittsburgh, and Cleveland. The renewal program has aroused a keener interest in urban disorders. Outside specialists have often been called in to take a look and prescribe. The interest of David Rockefeller in the redevelopment of New York City's downtown is one of the hopeful examples.

In 1948, when I was a housing columnist for the *New York Post* and tried to plug city planning, the city editor would tell me to get back to the subject of rats biting babies.[4] City planning now makes the front page if for no other reason than that the suburban threat to the department store has alerted the paper's business department to the link between downtown sales and newspaper profits. The *Washington Post* or the *Louisville Courier* will publicize, serialize, and editorialize anything on urban renewal, and the *New York Times* will give a tome on city or regional planning more attention than the fight over Fanny Hill.

IMPETUS TO CIVIC AND CULTURAL IMPROVEMENTS

Cities are perennially in need of new courthouses, parks, schools, administrative buildings, and other improvements which growing financial embarrassments have forced them to shelve. Urban renewal is far from being the wand that waves such improvements in, but it has sometimes been the persuader that goads officials into taking a second look at some of the fading blueprints in their pigeonholes.

One of the most important contributions has been the large number of public schools that have been generated by the credits the renewal program allows against the city's contribution to the write-down of land cost. While it is hard to determine precisely how many of these schools would have been built without the renewal inducement, there is little question that the program has been responsible for a good proportion.

Good civic and cultural centers (if there were a federal program that helped finance them) would be a gain for cities. Our own centers are far from rivaling the Forum and the Acropolis, nor do they compare with the examples of Venice and Stockholm, but

---

[4] This wasn't such a good idea either for an evening paper. The editor soon discovered that people stopped buying it because it spoiled their appetites for supper.

some have won the plaudits of architectural critics.[5] Norfolk's $15 million Civic Center will have a thirteen-story municipal building and four other structures as part of an extensive downtown development. Boston has started a government center with an estimated cost of $185 million. If more centers were properly located and if they included some skillful focuses of interest to which people would be drawn, civic spirit would get a sizable lift.

So with cultural improvements. Culture in the United States has depended largely on private support, and less than 4 percent of all corporate contributions go to the arts. In contrast to Europe, even public museums depend on hard-won gifts and on membership dues for survival, and the city's penchant has therefore been for the stadium, paying coliseum, and big auditorium. Less than a third of the cultural centers being built or on the drawing boards can accommodate more than one of the performing arts and many are little more than sports arenas or convention halls. A small town will build a costly swimming pool and do without a library. The promotion of the "progress of science and useful arts" encompassed in the federal constitution was only to protect copyrights, and not until the 1960s did the President designate a special consultant on the arts. His role, however, seemed to have been confined to making public statements, one of which was: "The American people have been slow to recognize that artistic and cultural expression is closely related to the vitality of institutions."[6] Federal interest in culture, meanwhile, has been confined mostly to agriculture.

The most dramatic cultural example is Lincoln Center in New York City. The project originated when Carnegie Hall was scheduled for demolition and the Metropolitan Opera decided to move. A site was available under the urban renewal program which "answered the real estate riddle of an adequate site at a reasonable price in the heart of skyscraper-crowded Manhattan."[7] Lincoln Center of the Performing Arts was born. "For me," said John D. Rockefeller, "new horizons began to open. Since the war my work had been concentrated in the international area. I had begun to think more seriously of my responsibilities as a citizen of New York."[8] His

[5] Lewis Mumford, "Civic Art," *Encyclopedia of the Social Sciences*, Macmillan, 1942, II, 493.
[6] August Heckscher, *New York Times Magazine*, September 23, 1962, p. 39.
[7] *New York Times*, Supplement, September 23, 1962.
[8] *Ibid.*, p. 14.

assumption of responsibility led to an investment by him and other sources of $170 million for the housing of the performing arts and a seating capacity for 12,000 patrons in six new buildings.

While urban renewal spurred both this citizen activity in New York and its new cultural center, the site for Lincoln Center was acquired not because culture was a public use authorizing the taking of $7.5 million in private land, but because the site was called a slum. To comply with the statute, high-rent housing had to be built on the site though it had no logical place in a cultural scheme. The statute also led to the building of a single center when a few smaller centers strategically placed in several sections of Manhattan—on the East Side, West Side, and lower Manhattan—would have reinforced existing entertainment clusters.

Lincoln Centers or at least their smaller cultural equivalents are needed in many cities. They should be authorized by state laws, and the power of eminent domain should be granted. Their fulfillment should depend neither on the provision of housing on the site nor on the selection of a slum area as a prerequisite. They are more within the range of public use than slum razing for high-rental project building. That urban renewal has spurred civic and cultural improvements that might have been stillborn is a big plus for the program.

BUTTRESSING INTEREST OF RELIGIOUS INSTITUTIONS

The multiplication of religious institutions and associations has been one of the most striking features of America's religious and social life. The church's influence, said James Bryce, was stronger and deeper in America than in European communities.

Bryce's observation was not unfounded. During the immigration period churches not only ministered to the poor but built homes for the aged, parochial and industrial schools, settlement houses, YMCAs, and immigrant aid societies. Social conscience combined with religious gospel to become a main force in the drive for municipal reform; it helped give urban issues an ethical focus. The recent shifts to suburbia, however, have effected a break with the city. They are confronting church (and synagogue) with some difficult choices.

The church could elect to remain—"Upon this rock I will build my church and the gates of Hell shall not prevail against it." And if it does, it might try to draw its constituency from a greater distance or resolve to win the new neighbors into its fold. It might also elect to retain the old seat while branching out to the suburb as well. It might resolve to do none of these and become a mobile church, laying a claim upon American engineering genius to build it a demountable chapel and spire so that it could follow the mobile trend and fulfill its mission on wheels.

The advent of urban renewal, public housing, public works, and federal aid to suburban growth has added not only new problems but new dimensions for the church. Thus far, too many churches have been destroyed and their people forced out of the neighborhoods in which these institutions had been a binding force. (The destruction by Stockton, California, of more than thirty Negro churches is an example of what should not be done.) But a number of churches have assumed leadership. They have spurred a greater social responsibility for the less privileged and influenced officialdom to revise their eviction and relocation policies. The 300-unit development under Section 221(d)(3) of the St. John Missionary Baptist Church in South Dallas and the 520-unit development of the Wheat Street Baptist Church in Atlanta are examples of constructive cooperation. The Presbyterian Synod in St. Louis not only chose to remain in the Mill Creek area but expanded its church and integrated it, so that it will play a more creative role in a new and extended neighborhood, part of which had been in an all-Negro renewal area. A few churches are building housing for their elderly and for their displaced poor [under Sections 202 and 221 (d) (3) of the housing acts] and more are becoming interested. This could become a major force in redevelopment, particularly if a national organization emerges—interdenominational if possible—that could guide the local churches in their operations or undertake the projects directly where necessary.

SPUR TO INSTITUTIONAL EXPANSION

The site locations of American universities and colleges have varied with the judgments of their founders. Oxford and Cambridge were built in isolated communities far from the turmoil of London, while universities in Paris, Cologne, Milan, Lima, Caracas, and Mexico City were built in the cities. So, too, in the United States, some universities chose urban locations and some the rustic hinterlands. New York University and Columbia located their buildings in New York City, the University of Pennsylvania in Philadelphia, the University of Chicago in Chicago, the University of California was sited at Berkeley, and Stanford at Palo Alto, while a host of institutions chose the backlands.

The desires of the founders, however, were not always respected as the surge of industry and people enlarged the urban orbit. Only a small bridge now separates Harvard and the Massachusetts Institute of Technology from Boston, while the city of Cambridge itself has burgeoned into a busy industrial center that has engulfed both institutions. Berkeley is now within the shadow of San Francisco.

Meanwhile institutional needs for space have swelled. Enrollments in the last three decades have tripled and are expected to accelerate in the three decades ahead. Some $15 billion is the estimated expenditure for new buildings to meet the needs of expansion and enrollments in the decade ending in 1970.

But as the need for expansion has grown, the university's ability to expand has become more restricted. Unlike a church housed on two or three lots, the university cannot move with its extensive chattels and classrooms to some secluded site in a suburb shielded from the pressures of the city.

Urban renewal not only sparked the university's interest in general planning, citizen education, and urban problems, but gave it the impetus for assuming responsibility in the replanning of its adjoining areas.[9] Write-downs of land cost provided cheap sites while below-market federal loans under the college housing program have helped them build student dormitories—by 1964 about $2.1 billion in low-interest loans had been approved by the Community Facilities Administration for such purposes.

Urban renewal's main benefit for the university was that it lent the power of eminent domain for acquisition of land. In 1962, sixty-

[9] Special provisions of the law have helped materially. Section 310 permits waiver of the predominantly residential requirement and permits a credit to the city for expenditures made by the university for acquiring and clearing the property in or around an urban renewal project.

four universities were proposing acquisition of 970 acres from local renewal agencies at an estimated cost of $28 million.[10]

The university, after all, is still part of the city's lifeblood, the seat of culture and enlightenment, the source of essential skills and professions, the fountainhead of research. A city suffers less from losing a major industry than from losing a university.

What may be said of universities may be said also of hospitals which are growing institutions vital to any city. Like the universities, they lacked the eminent domain power, and the advent of urban renewal has helped some of them acquire land at low cost for their expansion programs. Philadelphia and Chicago are outstanding examples of university interest and Boston, Chicago, New York, and Norfolk of hospital interest in renewal operations.

The "Town and Gown" problem, however, with its undercurrent of citizen suspicion, is aggravated when the tax-exempt institution becomes involved with the displacement of people. Though better public relations and greater interest in the community would help, the university has all too often isolated itself from the neighborhood's problems. New York University's support of a road through Washington Square Park is an example of how to make the town distrust the gown. (Recently NYU has shown a little more respect for the townsmen.) When MIT helped the beleaguered Cambridge renewal agency dispose of its vacant site by drawing industry into a research center, and when the University of Pennsylvania actively participated in Philadelphia's replanning, they set good examples of university cooperation.

INDUCEMENT TO INDUSTRY

One of the most pressing problems of cities is that of holding their industries or making room for new industries. The exodus of an industry not only brings unemployment but loss of purchasing power, foreclosures, emigration of people, and lower tax revenues. Inability to expand or to find suitable land is one of the reasons for exodus. High taxes and the inducements offered by other communities in the form of free land, low taxes, and easy financing are other reasons.

[10] "Universities, Their Role in Urban Renewal," Address by William L. Slayton at the University of Pennsylvania, September 20, 1962.

Urban renewal is one of the devices being employed by hard-pressed cities to induce industries to stay where they are. When the Cornell-Dubiler Electric Company contemplated leaving Providence for the South, Providence made land available to it in an industrial park. New Britain, Connecticut, was able to hang on to the American Hardware Company by offering to buy its land and buildings as part of an urban renewal project, demolishing the buildings, and reselling the cleared land to the company. When Sargent and Company threatened to move its lock manufacturing plant to Kentucky, New Haven induced the company to stay by buying a twenty-six acre industrial site on which the company will build a $4 million plant. A large food terminal will also be located on the site. An attractive site made possible by urban renewal may draw other industry to the city. Thus New Haven brought back the hardware firm of H. B. Ives Company which had already moved to suburban Hamden by offering it a square-block site in its Wooster Square renewal project. A number of other cities have been able to attract industries only by assembling the land on which ·factories could be built.

REBUILDING DOWNTOWN

Though urban renewal started as a measure to clear the city's slum towns, its emphasis has steadily veered toward rebuilding the city's downtowns. The growing need to salvage the city's threatened business centers coupled with the private redeveloper's enthusiasm for the still solvent downtown residential sites gradually brought pressure on Congress to broaden its purpose. "Over the years . . . it became clear that the construction of good neighborhoods was intimately tied to the economic health of the community. The revitalization of industrial, commercial, and downtown areas so as to attract job-creating private investment, was realized as a necessary goal to which urban renewal could make a substantial contribution."[11]

A 10 percent exception to the "predominantly residential" requirement of the law was put into the Housing Act of 1954; this was increased to 20 percent in 1959 and raised to 30 percent in 1961.

[11] *Housing Act of 1961* (H.R.6028), House Committee on Banking and Currency, 87th Cong., 1st Sess., June 1, 1961, pp. 25, 26.

570 / CHARLES ABRAMS

While 70 percent of the federal funds still had to be used for writing down land cost for slum clearance or residential building, the rest could be used for other types of developments. "The economic, institutional and cultural bases of community life are increasingly recognized as necessary to the creation and continuing existence of good homes in sound urban neighborhoods," said a Congressional committee.[12]

In addition to the funds available directly for downtown renewal, cities also increased their selection of the slum, pseudoslum or "nonslum but called slum" areas near downtowns, so that a majority of renewal sites have tended to be either in or near the business centers.

Where the designated downtown area was occupied by poorer families, they were detached from their well-located anchorages. In other cases, businesses were moved to make way for the better-paying enterprises that would brighten up trade and bring more people to the waning city centers. There have been some dramatic examples of downtown rebuilding spurred by urban renewal.

Providence proposes to transform its downtown into five cohesive precincts. The present New Haven Railroad terminal and tracks will be relocated, a new civic center will house a new state office building, a new city hall, and other civic improvements. Provision will be made for parking and for a new station; and there will be a new convention hall, garages, a bus terminal, and an arena, while a new office center and a pedestrian mall will serve as a thoroughfare between the large stores and the new Weybosset residential community.

In addition to its downtown Golden Gateway project, San Francisco's plans call for a billion-dollar rapid transit system, including a subway under Market Street and the abolition of all vehicular traffic (except some buses) to make way for a twenty-block-long pedestrian mall with intersecting malls and plazas.

Cleveland's Erieview project will link the waterfront and the retail office section, once separated by a group of old buildings, into a project which will ultimately entail $125 million of new investment. It is anticipated that new housing and offices around the commercial area will help support the new retail facilities. Other important downtown rebuilding is taking place in Pittsburgh, Sacra-

[12] *Ibid.*, p. 26.

mento, Philadelphia, Minneapolis, New Haven, Norfolk, and Boston.

Some major chain stores, whose presence pegs a new retail section, are often reluctant to make commitments in the declining areas. They have already established branches in nearby suburbia, find them profitable, and see no reason for supporting competition with investments they have already made. But urban renewal has challenged their continued outward drift. It has offered the big stores more space, parking, and a cohesive shopping center. As a result companies are taking a second look at the city and a growing number are electing to stay. Macy's will move into three renewal sites and calls its action a "new trend."

An official of the Sears, Roebuck Company told me that the downtown sites have advantages for the company, not the least of which is the built-in market of central city buyers who can walk to the stores. The main problems, he says, are getting the highway to feed into the downtown and providing ample parking for the suburban customers. New Haven, among other cities, exemplifies how cooperation between highway planning and urban renewal can salvage a city's downtown. The distance of suburbia from the store is less important than the number of traffic lights. But what often discourages the chains, the Sears official says, are the long delays in getting the program underway and the opposition of some local merchants fearing the competition.

However imperfect the effort, the move by cities to revitalize their main streets is at least an acknowledgment that something more than new housing and slum clearance is needed to restore the city's health and since regenerating a city's downtown is a vital part of its medication, this phase of the renewal program is one of its more important contributions.

PROVIDER OF HIGH-RENTAL HOUSING

Cities inhabited only by the poor are poor cities. A city is the crossway of the great unwashed and of those who have cleaned up; of the many both below mediocrity and above it. Homogeneity when voluntarily created in a single section of a city may be good and even colorful, but homogeneity in a whole city can be a bore, whether it be homogeneity of income, class, race, or age.

The suburban revolution has effected too sharp a class shakeout, leaving the poor in the central cities and too many of the upper-income families in the power-mower belt.

The result has been a loss of purchasing power for many establishments like art, craft, and antique shops, and the theaters, restaurants, and good hotels that add to a city's spirit. A city with nothing but chain groceries and a few five-and-dime stores hardly inspires tourists to circulate their money. A city with higher purchasing power helps the less privileged in employment and in opportunities. It may also bring more investment into the city from some of the better-heeled residents.

There should be no objection to building a string of multiple dwellings at $60 monthly per room, if there are customers for the product; and, if the market existed, some would be built even without urban renewal aid. But there is little question that many would not be built because the land could not be assembled and because the land cost would be too high. Nor would they be built where they serve the city's best interests. A well-planned project attracts high-income tenants who might otherwise shift to suburbia.

The main trouble with building for higher-income families has been the pushing around of the poor. If the low-income families could be adequately housed—and this does not mean confining their choices to public housing projects, other slums, or paying rents they cannot afford—the inconveniences inflicted upon them might at least be atoned for. But there is not yet an adequate program allowing use of renewal sites for the displaced families or for financing enough good housing elsewhere, particularly in suburbia.

PROP FOR LOWER-PRICED HOUSING

The flaws in one piece of legislation often lead to the shoring up of another. The renewal program has stimulated support for public housing appropriations that might otherwise have been defeated. It made no moral sense, even to opponents of public housing, to authorize ousting of low-income families without providing at least a compensatory alternative. The program has buttressed the public housing agencies in the 2,200 localities that have them; in the four years preceding 1965, the number of participating localities has increased by 700, mostly in smaller communities. A good number of these have organized as a result of existing or contemplated urban renewal programs.

So too, when it appeared that only a fraction of those evicted moved into public housing, $10 million was appropriated to finance experiments under a "Low-income Housing Demonstration Program"; in June 1963, there were twenty-three such demonstrations. On a very small scale, some of these experiments provide direct subsidies to families, others are experiments in design techniques or rehabilitation. Pilot schemes, when successful, sometimes serve as potent arguments before Congressional committees—public housing, for example, started as an experimental program. If the schemes affirm the validity of family subsidies and Congress can be persuaded to supplement the present public housing formula with a family rent subsidy for the lowest-income group, one of the most constructive devices for solving the slum problem might materialize.

The Section 221(d)(3) formula, with its 100 percent loans at below-market rates (3⅛–3⅞ percent), is another device spawned out of the renewal program and one of the most promising in its prospects. It enabled a reduction in normal market rents by 20 percent, which has been a help to some moderate (not low-income) families. It has also stimulated some rehabilitation and generated a widening interest by churches and civic organizations in building housing under a nonprofit arrangement.

The significance of the program is that it is the first step toward direct federal loans for low-income families. The second step—still to be taken—is to cut the interest rate to a level which would make it possible for families earning $3,000 a year to buy or rent homes built by private and nonprofit builders. The big question—and the big potential—for FHA, FNMA, and the entrepreneur under this profit-nonprofit formula is whether a realistic mean can be found which will afford the private builder a reasonable building fee and hold down his penchant for the windfall. The answer is: It is possible, if not yet probable.[13]

If a formula evolves under which a responsible building industry

---

[13] A ray of hope is shed in the experience of New York's Mitchell-Lama law in which the state and city make loans to builders at low interest rates and also grant tax exemption up to 50 percent of the normal real estate tax. The apartments rent at about $30 a room per month, which is well below market. The builder's incentive is a 7 percent contracting fee on cooperatives and 10 percent for limited dividend operations. Since the actual building fees may

will sponsor enterprises for a reasonable fee without having to stake any investment, federal housing policy could well take a turn toward private sponsorship of moderate- and low-rent housing operations. The know-how of private enterprise and the diversity of ownerships would be gains for these families. But to reach the lower-income families, particularly in the big cities, either the interest rate would have to be considerably lower or tenants would have to be subsidized directly.

If the arrangement works, 221(d)(3) may mark the evolution of a novel contractual arrangement between government and the responsible private entrepreneur under which the entrepreneur, for a limited fee, produces dwellings in line with improved government standards. If the process is to succeed, however, double bookkeeping must be removed from the operation; a realistic fee should be allowed the developer to spur his interest; a reasonable charge should be allowed for management; there should be no fictitious building fees and charges winked at by federal officials. Projects would have to be built at actual cost plus a fixed fee representing profit, and the profit should be made known to all parties and adequately certified.

Much will also depend on whether some of the larger corporations in American enterprise can be induced to enter the field under such an arrangement. At one time, company housing played a prominent part in home-building operations. The motives were not always pure, but the ethics of big business, while not yet to be confused with Christianity, have improved—there are generous hands as well as itching palms. The question is whether big industry will rise to the occasion. A real effort by the President after a White House conference of businessmen and insurance companies might induce more of them to take the giant step.

Section 221(d)(3) is not the only program authorizing liberal loans to private enterprise at below market rates. Congress also passed Section 202 of the Housing Act, authorizing the Community Facilities Administration to make fifty-year loans for almost the

---

amount to 3 percent or less, the difference is pocketed as profit. If the builder chooses the limited dividend formula, it should net him 12 percent or more on his cash investment, plus the depreciation advantage for income tax purposes. Builders of cooperatives under the law look to the 7 percent building fee for their profit. A $10 million project thus gives them a fee of $700,000 for their trouble.

total development cost at interest rates of a quarter of one percent above the government rate so as to encourage rental projects for the elderly. The sponsors were to be nonprofit agencies, and FNMA was to buy the mortgages which, under later legislation, could cover the entire cost.[14]

The nonprofit programs were no sooner launched than private entrepreneurs began to sidle into the areas reserved for nonprofit organizations. As the FHA administrator put it: "Because of well-intentioned but inexperienced and unsophisticated applicants, and private entrepreneurs posing as nonprofit sponsors, there has been need to move with caution." Yet it is hard to see how the profit element can be kept out of the nonprofit program; and when 100 percent loans were authorized, housing applications soared.

The big question in these operations is whether the entrepreneur will be satisfied with a good fee for his profit or will look for the bonanza. But the potential in the programs for a new kind of liaison between government and responsible entrepreneurs is there, and it is primarily the renewal program that exposed it.

SPUR TO COOPERATIVES

Until recently cooperatives were hard put to get started. Federal and state laws offered them little assistance except in New York. Single homes were often better buys than those built under co-operative legislation. Until the condominium arrangement was made feasible,[15] a cooperative usually depended upon the continued ability of all its members to meet fixed charges. If a few defaulted, the rest had to pick up the tab to keep the mortgage on the property from going into default.

Another handicap was the lack of a central cooperative that not

[14] Section 231 of the Housing Act of 1959 authorized FHA to insure mortgages on rental accommodations for elderly people built by "nonprofit-motivated" agencies. Where the sponsor was a public agency or a "nonprofit-motivated" entrepreneur, the mortgage could be for as much as 100 percent of replacement cost. The mortgage on profit-motivated projects could not exceed 90 percent with a maximum interest of 5½ percent. The 5½ percent rate dictated higher rents than most of the elderly could pay. The public housing program had already allocated a portion of its low-rent units for the aged, and some specially designed projects were built.

[15] One of the deterrents to cooperative investment had been the blanketing of the mortgages over all the units in a project. Under the condominium arrangement, each cooperator has title to his own unit, and default of others does not affect him. Loans on the individual units became possible when FHA was empowered to insure mortgages on them.

only understood the complicated problems of organizing, financing, building and managing, but could guide and build for its "daughter" co-ops as HSB (Hyresgästernas Sparkasse-och Byggnadsförening) is doing in Sweden. In the absence of know-how and leadership, the cooperator's advantages in cooperating were never impressive.[16] What was gained by the elimination of profit and other advantages was lost in conflicts, inexperience, and noncooperation by cooperators.

Greater interest was generated when FHA insured forty-year mortgages on cooperatives at 5¼ percent interest plus one-half percent for insurance. The loans could equal 97 percent of the replacement cost. Cooperatives were also authorized under Section 221(d)(3) for displacees and other families in the moderate-income group.[17] Cooperatives might also provide housing for the elderly with loans for the full development cost. Write-down of land cost in an urban renewal project and FNMA mortgage aid also helped.

With the 97–100 percent loans, the small downpayments required, and the favorable income tax deductions permitted to cooperative owners, cooperators showed more interest, and so did some labor unions. The ability of urban renewal agencies to supply the land to them at low cost has already spurred the International Longshoremen's and Warehousemen's Union in San Francisco to build a cooperative on cleared land; a project of 752 units on a renewal site in Paterson, New Jersey, has been built; and New York City has made a number of urban renewal sites available for cooperative development. While cooperatives still do not benefit the low-income families, legislation may some day permit subsidized cooperatives for their benefit. New York City's offer of cheap financing and substantial tax exemption for moderate-income projects may also spur other cities to follow suit.

[16] Some central leadership has now been supplied by the Foundation for Cooperative Housing and its subsidiary, the FCH Company. The FCH Company has a national office at 322 Main Street, Stamford, Connecticut. Two other cooperative organizations function; they are the United Housing Foundation and the Association for Middle Income Housing, Inc. Except for a Virgin Islands project sponsored by the latter, both organizations operate primarily in New York City.

[17] The forty-year financing at the original 3⅛ percent interest for debt service was $3.65 per $1,000. Thus on a $12,000 loan the monthly debt service would be about $44, or about 20 percent below the total monthly charges under the 213 program. (See David L. Krooth, "How Cooperative Housing Can Help Urban Renewal," *Federal Bar Journal*, Summer 1961, p. 340.)

If, through the stimulus of urban renewal, cooperatives emerge as important producers of nonprofit housing and perhaps even of subsidized housing for low-income groups, it would be a major advance.

INCREASED TAX REVENUES

Successful redevelopment of a site creates a substantial tax-paying asset which should compensate the city for its subsidy in five to eleven years. Thereafter the city enjoys a clear gain (see Appendix A, below, for the calculations). As the calculations in Appendix A show, through a contribution of $2 million for the land cost, the city could gain an extra $600,000 in annual revenue and thereby recoup its investment in a few years. When a city creates a new $600,000 annual income, the capitalized value of that gain is at least $10 million. This should far more than compensate for any losses during the development period when the buildings do not produce revenues. Urban Renewal Commissioner Slayton has estimated that the increase in assessed valuations on projects started or completed will be from $575 million to more than $3 billion, or a 427 percent increase. The San Francisco Redevelopment agency confirms that urban renewal can be "good business" for a city. Whether it is "good business," of course, depends on whether the project gets a sponsor, and a number of cities have been disappointed in their expectations. But despite one opinion to the contrary, the projects that are completed should prove profitable to the cities, even if it takes ten years to complete them.[18]

The cities have made no bones about the profitability of their renewal operations. They have publicized the new-found treasure in handsome brochures for citizen consumption and made it a leading argument for pushing more and bigger programs.[19] California renewal agencies have, in fact, been able to borrow the cost of their cities' contribution to the land subsidy by pledging future revenues.

[18] The statement by Martin Anderson (*The Federal Bulldozer*, M.I.T. Press, 1964, p. 172) to the effect that tax increases in cities with renewal programs are a "myth" and that "it is doubtful if the program will significantly increase tax revenues to any specific city" is not substantiated by the facts in a number of "specific" cities with completed programs.

[19] Typical quotations from urban renewal brochures are the following: "The Downtown Project in East Orange will cost an estimated $3,500,000. The re-

There is nothing wrong about a city making money as a dividend of its public operations (like profiting on marriage license fees), but the issue gets down to a finer logic:

The main purpose of a city is to act for the health and welfare of its people—which is the governmental function. The city also has proprietary functions, involved with the properties it owns for governmental purposes (sidewalks, asphalt plants, piers, etc.). The proprietary activities may not be extended into the real estate business; "municipal trading" as practiced in foreign countries has rarely been countenanced here. Although the city may profit as an incident of its authorized operations, private gain or speculation as a main aim is not within the contemplation of its charter. The traditional rule is that a city is organized not to make money but to spend it.

Urban renewal offered the opportunity to cash in on some of the builder's profits, and the cities reached for the money. In the absence of adequate state and federal aid to help meet their soaring commitments, they sought whatever revenues they could lay their hands on. The trouble is that when a city gets mixed up in its motives, it is apt to subordinate its social obligations to its financial prospects. This is what has happened in many renewal operations that have been called "successful." It became less important to clean up a slum than to clean up in tax collections. There are instances when both the public good and the public treasury have been enhanced, and in these a gain can be chalked up against the deficits of urban renewal. But it is a sad commentary that cities should have

---

turn for the sale of the land should reduce this cost to about $2,900,000 of which $966,000 will be contributed by the City in public improvements. The increased tax revenue should be nearly $200,000 more annually than is presently being returned. Within 5-6 years the City will have amortized its investment. Public funds will have been spent to give private funds the opportunity to work. In the long run this partnership will keep our economy healthy as well as help to stabilize the tax rate which is choking most of our large cities." (*East Orange, New Jersey, Urban Renewal Program*, Progress Report and Development Guide 1960–1961, Citizens Advisory Committee and Housing Authority, n.d., p. 14.)

"In 1953 the property tax revenue from Southwest was $553,409.77 ($592,-016.00 at current tax rates). It is estimated that the yearly tax revenue after completion of redevelopment will be $4,846,221.00. . . . Redevelopment offers one of the best methods for enhancing the value of the taxable property in the city. The increased property tax revenue from the redeveloped Southwest will repay the District's share of redevelopment in less than six years" (*Rebuilding Southwest Washington*, District of Columbia Redevelopment Land Agency, Annual Report, 1961, p. 13).

to look for profitable ventures to pay their costs of governing. It highlights the desperate plight of cities and the need for an overhaul of the federal-state-city tax system looking toward a more equitable distribution of revenues and aid.

ASSESSING URBAN RENEWAL

In assessing public programs, gains and losses cannot be quantified as in private operations to arrive at a precise profit or loss figure. Financial benefits cannot be offset against social costs nor an increase in revenues juxtaposed against the misery of people evicted from their homes. There are cities that can boast new downtowns and apartment houses, fresh revenues and other gains from the program; and if its faults and virtues could be put on the scales, what would tip the balance against it in a number of cities would be the uprooting of families, their increased rent burdens, and the numerous other hardships inflicted upon them. Yet the same objection could be made against demolition for streets, roads, traffic, bridges, and airports—why make some people flee to enable others to fly? Why should the people without cars be inconvenienced for the sake of those who can afford them?

By 1965, of 27,000 acres bought by cities since 1949, 10,439 had been resold; of the remainder, 7,400 acres were still uncleared, another 3,308 were cleared but lacked a sponsor. About 5,879 cleared acres were close to sale. Viewed from its inception in 1949, the record is not impressive, but viewed from its more recent acceleration, the progress is promising.

It takes time and effort to get projects underway, and while some may never see mortar, it would be rash to predict the program's failure. The renewal law confronted the cities with a task for which they were unprepared and which their officials had to learn the hard way. They had to win public support for a new program, master the involutions of the real estate enterprise, try to achieve good design while making it profitable for the renewers, replan whole sections, move people *en masse* while dealing with the racial issue, and do all these things while the federal officials were also groping with the program and changing the rules in the middle of the game. Moreover, the planning profession which was to supply these officials with the expert personnel is itself in embryo and the two-year graduate courses given at a few good universities have hardly equipped the candidates for the job. Yet all in all, considering the program's novelty and the obstacles, it is a miracle that so much was accomplished. It is a credit to the Weaver-Slayton administration that after years of stagnation, the program has begun to show more and better results.

Doubtless, the program has done many cities good and some more harm than good. However, the issue is not whether it has done more harm than good but whether its faults can be rectified so that it can do better.

From its inception, the program's shortcomings were acknowledged, and efforts were made to correct them. The 1950 act made forty revisions while the 1954 legislation gave it a major overhaul. New FHA aids, FNMA, Sections 220 and 221, (a), (b), (c), (d), (d)(1), (d)(2), (d)(3), and (d)(4) were rushed to its rescue. Thereafter, comprehensive planning and rehabilitation were emphasized and other programs brought in to supplement it. The widespread interest in planning which the program has generated is an important accomplishment. But Congress has been unwilling to face the real issues, and despite all these changes, the program's basic defects remain:

1. It overemphasizes slum clearance and lacks an adequate housing program for those it evicts and for those who live in the slums it proposes tearing down. It makes no provision for rehousing these people except in the cities.

2. It relies almost exclusively on the speculative profit motive for the clearance of these slums and the rebuilding of slum neighborhoods. Some of the projects cannot show a profit and should be developed for other purposes—more parks, playgrounds, etc.

3. It deals primarily with only one aspect of the city's predicament, i.e., housing and slums, while it ignores its others—poverty, social unrest, school problems, racial frictions, physical obsolescence, spatial restrictions, decline of its economic base, and the lack of financial resources to cope with its major difficulties. The poverty program is only a feeble start toward grappling with a few of these problems.

If the program continued its demolitions until every slum had been leveled, the housing problem would become incomparably worse and the housing conditions of low-income people would be aggravated with each demolition. The answer to a city's blight is not its destruction (without providing alternative shelter), but the removal of the causes and the improvement of the city so that it will become part of the better society.

The fundamental weakness of the renewal program is that it assumes that cities are sound for investment; that slum clearance and rebuilding in cities can make them sound if they are not; that the operations can even be profitable, if only the land cost is written down and the mortgage money is offered to the builders. Urban renewal puts the cart before the horse. If cities could have better schools, recreation, and environments, if they could cut their tax levies and provide their needed improvements from their revenues, and if they could be made pleasanter, safer, more interesting, and more convenient places in which to live and work, the demand for city living and housing would appear automatically in many areas. Mortgage money without FHA or FNMA assistance would become more plentiful, and private builders and merchants would scramble for the profit opportunities available. Urban renewal could then become a more constructive tool for assembling land, replanning obsolete layouts, and providing recreation, schools, housing, and other amenities to new, well-planned neighborhoods.

In sum, the urban renewal program is an important tool for cities and deserves continuance and expansion. But if it is to be a more useful component of a formula to regenerate cities, it must also do far more than it has done to date. It must be further implemented, be more selective in its authorizations, and sufficiently free of pressures to reject applications that are profit-motivated but not socially useful. It must show qualitative and not merely quantitative results. It must aim to improve cities, not simply speculative prospects.

America's vitality in the past was reinforced partly by its plurality of cultures and the contributions these cultures made to the American environment. These cultures are disappearing with the emergence of newer generations, and with their passing is also going the plurality of the environments which these varied cultures created. Diversity is giving way to a stagnant uniformity and a spiritual fatigue. Television in the parlor, automation and its routines, the monolithic additions to cities, the endless rows of duplicate suburbias and road programs are leading inevitably to an environmental homogenesis in the nation, the consequence of which will be a nationwide monotony. The urbanization and suburbanization of

American life is becoming a treadmill when it should be a frontier. This is the real challenge that urban renewal should be confronting. This goes for the housing program as well.

A young country is seeing its cities go to seed before they have borne their fruit. Its cities, not yet old enough to boast antiquity, are showing all the symptoms of senescence. They are losing population at a time when the nation is racing into urbanization. They are poor and becoming poorer, and the more they tax to meet their needs, the heavier become their burdens.

If urban renewal has accomplished nothing else, it has stimulated a new interest in cities and highlighted the need for doing something about them before it is too late. If its impositions upon individuals have been oppressive and if some of the cleared sites may never see brick and mortar rise over them, something hopeful may yet be discovered in the rubble. If Congress can be aroused to keep looking and searching for the real causes and cures of urban erosion, urban renewal and its concomitant programs will be a gain.

If the housing and urban renewal administrators were more forthright in confessing the incompleteness of what Congress has given them, were more willing to admit the hardships the programs have caused, and proposed the proper means for easing them, they would be less subject to criticism. If, instead of asking for statutory pittances and telling Congress that these will furnish the answers, they would proffer the remedies they know can be constructive, they might win wider public support. But they cannot be expected to carry the ball without the support of the President. In the long run, it is the prestige of his office and the leadership he gives to the issue that will determine the destiny of our cities and the contributions an urban renewal program can make to their progress.

Appendix A

Acquisition cost of site	$10,000,000
Resale price to redeveloper	4,000,000
Land subsidy required	6,000,000
Contribution by federal government	4,000,000
Required cash contribution by city	$ 2,000,000
Assessed value of private improvement and land	30,000,000
Annual tax rate at 3 percent of value	900,000
Less taxes previously received from slum	300,000
Tax increment to city from new improvement	$ 600,000

PART VIII

THE FUTURE OF URBAN RENEWAL

24 Policies for Rebuilding*

BERNARD FRIEDEN

PART 1: ALTERNATIVES FOR PUBLIC ACTION

The rebuilding of cities is now a matter of general public concern. Both the federal government and the cities are heavily involved in problems of housing and the future of declining neighborhoods, but the development of public policies that link housing concerns with rebuilding programs is a difficult task. Results of this study provide a sharp definition of some major issues involved in the choice of objectives for public policy and a number of guidelines for achieving housing goals while rebuilding the city.

If public policies are to serve broad social goals, there can be little justification for clearing away houses as long as they have a useful function. Big-city experience in the 1950's has demonstrated that the term "gray areas"—with its implications of abandonment and disuse —is a misnomer for the old neighborhoods. These areas serve rather as *zones of passage* for low-income groups new to urban life, and for other residents unable to afford higher rents or not yet prepared to leave the social surroundings of the old communities. Under

* Reprinted from *The Future of Old Neighborhoods*, Cambridge, published for the Joint Center for Urban Studies by The M.I.T. Press, 1964, pp. 120–157. Field surveys for this study were conducted in the spring of 1961, and information given for New York, Los Angeles, and Hartford is based on conditions at that time.

present conditions, the large-scale clearance of aging neighborhoods deprives people of valuable housing resources and in many cases brings on further hardship by uprooting people who have strong ties to a local community.

Despite the evident need for old housing, many cities have already cleared large residential areas for urban redevelopment projects. The search for additional real estate taxes, the political value of physical symbols of progress, aesthetic objections to decaying neighborhoods, and the application of current housing standards to structures built 50 or more years ago are rationales for such clearance programs. But the adverse social and political consequences of harnessing rebuilding policies to these approaches have become increasingly evident, and policy changes are clearly in order.

If the objective of public policy is to clear only *surplus* housing, what can be done with the declining neighborhoods? Major alternatives are:

1. Leave these areas untouched until they are virtually abandoned, then acquire the properties at reduced prices, clear them, and rebuild the cleared sites for new purposes.
2. Rebuild these areas gradually, replacing the old housing in small parcels as vacancy rates rise.

The first alternative raises serious problems of maintaining public services during the lengthy period of abandonment and dislocating remaining residents after population falls to a low level. The second is more difficult to achieve, but avoids these problems. Although neither alternative would force occupants of the old housing to leave in the near future, the first would eventually displace those that remained, and past experience suggests that a large number will remain even after occupancy has declined for many years. In addition, a gradual rebuilding will offer some people a chance to find new housing without leaving the community, and will widen the choices available to nonresidents who are in the market for new housing.

If these are the objectives—to limit clearance to structures that are no longer useful, and to promote a high degree of residential choice for the city's people—gradual rebuilding is a suitable technique. But how can public policies start this process? Public action can help create the preconditions for a gradual rebuilding, and public action is vital to establish necessary environmental conditions for rebuilding the older areas. This chapter will take a closer look at both types of action.

The three cities included in this study have all initiated programs to rebuild some of their older areas. In New York, new and interesting policies have been developed to bring about a planned rebuilding. In Los Angeles, certain basic policies are still being formulated for dealing with the old neighborhoods. In Hartford, where the preconditions for rebuilding are lacking, policymakers face particularly difficult obstacles. I shall review the current situations in all three cities to see how they relate to the findings of this study.

Urban Renewal and Low-Cost Housing

Public policy for rebuilding old areas of the city must recognize a large and continuing demand for low-cost housing. In the past decade, huge migrations of low-income groups from rural areas to the cities have kept steady pressure behind this demand. The greatest of these migrations, the movement of Negroes from the rural South to the urban North, reached near-peak levels in the 1950's. Yet the Negro population remaining in the South, an obvious source of future migrants, also grew to record levels by 1960. With large migrations likely to continue, and with high birth rates among recent arrivals, the pressure for low-priced housing is not likely to subside quickly.

It is obvious to observers of urban renewal practice in the United States that public officials have often been insensitive to this continuing need. Projects to clear old housing and develop high-cost apartments provide tangible symbols of civic progress, augment the property tax base, and enhance the appearance of formerly run-down sections. Policymakers justify such projects by pointing out the poor physical condition of the old housing and by urging the social objective of bringing "middle-class leadership" back to central areas. These approaches to urban renewal fail to take account of total housing needs in the community.

A recent study of capital requirements for urban renewal illustrates this fault in renewal policy in its review of the program of a representative medium-sized city. The renewal program for Case City (New Haven, apparently), based on an application of architectural standards to various parts of the city, calls for the redevelopment or rehabilitation of areas where two thirds of the population now live. The low-income groups now occupying these areas cannot afford the costs of new or rehabilitated housing and would have to be relocated elsewhere. Without a substantial low-income housing program, "Case City would be faced with the prospect of replacing the population of those areas where two thirds of the city's people now live with a market drawn from the stable areas where one fifth of the city's population lives, plus some suburban returnees."[1] The authors note that such a program is possible only if incomes rise for a large part of the population and if a substantial proportion of disposable income goes for housing expenditures.

Renewal programs of this kind would have highly destructive effects if they were put into effect in the near future. Fortunately, such programs have moved slowly in the past, so that they have not destroyed enough low-cost housing to affect the general improvement from 1950 to 1960, although they have certainly retarded improvement in New York. Despite the limited progress of most renewal programs to date, however, they have had many unfortunate effects. The very act of clearing an area and scattering its occupants often destroys valuable and unique social ties that have developed over the years.

As early as 1937, George Orwell found disturbing evidence that slum clearance in English cities disrupted many cherished features of personal and communal life. "When you walk through the smoke-dim slums of Manchester," he noted, "you think that nothing is needed except to tear down these abominations and build decent housing in their place. But the trouble is that in destroying the slum you destroy other things as well."[2]

Current renewal policies have barely caught up with Orwell's insights. A 1959 advisory report to the Mayor of New York examined City renewal practices of the 1950's and characterized relocation experience in very much the same way:

[1] John W. Dyckman and Reginald R. Isaacs, *Capital Requirements for Urban Development and Renewal* (New York: McGraw-Hill, 1961), p. 88.
[2] George Orwell, *The Road to Wigan Pier* (New York: Berkley Publishing Corp., 1961) (first published 1937), p. 69.

Forcing people to leave their old neighborhoods is probably the major source of bitterness and opposition to slum clearance. Slums, after all, are neighborhoods and communities. They teem with people who like the place in which they live for simple but deep-rooted reasons.[3]

Many careful studies have documented and detailed the intricate network of personal and social relationships that are often found in the old and declining communities.[4] If anything is to be learned from the bitter experience of large-scale clearance projects (some of which are chronicled in these studies), it is that any necessary rebuilding of such neighborhoods should be carried out slowly and displaced people should be offered relocation housing within remaining portions of the same community.

Recent experience with clearance projects argues for a policy that will enhance the individual's opportunity to choose his community, his housing, and the time when he wishes to move. Cities with active renewal and public works programs have disrupted the lives of many thousands of their residents in the last decade. Urban renewal projects from 1949 to 1961 encompassed areas containing 230,000 families, almost all with low incomes; and the majority were Negroes with particularly difficult problems in finding good housing.[5] In the face of this massive use of governmental coercion to disrupt residential neighborhoods, the reaction of an elderly woman in New York to a proposal to change the name of Third Avenue illustrates a

[3] J. Anthony Panuch, *Relocation in New York City: Special Report to Mayor Robert F. Wagner* (December 15, 1959), p. 18.

[4] See, for example, Elinor G. Black, *Manhattantown Two Years Later* (New York: Women's City Club of New York, Inc., April 1956); Marc Fried and Peggy Gleicher, "Some Sources of Residential Satisfaction in an Urban 'Slum,'" *Journal of the American Institute of Planners,* Vol. 27 (November 1961), pp. 305–315; Herbert J. Gans, *The Urban Villagers* (New York: Free Press of Glencoe, 1962); Sidney Goldstein and Basil G. Zimmer, *Residential Displacement and Resettlement of the Aged* (Providence: Rhode Island Division on Aging, 1960); Peter Marris, *Family and Social Change in an African City* (Chicago: Northwestern University Press, 1962); J. M. Mogey, *Family and Neighbourhood* (London: Oxford University Press, 1956); John R. Seeley, "The Slum: Its Nature, Use, and Users," *Journal of the American Institute of Planners,* Vol. 25 (February 1959), pp. 7–14; Peter Townsend, *The Family Life of Old People* (London: Routledge and Kegan Paul, 1957); United Community Services of Metropolitan Boston, *Housing Preferences of Older People, Follow-up Study No. 2: West End Couples* (January 1962); Charles Vereker and John Barron Mays, *Urban Redevelopment and Social Change* (Liverpool: Liverpool University Press, 1961); Michael Young and Peter Wilmott, *Family and Kinship in East London* (Glencoe: Free Press, 1957).

[5] U.S. Housing and Home Finance Agency, Urban Renewal Administration, *Urban Renewal Project Characteristics* (June 30, 1961), Table 3.

growing public attitude: "They should leave this city alone! They should keep their cotton-pickin' fingers off!"[6]

Effects of Population Decline

Two guidelines for the scale of rebuilding programs are clear so far:

1. Recent migration and housing trends indicate the desirability of limiting the total scope of rebuilding to the number of *surplus* low-cost dwelling units, in order to avoid removing needed housing from the market.

2. Numerous sociological analyses indicate the desirability of avoiding a forced displacement of low-income people from communities where they have strong ties. Where community life is strong, the scale of rebuilding should ideally be limited according to the amount of *locally* available relocation housing for people who wish to stay in the area. As the occupants gradually abandon the old housing in such an area, rebuilding should proceed in a series of stages.

These guidelines allow a first approximation to rebuilding policies —suggesting a slow rate of rebuilding under present conditions in most big cities—but the major policy alternatives for the old neighborhoods involve more complex considerations. These alternatives are (a) to postpone rebuilding until the areas are virtually abandoned, or (b) to maintain a steady rebuilding process, replacing the old structures as they deteriorate or become vacant.

The first of these alternatives, waiting for abandonment, is sure to be a process drawn out over several decades, with a great likelihood that much of the housing will still be occupied as long as it is available. Gradual abandonment has been the fate of many neighborhoods that once served as reception areas for the great waves of European immigrants at the turn of the century. The West End of Boston reached its population peak around 1910, when over 32,000 people lived there. The area declined steadily afterward, as the foreign-born population and their children moved on to newer locations. By 1950, population had fallen below 17,000, but the housing vacancy rate was only 5 percent. In 1950, a large part of this area

[6] "Elegant Name Proposed for Third Avenue," *The New York Times,* July 12, 1961, p. 33.

was earmarked for an urban redevelopment project. Official project designation came in 1952, and the impending clearance of the area was publicized repeatedly until the actual takeover in April 1958. Large-scale abandonment began, but the majority of units were still occupied at the time of land acquisition when the vacancy rate reached a peak of 38 percent.[7]

The Lower East Side of Manhattan had a similar process of decline, but without the threat of clearance. The area filled with immigrant Jews and Italians, reaching a population peak of 541,000 in 1910. As these occupants moved on to better housing, no further immigrant waves replaced them, with the exception of a small influx of Puerto Ricans. Population reached a low of 205,000 in 1940, and held at about the same level in 1950. During this long period of abandonment, the number of dwelling units shrank from a high of 108,000 to a low of 71,000—a proportionately smaller reduction for housing than for population—and the vacancy rate never exceeded 30 percent.[8]

After the process of abandonment is well advanced, the people who remain have special reasons to do so. Leo Grebler describes the Jews who stayed on the Lower East Side as "the poor, the orthodox, the servers of cultural needs, some of those having businesses in the area, and the aged."[9] Walter Firey, in his study of the North End of Boston, maintains that long-term residents of this area were those who wished to identify with Italian culture and the Italian community.[10] An analysis of occupants in a redevelopment area in Indianapolis characterizes the most persistent residents as the "indolent," the "adjusted poor," and the "social outcasts."[11] A long process of self-selection is at work here. When a majority of the population leaves an area, people who remain clearly have some special attachment to the place. Having chosen deliberately to

[7] Information on the West End from *U.S. Census of Population: 1910* and *U.S. Census of Population: 1950*, Boston tracts H-1, H-2, H-3, H-4; Gordon Gottsche, "Relocation: Goals, Implementation, and Evaluation of the Process with Reference to the West End Redevelopment Project in Boston, Massachusetts," unpublished master's dissertation, Massachusetts Institute of Technology, Department of City and Regional Planning, 1960.
[8] Information on the Lower East Side from Leo Grebler, *Housing Market Behavior in a Declining Area* (New York: Columbia University Press, 1952).
[9] *Ibid.*, p. 143.
[10] Walter Firey, *Land Use in Central Boston* (Cambridge: Harvard University Press, 1947), Chapter 5, pp. 170–225.
[11] John R. Seeley, *op. cit.*

remain, they are likely to be most severely affected by forced relocation. Thus, even at the end of a long waiting period, rebuilding an old neighborhood by large-scale clearance will still involve a considerable amount of forced uprooting and the destruction of remaining community life among a particularly vulnerable group of people.

This pattern of decline would also entail serious problems during the long process of abandonment. When population is thinning out while the physical equipment of the area remains intact, service costs would be high in relation to the number of people deriving any benefit from local facilities. As Raymond Vernon has pointed out,[12] streets and utilities would have to be maintained at previous levels for a dwindling population; police and fire protection could not be cut back; school structures would have to be maintained for small enrollments. Capital investments in modern facilities or environmental improvements would be difficult to justify against other claims for public funds, since the life of these facilities would be geared to the uncertain life expectancy of the old housing. Declining areas would probably receive minimum service and no new investment, despite the needs of the people who remain.

Gradual Rebuilding

The alternate approach is a process of continuous rebuilding, keeping pace with the gradual abandonment of old housing. Such a program would be difficult to manage, but the potential gains are significant. The pattern of change is evolutionary: new residents enter in small numbers each time a handful of new buildings is completed. This influx would prevent any problem of underutilization. Services and new facilities would be related to new housing as well as old. At no stage would it be necessary to force large numbers of residents out of the area. Rebuilding would proceed by small increments, with each stage depending first upon the voluntary abandonment of some old housing.

At each stage, some poor people would be displaced, even though clearance would be limited to deteriorated and predominantly vacant structures. But those displaced from their homes would have an opportunity to relocate within the same area, since an adequate *local*

[12] Raymond Vernon, "Some Reflections on Urban Decay," *Confluence*, Vol. 7 (Summer 1958), pp. 139–140.

vacancy reserve would be one cornerstone of the gradual rebuilding policy. The availability of some new housing within the community would widen residential choices for people in the area with rising incomes who might want better housing in the same locale and for outside people who would have an additional area in which to find some new housing. A possible fringe benefit is that gradual rebuilding would promote diversity in an area, rather than the homogeneity of a large-scale clearance project rebuilt all at once.

If new housing is to be attracted into the declining residential areas, their physical setting will have to be improved significantly, with new community facilities and a high level of public services. These environmental changes would also benefit occupants of the old housing. By making the area more desirable generally, environmental upgrading might slow the process of abandonment and might encourage more widespread rehabilitation of old housing. From a social point of view, these are desirable side effects, providing an improved environment for low-income people and prolonging the useful life of existing buildings. Such benefits may not please the municipal tax assessor if they slow the process of new development, but his perspective should not be decisive.

Environmental improvements, coupled with a steady process of rebuilding, may also raise the cost of site acquisition in the older areas. To the extent that a rise in price reflects increased utilization of the old structures, no conflicts with public objectives will arise, since rebuilding is not to be attempted while areas are still heavily utilized.

But site prices may rise because of speculative rebuilding values in an area where new development is active. If price increases threaten to block new development or to force up new densities to undesirable levels, the municipality may be able to forestall price inflation by a policy of advance property acquisition before rebuilding and environmental improvement are well under way. Early property acquisition need not influence the timing of clearance: buildings could be leased for operation or could be operated by the city until they are ready for replacement. Alternately, the city might obtain long-term options to buy properties at current prices before making major public investments in an area. Less directly, prompt reassessment to keep pace with rising values would discourage the holding of property on speculation.

In some circumstances, gradual rebuilding may be inconsistent with desired directions of change. Some old residential neighborhoods may be better suited for nonresidential functions in the future. Such transitions from residence to industry or large institutions, for example, may involve a general realignment of the street pattern, different utility systems, and a radically different land pattern. In such cases, rebuilding in small stages may be virtually impossible because of the sheer magnitude of physical change and reorganization. Some types of new development—heavy industry, truck terminals—may have a deteriorating effect on the environment for remaining residents rather than a positive effect on the quality of residential services.

These severe constraints on gradual rebuilding are not likely to be typical. Where residential areas are to remain residential in the future, slow rebuilding will indeed create more complex physical planning problems than complete clearance. But the advantages of gradual rebuilding are considerable in bypassing the problems of slow decline and eventual dislocation of the remaining community.

Creating the Conditions for Gradual Rebuilding

Policies to achieve a gradual rebuilding of the old residential areas consist of two separate phases: creating the preconditions for rebuilding, and establishing a setting that will attract new development. This study has focused considerable attention on the preconditions and the critical points at which public action can influence them. Less information is available about the final conditions for rebuilding; but the general nature of the problem is clear, and some useful conclusions can be drawn from those current renewal plans that aim at a gradual rebuilding process.

Two basic lines of attack are open for public action designed to strengthen the preconditions for attracting new development into the old residential areas: increase public preferences for these locations and reduce development and operating costs for the developer. The relationships that have been noted between metropolitan structure and locational preferences for new housing point the way for the first approach. To raise consumer demand, public action can be taken to *strengthen the downtown core* in terms of employment, service and recreational facilities; *increase the access advantages of the old areas* to downtown or to other activity centers; *remove competitive vacant land from the market;* and, of course, *improve the local environment in declining areas.*

Specific action to accomplish these objectives could take many different forms, depending upon local constraints and resources. Downtown renewal programs, improvements in the transportation system, the acquisition or regulation of vacant land—all offer opportunities to influence locational choices by manipulating the functional structure of the region. Such actions will produce complex effects, and none are likely to be undertaken solely to promote rebuilding of the declining areas. But these are illustrations of some ways in which public programs can conceivably increase demand for housing sites in the areas to be rebuilt.

Where costs and returns for new housing are out of line in the declining areas, the other approach is to lower costs. Direct financial subsidies are an obvious method: tax abatements and low-interest loans, for example. Less direct methods involve devaluing substandard properties by enforcing building and occupancy code requirements to reduce the profits of illegally operated housing, or formulating tax policies for the same purpose. All these methods are highly complex and generate many side effects; they cannot be undertaken without careful study of the housing market and analysis of the likely results of contemplated action. In a housing market where low-rent units are scarce, code enforcement measures may result in a transfer of maintenance costs from owners to tenants through rent increases. Where low-cost units are in large supply and vacancies are growing, prudent policy may simply involve waiting for vacancy rates to rise high enough to turn prices downward. Measures to expand the supply of sound low-cost housing, such as well-conceived public housing programs, are also likely to help devalue deteriorated structures in the declining areas.

An aspect of the abandonment of declining areas that appeared very clearly in the three regional analyses was the slowness of minority group dispersal from central locations. Where continued occupancy of the old housing represents the free choice of individuals who wish to remain in their communities, such decisions should be respected. To a certain extent, however, decisions to remain in the old areas result from discrimination in the private housing market or from fear of discrimination. The elimination of such barriers is an objective that needs no further justification. Fair housing legislation and other steps to open the suburban market to all groups in the population will widen the range of choice for minority families and will probably also speed the process of vacating substandard housing in the old areas.

The total demand for new apartments in a region is a critical factor in meeting the prerequisites for a gradual rebuilding of old neighborhoods. The importance of action at the national level in broadening the apartment market has already been noted. In addition, local actions that promote demand for inlying areas are likely to promote an acceptance of apartment densities as one condition of living near the center of the region. Local programs to reduce development and operating costs in rebuilding areas may also make possible a reduction in rents to levels competitive with the cost of owning a single-family house. Finally, local experiments with design innovations in multifamily structures may stimulate increased interest in this type of housing.

Local governments exert considerable power over the pattern of new apartment construction through the regulation of maximum densities in zoning legislation. Density regulations for areas to be rebuilt must steer a course between two conflicting objectives. In order to make new buildings feasible on expensive cleared sites, density regulations should permit fairly intensive development. But in order to use the limited apartment market as an effective force for rebuilding many old areas, maximum densities should not go so high as to exhaust the total potential for new apartments in just a few locations. Both criteria must enter into the choice of appropriate densities, for zoning itself is a tool for rebuilding and may reduce current land prices by controlling maximum development densities. The choice of densities should therefore reflect a careful consideration of the general demand for space for apartment housing in a region and the supply of feasible sites, as well as the economics of new development and the preferences of people who will live in the new housing.

Improving the Environment

In areas that meet the preconditions for rebuilding, attracting new development will require still further public action. Developers of new housing usually avoid the declining areas where deteriorated old housing is concentrated, although this is not inevitably the case.

A major task for public programs is to correct whatever environmental factors keep new development out of the old neighborhoods. Most current efforts in this direction emphasize the selective clearance of run-down properties, the provision of new community facilities (schools, parks, playgrounds), traffic improvements, redesigning of streets to enhance their appearance, and occasionally the development of a modern shopping plaza. An important feature in all these current plans is the rehabilitation of much of the older housing. Although most of these programs are too new to permit an evaluation of results, several general considerations are already clear:

1. Old residential areas differ markedly in their ability to attract new private housing, with important consequences for public programs. Some areas have special advantages for new housing: good accessibility to a center of activity, proximity to prestige locations, attractive views, or other special site characteristics. In such areas, little public action may be necessary to spur private rebuilding of cleared sites. In an area in Los Angeles, which will be described later in this chapter, the sole public expenditure required to set off a wave of rehabilitation and rebuilding was the administrative overhead for a series of building inspections and code enforcement orders.

   In contrast, some areas are so lacking in attractions that private building seems unlikely, even with environmental improvements. In such areas, private developers may have to receive special financial incentives, or perhaps some form of public housing is the only feasible type of new development. A successful rebuilding program is likely to encompass both extremes among old neighborhoods, as well as many in between. To cope with such a broad range of conditions will require more than mere reliance on private development: special inducements will have to be offered in some areas, and varying degrees and types of subsidy may be required in others.

2. One way to regard these differences is in terms of the differing multiplier effect of public investment in generating private expenditure in different areas. From the point of view of municipal finance, this relationship will be an important one, but a socially responsible rebuilding program will seek goals other than maximizing this multiplier effect. Investments in

public facilities and the community environment are more than techniques to attract new development; they are also means for providing good services and surroundings for people in the old neighborhoods.

3. Residential areas will also differ with respect to the amount of clearance and rehabilitation that is justified at any stage of a rebuilding program. Although the rate of rebuilding would be geared to the availability of vacant units within the area, the physical characteristics of existing structures will affect the types of treatment used in the rebuilding program. Certain types of structures, such as the brownstones in New York, are particularly suited to rehabilitation. Others may be of a structural type unsuitable for modern needs (old-law tenements), or may be uneconomical to renovate.

4. The use of renovation may have to be sharply limited in low-income areas unless subsidies are granted, for rehabilitated rental units are likely to be too expensive for many poor families. Under these circumstances, where rehabilitation would mean removing low-cost units from the market, government-induced renovation should move no faster than the growth of vacant relocation units in the area or the rise of incomes in the community. Present rebuilding programs generally call for extensive rehabilitation of older units, but these programs often envision a substantial amount of relocation out of the area. In some areas, however, moderate rehabilitation may be within the means of present occupants.

PART 2: NEW YORK, LOS ANGELES, AND HARTFORD

Renewal Policies in New York

Of the three study areas, New York has made the most use of urban renewal programs in recent years and offers the richest case material for an evaluation of public policy. The discussion here will be limited to renewal in the City of New York, where the bulk of the declining residential areas is concentrated, and where the most interesting programs in the region have developed. At first, government-sponsored renewal projects based on the Housing Act of 1949 were concentrated in and around central Manhattan, but the sphere of operations was soon extended to upper Manhattan (the upper

West Side, Harlem), areas of Brooklyn close to Manhattan, and a scattering of projects in outer Queens and the Bronx. The Housing and Redevelopment Board, which now administers urban renewal programs in New York, has already undertaken new developments in typical older residential locations of Manhattan, the Bronx, and Brooklyn, and has begun to plan still further incursions into such areas.

New York is no model of enlightened public policy working toward broad social objectives. Despite the severe shortage of low-cost housing in New York, redevelopment projects started between 1950 and 1960 demolished 22,000 low-cost dwelling units. Even this volume of destruction is only a small part of the total clearance resulting from all forms of public action including highway construction. Total public demolition displaced 15,000 families per year by 1960, and City projections assume no easing of this pace in the next few years.[13]

New York has continued to press on with the largest urban renewal effort in the country, but the program has provoked tremendous public opposition. It has already brought about two Congressional investigations and has stirred many pressures for change within the body politic. One indication of desperate citizen reaction to the untimely clearance of old housing is a recent proposal to forbid the demolition of all rent-controlled housing in sound condition. As a result of these pressures, the program is now being modified to give more emphasis to conservation and rehabilitation, to eliminate renewal projects intended solely for luxury housing, and to build more small public housing developments in neighborhoods that are being renewed.[14] Despite these concessions, much clearance is still contemplated.

[13] See City of New York Committee on Slum Clearance, *Title 1 Progress* (January 29, 1960), p. 25; J. Anthony Panuch, *Relocation in New York City: Special Report to Mayor Robert F. Wagner* (December 15, 1959), p. 24; "30,000 Families Face Relocation," *The New York Times*, June 26, 1961, p. 17.

[14] See "Luxury Housing Limited by City," *The New York Times*, March 6, 1962, p. 1; Milton Mollen (Chairman, City of New York Housing and Redevelopment Board), "For Urban Renewal," letter to the editor, *The New York Times*, March 17, 1962, p. 24; "More Low-Cost Housing Added to Plan for West Side Renewal," *The New York Times*, June 22, 1962, p. 11; Harris L. Present, "To Halt Destruction of Buildings," letter to the editor, *The New York Times*, February 9, 1962, p. 28. For a general review of urban renewal in New York, see "Title I and Slum Clearance: A Decade of Controversy," *The New York Times*, June 29, 1959, p. 1; and succeeding articles on June 30, July 1, and July 2, 1959.

600 / BERNARD FRIEDEN

Until recently, New York has been largely insensitive to the continued need for old housing, but it has pioneered boldly in using public programs to promote a rebuilding of old residential areas. Little governmental effort is needed to raise demand for inlying sites or to lower acquisition costs. These factors are currently in a favorable relationship with one another, and the large current volume of apartment construction provides a potential basis for re-using cleared sites. The current office-building boom in Manhattan seems to assure the maintenance of a strong core—an important factor promoting central housing preferences—without requiring direct governmental action. Improvements in the subway system— some of which are currently under way in Manhattan, such as the lengthening of stations and the acquisition of new equipment—will also help maintain the central orientation of New York's housing market. Other government action is likely to promote the voluntary abandonment of deteriorated housing: the City Housing Authority has announced plans to build 57,000 new public housing units during the next few years while City and State anti-bias legislation continues to widen the private housing market for minority groups now concentrated in the old neighborhoods.

With economic preconditions already favorable, New York is currently working to improve the social and physical environment of the declining areas. In areas where existing buildings still have a useful life ahead, City efforts have involved code enforcement, tax abatements to induce private rehabilitation, improvements in streets and street lighting, new community facilities, and a host of social services: English classes for adults, nursery schools, public health programs, and casework guidance.[15] But where plans call for rebuilding with some new private construction, the problem is one of attracting middle-income families into neighborhoods surrounded by poor people living in old housing. This problem may ease once an initial middle-income development helps diversify the character of the neighborhood, but the current task is to trigger the initial population change. New housing and new community facilities can accomplish physical change in the immediate environment, but run-

[15] See J. Anthony Panuch, *Building a Better New York: Final Report to Mayor Robert F. Wagner* (March 1, 1960), pp. 68–69; Gertrude Samuels, "To Brighten the 'Gray Areas,'" *The New York Times Magazine*, October 22, 1961, pp. 48, 72, 74; and "City to Spur Slum Conversions by Liberalizing Tax Benefits," *The New York Times*, July 6, 1962, p. 26.

down surroundings jeopardize the chances of attracting middle-income occupants to the new housing.

A policy emerging in New York seeks to overcome the reluctance of middle-income families to move to new apartments in the old areas by offering privately built housing at "bargain" rents.[16] The mechanism for this policy is a series of financial incentives to developers of rental or cooperative housing, authorized by the New York State Mitchell-Lama law. State or City loans are available to developers for terms up to 50 years at 4 to 4½ percent interest, covering up to 90 percent of development cost. In addition, the City grants abatements up to 50 percent in real estate taxes. (This program may also be combined with land write-downs in federally aided renewal areas.) The result is a substantial reduction in yearly financing and operating costs and a smaller equity share in new development in comparison with conventional financing and normal assessments. Rents are established by prior agreement between the sponsor and the City or State supervising agency. Under this program, rental units have come on the market for $25 to $30 per room; new apartments in conventionally financed private buildings rent for $40 per room or more. Mitchell-Lama cooperatives also offer advantageous prices to the public: down payments are generally $400 to $600 per room, with monthly carrying charges of $18 to $25 per room.

The Mitchell-Lama program has been in operation since 1946, but only recently has it become a tool used specifically to induce new construction for a middle-income market in the old and declining areas. The policy switch has taken the form of turning down applications of sponsors who propose new developments in areas where unsubsidized private construction is active. The rationale on the part of New York City officials is to avoid a situation in which new middle-income apartments in choice locations undercut the market for comparably priced units in the neglected areas. An additional objective of this policy is to safeguard the tax base of the City by avoiding subsidized building in areas where fully taxpaying property would otherwise develop.

Results of this policy are not yet evident. Two different phases of

---

[16] Much of the following discussion is based on an interview with Louis Winnick, Director, Planning and Program Research Division, City of New York Housing and Redevelopment Board, March 10, 1961. See also policy recommendations in John R. White and Edna L. Hebard, *The Manhattan Housing Market* (New York: Brown, Harris, Stevens, Inc., 1959), pp. 103–104.

the program will be interesting to watch. First is the question of whether the low rents of Mitchell-Lama developments will succeed in attracting an initial contingent of middle-income residents to a few bright islands set among a sea of obsolescent housing. The first new developments are sizable islands, however. An early venture in the Williamsburg section of Brooklyn will occupy 24 acres; another development is expected to use some 38 acres of land in the Brownsville area of Brooklyn.

If the scale of these initial developments is suitable for attracting the desired rental market, the second phase of the strategy must still be tested. Will the introduction of middle-income people into the old areas trigger later unsubsidized private development, or will rents have to be held below normal levels in order to continue rebuilding these areas? The problem at this stage will be to devise further changes in the environment that will allow the old areas to command rents consistent with their locational advantages, if the objective is to attract conventional private housing.

Gradual Rebuilding in New York

The large scale of these particular Mitchell-Lama developments is not really appropriate for the gradual rebuilding of old neighborhoods in accordance with objectives of avoiding forced relocation and clearing only surplus housing. Assembling land for a site of 25 or 30 acres will inevitably mean displacing many people and sweeping away a considerable amount of housing, including some that is neither surplus nor deteriorated. A gradual approach would require clearing smaller plots on a highly selective basis and introducing new buildings among old ones on the same street. An urban renewal project currently in progress on the West Side of Manhattan is closer to this model of gradual rebuilding and involves a number of interesting implementation techniques.

The West Side renewal area, however, does not conform to the general goal of replacing surplus, substandard housing in declining areas, for the area is not a declining one and its housing is over-utilized.[17] From 1950 to 1956, the population climbed from 33,000 to

---

[17] Information on West Side renewal area from New York City Planning Commission, *Urban Renewal: A Report on the West Side Urban Renewal Study to Mayor Robert F. Wagner and the Board of Estimate of the City of New York, and to the Urban Renewal Administration* (New York: 1958). Plan proposals cited are those of Plan A.

39,000, with a large influx of people from Puerto Rico and a smaller exodus of white non-Puerto Rican residents. By 1956, 20 percent of all living quarters were overcrowded (more than 1.5 persons per room); and with the conversion of many furnished rooms into family housing units, a third of all units lacked adequate bathroom facilities. The West Side program is nevertheless useful as an illustration of how gradual rebuilding might be accomplished in a more suitable area.

In this renewal area, sites cleared for new buildings are small, ranging from 7,200 square feet to 40,000 square feet. Over the four stages of the program, some entire street fronts are to be rebuilt, but at any one stage the new buildings are mainly noncontiguous. In the early stages, new development thus adjoins old buildings, some of which are in poor condition. Part of the program for attracting new development into this area is the eventual rehabilitation of most of the older structures that are to be retained. For some time, however, new buildings will have old and even substandard neighbors. Despite this potential drawback, developer interest in the project has been high, and both rehabilitation and new construction are already under way.

Another feature of the strategy for attracting new development is the addition of new community facilities. These include a new elementary school and playground, a new playground for an existing school, and various walkways and small open spaces.

In addition to physical improvements in the neighborhood, New York has an impressive set of tools in its varied programs for stimulating new building. As of 1960, plans for the West Side anticipated either conventional financing or FHA Section 220 mortgages for some new buildings and Mitchell-Lama financing for others. Rehabilitation can be undertaken through conventional or FHA financing. In addition, some low-income public housing is to be built in the area. At the end of the second stage, the ratio of new private housing units to new public units was expected to be 2.5 to 1, with private housing rising to a higher proportion in the remaining stages.

New York has still other programs for new private housing, involving various degrees of tax abatement and financing assistance and dependent upon a profit limitation of 6 percent. In the field of public housing, there are City programs for low- and middle-income projects, as well as state and federal low-income programs.[18] Other cities that wish to sponsor extensive rebuilding programs will have to develop similarly diversified tools to fit the highly individual character of different neighborhoods and different people.

Although many of these programs involve some public subsidy, the relationship of land cost to land value is basically satisfactory for new private housing in the West Side renewal area. No federally aided land write-downs are contemplated, and a considerable amount of new housing is expected under conventional or FHA financing, with no tax abatement or other City subsidy. Despite anticipated land costs as high as $16 per square foot, new apartments to rent at only $45 per room are considered feasible through FHA financing. One reason why actual site costs are not excessive for new development is that the densities follow normal levels for new construction in New York rather than the somewhat lower levels prevailing in large-scale urban renewal projects. Density for the total project area will remain about the same before and after rebuilding.

If the timing of various stages follows the suggested schedule of two and one-half years per stage, the rebuilding of this area will be far from gradual. Nevertheless, with more time allotted per stage, this plan could serve as a model for the gradual approach. Only the first two stages are worked out in detail. At the end of the second stage, about one third of all the living quarters in the area will be replaced with either new or rehabilitated housing.

Both rehabilitation and clearance will require the relocation of some former residents, but new public housing will be included within the area, and a number of families are expected to have incomes high enough for renovated or new units. Of 2,600 families expected to be relocated, about 1,300 are likely to be in the low-income category. With only 500 new public housing units in the area, at least 800 families will have to be relocated elsewhere.

With some modifications, this type of plan would be suitable for the gradual rebuilding of an old residential area. The most important change would be to postpone any clearance or rehabilitation until more vacancies are available in the area. Then, with slower staging and more public housing, the community could start a steady rebuilding process.

[18] See J. Anthony Panuch, *Building a Better New York, op. cit.*, pp. 47–48, 59.

The Double Standard in Urban Renewal

Urban renewal in New York has also raised serious questions about the purposes of public aid used for channeling private development into otherwise inactive parts of the City. Is the sole purpose to stimulate the rebuilding of old areas, or is there an additional objective of promoting higher quality housing developments than private builders provide elsewhere in the City? My economic analyses assumed that the rebuilding of declining neighborhoods would generally involve structural types and development densities similar to those currently in use elsewhere in the region. So far as densities are concerned, urban renewal in New York has departed considerably from normal development practice. Private housing developments in and near central Manhattan are usually built at densities of 300 to 500 dwelling units per net acre. Densities in large-scale Manhattan urban renewal projects have been less than half as high, ranging from 100 to 150 dwelling units per net acre. In the other boroughs of New York, where typical densities of private development are about 150 units per acre, urban renewal densities vary mainly between 50 and 100 units per net acre.[19]

From the point of view of public policy, a double standard is clearly involved here. Maximum densities of private development are controlled by zoning regulations. Thus the developer who builds at densities of 500 units per acre has governmental approval to do so. Yet when public subsidies are made available for urban renewal projects, maximum densities are set at levels far below usual practice. This is a costly procedure, requiring substantial subsidies to permit a normal profit when expensive land is to be developed according to exceptional density standards. The costliness of this approach results in large part from the inconsistency between zoning and renewal standards. Normal development densities, as regulated by zoning, strongly influence the value of land in areas where rebuilding is active or anticipated. Values resulting from expectations of normal development potential will almost certainly exceed values for re-use at lower densities. Subsidies are necessary if the gap is to be bridged at all.

A large part of New York's expenditures on urban renewal have gone to purchase nothing more than reduced development densities

19 City of New York Committee on Slum Clearance, *op. cit.*, p. 25.

in renewal areas. The Washington Square Southeast project is a particularly striking example. Located on the fringe of Greenwich Village, where private construction has accounted for a great deal of rebuilding in recent years, the project involved a land acquisition cost of $33 per square foot.[20] Typical land costs for privately developed housing nearby were between $30 and $40 per square foot. While unsubsidized developments nearby were built at densities exceeding 300 units per net acre, the Washington Square project has a density of 138 units per acre. Rent levels are about the same as those in new buildings nearby. Net project costs were 15.4 million dollars for a site of 14.5 acres, or over 1 million dollars per acre. Without public site assembly, new construction might not have been possible at this location, but the site could conceivably have been assembled and sold at cost for development at typical densities. Instead, the area was subsidized to the extent of 1 million dollars per acre to achieve a lower density. Some observers of renewal in New York point to an additional cause for high subsidies; they maintain that in the absence of competitive bids, the gap between project costs and resale prices has been unnecessarily high in many project areas, even after allowance for density restrictions.

Subsidies for lower densities may also serve other objectives. Most New York City projects differ from Washington Square Southeast in that they are not located in areas where private development has been active. Thus they initiate new construction in otherwise stagnant areas, and they may generate later unsubsidized building. A project currently contemplated for the Brownsville area of Brooklyn would have densities below those of private development as one means of attracting middle-income people into what is now a low-prestige neighborhood.

But the difficult question of double standards remains. If one objective of public policy is to change the standards of private development in the direction of lower densities, urban renewal is a costly tool and perhaps not a very effective one. Zoning can be a much more powerful way of changing development standards. New York has made an effort to reduce private development densities through its new zoning law, but the maximum permitted densities of 400 or more units per acre are still twice as high as those in renewal projects.

As long as this difference persists, the City is in effect attempting

[20] *Ibid.*

to reach high standards through renewal but willing to settle for lower standards in its more influential zoning regulations. This situation suggests a need for both clarifying the objectives of rebuilding and coordinating the various means of achieving these objectives. Reducing the density of new construction may be a highly desirable goal. My calculations indicated that with FHA financing, new housing can be built in the older parts of the Bronx, Brooklyn, and Queens at densities as low as 50 units per acre. Under present cost conditions, land write-downs are not necessary to permit moderate density construction in the old residential areas. But if zoning regulations allow higher densities, special incentives will probably be necessary to attract new housing at densities below the prevailing level.

Zoning measures should be tied more closely to rebuilding objectives in still another respect—to help divert new apartment construction from outlying parts of New York into the declining residential areas. A rapid rebuilding rate would be possible if new development could be drawn into the old neighborhoods. To do so on a broad scale would surely require the use of zoning restrictions to limit outlying apartment building, as well as the use of environmental improvements to make the old areas more attractive.

Zoning is but one example of public measures that should be coordinated with rebuilding programs. Tax policies and capital investment programs are other obvious spheres of public activity that can aid or hinder the rebuilding of declining areas. New York is far advanced in the measures it has devised to promote the rebuilding of its older sections, but many loose ends of public policy must still be tied together if this rebuilding is to succeed.

My major quarrel with New York's programs, however, is not with techniques but with basic policies. Despite some attempt at gradual rebuilding on the upper West Side and in a few other areas now in the planning stage, the City still appears committed to a large-scale project approach, even while the housing shortage persists. This policy is bound to create serious problems for dislocated low-income families, while it continues taking needed low-cost housing off the market.

The Setting for Renewal in Los Angeles

Los Angeles is in a favorable position for starting a rebuilding program. Vacancy reserves in the City of Los Angeles are at an ample level generally, with an estimated vacancy rate of 4.7 percent in the declining areas. Although the timeliness of large-scale clearance in Los Angeles is far from certain, the vacancy reserve exceeds the supply of deteriorated housing by a sizable margin in both the City and the region, so that a careful replacement of surplus housing could probably begin.

Economic conditions are highly favorable for rebuilding the older areas of Los Angeles. Although the demand for new housing gives few market advantages to central locations, development and operating costs in central areas are entirely consistent with current rent levels so long as the environment is satisfactory. Site acquisition costs are low; blighted areas in the Los Angeles region consist primarily of single-family houses, with only a handful of row houses or tenements. Even land assembly is no problem. Typical lot dimensions are 50 to 60 feet of street frontage and a depth of 120 or 125 feet. Apartment developers ordinarily require no more than a single lot of this size for a new structure with 8 to 10 units. Where the surrounding environment is unfavorable, however, each developer would probably need some assurance that others would rehabilitate or rebuild nearby property. Finally, the size of the rental market is no obstacle, with multifamily buildings accounting for almost half the new dwelling units in the region since 1957.

Under these circumstances, public action to create a favorable economic setting for rebuilding seems hardly necessary. Nevertheless, government programs presently contemplated for other purposes are likely to have the incidental effect of promoting greater demand for housing in central areas. These programs include a number of measures designed to strengthen the central business district through more intensive commercial development and a proposed mass transit rail system.[21] The mass transit system would start with a twelve-mile route from downtown Los Angeles along Wilshire Boulevard to the new Century City development in the west, and an eleven-mile route to El Monte in the east. Improved

[21] For a summary of central business district proposals, see Los Angeles Central City Committee and Los Angeles City Planning Department, "Economic Survey: Los Angeles: Centropolis 1980" (December 12, 1960), p. 36. Mass transit proposals are described in Daniel, Mann, Johnson, and Mendenhall, *Los Angeles Metropolitan Transit Authority Rapid Transit Program* (June 27, 1960). The full program described in this report was subsequently modified to an initial proposal for a single transit line; this immediate program is described in *The Los Angeles Times,* August 13, 1961, Section C.

accessibility to downtown along these two corridors is likely to strengthen demand for housing sites in inner areas adjacent to the transit routes, particularly if plans for expanding downtown activity are successful.

The first renewal projects in Los Angeles have been close to downtown, but even the limited experience in these prime locations illustrates the favorable economic conditions for urban renewal in this region. By 1961, land acquisition was under way for the Bunker Hill project, an area of 136 acres adjacent to the central business district and slated to be cleared primarily for business expansion. Advance appraisals indicated an average cost of $8.78 per square foot for land purchases and acquisition expenses.[22] Estimated returns from the resale of land average $7.23 per square foot, so that the anticipated land subsidy will amount to only $1.55 per square foot, or about $68,000 per acre. Other project expenses—relocation, site improvements, overhead—will constitute additional subsidies, but the combined net project cost or total subsidy is expected to be only $164,000 per acre. This is not an obscure declining neighborhood but choice commercial land. Comparable renewal projects near the commercial area of Manhattan (Columbus Circle, Lincoln Square, Pennsylvania Station South) have required total subsidies in the vicinity of 1 million dollars per acre.

Another Los Angeles project in the planning stage in 1961 was the Temple area about 5 minutes northwest of the central business district, intended for clearance and residential re-use. With an anticipated gross project cost—including land acquisition, site improvements, and all other expenditures—of only $4.45 per square foot, or $189,000 per acre, subsidies were expected to be still smaller than in the Bunker Hill project. According to resale estimates, the net project cost was expected to be $63,000 per acre. Again, New York clearance projects with comparable locations have required subsidies many times as great. The West Park, New York University –Bellevue, Cooper Square, and Washington Square Southeast projects are all residential areas quite close to the business center of Manhattan; subsidies for these projects ranged from $600,000 to 1 million dollars per acre.

[22] Information on Los Angeles renewal projects from Community Redevelopment Agency of the City of Los Angeles; financial estimates as of April 1961.

One small renewal project in Los Angeles has already been completed without any subsidy: the Ann project, formerly a residential area near downtown, has been cleared and put to industrial re-use without benefit of land write-down.

Although none of these initial projects have penetrated the old residential sections away from downtown, other areas officially designated for renewal study are scattered throughout the City of Los Angeles; and several outlying communities in the region have also started renewal programs. The first project in Santa Monica also presents an economic picture highly favorable for renewal, but it is by no means in a typical declining area. The Ocean Park project will use a choice site near the business center of Santa Monica, with an excellent view of the Pacific Ocean. As of 1961, real estate purchases and acquisition expenses for this site were expected to average $6.32 per square foot; and land resale value was appraised at $4.97 per square foot, for a mixture of new residential and commercial development.[23] Thus the expected land subsidy amounts to only $1.35 per square foot, or $59,000 per acre.

Official renewal efforts have not yet begun to cope with rebuilding typical old residential neighborhoods. As a result, policies have not yet been devised to take account of the special problems in such areas. The limited renewal experience in this region suggests, however, that public rebuilding programs will not require major subsidies for reducing land costs. The role of government in Los Angeles renewal is now largely that of assembling tracts of land on a scale suitable for rebuilding, investing in public improvements for renewal areas, and taking charge of relocation. The favorable economic setting for renewal in Los Angeles suggests that this role need not change when public programs begin to operate in the declining residential areas.

Mixing New and Old Housing in Residential Rebuilding

Rebuilding an area in small stages requires mixing new and old housing in a fine-grained pattern. To some observers of real estate practice, this pattern seems impossible to achieve when the old housing is in poor condition. Yet the upper West Side of New York is well on the way to achieving such a mixture, even before many of

[23] Information on Ocean Park Project from Redevelopment Agency of the City of Santa Monica; financial estimates are those of February 1, 1961.

the old buildings are rehabilitated. Los Angeles also has an area where public action has induced new development side by side with substandard old housing. In Los Angeles, developers of new housing had assurances that building and occupancy codes would be enforced to bring the neighboring old structures at least up to code standards.

Los Angeles has had an active code enforcement program operating largely outside the official urban renewal project areas.[24] One of the areas recently chosen for intensive code enforcement was the Sawtelle section of West Los Angeles located near several high-prestige areas of recent growth: Brentwood, Beverly Hills, and Santa Monica. Before the code enforcement program started, housing in the Sawtelle area consisted primarily of deteriorating single-family houses built in the late nineteenth century. Each property owner was given a list of repairs that would be necessary to bring his building up to code standards, with a thirty-day time limit to start work. Property owners were confronted with the alternatives of making repairs, having the City make repairs and assess their cost against the property, or selling the property. If rehabilitation costs were expected to exceed 50 percent of the replacement cost of the building, the City was to start demolition proceedings in the event of noncompliance.

The Federal Housing Administration in Los Angeles agreed to insure loans for new development in the Sawtelle area, and would-be developers soon appeared on the scene with offers to buy many of the properties. The net result of this code enforcement program was a wave of new apartment construction, as well as the rehabilitation of many original structures. The number of buildings demolished, however, almost equaled the number repaired: 386 were demolished and 397 repaired.[25]

This project differed from normal urban renewal approaches in a number of important respects. The City made no physical improvements in the area and gave no relocation assistance. Land subsidies were not involved; total costs to the City were the administrative expenses necessary to carry out code enforcement procedures.

[24] For a description of the code enforcement program, see City of Los Angeles Department of Building and Safety, *Conservation: A New Concept of Building Law Enforcement* (Los Angeles: 1958).

[25] Information from an interview with Fred Hoppe, Conservation Bureau, City of Los Angeles Department of Building and Safety, April 26, 1961.

What was accomplished? Social gains were dubious, with a large number of former residents leaving the area to make way for new construction. The physical change of the area alone is impressive. Experience in the Sawtelle neighborhood illustrates the favorable economic conditions for rebuilding in Los Angeles, as well as the possibility of mixing new and old housing even in an area that has long been bypassed by new development.

Other neglected areas in Los Angeles may not respond quite as easily to code enforcement programs. In less favorable locations, developers may be unwilling to bid for properties even when the owners are under some duress. In minority areas, the demand for new apartments may be less certain. When the surrounding neighborhoods are deteriorating, a larger scale of action may be necessary in order to attract new housing, and major public investments in local facilities may be a prerequisite for new private housing. In short, later attempts to rebuild blighted areas may have to incorporate approaches similar to those in New York, but the basic economic conditions are likely to be highly favorable in any case.

Old Housing and Minority Groups

Recent policy discussions within the federal housing agencies in Los Angeles have touched on another aspect of the declining areas that has been mentioned many times before: the extent to which old housing is an asset for disadvantaged groups in the City. Minorities in Los Angeles—Negroes, people of Mexican and Japanese background—cannot enter freely into the housing market despite the fact that many minority families have adequate incomes to buy new houses.[26] The nonwhite population (primarily Negroes and Orientals) constitutes about 9 percent of total population in the region; yet according to estimates of the Federal Housing Administration, only 1.9 percent of all new dwelling units constructed in the region between 1950 and 1956 were occupied by nonwhites. In the San Fernando Valley, a major boom area for new single-family developments since World War II, population soared from 155,000 in 1940

[26] Information on minority housing from Fred E. Case, "The Housing Status of Minority Families: Los Angeles, 1956" (University of California at Los Angeles Real Estate Research Program, January 1958); Los Angeles County Commission on Human Relations, Statement of John A. Buggs, Executive Secretary, January 16, 1960; Remi Nadeau, *Los Angeles: From Mission to Modern City* (New York: Longmans, Green, 1960), p. 247.

to 840,000 in 1960; yet aside from one segregated district in Pacoima with a Negro population of about 4,000, no more than a few dozen Negro families lived in the Valley in 1960.

Minority groups are now heavily concentrated in central areas of the region, and efforts to break down barriers of prejudice in the housing market are unlikely to produce sudden changes. The rate of decentralization among Negroes and, to a lesser extent, Mexicans and Japanese is likely to be slow for some time to come. In view of these unfortunate social characteristics of the suburban housing market, the Federal Housing Administration and Housing and Home Finance Agency offices in Los Angeles have been reconsidering their policies toward central areas where minority groups live.[27] Financing for home repairs has generally been difficult to obtain in these areas, and FHA assistance has only recently become available in a few of them. A position that has been advanced in these policy discussions is that many people would be eager to rehabilitate housing in the inner areas if financing were available on terms comparable to those for new housing. A reshaping of government policies to stimulate the flow of mortgage funds into these areas would, according to this view, represent a highly effective means of enabling minority groups to improve their housing conditions long before the suburbs are open to them.

The old housing is a strong social asset. Whether renovated or in its present condition, it provides living accommodations for groups unable to compete freely in the market for new housing. Economic calculations alone would reveal nothing of this special value that old housing has for minority groups. In Los Angeles, site acquisition costs are moderate and re-use values are high, but much of the old housing has a far greater social value than its acquisition cost would suggest. The Los Angeles situation calls attention once again to the danger of establishing public policy solely on economic terms. Declining areas are generally ambiguous in terms of their economic value, but public policy decisions should reflect an appraisal of the extent to which these areas are social as well as economic assets.

So far as Los Angeles is concerned, implementing policies for rebuilding the older areas—with new as well as rehabilitated housing —will call for approaches broader than those now in use in the

[27] Information from an interview with Arnold A. Wilken, Area Representative, Housing and Home Finance, Los Angeles, May 4, 1961.

region. To stimulate rehabilitation, public action will probably have to provide the same background conditions that are necessary to attract new housing. These conditions include public investment to provide facilities and services for upgrading the environment. Operations to improve declining Los Angeles neighborhoods will almost certainly have to combine elements of three separate programs: urban renewal, code enforcement, and favorable terms for financing home improvements. The main tasks of public policy in the region are to formulate clear objectives for the old areas and to weave together these separate techniques into an appropriate program for each area.

Renewal Policies in Hartford

Vacancy rates in Hartford have risen to the point where limited rebuilding could probably be started without depleting the supply of low-cost housing, but Hartford has problems of economic feasibility. A look at the choices confronting policymakers in Hartford will illustrate some of the difficulties in cities that do not meet the preconditions for rebuilding. My analysis of Hartford indicated a somewhat ambiguous situation with respect to the balance between land cost and land value in old residential areas. Although the apartment market displays some central preference in terms of rents as well as densities, land costs in the declining areas are slightly high in relation to likely rental returns. In many cases the gap can be bridged by FHA financing, but slight land subsidies may be required under some circumstances. The second precondition—a sufficient demand for housing sites in the older areas—is more clearly lacking since the total market for new apartments is small in Hartford.

Recent renewal activities in Hartford will probably strengthen central preferences in the housing market. In the mid-1950's, the decision of a major insurance company (Connecticut General) to move its headquarters from downtown Hartford to suburban Bloomfield gave an air of instability to downtown. Since then, an active renewal program has helped to safeguard the existing situation and to stimulate expansion in the central business district. Two renewal projects were in execution by 1960: one will provide a site for the new Phoenix Mutual headquarters building as well as other offices while the other is expected to be used for a mixture of business and light industry. Four more projects were in the planning stage by 1960, all in or near downtown. One will clear land for a convention hall, another will aim for retail expansion, a third for a combination of luxury apartments and offices, and the remaining project for new moderate-rental apartments overlooking the Connecticut River near downtown.

This program is likely to enhance the pulling power of downtown materially, both in a functional sense and in terms of improved appearance. The four projects within the central business district will rebuild more than 25 acres of downtown land with modern structures; two nearby projects will convert 100 acres to new uses. Central activity will increase, and the mixture of new uses will add variety to the core.

While these developments are likely to increase the attraction of downtown, other government action may divert housing demand from the inner areas to outlying vacant land. Concurrently with the downtown renewal projects, a major highway program has been under way in the Hartford region. Several new expressways now under construction or planned for the near future will improve access from many outlying locations to downtown Hartford. Since abundant vacant land is available only 7 or 8 miles from the core, much of the demand for housing sites readily accessible to downtown may be filled by new developments on open land rather than in the declining areas. Zoning restrictions in suburban communities will play a key role here, for a shortage of land zoned for apartments may shift development to alternate sites in the inner areas. Nevertheless, the availability of open sites within short driving times from central Hartford is likely to make single-family houses a most attractive alternative to in-town apartments, even when access to downtown is a prime consideration.

In contrast to Los Angeles, urban renewal in Hartford involves high land costs and substantial subsidies. As of 1961, site acquisition costs for three downtown clearance projects planned for the near future were expected to range from $17 to $24 per square foot, with total subsidies at levels comparable to those in New York: $780,000 to $946,000 per acre.[28] These are not sites in typical old residential

<hr/>

[28] Financial data for Hartford urban renewal projects from Rogers, Taliaferro, and Lamb, *Renewal Program for Downtown Hartford, Connecticut* (1960); and U.S. Housing and Home Finance Agency, Urban Renewal Administration, *Urban Renewal Project Characteristics* (December 31, 1960).

areas, however. Typical site costs in the old neighborhoods of Hartford range from $3 to $5 per square foot. Two clearance projects in areas near the core fall roughly within this range, with expected land acquisition costs between $3 and $4 per square foot.

In Hartford, land costs of $3 to $5 per square foot are slightly higher than site costs in locations where private rebuilding is currently in progress. Developers of new housing in the old-mansion territory of Asylum Hill rarely pay more than $2.50 per square foot for apartment sites. Resale value of land in the Riverview project, intended for moderate rental (nonluxury) apartment buildings, was estimated as $2 per square foot. The anticipated Riverview project re-use value is not a result of lowering normal densities; it simply reflects current market prices for apartment land elsewhere in the City of Hartford. Although the advantages of FHA financing can help close the gap between acquisition costs and re-use values in urban renewal areas, some subsidies will probably be necessary. In New York, land subsidies are likely to be needed in the older areas only if developers are required to build housing at densities lower than normal. In Los Angeles, land subsidies are likely to be unimportant. But in Hartford, present land costs are out of line with re-use values.

At current levels, the land subsidy in Hartford need not be very high. The expected gap between cost and resale price in Riverview was about $3 per square foot, or some $130,000 per acre. The net project cost anticipated for Riverview was $204,000 per acre, but 8 of the 24 acres in the project area are to be turned into a public park rather than sold as part of the apartment development. With some land subsidy needed in addition to expenditures for relocation and public improvements, rebuilding the old residential areas will be more expensive in Hartford than in Los Angeles, but much less expensive than in New York.

Size of the Apartment Market in Hartford

In addition to the imbalance between site costs and re-use values, Hartford faces a serious obstacle to rebuilding in the limited size of the market for new apartments. I have estimated the land utilization rate for new multifamily development as 5 to 7 acres per year in the City of Hartford. The Windsor Street renewal area in Hartford alone provides more than 70 acres of cleared land just outside the central business district. This project was originally intended for apartment development, but difficulties in finding apartment developers led to a change in plans in favor of new business and industrial development. According to the housing market study and my rough estimate, some 10 years of accumulated new apartment housing would be required to take over this 70-acre central site.

What can Hartford do to rebuild its declining areas, given the limitations of high acquisition costs and small demand for new apartments? Several general strategies seem worth considering. One is to spread the new construction rather than concentrate it in a few large clearance areas—a policy which has social merit in any case. New development can be parceled out to various areas, injecting some new life into each one. Even so, the potential rebuilding rate is so slow that 37 years would be required just to absorb sites cleared of housing now deteriorated.

An alternate strategy would be to broaden the demand for apartments. This could be done by providing types of multifamily housing that are new to the region. A recent housing market study suggests luxury apartments as one type of new housing that may extend the market by competing with upper levels of the single-family market.[29] This is the strategy of the proposed Bushnell Plaza renewal project, which will offer expensive apartments on a highly desirable site overlooking Bushnell Park close to the heart of downtown. Other possibilities are to experiment with row houses, town houses, or other forms of new housing that can be built at moderately high densities. Still another approach would be to broaden the market by producing apartments at rents below current levels. Counterparts of the New York Mitchell-Lama program might be devised for this purpose if subsidies are to be provided; or construction and financing methods might be manipulated to minimize production costs.

Another strategy would work at reducing acquisition costs of land in the declining areas, using measures already mentioned in this chapter, such as building subsidized housing to speed the depopulation of the old areas and enforcing housing codes or altering tax policies to chip away at operating profits in deteriorated housing.

[29] Real Estate Research Corporation, *Rental Housing Market Analysis: Downtown Hartford* (prepared for Department of Housing, City of Hartford, 1959).

Hartford may well represent a common situation among relatively small cities with vacant land available for development nearby. The inner parts of the city were developed at moderately high densities in the past, but tastes in the housing market have now changed. As the older parts wear out, private development cannot absorb the sites at current acquisition costs. Apartment developers can afford to pay almost as much for the land as present property is worth, but the total demand for apartments is too small to permit rebuilding more than a few acres a year, even if subsidies are available to close the gap between site costs and re-use values. The major housing demand is for new single-family homes, but developers cannot pay anything close to current land prices in the old residential areas for single-family sites.

Rebuilding with single-family houses would require large subsidies. With acquisition prices of $3 to $5 per square foot, clearing an acre will cost between $130,000 and $270,000 for land purchases alone, in addition to relocation and demolition expenses and environmental improvements. Resale value for single-family development would probably not exceed $10,000 per acre. Clearance for single-family re-use is not financially impossible: net project costs per acre for converting a Hartford neighborhood to single-family use would be far lower than typical net project costs per acre for the many New York City projects located near the business area of Manhattan. But where the demand for building sites is limited, as in Hartford, rebuilding programs must be weighed against inevitable land subsidies, as well as against other social and economic considerations.

General Policy Implications

This review of renewal experience in New York, Los Angeles, and Hartford raises a number of major issues involved in formulating public policies. First are the questions of when to replace existing housing and how much to replace. Decisions of this kind should depend upon the extent to which old housing is a social or economic asset. Economic value is likely to enter into rebuilding decisions through the influence of acquisition cost, but social value is not so readily apparent. Thus in Los Angeles, although site acquisition costs are reasonable for new apartment development, much of the old housing represents a scarce resource for minority groups. Elsewhere, the vacancy rate may be a good indicator of the need for retaining low-cost housing.

To govern the timing of new development, I propose that vacancy rates be determined on a local basis and that rebuilding should not begin in a neighborhood until the occupancy of the dwelling units falls off sufficiently to create a surplus. Each increment of new construction would depend upon the prior abandonment of other housing in the area.

Is a policy of gradual rebuilding feasible? Cities will find themselves confronting very different sets of policy choices, depending upon whether or not they meet the preconditions for rebuilding. If the prerequisites are weak or missing, public strategy can proceed along the lines that have been suggested to increase demand for housing sites in the old areas or to reduce their acquisition cost. A major vehicle for increasing demand is the physical planning program of the metropolitan region, particularly plans for the downtown core, the transportation system, and competitive vacant sites. Reducing acquisition costs implies devaluing the old housing through building alternative and superior low-cost housing, strictly enforcing building and occupancy codes, or instituting tax policies designed to reduce the profitability of deteriorated housing. Alternately, land costs may be reduced through subsidies or rebuilding may be attempted for nonresidential purposes.

If the economic background is favorable for rebuilding—as it is in New York and Los Angeles—the task of public policy is quite different. In this case, strategies must be devised to initiate and stage the actual rebuilding of declining areas, and public action must be shaped to attract new development into the old areas. Much experimentation will be necessary, but the techniques now in use for the upper West Side area in New York are probably a reasonable model. Components of this model are the improvement of the physical setting through public works and housing rehabilitation, the staging of limited clearance, and the implementation of a battery of housing programs to fit different situations. Housing alternatives should encompass different methods of financing, different degrees of public assistance, and public as well as private construction—all of which are represented in New York programs.

A successful program also involves coordinating rebuilding objectives with other spheres of public action, particularly with zoning and other regulation of private building outside renewal areas. Coordination is also necessary between rebuilding activities and the general apparatus of physical planning, including public works programming, highway construction, and over-all regional development. Even when the preconditions for rebuilding are present, regional growth must be guided so that the older areas become logical locations for new development.

The distinction between an economic situation favorable for rebuilding and one that is unfavorable is not sufficiently appreciated in recent discussions of urban renewal. Where the old areas of a city are stagnant, observers generally assume that economic costs and benefits are out of line for new development or that the demand for housing sites is very limited. Hence the frequent view that the root of the "gray areas" problem lies in acquisition costs that are too high for the level of demand. Clearly, this is not always the case. Even when costs and returns are in line, however, the old residential areas may remain inactive. Difficulties of site assembly, problems with the scale of operations, the effects of the surrounding environment, insufficient governmental commitments to improve old areas, and lack of entrepreneurial imagination may block rebuilding even when the economic situation is favorable.

For many cities with characteristics similar to either New York or Los Angeles, the problems of rebuilding declining areas may result much more from failure to capitalize upon favorable economic situations than from disparities in the economics of new development. Strategies for rebuilding these cities will have to focus on specific techniques for attracting new development into the old neighborhoods.

How difficult this job will be is far from clear. Some neighborhoods, such as the Sawtelle area of West Los Angeles, are located so favorably that a policing of minimum code standards in the old housing, together with the availability of FHA financing, is sufficient to attract large numbers of apartment builders. Most areas that are ripe for rebuilding, however, will show signs of long neglect and deterioration, both public and private. To attract new housing, considerable public investment in streets, landscaping, parks, schools, and other community facilities would be required—as in the West Side renewal area of New York.

Further improvements in the setting for new housing will be tied closely to the replacement of old housing. Public action will probably include the selective clearance of deteriorated buildings and either incentives or aid for the rehabilitation of usable old housing. Several reinforcing effects are likely to operate in such areas: environmental improvements provide an inducement to conserve and renovate the old structures, and as these structures acquire a new lease on life, the rebuilding process is held to a gradual pace.

Rising site acquisition costs may be part of this pattern, but they seem unlikely to pose a serious danger for a policy of gradual rebuilding. High prices for sound structures that are well utilized are of little consequence since such housing would not be scheduled for clearance. Prices for houses with high vacancy rates are likely to reflect re-use value of the land rather than the current earning power of the buildings, but the rebuilding program itself will establish re-use values. Housing that is deteriorated but still fully occupied—and therefore has high current earnings—may pose a problem, but not an insoluble one. Rebuilding should in any case be postponed until an expanded supply of low-cost housing creates local vacancies in deteriorated housing. In addition, code enforcement and tax policies could be employed to limit the earning power of substandard housing, or the city could acquire such property before undertaking environmental improvements in the area. The major threat to land prices in areas slated for gradual rebuilding will be a tendency of some property owners to hold out for speculative land values; but this inflationary force could also be checked by early acquisition, strict code enforcement for buildings on the property, and assessment increases to keep pace with rising values.

Social Obstacles to Rebuilding

The economics of rebuilding are probably more amenable to the influence of public programs than are the deeper social problems that underlie the reluctance of housing developers to build in old neighborhoods. The differences between people who can afford to live in new housing and those who live in the old buildings in declining neighborhoods are more than differences in income. They are often differences of social class, personal values, and ways of life. Various social welfare programs operating in the old neighborhoods —social casework, vocational training, adult education, youth guidance—may tend to level these distinctions in the long run, or at least to curb some of their outward signs. But for many years, they will play an important role in determining the chances of rebuilding old areas slowly, with new and old residents living near each other in the process.

If the driving force in the market for new housing today is a desire for social, economic, and racial segregation—as some critics of the suburban movement maintain—prospects are dim indeed for a gradual rebuilding of old neighborhoods, or for any socially oriented renewal policy. If the poor must always be kept out of sight, there are few alternatives to either abandoning the old neighborhoods to a long period of neglect or rebuilding them by clearance large enough to push out any unwanted neighbors.

But in fact very little is known of the extent or influence of social prejudice in the market for new housing. There are many examples of neighborhoods with mixed social composition, and these should be studied before hasty conclusions are put forth about the impact of social and racial prejudice upon housing choices.[30] New Yorkers, for example, have long been accustomed to the juxtaposition of luxury apartment houses with run-down brownstones in neighborhoods with locational advantages. Interracial areas are becoming more common as Negroes break out of their old ghettoes. Even when prejudices are strong, the complex operations of the housing market may nevertheless produce mixed social patterns. Not all groups who can afford new housing share the same social values: families without children may well regard many questions of neighborhood composition with indifference. And of those who hold strong social prejudices, not all have the resources to satisfy them, and not all will wish to sacrifice other values in order to do so.

These are the issues that will really determine the future of declining neighborhoods. This study has disagreed with recent interpretations that see the rebuilding problem as a product of powerful economic forces pushing land prices out of line with land values for renewal. As a minimum, this economic argument must be qualified carefully. In many cases, it is clearly wrong. Analyses of

[30] One recent study has made a notable start on this subject, setting forth a useful conceptual framework and interpreting the operation of the housing market in four racially mixed areas of Philadelphia. See Chester Rapkin and William G. Grigsby, *The Demand for Housing in Racially Mixed Areas* (Berkeley: University of California Press, 1960).

land costs and values in this study suggest that the fundamental problems are not economic but environmental and social. The ability of public programs to meet social objectives in the rebuilding of cities will depend to a large extent on learning more about these social and environmental constraints. Hopefully, future research in this area of public policy will move away from economic arguments that have clouded the basic issues and will approach more directly questions of how Americans want to live in cities, how they select neighborhood locations, and how determined they are to live apart from people who are different.

25 A General Strategy for Urban Renewal*

WILLIAM G. GRIGSBY

Despite the barriers to an early solution to the problem of sub-standard housing, it still seems possible that the previously projected rate of progress can be sharply accelerated. Much, however, depends on the strategy employed.

Renewal programs initiated by public agencies may, for analytical purposes, be thought of as conscious efforts to alter the dynamics of the private market. Unfortunately, these dynamics are little understood. The widespread recognition of the need to renew our cities has not been accompanied by an equal appreciation of the complexity of economic forces that surround the apparently simple task of tearing down the old and replacing it with something new and beautiful. The emphasis upon the purely physical aspects of redevelopment has obscured the fact that a renewal program so narrowly conceived may prove to be inordinately expensive and, even more serious, indirectly cause housing conditions of lower-income groups to become worse. At present no one really knows whether a given project will improve the total housing situation or merely create a better environment at one point while shifting and perhaps compounding the difficulty elsewhere. Clearly, "the close interrelationship of the several distinguishable parts of the housing

* Reprinted, with slight changes, from *Housing Markets and Public Policy*, Philadelphia, University of Pennsylvania Press, 1963, pp. 283–335.

market makes it imperative that public action to affect housing conditions not be decided in a partial frame of reference."[1]

There is an inherent danger in a program which involves the demolition of low-priced occupied housing units and their replacement with more expensive accommodations which the former residents cannot afford. The net results may easily be new housing which the free market would have added in any event, though possibly at a less favorable location; a housing shortage for those who can least afford to deal with such a situation; and overcrowding, blight, and higher rents in surrounding areas,[2] thus spreading slums and making their renewal more difficult by pushing up real estate prices and increasing the problem of relocation. The public can easily be penalized by its own expenditures. Moreover, these undesirable consequences can result from clearance projects of quite modest dimension, since the displacement of only a few thousand families would in most cities seriously reduce the vacancy rate among low-cost standard dwelling units.

It could be argued that, since the housing of lower quality would be replaced by better structures, the total stock after reconstruction would be improved and along with it the housing conditions of the lower-income families. Such a result, however, could be expected only if two conditions were met: (1) The demand for the new units came from families who would not otherwise have vacated their current residences, rather than from expansion in the number of households or from families who would have moved in any event. This, in turn, implies that at minimum the new units were superior in quality, location, or price to competitive structures being erected elsewhere in the urbanized area. (2) The dwelling units released by the families who were induced to move became available to lower-income households who in turn were drawn into the market and released their homes to still a lower income group, and that this process continued until finally the families originally displaced were served by dwelling units equal in number but superior in quality to

[1] Wallace F. Smith, "An Outline Theory of the Housing Market with Special Reference to Low-Income Housing and Urban Renewal," unpublished Ph.D. dissertation, University of Washington, 1958, p. 25.

[2] Relocation studies have shown that displaced families do indeed tend to favor adjacent districts even though somewhat better housing may be available at more distant locations. This phenomenon is one to which a renewal program should give considerably more attention.

those from which they had been evicted. Although this chain of events is potentially possible, what little is known of the filtering process would suggest that the desired result would actually occur only under highly particular circumstances. Some of the factors that could influence the outcome include the tenure, price or rent, and number of units per structure in the new development, as well as vacancies, prices and rents, and tenure and quality characteristics in the market generally. But regardless of the situation, unless the number of families drawn into the market by the renewal project were far greater than the number of families displaced, the filtering potential would dissipate itself in the higher price and rent brackets.

Clearly, housing conditions are not improved by demolishing *occupied* substandard housing if, in the process, the total supply of accommodations which the displaced families can afford is reduced.[3] To as great an extent as possible, demolition should be the consequence of abandonment, not the cause of it.[4] The complement of this rather elementary point was stressed in the early public housing legislation which provided that each new low-cost housing project must be accompanied by an equivalent amount of slum clearance. Both concepts seem to have been lost in most current residential renewal efforts. When, as is typically the case, housing in slum and blighted areas is replaced by new homes for higher-income groups, there is no assurance that the displaced families will be better or even equally well housed. Their fate hinges on the vagaries of the filtering process, which cannot function effectively when the excesses of supply over demand are being diminished rather than increased.

The foregoing discussion argues implicitly for the development of a strategy for residential renewal based on the realities of the

[3] According to the Urban Renewal Administrator, most families who were forced to relocate because of urban renewal projects have moved to better housing. There is some question as to whether the locally gathered statistics upon which this position is based are accurate. Granting the validity of the figures, however, this would seem to imply either that the pace of renewal was so modest as not to create any stringency in the market or that most of the families displaced had been spending less than they could afford for housing. Regardless of the reason, it is still possible that the total impact of the displacement on the market worked to the disadvantage of low-income families generally.

[4] The point has been recognized in nonresidential renewal. For example, the new Food Distribution Center in South Philadelphia was developed prior to the displacement of the food wholesaling complex from the Society Hill redevelopment area.

housing market. Market trends obviously cannot be permitted to dictate renewal goals, for in many instances it is these very trends which renewal seeks to alter. However, market forces do continue to operate regardless of the posture assumed by government. The function of leadership in renewal is, therefore, to channel funds in such a way that the private market mechanism will propel rather than retard public efforts. Regardless of the goals of a particular program, therefore, renewal strategy should be based on maximum utilization of developing market forces. More specifically, such a strategy should attempt to stimulate private investment, squeeze the false and inflated values out of low-quality housing, and hasten the voluntary abandonment of slum areas, thus accomplishing the task ahead without excessive burden on public resources. In some cases this very well might mean encouraging further migration to the suburbs.

The approach suggested here would free more public funds to solve problems which the private sector is incapable of handling, such as air and water pollution, transportation, and more space for recreation. Nevertheless, it involves problems so difficult to resolve that one might be led to prefer the present programs which, although they have solved little and may, in fact, create a more serious situation in the future, do at least convey the illusion of progress.[5] It must be said, moreover, that there is still some doubt that an old city ever can be genuinely renewed under any strategy. The pace of renewal necessary to eliminate the deteriorated parts of an urban structure is perhaps so great that we must become reconciled to living with a certain amount of decay and ugliness. It is, nevertheless, fruitful to pursue some of the possible lines of attack that would be included in a market-oriented strategy for residential renewal.

STIMULATION OF HOUSING EXPENDITURES

An explicit goal of urban renewal is the reduction of the number of occupied substandard housing accommodations. If at some future

[5] To make it perfectly clear, this is not a criticism of what is frequently referred to as "projectitis," for, increasingly in many cities, what appear to be isolated projects actually are parts of a master renewal plan. The objection here is to the master plan itself which does not include an entire market area, ignores the market consequences of demolition, and reflects no serious concern for the temporal and spatial ordering of the parts.

date all substandard accommodations are eliminated, this emphasis can be relaxed even though the need for residential renewal programs will, for reasons mentioned earlier, probably continue. At the present time, however, renewal is not a device simply for replacing capital assets as they become worn out, but a means of improving the average quality of the occupied stock. A major part of renewal strategy based on the market approach stems, therefore, from a self-evident truth that seems to have been submerged when the scope of urban renewal was extended beyond that of improving housing conditions. The quality of housing accommodations is below acceptable standards because insufficient amounts of money are spent to maintain, improve, and expand the stock of dwelling units. It follows that a major effort should be made to increase our residential wealth.

It has already been shown that tearing down substandard houses does not accomplish this end. Unless demolition is accompanied by increased housing expenditures or lower prices and rents, slums will never disappear but will simply shift from one location to another. Similarly, it was submitted that although replacing the demolished units with superior accommodations for higher-income groups may raise the average quality of the total inventory, it will not necessarily improve, and may in fact worsen, the housing condition of those who cannot afford new units. At best such a program, like demolition alone, may renew one area while at the same time inducing equivalent lack of maintenance and decline elsewhere. Barring the emergence of revolutionary technological innovations and associated gains in productivity, it is only by channeling more income into the housing inventory that housing conditions can be improved. This must be, but is not now, a primary aim of any residential renewal program.

Not all residential investment, of course, is necessarily helpful. In the case of expenditures for maintenance and renovation, for example, it obviously would be unwise to promote the improvement of structures soon to be razed. Equally, encouraging more outlays by residents of luxury neighborhoods does nothing to improve conditions in the slum sections ringing our central business districts. The question of where to stimulate added expenditures can become much more complex than is suggested by these simple illustrations, and will therefore be discussed in more detail in later sections of the chapter.

In general, there are five ways in which an increase in spending on housing can be induced: (1) through rising real incomes; (2) through larger expenditures by the federal, state, and local governments for the housing of special groups; (3) through a voluntary allocation of a larger proportion of income by the users of housing, i.e., a shift in consumer preferences in favor of housing; (4) through increased expenditures on the physical structures by investor-owners, particularly slum landlords; and (5) through net shifts of population among housing markets as a result of interurban and rural-urban migration. Each of the first four general paths to better housing suggests specific programs and problems which will be discussed in turn.

Rising Real Incomes

This is an area of concern which is for the most part peripheral to the question of renewal strategy. It will, therefore, be disposed of rather quickly with an observation that bears equally on the issue of income allocation. The principal contribution to better residential living conditions in the past has probably been general economic progress, not the various government housing programs. To the extent, however, that these programs furthered an economy of full employment, as well as greater investment in housing, they themselves helped to stimulate this general progress. It is difficult, unfortunately, to assess the results of federal participation, since it can never be known for certain what might have taken place in the absence of government intervention. Some observers feel, however, that regardless of how one views the past, there is a possible danger in programs designed to channel more investment into housing in the future, because such a shift could conceivably impair gains in productivity elsewhere in the economy.[6] This reasoning is of doubtful validity at the present time because, with the current slack in most industries, increases in residential wealth would not necessi-

[6] This question is discussed in John W. Dyckman and Reginald R. Isaacs, *Capital Requirements for Urban Development and Renewal* (New York: McGraw-Hill, 1961), pp. 113–116, and in Leo Grebler, David Blank, and Louis Winnick, *Capital Formation in Residential Real Estate* (Princeton: National Bureau of Economic Research, 1956).

tate a reduction in the rate of capital formation in other sectors. Nevertheless, the issue of resource allocation and its effect on productivity and economic growth does raise a basic question concerning renewal strategy. If the major bottleneck is low income, as has been argued here, and if low income is highly correlated with various forms of chronic unemployment, unskilled labor, etc., it might be wise to place relatively greater emphasis in national policy on the education and retraining of bypassed groups in the population. This does not imply that a choice must be made between human resources and housing resources. Programs in both areas would have to be vigorously pursued, since their benefits would not accrue concurrently nor always to the same individuals. If, however, there is recognition of the fact that substandard dwelling units are only one manifestation of a larger social problem, and housing programs only one of several approaches to this problem, it may be possible to achieve greater balance in our total renewal planning, as well as more rapid progress in the field of housing itself. At present, one could argue that there is a good deal of imbalance, but however the problem is seen, it merits more attention by those who make and influence renewal policy.

Increased Government Expenditures for the Housing of Special Groups

. . . Because of the complexity of [this] problem, it is rather hazardous to offer any specific solution. It may, nevertheless, be helpful to narrow the range of possible alternatives.

First, there seems to be no doubt that additional amounts of public housing will be necessary, even though the present government program is widely criticized by groups of all political persuasions. Equally, however, political realism dictates abandonment of the notion that public housing will be the major means of granting a subsidy for shelter. The principal market contribution of public housing has been and will continue to be as a relief valve restraining the upward pressure on prices and rents in the lower-quality stock, while at the same time creating a competitive situation conducive to higher levels of maintenance. In this role, an expanded program can be extremely useful as a servant not only of the low-income population, but of local redevelopment authorities as well. It may be noted in this connection that this view of public housing would seem to favor the creation of additional public units primarily by new construction rather than through purchases within the existing stock, as some observers advocate. The latter program may "produce" public accommodations at a lower unit cost; the former, however, adds dwellings to the total housing supply and at points where more dwellings are vitally needed to reduce monopoly powers of landlords.[7] The most suitable procedure, however, probably will vary from community to community depending upon vacancy rates, condition of the stock, broad redevelopment goals, and other factors. The market situation in each case must be thoroughly examined and adherents of one program or the other should not be too fixed in their predispositions.

Second, as has been pointed out by Fisher[8] and others, the departure from the traditional concept of public housing should be in the direction of several different programs, each of which is tailored to the requirements of a particular group and to local market conditions. Although the complexity of the issues makes it impossible to specify the various programs which might succeed where public housing has failed, one general proposal is presented here for further study and consideration.

Programs of assistance can take one or both of two general forms: subsidized rehabilitation or subsidized new construction. For reasons just mentioned, a program devoted exclusively to rehabilitation is not desirable. Part of the public subsidy must be directed toward an expansion of housing starts. With the home-building industry currently operating below full capacity, this approach would be desirable on other grounds as well.

An expanded program of assistance for new construction should attempt to include some provision for subsidized home ownership, or where this is not possible on a wide scale as in New York and perhaps Chicago and Washington, cooperative apartments. It was noted earlier that substandard housing is strongly correlated with rental occupancy. Although this is partly a function of income, it also relates to the higher levels of maintenance which owner-

[7] Assuming local authorities would purchase primarily low-quality units, which would then be rehabilitated, both programs would improve the quality of the occupied stock and reduce somewhat the monopoly position of slum landlords in this fashion.

[8] E. M. Fisher, *A Study of Housing Programs and Policies* (U.S. Housing and Home Finance Agency, 1960).

occupants are willing to undertake because of their dual role as both consumer and investor. Many repair bills which raise government contributions to public projects and push up rent levels in private developments are transformed into the expenditure of time and effort by middle- and lower-income owner-occupants. This could, of course, be regarded as an added cost to this group except that, in effect, it is also added income.

It might be protested that trying to foster more home ownership is effort poorly placed, since a huge shift to this type of tenure has already occurred, leaving a small reservoir of families still to be served in this fashion. The shift, however, has occurred only among those who can qualify for mortgage loans. There is still a large percentage who desire ownership status, but do not presently have the financial means to achieve it. In the Philadelphia SMA, for example, 73 percent of the families with children were homeowners in 1956, but this average figure varied considerably by income group. For those with incomes over $5,000 a year, the rate of ownership was almost 85 percent, whereas among those with lower earnings, it was only 56 percent. Assuming the underlying housing preferences of the two groups were the same, approximately 100,000 Philadelphia area families earning less than $5,000 would like to buy a home. For the country as a whole, several million would probably like to do so. Of course, many of these families already live in satisfactory accommodations, and might not be considered in need of outright government grants. A large number, however, would be eligible and could be better served by an ownership than by a rental program.

With respect to the form of assistance, whether for the purchase of new or used structures or for the construction of low-rent apartments or for the rehabilitation of owner-occupied homes, direct government first- or second-mortgage loans at below market rates would minimize costs to the taxpayer. In fact, the direct loan programs already in operation reach a considerable portion of the lower-income population at no public expense at all. As in public housing, the monthly payments required of a borrower under the proposed program would be increased as his income rose, and would in many instances eventually equal those paid by mortgagors in the private market.

A rough calculation indicates that the leverage provided by

subsidized interest rates is considerable. An annual government expenditure of less than half a billion dollars could support decent housing for the entire 2,500,000 low-income families who, it was estimated, would still be occupying substandard dwelling units in metropolitan areas in 1970. Such an accomplishment would far exceed that of urban renewal and public housing combined. This estimate assumes, however, either that the mortgage loans would be financed through current tax receipts or that, if borrowing were resorted to, such a policy would not force up interest rates and thus add to the costs of government borrowing generally. If interest rates were to rise even fractionally, the mortgage loan program would indeed be costly, since the government refinances billions of dollars of debt annually. That borrowing for the program could pose a threat in this respect may be seen by the fact that at least 25 billion dollars in mortgage funds would be required. If a substantial proportion of this amount were obtained from the bond market, it might require vigorous action by the Federal Reserve Board and the Federal National Mortgage Association to hold down interest rates. Of course, looking at the program even more broadly, the higher cost of money would be at least partially offset by lower writedown costs in clearance areas as large sectors of the substandard stock were abandoned by families moving into better housing.

Increasing Housing Expenditures by Users

This effort also presents a wide variety of difficult policy questions. The user group may be fruitfully classified into three categories according to the effect of their housing expenditures on the quantity and composition of residential investment: (1) buyers and renters of new housing, (2) owner-occupants of dwelling units in the standing stock, and (3) renters of dwelling units in the standing stock. The classification system is not completely satisfactory, since in the process of changing their expenditures for housing, families may shift from one category to another. It will, nevertheless, serve the purpose at hand.

Buyers and renters of new housing: Renewal policies directed toward this group quite obviously have as their purpose raising the level of demand for new construction, i.e., increasing the size of the group itself. The ultimate goals of such policies are the same as those of the subsidy programs—to expand the supply of and reduce rents in housing which is available to low-income families and also to force the depreciation of units that redevelopment authorities wish eventually to condemn. The possible scope of urban renewal programs is, however, widened to the extent that private enterprise can achieve these results without public financial assistance. . . . The discussion at this point is confined to three observations bearing directly on the relationship of construction output to renewal.

First, although it would require only a very small reallocation of income in favor of new housing to make a considerable dent in the substandard inventory, achieving even a small expansion of demand may be difficult. On the surface, the problem is deceptively simple. The vast majority of American families, including many living in substandard dwellings, spend much less on housing than they can afford. All that is required is that a few families, possibly 100,000 per year, or less than one five-hundredth of all households in the United States, make one additional move up the housing ladder during their lifetime. This incremental flow would, however, have to recur each year with a new group of families until 2,500,000 homes had been released for occupancy by the low-income population. Thus, as many as 5 percent of all households would ultimately have to make the extra move. Among families who could afford new homes, about 7 to 10 percent would have to do so. . . . However, most of these families would release homes in competition with new construction, thereby depressing homebuilding in other submarkets. Excluding these households, therefore, the proportion would probably be at least 25 to 35 percent. In brief, among the only group in which a shift in preference is both vaguely possible and also helpful, the change would have to be quite substantial. Since the additional move would represent a major decision for most families, inducing a preference shift of this magnitude would seem to be a formidable task. Clearly, expanding the volume of homebuilding even moderately will require action on many different fronts, and no individual program is likely to make a contribution large enough to be revealed by statistical measurement.

Second, much of the thinking on renewal is burdened by the erroneous assumption that residential renewal projects necessarily represent net additions to gross capital investment. In reality, many families moving into these projects have simply been diverted from other housing developments in the same urban area. If this is the sole or primary consequence, renewal will not have materially increased total investment, but only provided additional housing alternatives for those who are in the new construction market anyway.[9] Such a result should not be minimized because in the process other worthwhile planning objectives may have been achieved.[10] The true nature of the accomplishment, however, should be clearly understood.

If the new construction which is fostered by renewal is to contribute to the elimination of slums rather than merely shift them from one location to another, it must open up markets which formerly did not exist. Actually, it is probably impossible to determine whether a particular project has increased aggregate demand, but . . . some types of projects are more likely to do so than are others. Those with the greatest potential contribution in this direction draw primarily from families residing in lower-quality dwellings that are not competitive with new construction. In light of this fact, it is interesting to observe that in run-down neighborhoods in a number of cities there is evidence that the residents themselves constitute what may be a rather considerable market for new housing if it is constructed in the same general area.[11] Many evidently want and can afford a new home, but do not want to move from a familiar environment to obtain it. In this respect, they are no different from thousands of families who, because they cannot find both high quality and a good location in the same product, spend much less on housing than they can afford. Their behavior does, however, run counter to the widespread belief that a new environment must be provided in order to ensure a market for construction in clearance areas. Evidently this is so only if a different social class is to be attracted. For the resident population, elimination of nuisance factors, but not the basic characteristics of these areas, would seem to be what is most desired. Carefully planned spot redevelopment or rehabilitation of dilapidated struc-

9 This point is discussed in more detail by Louis Winnick, "Economic Questions in Urban Redevelopment," *American Economic Review*, LI (May, 1961), 292–295.

10 Unfortunately, we do not have very good criteria to judge whether the objectives are indeed as desirable as they are claimed to be, but this is another question.

11 Numerous examples could be cited. For a few illustrations, see Martin Millspaugh and Gurney Breckenfeld, *The Human Side of Urban Renewal* (Baltimore: Fight-Blight, Inc., 1958).

tures in old but otherwise reasonably stable areas might help fulfill this need and at the same time expand total demand for housing. This implies the possible demolition of occupied stock, a situation which, according to our own analysis, is not desirable. Since the new units would, however, be closer in value to the existing structures than is the case in most redevelopment projects, and since demand would come mostly from families in the immediate vicinity, the usual difficulties encountered by displaced families in finding suitable alternate quarters would be somewhat less.

As compared with luxury structures designed to attract upper-income families back to the city, new lower-cost dwellings have, then, two advantages: they are more likely to increase total expenditures for housing and to bring, indirectly, better living accommodations to the families which they have displaced. Here, therefore, is a situation where strategy and current goals may be in conflict, possibly because the strategy itself carries with it implicit goals of its own. The contradiction may be resolved by either abandoning the strategy or altering the goal. The important point is that by careful consideration of strategy, the feasibility and mutual compatibility of goals may be more fully tested.

Owner-occupants of housing in the standing stock: Approximately one third of the total substandard inventory inside SMA's is owner-occupied, but a much larger proportion of the homes in so-called conservation areas is in this category. Thus, between code enforcement programs and the broader efforts of neighborhood improvement, the owner-occupant is perhaps involved in renewal almost as much as the renter.

Two questions arise with respect to this group. First, if it is true . . . that relative to the investment standards of landlords, owner-occupants in general overmaintain their homes, why are even a small proportion[12] in substandard dwellings or units of marginal quality? Does the problem stem mainly from low income or from other factors? In formulating a strategy to deal with these families, it would be desirable to know more about the underlying reasons for the inadequacy of their housing expenditures. Since, however, a program of liberal government financing is already available to assist owner-occupants who wish to improve their homes, perhaps this deficiency of knowledge may not be too important. As the pro-

[12] Less than 7 percent inside SMA's.

gram, which is still relatively new, is put to more extensive use, the portion of the problem with which it is unable to cope will become apparent. At that time, the program can be adjusted accordingly.

The second question is more basic. Granting both the necessity and desirability of code enforcement, inexpensive painting and repairs, the removal of trash and junk from yards, and the elimination of neighborhood nuisances, how much beyond this minimal level of renewal should the improvement program in a particular area extend? Should owner-occupants necessarily be encouraged, as they are in some cities, to undertake extensive modernization, or would both their housing needs as well as those of the total community be better served in some instances if they invested instead in a more expensive new or used home elsewhere?

It is theoretically conceivable that greater expenditures for maintenance and repair by owner-occupants may in some circumstances divert demand from the new construction market, and in the process decrease total expenditures for housing, thereby lowering the average quality of the stock below the level it might otherwise have reached. This, of course, is the very result we wish to avoid. Of equal importance, even if emphasis on rehabilitation had no impact on aggregate residential investment, but merely shifted a portion of it from the new to the used sector of the supply, it is possible that families who must depend on cheaper units in the used supply of housing would be adversely affected. This is because the market impact of rehabilitation expenditures is quite different from that of outlays for new construction. The erection of new dwelling units creates a potential flow of housing to and reduced prices for lower-income groups. Rehabilitation has precisely the opposite effect. To the extent that it draws demand away from the new construction market, it retards the rate at which dwelling units are released to families of modest means.[13] Thus, the question of elevating the quality of the stock of existing houses *above code level* is central to the issue of creating an efficiently operating housing market. As long as a substantial segment of the population are prevented from purchasing new homes because of their income and

[13] The same possibilities also exist in the rental market, except that this sector has an internal self-regulator which tends to limit investment in the standing stock to a level considerably below that of owner-occupants. See Grigsby, *op. cit.*, Chapter VI.

asset position, the market, if it is to function in a satisfactory manner, must make dwelling units available to this group both in a volume commensurate with their requirements and at acceptable quality levels. If community renewal efforts, however worthwhile, should have the secondary effect of restraining mobility and placing a brake on the rate of depreciation in a large sector of the stock, programs to assist low-income families will have to be broadened. It is evident, then, that the problem of where and under what circumstances to encourage rehabilitation may go much beyond calculations of cost and the probable remaining economic life of the structures, which now form the bases for much of the thinking on the subject.

Is it really true, however, that the price of rehabilitating areas of blight and decay is a housing shortage for low-income groups? The question hangs on whether rehabilitation and new construction are complementary or competitive.[14] If the principal government weapon used to encourage home improvement continues to be liberal credit and if, as seems likely, the only families who take advantage of this financing are those who already have a long-term interest in their property, then the two areas of housing investment would seem to be definitely not in competition for the same demand group. The rehabilitation efforts of those who initially seek loans may, however, extend the investment horizon of their neighbors and thereby induce them to remain in the area longer, rather than move on to a higher-priced home elsewhere. Furthermore, public assistance is no longer being confined to credit aids, but has been expanded to include the strategic placement of parks, new schools, and other facilities, the introduction of which may tend to stimulate private expenditures and retard residential mobility. Still further, even homes that are not improved will command a higher price as their surroundings are upgraded, and thus either remain beyond or move out of the reach of lower-income households.

Whether these secondary effects of rehabilitation might materially reduce the volume of new construction and estop a large number of homes from passing to lower-income groups is not known. It may be that for every family diverted from the new

[14] This same issue presents itself in the rental as well as the owner-occupancy sector, but since the conclusions in both cases are the same, the discussion here is in terms of the latter submarket only.

home market to a conservation area, as many as ten or twenty existing homes would be materially elevated in quality by households who had no desire to move in the first place. If so, total housing investment would be greater than in the absence of a rehabilitation program, and the negative impact on filtering would be minimal. Even if the total volume of investment were not larger, however, it must be remembered that the expenditure of funds spread over a number of dwelling units will usually have a more favorable effect on environment than the same outlay on a single new home. In all, it appears that in neighborhoods where a large proportion of the families would prefer to remain where they are, renewal above code enforcement levels should be encouraged and that any potential adverse effects on either the rate of new construction or the housing situation of lower-income groups must be minimized through other housing programs.

Renters of housing in the standing stock: Increased expenditures by this group do not have an immediate effect on the quantity or quality of housing, but instead reduce the vacancy rate in and increase the profitability of the better rental units at the expense of other less desirable structures. In the second stage, there would be some tendency for owners of the vacated units to make improvements in order to remain competitive. There would also be some pressure for higher rents in the apartment buildings with zero vacancy rates. Finally, if the rents and rate of profit enjoyed by owners of the higher-quality used structures became excessive from an investment standpoint, new construction would occur. The translation of increased demand into more and better supply, however, is not a smooth one, and landlords may in some circumstances benefit more than either renters or the housing stock.

All this is common knowledge. The question is how families who rent units in the standing stock and who cannot afford new housing can be induced to spend more for shelter. For some, the answer may be an opportunity for owner-occupancy through more liberal mortgage financing, including well-regulated lease-purchase plans, for used homes. Others might respond to the chance for cooperative ownership of lower-priced structures which are now almost exclusively held by investors. Realistically, however, it must be recognized that here is a group comprised largely of families who either do not have the means to acquire better housing or do not have the desire to do so. As with the other groups, there is no magic formula which may be expected to have a marked impact on their expenditure patterns.

A final point concerns the general question of how a reallocation of income in favor of housing would affect other sectors of the economy. The problem can be viewed in one of two ways. First, which expenditures would families be most likely to curtail if their outlay for housing were increased? Would less money go toward an adequate diet, proper education, etc., or would luxury items disappear from the budget? Second, would it be possible to restrain selected nonhousing expenditures in order to release funds for the maintenance and expansion of residential wealth? Where and how might the restraint be applied and what would be the results? Although these questions have not been ignored by analysts,[15] they have not received the attention which they deserve by those concerned with the formulation of housing policy.

Increased Maintenance Expenditures by Investor-Owners

Particularly in the case of holders of slum properties, this constitutes the final and possibly most important path to satisfactory housing for all families. It is in the rental sector where most of the substandard accommodations in urban areas are to be found. Here, therefore, is where direct government intervention, if successful, has the greatest potential for improving quality and minimizing the public burden of renewal by shifting some of the costs to individual private owners.

Throughout this chapter, low income has been stressed as the principal cause of substandard housing. Satisfactory shelter simply costs too much for some families. It is possible that in an effort to demonstrate the futility of solving the housing problem of these families by destroying their homes, the role of inadequate earnings may have been overstated. A large number of low-income families who live in inadequate quarters must do so because government at both the federal and local levels has neither forced nor encouraged landlords to pursue a socially responsible maintenance policy nor created a market environment in which it would be profitable to do so. This situation is slowly changing, but much more vigorous

[15] See, for example, W. A. Morton, *Housing Taxation* (Madison: University of Wisconsin Press, 1955).

action is required. Compulsion, encouragement, and creation of a different market environment are all necessary and each would yield tangible results.

In the past, compulsion, i.e., enforcement of an adequate local housing code, has not been vigorously employed as a weapon against slum landlords, the view being that this would simply push families into the street. In fact, this has sometimes occurred. With rising vacancy rates in the lower-quality stock, however, has come the realization by many municipalities that codes can be enforced without either seriously depleting the supply of inexpensive dwellings or compelling families to accept even worse housing elsewhere.

It has been demonstrated by Schaaf[16] that there is much more leverage in a policy of code enforcement than is commonly realized. Under normal circumstances, an investor would not be expected to improve his property unless he anticipated that the cost would be covered by additional revenue or lower maintenance expenditures in the future. For example, if he were netting $1,000 annually and contemplating a capital outlay of $2,000, he would probably decide against the investment unless it would raise his net income to at least $1,200 or $1,300. If, however, he were told by the city to make the same improvements or close up his building, his choice would be entirely different. He would lose his entire current income of $1,000 unless he spent $2,000. Under these circumstances, the investment of $2,000 would not only be feasible, but highly attractive.

Obviously, vast numbers of investor-owners are not going to abandon their properties if cities choose to enforce the law. Moreover, even in instances where landlords refuse to make legally required improvements voluntarily, the local government may find it economically feasible to have the work performed under private contract, place a lien on the property, and recover the expense at some future date. This practice, already pursued in several cities, needs further encouragement at the national level through a revision in the kinds and conditions of federal assistance. No new legislation would be necessary. With the passage of the Housing Act of 1954, communities receiving aid were supposed to adopt and presumably

---

[16] A. H. Schaaf, *Economic Aspects of Urban Renewal: Theory, Policy, and Area Analysis*, Research Report No. 14, Real Estate Research Program, Institute of Business and Economic Research, University of California, Berkeley, 1960.

enforce adequate building and housing codes. However, this provision has been honored only on paper. Simply compelling cities to do what the law already demands would be a big step forward.

The huge potential gains offered by a policy of vigorous code enforcement can be increased still further if compulsion is accompanied by a fundamental change in real property taxation. Presently, there is a barrier to compliance with local codes because property tax assessments do not reflect the *loss* in net income and market value which may be caused by higher levels of maintenance and lower rates of occupancy.[17] Reducing assessments against dwelling units brought into conformance with the building and occupancy codes would, in correcting this deficiency in current assessment practice, increase the number of landlords who could fix up instead of board up.[18] Such a policy may be viewed, analytically, as the reciprocal of the proposal that cities tax the value out of slums. The wisdom of the latter policy may be questioned on the grounds that it may simply produce greater scarcities in the available low-rent stock and thereby create monopoly profits in adjacent sectors of the supply. Code enforcement, in contrast, partially "taxes" the value out of slums while at the same time pursuing a larger social purpose. The circumstances under which it should be accompanied by a downward revision of property assessments would be dictated by the specific goals for the area involved.

In arguing for better code enforcement, it is not intended to suggest that such a program yields only gains. One difficulty facing the slumlord is the problem family whom even public housing turns away. Another is a rent schedule so low that adequate maintenance is impossible. Moreover, . . . not all of the problem of substandard housing relates to inadequate structures. Part of it is overcrowding. Code enforcement will, therefore, result in the displacement of families, and cities must be prepared to meet this situation. This, however, is a minor objection. Code enforcement "produces" stand-

---

[17] A parallel problem, which will not be discussed here, concerns the complaint that owners contemplating improvement of their properties are frequently dissuaded from doing so because of the threat of being saddled with higher taxes. Whether the ad valorem tax is indeed a material deterrent to rehabilitation is not known. Except in the case of major renovation and repair, improvements to real property add very little, if anything, to market value, but may influence the tax assessor. The entire question merits study.

[18] This assumes, of course, that the properties in question are not already underassessed, as they sometimes are.

ard housing in the sector of the supply where such accommodations are most urgently needed. It does so at relatively modest public expense. We cannot ignore an approach that would cost tens of millions of dollars while pursuing programs that have been priced in the thousands of millions.

Turning now to the question of how higher levels of maintenance by slumlords might be encouraged rather than forced, the most potent weapon would seem to be liberal mortgage financing, which is already authorized in existing legislation.[19] Thus far, however, the federal program has not received wide acceptance. This has been said by some critics of government policy to be mainly due to the refusal of the FHA to give reasonable valuations in renewal areas to structures which owner-occupants and investors wish to rehabilitate. Presumably, this problem is now being resolved. It would be well to mention, however, other possible barriers, though at present there is no way of assessing their importance.

For the landlord in violation of a local code, recourse to a liberal mortgage loan may be the only alternative to closing his building. The loan is thus not only quite attractive to him, but also beneficial to the community since it minimizes the problem of displaced families. Enthusiasm for liberal credit may not, however, extend to those who must supply the funds. Institutional lenders are frequently reluctant to put money even into areas whose principal disability is age alone. Surely they may be expected to balk at risking their assets on the portions of the older inventory which have other deficiencies as well. Automatic "takeouts" by FNMA, or in other words, de facto direct government loans, are one, and possibly the only, solution to this problem.

It has been argued that lenders would assume a different attitude in the case of structures in a certified renewal area, since they could look to general appreciation of property values in the area to protect their collateral. This reasoning might be valid, with exceptions, in the case of improvements sufficiently above code level to attract higher-income groups to the rehabilitated buildings. It is doubtful, however, whether the argument would apply too well to

---

[19] It has also been alleged that federal income tax regulations exercise a significant influence on maintenance policies, but some difference of opinion exists on the question. See Arthur D. Sporn, "Some Contributions of the Income Tax Law to the Growth and Prevalence of Slums," *Columbia Law Review*, LIX (November, 1959), 1026–1063.

our discussion here which, to repeat, concerns expenditures that do no more than bring dwelling units into conformance with the code. Investment for this purpose cannot materially boost values, since the improved structures would still remain at the bottom of the quality scale and hence attract the same families as before. In fact, as previously pointed out, continuous compliance with local codes would in most cases probably reduce values by forcing up expenditures without altering current or expected revenues.[20] Thus, in considering loans for minimum improvements, institutions are unlikely to give much weight to the property appreciation thesis.

Expanding the analysis now to include an examination of the potential power of liberal mortgage terms in stimulating rehabilitation above code level, it may be seen that the focal point of resistance to easy credit shifts somewhat away from the lender and toward the landlord. With the element of compulsion largely absent,[21] the framework within which the investment decision must be made is considerably altered. Investor-owners will infrequently consider expenditures which do not add at least dollar for dollar to the value of the structure. This means that improvements must be followed by a boost in rents which in turn frequently means that higher-income families must replace the existing residents. Except in areas with unique location or extremely favorable environmental potential, however, the possibility of attracting wealthier households is remote. Where this does occur, the area is analytically the same as a clearance site, and the question arises as to whether the community or the families involved have gained anything by the exchange of populations.

Moreover, although liberal credit can greatly broaden the array of situations in which rehabilitation is financially feasible, it may not induce a corresponding response from owners. Investment alterna-

[20] In some instances, improvements to code level might lengthen the duration of the expected income stream, but this does not seem probable in the vast majority of cases.

[21] The phrase "largely absent" is used because in at least one instance—the Society Hill project in Philadelphia—owners were compelled to bring their buildings to a quality standard above code level or face legal condemnation proceedings. Their position was, however, much different from that of the owner in violation of a local code in that the threat of eminent domain, not the police power, was used to bring about this compliance. Moreover, it is not certain that the courts would uphold such a use of eminent domain in other situations.

tives among various components of the housing supply, and between housing and other assets, are continually shifting in nature and attractiveness. Changing interest rates, trends in the stock market, government tax policies, and even renewal programs themselves may cause a positive or negative change in the attitude of owners toward their real property holdings. Even with extremely attractive mortgage financing available to them, investors may, as a result of shifts in their own financial position or in the economy generally, move from a long- to a short-run point of view or be replaced by avaricious speculators, thus removing funds for the maintenance of housing from the market completely. Although this is well recognized as a theoretical proposition, too little is known of how large categories of investors might and do respond to various governmental and market stimuli. It was mentioned earlier that renewal policies directed toward maintenance should be based on improved knowledge of the occupants as well as the structures. This point can now be extended to include investor-owners, including slumlords. In programs directed at another sector of our national resources, the importance of tailoring programs to specific attributes of the investor, such as size and types of holdings and debt position, has already been demonstrated.[22]

All of the preceding remarks have been entered not as objections to liberal mortgage financing for rehabilitation, but in order to suggest possible difficulties and how to overcome them. In concluding this discussion, however, one problem that may emerge from the widespread use of this tool merits brief comment. Increasingly, rehabilitation and new construction must compete for the same supply of funds. In the past, the competition has not been serious. Institutional mortgagees have allowed liquid assets to remain idle rather than risk them on residential renewal. In effect, new construction was financed in one money market and rehabilitation, what there was of it, in another. As loans for renewal of the standing stock become more attractive to lending institutions and as an increasing number of such loans are sought, periods of stringency

[22] See Henry H. Webster and Carl H. Stoltenberg, "What Ownership Characteristics Are Useful in Predicting Response to Forestry Programs?" *Land Economics*, XXXV (August, 1959), 292–295. An even better example of the use of information on ownership characteristics might be in the debt management operations of the U.S. Treasury.

in the mortgage market sufficient to curtail housing starts may last longer and occur more frequently than before. This potentially adverse effect on the volume of new construction is not improbable and must be anticipated in formulating an over-all strategy for renewal.

Having examined the role of compulsion and encouragement in stimulating housing expenditures by investor-owners, we come finally to the possibility of achieving similar results through the creation of a market environment conducive to higher investment outlays. In a sense, liberal financing is a part of such an environment and perhaps so is the atmosphere created by vigorous code enforcement and a more favorable tax structure, but there are other elements as well. Two will be examined here.

First, it has frequently been said that public improvements undertaken by local governments will, through their favorable impact on environment, lengthen the investment horizon of private owners and in this manner induce them to spend money on their properties. This assumption is embodied in the federal programs pertaining to conservation areas. It implies, among other things, that cities may be able to accelerate the progress of renewal and minimize the cost to taxpayers through the strategic timing and placement of their capital expenditures. While this may be agreed upon in principle, a question arises in the present context as to whether the public spending might encourage speculation rather than investment. Intuitively, it would seem that there might be a systematic difference in the response of landlords and owner-occupants, with the former more likely simply to raise rents or sell out at a larger profit than would otherwise have been possible. Not enough is known about the dynamics of investment and speculation in real estate markets to conclude definitely that only homeowners would be persuaded to undertake rehabilitation as a consequence of public improvements in their neighborhoods. Nevertheless, with limited funds available for renewal, local communities should exercise more caution in the disbursement of seed money intended to produce a chain reaction of investment in the private sector. If speculation is the unanticipated result of public action, not only are tax funds wasted, but the renewal problem itself may be compounded. This possibility is analyzed in more detail in the next section of the chapter.

Second, a climate conducive to more responsible maintenance policies by landlords can be furthered to a small degree by establishing and preserving competition in the market for low-rent accommodations. Landlords will obviously not voluntarily incur expenditures for renovation and repair when they can achieve full occupancy at a satisfactory rent level without such outlays. Thus, maintenance will lag if either insufficient volumes of new construction or slum clearance without equivalent replacement induce a housing shortage and endow the landlord with monopoly powers. If vigorous code enforcement compels the investor to make improvements in such a situation, he will pass most of the costs on to his tenants.

Whether a competitive environment materially affects the maintenance programs of landlords can only be speculated upon. In one sense, competition has an impact analogous to that of code enforcement, which has already been shown to have immense potential. In both situations, failure to make necessary expenditures may completely stop the flow of income from the property. Code enforcement, however, influences primarily the policies of owners whose structures are occupied and producing income. The effect of competition, on the other hand, is mainly on the decisions of landlords whose dwelling units have been vacated. In the one case, therefore, income is preserved by spending; in the other, there is only the possibility that it may be restored. Moreover, in focusing on the vacant unit, the direct impact of greater competition is on only a small portion of the inventory. Still further, many slumlords watching their monopoly profits drain away as a result of rising vacancies may well choose to defer rather than increase maintenance expenditures or to accept successively lower rent schedules. As new construction renders the lower-quality stock increasingly obsolescent, potential tenants are too poor and too few to offer owners of unoccupied apartments much hope of recovering the outlays necessary to bring their units once more into demand. Of course, if these dwellings remain vacant, it is of little concern to the community whether maintenance and repairs are adequate or not. On the whole, it would seem that greater competition in the low-rent sector of the residential real estate market should have a generally favorable, but not extensive, impact on housing quality, particularly in so far as it facilitates enforcement of local building and housing codes.

MINIMIZATION OF WRITEDOWN

Although enlarging the volume of expenditures for housing is probably the primary component of a general strategy for renewal, there is a second element that may be of considerable importance, particularly at the local level where programs are initiated. This element has to do with the order in which various desired projects are scheduled, their scale, and even to some extent, their characteristics. It is defined here for purposes of discussion as minimization of the costs of writedown, though this may be an overly narrow description.

If only because potentially available public funds for renewal are more limited than those privately held, it is essential, if the goals of residential renewal are to be realized within a reasonable period of time, that the private sector of the economy assume as much of the cost as possible. Part of this burden takes the form of new investment and part, the depreciation of existing capital assets. These two components are highly complementary in that the creation of new wealth at a more rapid pace will usually mean a reduction in the market value of a segment of existing capital. It should be the aim of local public policy to intervene in the market process in such a way as to bring about some of these value declines in areas which the redevelopment authority wishes to condemn. Such an aim may be properly viewed as an element of strategy rather than as a subdivision of the goal of reducing values generally in the low-quality stock.

Possibly the idea of lowering writedown costs is wishful thinking. The constraints on public decision-making in renewal may be so great and the requisite knowledge so lacking as to preclude the integrated approach necessary to achieve this purpose. Conceivably, too, in the process of trying to minimize writedown, cities might jeopardize broader goals or increase public costs elsewhere. Nevertheless, it is useful to pursue the question briefly in order to suggest further lines of research.

Minimization of writedown could theoretically be accomplished in three ways: (1) avoiding planning decisions which will build value into areas which should be condemned, (2) "persuading" the market to reject areas which should be condemned, and (3) concentrating condemnation in areas rejected by the market, i.e., in sections where large declines in value have already occurred.

Each of these approaches poses special problems, but the injection of redevelopment criteria into planning decisions is probably the most difficult because of the inevitability of conflicting goals. Programs to increase industrial employment in inlying areas, for example, may raise values in run-down residential sections which should be razed and redeveloped. Highway construction may have the same effect. Nonresidential improvements must, of course, proceed on their own merit, but the timing could possibly be coordinated in such a way as to reduce total public outlays. With respect to residential redevelopment, there is at present a tendency for renewal projects to raise values speculatively in the adjacent areas next in line for treatment. This is exactly the situation which so frequently impairs the rational functioning of the private market.

Clearly, the new should take the value out of the old, or public renewal, like private renewal, will become trapped by a problem of its own making.[23] The solution lies partly in providing homes in redeveloped areas at prices and rents which residents of the adjacent old sections can afford. The current emphasis on programs to bring higher-income groups back to the city is obviously not so designed, and furnishes a neat illustration of one of many possible conflicts between strategy and goals.

The problem connected with a deliberate policy of inducing the market to reject areas selected for public acquisition is to some extent a moral one. Should particular owners and investors be segregated out of the total group and have capital losses forced upon them? This question must be answered strongly in the affirmative if the structures involved cannot be brought up to a quality level necessary for the health and safety of the occupants or if the owners refuse to do so. As for the problem of how to force rejection of areas by the private market, the most obvious procedure would be strict code enforcement, which would both accelerate depreciation of occupied structures and increase the rate of abandonment. If this policy did not have the desired effect, but instead resulted in larger

---

[23] Witness, for example, the huge increase in prices of slum properties in and close to downtown Philadelphia once the demand for rehabilitated units became manifest. This increase materially reduced the rate of improvement, according to informed real estate men in the area.

expenditures for maintenance and repair, it would suggest a need to reconsider the plan for the area.

Concentrating clearance in areas rejected by the market is perhaps the most simple and straightforward method of reducing writedown costs, though admittedly renewal must extend into other sections for the achievement of specific goals. Focusing efforts on rejected areas not only limits writedown, but recognizes that earning assets do perform a function which should not be minimized. Imperfect as the real estate market is in reflecting all the values of the community, it does afford some measure of utility. The question of condemnation in areas having low vacancy rates and more than minimal value, therefore, should be examined carefully, external appearances notwithstanding. Can it be certain that housing conditions will indeed be improved by the action? This caution of course does not apply where the structures will not be replaced by housing and where, therefore, the renewal goals are not residential in character. But if an occupied residential area is to be cleared and rebuilt with housing for a different and presumably higher-income group, a net gain to the community is, as pointed out in a previous section, by no means certain. Demolition, as a general rule, should be the logical consequence of improvement in housing rather than the means of attaining it. And high-priced clearance, which frequently stems from an attempt to reverse this sequence, will simply drain away money and make the problem of renewal more difficult.

The major problem in concentrating on neighborhoods rejected by the market is that even a small area is seldom completely rejected, i.e., vacated by *all* residential users. Prices and rents may decline, but occupancy rates seem to hold at fairly high levels. This fact results in a number of conflicts which seem almost impossible to resolve into a workable program. Ideally, if the market, with or without public assistance, were functioning well, there would be, as described earlier, mass abandonment of the old run-down areas. The substandard inventory would have a vacancy rate of 40 to 50 percent or even greater. Only the low-income families would remain, and many of these could be accommodated in public housing. Values would presumably sink to extremely low levels, and the redevelopment dollar could go two or three times as far as it does today.

Even if the private market were performing efficiently, however, the problem would not be so simple. In the absence of strict code enforcement and without major additions to the supply of public housing, it would take inordinately long to produce a 40 percent vacancy rate. Faced with the prospect of waiting a long period of time for the market to ripen an area for renewal, a city might well have to move in earlier and pay the higher costs of condemnation, rather than sit idly by watching the base for its tax revenues decline. Even with better code enforcement and more public housing, the market may be unable to raise vacancies to a level sufficient to depress prices as well as reduce significantly the problem of relocation. In some of the worst areas, no more than half of the individual units may be substandard. Assuming a much lower vacancy rate in the standard than in the substandard stock, as is the case today, the over-all vacancy rate might never reach a point where it would seriously affect prices[24] and also eliminate or minimize the adverse market effects of relocation. The only solution which seems to be suggested by this analysis is more spot redevelopment. Where extensive clearance is absolutely necessary, the problems described above will never be completely resolved.

With the increasing shift in emphasis from clearance to renewal, the problem of reducing writedown costs may become joined in importance by the task of minimizing speculative increases in prices in renewal areas. If neighborhood revivification above code level proceeds successfully, a point is reached prior to complete renovation where the new environment or expectation of it may be reflected in higher property values. This increase affects both the treated and untreated structures alike, but unrehabilitated buildings, like raw land in the suburbs, seem to appreciate the faster. As a result, the margin available for financially profitable rehabilitation diminishes, and the process of property improvement slows down. This phenomenon is typical of neighborhoods in which there is succession by higher-income groups. Whether it is also a problem in other areas is doubtful, since in these latter areas, marked inflation of prices and rents following rehabilitation has been noticeably absent. In fact, the knowledge that home improvements frequently do not push up values has been a barrier to renewal activity. At present,

---

[24] Since the size of the vacancy rate as well as the other market conditions needed to depress prices actually is not known, this point should be accepted with caution.

then, inordinate price increases are one of the annoying but not critical dilemmas faced by local redevelopment agencies.

OTHER ELEMENTS OF RENEWAL STRATEGY AND TACTICS

Maximization of housing investment and minimization of write-down costs are by no means the only components of a comprehensive strategy for renewal. Several others of either strategic or tactical importance merit brief mention.

Foremost among these is desegregation of the housing market, which is not only an element of strategy but a major goal as well. The abandonment of low-quality housing is intimately tied to the problem of race, for racial minorities typically account for a large percentage of the inhabitants of deteriorated sections of metropolitan areas. The housing dilemma of Negroes is a double problem, for it relates, as we all know, not only to income but also to market segregation. The market has not permitted nonwhite families to vacate bad housing as fast as rising incomes have provided them with the financial ability to do so. Middle- and upper-income Negroes are not able to release their homes at a rate sufficient to satisfy the housing requirements of lower-income nonwhites. The relocation of Negro families displaced by renewal projects becomes ever more difficult, as will also the acquisition of acceptable public housing sites. Fair housing legislation is meeting the problem in some states, but not as effectively as had been hoped. Unless bold steps are taken, renewal well might become impaled on this social thorn.

Another element of strategy has to do with paucity of building sites in the areas in which new housing, industry, and commerce are desired. This condition is certainly one of the principal reasons why redevelopment is so difficult. It is strange, therefore, that open space is the one urban commodity which is held inviolate in all renewal thinking. Homes can be destroyed, families displaced, shopkeepers thrown out of business, but open space not only cannot be decreased, it cannot even be moved. Philadelphia's beautiful and huge Fairmount Park, for example, is deemed to be as useful in its *precise* shape and location as it was sixty years ago, despite the fact that the entire urban structure has been radically transformed since the turn of the century. A potent tool would be provided if the sanctity of parks could be violated to the extent of realigning their boundaries without a reduction in their total area. But without this attack on virginity, some cities still have some open space that should figure far more importantly in their renewal strategy. Manipulation of this space might violate the senses of planners who judge the quality of cities from aerial photographs, but would certainly benefit the cities themselves.[25]

Still another element of strategy or tactics concerns the restrictive zoning practices of suburban communities. In many of these jurisdictions, medium- and low-cost housing is fast being legislated out of existence for status as well as financial reasons. This policy has limited the volume of new construction even where underlying demand is present and has thus retarded the rate at which the older, low-quality stock in the central cities can be abandoned. The potential impact on renewal costs and problems of relocation is obvious. The federal and state governments must somehow exert their influence to return zoning to its proper role.

In concluding, it should be reiterated that the renewal strategy employed is not independent of the goals sought. The assumption throughout the discussion has been that providing every American family with a decent home and suitable living environment is the most pressing need at the moment and ranks much higher than the objectives which have impelled cities to initiate renewal projects. By 1975 or 1980, however, it seems certain that our current residential renewal goals will have been achieved. Unlike peace, there definitely will be decent housing for all in our time. When that point is reached, new objectives will come to the front and with them, new strategies.

NEW CRITERIA FOR FEDERAL ASSISTANCE

. . . The principal barrier . . . to a solution of the housing problem . . . is the Housing Act of 1949 itself which, because of a loophole in its provisions, has permitted the subversion of its own national housing goals by local communities.

[25] For cities that do not wish to go this far, a similar though less comprehensive and effective device would be to give priority to clearance projects in which the reuse was at a higher density and thus added on balance to the total stock of housing.

The national goals, as enumerated in the Act, are a decent home and suitable living environment for every American family. Seldom, however, is that objective given even lip service at the municipal level where the federal program is implemented. Rather, what cities want and openly seek are the return of middle- and high-income families from the suburbs, more clean industry, and the revival of downtown. Thus there is a fundamental conflict between national and municipal goals. Unfortunately, the will of local officials has prevailed. Cities have been able to use the Act to pursue their own purposes, not those set forth by Congress.

How has this been possible? To achieve its stated objectives, the Act of '49 authorizes the federal government to make grants-in-aid to local communities on a project-by-project basis, the amount of aid being equal to a percentage (either two-thirds or three-fourths, depending on the circumstances) of the loss incurred by the local authority in condemning, clearing, and reselling the project area to private developers. This is the well-known "writedown" provision. The Act provides further that to be certified for assistance, a site must be predominantly residential *either before or after* redevelopment. To this general proscription, there is an exception which permits a portion of the money appropriated by Congress for capital grants to be used for nonresidential projects. In the original version of the Act, up to 10 percent of these funds could be so used. This figure was later raised to 20 and then 30 percent, and there is some pressure currently to remove it as a limitation entirely.

The argument for an increasing proportion of nonrestricted funds has been that the renewal program is tied too closely to housing and therefore lacks balance.[26] The experience under the Act completely contradicts this widely held position. Because of the "residential before or after" provision in the Act plus the 20 percent exemption clause, 85 percent of the areas certified for assistance from 1949 to 1959 have been predominantly residential before clearance, while only 50 percent will be primarily residential after redevelopment.[27] As would be inferred from these figures, there has been a large loss

[26] For example, see Richard H. Leach, "The Federal Urban Renewal Program: A Ten-Year Critique," *Law and Contemporary Problems* (School of Law, Duke University), XXV (Autumn, 1960), 778–779.

[27] 1959 *Annual Report* of the Housing and Home Finance Agency and *Urban Renewal Project Characteristics* (Housing and Home Finance Agency, Urban Renewal Administration, 1960).

of residential acreage. Even more alarming, in the majority of cases of residential reuse, the new structures have been for upper-income families.[28] Most cities have no renewal projects at all designed to help the low-income population.

Departure from the goals of the Act has been further assisted by some confusion as to whether the public purpose of a clearance project is the removal of blight and slums, as specified by Congress, or the creation of a new use. There are many instances where the openly acknowledged purpose is the latter, but where blight and slums have in effect been created administratively in order to obtain federal subsidies. Thus, slum clearance which was intended to be for the direct benefit of the residents of slum areas has been reduced to a tool for the achievement of other purposes, and a locality's very worst housing, if it does not occupy a site which can be put to another use, may be completely ignored.[29]

Nowhere in the record is there evidence of any major attempt to provide a decent home and suitable living environment for every American family. In fact, a neutral observer might conclude that the real effort has been to rid cities of slum families, not slum housing. For those who seek solace in the assumption that the future will be different, it should be pointed out that the record which has just been cited was compiled when only 10 or 20 percent of federal funds could be used for nonresidential projects. With the limit now up to 30 percent, the situation can only become more serious. Redevelopment, which was intended to focus upon families least able to cope with their urban environment, has instead distributed its largesse upon all but that group, and indeed forces upon those who need help the most a form of regressive taxation unequaled in recent American history.[30]

It is understandable that the plight of the low-income family is not of high priority in the renewal plans of municipalities, faced as they are with a multitude of other critical issues. Solving the

28 Thus adding little or nothing to total housing investment. See Grigsby, *op. cit.*, Chapter V.

29 Unpublished manuscript of Paul Davidoff, Institute for Urban Studies, on prescriptions for constraining administrative arbitrariness, January, 1961.

30 It could, of course, be argued that Congress did not intend that the provisions of the Act of 1949 pertaining to redevelopment would by themselves contribute to the goals of the Act, but that the total legislative package would do so. Even accepting this view, however, the criticisms made here would still seem to apply.

housing problem of the poor does not help to solve city financial problems; renewal for other purposes does. This is no justification, however, for the federal government abandoning its own goals and allowing each locality to substitute other objectives. The efforts of cities to renew themselves are vital to the survival of our urban areas, and the assistance of the federal government is surely necessary. But this aid should not extend to renewal projects which localities feel compelled to undertake in order to improve their own competitive position vis-à-vis the suburbs and other cities.[31] At best, such a policy diverts funds from projects which may be of greater social urgency, but which have no political or financial appeal. At worst, it may also facilitate the flow of ill-considered projects, rigidify the Balkanization of metropolitan areas, and inhibit orderly and balanced urban development.

During the years following the passage of the Housing Act of 1949, the concept of renewal has broadened and its projects have expanded and become more sophisticated. The original goals of the Act are, however, still as valid as they were more than a decade ago. They have simply been ignored.

In order to reassert the national purpose, the present formula for federal assistance must be completely changed. The writedown provision is, charitably, absurd, having no theoretical foundation or any other justification for existing except that it is simple to apply. Grants made under this clause bear no relationship to the effects of projects on the cost-revenue positions of recipient localities nor to the need of these communities for federal funds. Some of the wealthiest jurisdictions in the United States have qualified for aid, even though they have ample fiscal capacity to rebuild the few objectionable areas within their boundaries. Lacking a rational policy for distributing aid, the program is tending in the direction of pure pork barrel. Cities, as already pointed out, are able to confine their efforts to projects most profitable to themselves. Some of this redevelopment may be of no benefit at all to the urbanized area as a

---

[31] This principle has been quickly recognized and accepted when it applies in reverse, that is, to the detriment of a city. Recently, for example, the Philadelphia Industrial Development Corporation bitterly complained to the Pennsylvania Industrial Development Authority about the use of state funds to assist a firm wishing to move from Philadelphia to Bucks County. The argument of PIDC was that, since the move would result in no net gain to the Philadelphia area or to Pennsylvania, the intervention of the state agency "seems to run counter to the intent of the PIDA legislation and to be economically unsound."

whole, and might even be detrimental. More serious, a large number of projects which might bring a net loss to any individual municipality, but a net gain to the metropolitan area, go untouched. With each jurisdiction attempting to maximize only its own interest, a less than optimum solution is almost certain to result. For the federal government to continue to subsidize the existing chaotic arrangement without attempting to improve it does not make sense.

If the writedown principle is discarded, what criteria may be used in its stead? There are two potentially feasible alternatives, depending on whether aid is continued on a project basis or whether this approach too is thrown out. Assuming, first, the former possibility, the following line of reasoning could be adopted.

For all practical purposes, it is impossible with currently available techniques and data to determine, in most cases, whether a project has a favorable or unfavorable impact on a community's cost-revenue position. There are, however, certain classes of projects, namely those in which the reuse is high-rent apartments, commerce, or industry, which are undertaken with the implicit assumption that they will yield a profit to the city in terms of higher assessed values, increased business and employment, or less costly municipal services. They must, in fact, meet no other test except conformance with the master plan. If, however, they are indeed financially beneficial, as cities openly boast and as the record of both subsidized and unsubsidized projects also indicates, the local community should absorb the cost of writedown. Equally, if they would not be profitable in the absence of a subsidy, they should not be launched at all. In either case, then, the above types of projects are not worthy recipients of federal grants-in-aid. Currently, of course, they are the very types that comprise the bulk of the renewal program.

Continuing the argument, federal contributions should be confined to low-cost housing, parks, transit and transportation, and other public facilities. Assistance to commerce and industry need not go beyond a liberalized loan program.[32] A possible alternative to this general policy would be to continue aid to all types of projects, but

[32] If there were a master plan for the metropolitan area as well as an instrumentality with the power to execute the plan, and if the plan called for the dispersal or centralization of certain types of industries, subsidies might be granted to facilitate these movements. At present, however, the area master plans, the instrumentalities, and the knowledge that certain industries should definitely be relocated are all absent.

require that a portion of any added tax revenues derived from areas redeveloped for commerce, industry, or luxury housing be channeled back into a renewal fund. This fund would be used only for specified types of renewal activity. In implementing either of these two approaches, a method would have to be devised to avoid the possibility of local authorities gerrymandering project areas in order to qualify for federal aid. Currently this practice is widespread and is certainly unnecessary if not objectionable. To prevent it in connection with the above proposals, municipalities could be allowed to establish whatever project boundaries they desired, but be reimbursed only for that portion of the redeveloped acreage devoted to low-cost housing, parks, and other specified uses.

Still another possible formula for government assistance on a project basis would require the local government to stipulate whether a particular proposal was being undertaken to improve the housing conditions of families living in the redevelopment area or for some other purpose. If the former, very stringent conditions would be laid down to ensure that the residents were indeed the focus of the renewal or clearance effort. In the latter type of project, municipalities could proceed with much more freedom than is the case today. They would not have to demonstrate that the site was predominantly residential or, if it were residential, that it was blighted. Federal assistance for such projects would, however, be much more limited and could not exceed a given proportion of all funds allocated to a given community. In addition, there would have to be a redefinition of public purpose. This plan would eliminate some of the confusion, mentioned earlier, as to whether the goal of a particular project is the elimination of the current use or the establishment of a new one.[33]

All the above suggestions presume the retention of the policy of distributing capital grants on a project basis. There are, however, strong arguments for discontinuing this approach. The principal justification for the present form of assistance is probably that renewal activity is best organized on an area basis. Whether it be clearance or rehabilitation or code enforcement or open space reservations, the planning and effectuation ultimately focus on

[33] I am indebted to Paul Davidoff, Institute for Urban Studies, for helping me formulate this idea, though he may not wish to assume responsibility for it in its present form.

identifiable parcels of real estate. For federal assistance to be tied to the physical resurrection of scattered fragments of the urban structure is, however, quite another matter. Such a policy tends to cause local planners to concentrate on the micro- rather than the macro-aspects of renewal; to view the task as one of removing bits and pieces of blight and decay rather than of facilitating an orderly process of change involving the entire metropolitan area; and to preclude from their thinking a comprehensive approach to the problem. Aid that is tied to the physical improvement of an area has the equally serious consequence of almost invariably relegating the needs of the residents to a position of secondary importance. Materialization of an architectural rendering becomes the goal, and cajolery, threats, dispossession, and relocation the burdensome means. Even in rehabilitation projects, benefits to families on the site are sometimes only a fortuitous by-product. Pushing the renewal program out of its present mold would not completely overcome this bias nor eliminate the need for relocation. It might, however, force cities to give more attention to human values and cause local redevelopment authorities to take a somewhat broader view than that of a real estate speculator.

In jettisoning the project approach, the federal government would be well advised to develop a comprehensive strategy of its own before it decided upon the forms, amounts, recipients, and timing of the aid it bestowed. The various components of such a strategy as well as the criteria for assistance all should point toward correcting or compensating for the situation which caused the abandonment of national renewal goals in the first place—the multiplicity of taxing jurisdictions within urban areas. Even without a grand plan, however, grants for slum clearance, conservation programs, code enforcement, and the like could be effectively disbursed without requiring cities to specify the exact areas in which these funds would be used. Other government programs attest to this fact.

In brief, then, very little about the current urban renewal program is right and very much must be changed or federal expenditures may not only be largely wasted, but also compound some of the basic problems. Even in our affluence, we cannot afford to support an endeavor a large part of which is moving in the wrong direction.

SOME CONCLUSIONS

The general purpose of this chapter has not been to provide answers, but instead to pose questions and to induce some discomfort regarding the course and pace of urban renewal. On the one hand, the analysis has indicated that policy suggestions following from an assumption of spreading blight and slums are based on a false premise. In the past decade, there has been a vast improvement in housing conditions and with very little aid from public renewal programs. Although areas of physical decay may have become enlarged, these sections have substantially fewer residents than they did ten years ago. While these are encouraging signs, there are reasons for pessimism as well. The renewal of our cities cannot be accomplished solely by the private market mechanism, and it has long been accepted that various forms of public intervention are required. Yet the principal and potentially most powerful public program established by the Housing Act of 1949 itself rests on a questionable theoretical foundation which inherently limits its potential effectiveness much more than lack of funds. It is eminently clear that the criteria upon which public expenditures for renewal are based are in need of serious re-evaluation.

The principal objection from which nearly all the specific criticisms flow is that the present program gives inadequate consideration to the realities of the residential real estate market, particularly as they apply to the housing needs of the low-income population. As a consequence, it has produced rather little over-all improvement in living conditions per dollar of public investment. The market offers certain measures of social and economic usefulness. Its inability to reflect accurately at all times the entire array of values held by society has resulted in the rejection of many important market criteria in the planning and effectuation of urban renewal programs. Unfortunately, other measurable criteria have not been substituted for those displaced. Despite the postures assumed by planning and redevelopment agencies, however, market forces continue to operate and only too frequently produce unanticipated and undesirable consequences.

Redevelopment agencies are charged with achieving the maximum amount of renewal for each dollar of public contribution. In this effort, they must decide such questions as what to demolish, how fast, and in what time sequence; where to encourage rehabilitation; how to make the private sector assume more of the burden without deliberately penalizing particular individuals or groups; and, most important, how to facilitate the creation of decent housing for all families. These are largely market questions which are currently being decided largely on nonmarket considerations. Unless this emphasis shifts, more than token renewal will not be possible with the federal funds which are potentially available.

A major reason for the failure to consider market implications of urban renewal projects stems from the fact that the programs are, in the main, initiated by and geared to the problems of central cities of metropolitan areas. Understandably, these cities view the range of solutions in terms which reflect their own interest, rather than in the context of the needs of the total metropolitan area. They regard the so-called flight to the suburbs as undesirable, and their renewal plans focus on the problem of arresting and reversing this trend. It is not understood that, from the viewpoint of society as a whole, exodus from the city has produced a much higher standard of housing than could have otherwise been attained, and that the market forces that produced this shift should, therefore, be stimulated. These forces will hasten the voluntary rejection of the worst housing areas and produce a genuine return to the center at a much earlier date if they are guided, not impeded, by public policies. Exodus, therefore, should not be discouraged even in the face of declining central city populations. Rather, efforts should be directed to the problem of creating a healthful pattern of suburban growth in consonance with the needs of the total metropolitan area.

Above all, however, federal and local programs of residential renewal must redirect their emphasis to the needs of the low-income population. The key to better living accommodations for this group lies in several different areas, including a number which are outside the housing orbit. Thus, a large proportion of the occupants of substandard dwelling units are frequently unemployed, earn less than the minimum wage, are denied equal educational and employment opportunities, or are beset by unusually high medical expenses. Part of the solution to their housing dilemma lies in remedying these fundamental social problems.

Within the field of housing itself, current progress can be accelerated either by enlarging the volume of new construction or by raising the level of expenditures for the maintenance and rehabilitation of the standing stock. These two approaches should not, however, be thought of as close substitutes. Although both contribute to *better* housing, the former, by expanding the supply of dwelling units, leads additionally to *cheaper* shelter, an equally important goal. No estimate has ever been made of the amount by which home building would have to be increased in order to affect materially the structure of rents and values, but the economics of the market suggest strongly that only a modest annual increment would be required. . . . Virtually none of this needed increment is likely to be supplied by the current renewal program. With the residential construction industry operating far below capacity and with an explosion of family formation just around the corner, increasing the number of housing starts is a matter of some urgency at the present time.

In conclusion, it should be noted again that despite the many doleful commentaries about the urban environment, our cities manage to provide adequate housing for perhaps four-fifths of their population. Moreover, residential living conditions will continue to improve as incomes rise and as public intervention becomes more adept at triggering housing investment in the private sector. It is not too soon, therefore, to begin looking forward to the time, not over two decades hence, when slums will have been eradicated, and we are confronted with a new, and no doubt equally perplexing, set of problems. Greater knowledge, more imagination, and concerted effort will hasten the arrival of that much hoped-for day.

26 New Directions in Urban Renewal*

Robert C. Weaver

Although urban renewal is a vital tool for preserving our cities, we must modify it in light of sound analyses and experience. Thus there have been, and there will continue to be, new directions in the program. Moderate-income housing and rehabilitation of existing housing will be stressed.

Both moderate-income housing, as a form of redevelopment, and rehabilitation, which is designed to minimize family displacement and economic dislodgment, were inspired by economic necessity as well as social policy and political expediency. Similarly, both were in conflict with the goal of building primarily for upper-middle-class families and maximizing the tax returns to the city.

Thus, urban renewal has had to reconcile and broaden its stated and imputed objectives, recognizing that it must be concerned with social as well as economic returns. In the process, its economic gains will be less than was at first anticipated. The objective must be to get as much economic impact as possible while occasioning the least degree of social costs and upgrading the living conditions of all elements in the population.

The recent redirections in the program and those suggested in

* Reprinted by permission of the publishers from *Dilemmas of Urban America*, Cambridge, Harvard University Press, 1965. Copyright © 1965 by the President and Fellows of Harvard College.

President Johnson's message on "The Problems and Future of the Central City and Its Suburbs" (March 2, 1965) now offer a basis for redefining the functions of the program. They are as follows:

• Provide sites for new residential construction serving a variety of income groups. A limited amount of this will be higher-cost and serve to hold in, and attract to, central cities middle-class families. But most will be moderate-income and low-income housing.

• Continue to undertake downtown redevelopment. This will serve to strengthen the economic base of central cities. It will also make a contribution to increased tax revenue, but grants for social public facilities and for services will be a more direct and effective support to local government finance.

• Upgrade the quality of the existing supply of housing—especially in the dreary gray areas outside the central business districts—largely through new and expanded programs of rehabilitation and code enforcement.

• Demolish *some* of the dilapidated and substandard housing in the blighted areas.

• Afford sites for public institutions, particularly universities and hospitals.

• Provide sites for industrial redevelopment projects.

• Develop more attractive and better-planned cities.[1]

The volume of private expenditures and the amount of tax assistance to local government will be less than was previously contemplated, suggesting the need for other forms of revenue assistance to our cities. Hence the grants mentioned in the second point, above. To supplement indirect revenue assistance to cities via urban renewal, the federal government has proposed direct contributions. Included are the new program of matching grants for service facilities, such as neighborhood centers, and for acquisition

---

[1] The sequence of this list does not represent a system of priorities. In the first place, any one project or local program may well, and often does, perform several of these functions simultaneously. Secondly, in any city a project or a program may emphasize one or more of these objectives. It is imperative, therefore, that no system of inflexible priorities be established for urban renewal. However, as this analysis indicates, the main thrust of the program will be toward providing sites for residential redevelopment and rehabilitation and for revitalizing downtown areas. Urban renewal, of course, will involve slum clearance—either through demolition or rehabilitation—and it will serve to develop more attractive and better-planned cities.

of open spaces in congested neighborhoods. These will help cities carry out plans developed in connection with their community-action programs financed by the Economic Opportunity Act. In addition, federal funds are proposed to provide significant support for education, job training, and associated services.

These approaches recognize that cities need financial assistance to meet their required outlays for public facilities and services. They take the direct route and are more effective in assisting the provision of such facilities and services because they provide immediate financial relief without reducing tax revenue over the short run as urban renewal may well do.[2] Direct grants, however, are complementary to, and not a substitute for, urban renewal, which not only improves the local tax situation but supports the economic base of localities, upgrades the quality of housing, and serves to arrest blight and clear slums, at the same time that it encourages and facilitates orderly development of the localities. Direct grants can be, as they are, used primarily to assist the disadvantaged and the needy, providing services which are readily identified and politically accepted as those for which federal funds should be spent.

The goal of providing moderate-income housing in urban renewal areas is far from new. Apparently the early objective of urban renewal in many cities was to provide moderate-income housing on cleared sites. However, the existing tools of the federal government were inadequate for the task. An initial effort to meet the need was creation of Section 220 of the Federal Housing Act. This authorized the Federal Housing Administration (FHA) to provide mortgage insurance for residential developments in urban renewal areas and the purchase of such mortgages by the Federal National Mortgage Association (FNMA). The result was more and cheaper mortgage money for residential redevelopment; but moderate-income housing was not forthcoming. Thus, for the most part, even when, as in Chicago and Washington, the urban renewal plan specified moderate-income housing, it was impossible to produce it.

It was not until the Housing Act of 1961 was enacted that the situation improved. That legislation included still another new provision, Section 221(d)(3). This new provision authorized below-the-

2 Martin Anderson points this out, although by ignoring the time sequences he grossly overstates the issue. Martin Anderson, *The Federal Bulldozer* (Cambridge, Mass.: M.I.T. Press, 1964), pp. 163–172.

market-interest-rate mortgages, insured by FHA and purchased by FNMA. As a result, it was, for the first time, possible to construct moderate-income housing on a national scale.[3] Significantly, by the spring of 1965 the urban renewal projects in Chicago and Washington, referred to above, were in the process of adding a limited amount of moderate-income housing to the large inventory of higher-priced accommodations already in occupancy.

Prior to 1961, New York State had had experience with a middle-income housing program for six years. This program was one which utilized low-interest, long-term mortgages financed by the state or localities. It was designed to serve income groups slightly higher than those encompassed by the Section 221(d)(3) program. (For a four-person family, median income under the New York middle-income program was approximately $7,500; in the federal moderate-income program the figure was about $6,000.) And, until the federal moderate-income housing program became available, the middle-income housing program of New York was the only viable instrument to finance other than high-rent construction or public housing in urban redevelopment.

The impact of these two programs is reflected in recent statistics for urban redevelopment. As of June 1964, of the 61,777 residential units that had been completed in urban renewal sites, over 17 percent were developed under the middle-income program of New York State, 7.3 percent under the federal moderate-income program, and 8.5 percent for public housing. The remainder were for upper-income occupancy. On the vacant land conveyed or committed to a redeveloper in the fiscal year 1964, preliminary figures indicated that about 35 percent of the residential units would be developed under the federal moderate-income program, 9.4 percent under moderate-income sales' programs of the Federal Housing Administration, 6 percent under New York's middle-income program, 3 percent under the direct loan program for senior citizens, and 7.4 percent by public housing. Thus, whereas at the end of the fiscal year 1964 only one third of the residential units constructed in urban renewal areas were for lower-income occupancy, three fifths of the units scheduled for future development are planned for such occupancy.

[3] For a description of the Section 221(d) (3) program, see Robert Weaver, *The Urban Complex* (New York: Doubleday & Co., 1964), pp. 85–86, 114–118, 126, 252–254.

Most critics of urban renewal have emphasized its failure to recognize the human ingredients in the activity. The more objective among them also recognize the achievements of the program, but assert that it, like any slum clearance program, is vulnerable unless it is coordinated with, and facilitates, activity to augment the supply of housing available to groups displaced.[4] This indicates a major emphasis upon rehabilitation of the existing supply of housing, as one of the required tools.

But this rehabilitation must be cost-conscious—designed to accommodate approximately the same income groups as resided in the structures prior to their being improved. The Housing and Urban Development Bill of 1965 contains significant new tools to accomplish this. If they prove to be effective we shall be able to reduce the relocation load, preserve an increasing number of existing neighborhoods, and launch an effective attack upon the vast gray areas of our cities.

Rehabilitation which is cost-conscious is difficult to achieve. Even the new instruments in the 1965 legislation do not assure success. The principal problem is economic.

A given structure which may be appraised at $6,000 and requires $3,000 for rehabilitation is seldom worth $9,000 upon completion. To its owner, such an additional investment may be justified, but the security for a loan may be impaired by the lack of the property's liquidity or a low potential sales price. When and if the whole neighborhood is upgraded through widespread rehabilitation of properties, accompanied by the installation of additional and adequate community facilities and the upgrading of public services, the value of all properties will rise. This, however, takes time, and its prospect, though helpful, does not contribute enough to assure a sound economic basis for additional investments in individual structures.

An even more perplexing problem occurs in the instance of rental properties in blighted and slum areas. Some are operated by sophisti-

---

[4] For example: "Urban renewal has been used to increase the city's tax base, 'stabilize' the city's population, to beautify the city's face, to polish the city's image. It has not often been used to help those people of the city who need help most . . . urban renewal must be expanded, not cut back, but it must be expanded in its objectives as well as its extent. It must be directed at the rehabilitation of the urban poor, particularly the urban minorities, as well as the redevelopment of their dwellings." Donald Canty, "Architecture and the Urban Emergency," *Architectural Forum*, August-September 1964, pp. 173–178.

cated investors who milk them, and who are not enthusiastic about lessening their returns by putting more into properties which, because of the neighborhood surroundings, cannot sustain rental increases commensurate with the increase in investment. Also, of course, where there is an upgrading of a total neighborhood, it is possible, even probable, that by charging the maximum rentals the owners will place the rehabilitated structures far beyond the paying ability of existing tenants.

Another group of investors in low-income rental properties carries a different set of problems. These are the inexperienced operators who often have paid too much for their properties and use high-cost, short-term financing. For them, as well as for sophisticated small investors who are willing to put money into their properties and are satisfied with a reasonable return, there is no solution short of refinancing with a single, long-term mortgage. Assistance in management and operation will be required for the less knowledgeable in the group.

Recognition of all these difficulties has led to the greater utilization of existing government programs[5] and the development of the new tools already mentioned. These new tools include (1) low-interest direct loans, primarily to low-income and moderate-income homeowners; (2) direct grants to homeowners of the same economic group; and (3) capital grants to nonprofit redevelopers of rental housing.[6]

Even with these instruments rehabilitation in the gray areas will continue to present problems and its progress will be difficult. In addition to the economic factors outlined above, rehabilitation will be complicated by the hesitancy of local renewal officials to undertake it and the tendency of the Federal Housing Administration to resist new principles of underwriting. The hesitancy of the local officials will reflect two principal situations: the opposition to redirecting a program and the greater effort required to carry out rehabilitation as contrasted to clearance. These situations are indigenous to any bureaucracy: change takes time and entails repudiation of past commitments. My experience suggests that if rehabilita-

[5] "Little-Used Law Aids Remodeling," *New York Times*, Feb. 7, 1965, sec. 8, p. 1.

[6] For a more detailed analysis of rehabilitation, see M. Carter McFarland, *The Challenge of Urban Renewal*, Technical Bulletin No. 34 (Washington: Urban Land Institute, 1962), pp. 25–34, and "Residential Rehabilitation," in *Pioneering Urban Land Economics*, ed. James Gillies (Los Angeles: University of California Press, 1965).

tion is approached as a practical rather than an ideological issue, results can be obtained. But the case-by-case approach is time-consuming and frequently frustrating.

There are, however, some encouraging results in rehabilitation. In Boston, for example, three large areas have been designated for such treatment and one is well underway. Other cities, including Philadelphia, Pittsburgh, New Haven, and Chicago, have had successful experiences.

I have serious doubts about using urban renewal for rehabilitation that results in high-rent housing accommodations. Experience has shown that in prestige areas, such as the East Side of New York, Georgetown in Washington, and Beacon Hill in Boston, the forces of the private market do effect rehabilitation. Since, however, one of the generally-agreed-upon objectives of urban renewal is to encourage better land use and reflect good planning, there would be some legitimate employment of urban renewal for rehabilitation even if the result would be economic displacement. This would be justified where there were enclaves of blight destined for higher-income occupancy, in otherwise economically healthy areas of the city. The role of urban renewal assistance in these instances would be to accelerate the process of rehabilitation. Great care should be taken, however, not to use federal funds to eliminate economic diversity unless it is clear that market forces would result in a spread of blight and a decline in the neighborhood.

In much current discussion of rehabilitation versus the bulldozer there is great confusion relative to their impact upon the present occupants of blighted areas. Either approach, if the rehabilitated or new accommodations are priced beyond the pocketbooks of low-income and moderate-income families, causes displacement of the poor and minority groups. But in urban renewal projects those displaced are actually better off economically than families displaced by rehabilitation undertaken outside urban renewal areas. This follows because of the guaranteed relocation assistance. Well-motivated persons have objected to using subsidies to displace the poor and rehouse the affluent. What is lost sight of is that rehabilitation undertaken by private enterprise without public assistance (as well as new construction in blighted areas so financed) usually occasions the same type of displacement, without the mitigating effect of relocation benefits.

As rehabilitation is stressed in urban renewal, demolition will decline. It will, of course, occur within rehabilitation areas where structures, either because of their condition or because of the need for open spaces of public facilities, do not lend themselves to upgrading. Also, there are some whole neighborhoods which can only be upgraded through demolition. Fewer and fewer of them will be redeveloped for upper-income occupancy in the years immediately ahead. Code enforcement will result in some demolition; some of the redeveloped areas will be utilized for new low-rent construction; and others will be used for new moderate-income accommodations.

These new directions in urban renewal will have significant consequences. In the first place, they will minimize the disruptive impact of the program; consequently, the political opposition will be reduced. More significantly, this approach will yield greater results. For, with less potential for dislocation, it will be possible to deal with large segments of the gray areas, thereby providing a basis for more effective redevelopment and more of the economically sound rehabilitation.

Thus, the new directions of the program are realistic. They will not, in and of themselves, upgrade the housing conditions of all the poor. And, indeed, urban renewal was never structured to do that, despite the legislative intent at the time of its origin. Renewal will, however, improve the quality of shelter and urban living for an increasing number of the less affluent; and, when combined with the antipoverty program, provide meaningful assistance to many of the poor.

No one federal program can, by itself, solve the social problems of the nation. Urban renewal, in the past, has too frequently complicated rather than eased these problems; in the process, however, it revealed many social issues which had been ignored. Now it is attempting to make a continuing contribution to the economic health of the central city, make the city more attractive and livable, provide sites for the housing of a diversified economic segment of the population, and upgrade the shelter and physical environment of the poor and the discriminated against.[7]

[7] For an account of urban renewal programs in New Haven and Boston which reflect these new directives, see William Lee Miller and L. Thomas Appleby, " 'You Shove Out the Poor to Make Houses for the Rich,' " *New York Times Magazine*, April 11, 1965, which starts on p. 36, and John P. Reardon, "Urban Renewal—Another Look," *Harvard Today*, Spring 1965, pp. 2–6.

In retrospect, it seems obvious that urban renewal could never have been simultaneously the economic savior of the central city, an instrument for clearing all the slums, the means of attracting hordes of upper-middle-income families back into the central cities, and a tool for rehousing former slum dwellers in decent, safe, and sanitary housing, while generating a volume of construction involving private investments four to six times as great as the public expenditure. It could, and did, in its various aspects, do some of all of this. But the expectation that the total package would be realized through urban renewal was unrealistic from the start.

As I see it there are two dangers in the future.

The first is the existing tendency of some to cite the program's defects—real and imaginary—as a basis for doing away with it entirely. Unless there is a substitute to perform the functions that have been outlined above as the new directions of the program (and the opponents of urban renewal have no workable substitutes), we shall not save or revitalize our cities without urban renewal. (Nor, of course, will urban renewal alone perform that feat.)

The second danger, and in many ways a more serious one, is that we will attempt to freeze the form of what is still a young and evolving program. Those who feel that urban renewal should be primarily oriented to housing (and I am in agreement with them in this belief) often conclude that downtown renewal should be stopped. But the downtown section must be vital, exciting, and economically sound for the sake of the whole city. To date downtown urban redevelopment has been a major factor in sparking the renaissance of more than a score of American cities.[8] Even Raymond Vernon, a sophisticated student of urban problems who is dubious about the future of the central city, recognizes the potential for downtown redevelopment.[9]

Over a period of fifteen years urban renewal has changed a great deal. It is important that it remain flexible, and it is vital that we

---

[8] "New Spirit of St. Louis Sparks Renaissance," *Engineering News-Record,* Aug. 15, 1963, which starts on p. 30; Will Lissner, "Urban Renewal Reviving Centers of Nation's Cities," *New York Times,* April 6, 1964; "The City: Under the Knife, or All for Their Own Good," *Time,* Nov. 6, 1964; "Big Cities Try for a Comeback," *U.S. News and World Report,* Dec. 28, 1964, pp. 34–38. For a more recent description of downtown urban redevelopment undertakings, with special emphasis upon their aesthetics, see "Pedestrian Malls Brighten Up Downtowns Nationwide," *Journal of Housing,* January 1965, pp. 12–13.

[9] Raymond Vernon, *The Myth and Reality of Our Urban Problems* (Cambridge, Mass.: Joint Center for Urban Studies of M.I.T. and Harvard University, 1962), p. 42.

question constantly its assumptions and performances. It is not the magic some who are devoted to it would have us believe. It does not solve all the problems of the central cities in and of itself. Indeed, alone, it does not solve any one of these problems. But it does perform certain functions that are indispensable and it is beginning to perform others. Let us give more attention to defining its fundamental objectives. Let us realistically integrate it into the myriad of programs which affect the urban environment. And then let us evaluate, modify, and improve urban renewal.

Its task is to assist in preserving our cities. And they are worth preserving. Charles Abrams has eloquently expressed the issue: "Despite its losses of population and its setbacks, the city remains the concourse of the various—in faces, in trade, in the exchange of thought, and in the potentials for leadership. It continues to serve its role as a refuge for the underprivileged and for those seeking richer opportunities. It is still the citadel of American freedom, in which there is greater opportunity and where the greater variety of jobs enables one to select a skill and realize an aspiration."[10]

[10] Charles Abrams, "Downtown Decay and Revival," *Journal of the American Institute of Planners*, February 1961, p. 90.

Index

Abatement of taxes, 130, 137, 163, 263, 499, 600
Achievements, study by HHFA, 189–229
see also Advantages of urban renewal
ACIR, *see* Advisory Commission on Intergovernmental Relations
Adjacent blight, 25, 53, 147n., 153, 163, 191, 228, 407–421
Adjustment, *see* Relocated families
Advantages of urban renewal, 114, 305, 315, 385, 389, 398, 558–582
see also Arguments, pro and con
Advertising agencies, location of, 20
Advisory Commission on Intergovernmental Relations, report of, 357
Aesthetics, 454–487, 560–562
see also City planning; Design
Aged people, 47, 309n., 319, 518
Agents, public
counseling service of, 195–201, 312–315, 322, 325, 336–352, 518–520, 542
see also Local Public Agency (LPA)
Agriculture, *see* Farm aid
Aids to business, *see* Financing, federal; Local government; State aid; Subsidies
Air travel, effect on location, 22
Akron, O., 312, 317
Alcoa (Aluminum Co. of America), renewal projects, 278–290, 526–527
Aluminum companies, as developers, 278–290, 526–527

American Institute of Planners, 441
Apartments
market for, 272–275, 299–300, 340–344, 454–487, 596, 601, 616–618
rents of, 55, 263, 272, 315–320, 344, 466, 601
see also Cooperative apartments
Appraisal of property, 63, 138–145, 196–197, 207, 224–225, 262–263
Architects, role in renewal, 287–289, 454–487
Arguments, pro and con, 50–67, 491–582
see also Advantages of urban renewal; Faults
Assessment, 163–164, 262–263
see also Appraisal of property; Taxes
Atlantic City, N.J., relocation, 316
Attitude of relocated families, *see* Neighborhood associations; Neighborhoods; Participation; Psychological aspects; Relocated families
Attrition, *see* Clearance; Conservation; Rehabilitation; Relocated families; Substandard housing
Auctions, *see* Bidding
Automobiles
effect of, 5, 9–11, 388–389
see also Highway projects; Transportation and Transit

Background and goals, 71–229
Baltimore, Md.
job movement, 8, 11, 14
population changes, 6
renewal, 319–320

673

Banks, *see* Financial institutions

Benefits vs. cost, 43–48, 50–67, 325

Bettman, Alfred, 79n., 105–107

Bidding, competitive, 169, 224, 245, 459

Blight
adjacent, 25, 53, 147n., 153, 163, 191, 221, 407–421
definition of, 59
and price mechanism, 52–60

Boston, Mass.
community participation, 261, 270–271
federal financing, 260, 267–268, 275
job movement, 8, 11, 14
low-income homes, 272–273
minority problems, 271, 274, 293–335, 359–379
nonresidential projects, 267, 568
population changes, 6, 262
rehabilitation vs. clearance, 259–277
retail stores, 261, 270
tax problems, 262–263
transportation problems, 264, 268

Boston, Mass., urban renewal project (West End), 259–277
apartments as relocation destination, 272–275, 299–300
change in standard of living, 293–335
financing, 263
home ownership, 299–300, 316, 318, 328
Italians, 293–335, 359–379
outdoor space, 302–303
psychological costs of, 359–379
public vs. private housing, 305, 327
racial factors, 311
relocation aid by public agencies, 313–314
relocation sites, 295–299
rents, 306–311
spatial factors, 300–303, 361–366

Brooklyn, N.Y., 599, 602, 607

Buffalo, N.Y.
job movement, 8, 11, 14
population changes, 6
relocation, 310–311, 313, 320

Building codes, *see* Codes, building

Business
evictions of, 17, 380–403, 497, 541
losses from replacement, 153–155, 386–390, 445–446, 492, 498–499
rent-to-sales ratio, 383, 390
size as factor in nonsurvival, 382–383, 387, 390, 398, 497–498

stimulation of, 162, 241–248, 270, 278–290, 558–582, 597, 614–615, 664–665, 671–672
tax abatement, 130
and urban renewal, 3–23, 278–290
see also Small businessman and relocation; Subsidies

Business centers, *see* Central city

Calexico, Calif., tax benefits, 223

California
renewal laws, 142
use of tax-appreciation bonds by, 137
see also Los Angeles; Oakland; San Francisco

Cambridge, Mass., 568

Capital grants, 82, 85, 91, 94, 98, 100, 129, 200, 205, 221, 521, 658
see also Financing, federal; Local financing

Census Bureau, *see* United States Bureau of Census

Central city, the
effect of minority groups on markets, 395, 652
effect of transportation on, 3–4, 13, 23
federal vs. state relations, 422–434, 624–662
job movement in, 7–12
rebuilding at minimum costs, 569–571, 585–623
stimulation of business in, 241–248, 614–615, 664–665, 671–672
see also Cities; *specific cities*

Chain stores, 571

Chicago, Ill.
injunctions, 183
job movement, 8, 11, 14
population changes, 6
renewal projects, 312–314, 316–318, 331, 409–415, 568
tax benefits, 223

Churches, role in renewal, 227, 267–268, 351–352, 565–566

Cincinnati, O.
job movement, 8, 11, 14
population changes, 6

Cities
competition with suburbs, 3–23, 36–37, 189–190, 359–403, 423–424, 430, 450–453, 549–551
economics of, 3–67, 422–434
growth, decline, and change, 3–67, 189–191, 442–453, 558–582

Cities (*continued*)
  losses from business replacement, 386–390, 400–401, 445–446, 498–499
  remaking through urban renewal, 437–453, 585–623
  tax abatement by, 163, 263, 499, 600
  tax benefits and losses, 223, 386–387, 498–499
  see also Central city; *specific cities*
Citizen participation, 138, 172–176, 198–199, 227–228, 270, 287, 407–421, 563, 665
City government, *see* Local government; Municipal government
City planning, 197–199, 437–487, 558–582
  training for, 440
  see also Cities; Design
Civic associations, *see* Neighborhood associations; Participation, community
Civil Rights Act, 225, 538
  see also Discrimination; Minority groups
Clearance, 126–207, 219, 233–258, 359–379, 438, 493, 537–539, 545, 585–672 *passim*
  versus conservation, 171–176, 259–277
  see also Substandard housing
Cleveland, O.
  Erieview project, 472–476
  job movement, 8, 11, 14
  population changes, 6
Codes, building, 63, 157
  see also Zoning
Codes, housing, 63–64, 179–181, 611–612, 641–652
  sanctions, 182–185
  substantive standards, 177–181, 188
Coercive techniques, 176–186
Colleges, *see* Universities and schools
Collins, John F., 259–277 *passim*
Community life, and relocation, 293–403
Community participation, *see* Participation, community
Community Renewal Program (CRP), 198–199
Commuting problems, 264, 350
Compensation, 152, 154–156, 193–194, 200, 211, 386, 391, 535
  see also Write-downs
Competitive bidding, *see* Bidding, competitive

Condemnation
  compensation for, 152–156, 194, 211, 386, 391, 535
  versus conservation, 171–176
  delay in, 155–157
  illegalities in, 150–157
  judicial review of, 140–145
  legal issues, 140–157
  losses incident to, 153–157, 386–390, 400, 445, 492, 498
  see also Faults
Connecticut
  state grants in, 137
  see also Hartford; New Haven
Conservation
  versus clearance, 171–176, 259–277
  definition, 128
  expansion, 213–218
  participation, 172–176
  see also Rehabilitation
Control
  of existing areas, 171–186
  police-power, 146, 178, 471
  public versus private, 454–487
  of reuse of land, 162–171
Cooperative apartments, 166, 575–576, 601, 631, 639
Corporations, *see* Business; Small businessman and relocation
Cost, 30, 200–204, 248, 265–267, 281, 491–557 *passim*, 594–595, 609–610, 615–616, 618
  versus benefits, 43–48, 50–67, 325
  minimizing, 585–623
  psychological, 332, 359–379, 541–542
Counseling service, 195–201, 312–315, 322, 325, 336–352, 518–520, 542
CRP, *see* Community Renewal Program
Cultural centers, 243, 517, 563–565
  see also Nonresidential and nonindustrial projects

Dallas, Texas, renewal, 320
Danzig, Louis, 233–258 *passim*
Data-processing systems, effect upon relocation, 21–22
Declining areas, *see* Conservation; Rehabilitation; Relocated families; Substandard housing
Delay, *see* Time lag
Demand, *see* Market
Demolition, *see* Clearance; *specific cities*

Densities, 25, 37, 41, 300–303, 316–320, 339, 347, 605–607, 624, 642
Department stores, 7–9, 261, 270, 563
see also Retail stores
Design, role in redevelopment, 229, 287–290, 437–487
Destinations of relocated families, see Relocated families
Detroit, Mich.
Elmwood Park project, 233, 483–487
Gratiot project, 316, 456–471
job movement, 8, 11, 14
population changes, 6
Developers, see Private developers and redevelopers
Dilapidated dwellings, see Substandard housing
Disadvantages, see Faults
Discrimination
by race, 60, 225, 238
see also Minority groups
Displacement, see Business; Evictions; Relocated families
Downtown district, see Central city, the
Dwelling space, see Densities

Economic Opportunity Act, 665
Economics of cities and renewal, 3–67, 422–434, 620, 624–672
Educational institutions
aid to, 123–124, 242–244
see also Schools; Universities and schools, as redevelopers
Eminent domain, 64, 73, 101, 140, 145–150, 191, 425, 492, 500, 507, 512–515
see also Land, acquisition of
Emotions of relocated families, see Relocated families, attitude of
Employment, and relocation, 7–22, 41, 349–350, 384–387, 543–544, 550
Employment agencies, location of, 20
Enterprise, private, see Private developers and redevelopers
Environment, see Neighborhoods
Equitable Life Assurance Society, and Gateway project, 455n.
Ethnic groups, see Minority groups; Neighborhoods
Europe, low-income projects in, 545
Evictions
number of, 326, 496–497, 599, 611
see also Business; Relocated families; Small businessman and relocation

Examples of urban renewal projects, 233–290

Failure of programs, see Faults
Fair housing, see Minority groups
Farm aid, 87, 89, 428
Faults, 315–332, 386–388, 459–462, 491–508, 537–557, 624–662
Federal aid
versus free enterprise, 491–531
limitations of, 491–531
to local program, 509–531, 624–662
new criteria for, 624–662
statutory framework, 129–132, 509–531
see also Capital grants; Federal Housing Acts; Financing, federal; Mortgage insurance
Federal-city relations, 408, 422–434
Federal financing, see Federal aid; Financing, federal
Federal Housing Act of 1949, 31, 61, 72, 79–80, 91–96, 104, 128, 191–195, 208, 509–511, 518, 520, 653–655n.
Federal Housing Act of 1949, history of Title I, 191–195
Federal Housing Act of 1954, 61, 96–100, 109, 128, 175–176, 192–193, 213, 511, 641–642
Federal Housing Act of 1956, 100–101, 212
Federal Housing Act of 1959, 100–102, 110–111, 193–194, 228
Federal Housing Act of 1961, 194, 205, 228, 665–666
Federal Housing Act of 1964, 205, 288–289
Federal Housing Administration, see Federal Housing Acts
Federal legislation, 71–125
early origins of, 72–79
statutory framework, 129–132
struggle for enactment, 79–93
see also Federal Housing Acts
Federal-local sharing of costs, 113–125, 195–196, 200–203, 509–531
Federal National Mortgage Association (FNMA), 165–166, 522–524, 535, 665
see also Financing, federal; Mortgage insurance
FHA, see Federal Housing Administration
Federal-state relations, versus federal-city, 422–434

Finance, *see* Financing, federal; Local financing; Private developers and redevelopers; State financing
Financial institutions (banks, etc.)
    investment by, 269, 271, 285, 517
    relocation of, 17–20
Financing, federal, 233–258, 260
    arguments pro and con, 491–582
    cooperative apartments, 166, 575–576
    development of and debates on purposes, 71–125
    mass transit, 428
    sharing with local and private, 113–125, 191–203, 267, 275, 494, 517–524, 542–544
    see also Federal Housing Acts; Grants; Mortgage insurance; Rehabilitation; Subsidies
Food-related establishments, 381–403 *passim*
Free enterprise, *see* Private developers and redevelopers
Future of urban renewal, 37–44, 186–188, 203–205, 220–222, 585–672
    general strategy, 624–662
    policies for rebuilding, 585–623

GAO, *see* General Accounting Office
General Accounting Office, reports of, 357–358
General Neighborhood Renewal Plan, 100, 198–199, 455
    see also Neighborhoods; Participation, community
Goals and background, 71–229
Goods-handling, 10–12, 21–22
Government and legal issues, 126–188, 499–500, 512–515
    see also Eminent domain
Gradual abandonment, *see* Conservation; Rehabilitation
Gradual rebuilding, 586, 590–596, 602–605, 619–623
    see also Conservation; Hartford, Conn.; Los Angeles, Calif.; New York City; Rehabilitation
Grants
    capital, 85–86, 94, 100–103, 129, 200–206, 521, 658–659
    demonstration, 98
    direct, 665
    matching-plan, 98
    state, 137–138

see also Land grants; Noncash grants-in-aid
"Gray" areas, *see* Conservation; Rehabilitation; Substandard housing

Hartford, Conn., Bushnell Plaza, 477–480, 614–618
Hearings, public, 138–140, 196, 492
    see also Eminent domain
HHFA, *see* Housing and Home Finance Agency
High-rental housing, 263–264, 272, 280, 284, 446–447, 466, 495, 506, 538, 540, 571–572, 615, 617, 651, 657, 666, 669
Highway projects, 134, 264, 549–550, 615, 649
    and dislocation of business, 381–384, 391, 393, 395–396
    see also Transportation and transit
"Hiroshima flats," 283, 459
Historic preservation, 217–218, 561
History of urban renewal, 71–229
Home ownership, 25–30, 117, 172–176, 299–300, 315–320, 327–328, 348–349, 371–372, 374, 448, 456, 632
    see also Cooperative apartments
Hospitals
    as redevelopers, 227–228, 568
    federal aid to, 111, 125
Household densities, *see* Densities
Housing acts, *see* Federal Housing Acts
Housing and Home Finance Agency, 103, 129
    operation and achievement study, 189–229
    relocation study, 293–358
Housing codes, *see* Codes, housing
Housing, *see* Relocated families
Housing market, 3–23, 634–635
    free-market faults in allocation, 50–67
    and public policy, 24–49
    see also Market
Housing shortage, 31, 41–42, 45, 91–92, 324–326, 348, 638–639, 647

Illinois
    renewal legislation, 142
    see also Chicago, Ill.
Improvements brought about by urban renewal, 31–37, 203–218, 223, 268–276, 304–305, 315–320, 348–352, 389–390, 397–400, 504–

Improvements brought about by urban renewal (*continued*)
505, 509–531, 539, 558–582, 600–601
see also Conservation; Examples; Rehabilitation; Relocated families; Standard of living; Upgrading
Income, *see* High-rental housing; Low-income families; Low-income housing; Middle-income housing and families
Indianapolis, Ind., 317
Industrial corporations, *see* Business; Small businessman and relocation
Industrial district, *see* Central city
Insurance companies
outmigration of, 18–20
as redevelopers, 262–263, 285, 455n.
Interest rates, 77, 165, 216, 284, 288, 573, 576
Investments, *see* Private developers and redevelopers
Italians, 263–264, 294–313, 327–328, 330n., 591

Japanese, 612–613
Jersey City, N.J.
job movement, 8, 11, 14
population changes, 6
Jewelry manufacturers, displacement, 387, 390–392, 397–398
Jews, 271, 591
Job movement
manufacturing, 12–18
office, 18–22
retail, 7–9
wholesale, 10–12
Judicial review of condemnation, 140–145, 152, 188

Land
acquisition of, 74–116, 126–188, 206–207
control of, 146, 162–186, 454–487
disposition and new development of, 218–220
market for, 3–67, 220–222
prices, 207, 224, 494, 593, 604–610, 615–618
reuse of, 162–186, 585–623
see also Eminent domain; Land grants
Land grants, 94, 119–122, 134, 201–202,

227–228, 243–244, 268, 567–568, 601, 607
Lawrence, Mass., job movement, 8, 11, 14
Leasing versus purchasing, 167–168, 392–393, 448
Legal and governmental issues, 126–188, 499–500, 512–515
see also Eminent domain
Legislation, *see* Codes, building; Federal Housing Acts; Federal legislation; Zoning
Lehman, Jack, 246
Limitations of federal aid, 491–531
Little Rock, Ark., 319
Living standard, *see* Standard of living
Loans, *see* Financing, federal; Local financing; Mortgage insurance; State aid
Local-federal sharing of costs, *see* Local financing
Local financing, 61, 64–65, 163–164, 183–184, 250–255, 262–263, 267–270, 447
grants-in-aid, 43, 94–95, 119–122, 133–137, 191–192, 201–202, 227–228, 243–244, 268, 601, 607, 611, 633, 650, 654
sharing with federal, 77, 113–125, 195, 200–203, 267, 275, 447, 494, 507–524, 542, 654
state aid, 133–134, 494
tax gains and losses, 223, 284–285, 386–387, 498–499
see also Local Public Agency; Private developers and redevelopers; Taxes
Local government, and renewal policies, 422–434
Local legislation, *see* Codes, building; Zoning
Local Public Agency (LPA), 131, 195–201, 207, 312–315, 322, 325, 336–352, 518–520
see also Agents, public
Logue, Edward J., 265–277 *passim*
Los Angeles, Calif.
job movement, 8, 11, 14
minority problems, 612–613
population changes, 6
renewal policies in, 607–614
Low-cost housing, 624–662
see also Low-income housing
Low-income families, 39–48, 587, 655–656, 661

Low-income families (*continued*)
  rent subsidies to, 551, 572
  see also Low-income housing; Financing, federal; Mortgage insurance; Relocated families
Low-income housing, 226–227, 272–273, 572, 587–593, 624–662, 668
Lowell, Mass.
  job movement, 8, 11, 14
  population changes, 6
LPA, *see* Local Public Agency

Maintenance expenditures, 38, 63, 640–647
  see also Rehabilitation; Repairs
Manufacturing job movement, 12–18
Marginal business, 401–402
  see also Small businessman and relocation
Market
  effect of minority groups on, 395, 652
  for land and housing, 3–67, 220–222
  and public policy, 24–49, 428–432
  stimulation of, 585–672
  see also Apartments; Cooperative apartments; Housing market; Land, market for
Metropolitan government, *see* Local government; Municipal government
Mexicans, 448, 612–613
Middle-income housing and families, 23, 47, 226–227, 233–258, 411–413, 418, 427, 505, 545–550, 587, 600–603, 666
Minneapolis, Minn., 315n.–316, 320
Minnesota, use of tax-appreciation bonds by, 137
Minority groups, 30, 161–162, 271, 274, 295–304, 504, 612–613, 622
  discrimination against, 60, 225, 238, 496, 595
  effect on market, 395, 652
  and substandard housing, 161–162, 311
  see also Japanese; Jews; Negroes; Puerto Ricans
Mitchell-Lama financing, 601–603, 607
Mixed neighborhoods, 290, 315–320, 412, 466, 547–548, 600, 622
Moderate-income housing, *see* Middle-income housing and families
Moderate-income rehabilitation, *see* Rehabilitation

Morristown, N.J., renewal, 319
Mortgage insurance, xiii, 83, 97–98, 165–166, 193–194, 215–217, 272, 501, 503, 522–524, 535, 576, 581, 611, 633, 643–646, 665, 668
Municipal aid, *see* Local financing; *specific cities*
Municipal government, relations with federal, 422–434

National Association of Home Builders, 529
NAHRO, *see* National Association of Housing and Redevelopment Officials
National Association of Housing and Redevelopment Officials, critique of Anderson, 509–531
Negroes
  churches for, 566
  discrimination against, 48, 315–320, 543–544
  relocation of, 21, 239–241, 326, 408, 412–416, 426–427, 466, 530, 539, 552–555, 587, 589, 652
  rent-income ratio of, 354–355
  substandard housing of, 30, 33, 273
  see also Minority groups
Neighborhood associations, 100, 172–176, 198–199, 407–421, 455, 664
  see also Participation, community
Neighborhood stores, 381–382, 395–402
Neighborhoods
  mixed, 290, 315–320, 412, 466, 547–548, 600, 622
  see also Adjacent blight; Relocated families
Nevin, Joseph, 233–258 *passim*
Newark, N.J.
  job movement, 8, 11, 14
  population changes, 6
Newark, N.J., urban renewal project, 233–258
  Central Ward (redevelopment in ghetto), 239–241
  cost of, 248
  downtown program, 241–242, 246–248
  educational and cultural programs, 242–244, 252
  federal and municipal financing of, 234 *et passim*
  North Ward (adjustments in purpose), 237–239

Newark, N.J., urban renewal project (*continued*)
  politics in, 233–258 *passim*
  pragmatism and flexibility in, 233–258
  public relations (the press, etc.), 253–254
New Haven, Conn.
  cost of renewal, 265
  rehabilitation, 561, 588
New York City
  code violation, 184–186
  cultural centers, 517, 563–565
  finance, 601–608
  job movement, 8, 11, 14
  mixed neighborhoods, 622
  population changes, 4–6
  redevelopment by industrials, 278–285, 288, 290
  renewal projects, 310, 314–320, 538–539, 547, 549–550, 555, 568, 587–589, 591, 598–607, 618–623
  Washington Square Southeast, 606
  West Side, 602–603, 618
New York State, middle-income program, 666
Noncash grants-in-aid, 43, 94, 119–122, 134–137, 191–192, 201–202, 218, 237–238, 243–244, 268, 567–568, 591, 607, 611
  hidden factors in, 120
  prior-approval factor, 121, 136
Nonresidential and nonindustrial projects, 65–67, 102, 111, 119–125, 173, 205, 227–228, 240, 243–244, 267, 270, 278–279, 411–412, 563–565, 567–568, 570, 603
  federal aid to, 94, 102, 107–113, 125, 201, 205, 524, 655
Norfolk, Va.
  hospitals as developers, 568
  tax benefits, 223
Nuisance, abatement of, 185–186

Oakland, Calif.
  job movement, 8, 11, 14
  population changes, 6
  tax benefits, 223
Obsolescence, *see* Adjacent blight; Clearance; Substandard housing
Office job movement, 18–22
Oil companies, and real-estate development, 278
One-family dwellings, 7, 286–287, 299–300, 315–320, 340, 612–613
One-person households, 39, 354, 518

Outmigration, *see* Suburbs
Overcrowding, *see* Densities
Owner-occupied dwellings, *see* Cooperative apartments; Home ownership
Owning vs. renting
  of homes, 29–30, 46
  see also Home ownership; Rents

Pareto condition, 51–52, 58, 62, 67
Parking, improved, 389, 391
Parks, 66–67, 218
Participation, community, 138, 172–176, 198–199, 217, 227–228, 270, 287, 407–421, 563, 665
Philadelphia, Pa.
  density, 301–302
  home ownership, 632
  job movement, 8, 11, 14
  obsolescence, 7
  population changes, 6–7
  renewal in, 7, 116–118, 284–289, 301–302, 310, 316, 318, 330n., 568, 649n.
Pittsburgh, Pa.
  Gateway project, 455
  job movement, 8, 11, 14
  population changes, 6
Planning, *see* City planning
Playgrounds, 66–67
Police-power control, 146, 178, 471
Politics, 61–62, 233–277, 408–421, 426–427, 511
Population movement, 3–23, 189–190, 262, 445–446, 590–591
  see also Suburbs
Portland, Maine, replacement, 318–319
Pragmatism and flexibility, 233–258
Price competition, 169, 224, 245, 459
Price of land, 207, 224, 494, 593, 604–610, 615–618
Price mechanism, and urban blight, 52–60
Prior-approval factor, 102, 121–122, 136
Private developers and redevelopers
  attitude of, 278–290
  eminent-domain, rights of, 512–515
  grants to relocatees by, 555
  inducements for, 162–168, 597–598
  investments, 54–59, 162–168, 286, 520–527
  in Newark project, 233–258 *passim*
  versus public, 50–67, 191–195, 305, 327, 491–557, 605
  selection of, 168–170

Private developers and redevelopers (*continued*)
  sharing with federal, 220–221, 447, 494, 521, 525–527, 542–544
  state laws regarding, 130
  see also specific cities
Projects, number of, xii, 204, 407–408, 456, 494, 538, 543, 561, 567–568
Property, appraisal of, 63, 138–145, 196–197, 207, 224–225, 262–263
Providence, R.I.
  historic preservation in, 218
  relocation, 309n., 314, 319
  see also Small businessman and relocation
Psychological aspects, 259–277, 283, 324–325, 332, 359–379, 541–542, 588–589
  see also Neighborhood associations; Neighborhoods; Participation; Relocated families
Public developers, versus private, 50–67, 191–195, 491–557, 605
Public hearings, 138–140, 196, 492
  see also Eminent domain
Public housing, 24–49, 71–125, 226–227, 233–290, 336–352, 355, 426, 495, 518, 535, 545–546, 572–575, 604, 630–652
  versus private, 50–67, 191–195, 305, 327, 491–557, 605
Public policy, and housing market, 24–49
Public projects, *see* Nonresidential and nonindustrial projects
Public use of land, *see* Eminent domain
Public versus private control, 454–487
Puerto Ricans, 448, 496, 541, 591, 603
Purchasing versus leasing of land, 167–168, 448

Racial issues, *see* Minority groups
Railroads, and real-estate development, 278–279
Real estate, *see* Land; Market
Redevelopment, definition of, 128
Rehabilitation, 50–67, 74, 96–105, 128, 197, 213–217, 259–271, 275, 418–421, 543, 561, 588, 598–599, 613, 631–632, 635, 637, 659, 662–663, 667–669
  see also Conservation; Gradual rebuilding; Maintenance expenditures; Repairs

Relocated families, 293–335
  agency aid, 195–201, 209–211, 312–315, 322, 325, 336–352, 518–520, 542
  attitude of, 283, 324–325, 332, 359–379, 413–415
  Census report on, 336–357
  church, shopping, and transportation problems, 8, 350–352
  destinations, 295–299, 316–320, 340–347
  and employment, 7–22, 41, 349–350, 384–387, 543–544, 550
  housing of, 293–335
  objections to moving, 283, 322, 350–352, 589, 635–638
  racial factors, 311–313
  size of, 339, 347
  spatial aspects and densities, 25, 37, 41, 300–303, 316–320, 339, 347, 361–366, 605–607, 624, 642, 652
  statutory requirements, 157–162
  tenure, 299–300, 316–319
  time at previous addresses, 339–340
  see also Home ownership; Rents
Relocation of business, *see* Business
Renting versus owning
  of homes, 29–30, 46
  see also Home ownership; Rents
Rents, 17, 55, 263, 272, 315–320, 344, 393–395, 466, 495, 518, 520, 539–540, 626–627, 644
  business, 381–383, 390, 393–395, 498
  relation to income, 41, 307–308, 331, 344–347, 354–355, 390, 393–395, 540
  subsidies, 43–47, 273, 551, 601
Repairs, 38, 53, 63, 611–612
  see also Maintenance expenditures; Rehabilitation
Residential requirement, 104–113, 209–211
Retail job movement, 7–9
Retail stores, 261, 270, 571
  food-related units, 381–382, 397, 400
  losses from condemnation, 153, 308–403 *passim*
  service units, 390, 396–397, 400
Reuse of land, 162–186, 585–623
  control of, 162–171
  see also Redevelopment
Reynolds Aluminum, *see* Aluminum companies
Rural areas, substandard housing in, 46, 505

St. Louis, Mo.
"Hiroshima flats," 459
job movement, 8, 11, 14
population changes, 6
San Francisco, Calif.
Diamond Heights project, 310, 481
job movement, 8, 11, 14
population changes, 6
renewal, 319
Schools, 120–123, 563
in Newark project, 242–244, 252
see also Noncash grants-in-aid
Seattle, Wash., 311, 317
Security dealers, see Financial institutions
Segregation, see Minority groups
Self-relocation, 208, 210–211, 313–315, 337–346, 520
see also Relocated families
Service establishments, 20, 380–403 passim
Shortage, housing, see Housing shortage
Single-family dwellings, see One-family dwellings
Single-person households, see One-person households
Size of business, as factor in nonsurvival, 382–383, 387, 390, 398, 497–498
Slums, see Substandard housing
SMA, see Standard Metropolitan Areas
Small Business Administration, 497
Small business, see Compensation; Small businessman and relocation
Small businessman and relocation, 380–403, 541–542
advantages, 389–390, 397–398
city, losses to, 386–387, 400–403
cost of moving, 391–393
displacement payments to, 200
effect of highway projects, 381–384, 391, 393, 395–396
evictions, 17, 380–403, 497, 541
failures resulting from, 380–403 passim
food-related units, 381–382, 397, 400
improved parking, 390–391
jewelry manufacturers, 387, 390–392, 397–398
neighborhood stores, 381–382, 395–402
owning versus renting, 392–393

ratio of nonsurvivors to age of business, 384
rents, 381–384, 393
service establishments, 390, 396–397, 400
transportation advantages, 388–390
Social factors, 359–379, 588–623
see also Minority groups; Neighborhoods; Relocated families
Spatial factor, 300–303, 316–320, 361–366, 605–607, 652
Speculation, 645–646, 651
effect on land prices, 593
Standard of living, change in, 293–335, 495–496
Standard Metropolitan Areas, 27–45
State aid, 98, 116–118, 130–134, 137–138, 195, 494
State financing, federal aid in, 116–118, 137–138, 509–531
State legislation, 127, 130–134, 142, 154–158, 187
see also Eminent domain
Statutory framework for federal aid, 129–132, 509–531
Stimulation of market, 585–672
Strategy, general, 624–662
Subsidies
industrial, 263
land, 605–609, 614–616
for low- and middle-income families, 43–47, 273, 573, 624, 631
see also Financing, federal; Grants; Local financing; Mortgage insurance
Substandard housing, 24–49, 233–277, 304–305, 309–311, 315–320, 358, 438, 528–530
barriers to removal, 44–49, 161–162
changes in number of dwellings and inhabitants, 34–37
location of, 25–37
metropolitan versus suburban, 28
percentage of, 25–33, 283, 315–320, 326, 494, 501–505, 542
racial variations, 30–34, 504
regional differences, 28–33, 316–320, 504–505
tenure variations, 25–30
Substantive standards, in housing codes, 177–181, 188
Suburbs, move to, 3–23, 36–37, 189–190, 359–403, 423–424, 430, 450, 549–551

Successes, *see* Improvements brought about by urban renewal

Taft, Robert A., 76–92, 105–108, 191, 426
Taft-Ellender-Wagner bill, 83–92
Taxes
abatement, 130, 137, 163, 263, 499, 600
as affected by renewal, 167–168, 217, 222–223, 262–263, 386, 498–499, 516–517, 577–578, 582, 601, 617, 642
gains and losses of cities, 223, 284–285, 386–387, 498–499, 507, 517
versus profits, 283–285
Tenements, *see* Apartments
Tenure, *see* Cooperative apartments; Home ownership; Rents
Time lag, 71–72, 140, 154–157, 203–204, 253–256, 276, 283–287, 407–408, 475, 479, 499, 526, 534, 542, 571, 619, 668
Title I, history of, 191–195
see also Federal Housing Act of 1949
Toronto, Canada, 431, 434
Transportation and transit
effect on cities, 3–13, 17, 22, 264, 268, 350–351, 388–389, 608–609
federal financing of, 428
see also Automobiles; Highway projects

United States Bureau of Census, 9–20, 25–35, 41, 505–506, 526–530
relocated families, survey of, 336–358
United States Housing Act, *see* Federal Housing Acts
Universities and schools, as redevelopers, 102, 111, 227–228, 243–244, 411–412, 567–568
Upgrading, 39–40, 42, 177–178, 217, 272, 303–304, 552–554, 593, 628, 638, 663–670
see also High-rental housing; Improvements brought about by urban renewal; Relocated families; Standard of living
Upper-income housing, *see* High-rental housing
URA, *see* Urban Renewal Administration
Urban blight, and price mechanism, 52–60
Urban legislation, *see* Municipal government
Urban Renewal Administration, 189–229, 516–517

Vacancies, 31–32, 35, 41–42, 298–299, 504, 590–591, 607–608, 614, 619, 621, 625, 639, 647

Wagner-Ellender-Taft bill, *see* Taft-Ellender-Wagner bill
Warehouses, location changes, 11–12, 21–22
Washington, D.C., and taxable values, 223
Welfare economics, and urban renewal, 50–67, 547
West End urban renewal project, *see* Boston, Mass., urban renewal project (West End)
Wholesale job movement, 10–12
Wolcott bill, 83, 86
Women
in industry, 19, 21
and relocation, 360–376, 547
Write-downs, 43, 94–95, 119–122, 133–137, 191–192, 201–202, 268, 567–568, 601, 607, 611, 633, 648–651, 654–657

Zoning, 16, 126–127, 176–178, 439, 471, 596, 605–607, 653